The heraldry of York Minister; a key to the history of its builders and benefactors. As shewn in the stained-glass windows and in the carved work in stone

Arthur Perceval Purey- Cust

The Heraldry of York Minster.

Of this Book only 300 copies are printed, of which this is No 291

Arms of the Dean and Chapter
of the
Cathedral and Metropolitical Church of St. Peter. York.
South Transept, 2nd Window East.

THE HERALDRY

OF

York Minster:

A KEY TO THE HISTORY OF ITS

Builders and Benefactors.

As shewn in the Stained-Glass Windows, and in the Carved Work in Stone.

BY THE

VERY REVEREND A. P. PUREY-CUST, D.D., F.S.A.,

Dean of York

LEEDS:

RICHARD JACKSON, COMMERCIAL STREET.

1890.

LIBRARY
DEC 6 1968
UNIVERSITY OF TORONTO

TO

H.R.H. PRINCE ALBERT VICTOR OF WALES, K.G.

DUKE OF CLARENCE AND AVONDALE, &c. &c.,

CITIZEN OF YORK,

IN TOKEN OF LOYAL REGARD

AND

AS A REMEMBRANCE OF HIS SOJOURN

ERRATA.

Page 108,	*for*	Trehons	*read*	Trehous.
,, 175,	,,	Bridgeware	,,	Bridgeward.
,, 178,	,,	seusu	,,	sensu.
,, 186 } ,, 190 }	,,	Strafford	,,	Stafford.
,, 219,	,,	Fess	,,	chief.
,, 231,	,,	stork-fish	,,	stock-fish.
,, 234,	,,	interview	,,	interim.
,, 243,	,,	semblane	,,	semblance.
,, 244,	,,	Sir Thomas Marney	,,	Sir Henry Marney.
,, 261,	,,	forcet	,,	forest.
,, 263,	,,	George Clifton	,,	Gervys Clifton.
,, 280,	,,	Town	,,	Tower
,, 313,	,,	leader	,,	leaders.
,, 340,	,,	Burghesh	,,	Burghersh.

On Plate 7, *for* Crouchback, Earl of Gloucester, *read* Earl of Lancaster.

... ANCESTORS

... IVE LAND

... TED

... .S.A.,

DEAN OF YORK.

IO

H R H. PRINCE ALBERT VICTOR OF WALES, K G

DUKE OF CLARENCE AND AVONDALE, &c. &c.,

CITIZEN OF YORK,

IN TOKEN OF LOYAL REGARD

AND

AS A REMEMBRANCE OF HIS SOJOURN

IN A CITY

ASSOCIATED WITH THE MEMORIES OF MANY OF HIS ANCESTORS

AND

CELEBRATED IN THE PAST HISTORY OF HIS NATIVE LAND

This Volume

IS RESPECTFULLY AND CORDIALLY DEDICATED

(WITH HIS PERMISSION)

BY

ARTHUR P. PUREY-CUST, D D, F S A,

DEAN OF YORK

PREFACE.

THE following pages were not commenced with any idea of publication, but were originally the outcome of an ingrained interest in History, Heraldry and Archæology, which, in compliance with frequent requests, found its expression in the shape of lectures.

Having been invited to publish them, I have endeavoured to develop therein what I feel most strongly myself, viz., that Heraldry, rightly appreciated, is an invaluable stimulus and guide, not merely to the facts, but to the motives and causes of the history of the past.

I have had no intention of composing a mere grammar of Heraldry—of which many already exist,—neither a mere guide-book to the Heraldry of the Minster, which may some day be compiled.

I have endeavoured to do full justice, according to my own estimation thereof, to the several subjects in hand. That I have not exhausted them, is simply because the materials in York Minster are so considerable, and because there is a limit to every book.

That much more remains to be said, I candidly admit, but it seems presumptuous, in the last decade of human life, to make promises for the future; and it must also depend upon the favour with which this volume is received, whether it is but an instalment of further similar information—much of which is already in hand—or whether it remains a monograph.

I have endeavoured, as far as possible, to indicate the sources from whence my information has been derived. If I have in any respect failed to do so, I must plead inadvertence.

One thing I must admit, viz., the variety of spelling in the proper names. This seems to me, in such a work, simply unavoidable, as there exists no recognized standard of correctness amidst the diversities of Chroniclers and Historians in this respect. I have, therefore, for the most part, adopted the spelling in the text before me.

In conclusion, I desire to acknowledge my indebtedness to many kind friends who have helped me, especially to Canon RAINE for the generous information, sound guidance, and helpful criticism which he has given to me, without which I should have grievously failed in my undertaking.

I would also express my gratitude to Mr. KNOWLES, of Stonegate, York, for his careful and admirably executed coloured representations of the painted glass; and to Mr. BUCKLE and Mr. HARLAND, of York, and to Miss WOOLWARD, for their spirited drawings in "black and white."

If my book gives to any of my readers a tithe of the pleasure which it has given me to compile, and if it stimulate any in this or any other city to read History and examine the traces of the past for themselves, the pleasant recreation of eight years will be more than rewarded.

TABLE OF CONTENTS.

LIST OF COLOURED ILLUSTRATIONS.

THE

HERALDRY OF YORK MINSTER.

INTRODUCTION

The Origin, Progress, and Significance of Heraldry

I HAVE no doubt that to many the subject of Heraldry may appear utterly contemptible, something altogether beneath the notice of students of any kind, and fit only to be relegated to coach-painters, theatrical managers, and undertakers—mere effete mediæval rubbish, absolutely alien to the lofty intellectualism and transcendental motives of the nineteenth century And nineteenth century Heraldry is, I admit, all this, *i e*, the Heraldry which is simply the indulgence of that ignorant, vulgar ostentation which is only too prevalent, but which is simply a perversion, a parody, a burlesque of that with which I have to do

The conventional "gentleman," in search of his coat-of-arms, enters one of those many shops in London where "Armorial bearings are found" and "furnished" at a very small and reasonable charge He states his name, the *Dictionary of Arms* is produced and consulted, the name and arms found, copied, and supplied, and the purchaser having paid the fee goes away quite satisfied that because his name is the same as the name in the book, the arms there stated to belong to that name are his arms, *i e*, that he has a right to bear them Well, I suppose in this free country he has the right to do so, if he likes, only if that be Heraldry, I should not have troubled you, my gentle reader, with any remarks thereon, or given anything more than a very passing glance to the subject And if people regarded it simply as a purchase, there would also be an end of it, and they would use it like any other ornament they may buy But they don't, they invest it with an entirely fictitious value, and say, on the strength of their purchase, "O yes, I am related to So-and-so, because I bear the same arms" Like the lady in one of DuMaurier's charming cartoons in *Punch*, who, when asked to explain the relationship to another lady, of which she had boasted, naively replied, "We have the same monogram" And the absurdity of this is increased when it is remembered that anybody can take any name they please. It is said that a Mr. Bugg, naturally dissatisfied with his patronymic, assumed the name of Norfolk Howard, and then wrote to the Duke of Norfolk of that day, expressing his hope that he did not object to what he had done. "By no means," replied his Grace, "if you do not expect me to take the name of Bugg in return." But the association thus established between two things so widely different is not easily dissipated, for in a slang dictionary recently published you will find "Norfolk Howard" given as the *soubriquet* of that exceedingly unpleasant insect.

If Mr. Bugg had, however, been skilled in Heraldry, he would have known that his name had an historical and not entomological significance, being a corruption of budget or bouget, from the French word *bougette*, the diminutive of *bouge*, a leather bag or sack, the Gaelic word being *builg* or *bolg*, from whence are derived bellows and belly. The word *budge* is frequently used for a lamb's skin with the wool dressed outwardly, as we shall see when we come to speak of *furs*.

These leathern bottles or bags were slung on either side of the saddle like holsters, or hung at each end of a yoke over the shoulder, and thus gave a name to men who discharged a most useful duty in those days, viz., water-bearers to the army during the sultry marches of the Crusades.* Many distinguished families have been proud to bear the device of the water-bottles, indicating, no doubt, their origin, upon their shields, amongst many others the family of Bourchier, who formerly lived at Beningbrough, near York, whose arms were "Argent a cross engrailed gules between "four water-bougets sable"†; *Roos*, whose arms are to be found in many places in stone and glass through the Minster, viz., "Gules three water-"bougets argent." Planche, in his *Pursuivaunt of Arms*, says that a member of the family of De Roos, or probably a member of a family de Roos, *i.e.*, of Roos, a village in Holderness, married the daughter and heiress of Trusbut, Baron of Wartre in Holderness, who bore "Trois "boutes d'eau" as his arms, which with the heiress passed to her husband.

* Upon the font in Hook Norton Church there is a rude sculpture which shews the manner in which the bottles were carried.

† In an old political song referring to the wars in France, written about 1449, the badge of Lord Bouchier is described as "the water-"bowge."—*Cotton MS.*, 11, 23

The arms of Willoughby of Middleton, viz., "Or on two bars gules "three water-bougets argent," is the coat of the originator of that family, Ralph Bugge, of Nottingham, merchant of the staple, "the original ancestor," says Morton, "of "some good families." He amassed considerable wealth, and purchased lands at Willoughby on the wolds, in Nottinghamshire, which he left to his son Richard, who thereupon assumed the name of Willoughby. His son, Sir Richard, acquired the manor of Wollaton, and his son, again Sir Richard, was an eminent lawyer and Justice of the Court of Common Pleas, 1338.—*Notes on the Churches of Notts*, Godfrey (p. 315).

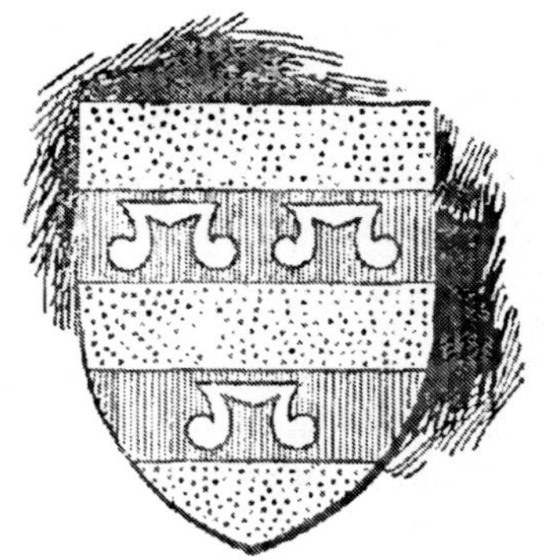

The family of Bugge carried, says Burke, "Azure three water-bougets or, two and one."

In Stowe's *Survey of London* reference is made to John Bugg, Esq., a rich merchant, who was mainly instrumental in rebuilding St. Dionis, Backchurch, in the choir of which church he was buried during the reign of Queen Elizabeth. In the following reign, when Mr. Seymour was brought before the Privy Council, February 20th, 1609–10, on suspicion of having held clandestine interviews with Arabella Stewart, he confessed "after that we had a second meeting at Mr. Bugge's, "his house in Fleet Street."

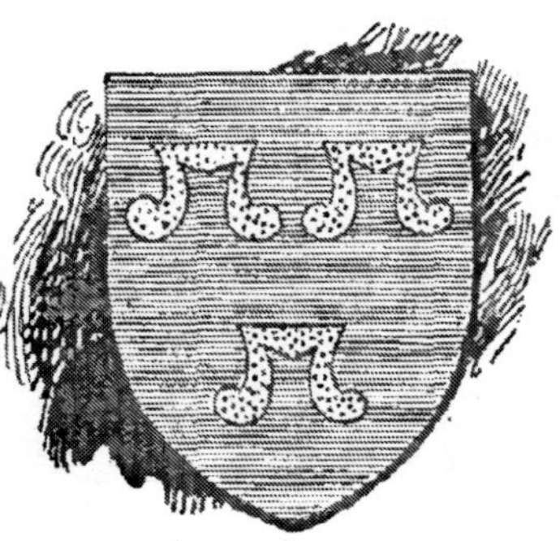

Heraldry, therefore, shows that the *etymology* of this name has nothing to do with *entomology;* indeed, "bug" the insect, is derived from a Welsh word, *bwg*, meaning a hobgoblin—so bogy, bogle. In this sense it is used in Psalm 91, in Taverner's version of the Bible, 1539: "So that thou shalt "not need to be afraid for any *bugs* by night nor for the arrow that flyeth "by day." In America the word is generally applied to beetles, *e.g.*, May-bug, lady-bug, land-bug, water-bug, house-bug.

But true Heraldry, albeit it flourished in the Middle Ages, is the exponent, the record, the language (if you will) of chivalry, *i.e.*, of a genuine noble effort to remedy wrong and mitigate suffering, to purify and keep pure society, and hold men together in lawful and loyal combinations by appealing to all the higher instincts of humanity, and by elevating all the features of true magnanimity, as worthy of reverence, protection, and imitation.

In those days, when might was right, and there was no public opinion to affect men's tyrannical or wanton gratification of their passions of anger, lust, or greed,—when legal justice was rude, difficult, and often biassed,—it was at any rate a great and noble ideal to elaborate Christian principles in a form at once so practical and popular as to produce a sentiment—an enthusiasm, I should rather say—which should not only hallow the natural ties of kindred or earthly interest, but should draw men together, give them mutual confidence in each other, and hold in subjection, yea, stamp with ignominy, those grosser impulses which nothing then existing could touch.

If you have patience to look through the outer film of poetic romance, or to study the tinsel of Heraldic ornament, you will find that there was an intense reality beneath of purpose and action.

What are mere empty titles now, mere vague forms, then expressed duties, which those who held them had bound themselves to discharge, or qualities which they had pledged themselves to cultivate.

Abstract legal power to control men scarcely existed, and abstract religious teaching or devotional habits would have influenced but few. Chivalry caught the fancy of the time, and exerted an influence which nothing else could have done.

For instance, to be a Knight represented not merely the unmeaning ceremony or the empty title of the present day, but the solemn dedication of self, after a period of retirement, meditation, and prayer, to a life of unselfishness and beneficence. "Be thou brave, true, and loyal," was the final charge delivered to him when the sword was laid upon his shoulder. The very word Knight (in its original Saxon "knecht") means a servant or pupil. To call oneself an Esquire comprised not merely the unmeaning affix of "Esq." after the name, but a period of discipline and subordination to another, required even of the noblest, by which alone he could become worthy of the higher degree. And to be a Retainer implied conduct consistent with his reputation whose service men entered and whose badge they bore.

Was this a foolish phantasy? Was it the baseless fabric of a vision? Nay! What subsequent period has put forth a higher aim or produced more substantial results?

"The period before us," says Charles Knight,* "is undoubtedly one "of the most grossly brutal in the history of European society; one in "which we find the greatest amount of crime and violence; in which the "public peace was most incessantly disturbed; in which the most dissolute "manners prevailed. But while the deeds are habitually detestable, while "crime and disorder of every description abound, yet we find dwelling in "the minds and imaginations of men nobler instincts and more exalted "aspirations. A brighter ideal of morality hovers, as it were, above that

* *English Cyclopædia*, "Chivalry."

"rude and stormy social state, attracting the view and commanding the "respect even of men whose lives are little conformable to it.

"Christianity must undoubtedly be ranked amongst the causes of this "fact. But, whatever the cause, the fact is indubitable. We find it every-"where in the Middle Ages; in the popular poetry as well as in the "exhortations of the priests. At no period, perhaps, has the intercourse "between the sexes been more licentious than in the age of chivalry; yet "never was purity of manners more strongly enjoined or more feelingly "described; and perhaps the fantastic elevation given to the female sex "by the laws of chivalry may have tended ultimately to place woman in "her true position as the equal companion of man.

"Nor was purity of manners a theme for poetic eulogy alone. We "find, from a multitude of testimonies, that the public thought in this "particular as the poet spoke, that the prevailing moral notions were pure "and noble, amidst all the rudeness and licentiousness of conduct."

This, then, was the grand moral characteristic of chivalry which entitles it to an important place in the history of modern civilization.

Is it too much to say that without it men would have lapsed into mere savages, or rather, never have been emancipated from the condition of savages; and if people in the present day, instead of thoughtlessly adopting the outward and visible signs, would study and endeavour to cultivate the things signified, the principles which underlay every sign therein (and which are just as necessary and as practical for our every-day life in this generation as they were in those), they would do much to remedy the evils which tarnish our social and individual life, and which we are so perplexed to control.

The issues of life are too momentous, and the dangers besetting humanity too many and complex, to allow of our ridiculing or ignoring any honest effort to grapple with them, even if it be, in our estimation, a little out of date. No doubt none are perfect, but at least they are worthy of our respectful attention, and of our endeavour to discover and disentangle the legitimate motive and purpose from the abuses with which they may have become surrounded, or the follies into which they may have degenerated, or the misconceptions and exaggerations which may have been circulated about them. I venture, as an old Freemason, to claim as much for Freemasonry; and, as a Fellow of the Society of Antiquaries, I ask the same for Heraldry. The aims of both were similar, though they adopted different illustrations; and, if quaint in conception, they are equally sound in principle, though the latter, from the far more modern date of its foundation, is more exclusively and distinctly Christian.

I know that it is the habit of many to regard chivalry as something frivolous while it lasted, and utterly effete now; but some at least, and they of no mean capacity, in subsequent ages thereto, who have thought it out, have come to a different conclusion

Spenser lived in Elizabethan times, after the age of chivalry had closed, but his *Fairie Queene* is an endeavour to stimulate the same high sentiments, by reviving the imagery of the past With what reverence does he draw the portrait of the ancient knight

"A gentle knight was pricking on the plaine,
Ycladd in mighty arms and silver shielde,
Wherein old dints of deep wounds did remaine,
And cruell marks of many a bloudy fielde
And on his breast a bloudie cross he bore,
The deare remembrance of his dying Lord,
For whose sweet sake that glorious badge he wore,
And dead, as living ever, Him adored
Upon his shielde the like was also scored,
For sovereign hope which in His helpe he had
Right faithful, true, he was in deede and worde,
But of his cheere did seem too solemn sad,
Yet nothing did he dred, but ever was y drad"

B 1, *c* 2, *st* 2

Dryden fully appreciated it, and would fain have attempted to revive by his pen the chivalrous sentiments of old, but (as he says in his letters to the Earl of Dorset) being "encouraged only with fair words by "Charles II, my little salary ill paid, and no prospect of a future sub-"sistence, I was then discouraged at the beginning of my attempt, and "now age has overtaken me, and want, a more insufferable evil, through "the change of the times has wholly disabled me"

Walter Scott alludes to this in his introduction to *Marmion*, where he apologises for venturing to

"Essay to break a feeble lance
In the fair fields of old romance"

And it is feeble (however graphic and poetic), for he seldom rises above the mere romance He says, however,

"The mightiest chiefs of British song
Scorned not such legends to prolong
They gleam in Spenser's elfin dream,
And muse in Milton's heavenly theme,
And Dryden in immortal strain
Had raised the Table Round again,
But that a ribald king and court
Bade him toil on to make them sport
Demanded for their niggard pay,
Fit for their souls, a looser lay,
Licentious satire, song and play
The world, defrauded of the high design,
Profaned the God-given strength and marred the lofty line"

Tennyson—one of England's sweetest poets, yes, and one of England's deepest thinkers of this nineteenth century—while he turns with rapture to old legends of chivalry in his *Idylls of the King* and *Holy Grail*, and fans the flickering flame until it beams with a fresh and brilliant radiance, yet shows that he values them also for their high moral (may I not say religious) significance. For when, as Poet Laureate, he would approach the Queen upon the occasion of her great sorrow, when surely to deal with it as a mere poetic theme would have been a mockery and an insult, he says of the late Prince Consort:—

"And indeed he seems to me
Scarce other than my own ideal knight,
Who reverenced his conscience as his king,
Whose glory was repressing human wrong,
Who spake no slander, no, nor listened to it,
Who loved one only and who clave to her."

But there has always been a strange fascination for the external, and therefore for the vulgar side of Heraldry, even by those who have vaunted themselves superior to such considerations.

Oliver Cromwell—whose name perhaps was more accurately Williams, for his paternal great-grandfather was the son of one Morgan Williams, of Wales, who assumed the name of Cromwell in consequence of his mother having been the sister of the famous (or infamous) Cromwell, Earl of Essex, in the days of Henry VIII. Indeed, "in his early days," says Carlisle, "he signed his name '*Cromwell alias Williams*,' as did his father "and grandfather before him."

Oliver, throughout the struggle with the Royalists, affected, with his adherents, to ridicule all earthly dignity; but as soon as he was firmly established as Protector, he assumed every kingly function—created peers by patents, on which he was depicted in royal robes; assumed the imperial crown, though he was never publicly invested with it; and adopted as his own private seal the new national arms, viz., the crosses of St. George and St. Andrew, with the Irish harp, charged with the lion rampant of Cromwell upon an inescutcheon, with the crowned lion of England and a sea-horse, as supporters. The helm, crown, crest, and mantling were borrowed from the royal seals. He also created one Bysshe Garter King of Arms, and, through him, made several grants of arms. From a MS. in the Harleian Collection in the British Museum, it appears that £1,600 was spent for banners, standards, pennons, &c., at his funeral, which cost, altogether, £28,000.

At the time, too, of the establishment of the American independence, those stout republicans (while they repudiated royalty and nobility, and professed to despise titles and dignities, &c.) yet stickled for heraldic achievements. For not only did the Union collectively adopt a shield which is familiar to all as "the star-spangled banner" (and which is nothing else than an adaptation of the arms of George Washington, descended from John Washington, who emigrated to North America during the time of the usurpation of Cromwell, and settled at Bridge Creek on the Potomac river, 1657, and which is thus heraldically described—Argent two bars gules, in chief three mullets of the second), but each separate State adopted a distinct armorial device, many of them heraldically correct enough, but some being pictures rather than arms, and when we remember that the very essence of an heraldic device is simplicity, utterly outrageous. What do you think of this for the State of Kansas?—

Arms of George Washington. *American Arms.*

"Five ox-teams and waggons, between a man ploughing in sinister "foreground, and Indians hunting buffaloes in dexter middle-distance. On "sinister, a river and double-funneled hurricane-decked steamer; behind, "mountains in distance, the sun rising; on sky, in half-circle, thirty-seven "stars, all proper."

That the *penchant* still lingers, is evident from the circumstance that when some few years ago Mr. Crampton, our Minister at Washington, sent his carriage to be repaired, he was surprised, on going to the coachmaker's shortly afterwards, to find that arms similar to his were painted upon every vehicle in the factory. In alarm he asked whether those were all intended for him? "I reckon not, sir," was the reply; "but, you see, "when your carriage was here some of our citizens admired the pattern "of your arms, and concluded to have them painted on their carriages too."

Heraldry, as a language, is, indeed, but the development and the organisation of a usage, universally prevalent amongst mankind, from the earliest period, for both individuals and communities to be distinguished by some sign, device, or cognisance.

A man's physical power or peculiarities as a warrior, or hunter, or the issue of some exploit in which he had been engaged, and with which he would like to be associated, would determine what this should be; and he would therefore adopt one or other of those objects, either animate or inanimate, which were recognised as symbolical or identified therewith, as an expressive device for himself. His son would feel a natural pride in preserving the memorial of his father's reputation by assuming and also transmitting this device. Thus a system of Heraldry would arise and become firmly established.

And such, indeed, has obtained in all countries and all ages. The Red Indian has from time immemorial delineated upon his person or property the "totem" of his people.* The Oriental has always revelled, and revels still, in symbolical blazonry. In the relics of the wonderful races which once peopled the Nile, and of the ancient Assyrians, this is everywhere present.

The Israelites had, we know, their divinely-appointed standards, under which each tribe had to march; and as regards the pitching of their tents, it was ordered in Numbers ii., verse 2:—"Every man of the children of "Israel shall pitch by his own standard, with the ensign of their father's "house."

Six hundred years before the Christian era, Æschylus described the heraldic blazonry of the chieftains who united their forces for the siege of Thebes. The well-known Roman eagle may be said to illustrate the Heraldry of Rome, and the dragon of China to shew that a similar custom has obtained from remote antiquity amongst the Chinese.

It is difficult, perhaps, to quote any definite heraldic charge earlier than 1164, when the device of a lion rampant was found on the seal of Philip Count of Flanders, or a figure resembling a fleur-de-lys on that of Stephen, Earl of Richmond, 1137. In England the earliest is that assigned to Edward the Confessor, viz., a cross patoncee surrounded by five martlets; and a shield so emblazoned is found on the tomb of Henry III. in Westminster Abbey. But this may possibly be taken from a coin struck by him; and the cross was possibly simply to indicate where it might be cut to provide small change, half-pennies and *four*-things being the current portions of real pennies. These arms were afterwards impaled by Richard II. when he made his expedition against the Irish, because Edward the Confessor was traditionally held in great esteem by them. They are carved in stone on the south side of the choir, near the organ, and also in the spandrels of the tower. The work of the former being completed, the latter probably commenced, in his reign.

* "And they painted on the graveposts
Each his own ancestral Totem,
Each the symbol of his household."
Song of Hiawatha, xiv.

Dallaway says the martlet was the ensign of the Saxon nation. Camden reports "that Geoffry de Bouillon, at one draught of his bow, "shooting against David's Tower in "*Jerusalem*, broched three feetless "birds, called allerions, upon his "arrow, and thereupon assumed in "'a shield or, three allerions argent "'upon a bend gules, which the "house of Loraine, descended from "his race, continue to this day."

Shakespeare mentions

"The temple-haunting martlet,"

and probably alludes to swallows, which, trusting so much to their wings, were depicted without legs, as an allegory of a restless, migratory disposition, and referring to those who left their own country to seek honour or sojourn in another land.

By the family of Arundel, of Tre-rice, in Cornwall, "sable six "swallows argent, three, two, and "one," appear to have been adopted from the furthest era of armorial ensigns. Guillaume le Briton notices them in the 3rd book of the *Philipeis*:—

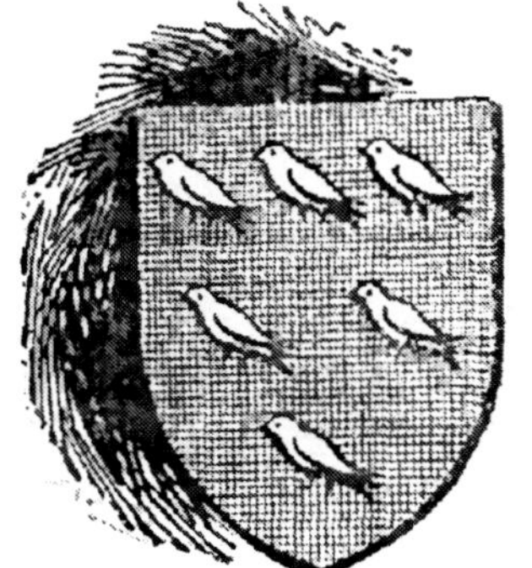

"Vidit hirundelam velocior alite quæ dat
Hoc agnomen ei, fert cujus in ægide signum."

In the famous Bayeux tapestry, *temp.* William I., there are many crude and rudimentary indications of Heraldry. The Conqueror appears with a small banner charged with a plain cross; and on the shields of the soldiers, as well as of Harold, there are devices representing dragons and crosses, as well as bosses.

Perhaps one of the oldest devices, viz., six lioncels rampant, is one which is displayed four times in the Minster in stone and once in glass, and which has been the object of many surmises. I venture to think that I have rightly identified it with the arms of Geoffrey Martel, who married Maude, daughter of Henry I., and was the founder of the great family of Plantagenet; for these arms are engraved on an enamel plate which once adorned his tomb in the Cathedral of Le Mans, and which is now in the Museum of that city. In an account written by John, a monk of Marmoustier in Touraine, about the year 1130, of the knighthood of Geoffry Martel, subsequent to his marriage with Maude, daughter of Henry I., it is stated that he was invested with a hauberk, chausses and gilt spurs, and a shield charged with little lions of gold was hung upon his neck.* They were also carried by Longespee, Earl of Salisbury, the illegitimate son of Henry II. by Fair Rosamond, and are emblazoned upon the shield of the recumbent effigy of him on his tomb in Salisbury Cathedral. His brother, Geoffrey Plantagenet (the only dutiful son, although "base born," of the unhappy Henry), was Archbishop of York from 1191 to 1207, *i.e.*, before any part of the now existing Minster was built. They are not likely to be his arms; but, as they are always found closely associated with the royal arms, it is possible that they may have been reckoned, at least amongst the earlier Plantagenets, as part of their family quarterings or as their initial coat.

Walford, in his introduction to the *Percy Reliques*, gives the following account of the acquisition by the King of the property of the Earl of Salisbury. "In the reign of King Richard I. the young heiress of D'Evreux,

* Cussans.

"Earl of Salisbury, had been carried abroad and secreted by her French "relations in Normandy. To discover the place of her concealment a "knight of the Talbot family spent two years in exploring that province "(at first under the guise of a pilgrim), till having found where she was "confined, he followed the example of the royal minstrel, Blondell de Nesle, "who thus detected the King's responsive voice from the dungeon of the "Duke of Austria, and having adopted the dress and character of a harper, "was gladly received into the family, whence he took an opportunity to "carry off the young lady, whom he presented to the King; and he "bestowed her, not on the adventurous Talbot, but on his natural brother, "William Longespee, son of Fair Rosamond, who became in her right "Earl of Salisbury."

These arms are also, however, borne by the family of Leyborne—Azure, six lioncels argent. In Dugdale's *Baronage*, Roger de Leyborne is recorded as having been made (49th year of the reign of Henry III., *i.e.*, 1265 A.D.) "Warden of all the forests beyond "Trent." Dugdale also tells us that he married Eleanor de Turnham, and Burke that he was ward of Stephen de Turnham, names which will be alluded to further on, and which seem to connect him with Yorkshire and the Yorkshire village Leyburn; but the Leybornes are principally identified with Leyborne Castle, and Leeds Castle in Kent, both of which belonged to them.

Roger Leyborne was succeeded by his eldest son, William, who was summoned amongst the Barons of the realm from 27th Edward I. to 3rd Edward III. Probably this is the name mentioned in the *Carlaverock Roll*, in words which seem so concisely and yet so graphically to set before us a truly sterling character:—

"Guillemes de Leybourne aussi
Vaillans homs sans mes, et sans si,
Baniere i ot o larges pans
Inde o sis blanc lyons rampans."

Thus translated:—"William de Leybourne, a valiant man, without *but*, "without *if*, had there a banner and a large pennon of blue, with six white "lions rampant."

The same charge, differently tinctured, viz., on a field argent six lioncels rampant, sable, was borne by the family of Savage. In Drake's *York* there are the following notices of the family of Savage, viz.:—

1317. 11th of Ed. II., Jordan Savage one of the City Bailiffs.

1356. 31st of Ed. III., William Savage one of the City Bailiffs.

1376. 51st of Ed. III., Robert Savage one of the City Bailiffs.

1369. 44th of Ed. III., William Savage, Mayor, and died in office.

1382 6th of Rd. II., William Savage one of the Members of Parliament for York.

1385. 9th of Rd. II., Robert Savage, Mayor.

1392. 15th ,, ,, ,,

1393. 16th ,, ,, ,,

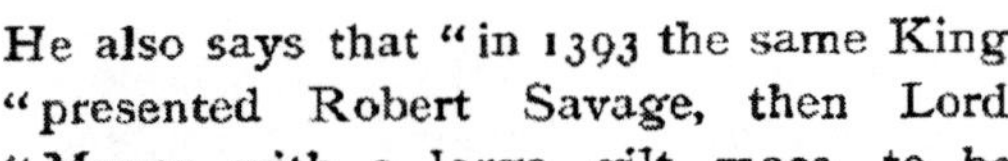

He also says that "in 1393 the same King "presented Robert Savage, then Lord "Mayor, with a large gilt mace, to be "borne likewise (*i.e.*, with the sword given in 1389) before him and his "successors."

Mr. Davies, in the *Yorkshire Phil. Soc. Annual Report*, 1849, says of this Robert Savage that he was a wealthy merchant, living in the parish of All Saints, North Street, and represented this city in Parliament 1386. He died 1398, and directed by his will that his body should be buried before the Altar of St. Michael's in the aforesaid Church.

The Savages, therefore, were people of great civic importance during the building of the Nave and Choir. That stone horn which is to be found sculptured close to these shields at the east end of the Nave and west end of the Choir, has been considered to be representative of the horn of Ulphus, and therefore these arms have been attributed to him; but he must have died many years before the Conquest, and, as I have shown, any heraldic device before that time was of the simplest character. Samuel Gale, in a paper on "The Antient Danish Horn kept in the Cathedral Church of York" (1718), says that Ulphus was a victorious general under Canute, and governor of the western part of Deira, and that "a little after the death of the King, viz., 1036, the contro-

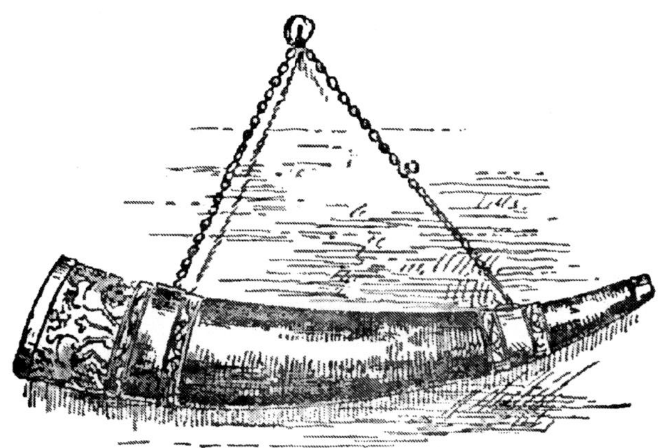

"versy arose between his sons about their sharing their father's lands, "which induced him to make the princely donation; and that he confirmed "the investiture not only by the delivery of the horn, but gave with it his "seal also. This manner of endowing land was usual amongst the Danes, "and specially in the time of King Canute, who gave lands at Pusey in "Berkshire to the family of that name, with a horn solemnly at that time "delivered as a confirmation of the grant, which, Camden saith, they held "in his time, and as I am informed, the horn is still there to be seen."

Mr. Pegge, in a paper read at the Society of Antiquaries, Feb. 6th, 1772 (*Archæologia*, vol. iii. p. 7), tells us that these horns were of "four "sorts: drinking horns, hunting horns, horns for summoning the people, "or of a mixed kind."

The horn of Ulphus was evidently the first; but the Pusey horn "served both the purposes of drinking and hunting, for the dog's-head at "the orifice or embouchure turned upon a joint, by which means the horn "could either be opened for blowing or shut in that part for the holding "of liquor." So Chaucer (*Frankl. Tale*, v. 2809)—

"Janus sits by the fire with double berde,
And drinketh of his bugle-horn the wine.",

But the horn was not only the certificate of the transfer of lands, but the emblem of special official duties. "Very anciently," says Dallaway, "the "bugle-horn was chosen as a device, with an obvious reference to the office "of Forester in fee; and it is easily to be collected (from the number of "forests in England which were extended to the depopulating whole "provinces), in how high a degree of honour those servants of the Crown "were held. In old romances very extraordinary effects were attributed to "the horns of giants and magicians. Spenser says (*Fairie Queene*, 61, lviii.):

> 'Was never wight that heard the shrilling sound
> But trembling fear did feel in every veine.'"

At Borstall, in the ancient Bernwood Forest in Bucks, there is (or was) a famous horn, which Edward the Confessor, who had a royal palace at Brill, gave to one Nigel, a huntsman, who presented the head of a wild boar ("by which the forest was much infested") to the King, and who was rewarded "with one hyde of arable land and the custody of the "forest." This horn was in the possession of Sir John Aubrey, with "wreaths of leather to hang on the neck, and several plates of brass with "flower de luces, which were the arms of Lisures, who intruded into the "state and office during the reign of William the Conqueror. From "this pretended title one of that family had it certified that, being forester "of fee to the King, he was by his office obliged to attend him in his "army, well fitted with horse and arms, his horn hanging about his neck." —*Archæologia*, vol. iii. p. 17.

At Ripon the horn is to this day carried before the mayor, three blasts of which were sounded nightly before the mayor's door at 9 o'clock, and one afterwards at the Market Cross. The horn itself is decorated with silver badges and with the insignia of trading companies belonging to the town.

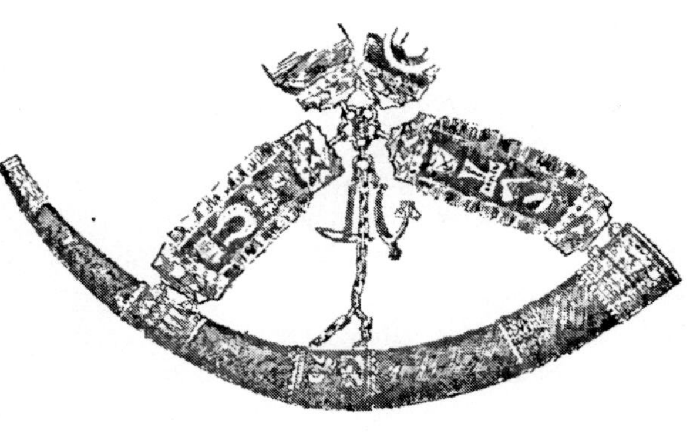

In the Museum at York are two very curious horns: one of metal, until 1839 always worn, and I believe blown, by the sheriff's officer, and a horn of ivory, which was evidently used only as a badge.

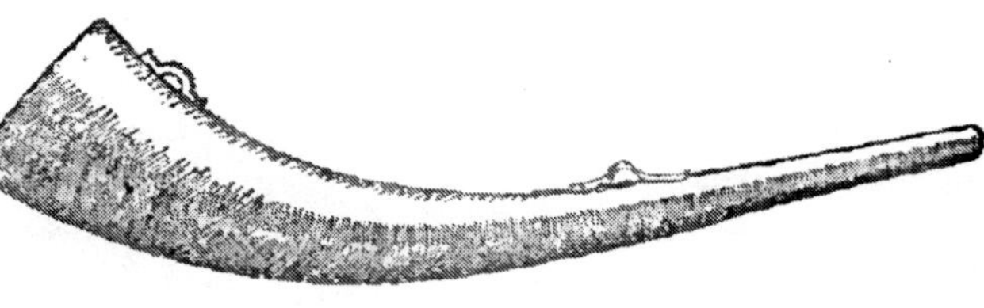

Collins, in his *Peerage*, says of Henry Percy, third Earl of Northumberland—"In 38th Henry VI. he was constituted justice of all forests beyond "Trent." Longstaffe, in his book, *The Old Heraldry of the Percys*, mentions "a bugle-horn, unstrung end to the dexter, mounted with coronal ornaments,"

as the arms of Bryan, and gives the following amongst the pennons and pennoncelles of Percy —"Bryan—Rosset, gold and tawny, the bugle-horn "as before"

Henry Percy, third Earl of Northumberland, married Eleanor, granddaughter and heir of Richard Poynings, Lord Poynings, Fitz-Payne, and Bryan, so he may have inherited the badge from him and the office also

It therefore by no means follows that the horn, being so common a badge, should necessarily be the horn of Ulphus My own opinion at present is that the horn and arms together represent either Plantagenet and the royal supremacy over the northern forests generally, or the royal rangership of the forest of Galtres, by which York was nearly surrounded, or, it may be, the arms of Savage, and the horn, as it is at Ripon now, the civic badge before the mace was given by Richard II

From the position of the shield and horn in the Choir, they would seem to have been placed there at the completion of the building, which, is known, was commenced by Archbishop Thoresby, at the east end And we may, therefore, assume that the shield and arms in the Nave mark the completion of that portion of the Church These dates, about 1345 and 1400, tally with the official existence of William and Robert Savage The last Baron Leyborne died in 1309, which would prevent these shields being attributed to them

But no doubt the great impetus to this ingrained taste for distinctive devices was given by the Crusades, which commenced in 1095, when the Council of Clermont, having determined to recover the Holy Land from the Saracens, Peter the Hermit, animated by religious enthusiasm, roused the sovereigns and nobles throughout Europe to take up arms against the Moslem

In the following year an immense army was collected from every corner of Europe, under the magnanimous Godfrey de Bouillon, since immortalized by Tasso, and being composed of so many nationalities, it was necessary to adopt certain distinctive insignia

Thus the English had a white cross sewn or embroidered on the right shoulder of their surcoats, the French were distinguished in a similar manner by a red cross, the Flemings adopted a green cross, and the Crusaders from the Roman States bore two keys in saltire The French bore also the banner of St Dennis, viz, a square flag of a red or flaming colour, which was called the oriflamme, and was carried at the head of the French armies from the 12th to the 15th century

The English on their side had also their distinctive flag, according to Tasso, thus translated by Fairfax*—

* This was Edward Fairfax, born 1568, who may have been a son of the great grandfather of that famous Parliamentary General, Thomas Fairfax, who lived in York, whose son Henry restored the horn of Ulphus to us, which had been "taken away," says Drake, at the time of the Reformation

"Loose in the winde waived their banner light,
Their standard Roial towards Heaven they spread,
The Cross triumphant o'er the Pagan dead."

There have been some translations of Tasso since, but none, I think, better. Tasso is no authority on chivalry, as he lived after its date, 1544–95; but his poem is grand and stirring, and his description of the Crusaders falling on their knees, bareheaded, when they first saw Jerusalem, is, if imaginary, very touching and effective.

The second Crusade was excited by the preaching of St. Bernard, 1147. The third, in which Richard I. joined, was commenced 1191. Altogether these futile wars lasted two hundred years, and, Voltaire says, cost the lives of two millions of men.

This contact with the Saracens, however, produced two definite results: 1st, that attention to the breeding of horses, and that extraordinary love and care for them which have always marked Orientals, and which may specially be noted in the Middle Ages in England; and the other, the development of Heraldry, for the Saracens abounded in every magnificent decoration so peculiar to Asiatics. Their military attire exhibited a profusion of ornament which the treasures of the East could alone have supplied, and this naturally attracted the admiration and excited the emulation and imitation of their adversaries.

For the Christian soldiers were encouraged to deeds of valour by being permitted to assume whatever device their fancies might dictate as the memento of a gallant exploit, and specially some portion of the accoutrements or arms of a vanquished enemy; and hence arose a multi-

tude of charges hitherto unknown in Heraldry, such as:—escallop shells, bezants (gold coins of Byzantium), water-bougets (leathern vessels for carrying water), Palmers' staves, passion nails, Saracens' heads, crescents, scimitars, &c. But the cross, being the object of the greatest veneration, was naturally more in favour as a device than any other, and numberless modifications of its form were devised for this purpose.

On the final return of the warriors to their homes, the unsettled state of their countries not only did not suffer their military ardour to cool down, but seemed to demand for many generations the consolidation of those principles and the elaboration of those theories of which the rudiments had been founded in the East.

In England, during the reigns of Edward I. and Edward II., there were incessant demands for men to fight against the French and the Scotch; and then, from the reign of Edward III. to that of Henry VII., a period of more than 150 years, viz., from 1377 to 1485, were waged the Wars of the Roses, that unhappy, cruel internecine strife which caused the death of innumerable Englishmen—embittered them against each other into acts so savage and ruthless that they seem almost incredible, and rendered the condition of the country so unsettled from the constant change of government swaying from one family to another, that any stable, central authority was impossible; and it seems almost providential that such a system as chivalry should have been established, which, expressed by Heraldry, appealed to the higher instincts of honour and courage and magnanimity, and therefore held those who differed diametrically on other matters bound to a certain code of laws, and subservient to certain mutually recognised principles, without which the deeds of those days, cruel as they were, would have been far surpassed in ferocity and brutality.

And thus, Heraldry having become popularly adopted, was in due course established, as matters became more settled, as a recognised department of the national government. Of the practice of the Curia Militaris (or Court of the Earl Marshal) in the early centuries, no satisfactory documents have reached us, though it may be presumed, says Dallaway, that precedents of it were followed as scrupulously as the memory of man or oral traditions could warrant. It was usually held within the verge of the royal Court by the High Constable and Earl Marshal, who called to their assistance as many of their peers as they thought expedient, and the processes were conducted by the Heralds, Doctors of Civil Laws (who were assessors by commission), and their inferior officers. Appeals were sometimes made to the Court of Queen's Bench.

On January 10th, 1386 (9th Richard II.), this duty was restricted to the Earl Marshal alone; and Thomas Mowbray, Earl of Nottingham, was invested with authority to preside as Earl Marshal in the Court of Chivalry. The Earl Marshal is the highest great officer of State; and until the office was made hereditary by Charles II. to Henry Lord Howard, and the heirs male of his body lawfully begotten, it always passed from the King, and was never held by tenure or serjeanty. To him was given the privilege to bear in his hand a gold truncheon enamelled with black at each end, having at the upper end of it the King's arms engraven thereon, and at the lower end his own arms. This Court still is the fountain of the Marshal law, and grants coats armorial and supporters to the same to such as are duly qualified to wear them. The Heralds appear there as advocates—support arguments in matters of controversy—and the decision of the Earl Marshal is final.

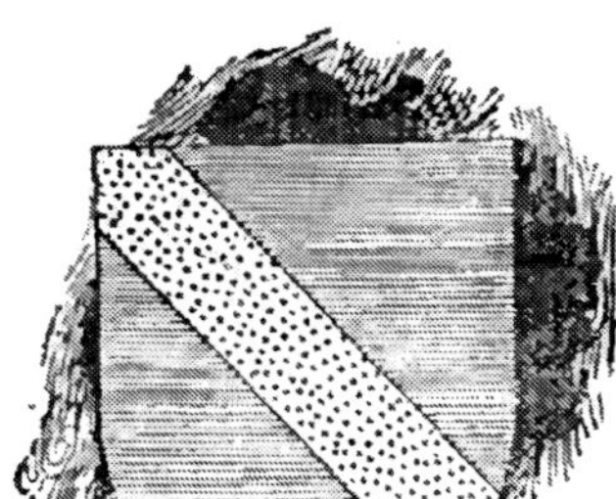

One famous cause at least has come down to us from these ancient times, viz., that between the families of Scrope and Grosvenor, for the right to bear as a coat-of-arms "Azure a bend "or," and the proceedings of which are still extant in the Scrope and Grosvenor Roll, a copy of which is in our Library.

It seems incredible to us, but this cause lasted three years, during which more than two hundred witnesses were examined, amongst them John of Gaunt and Geoffry Chaucer; and its decision was ultimately in favour of the former, with a recognition of the claim of the family of Carmenow, of Carmenow in Cornwall.

The case of Hastings will be mentioned further on; but there was also another case, when Sir John Sitsilt (Sicelt or Cyssel *temp.* Henry VIII., Cecil *temp.* Queen Elizabeth), being at Halidown Hill, near Berwick, in 1333, there arose a great controversy between him and Sir Wm. Faknaham concerning a banner charged with this coat, viz., "a field barry of ten pieces, argent and azure, "on six escutcheons, three, two, and one, sable "as many lions rampant of the first;" which arms each challenged as their right, and offered to maintain the same by a combat in their proper persons. But the King, Edward III., was pleased to forbid it; and ordering the Heralds to decide the affair by law and justice, they solemnly adjudged the right of bearing those arms to Sir John Sitsilt, as heir of blood lineally descended from the body of James Sitsilt, Baron of Beaufort, slain at the siege of Wallingford Castle in the 4th of King Stephen (see Collins's *Peerage*). Which arms are still borne by the families of the Marquises of Exeter and Salisbury.

Garter, principal King of Arms

Henry V. gave the title of Garter King of Arms to the principal officer of the court, and in 1419 issued an edict to the sheriffs of each county to summon all persons bearing arms to prove and establish their right to them. The first regular chapter of the court was held at the siege of Rouen in the following year, 1420.

The outlines of a code of laws and observances were thus formed and approved of, and the officers of the institute recognised, not merely as personal servants, but as officers of the King. In the reign of Richard III. they were incorporated by royal charter, and two additional subordinate Kings of Arms were appointed, viz., Clarenceux, with jurisdiction south of the Trent; Norroy, or North King, north thereof.

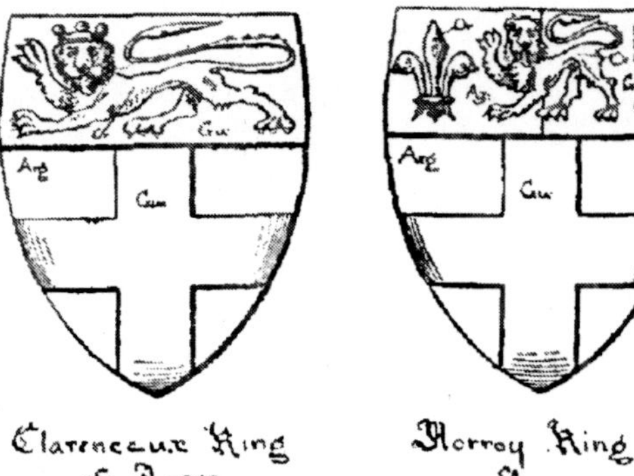

Clarenceux King of Arms. Norroy King of Arms

Under these were appointed six assistant officers, called Heralds, and thus styled—Lancaster, Somerset, Richmond, Windsor, York, Chester; and four Pursuivants—Rouge-Croix, Blue Mantle, Portcullis, Rouge-Dragon. They were also called Chevaliers of Arms, or Knight Riders, and their service was originally of high trust and great consideration, viz., the bearing of letters and messages to sovereign princes and persons of great authority. In fact, they were the predecessors of the modern Queen's Messengers; but their duty, if not more honourable, was at least more delicate and difficult than the latter, as the messages would often be by word of mouth, and the delivery thereof involve considerable personal risk as well as great fatigue.

In Ireland (see Clarke's *Heraldry*) there was an Ulster King of Arms, with two Heralds (Cork and Dublin) and six Pursuivants. For Scotland, the Lyon King of Arms, with a Deputy, Clerk, and Keeper of the Records; six Heralds—Rothesay, Marchmont, Islay, Albany, Snowdon, and Ross; and six Pursuivants—Dingwall, Bute, Carrick, Ormond, Kintyre, and Unicorn.

Ulster King of Arms. Lyon King of Arms.

In his poem of *Marmion* (canto iv., st. vii.), Sir Walter Scott has given us a charming picture of one of those Lyon Kings of Arms, and has shewn what dignified personages they were, and in what estimation they were held.

"First came the trumpets, at whose clang
So late the forest-echoes rang;
On prancing steeds they forward pressed,
With scarlet mantle, azure vest;
Each at his trump a banner wore
Which Scotland's royal 'scutcheon bore.
Heralds and Pursuivants, by name
Bute, Islay, Marchmont, Rothsay, came,
In painted tabards, proudly shewing
Gules, argent, or, and azure glowing:
  Attendants on a King at Arms,
Whose hand the armorial truncheon held,
That feudal strife had often quelled,
  When wildest its alarms.
He was a man of middle age;
In aspect manly, grave, and sage,
  As on King's errand come:
But in the glances of his eye
A penetrating, keen and sly
  Expression found its home;—
The flash of that satiric rage,
Which, bursting on the early stage,
Branded the vices of the age,
  And broke the Keys of Rome.
On milk-white palfrey forth he paced;
His cap of maintenance was graced
  With the proud heron's plume;
From his steed's shoulder, loin and breast,
  Silk housings swept the ground,
With Scotland's arms, device and crest,
  Embroidered round and round.
The double tressure might you see,
  First by Achaius borne,
The Thistle and the Fleur-de-lys,
  And gallant Unicorn.
So bright the King's armorial coat,
That scarce the dazzled eye could note,
In living colours, blazoned brave,
The lion which his title gave;
A train, which well beseemed his state,
But all unarmed, around him wait.
Still is thy name of high account,
  And still thy verse has charms,
Sir David Lindesay of the Mount,
  Lord Lion King-at-Arms."

And Lancaster Herald gives a very quaint and graphic account of the estimation in which his office was held when, in 1536, he went to Pontefract to read the King's proclamation to Aske and those associated with him in the Pilgrimage of Grace. He tells us how he passed through "certen companyes of the said rebelious, beinge comon people of husbandrye, "who saluted me gentilly, and gave gret honour to the King's coote of "arms, which I ware;" and how, when he came to the Market Cross, he "founde many in harness of very cruell fellowes," who yet did not molest him. He was then brought to the great hall, where he stood at the high table and shewed the people the cause of his coming. Then he continues: "The saide Haske sent for me into his chamber, and keeping his porte "and countenance as though he had been a grett prince, with grett rigor "and like a tiraunte."

Richard III., by letters patent dated March 21st, 1483, the first year of his reign, directed the incorporation of Heralds, and assigned for their habitation "a messuage with the appurtenances, in "London, in the parish of All Saints, called Pul-"teney's Inn or Cold Harbour;" so called from Sir John Pulteney, who had lived there, and been four times Lord Mayor of London. It had, however, by marriage become the property of the King, and according to Stowe, was a "right fayre and stately "house" when Richard gave it to Sir John Wryth or Wriothesley, Garter King at Arms, in trust for the residence and assembling of Heralds. The College of Arms, considering him as their founder, adopted his armorial bearings upon their seal (Dallaway).

College of Arms.

But his penurious successor, Henry VII., dispossessed the Heralds of their property, and they were glad to take refuge, upon sufferance of the Crown, at the Hospital of our Lady of Roncival, at Charing Cross, where Northumberland House lately stood.

In the reign of Philip and Mary, Thomas Duke of Norfolk, Earl Marshal, purchased Derby or Stanley House, on St. Benet's Hill, from Sir Richard Sackville, to whom it had been mortgaged by the Earl of Derby; and he, having transferred it to the Crown, it was instantly regranted by charter to Sir Gilbert Dethick, Garter King of Arms, and his associates in office, July 18th, 1535.

In the great fire of London, 1666, Derby House was destroyed; and the present building was erected on the old site, after the design of Sir Christopher Wren, assisted by Sir William Dugdale, who built the north-west corner of the College at his own expense.

The most severe punishment that could be inflicted by this court was that of degradation from the honour of knighthood, of which only three instances are recorded during three centuries, shewing the reluctance with which it was decreed, viz., Sir Andrew Harclay, 1322; Sir Ralph Grey, 1464; Sir Francis Michell, 1621. The last named, we are told, being brought into Court without the bar, there sat upon a standing while sentence was pronounced by the Somerset Herald; in compliance with which one of the Knight Marshal's men, "standing on the scaffold with "him, did cut his belt whereby his sworde did hang, and soe let it fall to "the grounde: then he cut his spurres off from his heels, and hurled the "one one way into the hall, and the other another way. That done he "drew his sword out of his scabbard and with his hands broke it over his "head, and threw the one piece the one way, and the other the other way. "Then the rest of the writing was read and pronounced aloud, viz., 'That "'he be from henceforth reputed, taken, and styled an infamous, errant "'knave. God save the King!'"*

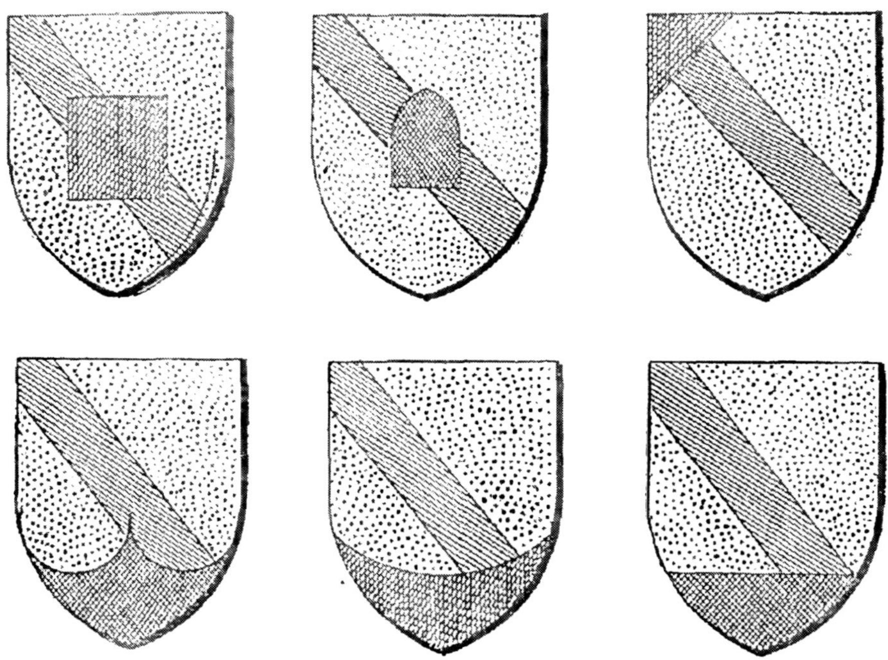

But there were other punishments, which if less severe than this were equally degrading and disgraceful. These were effected by "abatements," as they were called, or accidental marks upon the coat-armour, denoting some "ungentlemanlike, dishonourable, or disloyal demeanour, quality, or "stain in the bearer, whereby the dignity of the coat-armour is greatly "abused."

"To him that revoketh his own challenge" (or as we call it, eats his own words), a delf or square patch of tinne or orange was placed on his escutcheon.

* Dallaway.

"To him that discourteously entreateth either maid or widow against "their will, or to such an one as flyeth from his Sovereign's banner—until "such time as he have done some valiant exploit worthy to be noted by "the Heralds, upon whose true report it may please the Sovereign to "restore him to his former bearing"—an escutcheon reversed, sanguine (crimson), was placed on his shield.

"To him that overmuch boasteth himself of his martial acts,"—a dexter point parted (*i.e.* a corner of his shield was cut off). "If a man has "performed any praiseworthy action," adds the old Herald, "the self-deed "will sufficiently commend him, though he hold his peace."

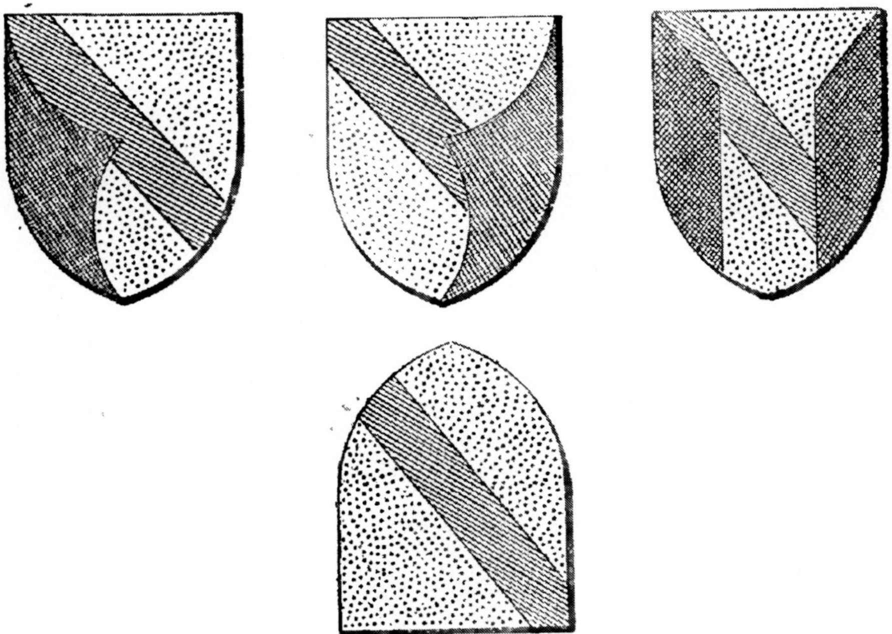

If a soldier demean himself, not while in fight, the Judge Martial may "cause his escutcheon to be pierced. If the dastard dares not come so "near the enemy to bear the strokes on his shield, he must be content to "take this piercing of some of his own side in arms."

The base of the shield was effaced with a curved line "unto him that "killeth his prisonner (humbly submitting himself) with his own hands," and with a straight line "to him that telleth lies or other false tales to his "Sovereign; for if light ears incline to light lips, harm ensueth."

To the immoral man was adjudged a gusset on the dexter side of the shield; to the intemperate one on the sinister side. "If he be faulty "in both, he shall bear both."

And finally, to the traitor was awarded the indignity of carrying his shield upside down, and this was imposed on "Sir Armery of Pavie, a "Lombard born, an unworthy captain of Calais, and traitor to King "Edward III in selling the same to Sir Geffrey Charney for 20,000 crowns"*

And so, doubtless, you will remember how the Herald, when he announces the entry of Lord Marmion, recounts his triumph over the luckless Ralph de Wilton, and says

"We saw Lord Marmion pierce his shield
And saw his saddle bare,
We saw the victor win the crest
He wears with worthy pride
And on the gibbet-tree reversed
His foeman's 'scutcheon tied"
Canto 2, *st* XI

In Meyrick's *Ancient Armour* (vol III, glossary), under "arma rever-"sata," is the following —"The chronicle of Bertrand du Guescelin has

"Oy, dist l'escuier, regardes la douleur,
Les armes de Bertrand, où tant de vigeur,
Ont pendué laidement, ainsi come trahiteur,
Et traisnée aussi au long d un quarrefort,
Et les ont enversée, et monstrant par frenour
Que Bertrand de Glaiequin a cuer de boisoeur"

Thomas Walsingham says "Inter probra vero quæ duci intulerat, "arma ejus in foro sunt publice reversata"

So you see that the Court dealt with moral and social, rather than criminal offences, and admitting that the Court itself may be out of date, we cannot deny the wisdom of it, or, alas! the need of some substitute for it, now

But in due course of time, as is the case with everything in this world, the primitive spirit of Heraldry waned, because distorted, perverted, abused, exaggerated Perhaps the very effort to secure its permanence, by the establishment of a College, hastened its dissolution, for large fees accompanied all heraldic proceedings, and these attract unworthy persons, not only dishonest, but those who try by puffing to increase their gains. And so the unhappy ambition of the Heralds in the Middle Ages to exalt their science in the eyes of the commonalty, and a less excusable desire to pander to the vanity of those who had inherited ancient armorial devices, caused them to found the most preposterous stories on the simplest "charges," to adopt the wildest legends, and the most unsupported assertions and ludicrous applications as to the arms on the shields or the badges on the standards, so that Heraldry, pure and simple, scarcely survived to the accession of the Tudors

* Guillim's *Heraldry*

That it had become, in some respects, an object of ridicule in Queen Elizabeth's time is evident; for Shakespeare, in the first scene of the *Merry Wives of Windsor*, thus plays with the luces (*i.e.* fish, pike), which were the charges of the Lucy family, one of whom had imprisoned him, it is said, for deer-stealing, and whom he characterised as Justice Shallow:—

"*Shallow.*—Sir Hugh, persuade me not: I will make a Star Chamber matter of it. If he were twenty Sir John Falstaffs, he should not abuse Robert Shallow, Esquire.

"*Slender.*—In the county of Gloster, justice of peace, and *coram.*

"*Shallow.*—Ay, Cousin Slender, and *custalorum.*

"*Slender.*—Ay, and *ratolorum* too: and a gentleman born, Master Parson, who writes himself *armigero*, in any bill, warrant, quittance, or obligation, *armigero.*

"*Shallow.*—Ay, that we do; and have done any time these three hundred years.

"*Slender.*—All his successors gone before him have done it, and all his ancestors that come after him may: they may give the dozen white luces in their coat.

"*Shallow.*—It is an old coat.

"*Sir Hugh Evans.*—The double white louses do become an old coat well: it agrees well, passant. It is a familiar beast to man, and signifies love.

"*Shallow.*—The luce is the fresh fish: the salt fish is an old coat.

"*Slender.*—I may quarter, coz?

"*Shallow.*—You may by marrying.

"*Evans.*—It is marring indeed if he quarter it.

"*Shallow.*—Not a whit.

"*Evans.*—Yes, by'r lady: if he has a quarter of your coat, there is just three skirts for yourself."

Ben Johnson, in a dialogue between Lovel and Goodstock, thus displays the decadence of chivalry. The former has offered to take Goodstock's son for his page, which the latter declares to be a desperate course of life.

"*Lovell.*—Call you that desperate, which by a line
Of institution from our ancestors
Hath been derived down to us, and received
In a succession, for the noblest way
Of breeding up our youth, in letters, arms,
Fair mien, discourses, civil exercise,
And all the blazon of a gentleman?
Where can he learn to vault, to ride, to fence,
To move his body gracefully: to speak
His language purer: or to tune his mind
Or manners more to the harmony of nature,
Than in the nurseries of nobility?

"*Goodstock.*—Ay: that was when the nursery's self was noble,
And only virtue made it, not the market.
Those titles were not vented at the drum
Or common outcry. Goodness gave the greatness,

And greatness worship. Every house became
An academy of honour, and those parts we see
Departed, in the practice, now,
Quite from the institution." *

In the sixteenth century, indeed, Heralds' College had subsided into an institution for the registering or recording of the gentry allowed to bear arms, thus providing archives invaluable for genealogical purposes, and tracing the descent or relationship for those who were possessed of or laid claim to property.

This sphere of duty had indeed not been altogether neglected in the earliest times; but it survived when the more æsthetic fell into disrepute. That such investigations might be as extensive as possible, a visitation of each county was decreed by the Earl Marshal, and confirmed by a warrant under the privy seal.

The most ancient visitation of which any account is recorded was made by Norroy King of Arms, *temp.* Henry IV., A.D. 1412; and others are said to have been made in the reigns of Edward IV. and Henry VII.

But in 1528 a commission was granted and executed by Thomas Benoilt, Clarenceux for the counties of Gloucester, Worcester, Oxford, Wiltshire, Berks, and Stafford; and from that period visitations were regularly made every twenty-five or thirty years. "It is probable," says Dallaway, "that by them the ordinance of parochial registers was suggested "to Cromwell, Lord Essex, the Vicar-General, who in 1536 caused his "mandate to be circulated for that purpose." In 1555 a similar commission was issued; and in 1566 the freedom of a Pursuivant from arrest was contested and proved.

In 1622 the Earl Marshal contested before the Star Chamber his right to hold a "Court of Chivalry," and obtained a judgment in his favour. Indeed, so pleased was the King (James I.), that he issued a commission under the great seal, renewing and confirming all his former privileges, and the peculiar jurisdiction of his court.

During the Commonwealth the Court was, as I have said, not discontinued; but after the Restoration, the decline of the Court of Chivalry, which had been gradual in former years, was hastened by the growing dislike of the canon law, and the arbitrary decisions and penalties which frequently occurred on very frivolous excuses. Mr. Hyde, afterwards Lord Chancellor Clarendon, proposed its dissolution, saying "that a citizen of "good quality, a merchant, was by that Court ruined in his estate, and his "body imprisoned, for calling a swan a goose." It was suspected that he thus alluded to a near relative, who had incurred the censure of the Heralds in their visitation in 1623, and been branded as a usurper of armorial distinctions.

* *New Inn*, act i., scene iii.

The effort was, however, unsuccessful, for the Court dragged on its existence for many years, the last cause concerning the bearing of arms being that between *Blount* and *Blunt*, in 1720.

But a significance was still attributed to Heraldry, and even an unintentional and imaginary reference thereto was likely to result in serious consequences, for Bishop Burnet, in the *History of His Own Times*, tells us that "on November 6th, 1684, at the Rolls Chapel, I chose for my "text these words: 'Save me from the lion's mouth; thou hast heard me "'from the horns of the unicorns.' I made no reflection in my thoughts "on the lion and the unicorn as being the two supporters of the King's "escutcheon—for I ever hated all points of that sort as a profanation of "Scripture—but I shewed how Popery might be compared to the lion's "mouth, thus opened to devour us, and I compared our former deliverance "from the extremities of danger to the being on the horn of a rhinoceros; "and thus leading me to the subject of the day, I mentioned that wish of "King James against any of his posterity that should endeavour to bring "that religion in amongst us. This was immediately carried to the Court, "but it only raised more anger against me, for nothing could be made of "it. They talked most of the choice of the text, as levelled against the "King's coat-of-arms. That had never been once in my thoughts. Lord "Keeper North diverted the King from doing anything on account of my "sermon, and so the matter slept until the end of term. And then North "writ to the Master of the Rolls that the King considered the Chapel of "the Rolls as one of his own Chapels; and since he looked on me as a "person disaffected to the Government, and had for that reason dismissed "me from his own service, he therefore required him not to suffer me to "serve any longer in that Chapel, and thus all my service in the Chapel "was now stopped."

Heralds' College has, however, even in its more degenerate days, contained worthies who have shed a lustre on the institution, and are also ornaments of the general literature of Great Britain.

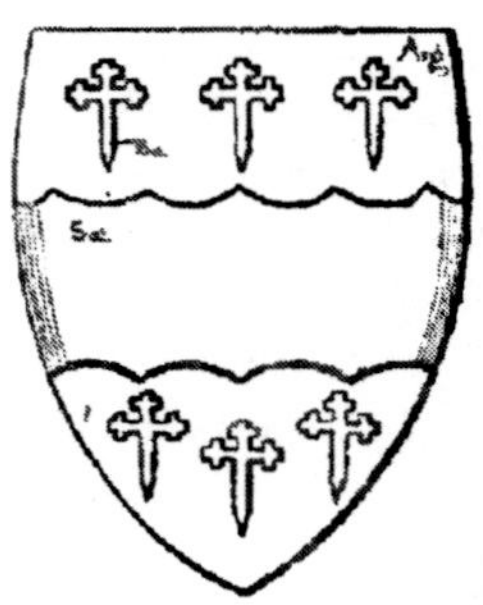

Camden.

Earliest, and highest perhaps, stands the learned Camden, the son of a paper-stainer in the Old Bailey, and educated at Christ's Hospital, St. Paul's School, and Magdalen College, Oxford. He was head-master of Westminster School, 1592; Clarenceux King of Arms, 1597, "by the singular favour of Queen "Elizabeth." His *Britannia*, his *Annals of Queen Elizabeth*, and his *Remains concerning Britain*, will ever enable posterity to ratify what was said of him by his contemporaries, that he was "worthily admired for his great learning, "wisdom, and virtue, throughout the Christian world."

Sir William Dugdale, author of the celebrated *Monasticon* and the *Antiquities of Warwickshire*, is another equally remarkable man. Born in 1605, the friend of Sir Christopher Hatton and Sir Henry Spelman, he became Chester Herald, 1644. He attended Charles I. at the battle of Edgehill, and remained with him till the surrender of Oxford to the Parliament, 1646. Charles II. made him first Norroy, and finally Garter King of Arms; and he died 1686, aged 80.

Dugdale

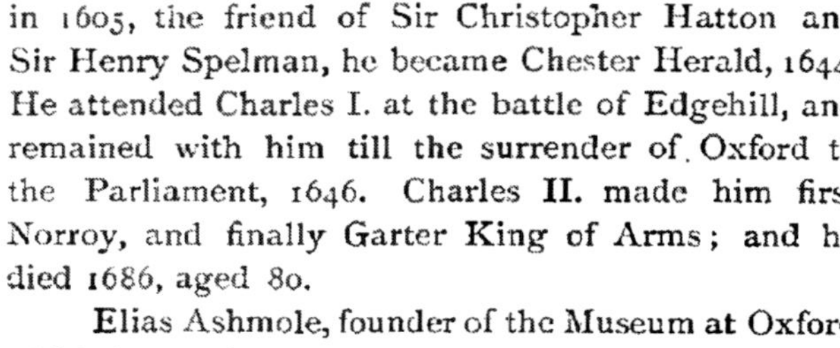

Elias Ashmole, founder of the Museum at Oxford which bears his name, was another. He was the son of Simon Ashmole, a saddler at Lichfield, an improvident man, who, it is said, "loved war better than "making saddles and bridles."

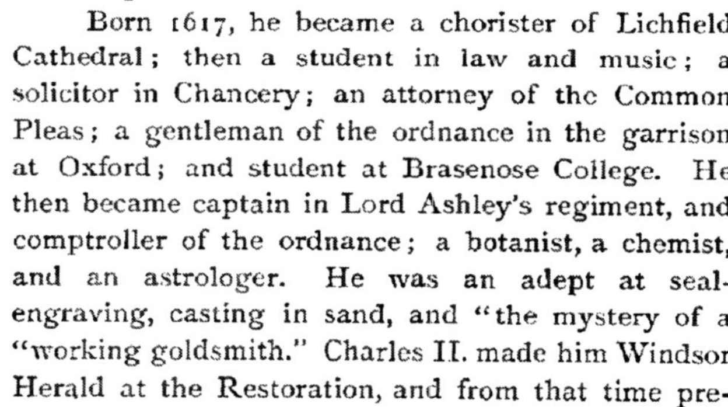

Born 1617, he became a chorister of Lichfield Cathedral; then a student in law and music; a solicitor in Chancery; an attorney of the Common Pleas; a gentleman of the ordnance in the garrison at Oxford; and student at Brasenose College. He then became captain in Lord Ashley's regiment, and comptroller of the ordnance; a botanist, a chemist, and an astrologer. He was an adept at seal-engraving, casting in sand, and "the mystery of a "working goldsmith." Charles II. made him Windsor Herald at the Restoration, and from that time preferment followed preferment, he becoming a barrister, F.R.S., M.D.; refusing twice the office of Garter, and the honour of representing Lichfield in Parliament. He died 1692, aged 76.

Ashmole

Edmondson.

Guillim.

And others there are of whom I can only give a passing mention: John Guillim, the author of the famous *Display of Heraldry*: John Edmondson, Mowbray Herald, also author of one of the standard works on this subject: Sir John Vanbrugh, Clarenceux King of Arms, a well-known dramatic author, and the architect of Blenheim, Castle Howard, Grimsthorpe, and other very massive and ponderous edifices; for whom a wag proposed this epitaph:—

> "Lie heavy on him, earth, for he
> Laid many a heavy load on thee."

And lastly, Edmund Lodge, Lancaster Herald, whose name will ever be associated in our minds with the most beautiful and interesting series of *Portraits of Illustrious British Personages* ever published.

One of the fraternity, William Oldys, Norroy King of Arms, *temp.* George II., was author of the life of Sir Walter Raleigh, and several others, in the *Biographia Britannica*; but he was also the author of a pretty Anacreontic, very familiar to us all, which he wrote on a fly drinking out of his cup (I am afraid I must not say of tea, for he was anything but a teetotaller):

"Busy, curious, thirsty fly,
Drink with me, and drink as I:
Freely welcome to my cup,
Couldst thou sip and sip it up.
Make the most of life you may:
Life is short, and wears away.

"Both alike are mine and thine,
Hastening quick to their decline:
Thine's a summer, mine's no more,
Though repeated to three score.
Three score summers, when they're gone,
Will appear as short as one."

Old and New London, Walter Thornbury.

But I am not going to dwell on the more prosaic side of our subject, though, perhaps, in this matter-of-fact age it would be deemed the more practical and useful.

There are some who treat with lofty contempt the idea of any hereditary transmission of intellectual riches, but I never heard of any scepticism as to a similar succession to earthly wealth; and if any time you should notice your own surname in some published list of those who have died intestate, and for whose estate the next-of-kin is invited to apply, you may be seized with a greater genealogical interest in your own progenitors than you have yet experienced; and should you be fired with a commendable enthusiasm to prove your descent to the illustrious deceased, let me advise you to pay a visit to Heralds' College, now situated in Queen Victoria Street, London, where you will find every assistance from the present York Herald, Alfred Scott Gatty, Esq., the able and genial son of the present Sub-Dean of York Minster.

But I would rather dwell upon the more visionary, perhaps, but more elevating side of the subject—upon the primitive Heraldry, the Heraldry begotten by, and expressing grand, true, noble aspirations for goodness, purity, courage—the Heraldry of York Minster. For that is indeed the Heraldry which adorns its walls and glistens in its windows; and in the varied beauty of its colouring, and the quaint mediævalism of its devices, seems to me at least to speak with a thousand tongues, and to say:—
"*Whatever* thy age, *whatever* thy surroundings, strive to keep thyself
"unspotted from the world. Be *brave*, *true*, *noble*, *loving*, *pure*, *humble*; fear
"NOTHING but dishonour, and *no one* but GOD; and let death find thee
"striving against wrong, in whatever shape it may be around thee, and so
"a faithful Soldier of the Cross."

Doubtless this is not "a language understanded of the people;" a dead language very likely, but a *genuine language* nevertheless—a language as true as that which in cuneiform characters or quaint hieroglyphics adorns the cliffs of Sinai, or the walls of Thebes and Nineveh; a language as true as that in the pages of Thucydides or Æschylus, Cicero or Horace; a language not speaking, perhaps, nineteenth century truths in nineteenth century phraseology, but that which men, then as now, were trying to understand and to communicate, and which then, perhaps, they comprehended as much as men do now, or will at any future time.

But there is all the difference between these coats-of-arms and the arms which adorn the monuments which cumber our aisles, or which are painted on the panels of carriages, or engraved on plate, at the present day.

Just the difference between the Latin of Cicero and the Latin of the chemist or the botanist—the one the natural expression, the other the pedantic adaptation.

Now you can no more learn this language in one chapter than you can learn any other language, or even the grammar thereof.

I can but satisfy you that it is a language which perhaps you have never realized before, and very briefly set before you some of the characters thereof written on our Minster walls and windows, and mention one or two incidents connected therewith as illustrations. I must leave you to decide for yourselves whether you think it worth your while to pursue the subject any further.

What should I get by so doing? you may ask. Well, I answer, a mine of interest, full of the sweetest poetry and romance, and a more thorough knowledge of English history, of the motives and causes which underlie that history, and of the principles of a philosophy founded on, developing, and in harmony with the principles of God's Word—a philosophy which was not altogether fatuous, which had its day (though like everything else its day was very brief), and which has been succeeded by numberless similar efforts, which may, perhaps, have been more pretentious, but I doubt whether more successful.

Heraldic charges or devices were originally emblazoned upon the shield only, which was made of wood and covered with hide—in Latin, *scutum;* hence the word "escutcheon."

In the thirteenth century they were also displayed upon the surcoat, a long white garment of linen or silk, without sleeves, intended to protect the wearer from the great heat of the sun upon his armour; hence "cote-armure" or "coat-of-arms." So Chaucer speaks in his *Book of Fame*—

> A vesture
> Which men clepe a cote armure,
> Embroidered wonderly riche,
> As though thei weren not yleche
> But though will I, (so mought I thrive)
> Be abouten to descrive
> All these armes that they weren
> For to me were impossible
> Men might make of hem a Bible "

In the succeeding century it was cut short in front and called a "cyclas," and eventually the hinder skirt was also reduced, when it was called a "jupon" This in the fifteenth century was succeeded by the tabard, not unlike the jupon, but it had short sleeves, on which the arms were also emblazoned Every knight had also his banner (differently shaped, according to his degree) similarly adorned, while on his helmet he carried his crest, a separate device, of later origin than coats-of-arms, but esteemed of even greater honour

Badges or figures totally distinct from crests or arms, seem to have been assumed very much at pleasure

Geoffry Martel, whom I have already mentioned, adopted the *planta genesta* or *plant genet*, the yellow broom, a sprig of which he used to wear in his cap, and from which his family derived their name of Plantagenet

Eleanor of Provence, on her marriage with Henry III, seems to have introduced the Provence rose into England Her eldest son, Edward I, very naturally adopted that which had by its beauty so completely eclipsed the wild rose of England He assumed as his badge, "A rose or, stalked "proper" And the tomb of his brother, her second son, Edmund, surnamed Crouchback, Earl of Lancaster, was carved with red roses

His children, Thomas and Henry, inherited the county of Provence, and the latter, the first Duke of Lancaster, bore on his seal a branch of roses beside his crest On the death of Maude, his eldest daughter, the rights of Provence devolved on John of Gaunt, who had married Blanche, her younger sister He bequeathed to St Paul's Cathedral his bed, "powdered with roses" When he thus adopted the rose of Provence, *i e* the red rose, his youngest brother, Edmund Langley, Duke of York, assumed the white rose (which Palliser says was derived from the Castle of Clifford)

Sandford, in his *Genealogical History of England*, simply mentions the fact, without assigning any reason This, however, explains the scene in Shakespeare's *Henry VI* (part I, scene iv), where Richard Plantagenet, Earl of Cambridge, grandson of Edmund, and Beaufort, Duke of Somerset, grandson of John of Gaunt and Catherine Swinford, are introduced walking in the Temple gardens Henry VI was at that time childless, and the succession in doubt, viz, whether the descendant of John of Gaunt or of his brother should succeed

Richard says, with perhaps a sneering allusion to the fact that Catherine Swinford's children were born before marriage, and legitimatised by Act of Parliament afterwards,—

> "Let him that is a TRUE-BORN gentleman,
> And stands upon the honour of his birth,
> If he suppose that I have pleaded truth
> From off this briar pluck a *white* rose with me"

To which Beaufort, Duke of Somerset, rejoins (I suppose insinuating his belief in the story that Edmund Crouchback had been really the eldest son of Henry III, and suppressed on account of his humped back in favour of his brother Edward, and that therefore Richard had no *true* right to the throne) —

> "Let him that is no coward, nor no flatterer,
> But dare maintain the party of the truth,
> Pluck a *red* rose from off this thorn with me"

The Prince of Wales' plume is another badge, erroneously attributed to the plume of the King of Bohemia, said to have been taken by the Black Prince at the battle of Cresy, with the motto "Ich dien," translated "I serve," a token of royal humility

Really, the ostrich plume was originally borne by King Stephen, who adopted two devices, one a Sagittarius, under which sign of the Zodiac he had entered England and triumphed by the aid of his archers, and the other a plume of three ostrich feathers, with this motto, "Vi nulla invertitur ordo," *i e* "My determination once taken, nothing alters it," illustrated by the stability of the quill, which, once fixed, will withstand great pressure from the wind, and if bent a little while the blast lasts, is not easily broken

This was not only his policy but his character He had perhaps reasonably assumed that when his cousin, Prince Henry, was drowned, Henry I, his uncle, would recognise him as heir to the throne Instead of which he sent for his daughter Matilda, the widowed Empress, and compelled the Barons of England to swear fealty to her, and married her to Geoffry Martel Stephen therefore determined to gain his legitimate rights, as being male heir, female succession being unknown in England at that time, and, in spite of the tremendous odds against him, to acquire the kingdom He did so, and,—notwithstanding the vigorous opposition of Robert of Gloucester, Matilda's natural brother and general,—attained the throne and remained King of England to his death He is not generally a very attractive personality in history, but his character is thus very favourably drawn by the historian Stowe —"This was a noble man and hardy, of "passing comely favour and personage—he excelled in martial policy, "gentleness and liberality towards all men, and although he had continual "war, yet did he never burden his Commons with exactions"

The ostrich plume was adopted by Edward III. as a badge, and carried by all the Plantagenets. The motto does not belong to the feathers, but to the *title* of Prince of Wales.

When Edward I. killed Llewellyn, the last independent Prince of Wales, and hanged his brother David of Snowdon, whom he had taken captive at Shrewsbury, he annexed the Principality to the English Crown, made his infant son prince, but gave him the Welsh motto, "Eich dyn," *your man*, which he was to bear, to remind himself and the people that he was not an independent, but a suzerain Prince to England.

Three single feathers, their quills passing through scrolls with the motto, appear on shields on the tomb of the Black Prince at Canterbury, and as such we know them at the present day. All the sons of Edward III. used the ostrich feather as a badge, differenced in various ways. On the tomb of Prince Arthur, eldest son of Henry VIII., at Worcester Cathedral, three feathers, united, are thrust through one scroll. Prince Henry, eldest son of James I., thrust the three feathers through his prince's coronet in place of the scroll, as the ensign of the Prince of Wales.

Edmond Langley (first Duke of York, fifth son of Edward III.) adopted the falcon, a *white* falcon having been the device of his grandmother, Isabella de Valois, daughter of Philip IV. King of France, from whom also his father Edward derived his claim to quarter the fleurs-de-lis of France in his arms, and his claims to the French Crown. The hawk upon the fist was a mark of great nobility. Harold, in the Bayeux tapestry, is thus depicted. So sacred was the bird esteemed, that we find it prohibited in the ancient laws for any one to give his hawk or his sword as part of his ransom. To the falcon Edward added the fetter-

lock, which was symbolical of his caution. "Hic, hæc, hoc taceatis," he said to his sons; when they asked its meaning—Be silent and quiet, as God knoweth what may "come to pass." Or perhaps he may have inherited the falcon from his father, who adopted the *golden* falcon (as you may see in the east window of the Chapter-house), because Louis of Bavaria, Emperor of Germany, created him Vicar of the empire.

Richard II. adopted a white hart, "lodged," *i.e.* kneeling, with a crown about his neck, and a chain of gold, as you may see on the cap of the pillar at the entrance of the South Choir aisle.

This he is supposed to have adopted from his mother Joan, "the Fair "Maid of Kent," daughter of Thomas Wake, created Earl of Kent, "per "cincturam gladii," by Edward III. The Earl's cognisance was a white hind; and I shall have much to say about him and his family when in another chapter we come to speak of the arms of Wake in the Minster. I must also defer the further consideration of the royal badges until I can deal at length with the *Royal Heraldry* of the Minster.

Badges also sometimes expressed the name, and were called "rebus." An ash tree growing out of a tun, Ashton; an arrow or bird-bolt through a tun or barrel, for Bolton; a deer and a ring, for Dering. On the organ-screen a hind's head may be noticed immediately under one of the niches. This is the rebus of Hyndley, master-mason, 1479, the time of its erection.

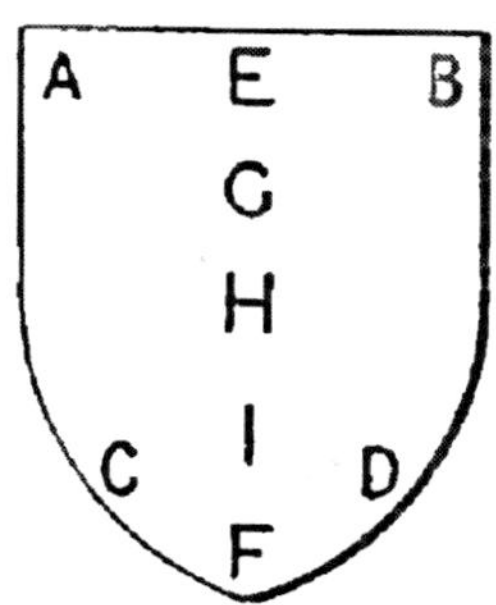

But the shield was the principal exponent of arms, and was divided into nine points:—

A. Dexter chief	D. Sinister base	G. Honour point
B. Sinister chief	E. Middle chief	H. Tesse point
C. Dexter base	F. Middle base	I. Nombril point

The surface of the shield was called "the field." The colours which covered or adorned the shield are called "tinctures," and are divided into two metals, five colours, and eight furs, each of them having originally a moral significance.

The metals are silver and gold, or *argent* and *or*, the former representing innocency and humility, the latter worth and generosity. Of the seven colours—*azure* (blue), charity; *gules* (red), courage; *sable* (black), grief and prudence; *vert* (green), youth; and so on. *Purpure*, *orange* or *tinne* or *tawny*, and *sanguin* or blood colour, completing them.

The introduction of furs into Heraldry probably arose from the ancient custom of covering shields with the skins of beasts, which formed a valuable additional protection against arrows and other missiles. But fur seems also to have been from very early times an emblem of honour or dignity. There were eight furs, but they are really varieties of two. The one the *ermine*, *i.e.* the skin of the "mustela erminea,"—a sort of weasel, which, brown in summer, is white in winter, and its tail always black. Ermine is indeed generally worn as it is depicted in Heraldry, white, with the black tail on each skin. The other a delicate white and grey fur, called *vair* in French; and there seems to have been two sorts, the great and the little, or the *gros-vair* and the *menu-vair*, or *miniver* as it was corrupted into English.

We have all been acquainted from childhood with the story of Cinderella and her glass slipper, and often thought, perhaps, what a strange and uncomfortable covering it must have been for her foot. The fact is that the *Cenerentola* is an ancient tradition of Pisa, where the old witch clad

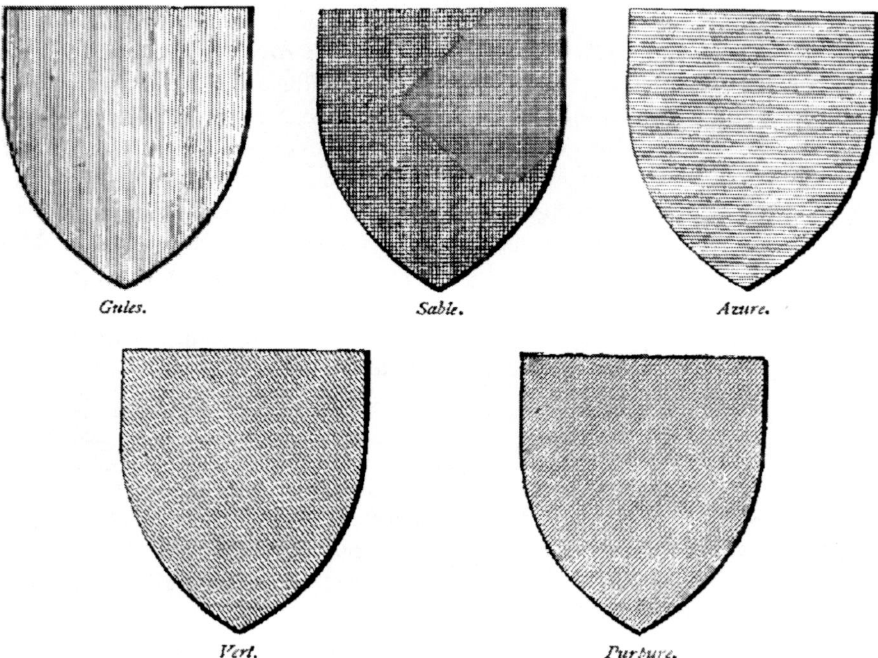

Gules. *Sable.* *Azure.*

Vert. *Purpure.*

the neglected damsel of Tuscany in rich apparel, with slippers of cloth of gold. But it was adopted by the people of Brittany, having probably penetrated there through the songs of minstrels; and the courtly Frenchmen arrayed the heroine in slippers of fur—*menu-vair*—the most delicate and honourable covering for her feet; but the legend being transcribed, *vair* became *verre, i.e.* glass. Vair is always depicted by alternate escutcheons of blue and white, which at a distance would give a silvery-grey appearance.

In these days, when fur is seldom worn—and only those kinds which are, or which profess to be, brought from other countries are valued—it is curious to notice how much the furs of our own native island were used and appreciated in days gone by. Riley, in his *Memorials of London Life*, gives two charters granted by Edward III., viz., first, 1327, and thirty-ninth, 1365, addressed to "our well-beloved men of the city of London called Pellipers" (or Pilterers: the Church of St. Mary Axe was called St. Mary Pelliper, from a plot of ground near, where the Pellipers dressed their skins). In

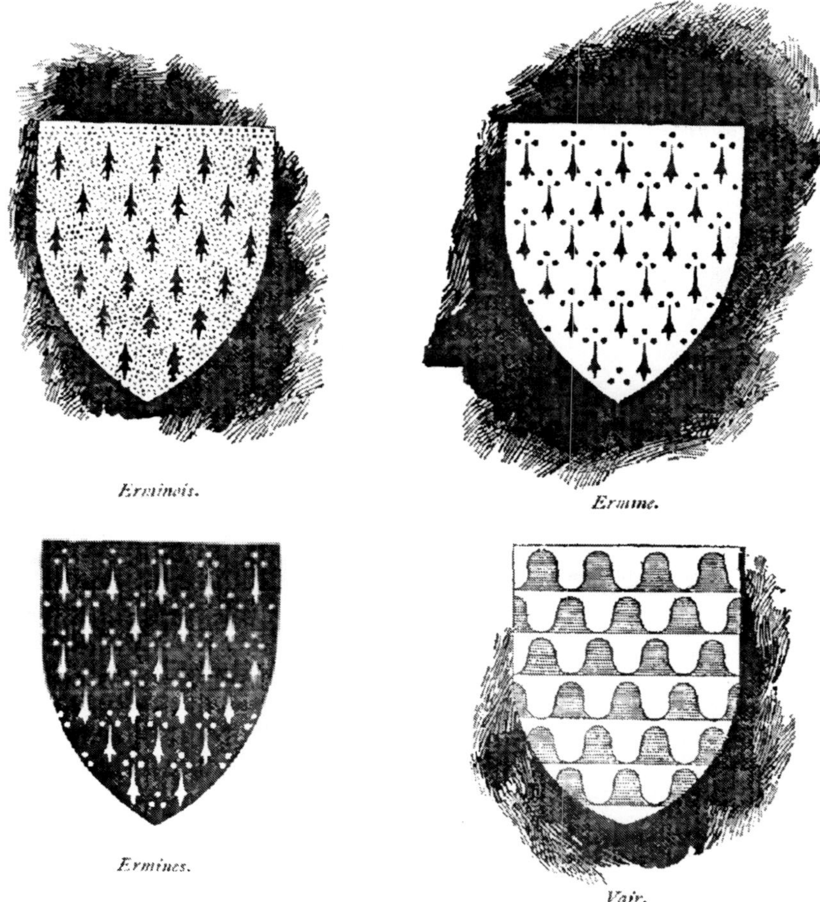

Erminois. *Ermine.*

Ermines. *Vair.*

the former it is stipulated that every fur (*i.e.* set of furs) should contain a certain measure, viz., every fur of minever of eight tiers should contain 120 bellies; a fur of bishes (a fur made from some part of the skin of the hind) of seven tiers, 60 beasts; a fur of popelle (*i.e.* the back of the squirrel in spring) of seven tiers, 60 beasts; a fur of stranlynge (*i.e.* fur of the squirrel between Michaelmas and winter) of six tiers, 22 beasts; a fur of scurella (*i.e.* squirrels of other kinds than those named), 60 beasts; a fur of beaveret or lambskin should be $1\frac{1}{4}$ ells in length and $1\frac{1}{2}$ in breadth in one part, and one ell in breadth in the middle of the fur. No pheliper (or frippever, dealer in second-hand clothes) is to sell old furs otherwise than as taken off the garment.

In the second charter it is "ordained" that old and new materials are not to be worked together; that no one shall mingle bellies of calabre (an inferior sort of fur) with furs of puree (*i.e.* cleaned fur), or minever, or bishes; that no one shall mingle roskyn (*i.e.* the fur of the squirrel in summer) with popelle; also that the bellies of calabre are to be made up in their natural way, *i.e.* that the belly must have its black side, so that the people may not be taken in. The penalty for non-observance of the above was to be fourteen days' imprisonment in Newgate; on coming out of prison a fine of 13*s.* 4*d.* to the Chamber of the Guildhall, and 6*s.* 8*d.* to the trade.

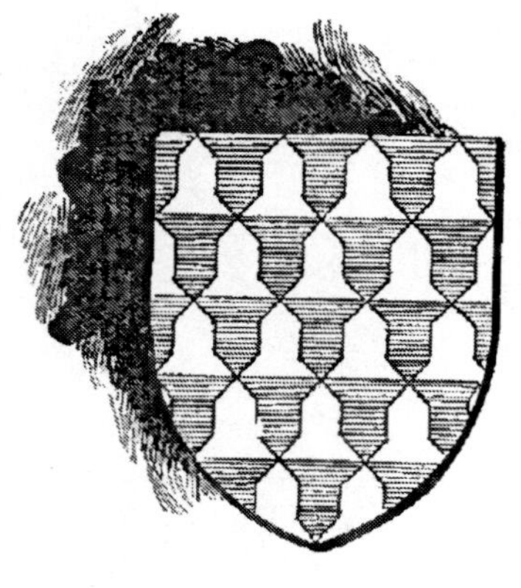

Vair.

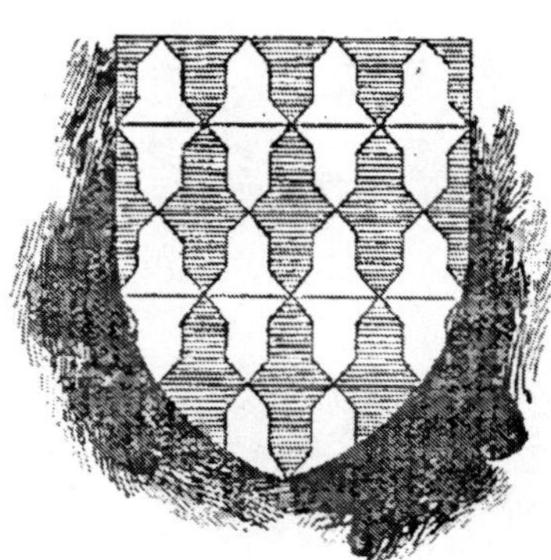

Counter Vair.

No furs also were to be beaten in the streets; and no fellmongers should carry any furs of wildewerk (*i.e.* fur of wild rabbits) out of the city before the rulers of the trade had surveyed them. No one to sell furs of greywerk (*i.e.* badger skin) from Flanders before surveyed by the trade, because "for the most part so stuffed with chalk that persons can hardly "know them." If any dealer, native or stranger, selling ermynes lettis (a kind of grey fur from Leltowe, of Liltmania) or greywerk, shall make any pakkure (*i.e.* padding) but what is good and lawful, he shall be arrested and the fault redressed.

All freemen of the trade to dwell in Walbroke, Cornhill, Bogerowe (Budge Row—so called from the sale of the fur called budge there prepared, lambskins or goatskins), and not in any foreign streets (*i.e.* not frequented by the trade), that the owners may be able to oversee them.

In the 9th of Edward I., 1281, it is provided and commanded that no woman of the city shall go to market, or in the King's highway, out of her house, with a hood furred with other than lambskin or rabbitskin, on pain of losing her hood to the use of the sheriffs. Ladies who wear furred capes may have on the hoods such furs as they think proper; and this because the regeatresses (females who sold articles by retail), nurses and other servants, and women of loose life, bedizen themselves, and wear hoods furred with gros-vair and minever, in guise of good ladies.

By 24th of Edward III., 1351, it is provided and ordered by the mayor, sheriffs, aldermen, and commoners of the said city, that women of immoral character shall not "be so daring as to be attired by day or night in any "kind of vesture trimmed with fur, such as menevyer, grey-purree of "stranlyng, popelle of squirrels, bys (*i.e.* brown hue) of rabbits or hares, or "any other manner of noble budge, or lined with seradale, bokerames, "samytes (samite, a rich texture of silk), or any other noble lining," on pain of forfeiture.

In the 3rd of Richard II., 1382, it is ordered that such women shall have and use hoods of ray only, and should not wear any manner of budge, or perreie (purree), or revers (some kind of fur specially used for trimmings and linings)—any one transgressing to be brought to the compter, and the furs forfeited.

Edward II., 1310, forbids tailors to scour fur in the Chepe—"that so "the great lords and good folks passing through . . . might not by "such manner of scouring be disturbed or delayed in passing." They are to be scoured in some "dead lane, where no great lords are passing, either "going or coming, and whereby no dispute may arise."

The ermine holds, perhaps, the chief place in popular estimation amongst furs, not so much from the finish of its quality, but because of its assumed significance.

Anne of Bretagne (says Palliser, p. 113), 1513, Queen of Charles VIII., and afterwards of Louis XII., adopted the ermine, the ancient hereditary device of her duchy, with the motto, "Malo mori quam fœdari"—"Better "to die than be sullied"—or as the French render it, "Plutot mourir "que souiller."

Anne appears more frequently to have used the motto of the Breton order of the ermine, "A ma vie." It was placed on the herse erected at Nantes after her death to receive her heart; and on a fountain of the market-place of Tours may still be seen on one side the porcupine of Louis XII., and on the other the ermine of Queen Anne, with the motto, "A ma vie."

After the death of Charles VIII. she encircled her arms with the cordeliere or cord of St. Francis, which she afterwards converted into an order for widow ladies.

The Chevaliers de la Cordeliere were instituted 1498. Anne adopted this name in honour of St. Francis, the patron saint of her father. The badge, a silver cord of true-lovers' knots, with large knots between, was worn around their arms. The motto, a rebus, "J'ai le corps delié."

Ferdinand I., 1494, the illegitimate son of Alfonso—when the Duke of Sessa, who had joined the party of John of Anjou, son of René, was in his power—refused to put him to death, but condemned him to imprisonment, saying that he could not imbrue his hands in the blood of his relations. He then took for his device the ermine, surrounded with a wall of mud, with the motto, "Malo mori quam fœdari." In a MS. book of Ferdinand, the motto "Probanda" is used with the ermine, also "Nunquam," never.

Sylvanus Morgan, in his *Sphere of Gentry*, says, "The ermine is a "creature of so pure a nature that it will choose rather to be taken than "defile its skin." It is said that hunters surround it with a wall of mud, which it will not attempt to cross, and therefore becomes an easy prey.

Hence the ermine is the emblem of purity and of honour without stain. The robes of royal and noble persons are lined with ermine, to signify the internal purity that should regulate their conduct. I have been given the following stanza, without name, expressing the same idea:—

"To miry places me the hunters drive,
That I my robes of purest white may stain;
Then yield I, nor will further strive,
For spotless death, ere spotted life, is gain."

Joan of Navarre, daughter of Charles II., King of Navarre, and second wife of Henry IV., King of England, also bore this badge. The canopy of her tomb at Canterbury is dignified with this device—the ermine collared and chained, with the motto, "A tamperance," subscribed in golden characters.*

I should exhaust your patience, and to little purpose, if I were to go into all the ways of dividing the shield—per fesse, per saltire, per bend, &c.—and all the varieties of lines used—engrailed, indented, wavy, dancetté, embattled, and what not.

I will not trouble you with a long dissertation about ordinaries and subordinaries, blazoning or marshalling (the former of which signifies the right description of the arms, the latter the correct arrangement); nor need I dwell at length upon impaling, quartering, and inescutcheons, suffice it to say that the first describes the position of a wife's arms (if one of many children) on her husband's shield, the last the position thereof if she were an heiress (*i.e.* had no brothers), and the second the incorporation of her arms by her children with their father's coat.

---

* *Sandford's Genealogical History.*

It may interest the ladies to know that their predecessors in those ancient days carried their arms, when unmarried, not on a shield, but on a lozenge or diamond shaped figure, said to be emblematical of female worth, either because intended to represent a diamond or jewel, or because it was composed of two equilateral triangles, the most perfect mathematical figures, as well as having a very sacred significance. Others have said that they were intended to represent spindles used in spinning: many estates, Blount says in his *Tenures*, being held in "*petit serjeantry*" of the King by presenting him "fusillam fili crudi."

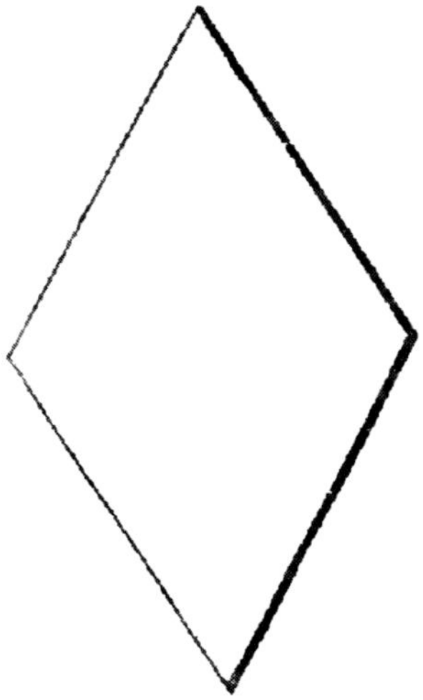

Probably this phrase, "petit serjeantry," is new to many. It refers to the ancient tenure of land, and was used when a man held his land of the King to yield him yearly a bow, or a sword, or a dagger, or a pair of gloves, or such small things belonging to war.

So the Duke of Marlborough holds his property on which his palace of Blenheim was built, and which was formerly the royal manor of Woodstock, in petit serjeantry, viz., by presenting to the sovereign every year, on August 2nd, the anniversary of the battle of Blenheim, a Flemish flag. And the Duke of Wellington holds Strathfieldsaye in like manner, viz., by presenting on June 18th, the anniversary of the battle of Waterloo, a French flag.

There was also "grand serjeantry," which Spelman calls "the highest "and most illustrious feudal service," *i.e.* when a man holds his lands and tenements of the King by such services as he ought to do in his proper person to the King—carry his banner or lance, lead his army, bear his sword before him at his coronation, or be his server, butler, or carver.

John Baker, says Madox, held certain lands in Kent for holding the King's head in the ship which carried him in his passage between Dover and Whitesand (Lord Lyttleton's *Life of Henry II.*). So you see no age and no quality have ever been exempt from that particular inconvenience so well known to all travellers who have to cross the "silver streak" which separates us from our foreign neighbours.

I have been told that it is a common proverbial expression in France, when a property has passed to an heiress, to speak of it as "tombe en "quenouille," *i.e.* fallen to the spindle.

And this expression refers to an incident so deeply interesting and so honourable to all parties concerned that I must detain you to relate it, feeling sure that the ladies will be quite satisfied with such an explanation of the origin of the peculiar figure on which they bear their arms.

Bertrand du Guesclin, born 1320, was the most famous French warrior of his age. As he was not a great baron, with a body of vassals at his command, he joined the Free Companions of France, as they were called, a body of between 50,000 and 60,000 men, soldiers of fortune, accustomed to desultory warfare, and always ready to act as mercenaries for those who were willing to pay them. Bertrand du Guesclin soon attained a high command amongst them, and fought on the side of Charles and of France against the English.

When Rennes was besieged by the Duke of Lancaster, 1356, he forced his way with a handful of men into the town, and successfully defended it till June, 1357, when the siege was raised. At the siege of Dinan, 1359, he engaged in single combat with Sir Thomas Canterbury, captain in the army of the Duke of Lancaster (John of Gaunt), at whose intercession he spared his defeated foeman's life. In 1364, in conjunction with Boucicaut, he recovered Mantes and Meulan from the King of Navarre; and in May of the same year he defeated the Navarrese under Captol de Buch at Cocherel. Created now Marshal of Normandy and Count of Longueville, he commanded at the battle of Auray, where Charles of Blois was killed, his army defeated, and he himself taken prisoner by Sir John Chandos. (*James' History of the Black Prince*, vol. ii. 357.)

A sum of 100,000 francs was demanded as his ransom, and this was willingly paid by the Pope, the King of France, and the aspirant to the throne of Castile (Henry of Transtamare), for the deliverance of a man who not long before had appeared as one of the poorest and most insignificant squires in the train of Charles of Blois. By them he was placed at the head of a considerable company of the French knights and men-at-arms, joined to a large force of the Free Companies, with the object of dethroning the savage tyrant "Pedro the Cruel," and making his brother, Henry of Transtamare, King of Castile in his place.

It is impossible to describe the enthusiasm which not only pervaded France, but the whole principality of Aquitaine. L'Ambrecicout, Calverly, Sir Walter Hewet, Sir John Devereux, Sir Matthew Gournay, Sir John Nevill, and several other distinguished knights, with a large train of men-at-arms, joined the adventurers under Du Guesclin. The people flocked round his standard, hailing him as their deliverer. Knights and nobles abandoned the court of the hated and dreaded Pedro, and swelled the train of his rival.

Don Pedro's cause seemed lost. In his extremity he appealed to Edward III. on the alliance which he had already formed with him. And the Black Prince, generously believing that Don Pedro had already been chastened sufficiently for his past conduct, came to his assistance with John of Gaunt (who afterwards married his daughter) and a large body of men.

The great name of the Black Prince acted like magic, and 10,000 men of the Free Companies deserted and joined his standard; the Lord of Albret offered 1,000 lances, and the Comte de Foix promised support. The high tide of popularity which had carried Don Henry to the summit of power began to ebb; and when Du Guesclin and the Black Prince confronted each other at Najarra, the former had but a collection of 60,000 men to face 30,000 trained and disciplined warriors of the latter.

The battle was obstinately contested on both sides, and at last decided for the English. At the close of the day Don Pedro, heated with pursuit, and dripping with gore, galloped up to the Black Prince, and springing from his charger to the ground, thanked him for a victory which would restore him to his throne. "Give thanks and praise to God, and not to me," replied the chivalrous Prince, "for from Him, not me, you have received "the victory."

Amongst many prisoners whom Don Pedro, but for the interference of the Black Prince, would have immediately massacred, was Bertrand du Guesclin. In Meyrick's *Ancient Armour* (vol. i. p. 106) the following stanza is given :—

> "Bertrand de Glayequin fie ou champ pleiner
> Ou il assaut Anglois a un martel d'acier
> Tout ainsy les about come fait le Bouchier."

"Bertrand de Glayequin was everywhere in the field, where he assaulted "the English with a martel of steel, and beat them down as a butcher "would." The "martel de fer" had one blunt projection, while the other was sharpened to an edge, often to a point.

Some days after, seeing Du Guesclin standing near, the Black Prince called him, and asked after his health. "I never was better, my Lord," replied the Breton, "and well I ought to be, for though I am your prisoner, "I feel myself the most honoured knight in the world; and I will tell you "why. They say in France, and other countries too, that you are afraid "of me, and dare not set me free."

"Ha, Sir Bertrand," replied the Prince, "do you think, then, for your "renown I keep you in prison? No, by St. George! Pay a ransom of "100,000 francs," he continued, laughing, "and you are free."

His councillors, standing near, and knowing the power of Du Guesclin, thought that the jest need not be carried any further; but the Prince was firm, declined to swerve from his word, and allowed the bold Breton to depart, in order to seek his ransom in his own country.

Bertrand du Guesclin was himself poor, and his countrymen terribly reduced by the war. The joy of their faces changed into blank despair when they heard the terms of his liberty, and they hung their heads in dismay as to whence they should raise so large a sum. But then, as is always the case when the men are cast down and desponding, the women came to the rescue. "Fear not," they exclaimed, brandishing their distaffs, "we will spin him out"—meaning, of course, that by their industry and skill they would soon produce and sell enough yarn to provide the greater part of the sum required. They set to work at once. Charles V. contributed a large portion. Before the close of the year 1367 the money was paid, and Du Guesclin once more drew his sword in favour of Henry of Transtamare for the throne of Castile.

Surely such gallant and patriotic deeds deserve commemoration; and the following refrain of an old Breton ballad shews that it was speedily enshrined in that surest token of national appreciation—a nation's song:

"Filez, filez, femmes de la Bretayne;
Filez vos quenouilles de lin;
Pour rendre à la France et à l'Espagne
Bertrand du Guesclin."

Of which the following is a rough rendering:—

"Women of Brittany, spin, spin again;
Your flaxen distaffs spin;
To give to France and unto Spain
Bertrand du Guesclin."

While the charming poem which I also append, from the graceful and cultured pen of one of our own Yorkshire poets, the late Lord Houghton, shews that the capacity to appreciate gallant deeds, even though they be "ancient history," has not passed away.

"'Twas on the field of Navarrete,
While Trastamara sought
From English arms a safe retreat,
Du Guesclin stood and fought;
And to the brave Black Prince alone
He yielded up his sword:—
So we must sing in mournful tone,
Until it be restored:—

CHORUS:

"Spin, spin, maidens of Brittany;
And let not your litany
Come to an end,
Before you have prayed
The Virgin to aid
Bertrand du Guesclin, our hero and friend.

"The Black Prince is a gentle knight,
And bade Du Guesclin name
What ransom would be fit and right
For his renown and fame.
'A question hard,' says he, 'yet since
Hard fortune on me frowns,
I could not tell you less, good Prince,
Than twenty thousand crowns.'
Spin, spin, &c.

"'Where find you all that gold, Sir Knight?
I would not have you end
Your days in sloth or undelight,
Away from home and friend.'
'O Prince of generous heart, and just,
Let all your fear be stayed,
For my twenty thousand crowns I trust
To every Breton maid!'
Spin, spin, &c.

"And he is not deceived, for we
Will never let him pine
In stranger towns beyond the sea,
Like a jewel in the mine.
No work but this shall be begun,
We will not rest nor dream,
Till twenty thousand crowns are spun,
Du Guesclin to redeem.
Spin, spin, &c.

"The bride shall grudge the marriage morn,
And feel her joy a crime;
The mother shall wean her eldest born
A month before its time.
No festal day shall idle be,
No hour uncounted stand;
The grandame in her bed shall die
With the spindle in her hand.
Spin, spin, &c."

Can we not also appreciate the adoption of such a token of feminine magnanimity, and approve that the outline of a distaff full of flax should be the form on which women should ever after carry their family honours.

You will like, I think, to hear in a very few words the rest of the history of the Breton hero. He continued to fight against the English for the next ten years, and powerfully contributed to the establishment of a united France.

In 1370 he laid siege to the fortress of Chateau-neuf Randon, held by the English, strongly garrisoned, and well provisioned. A day was fixed for capitulation, should succour not arrive. In the meantime the great warrior was smitten with a mortal disease, and died July 13th, 1380. The Commander led out the garrison on the day appointed, and deposited the keys of the castle on the coffin of his brave and generous foe.

His body was buried amongst the kings of France, at St. Denys. His heart, in a leaden casket, was placed in the Church of Dinan; and his life is commemorated by a plaster statue, erected on the esplanade which bears his name, in 1823.

THE sons carried their father's arms, but they bore certain marks to distinguish the members or branches of a family from each other. Sometimes it was a variety in the charges; sometimes by adding a bordure (*i.e.* border) round the arms; sometimes by changing the tinctures (or colours); sometimes by drawing a ribbon (*i.e.* a very narrow bend) across the arms; but, more commonly, by one of the following figures:—

For the eldest son—a label or file (*i.e.* fillet), interpreted by some to represent the parchment tags of the family title-deeds, on which the seal of the owner would be affixed; by others, that he should be a crown to his family.

For the second son—a crescent, to indicate that he is to increase, or make a position for himself.

For the third son—a mullet (*i.e.* a five-pointed star, or the rowel of the spur), to indicate that he must exert himself.

For the fourth son—a martlet (or bird without feet), to indicate that he must expect no landed inheritance, but live by his head or his wits.

For the fifth son—the annulet or ring (not a finger-ring, but a ring or link of the chain-armour), shewing that he was to take his share in protecting the family.

For the sixth son—the fleur-de-lis (probably the spearhead), indicating that he must defend his family also—perhaps by offensive, as his brother by defensive, means.

For the seventh son—the wayside rose, the humblest blossom amongst natural plants, but yet one of the chiefest ornaments of the forest glade—so the youngest and lowliest of the family may hope to adorn his race.

For the eighth son—the fer de moline, or the mill-rind (*i.e.* the iron cruciform plate in the mill-stone through which the spindle passes, and by means of which the heavy stone is whirled round and the grain crushed into flour), a rough, lowly, unobserved place, yet not to be despised, for the nourishment of man depends upon it, so the welfare of every household depends on even its meanest members, though the position assigned by Providence seem a hard cross to bear.

When an heiress married, her arms were borne by her husband on a smaller shield (not a lozenge) placed upon his, and called an inescutcheon or shield of pretence, thereby acknowledging that he had a pretence to her hereditaments. Usually their children quartered (*i.e.* incorporated) their mother's arms with their father's, but there are many instances in which the arms so acquired remained in the same position on the family shield. The custom of quartering was only introduced in the reign of Edward I., and not generally adopted until the end of the fourteenth century. The earliest known example of a quartered shield occurs in the arms of Eleanor, daughter of Ferdinand III., King of Castile, and Leon, the son of Alphonso, King of Leon, by Berengaria, daughter of Alphonso, King of Castile. He probably carried his arms thus—Leon, on an escutcheon of pretence, Castile. His daughter quartered the arms of Castile with Leon, giving the preference (*i.e.* the first quarter) to Castile, as the greater dignity. We have an instance of this in the first west window, North aisle, called the Dene window, which was probably erected in this reign.

The inescutcheon, however, is what is termed in Heraldry an "augmentation," which is thus defined by Mr. Boutell:—"An honourable addition "to an heraldic composition." Probably for that reason the lady's arms were so treated in an age when "Place aux dames" was the ideal in everything—perhaps also in honour of her family, which by her marriage was now absorbed into her husband's family, her property, and, in the case of a peerage, her title passing into it.

Sometimes, however, the husband seems to have placed his own arms as an inescutcheon on the lady's shield, which were either eventually effaced or perpetuated thereon. This seems to have been the case in the ancient families of Warren and Mortimer, which were both descended from Walterus or William de Sancto Martino, Earl of Warrenne in Normandy. He accompanied William the Conqueror, Dugdale tells us, to England, and received in recognition of his services large grants of land, together with the castle of Conisburgh in Yorkshire, and the castle of Mortimer (Mortuo Mare) in Normandy. Roger de Mortimer, (Dugdale thinks) his own brother, being dispossessed for treachery. The arms of De Sancto Martino were probably a simple shield argent, without any charge.

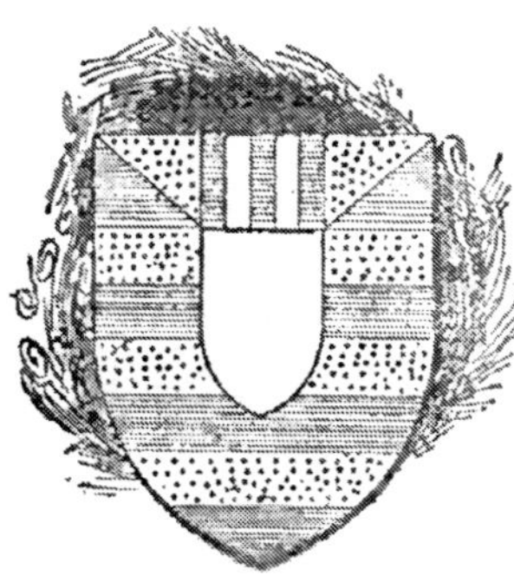

The eldest son, Gualterius de Sancto Martino, Earl of Warrenne, was created by William Rufus Earl of Surrey, and married Elizabeth, daughter of Hugh, Earl of Vermandois, and placed upon her arms, or and azure checky, "the proper coat-"armour of the princely house of Vermandois, an "inescutcheon argent, with a bend thereon gules," probably added for difference. "Vincent says—"They probably dropped part of their arms, *i.e.* the bend gules, on account "of the house of Vermandois being more honourable than their own." *

And so the shield of Warren has always appeared, as it appears in the windows of York Minster, checky or and azure. But in one of the windows of the parish church of Selby, and also of Dewsbury, which manor belonged to the Warrens, the arms appear with the inescutcheon.

The second son, Ralph, seems to have inherited the barony of Mortimer, and having subdued the castle of Wigmore for the Conqueror, he received it as a reward for his services. He seems also to have acquired vast estates in different parts of the kingdom, possibly by marriage, though as Dugdale only tells us that his wife was "Milicent, daughter of . . . ," we cannot say for certain. However, she was possibly an heiress; and he, like his gallant brother, placed his shield upon hers, where it has ever remained.

---

* *Memoirs of the Ancient Earls of Warrenne and Surrey.* Rev. F. Watson.

In royal armoury, inescutcheons are frequently perpetuated, and even multiplied. On the stall plate in St. George's Chapel, Windsor, of Frederick II., King of Denmark, the father of Anne of Denmark, Queen of James I., the arms of Denmark appear with an inescutcheon of the arms of Holstein, upon which there is another inescutcheon of the arms of Oldenburg; while at Holyrood there is a contemporary painting of James of Scotland and his Queen Margaret, daughter of Christian I., King of Denmark, on which is emblazoned a lozenge containing the arms of Scotland impaling Denmark, on which there is an inescutcheon of Holstein, over all a second inescutcheon of Oldenburg. And the authorized arrangement of the arms of the Prince of Wales consists of the royal arms of England differenced with a label of three points argent, over all an inescutcheon of Saxony.

Such augmentations and honours have been granted from time to time. Henry VIII. granted, "for merit," to Thomas, Duke of Norfolk, and his posterity, for his victory at Flodden Field, September 9th, 1513, as a commemorative augmentation, the royal shield of Scotland, having a demi-lion argent, which is pierced through the mouth with an arrow; to be placed on the silver bend of the Howards.

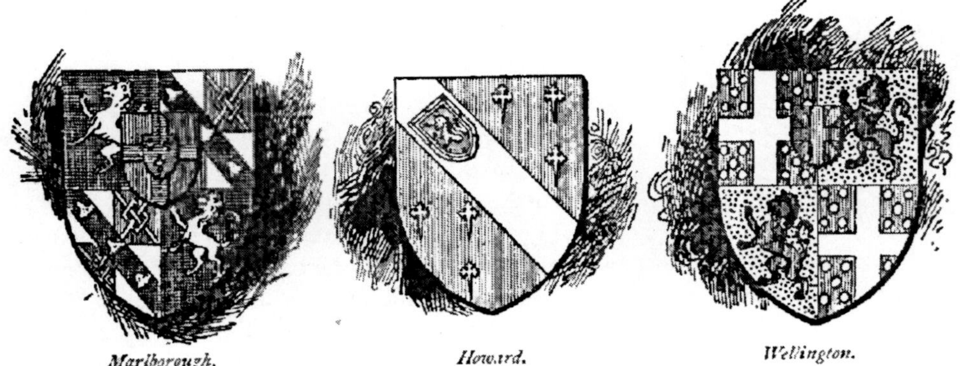

Marlborough. *Howard.* *Wellington.*

In modern days there have been granted similar augmentations of honour to the two great military heroes of the eighteenth and nineteenth centuries. To Marlborough, an inescutcheon argent, charged with the cross of St. George gules, and therefore an inescutcheon of the arms of France.

To Wellington, an inescutcheon charged with the crosses of St. George, St. Andrew, and St. Patrick conjoined, being the union badge of the United Kingdom of Great Britain and Ireland.

When a lady was not an heiress (*i.e.* one of a family of brothers and sisters), her arms were borne on the sinister side of her husband's shield.

Originally these were "dimidiated," as it was called, *i.e.* each shield was cut exactly in half. Edmund, Earl of Cornwall, son of Richard, the brother of Henry III., married Margaret, daughter of Richard de Clare, and on his seal, given in Sandford's *Genealogical History*, carried the arms of the Earls of Cornwall, argent a lion rampant gules crowned or, within a bordure sable bezanté, dimidiated with the arms of Clare, or three chevronels gules. In the same book we find the arms of Eleanor de Bohun, wife of Thomas, Duke of Gloucester, youngest son of Edward III., impaled with those of

her husband (p. 125), by which the arms on both sides of the shield, though reduced in size, are kept entire. This has been invariably the subsequent practice, though on the seal of Mary, Queen of Scots, her marriage with the Dauphin of France is dimidiated with the entire shield of Scotland.

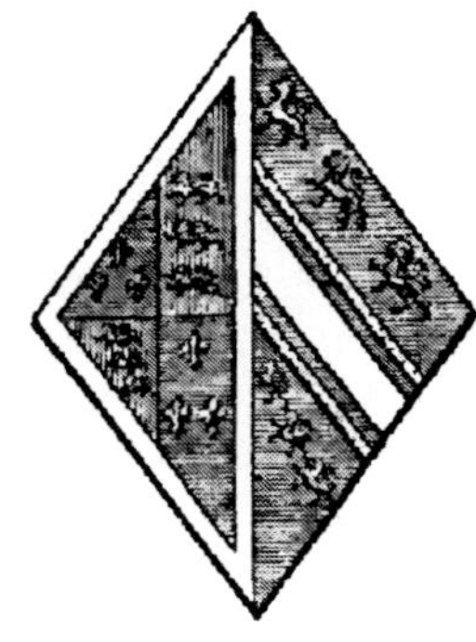

Of crests there is not one illustration in the Minster. Dallaway tells us that such an appendage was unknown to the Normans, who, on the authority of Montfaucon, denoted the rank of the individual by the number of bars of which the beauvoir or visor of the helmet consisted. The ancient Norman casque was composed of an iron frame-work, covered with leather, and quite flat at the top. Such we find on the seal of Richard, Earl of Cornwall, brother of Henry III., 1209–1271. The seal of his son Edmund, Earl of Cornwall, shews the helmet conical; whereas the seal of Thomas, son of Edward Crouchback, Earl of Lancaster, 1245–1296, shews a crest of a dragon, which Dallaway says is "the first instance." Crests were originally used in jousts, when the shield was not borne, or by the chief commanders in battle, and conceded by royal grant, confined to very few persons. In process of time the assumption of them has become universal. They are not held to be absolutely hereditable, but may be assumed. As women did not wear helmets, they were not deemed entitled to crests; and indeed, in the fourth year of Queen Elizabeth, at a Chapter of Heralds held at Broiderers' Hall in London, it was expressly decreed that they should not assume them.

The origin of *supporters* has been attributed by some* to the practice of tournaments, when the adventurers did not use their shields, which were generally suspended upon the barriers and pavilions within the lists.

* Dallaway's *Heraldic Enquiries*.

The attendant armour-bearers and esquires, being dressed in fantastic habits, guarded their masters' escutcheons, and reported the name and quality of the challenger, whose defiance was signified by the act of touching the shield with the point of a spear Others* have attributed them entirely to seal engravers, who on cutting, on seals, shields of arms, which were in a triangular form, and placed on a circle, finding a vacant space at each side and at the top, thought it an ornament to fill them up with olive-branches, garbs, trees, fretwork, lions, unicorns, or some other animals, according to fancy These surmises are probably both true—the former being the development of the latter indeed, we can trace its gradual growth in the royal seals, as given in Sandford's *Genealogical History* On the seal of Edmund, Earl of Cornwall, his shield is represented as held up by a strap passing through the beak of an eagle On the seal of Thomas, Duke of Lancaster, the eldest son of Crouchback, the shield is hung by a strap to a hook, but on each side is a small dragon, the same as on the crest of his helmet On the great seal of Edward III, eight lions are represented on each side of the King, and two under his feet On the great seal of Richard II, shields bearing the arms of England are represented on either side of him, hanging on trees, with a greyhound beneath them, while a lion sejeant supports the effigy of the King on either side In his reign, Dallaway says, the ample field of heraldic invention was expanded, crests and cognizances were multiplied, and supporters generally introduced Richard—effeminate and luxurious—indulged himself in the fopperies of dress, and armorial devices were no longer confined to warriors completely armed, but embossed and embroidered on the habits, mantles, and surcoats of those who attended his sumptuous Court, and we can well imagine that, not content with bearing his cognizances, they were actually arrayed so as to personify the figures or animals which he had already associated with his arms The fashion would soon spread, and the shield be deemed incomplete without them Indeed, the stone shields in York Minster furnish illustrations of this In the Nave, built 1291–1345, i e during the reigns of Edward I, II and III, the shields are represented as hanging from hooks In the Choir, built 1373–1400, i e during the reign of Richard II, they hang from the necks of figures, i e supporters

But there seems to have been no written precedent for the ordering, bearing, or limiting of supporters Custom and practice have reduced the use of bearing supporters to "the major nobility," and no one of inferior degree is *entitled* to assume them without a special grant from the Heralds' College, which is rarely given, but there are certain families whose ancestors have used supporters from very ancient times, and who therefore continue to do so, viz —

* Edmonson's *Heraldry*

Heavingham	- *Suffolk*	Popham -	- *Hants*	Sherard -	- *Leicester*
Stawell -	- *Somerset*	Covert -	- *Sussex*	Paston -	- *Norfolk*
Lutterell -	- ,,	Savage -	- *Cheshire*	Carew -	- *Surrey*
Wallop -	- *Hants*	Porter -	- ,,	St. Leger -	- *Kent*
		Pierpoint -	- *Notts*		

Hilton	Napier	Chudleigh	Foljambe	Hele
Gardiner	Pomeroy	Vaughan	Heskett	Shireborne
	Houghton	Baynard	Balfour	

Amongst these is the family of *Savage*, of which we have a member buried within the Minster, viz., Archbishop Savage, 1501–1507. His monument, which contains his recumbent figure, is only a fragment of what must have been a much larger edifice. There are traces of a doorway, and a piscina is just beyond the figure, showing that there was probably a

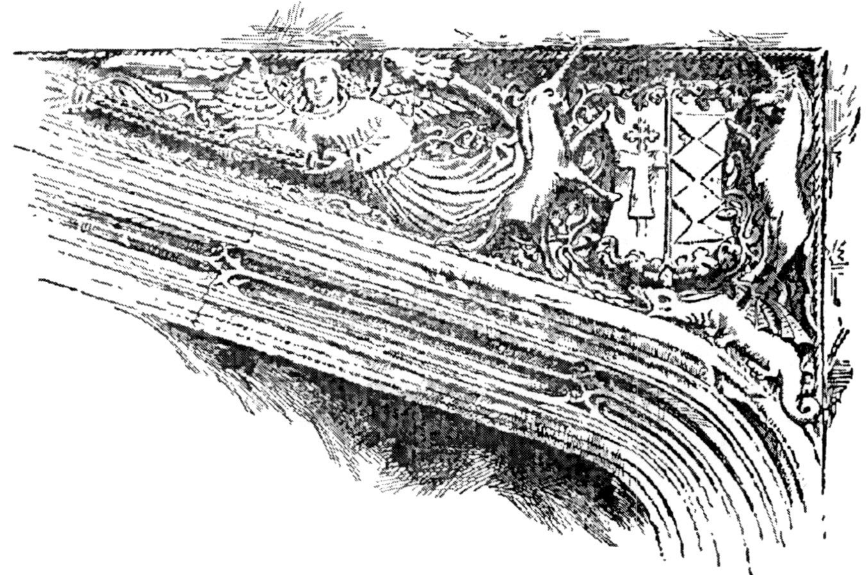

small oratory there; and above there is said to have been a wooden chantry. But the details of what remains are full of heraldic interest, for the cornice of the tomb is decorated with angels bearing shields containing the arms of the Archbishop, and the arms of the official positions which the Archbishop had previously held, and at the north-west corner an angel bearing the arms of Thomas Dalby, his domestic Chaplain, Archdeacon of Richmond, who, it is said, erected his patron's tomb; while on the splay of the arch above the recumbent figure, on either side, are shields, supported by unicorns, charged with the ancient coat of the Archbishopric, viz., the pall, impaling a pale lozengy. One of the unicorns on each side of the arch seems to be standing on a dragon On the panels under the recumbent figure beneath, the Archbishop's arms are emblazoned on four shields No 1, the pale alone, for Savage, *i e* the individual, 2, the pale impaled with the saltire cross of Rochester, *i e* his first bishopric, 3, impaled with the keys in saltire and crown, for the diocese of York, 4, impaled with the pall, for the province of York And this furnishes a subject alike of historical and heraldic interest, for the coat is not the family coat of Savage, which as I have already shewn is argent six lioncels sable, it is the coat of Danvers, or De Anvers, after Edward II written Daniell *

It would appear that John Savage, the great-great-grandfather of the Archbishop, who died in 1386, married Margaret, daughter and heiress of Sir Thomas Danvers, of Bradley and Clifton in Cheshire She was married three times First to John Radcliffe, secondly, to John Savage, and, after his death, to Piers Legh, of Maxfield, younger son of Robert Legh, of Adlington By her second husband she had one son, John Savage, and by her last husband a son, Piers Legh She survived them all, but when she died, in 1427, she specially directed in her will that her son, John Savage, should bear her coat-of-arms, which she inherited from her father

And this was according to the custom of those days, for not only did the nobility claim the privilege of granting arms to their esquires, which were afterwards confirmed by the Earl Marshal, but arms appear likewise to have been conceded by one knight to another, and they might be assigned by a female, who was an heir general, to her own husband, or the husband of her daughter, who inherited her lands, and therefore certainly to her son, who even without that stipulation would have been entitled to quarter them And I think that we can understand the reason for what she did, for her husband, John Savage, was simply a member of that family, then located at Sarcliffe in Derbyshire But her father, Sir Thomas Danvers, was a distinguished warrior He was one of the flower of Cheshire chivalry who were engaged under their Earl, the Black Prince, when only sixteen years of age, at the battle of Crescy

Stowe, in his terse account of this bloody battle, which lasted two days, says that at the commencement "the French King caused his banner, "called 'auriflaime,' to be set up, after which time it was not lawfull, under "paine of death, to take any man to save his life This banner, that it "might differ from his standert, had in it Lilies of gold very broad On "the other side, King Edward commanded his banner to be erected of "the Dragon, which signified fiercenesse and cruelty to be turned against "the Lillies"

So that no quarter was given on either side The principal division of the English army, some 10,800, was entrusted to the young Prince, who

* Ormerod's *History of Cheshire*

manipulated his force with great skill and gallantry.* At one time, beset by nearly 40,000 of the enemy, a knight was despatched to the King by the Earl of Warwick, urging him to advance to his son's support. "Go "back to those who sent you," was the stern reply; "tell them from me "that whatever happens, to require no aid from me as long as my son is "in life. Tell them, also, that I command them to let my boy win his "spurs; for, God willing, the day shall be his, and the honour shall rest "with him and those to whose charge I have given him." This message inspired the Prince and those around him with renewed ardour, and the French men-at-arms dashed down upon the English ranks only to fall wounded, or die in heaps before them. The Count of Harcourt, the Count d'Aumale with his two gallant sons, were slain; Charles of Luxemburg turned his rein and fled, casting off the rich surcoat of his arms, to avoid being recognised. His father, the blind King of Bohemia, learning from those around him that the day was well-nigh lost, heroically exclaimed, "Lords! you are my vassals, my friends, and my companions; and on this "day I command and beseech you to lead me so far forward that I may "deal one blow of my sword in the battle." And tying his horse's bridle to theirs, they galloped into the midst of the thickest strife, in front of the Prince of Wales, fighting gallantly, till at length the standard of Bohemia went down; and John of Luxemburg was found next day dead upon the field, with all his friends round him, and their horses still linked together with their bridles.

Night only closed the carnage, amidst the shades of which the routed forces of France fled away. By the light of blazing torches the young Prince was brought to his father. "Sweet son," said the King, when he had embraced him in his arms and kissed him, "God give you good "perseverance, for most loyally have you acquitted yourself this day: you "are worthy to be a sovereign."

The young Prince generously recognised the support which he had received from Sir Thomas Danvers in the most hazardous part of the battle; for we are told that "the said Sir Thomas relieved the banner of "his Earl, and took prisoner the Chamberlain of France, Tankerville."† For this service, as Earl of Chester, he settled on him an annuity of forty marks out of his manor of Frodsham, until a convenient grant of land could be made, which (21st Richard II.) was apportioned from the lands of Hanley in Macclesfield Forest, called Lyme, because situated on the limes or borders of Cheshire. He also granted him, as an augmentation of honour to his arms, an escutcheon of pretence sable, semée of mullets argent, an arm embowed, armed, and couped proper, bearing a pennon argent.

* Froissart and Barnes. James' *History of the Black Prince*, vol. i. p. 435.

† Ormerod's *History of Cheshire*.

Margaret Savage seems, therefore, to have divided her arms and lands between her two sons. To the son of her second husband, John Savage, she bequeathed the estate of Clifton, which she had inherited from her mother, daughter and heir of William Baggily, who had married the co-heir of Sir Roger Dutton, Lord of Chedhill and Clifton,—and with it the coat and crest of Danvers, viz., argent a pale fusilly sable; crest, a unicorn's head couped argent,—and probably the supporters, unicorns, which harmonize with the crest, and which may have been granted about this time. These arms were borne by his descendants until the year 1547, when Sir John Savage, who married Elizabeth Manners, daughter of the Earl of Rutland, resumed the ancient coat of his family, the six lioncels sable, simply quartering the arms of Danvers.

Legh of Lyme.

To the son of her third husband, Piers Legh, she bequeathed the estate at Lyme, granted to her father by the Black Prince, and with it the augmentation of honour granted at the same time, as a separate coat-of-arms, which is still borne by the family of Leigh of Lyme.

Her son, John Savage, inherited also his father's gallantry, for he was knighted at the battle of Agincourt, 3rd Henry V., and died 25th Henry VI., 1450.

His grandson, Sir John, knighted 17th Edward IV., 1477, married Catherine,* daughter of Sir Thomas Stanley, afterwards Lord Stanley, and sister to Thomas Stanley, Earl of Derby, who married Eleanor, sister to Richard Nevill, Earl of Warwick, nicknamed the King-maker. He, however, refused his importunity to desert with him to the cause of Henry VI., and remained faithful to Edward IV. during his life, and to his son Edward V. after his death.

He was present at the Council in the Tower where Hastings was denounced by Richard and ordered to immediate execution. Indeed, he seems to have had a presentiment, in a dream the night before, that evil was intended by Richard, for he had counselled Hastings to ride away with him, and he only escaped himself with life by creeping under the table when a man struck at him with a halbert.

He was imprisoned as soon as Richard ascended the throne; but his son, Lord Strange, was, however, so powerful in Lincolnshire that it was evidently more expedient to conciliate him, so he was set at liberty, and created Lord Steward of the Household. His second marriage, however, with Margaret, widow of Edmund Tudor, and mother of Henry, Earl of Richmond, again made him an object of suspicion; and he now found it

* Collins' *Peerage*.

convenient to temporise, as his son, Lord Strange, was now a hostage in the King's hands

"For some time," Stowe says, "he inclined to neither party," but the day before Bosworth, with his brother William, he had an interview at Adderstone with the Earl of Richmond, secretly, in consequence of Richard's threat to kill his son His nephew, Sir John Savage, joined the Earl at the same time, and to him was assigned the command of the left wing of his army

On the following day Lord Stanley, with his brother, Sir William, with 3,000 men, accompanied Henry, and Stowe records that "the armies "joyned and came to hand stroke, at which encounter the Lord Stanley "joyned with the Earl" Indeed, his forces ultimately decided the fortunes of the day, for Stowe adds that Henry's army, "being almost in despair "of victory, were suddenly recomforted by Sir William Stanley, which came "to succour with 3,000 tall men" The whole conflict endured little above "two hours," and then Richard was slain, and the crown which he had worn on his helmet being found in a bush, was placed by Lord Stanley on his head amidst the shouts of the victorious army

King Henry VII was neither slow nor niggardly in recompensing those who had so opportunely and efficiently served him Lord Stanley was made Earl of Derby, Lord High Steward at the King's coronation, and Constable of England for life, besides being godfather at the christening of the young Prince Arthur To Sir John Savage were granted the manors and estates in Derby, Nottingham, Leicester, and Shropshire, which had until then belonged to Francis, Viscount Lovel He had been conspicuous for his attachment to the late King, for Stowe says, "In these "daies were chief rulers about the King, the Lord Lovel and two gentle-"men, being named Sir Richard Radcliffe and Sir William Catesby, of "the which persons was made a seditious rime, and fastened upon the "crosse in Cheape and other places of the city, whereof the sentence was "as followeth —

'The cat, the rat, and Lovel our dogge,
Rulen all England under an hogge'"

Lovel, however, is mentioned by Stowe as "amongst them that ran "away" at Bosworth For the time he saved his life, but, if tradition be true, only for a worse and ignoble fate, for it is said that in 1708,* upon occasion of new laying a chimney at Minster Lovel, there was discovered a large vault underground, in which was the entire skeleton of a man, as having been sitting at a table which was before him, with a book, paper, pen, &c, in another part of the room lay a cap, all much mouldered and decayed, which the family and others judged to be this Lord Lovel whose exit has hitherto been so uncertain Hence it has been concluded that it

* Burke's *Extinct Peerage*

was the fate of this unhappy Lord to have retired to his own house after the battle, and there to have entrusted himself to some servant, by whom he was immured and afterwards neglected, either through treachery, fear, or some accident which befel that person.

In the Savage chapel in Macclesfield church there are two altar tombs under Gothic arches, one of a recumbent alabaster figure of a warrior in plate armour, his head resting on his helmet, and his feet on a dog, a chain being suspended round his neck; the countenance very aged. The other contains another recumbent figure of a warrior in plate armour, the face having a much more youthful expression; his collar is composed of *SS.*, and his belt for sword and dagger are richly studded; his head rests on a helmet, and his feet on a lion. The effigies, probably, of Sir John and his father.

Sir John Savage, however, did not long enjoy his riches, for in the eighth of Henry VII., 1492, he was slain at the siege of Boulogne. He married, and from him were descended the Viscounts Savage and Colchester, eventually Earls Rivers, which titles became extinct in 1728, the estate of Clifton (*temp.* Elizabeth, called Rock Savage*) passing by marriage to the Cholmondeleys.

Sir John had, however, an illegitimate son, named George, who was "Parson of Davenham," and who seems to have developed his father's immorality to an excess of profligacy, for he had several illegitimate children. One, George Savage, a priest, became Chancellor of Chester; another, John Wimslow, became Archdeacon of Middlesex; and a third, Edmund Bonner, became first Dean of Leicester, and afterwards twice Bishop of London,—only to render himself notorious for his bigotry and cruelty as the ruthless time-server to the fanatical Mary, Queen of England, and the self-interested, hypocritical members of her Council and Parliament.

The royal gratitude was extended also to yet another member of the Savage family. Thomas, younger brother of Sir John, was, Drake tells us, "Doctor of Laws in Cambridge, though of a moderate character for learning, "his genius leading more to a Court life. Notwithstanding his deficiency in "this point, he was by Henry VII., a prince well read in mankind, first "made Bishop of Rochester, then of London, and lastly translated to York," though he seems not to have been "elected to the see of York after the "ancient custom, but nominated by the King and confirmed by the Pope."

"Our prelate," adds Drake, "is said to have been too much employed "in temporal affairs when at Court, and in the country in hunting,—a "diversion he was passionately fond of, to mind the business of his see." He affected much grandeur, having, according to old Stowe, "many tall "yeomen for his guard." He seems to have kept up his palaces at Cawood

* Ormerod.

L

and Scrooby in proper repair, and has left this record behind him —"He "was a man, beside the worthiness of his birth, highlie esteemed with his "prince for his fast fidelitie and great wisdome" He died at Cawood on September 2nd, 1507, having only held the Archbishopric for seven years

His monument, as I have said, was erected to his memory by Thomas Dalby, his chaplain He seems to have been buried near his patron, and to have survived him eighteen years, dying in 1525 Formerly there was a brass on the floor, of which there is an illustration in Drake, to his memory

He was Prebendary of North Leverton in the Cathedral of Southwell, 1505, and of South Newbald in York Minster the same year The year following he was collated to the Prebend of Stillington, and to the Archdeaconry of Richmond

At the south-west corner of the monument to Archbishop Savage there is a figure of an angel holding a shield emblazoned with arms similar to those which were on Thomas Dalby's monumental tablet, viz, a garb impaling a chevron ermine between three buckles The latter is the cognizance of Dalby, but it is difficult to identify the former accurately Torre, in his MS history of the Minster and its property, mentions this coat as existing in the prebendal house of Stillington, "in the hall window," "in the window "of the dining-room above stairs," and carved in stone on the chimney-piece of the same, with another shield containing a garb only He thus labels them—"Richmond Archdeaconry impaling Dalby" For want of more definite information I must accept his statement, but neither in the Diocesan Record Offices of York or Chester, nor in the British Museum, can I find any seal shewing what the device of the Archdeaconry of Richmond actually was

There is also an uncertainty as to the meaning of the dragons on which the supporters of the arms of Savage, in the spandrels of the arch above the tomb, stand Perhaps they are intended to represent the dragon on the banner of Edward III, which "signified fierceness and cruelty" memorials, therefore, of Crescy and brave Sir Thomas Danvers Perhaps they represent "the red dragon, ensign of Cadwalader, last King of the "Britons, from whom, by a male line, Henry VII is said to have derived "his pedigree, and which, painted upon white and green silk, was his "banner at Bosworth, and afterwards affixed up, amongst other trophies "of his victory, at St Paul's, and commemorated by the institution of a "Pursuivant of Arms called Rouge Dragon'* Memorials, therefore, of that brilliant victory, and gallant young Sir John Savage Perhaps they represent both Who can say? But who can regard them otherwise than as tokens of the heroic deeds done

"In the brave days of old"

---

* Sandford's *Genealogical History*

THE BEND.

HAVING now considered the subject of Heraldry generally, I propose to notice some, at least, of the charges, with the family histories and national incidents to which they are the keys. And first I would call your attention to those portions of the dress or accoutrements which were originally adopted as charges; sometimes, perhaps, as memorials of a conquered enemy, sometimes as tokens of honour conferred, and sometimes as compliments to those who had the highest esteem and the tenderest regard of the warrior.

These charges are many. Let us commence with the Bend.

The bend is a stripe passing diagonally across the shield. When drawn from the dexter corner or chief to the sinister base, it is termed a bend dexter; when issuing from the sinister instead of the dexter chief, it is called a bend sinister. It is sometimes imagined that the bend sinister is the mark of illegitimacy; which is an error arising from confusing the bend with the *baton*, which is one-fourth of the bend in width, and is couped, or cut off at both ends. As such it is a token of illegitimacy, and is so used in the third quartering of the arms of the Duke of Cleveland, which consist of, quarterly; first and fourth quarterly, France and England; second, Scotland; third, Ireland; charged in the centre with a sinister baton, ermine and azure, for Fitz-Roy, being the arms of Charles II. Henry Vane, third Baron Barnard, having married, 1725, Lady Grace Fitzroy, daughter of Charles, first Duke of Cleveland, son of Charles II. by Barbara Villiers, daughter and heir of Viscount Grandison. There is another way of marking the same blemish in the family escutcheon, viz., by a bordure, which may either be an "augmentation of honour," as in the arms of Archbishop Scrope; or an "abatement of honour," *e.g.* the great family of Beaufort have always borne—quarterly France, azure, three fleurs-de-lis or, and England, gules, three lions passant guardant, all within a bordure componé argent and azure. This shield may be found in the eighth window on the south side of the Choir; but it has there this peculiarity, viz., that the "abatement" has been changed into an "augmentation" without altering the bordure, for it is charged with ermine alternately * This is probably the coat of Henry de Beaufort, second son of Thomas de Beaufort, Duke of Exeter, third son of John of Gaunt and Catherine Swinford Henry de Beaufort was Prebendary of Riccall in York Minster, 1390, and Bishop of Lincoln 1397, Bishop of Winchester 1426, and afterwards Cardinal of St Eusebius Torre mentions in the east window of the south transept of the Choir, the arms of Scrope of Masham, with a bordure componé or and gules, probably being the achievement of some illegitimate member of that house, but the shield does not exist now

The bend, however, is probably the representation of the baldrick, a broad belt or scarf worn over the right or left shoulder, either simply as an ornament or to carry a weapon or a horn As the former, it was often the gift of the lady-love of the gallant knight—perhaps her own scarf—and sometimes a token of honour conferred by the King Spenser, in his *Fairie Queene* (book 1, chapter 9, stanzas 29, 30), represents Prince Arthur as thus adorned —

'Athwart his breast a bauldrick brave he wore,
That shined like twinkling stars with stones most precious rare,
And in the midst thereof one pretious stone
Of wondrous worth, and eke of wondrous mighte,
Shaped like a lady s head, exceeding shone,
Like Hesperus amongst the lesser lights,
And strove for to amaze the weaker sight"

Planché, in his *Cyclopædia of Costume*, gives some illustrations of this, viz, a figure from the book of Cæsare Vicellio, carrying a hawk on his wrist, and wearing the baldrick, probably as the badge of his master in whose household he is a member 2 A figure from the military costumes of Flanders and Holland, by Michael Vosmer, 1578, probably one of the Counts of Holland He is in full armour, carrying his shield round his neck, and wearing a long vestment with ample sleeves, his right hand leans upon a long two-handed sword, and across his breast, nearly down to his left knee, hangs a broad baldrick, evidently of costly material and workmanship, to which is suspended a jewel 3 A figure of a nobleman of the close of the fourteenth century bearing a baldrick over the left shoulder, decorated with bells

The baldrick, or a broad strap worn like the baldrick, sometimes bore the shield when it was carried at the back Meyrick, in his *Ancient Armour*, gives a fancy illustration, suggested by a tomb in Ash Church, Kent, of Aymer de Valence so adorned Hewitt, in his *Ancient Armour and Weapons in Europe*, gives an illustration of the brass of Sir Roger de Trumpington, representing a recumbent figure, with the shield slung over the left arm by a strap or baldrick, which passes over the right

* See coloured illustration

shoulder. Planché also gives two illustrations of baldricks used for supporting the horn. 1. A group of huntsmen from the *Livre de Chasse* of Gaston Phœbus, MS. fifteenth century at Paris; and the effigy of Sir John Corpe, from his brass in Stoke Heming Church, Devon, 1361 A.D.; where the baldrick bears a short dagger in a sheath. 2. A figure of a German noble in hunting costume, from a painting by Albert Durer. The yeoman in Chaucer's *Canterbury Tales* is described as having his horn slung from a green baldrick, and the ploughman upbraids the clergy for wearing baldricks with keen basilards or daggers.

I cannot find, however, that in ancient days the military sword was ever carried by a baldrick. Certainly on all the mediæval tombs of men of war the recumbent figures carry their swords from a belt round the loins, and I notice the same in all mediæval illustrations. This seems, however, gradually to have become the practice in later times. Meyrick, in his *Ancient Armour*, gives an illustration of a harquebusier, 1556 A.D., who carries his weapon over his right shoulder, and his powder-horn round his neck, suspended by a band; a broad baldrick of leather hangs across his breast from his right shoulder, with cartridges or cases containing charges for his gun dependant therefrom, called a bandilier. An order of Council of War, Charles I., contains this entry—"For a new bandelier, with "twelve charges, a primer, a priming wire, a bullet bag, and a strap or belt "of two inches in breadth, 2*s*. 6*d*." Turner, in his *Pallas Armata*, says—"To a musketeer belongs also a bandelier of leather, at which he shall "have hanging eleven or twelve shot of powder, a bag for his ball, a "primer, and a cleanser."

Another, of a later date, viz. 1579, wears a vest of silk, covering probably armour, which appears on his shoulders and arms, trunk hose, and a scarf or baldrick across his breast from his right shoulder, under which appears his sword-belt. In the time of the Stuarts, however, the sword is represented as attached to the baldrick, and an illustration is given of this, viz. a cuirassier, date 1650, who has his sword suspended by a large fringed baldrick.

Planché (vol. 2, p. 285) represents the French infantry, *temp.* Louis XIII., as so accoutred; but there are two illustrations (287, 288) where the baldrick is worn over the left shoulder, evidently only as an ornament or badge of authority. In Queen Anne's time the cartouch-box supplied the place of the bandelier, and a second baldrick or band from the other shoulder, crossing it on the breast, sustained the sword. I think that I am right in saying that now the sword is universally carried from the belt; that in the infantry the officers wear a baldrick of silk interwoven with gold, according to their rank, from the shoulder; in the cavalry a baldrick of leather, carrying a cartouch-box behind the back. I may also add that the ribbons of the orders of knighthood which first appeared towards the end of the seventeenth century (Planché), are practically baldricks. The blue ribbon of the Garter, and the green ribbon of St. Andrew, are worn over the left shoulder, supporting the jewel of the order under the right arm. The red ribbon of the Bath is worn by Knight-Grand-Crosses over the right shoulder.

Of the bend we have many instances in the Minster, indicating honoured names and stirring scenes in the annals of the past. Let us commence with Scrope—a household word to all who know Yorkshire, may I not say English, History.

THE SCROPES.

The family of Scrope, probably of Norman origin, is said to be descended from one Richard le Scrupe, or Le Scrap, the ancient name for a crab, who held lands in Worcestershire, Herefordshire, and Shropshire, *temp.* Edward the Confessor, and who is recorded by historians of the period as one of the King's foreign favourites. This would account for his not being dispossessed by the Conqueror, and for the increasing prosperity of his family under that dynasty. In the reign of Richard I., Simon le Scrope seems to have inherited lands at Flotmanby in Yorkshire from his nieces; and in the reign of Edward I., Sir William le Scrope is mentioned as possessing lands in West Bolton and Bolton Parva in this county. He left two sons, Henry and Geoffry, from whom two great and distinct baronial families were descended.

The elder, Henry, acquired the property at Bolton from his father. He seems to have been an eminent person, as he was made Chief Justice of the King's Bench by Edward II., and, by Edward III., Chief Baron of the Exchequer. Sir Henry Scrope was also a knight banneret, and his arms, azure a bend or, charged in the upper part with a lion passant purpure (in recognition of a grant received by him from the Earl of Lincoln), appear in the roll of arms of the bannerets, between 2nd and 7th of Edward II. He died in 1336, and was buried at the abbey of St. Agatha, near Richmond, of which he was the founder or patron.

His eldest son, William, survived him for only a few years, when he was succeeded by his brother, Sir Richard. He served under Edward III. at the battle of Crescy, and was knighted at the battle of Durham, 1346. In 1371, 44th Edward III., he was summoned to Parliament as a baron of the realm, and made Treasurer of the King's Household; on the accession of Richard II., Steward of the King's Household—"Senescallus Hospitii "Regis"—and twice Lord Chancellor; besides which he was entrusted with several important and delicate matters of state, for Walsingham says of

PLATE 1.

SCROPE AND CHAWORTH.

SCROPE OF BOLTON.

SCROPE OF MASHAM.

SIR HENRY SCROPE.

SCROPE AND WELLES.

ARCHBISHOP SCROPE.

him that he was distinguished for his extraordinary wisdom and integrity. Some traits of his character are specially interesting to us, indicating his appreciation of the value of the heraldic cognizance of his house, and his energy in protecting that which affected the honour and dignity of his family.

In September, 1346, when present at the siege of Calais, he maintained his right to his crest, a crab issuing from a ducal coronet, which, much to the astonishment of Robert de Ufford, Earl of Suffolk, who knew the antiquity of his family, had been challenged.

In 1359, when serving under John of Gaunt before Paris, an esquire from Cornwall, named Carminow, challenged him as to his right to bear the arms—azure a bend or; and he successfully defended his claim before the Duke of Lancaster, the Earl of Northampton, the Constable, and the Earl of Warwick, the Marshal of the army, who adjudged that they might both bear the said arms entire, on the ground that Carminow was of Cornwall, which was a large county, and was formerly a kingdom, and that the Scropes had borne them since the Conquest.

In 1384, however, another difference on the same subject arose, in which Scrope was the aggressor. For, being Warden of the Marches, he was ordered by the King to review a large army under the command of the Duke of Lancaster, levied to invade Scotland, and report the efficiency and number of the troops to the King. In so doing he observed Sir Robert Grosvenor bearing as his arms, azure a bend or, and at once challenged his right to do so. In August, 1385, a general proclamation was made throughout the host in Scotland that all who were interested in the dispute should appear at Newcastle-on-Tyne on the 20th of that month. Lord Scrope attended accordingly; but the further consideration of the matter was adjourned, and the suit was continued for upwards of four years. A long time: but when we consider the number of witnesses and the difficulties of procuring their evidence, it is easily explained. Sir Harris Nicolas, in his *Scrope and Grosvenor Controversy*, has published the depositions of two hundred and twelve witnesses, and promises another volume, which, alas! has never appeared, but which, he says, shall contain the remainder of the deponents in behalf of Sir Richard Scrope, "and notices of all the "witnesses who gave their testimony in favour of Sir Robert Grosvenor." So that we have some idea of the large number who gave evidence; and when we remember the difficulties of travelling, and that they resided in different parts of the country, the labour appears very great.

Commissioners seem to have attended at different towns of England for this purpose. Lord Fitz-Walter, Sir John Marmion, and Sir John Kentwode, at the palace of John of Gaunt, King of Castile and Leon, in the Friars Carmelites, at Plymouth. Here "time-honoured Lancaster" and his son, Henry, Earl of Derby, afterwards Henry IV, and many others, gave their testimony before sailing upon an expedition to recover the kingdom of Castile and Leon, which the Duke claimed in right of his wife Sir John Kentwode attended for a similar purpose at Tiverton, in the manor of the Earl of Devonshire, and in the parish church of Edesleigh, Sir Stephen de Derby in the refectory of the abbey of Abbotsbury, in the county of Dorset, Sir Nicholas de Haryngton, Knight, in the church of St John, within the walls of West Chester, the abbot of the abbey of Our Lady of York, and Sir John Derwentwater, at the chapter-house of the cathedral church of St Peter, of York, September 17th, 1386 Here the witnesses were chiefly ecclesiastics —the abbots of Selby, Rievaulx, Jervaux, St Agatha, Byland, Roche, Coverham, the priors of Gisburgh, Lanercost, the sub-prior of Wartre, the prior of Newburgh, the canon and cellarer, and canon and sacristan, of the priory of Bridlington, Sir Ralph Hastings, Sir Bryan Stapleton, Sir Robert Roos, Sir Gerard Grymston, Sir Robert Neville of Hornby, Sir John Bosville, Sir John Constable, Sir John Mauleverer, Sir William Melton, Sir John Savile, Sir John Hotham, Sir Thomas Reresby, Sir Thomas Rokeby, Sir Thomas Boynton, Sir Ralph Eure, Sir Robert Conyers, and many other good Yorkshire names

On the two following days, also, the enquiry was continued, when Thomas de Saltmersshe, John de Feryby (under-treasurer of the cathedral church), and the parson of the church of St Mary-sur-Bychille, in York, deposed Sir James de Pykerynge attended at Nottingham, Commissioners at Leicester, and Sir John Derwentwater attended in October in the church of St Margaret, at Westminster, and there were probably many other "centres" for enquiry besides How many deposed in favour of Sir Richard Grosvenor I cannot say, but with very few exceptions those whose names are recorded testified in favour of Scrope

There is not much variety in their depositions, but they are curious, as throwing some light upon the habits and manners of those days Their testimony is derived from observation in the field of shields, banners, pennons, and coat-armour, with, I think, a single exception, viz, Geoffry Chaucer, who though he had been "in arms," was more of a civilian than a soldier, having been King's valet (his wife was sister of Catherine Swynford), comptroller of the customs, clerk of the works at Westminster and Windsor, &c He said that he was once in Friday Street, London, and walking through the street he observed a new sign hanging out with these arms thereon, and enquired "what inn that was which had hung out these "arms of Scrope" and one answered him, saying, "They are not hung "out, sir, for the arms of Scrope, nor painted there for those arms, but "they are painted and put there by a knight of the county of Chester, "called Sir Robert Grosvenor," and that was the first time he ever heard speak of Sir Robert Grosvenor or his ancestors, or of anyone bearing the name of Grosvenor.

Two of those summoned, viz., John Leycester and Sir John Pole, could not or would not remember anything. Sir John Brereton was stoutly contumacious, refused to give any evidence, and was fined £20.

It is interesting, too, to notice the early age at which many of them were "armed," *i.e.* entered on service in the field; some as early as ten years of age, many at fourteen or sixteen, while the majority were under twenty. Many, on the other hand, had attained a great age. Many over sixty years; indeed, John Thirlewalle deposed that his father, when he died, was of the age of seven score and five ("$\overset{\text{xx}}{\text{vii.}}$ ans and v.") *i.e.* 145, and had been armed during sixty-nine years. But Sir Harris Nicolas thinks "either that the "deponent was mistaken about his father's age, or that the person who "took down his statement, or he who copied it on the roll in the Tower, "committed an error on the subject." Sir R. Roos, 76; Sir Thomas Roos of Kendal, 80; William Heselrigg, 70; Sir John Chydioke, 100 and upwards; Sir John Sully of Iddesleigh, Devon, 105 years. He had passed the greater part of his life in the field, and was the hero of a hundred battles; but now, overcome with the infirmities of advanced years, his evidence, together with that of his old and faithful squire, Richard Baker, was taken at his own home.

Eventually the Constable gave judgment in favour of "Mr. Scrope," and allowed "Mr. Grosvenor" the same arms, with a white border, adjudging him to pay the costs. But he utterly refused both arms and judgment, and appealed to the King, who on 27th May, 1390, gave judgment in the great chamber of Parliament, in his palace at Westminster, to the same effect. The bill for the expenses, amounting to £466 13*s.* 4*d.*, was reduced by the "comyssaryes" appointed for the purpose to fifty marks. But as the said Robert would not appear, and was obstinate, it was again assessed by the King, on Monday, 3rd of October, first day of Parliament, at 500 marks. "Wch seid som' of v$^{c.}$ m'ks the seyd Sir Robert Grosvenor "requested the seyd Sir Rychard Scrope to forgive him, who agayne "awnsweryd that he had so ivell usyd hym and belyed hym in his answers, "that he des'vyd no courtesye. Who agayne aunswered that hyt was not "his doings, but his counsellors, to make his mattre seame the bettre, "and that he knewe he dyd not well nor seyd trewle therein. Wheruppon "he agayne aunsweryd that yf he wolde so openlye declare, pr'fesse, and "confesse, and be content, it shuld be so enteryd of recourde, wch he "requestyd the Kinge hit myght be, that then he wold forgyve hym; wch "was done accordinglye, and the som forgeven, and they made frynds "afor the Kinge in the P'lyament howsse." And so the great *cause celebre* of Heraldry concluded.

Another great achievement was the rebuilding of his manor of Bolton, which he obtained the King's license to castellate, and 18,000 marks and eighteen years of labour were consumed thereon The building, with its four square towers at the angles, enclosing a spacious court, measured on the north and south sides 185 feet, and 125 on the east and west, with three entrances Leland, *temp* Henry VIII, describes it, and says—"One thing I much notyd in the haulle of Bolton, how chimeneys "were conveyed by tunneles made on the sides of the walls, betwixt the "lights in the hawll, and by this means and by no covers is the smoke "of the harthe in the hawle wonder strangly convayed"

So Lord Scrope was a great and prosperous man, but his prosperity was eventually clouded by a trouble which saddened and embittered his closing years His eldest son, Sir William, seems to have been a man of brilliant ability and success Having distinguished himself by his gallantry under the Duke of Lancaster in France, he was knighted, and appointed seneschal of Aquitaine His success in that office commended him to the notice of Richard II, who made him Vice-Chamberlain, then Chamberlain, employed him to negotiate his marriage with Isabel of France, sent him on diplomatic missions, made him governor of Beaumaris and Queensburgh castles and Chamberlain of Ireland, created him, 1397, Earl of Wilts, without ever having been a baron, and, soon after, Knight of the Garter, justice of Chester and North Wales, captain of Calais, and constable of Guisnes, and eventually Treasurer of England He purchased the sovereignty of the Isle of Man from the Earl of Salisbury, and when the truce was confirmed with France, assented to the proceedings "pour le seigneurie de Man," as one of the allies of the King of England Well might Lord Roos exclaim (*Richard II.*, act ii scene i)—

"The Earl of Wilts hath the realm in farm!"

But dark days were at hand The people were becoming weary of Richard's strange combination of vigour and lassitude, despotic tyranny and lavish prodigality, love of idle show and magnificence, devotion to favourites and pursuit of pleasure, which had alienated all classes from him, and their hearts turned to the exiled Henry, now, by John of Gaunt's death, Duke of Lancaster, and he, taking advantage of Richard's absence in Ireland, came over to England, and the nation was at his feet Of course the late King's favourites were the first to fall, and the Earl of Wilts, compelled to abandon Wallingford Castle, where the young Queen had been placed under his care for security, sought shelter in the castle of Bristol, where he was compelled to surrender, and was immediately beheaded by popular clamour, without even the form of a trial

His aged father, then past seventy, never recovered the blow Under the plea of State necessity he had assented to the deposition and imprisonment of the unfortunate Richard, who had loaded himself and his son with honours, but he does not appear to have taken part in public affairs again. Once he attended Parliament, when the attainder of his son, the Earl of Wilts, was confirmed. Rising from his seat, his eyes streaming with tears, the venerable peer, while he admitted the justice of the sentence and deplored the conduct of his son, besought that the proceedings might not affect the inheritance of himself and his other children. Was it a consolation, unmixed with bitterness, that King Henry comforted him with the assurance that he had always considered him a loyal knight?

One other member of this branch of the family deserves our attention as connected with the Minster, viz., his grandson, another Sir Richard Scrope, third Baron Scrope of Bolton. He seems, on 7th February, 1418, with his servants and a certain John Hoton, to have "attacked one Richard "Hemmingburgh, a serving-man, and one of the family of the Reverend "Master Richard Cawood, canon residentiary of the church of York afore-"said, did savagely wound him, and him so wounded did leave half dead." Sir Thomas Haxey, the treasurer, with Master William Cawood and Master William Pelleson, the canons residentiary, met together in chapter at once, and pronounced "the greater excommunication" against Sir Richard and his friends. Moreover, they decreed that divine service should cease to be celebrated in the Choir, and take place in the chapel of St. Mary and Holy Angels, "in a low voice, without the melody of organ "or free chanting whatsoever, until the time of the humiliation and sub-"mission of the said violators, and the parsons and vicars of the Cathedral "Church, from the impulse of their own conscience, desisting or refraining "from the celebration of their masses in the said Cathedral Church." Also every day they "went down into the Nave to denounce as excom-"municated persons the violators aforesaid." On the Sunday following they went in procession through the passage leading to the palace as far as the Archbishop's hall, and round the garden of the palace; and "all "the doors of the church were strongly bolted, except one valve of the "south door." On the 15th February following, the chapter assembled again, and commissioned "that religious man, Brother Thomas de Spofford, "abbot of the monasterie of St. Mary of York, to absolve in form of law "Sir Richard Scrope, John Hoton, together with their accomplices," who on the same day appeared and submitted themselves, swearing on the gospels that they would abide by the commands of the Church and humbly fulfil the penance to be imposed upon them. Upon which the abbot enjoined Sir Richard to make sufficient reparation to the person injured, and then to enter by the western door, having laid aside his belt, carrying aloft and publicly in his hand his dagger drawn, the handle thereof being held aloft, and uncovered in the midst before the Archbishop in the procession; and when the procession returned to the Choir, to come to the altar, and there on his bended knees three times devoutly say the Lord's Prayer and the angelical salutation, and offer upon the high altar the dagger aforesaid; and then, withdrawing to a certain fald-stool, there to await the finishing of the mass, humbly and devoutly saying his prayers; and the next year to offer an image of silver-gilt of the value of ten marks, made to the likeness of St. Stephen. A similar sentence was pronounced on all the others, and was obediently conformed to. Truly "the Power of "the Keys" was no *brutum fulmen* in those days.

But it is no part of our purpose to pursue the fortunes of this branch of the family further, for they have no other connection with the Minster, where the interest seems to centre in Richard Scrope, Archbishop of York, grandson of Geoffry Scrope, the younger son of old Sir William le Scrope. Sir Geoffry, like his elder brother, Sir Henry, seems to have been a distinguished lawyer, and equally skilful as a knight: whether in the courts or lists he was *facile princeps*. He was Chief Justice of the King's Bench and Chief Justice of the Common Pleas. He accompanied Edward III. in his invasion of Scotland, where his banner and pennon were displayed; and as for his prowess in the tournament, both Sir Thomas Roos and Sir William Aton stated in their depositions on the famous trial that they had seen him "tournayer" both at Guildford and Newmarket, and that he "performed his part most nobly."

He purchased the manor of Masham from Joan Hepham, daughter and heir of John de Wanton, and differenced his coat-of-arms with a label, which again was tinctured for difference by his descendants. His son, Sir Thomas, carried it white, with three crescents on the bend; Sir Wm., a younger brother, bore it ermine; another brother, Geoffry, a priest, bore it with the first and third point argent, the centre gules; Sir Geoffry, his grandson, bore it gobonné, argent and gules; while the Archbishop carried it red. He died in 1340, and was buried at Coverham.

His son, Sir Henry, was an enthusiastic companion in arms of Edward III., served with him in the wars of France and Scotland, was knighted at the siege of Berwick, fought at Halidon Hill, Crescy, Durham, the sea-fight with the Spaniards at Espagnoles-sur-Mer, and at the siege of Calais. In 1350 he was summoned to Parliament as a baron; and until the King's death, in 1377, filled many positions of trust—ambassador to Scotland and to Flanders, governor of Guisnes, warden of the Marches. He lived to be seventy-eight years of age, but took no part in public affairs during the sixteen years which elapsed after the death of the King.

Under such circumstances it is not surprising that his son Richard rose rapidly in the scale of ecclesiastical promotion. From 1367–86 he was rector of Ainderby Steeple, then chancellor of Cambridge, then, 1383, dean of Chichester; six years afterwards he was consecrated Bishop of Lichfield and Coventry, Richard II. being present at his installation, and in 1398, on the death of Robert Waldby, he was translated to the Archbishopric of York. The entries in the fabric rolls of the Minster at this time shew that much large timber had been procured, also "3,000 stones of lead, with 100 "pounds of sodder and 5,000 lead nails;" so that the good work of rebuilding the Choir, commenced by Archbishop Thoresby, was going on. On the 10th of August, 1603, the Archbishop is recorded to have "celebrated "high mass at the great altar in the Cathedral Church, in the presence of "the illustrious Prince Henry, by the grace of God King of England and "France, who at the said mass, and at the accustomed time, offered in "gold 5*s*. 8*d*." Probably this was the occasion of the opening of the middle Choir, after the completion of the roof. Most of the windows in the side aisles in the eastern portion of the new Choir were probably by this time glazed, and the altars on the south of the Holy Innocents and the north of St. Stephen, had been duly restored for use.

Stephen, second Lord Scrope, of Masham, the Archbishop's brother, directed in his will, January, 1405, that his body might be interred in a part of the new work, viz., in the middle of the chantry chapel of St. Stephen, just below the steps, which was the commencement of the family sepulchre at that part. Large stores of glass also had been accumulated for the great east window, and in the same year a contract was made between the dean and chapter and Master John Thornton, of Coventry, glazier, to "pourtray the said window with his own hands, and the historic images "and other things to be painted on the same." "And the said John shall "receive of the dean and chapter for every week he shall work in his art "during the said three years, four shillings; and each year of the same "three years, five pounds sterling; and after the work is completed, ten "pounds for his reward." So that Archbishop Scrope's tenure of office is associated with much work going on in the Minster just at the part where we find heraldic memorials of his family and himself, viz., the high altar and the chapels north and south. So far had the work, commenced at the east end, advanced towards the west.

But his rule came to a sudden and violent end. Richard II., in spite of all his frivolities and excesses, must have been a fascinating person, for he had some grand traits of character, and was graceful and cultured. The Archbishop must have been intimately associated with him, and, together with other members of his family, had derived great benefits from him. As a statesman he could not but feel that his continuance upon the throne was detrimental to the tranquillity and prosperity of the country. His purpose, according to the proclamation afterwards made, evidently was to establish a strong regency during Richard's life, and preserve the throne for the infant son of Roger, Earl of March, the grandson of the Duke of Clarence, whom Richard had declared to be his heir-apparent. He had welcomed Henry when he had landed at Ravenspur as a means to that end, and concurred in Richard's deposition. According to Fabyan, he was present in the Tower when he solemnly made his formal renunciation of his claims to be King, and on the following day read the same to the Parliament assembled in Westminster hall, standing by the empty throne, dressed in cloth of gold. Perhaps he felt it expedient to dissemble his opposition when Henry, Earl of Hereford, rose up and, crossing himself, boldly claimed the throne, and the whole assembly unanimously acceded thereto.

But time went on. Richard had died at Pontefract; how, no one knew, or ever will know. The secrets of that dark prison-house were seldom revealed; and it is still only a matter of conjecture under what dark cloud that bright, careless life was extinguished. The great expectations formed on Henry's accession were, as usual, not universally fulfilled. Dissatisfaction and discontent arose, culminating in the open rebellion of the great Earl of Northumberland, the Constable of England. His son, Hotspur, had had an altercation with the King about allowing his brother-in-law, Edmund Mortimer, to ransom himself from captivity. Henry struck him in the face and called him "traitor," and drew his sword. "Not here," said Hotspur, "but in the field;" and he kept his word.

A formal defiance was immediately issued, charging Henry, *inter alia*, "That he had sworn to them at Doncaster in 1398 that he would not "claim the kingdom, but only his inheritance and land, but that Richard "should still reign under the control of a council of prelates and barons. "Yet he had imprisoned him, taken his crown, starved him to death in "Pontefract, after fifteen days and nights of hunger, thirst, and cold. He "had refused to allow Edmund Mortimer to ransom himself from captivity, "and had kept the young Earl of March from his rightful succession to "the throne."

The battle of Shrewsbury followed, where Percy fell, and his head was fixed on the gate of York. There, on St. Lawrence day, Henry himself received the abject submission of the Earl, and the poor old man was quite broken down when his eyes saw the ghastly head of his favourite son upon the gate.*

By the end of the year the rebellion seemed, for the time, suppressed. Elizabeth, widow of "Harry Hotspur," and sister of Edmund Mortimer, was released from arrest, and her husband's head taken down from the walls of York and given to her, November 3rd. The Earl of Northumberland

* Wylie's *History of Henry IV.*

having been kept under close guard at Baginton in Warwickshire, and deprived of his office of Constable, received his pardon, and having taken the oath of allegiance, returned to his northern home. William Clifford, however, the guardian of Hotspur's son, young Henry Percy, still held the castles of Berwick, Warkworth, and Alnwick, until his father's confiscated estates should be restored. Badges of the white hart were being widely distributed in Essex, and word was despatched to the King, who was absent in the west, urging his presence in the north. He came at once to Pontefract, and thence to Thorp, near York.*

I suppose the unsettled state of things seemed to indicate a good opportunity, and accordingly another effort was made, Hardyng says, "by "good advyse and counseill of Master Richard Scrope," together with Thomas Mowbray, the Earl Marshal. He was the eldest son of the Duke of Norfolk, one of "the five lords appelant" in Richard II.'s reign who had initiated revolutionary proceedings against him in Parliament, 1356, and in dealing with whom Richard had, for once, exhibited his father's vigour and courage, arresting the Duke of Gloucester, the Earls of Arundel and Warwick, and banishing Hereford (now Henry IV.) and the Duke of Norfolk, when, on the trumpery plea of a quarrel concerning loyalty to him, they entered the lists to settle their differences. Norfolk died in exile.† His son, therefore, would perhaps have naturally sided with Henry IV.; but he married Constance, daughter of John Holland, Duke of Exeter, brother of Thomas, Earl of Kent. She was also cousin to Joan, wife of Henry Lord Scrope, while Margaret Welles, mother of Margaret, wife of Stephen Lord Scrope, was Mowbray's father's sister. So that there is ample reason why he should be found associated with the house of Scrope in aid of the house of Mortimer.

Northumberland favoured the movement, but remained at home, excusing himself to Henry, who required his presence with him, on the plea of illness and old age.‡ Archbishop Scrope caused an instrument of ten articles against Henry to be affixed to the doors of the churches of York, and having preached a sermon to the same effect in the Minster,§ joined Mowbray, who had gathered a considerable force at Shipton, in the forest of Galtres, near York. The Earl of Westmoreland met them with an inferior force, and feeling his inability to cope with them, had recourse to stratagem. He invited a conference, heard their grievances, assured them that they should be attended to, and then suggested that, as their object was attained, their forces should be at once disbanded. The unsuspecting Archbishop, anxious for peace, fell into the trap. The armed

---

* Wylie's *History of Henry IV.* *History of the Percies.*

† Taswell Langmead's *Constitutional History.*

‡ *History of the Percies*, vol. i. p. 234. § Browne's *History of York Minster.*

men were dismissed; and he and Mowbray were immediately seized and carried to the King at Bishopthorpe, who was advancing by hasty marches to suppress the insurrection.

Two years before, Henry had received from Scrope's hands the blessed Sacrament at the Minster; now the exasperated and triumphant King insisted on his instant execution. The just and brave Judge Gascoigne, one of Yorkshire's noblest heroes, refused to pass sentence upon him. "Neither you, my lord, nor any of your subjects, can legally, "according to the law of the realm, sentence any bishop to death." But "Sir William Fulthorpe, Knight, learned in the laws" (Stowe), hesitated not for a moment to obey the King's commands. Sentence was pronounced, and on the same day, mounted on a "sorry nag," worth 40*s.*, and clad in a blood-coloured garment with purple cord, he was taken to the river-bank, at Clementhorpe, in sight of his Cathedral Church. "Son," he meekly said to Thomas Alman, who was to be his executioner, "may God forgive "thee my death, as I forgive thee. But I pray thee that thou wilt give "me with the sword five wounds in the neck, which I desire to bear for "the love of my Lord Jesus Christ, who being for me obedient unto His "Father until death, bore five principal wounds." Then he three times kissed him, and kneeling down, with his hands joined and his eyes raised to heaven, prayed—"Into Thy hands, most sweet Jesus, I commend my "spirit;" then, stretching out his neck, and folding his hands over his breast, the executioner at five strokes severed his head from his body. The Earl of Nottingham was condemned and executed in a similar summary manner, and the Earl of Northumberland, on receiving the intelligence, fled into Scotland.

"The next day following, four vicars choral of the Cathedral Church "of York did unto the same Church, five or more accompanying them, in "fear and silence, not without fear and trembling, convey the body of the "venerable prelate, where at the east end of the new work of the said "Church, but with moderate ceremony, as the circumstances of the time "permitted, that sacred body rests in the earth."* And there, when the grave was opened March 28th, 1844, the remains were discovered, and left undisturbed.

It was a pious end to a holy life. It was an act of arbitrary power unique in the history of England. Becket had been murdered by obsequious courtiers; Simon Sudbury had been beheaded by the Wat Tyler's mob; and in after days, Laud was condemned and executed by the supreme judicature of the land. But here the King himself usurped a power which the chief exponent of law told him he did not possess, and which, therefore, nothing could justify. Treacherously taken, unlawfully condemned,—it was a cold-blooded murder.

* *Barlow MS.* Browne's *History.*

Life was lightly valued in those days, and "Sic volo sic jubeo" often the policy of kings, but such an act as this could not be tamely submitted to. In vain were logs of wood laid upon the grave. The people flocked in numbers to offer prayers as at a shrine of a saint; and doubtless they but expressed the wide-spread feeling amongst those whose sentiments it would be dangerous policy to disregard. The Scropes were amongst the most powerful families in the land, and certainly they, and the members of the other noble houses with whom they were related, would resent that the distinguished son of the head of the branch of Bolton, and the no less distinguished brother of the head of the branch of Masham, should, by the same hand, be laid in bloody graves.

Then there were the clergy to be reckoned with. John of Gaunt, his father, had been more than suspected of favouring John Wycliffe and the Lollards. Henry had lately found it expedient, therefore, to consent to the burning of William Sawtre, or Chatrys, on that charge, a penalty never before heard of in England. The ecclesiastical spirit was not to be trifled with. Such an event as Scrope's death might well seem to indicate a reactionary policy.

And therefore he may have deemed it wise to temporise, and to seek to reconcile his aggrieved and angry subjects in the north by honouring the persons and the memories of the houses which they loved. Perhaps, too, he remembered the trouble and dishonour to which his predecessor, Henry II., had had to submit for the death of Becket.

And so young Henry Scrope, now third Baron of Masham, the nephew of the Archbishop, was received into royal favour, and sent as ambassador to Denmark the following year, 1406, and to France in 1408. His wife, Philippa, daughter of Sir Guy de Bryan, had died in 1406, and this year he married Joan Holland, second wife and widow of Edmund, Duke of York and Earl of Cambridge, the King's uncle. Surely the house of Scrope must have seemed to be again in the ascendant by such a brilliant alliance. Additional tokens of royal confidence followed. In 1409 he was made Treasurer of England. In 1413 he was again sent as ambassador to the Duke of Burgundy, and the year following to France, perhaps to communicate to the King the accession of Henry V. to the throne, for Henry IV. died that year. At any rate it is evident that he was in his favour, for the year following he was employed by him as one of the ambassadors sent to Charles VI. demanding the crown of France as the heir of Isabella, mother of his great-grandfather, Edward III., with the quaint but characteristic alternative that he would marry his daughter Catherine if he consented, or fight him if he did not.

The King of France naturally chose the latter; and after many fruitless negotiations, war was declared, and Henry, with his customary energy, set about his preparations at once, raising money in every way in his power, sparing no expense in making his army as efficient as possible, until he had raised and equipped 6,000 men-at-arms, 2,400 archers, with cannons as effective as the manufacturing skill of that day could produce, and other engines of war; and, for the first time in history, a hospital staff for the sick and wounded, under the charge of his physician, Nicholas Colnet, and his surgeon, Thomas Morstede, each of whom was to receive the daily pay of twelve pence, and twelve assistants of their own craft, each of whom was to receive the daily pay of an archer, *i.e.* eightpence.*

Up to this time the revived prosperity of the Scropes seems to have been in its zenith; and, if I mistake not, this is indicated in the Heraldry of York Minster in the windows and on the walls of the new Choir, which must then have been just ready for glazing and adorning. Much still remains, but much has been defaced and much has passed away.

In the north aisle of the Choir is a large window of three lights, too mutilated to enable us to form any idea of the subject; and Torre's account of the window in his time is too vague to give us more than a general idea. It seems to have had three large female figures, one in the centre of each light, and each of those in the outside lights bearing a child in her arms. The pedestals on which they stood are destroyed, but there are traces of splendid canopies over them, enriched with figures, one or two of which remain. And beneath the pedestals of the figures was a predella with, Torre says, many figures. The lower tracery lights were, he also says, filled with the arms of Scrope, and figures in the lights above. The border is still fairly perfect, and that is composed of "the bend or" alternating with the letters R. and S., the initials of the Archbishop's name. Doubtless in its integrity it was a splendid window. From its position at the west end of the Lady Chapel, I should fancy that it was an offering from the Archbishop himself to the work which he found almost completed when he attained the see.

Other memorials are there of him, which indicate special honour. In the north transept of the Nave, third window, east, and in the south Choir transept, east, there are shields containing the arms of Scrope of Masham, with a red bordure set with mitres,† and the same carved in stone may be noticed on the south side of the Choir, above the arch opening into the south transept. This bordure is known in Heraldry as "an augmentation of "honour," and was probably granted for this purpose, to efface any stain on his reputation which might be caused by his execution, and to indicate that the charge of high treason, for which he was beheaded, was annulled.

The shield in the Nave transept is probably out of its original place, and doubtless, like the other, originally formed part of one of the new

* *Life of Henry V.* Rev. A. J. Church. † See coloured illustration.

Choir windows. The shield on stone is of course in its original place. And how significant and appropriate is that place! It probably marks the portion of the Choir on the building of which Scrope concentrated his efforts during his short tenure of office. Next to it are the arms of Skirlaw, a cross of six bastions or willow withies, which he adopted in allusion to his father having been a basket-maker. Walter Skirlawe was prebendary of Fenton in this Minster, 1370, and archdeacon of the East Riding. In 1385 he became Bishop of Lichfield and Coventry, and was translated to Durham 1388. During his tenure of office here he certainly liberally co-operated with Scrope in benefactions towards, if indeed he were not the actual architect of, the new Choir. He bequeathed money for the building of the Lantern Tower, which is commemorated by his arms above the spandrils. Many of the surrounding shields in glass and stone represent relatives or friends of the late Archbishop, either put up to do them honour, or in acknowledgment of donations which they had given.

In the northern transept of the Choir aisle we find in stone on the west wall the shields of Scrope and Neville, probably Sir Geoffry, the Archbishop's brother, killed in Lithuania, and Eleanor, his widow, daughter of Ralph, Lord Neville, who eventually became abbess of the Minories in London, or, as seems indicated by the bird on the saltire, Maud, daughter of Thomas Nevill, Lord Furnival, who, Burke says, "married William, "Lord Scrope." Facing them, on the east wall, are Scrope and Fitz-Hugh, probably commemorating Henry, Lord Fitz-Hugh, who married the Archbishop's sister Joan.

On the south wall, in stone, Clifford, perhaps Sir Lewis Clifford, younger son of Robert, third Lord Clifford, surnamed "the King's knight," I suppose from his close attendance on Henry IV., or perhaps Roger, Lord Clifford, his cousin; and a shield bearing a cross patonce, either Sir Thomas Marshall—or a cross patonce gules,—or Sir William Melton, azure a cross patonce argent.

And then the windows, now so bare, were thick set, according to Torre, with the armorial devices of Percy, Mowbray, Neville, Clifford, Fitz-Hugh, Darcy, Hastings, Roos, Thoresby—all names recorded as companions in arms of the great house of Scrope, in the Scrope and Grosvenor roll.

The third west window in the clerestory above may have been put up by Sir Henry Scrope, in commemoration of himself and his own immediate family. In the tracery lights we find Scrope impaling or, a lion rampant sable, probably the coat of Sir Stephen Scrope, the second baron, his father, brother to the Archbishop, who married Margaret, daughter of Lord Welles.* Another shield, probably that of Sir Henry himself.

* See coloured plate.

Six other shields are in lower parts of the six lights, each having the family coat, but they are not sufficiently perfect to enable me to ascertain accurately whether they are differenced or not. If so, they represent the other members of his family. Sir Geoffry, the second son, who was knighted, and received a grant of £20 per annum for his services in the field; Stephen, another brother, prebendary of Langtoft in the Minster, archdeacon of Richmond, and chancellor of Cambridge; William Scrope, his younger brother, prebendary of Skipwith and archdeacon of Durham; with their sisters—Maud, who died a nun, Elizabeth, who married Lord Greystock, whose arms in stone are on the wall beyond, and another, who married Sir Baldwin de Frevyll.

And on the bend in each is to be noticed an interesting and significant feature, a lion passant in outline.* What does it mean? That it was valued is indicated by a provision in Sir Henry's will (dated June 23rd, 1415), who directed concerning his sepulchre:—"Fiat tumba mea habens "nomen meum et obitum scriptum in illa parte tumbæ meæ versus "ecclesiam, et imaginem mei super dictam tumbam armatam in armis meis "cum *umbra leonis* in le bende prout vivens utor." What does it mean?

Dallaway quotes from the "Boke of St. Albans":—"There be certain "nobuls and gentilmen in Englande the which beere shadys diverse in "theyr armys, as lyon, antlope, and other, and men say that such personys "as beer theyr umbrated armys had theyr progenitors beryng the same, not "umbrated, but hole. Bot the possessionis and the patrimonyes descended "to other men," *i.e.* that when arms represented no substantial value they were carried in outline only; and so, doubtless, this was purposely so given that Scrope might understand that it did not recognise him as received into the family of Plantagenet, but that it was simply another additional token of royal favour and friendship from the King (granted to him, perhaps, when he married his uncle's widow, and thus became almost a relative to the royal house), viz., the privilege of bearing the *form* of a lion of England, the royal cognizance of Plantagenet, upon his ancestral bend; and the favour may have been extended to each member of his family, as though they all shared the royal goodwill. What a climax of prosperity! The last vestige of the cloud seemed to have passed away, and the glory of the race seemed complete. Alas! for the frailty of human prosperity and human intentions; that tomb was never made; that body never rested in these hallowed aisles; in less than twelve months from the date thereof it was consigned, headless and dishonoured, to a far distant grave.

Sir Henry's brilliant marriage had acquired for him many advantages, but it also involved him in many dangers, for he became not only step-great-uncle to the King, but step-uncle to Edward, Duke of York, and

* See coloured plate.

Richard, Earl of Cambridge; while his wife's sister, Alianore Holland, having married Roger Mortimer, he became uncle to Edmund Mortimer, who was still languishing in prison, and to his sister Anne, who had married Richard, Earl of Cambridge. Thus he was, naturally, entangled in the conspiracy promoted by the latter, thus expressed in the record of his trial:—"He intended to kill the usurper, Henry of Lancaster, and to set the "Earl of March upon the throne." And as he was married and had no children, the Earl of Cambridge calculated that the succession would at his death come to his own son Richard. It was, in fact, very much of a revival of the conspiracy for which the Archbishop had suffered in favour of the house of Mortimer. Eventually, though neither in his way nor in his life, his wishes were fulfilled, for that son Richard was the Duke of York who was killed at the battle of Wakefield—whose son was Edward IV.

But when the army was on the point of embarking, and Henry himself had arrived at Southampton to superintend the operation, the conspiracy was discovered, and the Earl of Cambridge, Lord Scrope, and Thomas Grey, of Heton, in Northumberland, were arrested. Henry's action was prompt, but legal. A jury of Commoners was summoned, and the three conspirators were indicted before them. The Constable of Southampton Castle swore that they had each confessed their guilt. Sir Thomas Grey was at once condemned and executed. The Earl of Cambridge and Lord Scrope pleaded the privilege of peerage. A Court of eighteen Barons, presided over by the Duke of Clarence, was summoned; the evidence given to the jury was read to them; the prisoners were neither produced in court nor examined nor heard in their own defence, but received sentence of death, which was soon after executed.

Shakespeare has graphically represented, in *Henry V.*, act 2, scene 1, the exposure of this conspiracy. Henry's words to Scrope are indignant and severe, but not more than his act of unmerited treachery had deserved:—

> "But, O! what shall I say to thee, Lord Scroop; thou cruel,
> Ingrateful, savage, and inhuman creature!
> Thou that didst bear the key of all my counsels,
> That knewest the very bottom of my soul,
> That almost might'st have coined me into gold,
> Would'st thou have practised on me for thy use?"

I know not on what authority Shakespeare has put this speech (which extends some eighty lines more) into the mouth of Henry. It is full of deep pathos, and such as a gallant man, stung to the quick by the unexpected treachery of a trusted friend, could utter—indignant at his perfidy, but yet scarcely able to renounce his affection for him. His concluding words express deep sorrow rather than passionate anger, and are at least in harmony with the chivalrous nature of Henry V.:—

"I will weep for thee
For this revolt of thine, methinks, is like
Another fall of man"

And Scrope's words are at least what he ought to have said, and what, let us hope, he did say, for they express the only reparation which he could make for his conduct —

"Our purposes God justly hath discovered!
And I repent my fault more than my death,
Which I beseech your highness to forgive,
Although my body pay the price of it"

He left no children, but his heir was his younger brother, Sir John Scrope, who was restored to the barony eleven years afterwards, 1426, by Henry VI, who seems to have taken him into favour He was made a Privy Councillor, Ambassador to the King of Spain and King of the Romans, 1420, to Scotland, 1429, and was employed in diplomatic missions on many subsequent occasions Eventually he became Treasurer of England, and died six years before the unhappy end of that King, 1455 His arms are in the south transept of the Choir, impaling those of his second wife, Elizabeth, daughter of Sir Thomas Chaworth, of Wiverton, by his wife Nicholaa, daughter and heiress of Sir Gerard Braybrook *

Why the Chaworths carried the quarterings of Aufreton (azure two bendelets, or) and Caltoft (argent, an inescutcheon within an orle of ten cinquefoils, sable) into which families they had intermarried, instead of their own coat (Barry of ten, gules and argent, an orle of martletts sable) I cannot say Thoroton, in his *History of Nottinghamshire*, has little of interest to record about them, though one member of the family is, at least, closely associated with English history, viz, Maud, daughter of Sir Patrick Chaworth, who married Henry, younger son of Edmund Crouchback, second son of Henry III, and younger brother of Thomas, Duke of Lancaster, beheaded at Pontefract, and her grand-daughter Blanche married John o' Gaunt The name of Chaworth is, however, intimately associated with a tragic episode in very modern history—William Chaworth, the last of his race, being killed by his cousin, William, fifth Lord Byron, great uncle of the poet It could hardly be said in a duel † They were dining with a large party at the Star and Garter Tavern, in Pall Mall, Jan 26th, 1765, when an altercation arose between them on the subject of preserving game Heated with wine, they accidentally met after dinner on the staircase, resumed their altercation, and retired together into a private room, lighted by one tallow candle, wrangling as they went Very soon the bell was violently rung, and the waiter entering, found Lord Byron supporting Mr Chaworth, their swords drawn, and the latter mortally wounded What had actually happened was never

* See coloured illustrations † *Annual Register*

STONE SHIELDS IN THE CHOIR AND NORTH & SOUTH CHOIR TRANSEPTS.
YORK MINSTER.

clearly established, perhaps those most deeply interested scarcely knew themselves Lord Byron was tried by his peers for manslaughter, and pronounced guilty, but claiming exemption from sentence as a peer, under a statute of Edward VI, he was dismissed on paying the fees, and retired to Newstead, where he lived a secluded life for 30 years, dying 1798 Mary Ann, the only child of William Chaworth, married John Musters, of Colwick Hall, and is commemorated in the poems of Lord Byron as

> "Herself the solitary scion left
> Of a time-honoured race"

On the window immediately beside the arms of Scrope and Chaworth are two shields of Scrope of Masham The one has simply a bend or and label, the other the bordure of mitres already mentioned There is also another shield, bearing on a bend sable three mullets or, probably the arms of John Hotham, who married Ivetta, daughter of Sir Geoffry Scrope One of the shields over the west arch bears a fesse dancetté, probably Sir Wm Vavasour, whose name appears on the Scrope and Grosvenor Roll

Other shields there are in the south transept, which are probably connected with Scrope The escallops of Dacre, and a fesse between six crosslets in stone above the north arch, are perhaps the cognizances of Margaret, daughter of the sixth Lord Dacre, who married John, a younger son of Sir John Scrope, he died in 1452, leaving no children, and was buried in the Minster The other shield may be the arms of Beauchamp, but I think are probably those of Sir Robert Laton, who held lands at Laton and Melsonby, *temp* Richard II, and who appears, by his deposition in the Scrope and Grosvenor roll, to have been for many years a companion-in-arms of the Scrope family The lions rampant on the stone shields above the east arch represent, no doubt, Mowbray and Percy, so intimately associated, as we have seen, with the house of Scrope

The stone shields on the north and south sides of the Choir, between the transept and the nave (*i e* the part probably built by the Archbishop) seem to carry out the same story The altar then stood one bay nearer the west than now On the north side, then, we have five shields representing the sacredness and dignity of the Archbishopric of York —(1) The emblems of the Passion, (2) the seven pointed stars of St Wilfrid, (3) the keys, (4) the swords, of St Peter, (5) the seven mascles of St William Then follow (1) Sir Henry Scrope, the bend charged with a very substantial "umbra leonis" (2) a chief, three chevrons in base, possibly the arms of Henry, Lord FitzHugh, whom Sir Henry Scrope in his will calls "consanguineo meo," *i e*, as we have seen, his uncle, and to whom he leaves two books, "pro remembrancia", (3) a saltire charged with a crescent, possibly Sir William Nevill, second son of Ralph, second Baron Nevill, a distinguished soldier, gentleman of the bedchamber to Richard II, and a staunch adherent to him in his family difficulties, (4) a saltire, possibly John, Lord Nevill, son of Ralph, Earl of Westmoreland, by whose treachery the Archbishop was captured, but as he married Lady Elizabeth Holland, daughter of Thomas, Earl of Kent, he would be brother-in-law to Sir Henry Scrope, and thus drawn into the same political intrigue, (5) a fesse dancette, Vavasour repeated, the fesse highly ornamented, doubtless because he allowed the stone necessary for the building to be quarried on his land, and therefore his shield is thus appropriately placed at the completion of the Choir

On the south side we commence with the shield of Archbishop Scrope, with the augmentation of honour, the bordure of mitres, immediately above the altar Next to him his colleague and helpmeet, Bishop Skirlaw, who had the moral courage to acknowledge that his father was a basket-maker, and carry three osiers crossed Then the shields of the three principal actors in the great drama Scrope, where the label denotes, I think, not only Masham, but primogeniture, and marks, therefore, the Earl of Wilts, slain at Bristol, then a shield having quarterly Percy and Lucy, the arms of the great Earl of Northumberland, father of the gallant Hotspur, and chief of the rising in the north, and then the lion rampant of Mowbray, who was beheaded at the same time as the Archbishop The remaining shields are, I think, official, or royal First the lioncels and horn, which, as I have already pointed out (page 36), may be the cognizance of the Lord Mayor of the time here, or the initial quartering of Plantagenet Next to it the shield of the house of Mortimer, for which so much was dared and suffered, and representing the senior claim of the house of York Then the three crowns of Edwin of Northumbria, the arms of the ancient kingdom in which York is situated, and therefore the token of sovereignty over it Next to it the cross and martlets of Edward the Confessor, which had been specially adopted by Richard II and impaled with his own arms And finally the last shield, bearing a cross, probably or a cross gules The arms of De Burgh, quartered by Edward IV from his grandmother, Anne Mortimer, whose grandmother, Philippa Plantagenet, wife of Edmund Mortimer, was the daughter of Elizabeth de Burgh, only daughter and heiress of William de Burgh, Earl of Ulster, by Lionel, Duke of Clarence

Edmund Mortimer quartered these arms on his seal, viz, 1 and 4, Mortimer, 2 and 3, De Burgh

On the capital of the pillar just outside, at the entrance of the Choir, and also high up above it on the capital of the pillar supporting the south tower arch, may be seen the white hart couched, to which I have already alluded (page 56) as the badge of Richard II, and which was adopted by Edward IV Sandford tells us—"Generally with a scroll inscribed 'Rege "'Richardo,' *i e* 'In honour of Richard II,' whose device it was, and who

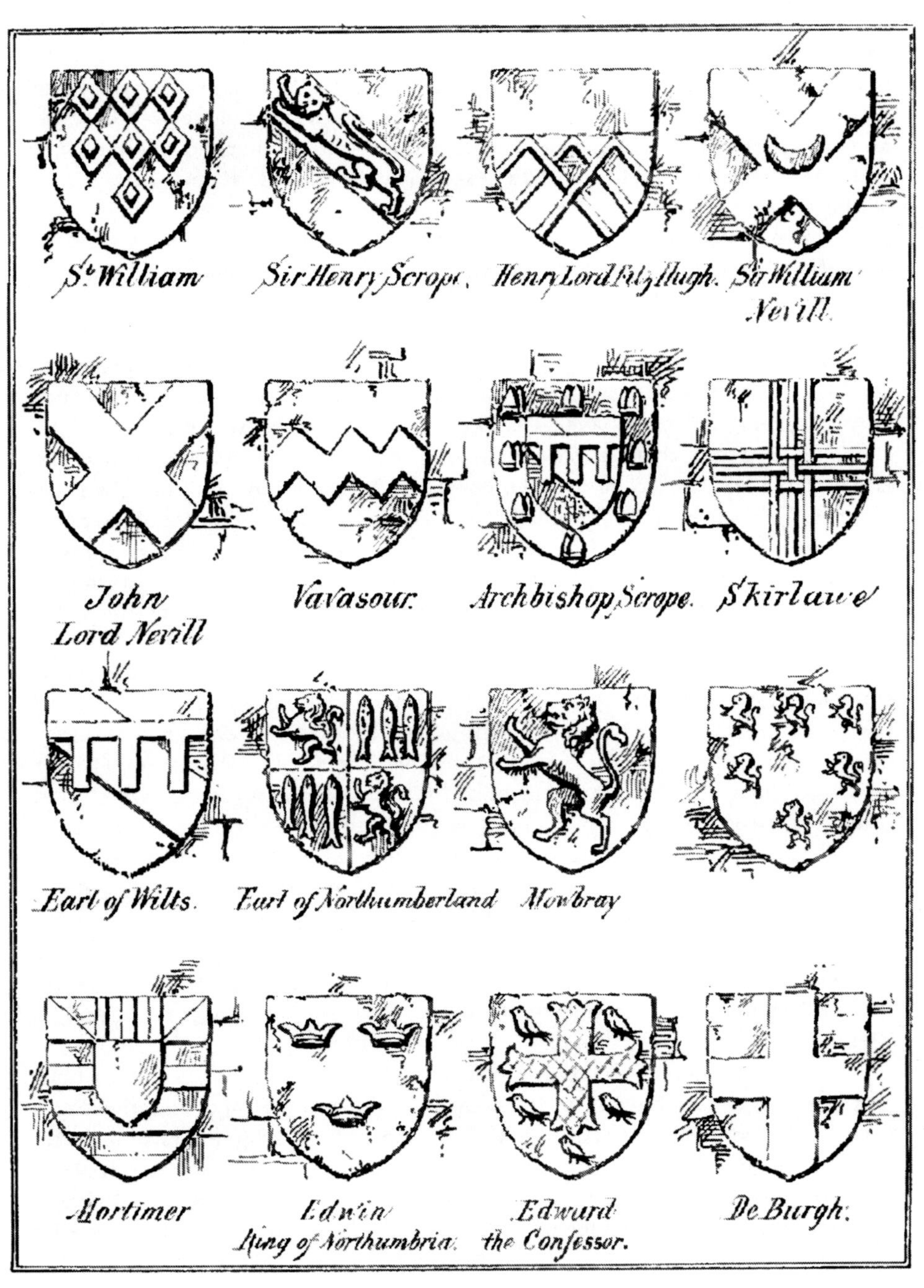

STONE SHIELDS IN THE CHOIR AND NORTH & SOUTH CHOIR TRANSEPTS.
YORK MINSTER.

"in 1387 had nominated Roger Mortimer, Earl of March, his successor in "the kingdom of England, which Roger was great-grandfather to this King "Edward IV" Indeed, the shields round the tower are very much repetitions of the shields in the Choir, for the perpendicular lining of ashlar work to the old Norman tower, and the raising of the lantern above, were done about the same time Close to the hart lodged, on the lower capital, may be observed the stag's head cabossed, the cognizance of Archbishop Bowet, who was a munificent benefactor towards the completion of the Choir

Possibly these shields may not have been carved until the accession of Edward IV We know how cordially he recognised the value of the services which the Archbishop had rendered to his family, for in his proclamation, April, 1471, immediately after the battle of Barnet, after adducing the success which had attended the house of York on that occasion as evidence of the justice of his cause, the King says—"Yet "natheless no consideraci'n had to the p'misses, nother to thauthorite of "that holy fader, Richard Scrope, somtyme Archbis'shop of Yorke, which "for the right and title of our auncestrie, whos estate we nowe bere, and "have, died and suffred deth and martyrdom"* It is very probable, therefore, that he added to the emblems in the Minster commemorating his life and death Possibly the tomb of the Archbishop was at this time erected by his direction It is of late Perpendicular date, and corresponds with the style of this reign Up to this time, no doubt, the Archbishop's body had remained marked only by the rough logs of wood cast on his grave by Henry IV's order. The tomb is massive and handsome, but it would be scarcely of sufficient dignity for so important a character in English history, if we did not consider the completion and decoration of the Choir as Scrope's monument Indeed, the amount raised by "oblations at the "tomb of Master Richard le Scrope, late Archbishop of York," materially assisted in providing funds for its completion One year they reached £62 8*s*, while the oblations at the shrine of St William amounted to only 14*s* 2½*d* †

Henry VI, during his reign, on several occasions shewed his desire to conciliate the Scrope family Besides conferring the honours which I have already mentioned on Sir John Scrope, he restored to him the dower of Margery, his mother, and the lands forfeited by his brother, Sir Henry, third Lord Scrope. He allowed his son Thomas, fifth Lord Scrope, to build a chantry, where prayers might be offered for the souls of his deceased relatives, Sir Henry and the Archbishop included

But the death of the Archbishop, and the cause for which he suffered, were not allowed to be forgotten On the capitals of the south-west column of the north Choir aisle, and fourth and fifth columns eastward, may be

* *Scrope and Grosvenor Roll*, vol ii p 161 † Browne's *York Minster*

noticed figures introduced amidst the foliage, which Mr Browne has ingeniously demonstrated to be the history of the imprisonment of Edmund Mortimer and the murder of Scrope I have not space to enter into them at length here, but, though coarse, they are vigorous and full of significance, and in those days, when few could read books, we can well imagine how the savage representations of Henry and his myrmidons, and the quaint and touching, though rude, figure of the young Edmund in captivity, must have gone to the hearts of those who glanced at them as they passed by to lay their offerings on the grave of Archbishop Scrope, and returned only the more resolute to remain faithful to the interest of the house of Mortimer and York, and revenge on the house of Lancaster the violent and impious act of the fourth Henry

In 1461 Henry VI was deposed, and by the accession of Edward IV the house of Mortimer became at last supreme, and an early effort was made by, I suppose, the Yorkist sympathisers in the Chapter, to do distinguished honour to the Archbishop's memory For on Monday, March 21st, the Chapter was summoned to "consider the holy work of "canonization and translation of Richard, of blessed and pious memory, "sometime Archbishop of York," when, "having held a long and earnest "deliberation of and concerning the matter for which the convocation was "made," it was adjourned to the following day, and then further adjourned, and then, after several adjournments, it was finally determined that the Chapter should assemble on the 16th of August next ensuing, but then no mention was made of the matter—in fact, it was evidently allowed to drop * And the solution of this is not far to seek, for, on the one hand, I find amongst those who called the first Chapter the name of John Pakenham as treasurer of the Cathedral Church, who was probably the moving spirit in the transaction, for the only daughter and heir of Sir John Pakenham, of Lordington, had married Sir Geoffrey Pole, second son of Sir Richard Pole by the Lady Margaret Plantagenet, Countess of Salisbury, daughter of George, Duke of Clarence, brother of Edward IV On the other hand, Richard Andrew, the Dean, had been private secretary to Henry VI—indeed, had erected the Choir screen, and placed the statue of that monarch therein, and therefore, while he did not openly oppose the new regime, he would be scarcely prepared to agree to that which would be most offensive to the Lancastrians *

But, nevertheless, the time-serving Archbishop, Lawrence Booth (who had changed sides more than once, and who succeeded George Nevill as Archbishop, 1476, the 15th year of Edward IV, and was for the moment a partisan of that King), professed to be very much scandalized at the veneration paid to the statue, and directed Master William Poteman, his

* Browne's *York Minster*

official "of our Consistorial Court at York, to admonish all and singular the "(Rural) Deans of the whole diocese of York, in order that the Deans may "each of them, all and singular, in his or their deanery or deaneries, "admonish with effect, whom we also admonish by these presents, that they "each of them refrain themselves, under penalty of the law, from this kind "of reverence of the said place "*

Dean Stanley thinks that the Dean and Chapter paid no attention to this stilted admonition, and that the observance was allowed to continue, though eventually, perhaps at the Reformation, the statue was removed and destroyed

However, the conflicting animosities of York and Lancaster went smouldering on for another twenty years, until, in 1485, Henry VII, by his marriage with Elizabeth, daughter of Edward IV, united the rival factions, and their sanguinary feuds ceased for ever

---

THE DE MAULEYS

The next cluster of shields illustrating the Bend is in the south aisle of the Nave, fourth window from the east, and represents the achievements of several members of the family of De Mauley, at the time when this Nave was built the owner of Mulgrave Castle, and one of the most powerful baronial houses in the north The window itself has suffered much by lapse of time, so we must turn to the invaluable manuscript history of the Minster, drawn up with indefatigable labour by James Torre, the learned antiquary, who lived 1649–99, and to whom we are indebted for much information concerning the property or buildings of the Minster, many traces of which would otherwise have been obliterated

By his help we can discern that the confused mass of coloured glass at the lower part of the middle light represents "an archdeacon in a chair, "habited sang, B, and gules," and on the same authority we can accept what no longer exists, viz that "At his feet is written

" . . en de Mauley, Arche D "

i e Stephen de Mauley, Archdeacon He held that dignity in 1289, and also possessed it in 1306 In 1298 he was instituted to the prebend of Bugthorpe, so that he was in office during part, at least, of the time of the erection of the Nave, and the window may therefore have been erected by him during his life, or by his friends after his death, to commemorate his tenure of office and the dignity of the family of which he was a member For, unless I mistake, the shields depicted hereon indicate the several members of his generation, both by kindred and alliance

* *Memorials of Westminster Abbey* (p 522), by Dean Stanley

It would be difficult to give an illustration of the entire window, but the several coats-of-arms thereon are engraved in the order in which they occur.* He himself holds up (or perhaps I should say held up, for nothing remains of his figure except his face) a shield, now defaced. Torre tells us that it was, or a bend sable charged with three dolphins argent. To his left are the remains of a leg and arm, mixed up in a confused *debris* of fragments, which evidently formed part of a figure of a mailed warrior kneeling, holding up a shield, still perfect, charged with vaire a maunche gules.

In the light beyond are fragments of the other kneeling figures, holding up shields. The nearest, utterly defaced now, was, according to Torre, or, a bend sable charged with a dragon argent, that beyond showing still the bend sable charged with three dolphins argent. In the light on the right of the figure of the archdeacon are two kneeling figures, that furthest east clad in armour, with a tunic of gold colour with broad stripes of black, charged with three eagles displayed argent, and holding a shield, or on a bend sable three eagles displayed argent.

Between him and the archdeacon there is another figure, similarly clad in armour, with tunic of yellow and red stripe, holding above his head a shield, bearing Or a bend gules.

Now, of course, it is very difficult absolutely to appropriate these figures and shields to the individuals they were intended to represent; but my conjecture is that they represent the sons of Peter de Mauley, third baron. Sir Harris Nicolas,† in a blazon of arms in a roll of the time of Edward II., gives the following bearings of the De Mauleys:—Sir Peter de Maulie, or a une bende de sable; Sir Robert, or a bend sable, and in the bend three eagles argent; Sir John de Mauley, or a bend sable, and in the bend three dolphins argent; Sir Edmund, a bend sable, and in the bend three wyvres or vipers argent. In the 32nd of Edward, viz. 1304, "Mons. "Pieres de Mauley" is mentioned as "en la compaignie de Roi, and de la "compaignie Mons. Pierre de Mauley, Mons. Robert, son frere, and Mons. "Johan, son frere."

It is, I admit, an assumption that they were brothers; but I ground it first upon their being represented in this particular manner together, and secondly upon the fact that they must have been living about the same time. Peter de Mauley, fourth, died in the third year of Edward II., viz. 1310. Edmund was killed at Bannockburn, 1314. Robert was alive in 1306 we know, for in that year, viz. 34th Edward I., in the "further orders "for the safe custody of certain Scottish prisoners," is the following:— "La feme Mons. William Wysman . . . soit envee a Rokesburgh, pr. garder "y en chastel, et soit livrée a Mons. R. de Mauley, Viscount de Rokesburgh."

* See illustration. † *Archæologia*, vol. xxxi. page 247.

PLATE 2.

TREHOUS.

BEK OR GANT.

FOSSARD.

SIR ROBERT DE MAULEY. SIR PETER DE MAULEY.

STEPHEN DE MAULEY, ARCHDEACON OF CLEVELAND.

FURNIVAL OF BLAGSDON

SIR EDMUND DE MAULEY. SIR JOHN DE MAULEY.

MALBIS.

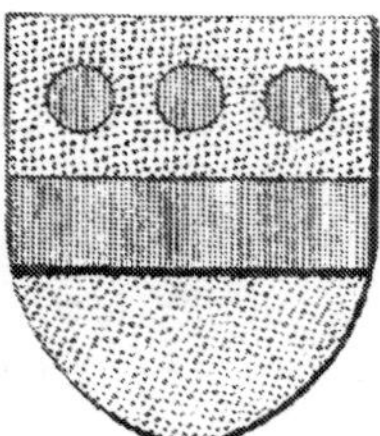
COLVIL.

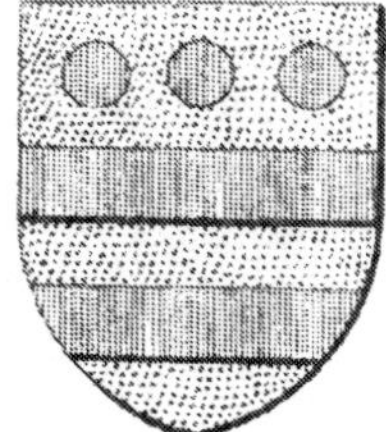
WAKE.

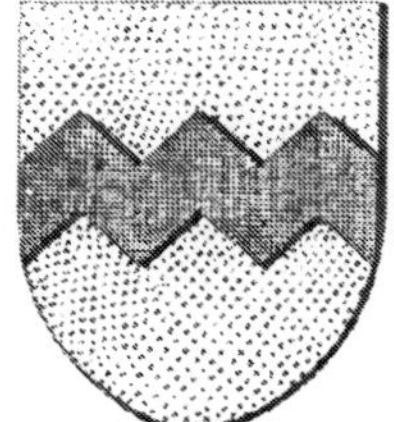
VAVASOUR.

FOURTH WINDOW FROM THE EAST. SOUTH AISLE OF NAVE,
COLOURED SHIELDS STILL EXISTING. PLAIN SHIELDS MENTIONED BY TORRE.

He was probably buried in the Minster, for in Torre's account of the "funeral monuments in the south aisle" (p 148) he says—"On the north "side, last under the south-west pillar of the lanthorn, lyes an old "monument, cutt in white stone, with the effigy of a knight in a coat of "mail, and other compleat armour, a sword by his side, and military bend "charged with three eagletts, his hands conjoyned at prayer, and his legs "across, with a lyon dormant at his feet And on his left side is a large "shield of his arms, viz or a bend three eaglets displayed"

There is a paper in the *Archæologia* (vol xxvi p 238) about this stone, which seems to have been given by Mr Thiselton, the then chapter-clerk, in whose garden it had been placed after the fire in 1829, to Sir Samuel Meyrick, who had deposited it in the chapel of Goodrich Court

Stephen de Mauley, the archdeacon, died, according to an entry in the Archbishop's registry, in 1317 And we may conclude that John, the remaining one mentioned, was also a brother Why the archdeacon should hold up what seems to be John's shield, charged with three eagles, I cannot say, possibly the shields may have been changed before Torre's time, and the shield with the red bend (the tincture changed for difference) has been placed in the hands of another figure I cannot discern any trace of that shield having been moved, and it seems to harmonize with the dress of the figure which holds it But the figure next to the archdeacon, holding the shield, vaire a maunche gules, I fancy to be the figure of Peter, fourth baron, as this, as I will shew by and by, would be the principal quartering of the family

According to Torre, three shields, since destroyed, were in the window beneath, *i e* in the north-eastern light, now occupied by the shield of Fenton (azure, six hawks' heads or), the arms of Malbis, argent, a chevron between three hinds' heads gules, in the centre light, or, a fesse gules, three torteaux in chief, and in the western light, or a fesse dancetté sable, Vavasour I venture to think that Torre was mistaken as to the two former, in consequence of the similarity of the coats, and that they should have been described as (1) argent, a chevron between three fowls' heads, Furnival, which difference in the ordinary coat seems to be still carried by one branch of the family, viz, Furnival of Blagsdon (Burke), (2) or, two bars gules, in chief two torteaux, Wake

This would make their significance quite clear, viz, the alliances formed by the only two of this generation who married Wake being the shield of Baldwin, Lord de Wake, whose daughter, we are told in the Hotham pedigree, married John de Mauley, who inherited the lands, and therefore acquired the name of Hotham Furnival being the coat of Eleanor, daughter of Thomas, Lord Furnival, who married Peter, fourth Baron de Mauley, and Vavasour that of Walter de Vavasour, who married her sister, Alyne or Alianora

If so, they were certainly a distinguished generation, the head of the house, perhaps, more for evil deeds than good, for we are told that he was a man of dreadful immorality, and had an intrigue with his wife's sister Alyna, for which he was admonished by the Archbishop of York, and absolved "on condition that he pays one hundred marks to the fabric "of York Minster"*

Two years later he was in more serious trouble with the King, for opening a cart belonging to the prioress of Walton, and carrying off seven nuns he found therein Eventually he was sentenced for his excesses to a severe penance, viz, that every Friday in Lent, the Ember days, and Advent, for seven years, he is to fast on bread and small beer, and on Good Friday and the vigil of the Festival of All Saints to use only bread and water He is to make a pilgrimage to the shrines of St William of York, St Thomas of Hereford, the Blessed Mary at Southwell, St John of Beverley, and St Wilfrid of Ripon, and is to be "fustigated seven times "before a procession in the church of York, in sola basna capucio deposito," *i e* well stripped † He seems, however, in spite of his peccadilloes, to have been exemplary in matters political and social,—a firm supporter of the Earl of Lancaster Probably for that reason he was excused from attending the Parliament of 1315, together with Walter Vavasour, Walter de Fauconberge, and others, and to that exemption has been attributed the result of Bannockburn and the regal imbecility In 1324 he was ordered for service in Germany, and died 1333 (*Archæologia*, xxxi 224)

Edmund de Mauley behaved so valiantly in the wars of Edward I that Edward II made him "Seneschallus hospitii," *i e* steward of the household In the 32nd year of the previous reign he had obtained a grant of the manor of Seton in Whitby-strand, and in the fifth year of Edward II he was appointed governor of Bridgnorth, and also of the castle town and bar town of Bristol Two years after, he had conferred on him for life the governorship of Cockermouth Castle, and in the next year "he was slain at the battle of Bannockburn," says Dugdale Vincent uses the expression "submersus,"‡ which probably means that he and his horse fell into one of the pits with which the Bruce had so craftily fortified his lines Robert de Mauley seems also to have been under-sheriff of Roxburgh, or as he is described in "the further orders" already alluded to, "Viscount de Rokesburgh"

We are also told § concerning Peter, that when Sir Edmund de Mortimer, of Wigmore, was ordered to march against Rhys ap Meredyth in South Wales, this Peter was retained to serve with him, and provide ten horses "cooperti," *i e* completely armed in mail under their housings They were to be—one black with a white foot, valued at 60 marks, or £40

* *Fasti Ebor* (Canon Raine), p 383. † Wheater *Archæologia* xxxi, ‡ p 245, § p 243

(this sum, according to the price of wheat, equalled £820), one black, price 40 marks, another black with two white feet, estimated at 30 marks, one dun, worth 20 marks, one bay, 18 marks, one iron-grey, 40 marks, one sorrell, 18 marks, one lyard (mottled-grey), 18 marks, one grey, 14 marks, and one colt, value 100 shillings Such as died in the service to be paid for according to this valuation

John de Mauley seems to have acquired the estates of Hotham, according to the manuscript pedigree of that family at Dalton If the position of these shields in the window indicates that they are brothers, it would certainly demonstrate that the Archdeacon Stephen was one of them

It is equally certain that there was a Stephen de Mauley, who was the son of Peter, the first Baron de Mauley, for in Roberts' *Calendarium Genealogicum*, p 278, we find under date of 7th Edward I, *i e* 1279, the mention of Stephen de Malolacu, brother of the said Peter, deceased, who (*i e* the said Peter) gives to his son and heir, and Nicholaa his wife, certain moneys Now Peter, third baron, married Nicholaa, daughter of Gilbert de Gant, and Stephen, therefore, would be the brother of the second baron, and son of the first, who was betrothed to Isabel de Turnham, 1214, and paid 7,000 marks, for her marriage, to King John in 1221 The archdeacon died in 1317, and supposing that he was this Stephen, and was born about 1230, he would have been eighty-seven at the time of his death, a great, but still a possible age Or there may have been two Stephens de Mauley—one the younger son of the first baron, born circa 1230, the other the son of the third baron, and eventually archdeacon

Another interesting question is suggested by the arms immediately above the row which I have been describing The centre shield, now destroyed, Torre tells us was gules a cross moline argent, which he names as Bek

Now Browne tells us that Archbishop William Fitzherbert (St William) died June, 1154, and was canonised by Pope Honorius, 1226 In 1284, his bones were translated from the place where they were first laid to the shrine prepared for them behind the high altar, on the day of the consecration of Anthony Bek, who paid all the expenses It is said that the translation took place at the urgent request of Stephen de Mauley, archdeacon of Cleveland Edward I, who assisted to carry the feretory, his Queen, eleven other bishops, Archbishop Wickwane, and the whole court attending Stephen was a cousin, and is reputed to have been a great friend of Bek's, which may account for the appearance of this coat in the window

But there is another possible, and to my mind very probable, solution Burke mentions this coat as carried also by the family of Gaunt or Gant Now Peter the third married Nicholaa, daughter of Gilbert de Gant, and Peter the fourth and his brothers Edmund, Robert, John, and (perhaps)

Stephen, were her sons. What more likely than that the Archdeacon should have placed in the window his mother's arms; while the coats on either side would be his father's? They remain unto this day. That shield on the east side contains vaire a maunche gules, that on the west side, or a bend sable. In the Hotham pedigree at Dalton it is stated (on I know not what authority) that the latter were the arms of Nigel Fossard, whose daughter, Johanna, married Robert de Turnham, and that the former are the arms of Peter de Trehons, Esquire to King John, who married Isabella, only child and heiress of Robert de Turnham. It is somewhat remarkable that the arms of Turnham are nowhere emblazoned on the window; but if history is to be trusted, there may have been good reason why the descendants of Peter de Trehons and Isabella de Turnham did not perpetuate the shield of the former; and why the Mauleys, who were the elder branch, and the Hothams, who were the younger, preferred to bear only the arms of Fossard "differenced." Indeed, the associations with the arms of Fossard are all agreeable, those with the arms of Trehons as distinctly painful.

Any one who has visited Mulgrave Castle, and driven through the picturesque domain of undulating woodland, carpeted with luxuriant undergrowth, and bounded on the south side by the vast expanse of moorland, and on the north by the beetling cliffs and stormy waters of the North Sea, cannot be at any loss to decipher and appreciate the selection made by the brothers for the "differences" of their coats of arms. It is even now a spot to kindle romantic sentiments in the hearts of the most callous tourists, and one can well imagine the enthusiasm which would be aroused by these scenes in the hearts of those who, in days when the present moor and woodland formed only a part of a vast forest, spent their lives amidst its glades in the exciting occupation of the chase, or embarked from the shore to gather "the harvest of the sea." How attractive to them each bird that sojourned amidst the branches, or reptile that crept beneath the brushwood, or fish that infested the sea—tokens in their eyes perhaps of mysteries which they had not unravelled, and types of characteristics which they would fain imitate in their future lives. Reared from childhood amidst such associations, what wonder that one chose the eagle which soared above his head; another the viper that crept beneath his feet; another the dolphin or porpoise that swam in the sea. Types of powerful soaring ambition,—quiet, unostentatious, yet deadly and successful craft,—and of buoyant vigour never extinguished under the waves and storms of life, but able to ride triumphant over them.

John de Mauley, or Hotham, carried also or, a bend sable differenced by three mullets argent*, which shield was borne by his descendants, for it appears in the east window of the south transept in the Choir, where it is probably the shield of John de Hotham, Prebendary of Stillington, 1310, or of

* See illustration.

John de Hotham, 1353, who married Ivetta, daughter of Sir Geoffry Scrope, probably the latter, as shields bearing the Scrope arms are on each side of it But this shield was discontinued, according to the MS family history in the possession of Lord Hotham, when Hugh le de Spencer the younger, the favourite of Edward II, who had married Alice, heiress of Sir John Hotham, was hung at Hereford His cousin and heir, Thomas Hotham of Scorborough, considering the family arms thus disgraced, abandoned them, with the advice of his great uncle, John, Bishop of Ely, the rebuilder of the Choir of that Cathedral Thomas Hotham assumed for his arms the present coat, viz, barry of ten, argent and azure, on a canton of the first, a Cornish chough sable, possibly with reference to the distinguished lineage of his mother, who was the daughter of Robert Baron of Hilton (argent two bars azure), by Margaret, sister and co-heir of Baron Thweng (argent between three popinjays vert, a fesse gules)

According to the Hotham pedigree, the coat, Or a bend sable, was originally the bearing of Nigel Fossard, a follower of the Conqueror, who, at the distribution of the land amongst his followers, received the plot of land called by the Celts Moel-graf (or Bere-hill, grave or moat), *i e* the moat at the barehill, or perhaps "the bare hill moated," in order to preserve it from the invasions of troublesome and unscrupulous neighbours In *Domesday Book* Mulgrave is simply called the Grif The manor had been held by Sunen in the English days, and was tilled by three ploughs Nigel Fossard held it of the Earl of Morton One of the family, William Fossard, is mentioned by Richard of Hexham in his narrative of the Battle of the Standard, fought near Northallerton, August 24th, 1138, amongst "the chiefs of the English who fought against the Scotch" The ruins of the Castle, which was probably originally the work of the Fossards, and indicate a position of great strength, are very picturesque It was probably remodelled and partly rebuilt by the De Mauleys, and occupies the entire width of a ridge extending to the cliffs, with deep valleys now clothed with wood on each side Leland speaks of it thus "Mongreve Castle stondeth upon "a craggy hille, and on each side of it is an hille far higher than that "whereon the Castelle stondeth"* The Fossards were a powerful stock They were lords of Doncaster, of Bramham, and of much land in the East Riding

There was a small Priory at Grosmont, near Whitby, founded about 1200 by Johanna de Turnham, attached to the Abbey of Grosmont or Grandimont in Normandy—a branch of the Benedictine order—and further endowed by the Fossards and Mauleys

The male line became extinct before the reign of Cœur de Lion, when Joan, the daughter and heiress of William Fossard, married Robert de

* *Abbeys and Castles of England*—Timbs

Turnham, one of Richard's chief lieutenants and a commander Wheater* gives a stirring account of his prowess with a powerful Yorkshire contingent, led by De Ros of Hamlec, Ralph de Granville, Roger de Granville, and others, who made a desperate and unsuccessful assault on Acre, Nov 30th, 1190 His name is mentioned by Matthew Paris (*Hist Anglorum*, vol ii, p 510) in a list headed *Clipei in Anglia, heu! prostrati* A D 1245, in which year therefore I conclude he died Robert de Turnham, in the time of Henry II, was lord of Turnham or Thurnham Castle, which he rebuilt on the site of an ancient British camp, which crowned the high point of a very steep spur, which juts out between a depression on the one side and a very deep combe on the other, in the great escarpment of the lower chalk, about four miles east north-east of Maidstone, and which is also called "Godard's Castle"

Turnham occurs in *Domesday*, and was one of the numerous manors given by the Conqueror to Bishop Odo, on whose fall it was granted to Gilbert Maminot, by the tenure of "Castle guard" in Dover Castle

In *Archæologia Cantiana*, vol v, p 196, two charters are given containing the confirmation by Walkelin de Maminot, Superior Lord of Cumbwell Abbey, of the grant of Robert de Turnham to the Abbey of Cumbwell So it is possible that Robert or his father may have married a daughter of Gilbert Maminot, and thereby acquiring the manor of Turnham, become Robert de Turnham Cumbwell Abbey, of which more presently, seems to have been situated at a spot called Henlie, in the parish of Goudhurst, in Sussex, and was founded by Robert de Turnham for canons of the order of St Augustine, and endowed not only with the manor of Cumbwell but with lands also in Turnham, and with the advowsons of the churches of Turnham, and of Brickhill in Buckinghamshire

Dugdale, in his account of the Priory of Cumbwell, gives a charter of inspeximus of Henry III, dated July 6th, the eleventh year of his reign, which recites *in extenso* a Deed of Confirmation by Stephen de Turnham, son of Robert, the founder of all the grants made by his father and himself to the Abbey It seems, however, that the value of these endowments was by no means great, and about the year 1216, some fifty years after the foundation of the Abbey, it was thought advisable to reduce it to the less expensive dignity of a Priory, which was accordingly done, with the consent of Stephen de Langton, the Archbishop, and Mabel, then patroness, the eldest daughter of Stephen Turnham, and the wife of Hamo de Gatton We learn from Dugdale that 170 years later, in the eighth year of the reign of Richard II, the revenues of the Priory amounted to no more than £66 *2s 6d*, and when the crash came at the Reformation, in spite of large benefactions lately made by one of the Lords Dacre, it was amongst the

* *Mansions of Yorkshire*

small monasteries first suppressed by Henry VIII, the gross income as returned by the Prior to one of the King's Commissions being only £128 1s 9½d (*Arch Cant*, vol v p 205*n*)

Robert de Turnham had two sons The eldest, Stephen, seems to have held the office of Seneschal of Anjou, 1186, and his name is connected with one of the most romantic episodes in English history *

Johanna, youngest daughter of Eleanor and Henry II, was affianced to William the Good, King of Sicily When his bride arrived, he was so much impressed with her beauty and sweet temper, so far exceeding anything that Peter of Blois (his old tutor and her father's chaplain) had described, that he greatly augmented the already immense dower which he had promised

He seems to have been, however, an old man, and soon died childless, leaving her large legacies in his will On these, his successor, King Tancred, immediately laid violent hands, and, to prevent her complaints, shut her up in prison at Messina

The fair widow, however, contrived to communicate with her brother, Richard I, and he at once hastened to his sister's rescue, liberated her from the power of the tyrant, and forced him to disgorge some part, at least, of the spoil An arm-chair of solid gold, footstools of gold, an embroidered tent, a table of the same, with tressels twelve feet long, with urns and vases of same precious materials, formed, we are told by Piers of Langtoft and others, part of her household chattels so recovered Moreover, Tancred was compelled to compound for her dower and legacies with the enormous payment of 40,000 ounces of gold

Richard, however, as some acknowledgment, presented Tancred with the famous sword, "Escalibert," the brand of the great King Arthur, lately found at Glastonbury during his father's antiquarian researches for the tomb of that king —

"And Richard at that time gave him a fair juelle,
The good sword Caliburn, which Arthur luffed so well" †

Richard was also rewarded for his zealous care of his sister by the arrival of his mother Eleanor with the fair Berengaria, daughter of Sancho the Wise, King of Navarre, with whom the lion-hearted King had been much smitten at a tournament at Pampeluna, her native city, and whom he would long ago have married but for his compulsory betrothal to the fair and frail Alice of France

Eleanor, now 70 years of age, was anxious to see her son married, and therefore exerted herself to accomplish this object, but the same reason made her anxious to return home, and she gladly committed the destined bride to her daughter Johanna, as a chaperon, and then sailed for Rome

* Agnes Strickland's *Lives of the Queens of England Berengaria* † Robert of Brune

The season of Lent prevented the immediate marriage, and therefore Richard embarked in his favourite galley, "Tranc-the-mer" ("cut the sea,") attended by 150 ships and 50 galleys, filled with armed men and gallant knights, to join Philip Augustus, who had already indolently commenced the siege of Acre, the walls of which they had pledged themselves to scale. Indeed, each man, in token thereof, wore on his left leg a blue band of leather, and were termed "knights of the blue thong." Richard led the van, bearing a huge lantern on the poop of his galley to rally the fleet in the darkness of the night, and close to him sailed his sister Johanna and his bride-elect, Berengaria, in one of the strongest ships, under the care of a brave knight, Stephen de Turnham.

But the weather was not propitious, and Piers of Langtoft quaintly describes the storm which arose and submerged the ship on board of which was the Chancellor:—

"Roger Mansel,
The Chancellor so hight,
His tide fell not well,
A tempest on him light,
His ship was down borne,
Himself there to die,
The seal was lost
With other galleys tway.

"Lady Johanna she
The Lord Jesus besought,
In Cyprus she might be
To haven quickly brought:
The maid Berengare,
She was soon afright,
That neither far nor near
Her king rode in sight."

This seems to have scattered the little fleet, and Queen Johanna's galley found shelter in the harbour of Limoussa. Isaac (the Lord of Cyprus) sent two boats, and demanded if the Queen would land, but she declined the offer; upon which Isaac himself came on board with a great suite, and was so much smitten with Berengaria, and so angry when he heard that she was the affianced bride of the King of England, that, as soon as he departed, Stephen de Turnham, fearing for the safety of his charge, gave signal to heave up the anchor, and the Queen's galley rowed with all speed into the offing. Here the anxious Richard (who had been eagerly searching for the vessel with her precious freight) found the galley tossing and labouring heavily in the still rough sea, and great was his indignation when, with some difficulty, getting on board, he learned that they had quitted the snug harbour through fear of the Greek despot.

With his customary impetuosity, Richard, armed and battle-axe in hand, proceeded to demand redress, and found the interesting monarch busily engaged in plundering the wrecks of the English vessels. In reply to Richard's remonstrance, he said that whatever goods the sea "threw on "his island, he should take without asking leave of any one." Upon which Richard exclaimed, "They shall be bought full dear, by Jesu, heaven's "King"; and, leading his crusaders to the rescue, soon put the Emperor and his Cypriots to flight into Limoussa. Johanna's galley then entered, the royal ladies were landed half dead with fatigue and terror, when, says the chronicler, "there was joy and love enow" Isaac, however, continued implacable and tiresome, vapouring and boasting from behind his defences, until Richard, exasperated, expressed himself in the only English he was ever known to utter, "Ha! de debil! he speak like a fole Briton!" and immediately attacking Limoussa, made himself master thereof

Then ensued the long delayed fulfilment of all his hopes, and Richard and Beringaria were made man and wife It must have been a brilliant and beautiful espousal The bridegroom, a perfect model of military and manly grace, with his bright complexion and yellow curls, clad in a satin tunic of rose colour, with a mantle of striped silver tissue, brocaded with silver half-moons, his sword of Damascus steel, with a hilt of gold, and silver-scaled sheath, on his head a scarlet bonnet, brocaded in gold, with figures of animals. The fair bride, with her hair parted (*a la vierge*) upon her brow, a transparent veil open on each side covering her rich tresses of hair, on her head a regal diadem studded with several bands of gems, and surmounted by *fleurs-de-lys*

"There, in the joyous month of May, 1191," says an ancient writer, "in the flourishing and spacious island of Cyprus, celebrated as the very "abode of the goddess of love, did King Richard solemnly take to wife his "beloved Berengaria"

By the consent of the Cypriots, wearied of Isaac's tyranny, and by the advice of the allied Crusaders who came to assist at his nuptials, Richard was also crowned King of Cyprus, and his wife Queen of England and Cyprus

Bishop Bernard of Bayonne seems to have been "the officiating "minister", and the climax of the ceremonial was the self-surrender to the King of the daughter of Isaac, who henceforth became the inseparable companion of the Queen, and also of the vanquished Isaac himself, who, bound in chains of silver richly gilt, was presented to the Queen as her captive

Was ever such a wedding seen on earth! Who would not gladly have a brief vision of that graceful and dignified pageant—but one glance at a scene where so much power and beauty were assembled? with the glad sun from a cloudless sky irradiating the brilliant dresses and glittering jewels and flashing arms with his brightest beams!

At the conclusion of the nuptials and coronation, the illustrious party once more embarked The bridegroom in his good ship "Tranc-the-mer," the bride and Queen Johanna again under the charge of Sir Stephen de Turnham Their arrival at Acre on the festival of S Barnabas was another triumph, for the whole allied army marched to the beach to welcome their champion, and "the earth shook with the footsteps of the Christians and "the sound of their shouts"

During the whole of the Syrian campaign the two Queens remained at Acre, and after the final truce between Richard and Saladin was concluded, we are told, in a fair flowing meadow near Mount Tabor, Richard bade farewell to his Queen and sister, confiding them to the care of Stephen de Turnham for their voyage to Naples, while he started on that solitary journey which resulted in his capture by Leopold of Austria, his imprisonment for more than two months in the fortress of Tenebreuse, his discovery by his minstrel, Blondel, and his eventual ransom at 100,000 marks of silver.

The chronicle of Roger Hoveden thus particularises their route:—"Eodem Anno (1193) Berengaria Regina Angliæ et Johanna quondam "Regina Siciliæ, et filia Imperatoris Cypri, venerunt Romam sub custodia "Stephani de Thurnham . . . et moram fecerunt ibi fere per dimidium "anni spatium propter metum Imperatoris . . . Et perrexerunt usque "Pisam, deinde usque Genoam, deinde usque Marsilliam. Apud Marsilliam "suscipit eas Rex Arragoniœ et conduxit eas usque ad fines regni sui. Et "comes de Sancto Egidio conduxit eas per terram suam, et sic pervenerunt "Pictaviam"—*i.e.* Poitou—where the Castle of Chinon stood on the borders of Poitou and Tourraine, so that it is sometimes said by the chroniclers to be in one, sometimes in the other. It was one of the strongest of the English fortresses in France, and much used as a royal residence for those provinces—a castle, as Gulielmus Armoricus tells us, "non solum munitione, "verum et ædificiis et habitatoribus, et situ amœnissimo, prœclarum" (*Recueil des Hist.* xvii. 80*d*).

Hither Henry II. had retired to die, in the middle of a campaign with Philip (*Chroniques de St. Denis*, *An.* 1190). Here Richard kept his treasure, which, on his death, Robert de Turnham, the then custodian, handed over to John; and hither, two years later, came Berengaria, again to receive her dower from John, who was holding his court here (*Roger Hoveden*, *Savile's "Scriptores,"* pp. 451, 466).

This, then, was no doubt the very point of safety for which Stephen had been making with his anxious charge through the whole of their long and perilous journey; and here then they were safe at last on English territory, in one of Richard's strongest castles, and under the charge of a Governor whom he could trust for loyalty to his King and fidelity to himself—his own brother Robert. We can well understand that such an occasion would be one which a Christian knight would, according to the custom of those days, be anxious to mark with some special offering to the service of God; and amongst the original charters of the Priory of Cumbwell existing in the archives of Heralds' College, and published by Sir Charles Young, Garter King of Arms, there is one which evidently bears this character. It was granted by Stephen de Turnham, about a month after the coronation of Richard I., on his return from captivity. It makes special mention of the safety of Richard's body, as well as of his soul, for one of the objects of his gift—no unseasonable addition, when we remember the state of rebellion in which he found his kingdom It is dated "In castello de "Chinon, anno ab incarnatione Domini m°c°lxxx°iiij° mense Maii," and it grants to the abbey of Cumbwell the denne called Lechinese (Dennam que dicta est Lechinese cum pertinentiis suis), without prejudice therein to the right of the Prior of the Holy Trinity at Canterbury It is sealed with his seal, bearing a figure of a knight on horseback, with the legend, "Sigil "Stephani Thorneham," and with his counterseal, bearing a head in profile, the legend being, "Deus salvet cui mittor," probably in allusion to this honourable service—"God save her to whom I am sent" (as a protector)

Stephen de Turnham married Edeline de Broc, whose name appears attached to one of the charters granting to the abbey of Cumbwell the lands which she holds of the King at Hamwold She evidently survived him, for in 1215 she gives 300 marks for liberty to re-marry They had no son, but five daughters The eldest, Mabel, married Hamo de Gatton, as I have already stated Clemencia married Henry de Braibœuf, Alice married Adam de Bending, Beatrice married Ralph de Fay, Alianora married Roger de Leybourne, whose family history has been already noticed

And so the male line of Turnham seems to have ended I can only find mention of two others, who seem to have been uncles of the brothers whose history we have traced,* viz, Michael, who granted to the abbey of Cumbwell his land of Racchele (the seal to this charter is lost, but it is endorsed in a contemporary hand, "Michael de Torneham de Rachel," to which Le Neve adds "Canonicis de Cumbwell Kanc 1168," so I conclude that he died unmarried), the other, John Turnham, is a witness, with Michael, and described as "frater ejus," to a charter by Walkelin Maminot, granting to the abbey of Cumbwell his land called Selketinsell—but I can find no trace of any wife or descendants, so I conclude that he died unmarried also

Burke, in his *General Armory*, gives—Turnham, cos Kent and Surrey, time of King John, gules a lion passant or between two masceles argent, but at present I can find no trace thereof.

The family history is indeed short but brilliant, and few genealogical trees can boast greater ornaments than Stephen and Robert, the loyal, brave, and chivalrous brethren of the house of Turnham

But the descendants of Stephen de Turnham continued for several generations through the marriage of his daughter, Alianora, with Roger de Leyborne I have already mentioned some members of the family when discussing the possibility of the stone shield with the horn in the Minster

* *Arch Cant*, vol v p 134

bearing their arms (see page 32). I must not dismiss the family finally from our consideration without making the memoir complete.

According to the quaint custom of those days, Stephen de Turnham gave 300 marks fine for his wardship and marriage, and in due time united him to his daughter Eleanor.

In the 17th year of King John, when he was, I suppose, about eighteen or twenty, he was taken prisoner amongst the rebellious barons, then in arms, and committed for a time to Rochester Castle. The next mention of him is 36th year of Henry III., when he must have been fifty-six. He took part in a notable tournament held at Walden, and encountered Ernald de Mountenci, "a valiant knight, and ran his lance into his throat "under his helmet, it wanting a collar, whereupon Mountenci fell from his "horse and died presently." Dugdale adds, "As it was supposed by some, that "in regard his lance had not a socket on the point, he did it purposely, in "revenge of a broken leg he had received from Mountenci tilting with him "in a former tournament."

The next year he accompanied the King into Gascony, and seven years after was made constable of the castle of Bristol. But in two years, his loyalty becoming suspected by his favouring the turbulent barons, the King forbade him to take part in any tournament without his special license. This seems to have exasperated him, so that he openly took their side at Oxford, and was excommunicated by the Archbishop of Canterbury. "But not long after this, being drawn off by rewards, as was said, he "forsook them," and was made warden of the Cinque Ports, and in the following December appointed a commissioner, with Prince Edward, to treat with these rebellious nobles; and, on their refusal, he testified his fidelity to the King in the war which ensued against them, assisting in their defeat at the battle of Northampton, and afterwards at the assault upon Rochester Castle, where he was dangerously wounded. Before the end of the year he also took part in the battle of Lewes, where the royal army was defeated; upon which he fled into Wales, and took part with Lord Mortimer against the barons there. After the victory of Evesham, he was rewarded by the King with the wardenship of all the forests beyond Trent (which might mean that the arms and horn in the Minster belong to him), and was also made sheriff of Cumberland, warden of the Cinque Ports, and sheriff of Kent, with other substantial grants. These honours were annually renewed to him during the next two years, with the addition of the governorship of the castle of Carlisle. In the 52nd year of Henry III. he was "signed with the cross," in order to his going to the Holy Land with Prince Edward.

Indeed, his character seems well expressed in the following metrical translation of the song of Hybrias the Cretan, which the late Rev. Lambert

Larking, from whose article in *Arch Cant*, vol v, I am quoting, adopts as his portrait —

"My wealth's a burly spear and brand,
And a right good shield of hide untanned,
Which on my arm I buckle,
With these I plough, I reap, I sow,
With these I make the sweet vintage flow,
And all around me truckle
But your wights that take no pride to wield
A massy spear and well-made shield,
Nor joy to draw the sword,
Oh, I bring those heartless, hapless drones
Down, in a trice, on their marrow bones,
To call me 'king' and 'lord'"

Amongst the records of the Exchequer is the copy of a convention, dated 27th August, 1269, 53rd Henry III, between the King of France and Prince Edward, eldest son of Henry III, concerning their joint crusade to the Holy Land To this convention Roger, with four others, is a party, binding himself to the Prince's faithful observance of the contract He is also mentioned in the Patent Roll, 54th Henry III, 12th May, 1270, among the Crusaders to whom the Crown issued letters of protection during their absence, with privilege and exemption from all suits for four years, while attending in the suite of his son, Prince Edward, in the Holy Land

The expedition left Dover August 19th, 1270, arrived at Aigue Morte about Michaelmas, and Tunis ten days after On the taking of Tunis the Prince forbade the English to seize any of the spoil, but the French, says Fuller, "glutted themselves with the stolen honey which they found in this "hive of drones, and, which was worse, now their bellies were filled, they "would go to bed, return home, go no further Yea, the young King of "France, called Philip the Bold, was fearful to prosecute his journey to "Palestine Whereas Prince Edward struck his breast, and swore that "though all his friends forsook him, yet he would enter Ptolemais, though "but onely with Fowin, his horsekeeper, by which speech he incensed the "English to go on with him" The French returned, but experienced terrible weather "Their ships being wrecked, and the goods therein cast "into the sea, with which the waves played a little, and then chopped them "up at a morsel" The weather, however, smiled on the English Prince Edward, no whit "dammified, either in his men or ships, with Eleanor, his "tender consort, then young with child, safely arrived at Ptolemais, to the "great solace and comfort of the Christians there" *

Roger de Leybourne reached Acre (*i e* Ptolemais) in the quindam of Easter, A D 1271 But on the Fine Roll of that year is entered the homage of his son and heir, William, and the appointment of dower to his widow, Alianore, Countess of Winchester—shewing that Roger must have died

* Fuller's *Holy Wars*, b iv ch 28

either of sickness, or in the field of battle Whichever it was, we cannot doubt that he remained true until death to his royal master

Mr Larking also mentions an archæological discovery which seems to acquire much pathos when regarded in connection with this On the north wall of the north aisle of Leybourne Church, which stands under the very shadow of the ruins of Leybourne Castle, once the stronghold of this ancient race, he found, on clearing away the plaster and executing some trifling repairs, two little stone shrines, shaped like chapels, standing within a double niche Lifting that on the dexter side, it was found to form the covering of a leaden cylindrical box containing an embalmed heart, but without any lid The edges of the lead were quite smooth, and the bottom ornamented with a sort of Greek cross within a quarterfoil, surrounded with a border, and this inscription—"✠ AVE MARIA GRACIA PLENA DNS" After taking drawings and measurements, the leaden box and its contents were carefully replaced and covered as before On lifting the sinister shrine, however, it was found to be perfectly solid—evidently intended to be one day the depository of a heart-case, but none ever inserted, nor the hole cut for its reception

Of course there is no direct evidence to identify that heart with the heart of Sir Roger, still the date of the architecture of the double niche coincides with the period of his death, and as it was customary in those days to send back the hearts of the fallen warriors, like the heart of the Bruce, and the heart of Percy in Whitby Abbey, what more likely than that the chivalrous Edward should have sent back the heart of his faithful servant and comrade to the widowed Countess of Winchester, and that she, receiving it, should have placed it in the church close by, intending that when she passed away her heart should be enshrined beside it? But she had been already married twice before—first to William de Vaux, and second to Roger de Quincy, Earl of Winchester By Sir Roger de Leybourne she had no child, so, probably, when her husband, Sir Roger, died, she left Leybourne, to live amongst her own people, and when she died her body was laid in some other church

But yet the heart of the great Crusader, and friend and companion of Prince Edward, still rests—in the land of which he was so high an ornament—the home he loved,—the church in which he worshipped

In three generations, however, the inheritance had passed away from his race and name for ever His son, Sir William, was summoned amongst the barons of the realm from 27th Edward I to 3rd Edward III Probably this is the man mentioned in the *Caerlaverock Roll* in words already quoted —

"Guillelmus de Leybourne aussi
Vaillans homs sans mes et sans si
Baniere i ot, larges pans
Inde o sis blanc lyons rampans"

Thus translated —"William de Leybourne, a valiant man, without *but*, without *if*, had there a banner, and a large pennon of blue with six white lions rampant"

He married Juliana, the daughter of Sir Henry de Sandwich, of Preston, near Wingham, in Kent ("a wealthy Kentish gentleman," who supported Archdeacon Langton in receiving the first body of Franciscans at Canterbury, 1224 —"*The Coming of the Friars*," Rev A Jessop), and seems to have removed there, leaving Leybourne Castle to his son Sir William died in 1309, leaving two sons, Sir Thomas and Sir Henry The latter was outlawed, the former married Alice, sister and heiress of Robert de Tong, and died "vit patris," 1307, leaving one daughter, Juliana, an heiress of so great dignity and possessions that she acquired the soubriquet of "the Infanta of Kent" She made two great marriages, her first husband being John Lord Hastings and Abergavenny, son of Isabel, the eldest sister and co-heir of Aymer de Valenče, Earl of Pembroke Her second husband was Thomas de Blount (Burke) Her third husband was William de Clinton, Earl of Huntingdon, who left a daughter (Burke), married to Sir John Fitzwilliam, of Sprotborough, but as she did not inherit the barony of Clinton, she was probably illegitimate, and not by Juliana It would naturally be expected that all her great wealth would have passed to her son, but by an entry on the Close Rolls it appears that on Feb 20th, 36 Edward III, she conferred divers manors in Kent and elsewhere (amongst them the manor of Preston) to trustees, who, on March 15 of the same year, conveyed them to her for life, with remainder to the King for subsequent grants to religious houses This appears to have been a not uncommon "modus operandi" in effecting religious endowments, and though the King did not always carry out the donors' intentions, eventually the endowments seem to have reached their destination The amount must have been very great, for it comprised twelve manors in Kent, besides manors in Norfolk She seems, however, to have retained the chattels in her manor-houses as her own property, and by will on October 30, 1367, she bequeathed them to Sir Alexander Wayte, canon of Wyngham, Sir John Amublee, rector of the church of Harrietsham, and John de Middleton, "that they may dispose" of them "for my soul, in rewards to my servants, and other works of charity, as to them may seem most expedient" She died the following day, November 1st, and the inventories of the chattels in her houses, which seem to have been thirteen in number, have been preserved in the Surrenden Collection

In the "*Archæologia Cantiana*," vol 1, that in the houses at Preston is printed, and contains some curious items, casting a light upon the manners and customs of those days "Pecunia numerata," *i e*, ready money, £1,241 6*s* 8*d*—a large sum to keep in the house, even according to the computation of those days, but there were no banks Vessels and jewels of gold and silver £410, four cloths of gold £26 13*s* 4*d* *The Chapel* "divers vestments, books, and other ornaments for my lady's chapel, £34 0*s* 8*d*" *The Chamber* "divers ornaments for my lady's head, £10 8*s*" "Item, divers my lady's vestments, with fur, buttons, and other apparel for my lady's body, £37 5*s* 4*d*" "Item, divers beds, with their furniture, £48 16*s* 2*d*" *The Hall* "item, one dorser of the work of Befs de Hampton," *i e*, a hanging for the wall at the back of the sitter, worked with the legend of Bevis de Hampton "Item, three bankers, 5*s*," *i e*, coverings of the benches *Pantry* "item, one pipe of red wine, value £2 18*s* 4*d*" *The Larder* gives us some idea of the amount of provisions required to be laid by, *salted*, for the winter use of the household Remember this inventory is dated November, the beginning of winter, when the larder would be full

		£	s	d
Item,	10 carcases of oxen for my lady's larder	£16	0	0
,,	2 boars and 200 hogs for the same larder	33	0	0
,,	280 muttons and other sheep for the same larder	14	0	0
,,	16 fat bucks salted for the same larder	5	0	0
,,	Salmon, melewell (codfish), stock fish, and other fish	32	0	0

The corn and malt in the bakery and brewery are estimated at £21 In the stable are as follows

			£	s	d				£	s	d
Item,	1 horse,	value	£13	6	8	Item,	3 horses	value	£10	0	0
,,	1	,,	10	0	0	,,	10	,,	20	0	0

The sum total of the house £2,062 12*s* 8*d*, with a few other items amounting to £139 The chattels in the other twelve houses, which I conclude must have been small, only amounted in value altogether to £849 3*s* 10*d*

"Even so, the lady of Leybourne, owner, it seems, of more numerous domains and wider far than any held by one lord within the bounds of Kent since the days of Odo, is ready for her hour The settlement of her estates has long been made, 'the day is far spent,' and, as the shadows of evening gather round, her worldly task is done" She was three years old when her father died in 1307, and expired just sixty years after She directs in her will that her body shall be buried "in the church of the monastery of St Augustine of Canterbury, in the new chapel (which was her own foundation) on the south side of the church"

"With this noble lady passed away the baronial and illustrious name of De Leybourne The palace at Preston soon degenerated into a mere monastic farmhouse," the old castle at Leybourne is in ruins, "and not a trace now remains of the grandeur which must once have there existed"

TREHOUS

But now for the other shield in this window, mentioned on page 108, viz, a maunch (i e a sleeve) gules, upon a field of vair

The old song says—

"When Arthur first in Court began
To wear long hanging sleeves,
He entertained three serving-men,
And all of them were thieves"

Drake, quoting from "the chroniclers of those times," tells us (vol 1 p 104) that King Arthur held his jovial court in York, Christmas, A D. 521, but reliable history, while it does not substantiate the romances of that mythical monarch, shews us that this is a quaint illustration of the fashion, prevalent in the reigns of Rufus and Henry I, and indeed throughout the twelfth century, to elongate the sleeves to an extraordinary degree

These sleeves went out of fashion in the thirteenth century, but were revived in the days of Richard II and succeeding kings

Occleve the poet, *temp* Henry IV, thus sings—

"But this methinks an abusion
To see one walk in a robe of scarlet
Twelve yards wide, with pendant sleeves down
On the ground, and the furrur therein set,
Amounting unto twenty pounds or bett [better],
And if he for it paid, hath he no good
Left him wherewith to buy himself a hood
* * * * * *
Now have these lords little need of brooms
To sweep away the filth out of the street,
Since side sleeves of penniless grooms
Will up it lick, be it dry or wet"

In the third niche of the Choir-screen there is a figure of King Stephen, which gives as good an idea as we could desire of the sleeve from which the maunch was taken The date of the screen is about Henry VI, and the figures are clad in the costumes of that epoch

*The maunch, indeed, seems to be rather the combination of two sleeves, viz, the long, wide sleeve of the "houpeland" or outer garment, which was highly fashionable in the reign of Richard II (Strutt calls it a loose upper garment of the super tunic kind), and the sleeve of the under dress, tunic or kirtle, often with buttons set close from the wrist to the shoulder, which would be thrust through it

In the 16th century the sleeves were generally distinct from the dress, to be added to or taken from at pleasure Amongst the Harleian MSS is an inventory of apparel left in the wardrobe of Henry VIII at the time of his decease, 1547 Therein are entries of "a pair of sleeves of green "velvet, richly embroidered with flowers of damaske gold of Morisco work,

* Planché's *Encyclopædia of Costume*

"with knops of Venice gold cordian raised, each sleeve having six small "buttons of gold, and in every button a pearl, and the branches of the "flowers set with pearles."

An Act, passed in the fourth of Richard II., forbade any man, not being a banneret or person of high estate, to wear long hanging sleeves, open or closed, except only "Gens d'armes quand sont armez." This alludes to the fact of nobles and knights wearing sleeves even on their military surcoats; and such we find in the effigy of Brian Fitzalan, A.D. 1302, in Bedale Church, in which case, however, the sleeves were often "dagged," as it was called, *i.e.* slashed. So that the sleeve was at once highly ornamented, a badge of distinction, and an independent portion of the military and civil dress—which would render it likely to be adopted as an heraldic charge, with reference possibly in its colour to the individual in whose honour it was borne.

The military surcoats were first used by the Crusaders, in order to mitigate the discomfort of the metal hauberk, so apt to get heated under a Syrian sun or injured by the rain. In the "Avowynge" of King Arthur, stanza 39, the following lines occur:—

"With scharpe weppun and schene,
Gay gownas of grene,
To hold thayre armur clene,
And were [protect] hitte from the wette."

The surcoats were both sleeveless and sleeved, though the latter is not found till the second half of the thirteenth century. King John is the first monarch who appears in his great seal in the sleeveless surcoat.*

In the pedigree of the Hotham family at Dalton Holme, these arms are given as the bearings of Peter de Trehous, the great-grandson of Sir John Trehous, who served under William the Conqueror at the battle of Hastings, and had a grant of the manor of Hotham, county York. He is also therein described as the husband of Isabella de Turnham; and so it is said that he was rewarded with the hand of the heiress of the barony of Mulgrave by King John for murdering his nephew, Arthur, Duke of Brittany. The rapacious "Lackland," however, did not give up the heiress and her broad acres without charge upon the latter; and he bound Trehous, "De Malolacu," or De Mauley, to pay 7,000 marks as a consideration for her and her lands—an enormous sum of money, equivalent to £150,000 of present money.

There are, however, various accounts as to the death of this unfortunate Prince. Historians are united so far that, as Matthew Paris relates on the authority of Roger of Wendover, King Philip and King John having quarrelled, the former delivered a body of two hundred

* Hewitt's *Ancient Armour*, p. 274.

soldiers to Arthur, a lad of sixteen (according to Hall), and still in *statu pupillari*, though already affianced to the daughter of Tancred, King of Sicily, and directed him to march into Poitou There Arthur at once attacked the castle of Mirabel, where Eleanor the Queen was residing with a scanty guard They seem to have speedily captured the castle, but the tower in which the Queen and her attendants had intrenched themselves withstood all their assaults The principal nobles of Poitou, including the Count of Marchia (?), Hugo Brunnes, came to his assistance, and the Queen, finding that her cause was desperate, sent to King John in Normandy, urging him to come to her rescue—which he did, marching day and night with incredible speed Arthur at once drew out his forces to fight with his uncle, but was speedily overcome, his men beaten back to the castle, and so hotly pressed by the King that he entered into the gate with his retreating foes There Arthur and all his force were taken captive, bound hand and foot with fetters, and sent on two-horse carts (an unaccustomed mode of carrying in those days), some into Normandy and some to England Arthur himself was imprisoned under a strong and trusty guard at Falaise After some time, John followed him there, and had an interview with his nephew, which seems to have been of a conciliatory character on the part of the King, who urged him to abandon the King of France and identify himself with him Arthur, however, in the pride and impetuosity of his nature, replied in threatening language, claiming all the territory which had belonged to King Richard, and, drawing himself up, declared with an oath that unless his demands were speedily complied with, there should not be a day's peace John was very much disturbed at this, and sent him to Rouen, to be kept in stricter custody than ever

As to what happened after that, the chronicler says, is almost entirely unknown Some said that, in endeavouring to escape, he was drowned in the Seine—others that he died of a broken heart The French, however, declared that he was killed, if not by John's own hands, at least by his orders

Hall says that he was put in the tower at Rouen, "under the custodie "of Robert de Veypont, where shortly after he was despatched of his life, "some say by the hands of his uncle John"

The Lanercost chronicler gives this version, in Latin, of the transaction "The King John had an elder brother, by name Geoffry, Earl of Bretayne, "who dying during the lifetime of Henry their father, and in the thirty- "third year of his reign, left as the representative of his family a son, by "name Arthur, and a daughter named Aleanor On the death of their "grandfather, the kingdom having at length devolved on John, King Philip "committed them to the charge of the King of England for their education, "and to be brought up according to their name and rank in England "But because riches and honours too often destroy fidelity amongst the "nobility, the perfidious King, knowing that the youth—now eighteen, "fair in countenance, stalwart in body, and acceptable to the people— "had more right to the kingdom than he had, as being the son of his "elder brother, and could easily acquire this on account of the hatred "entertained as regards himself by Bretons and Angles alike, began to "plot against the young man, that he might eradicate him from the midst. "As therefore Saul treacherously treated the holy David, so that he might "transfix him to the wall with a lance, so he ordered the boy, at supper "with him, to stand in a narrow place between the table and the fire, in "order that he might secretly stab him and drive him into the fire. But "the spirit of innocence gave him a token of what the other was purposing, "and for the time he escaped from the angry tyrant, half-burned.

"The impious man, therefore, purposing to carry out his conceived "treachery so that it might not be discovered, and careful so to do it that "it might not be noised abroad, took out one evening for a walk the young "man instead of his esquire, and with him William de Vipont, Baron and "Lord of Westmoreland, and, as the story goes, a miller. They embarked "in a boat on the sea, and when far away from human habitation, the "wicked purpose was carried out by I know not whose hand.

"So, from his own land, as it were, cast out of the vineyard, was the "true heir of England cast out and destroyed. His sister Alianore shared "a similar fate, being first in the custody of William de Vipont at the "castle of Burgh in Westmoreland, then at Bowes, and afterwards at Corfe "Castle, until her death."

Henry Knyghton, canon of Leicester, whose *Chronicle* extends to the year 1395, says—"He (John) kept possession of Arthur, the son of his "elder brother, Geoffry, Duke of Brittany, whom he had captured by "stratagem when in Aquitaine, and killed him by the hand of his squire, "Peter de Malolacu, to whom he afterwards gave the heiress of the barony "of Mulgrave in marriage as the reward of his iniquity." This is quoted by Dugdale in his *Baronage*.

In his *Chronicon Anglicanum*, Radulp de Coggeshall gives the following account, in Latin (p. 139);—"The councillors of the King perceiving "that the Bretons would make much slaughter and sedition on all sides "for their Lord Arthur, and that no sound agreement of peace could be "concluded as long as Arthur survived, suggested to the King how far "he might approve of it, that the noble young man might be blinded and "mutilated, and thus rendered henceforth unfit for governing, so that the "opposing faction might be quieted from the madness of vigorous warfare, "and submit themselves to the King. Exasperated, therefore, by incessant "gatherings of his adversaries, and harrassed by their threats and seditious "acts, he charged, at length, three of his servants to go to Falaise as "quickly as possible and carry out this detestable work Two, however, "of these servants, recoiling from the commission of such a detestable act "against so noble a young man, fled away from the palace of their lord "and King The third, however, came to the castle in which the royal "boy was kept by Lord Hubert de Burgh, the King's Chamberlain, having "triple fetters round his feet And when he had delivered the orders of "the King his master to Hubert, there arose exceeding bewailings and "lamentations amongst the soldiers, as moved by their exceeding pity for "the noble young man But Arthur, hearing the dreadful sentence of his "uncle passed upon him, and utterly hopeless for his own deliverance, "burst into tears and piteous complaints But when he who had been sent "by the King to carry out the work happened to be standing by, and his "presence became known to the groaning and weeping boy, suddenly "aroused, he started up in the midst of his lamentations, and violently laid "his hands, lately hanging down in despondency, upon him for revenge, "crying out in a lamentable voice to the soldiers standing round, 'O my "'dearest lords, for the love of God forbear for a short space, that I may "'revenge myself upon this evil-doer before he takes away my eyes, for "'he is the last person whom I shall see in this present life' But the "soldiers immediately sprang up to stop the tumult, and seized the hands "of both of them, and at the command of the Lord Hubert, the young "man who had come was turned out of the room From whose expulsion, "as well as from the comforting words of those assisting him, Arthur, the "sadness of his heart being appeased, received a little consolation

"But Hubert, the King's Chamberlain, wishing to consult the "character and reputation of the King, and foreseeing that he would be "pardoned for so doing, kept the royal boy uninjured, persuaded that his "lord the King would speedily repent of such an edict, and ever after-"wards hold him immeasurably excused because he had ventured to "mitigate so cruel a command, in the belief that it had emanated rather "from a sudden fury than from a well-balanced decision of equity and "justice Wishing, therefore, to mitigate the King's wrath for the time, "and to restrain the fury of the Bretons, he caused a report to be circulated "throughout the castle and the whole province that the King's sentence "had been deferred, and that Arthur had died from a broken heart and "the severity of his wounds Which report was incessantly circulated for "fifteen days Lastly, the bell was tolled, as though for his soul, through-"out the villages and the castle, and his clothing was distributed in a "hospital of lepers It was announced, also, that his body had been taken "to the abbey of St Andrew, of the Cistercian order, and there buried

"But by such rumours the minds of the Bretons not being calmed, but "more and more embittered, they abandoned themselves to greater violence, "if possible, than before, swearing that they would never henceforth rest "from fighting against the King of England, who had permitted such a "detestable wickedness to be perpetrated against his own lord and nephew "And so it came to pass that it was necessary to proclaim that Arthur "was still alive and safe, whom they had everywhere pronounced to be "dead, so that thus the unbridled ferocity of the Bretons might be a little "mitigated When this was reported to the King, he was by no means "displeased for the present that his order had not been carried out Some "of the soldiers even said to the King their master that he would no "longer have found soldiers ready to guard his castles if he had persisted "in executing such a nefarious sentence against Lord Arthur, his own "nephew, for if it had chanced that any soldiers after that had been taken "by the King of France, or by their enemies, they would immediately, "without any mercy, have met with a similar fate out of revenge"

What ultimately took place he does not record, but a little further describes Philip, as exceeding wroth for the death of Arthur, who he had heard had been drowned in the Seine, and as being reported to have sworn that he would, in consequence, never desist throughout his whole life from attacking King John, until he had deprived him of all his kingdom

Shakespeare, founding his play of *King John*, more or less, upon some one or more of the above chronicles, represents Arthur as taken prisoner by John at Angers (act iii scene 2), where his mother had been "assailed "in her tent," and committed to Hubert de Burgh, his Chamberlain, who is charged to take him to England

Shakespeare then represents that Arthur has been taken to Northampton, and the first scene in act iv, in which the famous scene between Hubert and Arthur about the young Prince having his eyes put out, is laid at "Northampton, a room in the castle" The conclusion to which is that Hubert spares his eyes, but says—

"Your uncle must not know but you are dead"

In the next scene Arthur appears upon the walls disguised as a ship-boy, and leaping down in his attempt to escape, is killed

Hume, in his *History of England*, quoting from M West, p 264, says that the King first proposed to William de Bray, one of his servants, to despatch Arthur, but William replied that he was a gentleman, and not a hangman Upon which another individual was chosen for the work, who was sent back by Hubert with the report that the young Prince was dead, and a funeral was performed The Bretons were so incensed at this, however, that they vowed revenge, and the barons continued their insurrection

Hubert, therefore, thought it prudent to admit that the boy was alive Upon which John moved him from Falaise to Rouen, and coming to the castle in a boat during the night-time, ordered him to be brought forth The young Prince, aware of his danger, and now more subdued by his misfortune, threw himself on his knees before his uncle and begged for mercy, but the barbarous tyrant, making no reply, stabbed him with his own hands, and fastening a stone to the dead body, threw it into the Seine

In whatever manner, however, Arthur met his death, John seems to have been universally credited with the responsibility of it Matilda de Braose, wife of William de Braose (Matthew Paris tells us, ii, 523) when the King's soldiers came to her demanding her sons as hostages for the fidelity of their father in case the Pope should put the country under an interdict, uttered these taunting words "I will not give up my children "to your King John, because he basely murdered his nephew Arthur, whom "he ought honourably to have guarded" Her husband tried in vain to palliate such an incautious utterance, and John, in a fury, as soon as it was reported to him, sent off secretly in hot haste a large body of soldiers and retainers to seize William de Braose and all his family—who only saved themselves by precipitate flight into Ireland But John had his revenge, for two years afterwards (1210) he seized them in Meath, and on their escaping to the Isle of Man, recaptured them and sent them heavily ironed to Windsor Castle, where, by his orders, Matilda and her eldest son, William, were starved to death One of the soldiers of King Louis, at a conference between Louis and the Papal legate, Waldo (651), openly charged John with his nephew's death, as a thing well known by all (*res notissima est omnibus*), and King Louis's ambassadors to Pope Innocent gave as their reason for dethroning John, "that he had killed his nephew "treacherously, with his own hands—by that sort of death which the "English call murder"

Innocent, however, whom John had conciliated by appealing to him to interpose his authority between him and the French monarch (Hume, vol i, 447), seems to have taken a more lenient view of the proceeding, and replied (Matthew Paris, p 659) that "many Emperors and Princes, and "even Kings of France, are said in their annals to have killed many "innocent people, but we do not read that any of them were sentenced to "death, and when Arthur was taken at the Castle of Mirabel, not as an "innocent man, but as a guilty man and traitor to his lord and uncle, to "whom he had done homage and fealty, he could have been condemned "by right to even the gravest death without condemnation"

However, this friendly intercourse did not last long, and the Holy Father, who could condone murder and cruelty when employed to further a matter of State policy, could not so regard any lack of submission to his will, and therefore, when King John shortly after declined to recognise Cardinal Langton, whom he had appointed Archbishop of Canterbury, without any previous writ from the King, he at once laid the country under an interdict.

Fabyan gives a very short notice of Prince Arthur in his *Chronicles*, but he is the only one who supplies any foundation for Shakespeare's representations of Prince Arthur having been sent to England. He says, after simply mentioning the capture of Arthur and others at Mirabel, "in "which season also King John returned with his prisoners into England."

John Hardyng, the rhyming chronicler, who was born in 1378, and was a page in the family of Sir Henry Percy, eldest son of the Earl of Northumberland, and who lived to be at least 87 years of age, says:

"The Kyng Philip confered with Arthure
To rebell sore agayne his eme Kyng John,
And graunte hym men and power, stronge and sure,
To gette Guyan, Poyton, and Anjeou anon:
Wherefore Kyng John to Normandy gan gone,
And there he tooke Arthure, Duke of Britayne,
In Castell Mirable dyed, in mykell payne.

"Dame Isabell, the sister also of Arthure,
In the Castelle of Bristowe was then holde,
And dyed there in pryson then full sure,
As King John, her uncle, so it wolde:
A lady of great beautee, she was hold
Beshet in pryson in paynes strong,
So ended her life, for sorrow lives not long.

"Thus slew he both Arthure and Isabell,
The children of his brother, Duke Geffry,
To joye the croune of Englande, as men tell;
Wherefore most parte of all his landes that daye
Beyond the sea forsook him then for ay,
Returning to the Kyng of France in hye,
To hold of hym and his perpetually."

Holinshed, who dedicates his *Chronicles* to "The Right Honourable "and singular good Lord Sir William Cecil, Baron of Burleigh, Knight "of the most noble Order of the Garter, Lord High Treasurer of England, "Maister of the Courts of Wards and Liveries, and one of the Queenes "Majesties Privie Councell," *i.e.*, Queen Elizabeth, after quoting from Matthew Paris the greater part of the passages which I have already transcribed, thus concludes:—"But now touching the maner in verie deed "of the end of this Arthur, writers make sundrie reports. Neverthelesse, "certaine it is that in the year next insuing he was removed from Falais "unto the Castell or Tower of Rouen, out of the which there was not any "that would confesse that ever he saw him go alive. Some have written "that as he assaied to have escaped out of prison, and prooving to "clime over the walls of the castell, he fell into the river of Saine and "so was drowned Others write that through very grief and languour he "pined awaie and died of naturalle sicknesse But some affirme that "King John secretlie caused him to be murthered and made awaye, so "as it is not throughlie agreed upon in what sorte he finished his daies "but verelie King John was had in great suspicion—whether worthily or "not, the Lord knoweth"

Shakespeare represents that the subject created a great sensation Hubert, mentioning to King John (act 4, scene 2) that "five moons "were seen to night," adds

"Old men, and beldames in the street,
Do prophesy upon it dangerously
Young Arthur's death is common in their mouths,
And when they talk of him they shake their heads
And whisper one another in the ear
And he that speaks doth gripe the hearer's wrist,
Whilst he that hears makes fearful action,
With wrinkled brows, with nods, with rolling eyes
I saw a smith stand with his hammer thus,
The whilst his iron did on the anvil cool,
With open mouth swallowing a tailor's news,
Who, with his shears and measure in his hand,
Standing on slippers, which his nimble haste
Had falsely thrust upon contrary feet,
Told of a many thousand warlike French
That were embattled and rank'd in Kent,
Another lean, unwash'd artificer
Cuts off his tale, and talks of Arthur's death"

It has even been suggested that so evil was the reputation which Peter de Trehous had acquired, in consequence of his share in the transaction, amongst the good people of Yorkshire, that they changed the name of the place from Moultgrace to Moultgrave This, however, as well as Shakespeare's description, I regard as purely apocryphal In Canon Raine's *Lives of the Archbishops of York* it is stated that King John came to York in March, 1205, about the date when the murder took place He seems to have had a quarrel with his illegitimate brother, Geoffrey, son of Fair Rosamond, then Archbishop of York, to whom he was not reconciled until "the spring of 1207" "We are unacquainted," says Canon Raine, "with "the causes of the quarrel which was thus terminated" Could it have been on the late tragic event? Canon Raine says of Geoffrey that, "though passionate and regardless of consequences, he was capable of "generous and patriotic actions, and his filial affection is not to be "forgotten" It is quite possible that such a character would not hesitate to speak plainly, and perhaps strongly, to a guilty sinner, even though he were his near relation, and King of England But neither here nor anywhere else can I discern any public manifestation of ill-feeling against him on this account Such events in those days travelled very slowly, and possibly the news of the murder never reached this part of the country until sung by troubadours or wandering minstrels, long after the actors therein had gone to their account It is very possible, also, that in those rough times the participation in even such a dark and bloody deed could not have been deemed an unpardonable offence, we have seen that even a Pope could look indulgently upon it Besides, in this world, "so long "as thou doest well unto thyself men will speak good of thee"

Peter de Trehous was in high favour with the King He had received from him, as a token of his confidence and regard, the hand of Isabel, the daughter of Robert de Turnham, heiress of the barony of Mulgref Other honours were added, including the custody of the regalia which he kept in Corfe Castle, where the unfortunate Alinore, sister of the murdered Arthur, was still immured And Henry III continued to him the favour which his father had always shewn towards him Moreover, when his wife Isabel died he gave large benefactions to the monks of the Abbey of Meaux, in Holdernesse, where her body was buried So the circumstances of his advancement, if known, would not be very unfavourably criticised And we can appreciate the appropriate recognition of his "fount of honour" adopted for his armorial bearings—one of royal sleeves resting upon the most delicate and honourable of furs

Well, at any rate he remained faithful to his master, for, as far as I can discover, he never failed him, but, as Dugdale says, "stood firm to "him on all occasions, though many of his barons reverted from him, and "the Pope excommunicated him"

Hastings

There is another sleeve in the *first west window of the Clerestory* of the nave, but this is black (sable) on a white (argent) field * This is the arms of Hastings, Earl of Huntingdon The family of Hastings originally carried the red sleeve also, upon a gold ground, and perhaps, therefore, received it at the same time though under different circumstances to Peter de Trehous Henry, third Earl of Huntingdon, was Lord President of the North during the reign of Queen Elizabeth, and this particular shield may be his arms He built a considerable portion of "the Manor House" here, where he probably died

You will not find his arms there, but you will find the bear and ragged staff, embossed on the cornice of the rooms, which was the badge of the Earls of Warwick, or owners of Warwick Castle, and which he

* See illustration

PLATE 3.

HOTHAM.

HASTINGS.

EURE.

CONSTABLE.

CONSTABLE.

CONSTABLE.

assumed, not, as Mr Davies says, because his wife was a Dudley, *but* because his mother was a Pole, grand-daughter of Margaret, Countess of Salisbury, sister of Edward, Earl of Warwick, and daughter of George, Duke of Clarence, and his wife Isabel, daughter of Richard Nevill, Earl of Warwick. This Earl of Huntingdon married Catherine, sister of Lord Guildford Dudley, and her father was created Earl of Warwick by Edward VI, and eventually Duke of Northumberland.

But Huntingdon was (I think) more likely to carry the badge in right of his own inheritance than of his wife's.

But why did the Earls of Huntingdon change the colour of their sleeve, and bear it black instead of red? It may be simply what is called in heraldry "a difference," viz, to distinguish one branch of the family from another. It may be (and I think it is) to record a tragic (but at the same time honourable) incident in the family history (narrated in Hume's *History of England*, and represented in *Richard III*, act 2, scene 4).

Sir William de Hastings, created Baron Hastings by Edward IV, Knight of the Garter, and Master of the Mint, was one of the most powerful men of his day. Fuller the historian speaks of him as an "illustrious person," and therefore, when Edward was dead, Richard, Duke of Gloucester, was anxious to secure his influence to enable him to obtain the crown for himself and dispose of his nephews, Edward V and Richard, Duke of York.

He therefore sounded his sentiments through Catesby, a lawyer who lived in great intimacy with him, but found him impregnable in his allegiance and fidelity to the children of Edward, who had ever honoured him with his friendship. He says to the Duke of Buckingham—

> "Catesby hath sounded Hastings in our business,
> And finds the testy gentleman so hot
> That he will lose his head, ere give consent
> His master's child (as worshipfully he terms it)
> Shall lose the royalty of England's throne."

And Richard determined, therefore, on his death.

A meeting of the Council was summoned at the Tower, where Richard for a long time appeared in a most easy and jovial humour. Then suddenly demanding what they deserve who conspired his "death with devilish plots "of damned witchcraft," he tore up his sleeve, and shewed a withered arm, which he accused the Queen and Jane Shore of having caused, and, on Hastings commencing—

> "If they have done this deed, my noble lord,"

he cried—

> "Talkst thou to me of ifs? Thou art a traitor.
> Off with his head. Now by St Paul I swear
> I will not dine until I see the same."

At a sign from Gloucester, bands of soldiers rushed in from the corridor. Hastings was seized, hurried away, and instantly beheaded on a timber log which lay in the court of the Tower.

What wonder, then, if in those days of eloquent heraldic significance, the family changed the red sleeve to the black—the token of royal favour to the commemoration of royal displeasure, when the latter had become the token of unswerving fidelity and courage, and of a determination to defend the rights of fatherless children, even at the sacrifice of life. When next you go up the Nave, look up to the black sleeve, and then ask God to give you grace, at all hazards, to do what is right also.

But there were other members of the same race, who were as staunch to what they deemed right, and one especially, whose name may be fittingly commemorated in a disquisition on Heraldry.

There were, and indeed there are, two distinct families of Hastings, viz., Hastings, Baron Hastings, Earls of Pembroke; and Hastings, Baron Hastings, Earls of Huntingdon—both descended from one common ancestor, Robert de Hastings, who was portgrave of that place, and steward to William the Conqueror. His son, Walter, was steward to Henry I., and had a grant of the manor of Ashill, Norfolk, for taking care of the naperie (table-linen) at the Coronation.

On the death of John, sixth Lord Hastings and third Earl of Pembroke, 1389 (who was killed in a tournament, while yet a lad of sixteen, by Sir John St. John, who by an unlucky slip of his lance mortally wounded him in the abdomen), a controversy arose as to the right to bear the arms of Hastings, without a mark of difference or abatement, between Reginald, Lord Grey de Ruthyn, and Sir Edward Hastings.

They were descended from the second Baron Hastings, who died in 1313, and was great-great-grandfather of the unfortunate young man.

Lord Grey de Ruthyn claimed the privilege because his grandfather, Roger, Lord Grey, had married Elizabeth, the daughter of Lord Hastings by his first wife, Isabel de Valence.

Sir Edward Hastings, because he was descended from the eldest son of the said Lord Hastings by his second wife, Margery de Foliot. Each assumed the title of Lord Hastings. The cause was tried before the House of Lords, and referred by them to the judges. On their report, the Lords decided in favour of Lord Grey de Ruthyn.

But Sir Edward Hastings appealed against this decision; and, on the accession of Henry V., several commissions were issued for hearing it.

The proceedings were protracted for some years; and in 1421, before any judgment had been given, Sir Edward Hastings was arrested by Lord Grey for the sum of £987, the cost of the original suit, and was thrown into the Marshalsea.

But the stout old knight would not submit, and fearing that the payment of these costs would be deemed an acknowledgment of Lord Grey's right to the honour and arms of his family, he continued a prisoner for twenty-six years, part of which time he was, he says in some pathetic documents on the subject, "boundyn in fetters of iron like a thief or a "traitor, than like a gentleman of birth"

Imprisonment and chains, the destruction of his own health, and the death of his wife and children, could not shake his firmness

He steadily refused Lord Grey's offer to release him from the debt if he would admit his superior right to the objects in dispute The only compromise to which he could be induced to consent was a marriage, either in his own person or in that of one of his children, with one of those of his adversary And in case his eldest son, John Hastings, should marry one of Lord Grey's daughters, he said that he would relinquish to him and the heirs of that marriage the name, right, inheritance, and arms which he claimed as heir of John, last Earl of Pembroke, which offer he concluded with this uncompromising vituperation—"God's curse and mine "have all mine heirs that will not sue the right and inheritance after me"

This was probably written about 1420 Whether from the personal antipathy of the parents, or lack of inclination on the part of the young people, the matrimonial alliance never came to pass

In 1433 Sir Edward Hastings was still in prison, and, as before, styled himself "Edward, Lord Hastings" In 1437 he died After his death his son, John Hastings, warned, perhaps, by his father's unhappy fate, yielded to the usurpation of his rights by the Lords Grey of Ruthyn, and in the reign of King Henry VIII, the representation of the house of Hastings fell amongst co-heirs

In 1641, Charles Longueville, Esq, nephew and heir of Henry Grey, eighth Earl of Kent, presented a petition to Charles I, claiming that the dignities of Lord Hastings and Ruthyn belonged to him The petition was referred to the Lords, where he was opposed by Anthony, ninth Earl of Kent, who had for his advocate the learned Selden The Lords referred it to the judges, and after counsel had been heard on both sides, Lord Chief Justice Brampton delivered judgment according to their opinions—practically confirming the previous decision, and allowing his claim to the barony of Grey de Ruthyn, but not of Hastings *See case prepared by Sir Harris Nicolas*, 1844

But after a lapse of four centuries, Sir Jacob Astley, one of the co-heirs of Sir Edward Hastings, redeemed the curse, and "sued the right "and inheritance after him" successfully The House of Peers having decided in his favour, between him and Henry L'Estrange Styleman L'Estrange, Esq, of Hunstanton, Norfolk, another of the co heirs, on the 18th of May, 1841, he was summoned to Parliament by writ as Baron Hastings, in his right as a co-heir of Sir Henry Hastings, summoned to Parliament in the 49th year of Henry III, thus reversing the two previous decisions, and confirming the claim for which Sir Edward had contended so stoutly and suffered so much.*

Is any one disposed to regard with pity and contempt so much endured for a mere empty title? On the contrary, let us rather reverence the memory of one who was willing to submit to so much rather than give place to what, in his conscience, he felt to be wrong, or to forego, from any motives of personal advantage, what he honestly believed to be the lawful right and inheritance of his children. Such resolute, undaunted suffering for conscience sake should never be depreciated or lost sight of. Truly "there were giants on the earth in those days."

But there are other sleeves which specially belong to Yorkshire, though not actually in the Minster. The family of Wharton, famous at least in two members, viz., the sixth baron, a pious man and a Puritan, who bequeathed the legacy of Bibles annually distributed both here and in Bucks, and his son, the madcap duke, who, having attained the highest honours which Queen Anne could give, went over to the Pretender, and was attainted, his estates being sold by the Crown, and purchased by the rising favourite, John, Duke of Marlborough. The Whartons carry the sleeve white on a field black or sable.

The family of Norton, also, of Rylston in Craven, immortalized in Wordsworth's *White Doe of Rylstone* and *The Rising in the North*, carry a sleeve ermine on an azure field, debruised by a bend gules.

The Eures

In the third window on the north side of the Nave is another variety of the Bend, viz., quarterly or and gules, on a bend sable three escallops argent. These are the arms of the family of Eure,† and as they are of *historical* as well as heraldic interest, reminding us of many who took prominent and active part in the events of days gone by, as well as supplying good illustrations of "differencing by the bend," I purpose to give some account of their ancient lineage.

Dugdale says "that the name was first assumed from the lordship of "Evre, in county Bucks, where Hugh, a younger son to one of the Barons "of Werkworth, in county Northumberland (which barons were afterwards "known by the name of Clavering), did seat himself in the time of King "Henry III., is out of doubt."

* *Grey and Hastings Controversy*, by Sir Charles Young, 1841.   † See coloured illustration.

According to the pedigree contained among the "Additional pedi-"grees" at the end of Glover's *Visitation of Yorkshire*, 1575, edited by Joseph Foster, and for which he says he is indebted to John H. Matthews, Esq., of Lincolnshire, the worthy knight seems to have had, even in those ancient days, a distinguished lineage and illustrious family history; indeed, we must go back to the time of the Roman occupation, when the hill on which the town of Malton now stands, and which is the extreme end of a spur of the Yorkshire wolds, was surrounded by a belt of low marsh skirting the river Derwent, a totally impassable morass for many miles, except at this point, where there was a long, but easy ford. To command this, a Roman station was established at the junction of the great roads running to Whitby, Flamborough, Londesborough, and York. During the Heptarchy it became the royal villa of the Kings of Northumbria—and here Edwin probably lived. The lords of it were Torchil, and Siward, Earl of Northumberland, the mighty warrior who overthrew Macbeth, and eventually (dying peacefully, clad in armour, on his bed) was buried in St. Olave's Minster, York, which he had founded.

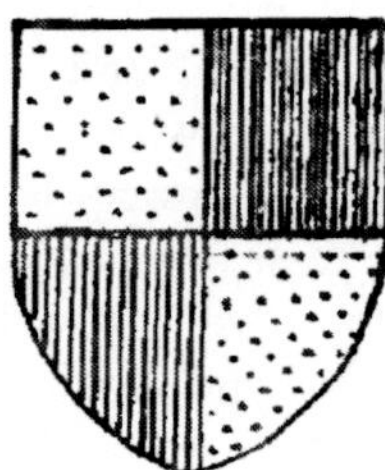

At the Conquest it was held by Gilbert Tyson, who fell at the battle of Hastings, fighting under the Anglo-Saxon banner, and was afterwards granted to his son William, whose only daughter carried it in marriage to Ivo de Vesci, who built a castle here. Their only daughter, Beatrix, married Eustace Fitz-John, son of John Monoculus, lord of Knaresborough, the younger son of Eustace de Burgh, a noble Norman, whose arms were—quarterly or and gules.

FitzJohn sided with Henry I. and held the castle against Stephen—indeed, commanded a division of the Scotch army against him at the battle of the Standard. "However, on the accession of Stephen, he was "received into favour, and founded and endowed the priory of St. Mary's, "Malton, committing it to the charge of the canons of the order of Sem-"pringham," whose superior, Gilbert, had established the order of the Premonstratensians or Gilbertines, a mixed community of men and women, of which eventually there were as many as forty throughout England. Little, however, now remains of it except a portion of the nave of the church, which has been lately beautifully restored (as far as restoration is possible) by the Rev. E. Pitman, under the direction of Mr. Temple Moore, the architect.

FitzJohn was slain in the wars against the Welsh, 1157. By his first wife, Beatrix, daughter of Ivo de Vesci, Lord of Alnwick and Malton, he had a son, William FitzEustace, Lord de Vesci in right of his mother, whose great-granddaughter, Margery, married Gilbert De Aton in Pickering-lythe *circa* 1200, and her great-grandson, Sir William de Aton, *circa* 1350, succeeded to Malton Castle in right of his ancestor, Lord de Vesci. His granddaughter, Catherine, as co-heir with her sister, carried it eventually to the family of the Eures by her marrying with Sir Ralph Eure, *circa* 1400, of which more anon. For his second wife Eustace FitzJohn married Agnes, sister and co-heir to William FitzNigel, and their grandson, Roger FitzRichard, was made Baron of Warkworth, Northumberland, by Henry II. His elder brother, John, succeeded to the barony of Laci, Halton, and Pontefract, by right of his mother, Albreda de Lisours, daughter and heiress of Albreda de Laci. John of course retained the family coat, and Roger, therefore, when made a baron, differenced his with a bend sable.

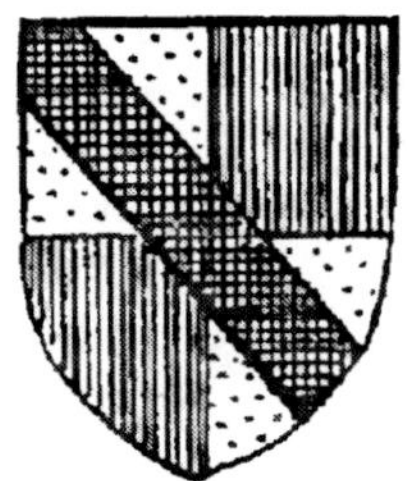

Roger married Adeliza, daughter and co-heir of Henry de Essex; and his son Robert, second Baron of Warkworth, received the lordship of Clavering from Henry II., and of Eure from Richard I. His son John, the third baron, married Ada, sister of John de Baliol, the founder of Baliol College, Oxford, and aunt to John de Baliol, King of Scotland.

The barony of Stokesley had been granted to the Baliols by William II., and we find that John Baliol, afterwards King of Scotland, held the signorial rights as lord paramount in 1286. In 1290 they were, however, granted to Hugh de Eure; and in 1315 Sir John de Eure is certified as lord of the township of Stokesley, Ingelby, Easeby, Battersby, and Kirby.

As they had three sons, the property was divided amongst them, and the arms differenced again. The eldest, Roger, became fourth Baron of Warkworth and Clavering, and retained the family coat. The second son, Sir Hugh, took the estate and title of Eure, with Stokesley and Ingelby in Yorkshire, and differenced his bend with three escallops. The motive for so doing can, of course, be only a matter of conjecture. The escallop was generally the badge of having been to the Holy Land; as the last crusade, under Richard I., took place in 1191, he must have gone there as a pilgrim. His younger brother, Robert, took three fleurs-de-lis, probably in consequence of being engaged in some of the wars with France which raged towards the close of the thirteenth century. Perhaps he was amongst the 7,000 men who (under the command of the Earl of Lancaster) defeated the French at Bordeaux, 1296, in attempting to recover Guienne.

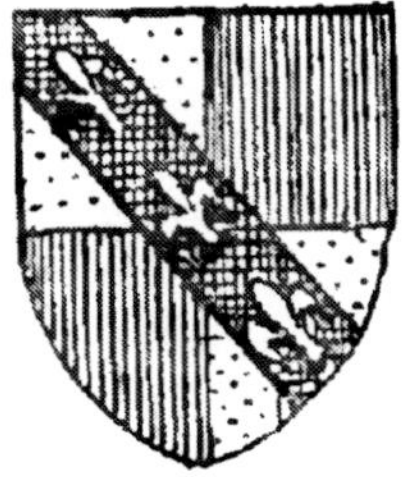

In *Old Yorkshire*, vol iv p 199, Richard de Eure is mentioned as Vicar of Bradford, who died 1309, and was probably also a son.

Sir Hugh de Eure appears to have been executor to John de Baliol, and in that capacity his seal is attached to a deed, on that the bend has no escallops, but he may have adopted them later

Perhaps it is of him that Stowe, in his *Annals* (p 210) says — "I have seen under the broad-seale of the said King Edward I a manor "called Ketness, in the county of Forfar, in Scotland, and neere the "furthest part of the same nation northward, given to John Ure and his "heires, ancestor to the Lord Ure that now is, for his service done in "these partes, with market, dated Lanercost, 20th day of Oct, regis 34"

At any rate his son John (by a daughter of Bertram, Baron Mitford) used the escallops, for they are on his seal still attached to a deed at Durham He was engaged with Edward I and Edward II in the Scotch wars, and died, leaving another Sir John as his eldest son His wife Margaret is supposed to have been a Lumley or Heron Her will, dated 1378, is published in the *Durham Wills*, vol i, and contains many quaint provisions peculiar to that time To her son Ranulph she leaves "aulam "meam novo paratam," *i e* "My newly made hangings (or hallings) for "the hall," but she adds this very practical condition "Si voluerit solvere "pro tectura"—"If he is willing to pay for putting them up" To her grandson Ralph she leaves a cup of silver gilt, and to his sister Margaret a cup of silver To Margaret Lumley she leaves "ij pecias argenti, cum xij "coclearibus argenti," and Robert Heron is her executor

Her eldest son, John (one of the principal warriors of his time), died Constable of Dover Castle and Lord Steward of the King's House His name appears as a witness in the famous Scrope and Grosvenor controversy He made a great alliance by marrying Isabella, daughter of Robert, Lord Clifford, and his son, Sir Ralph, having married, first, Isabel, daughter of Sir Adomar de Athol, married, second, Catherine, daughter of Sir William de Aton, to whom I have already alluded By her he obtained the estate at Malton He was sheriff of Yorkshire, constable of Newcastle-upon-Tyne, and constable of York Castle The castle at Malton had been destroyed by Henry II, and he did not rebuild it

He seems to have been a person of some consideration, for he served in the campaigns in Scotland under the Duke of Lancaster in 1383, and under King Richard II in 1385, when the canny Scots allowed the English army to march unopposed into their country, but soon to become embarrassed and distressed for want of provisions—finding little to destroy and nothing to subsist on, for the people had driven the cattle to the woods and hills, and their houses were mere huts—while the Douglas, with a numerous body of light cavalry, burst into the western counties of

England, and by ravage and plunder did more damage than their invaders could have done had they burned all Scotland from the Border to Aberdeen

After this disastrous expedition Sir Ralph was frequently employed by the King in matters requiring sagacity and tact rather than courage He it was who was appointed to settle some disputed rights as to prisoners taken at the battle of Hambledon, to treat with the Kings of Scotland for a truce on three separate occasions, 1404, 1405, 1407, and, in 1415, to treat for the ransom of Murdoc, son of Robert, Duke of Albany, in exchange for Henry Percy, the renowned "Hotspur" Murdoc returned to Scotland—for what a chequered career! In four years he succeeded his father as regent, and then,—after having accomplished the restoration of James, who had been taken captive as a child and imprisoned in the Tower of London since 1405,—as soon as the young King and his wife (Joan, daughter of the Earl of Somerset) had been crowned at Scone, he was beheaded with his two sons on the castle hill at Stirling, on the pretext of abusing the King's authority

Sir Ralph probably died soon after his mission, as he must then have been sixty-five By his first wife he had one daughter, Katherine, who married Sir John Pudsey of Bolton

In 1410 he had license from Langley, Bishop of Durham, to fortify his castle at Witton in Durham Nothing remains of that stronghold now, and what little interest lingers in the village centres in the ruins of the house of the Derwentwaters, so intimately associated with the last rising in England in favour of the Pretender, and the secret chamber is still shewn where the luckless Lord Lovat was taken If the dimensions given are correct—eight feet long, by three feet broad, and ten feet high—he must have been cruelly squeezed, as he was very corpulent, and death itself would, I should think, be preferable to life under such circumstances

Sir William Eure, his eldest son, when a lad of fifteen, in his father's lifetime, married Matilda, daughter of Henry, Lord FitzHugh, of Ravensworth, in whose retinue he went to the battle of Agincourt four years after, October 25th, 1415, and died about 1460

There is something more than quaint and curious in these old wills—they seem to bring us into very close communion with the personal feelings and family life of days gone by, something very touching in the disposition of cherished articles of family plate to beloved relations, not long to tarry after them, and quaint illustrations of the simple family life in those days, partly agricultural, partly sylvan, when the household was dependent not only on their own labours in the farm, but on the chase in the forests and wild country around I shall quote a few of them from the *Test Ebor*, *Surtees Society* First, that of the widow of Sir William, Maude de Eure, dated the same year

She speaks of herself therein as a widow, and desires to be buried in the abbey of Malton, by the side of her husband. To her daughter Margery, wife of Sir Christopher Conyers of Sockburn, she leaves "one "standyng piece gilted." To Catherine, wife of Sir Robert Ughtred of Kexby (who was her second cousin, their grandmothers being sisters and co-heiresses of the Atons—a dispensation being obtained for the purpose from Pope Eugenius IV., 1432, which was ratified by Langley, bishop of Durham), "one pece of silver coverde." To her daughter Johan, wife of Sir John Ogle of Bothal, she leaves "one piece of silver coverde and xx[ti] "zows" (ewes). "Also," the will goes on to say, "I will to Herre my son all "my husbandry at Malton, that is to say, vj. oxen with the ploght and wayne "and all oder gere thereto belonging, with two staggs that are at Wotton."

This same Henry married Catherine Danby, widow of Robert Lascelles of Sowerby, and his will also is extant, dated October, 1476. He is there described as "of Olde Malton, esquire," and desires his "body to be beryd "in the monastery of Our Lady in Olde Malton, before the medys of the "alter of Seynt John the Baptist, where the prest useth to say confiteor." He bequeaths "to my said wiff all my housald as it stands within my manor "of Olde Malton, with ij. wanes, ij. pleughes, et xvj. oxyn, a pece of silver "di-gilt covered, with ij. law cuppes of silver, called le beyl cuppes, the "which are at Sowerby, whereof on of thame is covered."

"Also I will that my said wiff have the use of ij. saltis of silver "during her liffe, and after her dissese, I bequeathe thame to my daughter "Marjory." Also to his said daughter he bequeaths "a pece gilt called "*le fale;* also a pece of silver with a rose in the mydes covered; also j. "basyn of silver, with iij. saltes of silver and gilte." He also states that he has "delivered to my said wife xx. nobilis of olde gold to make xx. "rings, the price of every ring vj*s.* viij*d.*, of the which ringes I will that "ichon of my brether and susters have on."

Both Matilda Eure and Henry Eure appoint William Eure, one of the younger sons of the former, to be an executor. He was S.T.B., in holy orders, and had the following preferment:—On Jan. 31, 1447–8, he was instituted to the rectory of Brompton, in Pickering-lithe, and received license of non-residence for a year. Dec. 1st, 1453, he was instituted, on the presentation of Sir William Eure, Knight, to the Mastership of the Hospital of the Blessed Virgin, in Bootham, York; and in 1460 he exchanged his rectory of Brompton with John Gisburgh for the precentorship of York Minster, to which he was collated Nov. 14th, 1460. On July 25th following he had leave to be non-resident in that office, as the King had ordered him not to leave the city of London. On the 9th March, 1462–3, he exchanged with Lawrence Roche the rectory of Wem, in Shropshire, for the rectory of Workington. He gave up the latter in 1470; and in November, 1471, he was collated to the archdeaconry of Salisbury, which he held for six years.

In 1473 he was instituted to the vicarage of Leeds, where he founded the chantry of St. Mary Magdalene, "the corner building on the west side of "the great street." He seems to have died in 1483, and was buried in York Minster. No memorial of him exists, but Torre records that "in the "south quire, on the north side east, lyes a blue stone about three yards "long, whereon has been a square plate at the head, about three inches "broad, which I perceive bore this inscription: 'Orate pro añi dñi Will'mi "'Evers, nuper unus personarum hujus alme Eccles, et Rectoris Eccle "'omnium storum in Marisco.'"

Drake gives this inscription, and adds: "Civit Ebor, qui obiit xxiij "die mensis Maii, An. Dom. 1419." This seems, however, to point to another William, who lived and died several generations before. Nevertheless I cannot but fancy that Drake must have printed 1419 for 1490; for in the roll of the Guild of Corpus Christi in York, we find, 1475, "Dom Will "Evers, Rector Ecclesiæ Omnium Sanctorum in Peseholme;" and Drake speaks of the parish church of All Saints, or All Hallows, having stood in "Peaseholme, Havergate, all in Marisco;" while in the same roll, under date 1475, "Magister Will: Eure, eccl. Cath. Ebor Precentor," is mentioned. So, evidently, there were two William Eures, ecclesiastics (probably kinsmen or cousins) living about the same time.

John Eure (the precentor's younger brother) died 1492, and his will has come down to us, in which he is described as armiger, and that he was to be buried in the churchyard of Hoton-Bushell. It is a very brief document, containing little more than two bequests—one a gift of xl*s*. to the fabric of the bridge over the Derwent, and remission of xxvj*s*. viii*d*. which he had spent from his own property at the time of the building of the said bridge. He also gives vi*s*. viij*d*. to the building of the chapel of the Blessed Virgin on the east side of the Derwent.

Sir Ralph Eure, eldest son of Sir William Eure, married Eleanor, daughter of Baron Greystock, and was killed at Towton field on Palm Sunday, March 9th, 1461. His eldest son, Sir William, was Sheriff of Yorkshire (Richard III., 1483), and married twice—first, Margaret, the daughter of old Sir Ralph Constable, of Flamborough; and second, Constance, widow of Sir Henry Percy, of Bamboro'.

He is probably the Sir W. Eure mentioned in the following quaint entry (quoted in *Old Yorkshire*, 2nd series, p. 105):—On Feb. 20th, 1489, the King directs a writ to the Master Forester of Pykering, directing 300 "trees of oke" called "scobbs and stobbs," in the woods called Elysclore, to be delivered to the bailiffs of the town of Scarborrow, for the repairing of the "gayle and key" thereof, which are "in grete ruign, and without "brieff remedy likely to be to thimportable charge of our said towne;" to be used under the oversight of "thurle of Northumberland, Sir W. Euer, "W. Tunstal, Esq., and Robert Wauton."

The Eures appear to have inherited property near Scarborough from the Aitons, for Leyland, in his *Itinerary*, says "From Scarborough to "Aiton three miles, when coming over Derwent I saw a manor-place, some-"time longing to a knight called Aiton, now to the best of the Eures"

His younger brother, Hugh, LL D, was instituted rector of Huggate, 1485, and of Brompton "on the resignation of William Eure, 1506" So says the pedigree, which seems to point to another William besides the two whom we have already mentioned The rector of Huggate died 1522, and his will has also been preserved (*Test Ebor*, vol liii p 83) It is interesting, as characteristic of an ecclesiastic, and indicating some details of clerical life and thought in those days He gives "to the church and "chauncel of Hugate, aither of them, 10*s*, to the reparell of the bells "there, x*s*, to the House of Saynctie Roberte of Knaresburgh, for my "broderhede, iij*s*. iiij*d*, to Robert Rocliffe al such dettes as he awe me, "I forgif Rauf Hastynges al such dettes as he awe me, to Guy Rowclif a "horse, to my cousyng Matilde a fillye stag, which at this tyme rynneth in "Barleby Carre, to Thomas Rauf, Brian, Kateryne, Agnes, and Margery, "childer of Robert Rowclif, ij yowes each, to Rauf Ellercar a young stag in "Barleby Carre, to the House of Saynctie Mary Abbey, ij hundredth and iiij "score wedders I will that my cosynge Matilde childer have to be skifted "amongst them xl wedders, xl yowes, xl hogges To Sir William Eure "[his brother] the best silver salte, gilted The residue to Sir William "Eure, knight, Maister Henry Machell, doctor, Sir William Thomson, and "Sir John Eure [his nephew, buried at Leeds, 1524], preistes my executors, "I bequeath to every oon of them an hundred shepe withoute grugeyng "of conscience"

Sir William's eldest son, Sir Ralph, succeeded him, and was twice married—first to Muriel, daughter of Sir Hugh Hastings, of Fenwick, second, to Agnes, daughter of Robert Constable, of Dromondby, and widow of Sir Ralph Bigod He had three children by each wife, of whom probably were two whose names are associated with York, viz. Will Eure, whose will was proved in April, 1523, and who desired to be buried near John Reynolds at the east end, and George Eure, buried (according to Drake, p. 339) in Belfry Church, Scriba, Registrarius dum vixit Curiæ Ebor, Oct 21, 1520 The eldest son, by his first wife, Sir William Eure, who married Elizabeth, daughter of Lord Willoughby d'Eresby, and aunt to the Duchess of Suffolk, was Sheriff of Northumberland, 1527, and captain of the town and castle of Berwick-upon-Tweed, 1539 He was afterwards warden of the East Marches towards Scotland, and was created Lord Eure of Witton by letters patent, February 24th, 1544

In these days, when the Borders have become so completely a figure of speech, it is difficult to imagine that the office of Warden of the Borders (or Marches, as they were termed) was anything but an honorary or unnecessary office of title or dignity; but in ancient days the border counties were for many centuries in a state little favourable to quiet or peaceful government. On the northern side of the Tweed, the Scottish border counties were thronged with inhabitants divided into clans of Scott, Kerr, Hume, Douglas, Cranstoun, Beeton, &c., and having chiefs whom they obeyed in preference to the King or his officers placed amongst them—rough, unruly people, dwelling in a land of dales and valleys, morass and forests, living by hunting or by plunder, sometimes on the English, sometimes on each other, and sometimes on the more civilized country which lay behind them, always going armed with shields of wood, bows and arrows, large swords called claymores, poleaxes, daggers, and invariably horsemen, "and with jedwood axe at saddle bow," for, says Froissart, "Of a truth the Scottish cannot boast great skill with the bow, but rather "bear axes, with which in time of need they give heavy strokes." On the other side, the English Borderers, consisting of the great families of Dacre, Fenwick, Lisle, Percy, Swinburne, the Herons of Ford, Chipchase and Simondburn Castles, and many others equally unsettled and equally warlike, were always ready to resort to similar measures. The ancient chronicles are full of laments over the desolation and misery of the land, and the ruin of the lords and people which reduced Northumberland to a desert. A prior of Alnwick quaintly says:—

"Lugeat Northumbria nimis desolata,
Facta est ut vidua filiis orbata;
Vesce, Merley, Somerville, Bertram, sunt in fata,
O quibus et quantis et qualibet viduata."

A bitter retaliation followed upon each successful raid. Wholesale plunder, wanton destruction, indiscriminate burning and slaying became the object on each side, and (in the absence of resistance) fire and sword were turned against peaceful villages, and defenceless women and children—so much so that when we contemplate the continuous raids and counter-raids we can but marvel how the population on either side escaped starvation. Each side, of course, charges the other with atrocity, but there was probably no greater leaning to humanity and mercy on the one side than the other. If the English prior wrote so plaintively of Scotch barbarity, the Scotch poet is equally pathetic of English. In 1296, when Berwick had been taken by assault, he says:—

"The nobilis, all that war within the town,
And also thereout, were haillelie slaine down;
Five thousand men that mickle were of thaine,
Within the towne that samye day war slain;
Women and bairns, also young and old,
*War slain that day out of numbers untold."

* Hutchinson's *History of Cumberland*, vol. i. p. 26.

Sir Thomas Carlton, of Carlton Hall, 1547, gives a most placid report of spoliation and barbarities committed by him in a raid through Teviotdale and Dumfries

Robert Bruce, in 1312, entered Cumberland by the Solway Firth, ravaged Gillesland to the value of £2,000, and pillaged the abbey of Lanercost In Haines's *State Papers* a record is given of a raid in 1543, when 10,386 horned cattle, 12,492 sheep, and 260 nags were "lifted," besides 192 buildings destroyed, 403 Scots slain, and 816 prisoners taken

In 1545 the Earl of Hertford boasts of having destroyed 7 monasteries, 25 castles, 5 towns, 243 villages, 13 mills, and 3 hospitals

In the *Annals of the House of Percy* (vol ii p 197) there is a letter (too long to transcribe here) from Lord Eure to the Earl of Northumberland, giving a lamentable account of an onslaught by the Burnes, Younges, and Mawes upon two of his tenants, and the state of expectation and preparation for such events in which they lived, is graphically set before us in Scott's *Lay of the Last Minstrel*, where (canto i)—

"Nine and twenty knights of fame
Hung their shields in Branksome Hall,
Nine and twenty squires of name
Brought their steeds to tower from stall,
Nine and twenty yeomen tall
Waited duteous on them all
Ten of them were sheathed in steel,
With belted sword, and spur on heel,
They quitted not their armour bright
Neither by day nor yet by night
They lay down to rest
With corslet laced,
Pillowed on buckler cold and hard,
They carved at the meal
With gloves of steel,
And they drank the red wine through the helmet barred
Ten squires, ten yeomen, mail-clad men,
Waited the beck of the wardens ten
Thirty steeds both fleet and wight
Stood saddled in stable day and night
Barbed with frontlet of steel, I trow,
And with Jedwood axe at saddle-bow,
A hundred more fed free in stall,—
And such was the custom in Branksome Hall
Why do these steeds stand ready dight?
Why watch these warriors armed by night?
They watch to hear the bloodhound baying,
They watch to hear the war-horn braying,
To see St George's red cross streaming,
To see the midnight beacon gleaming
They watch 'gainst southron force and guile,
Lest Scroop, or Howard, or Percy's powers,
Threaten Branksome's lordly towers,
From Warkworth, or Naworth, or merry Carlisle"

And the occasions which led to these sanguinary results were often as trivial as they were unpremeditated.

In 1370 a drunken brawl at Roxburgh fair led to an indiscriminate attack upon the Scotch there assembled, and some of the servants of Patrick Dunbar, Earl of March, were slain. Failing to recover the redress he demanded of Lord Percy, he ravaged the country round Carlisle, and carried off some hundreds of English, as well as great booty in horse and cattle; and a series of retaliatory raids ensued on both sides.*

The battle of Chevy-Chase, when

> "To drive the deer with hound and horn
> Earl Percy took his way:
> The child may rue that is unborn
> The hunting of that day,"

whether an actual or apocryphal incident, is simply an illustration of the quarrels which ensued then, as now, on the vexed question of "game;" and the battle of Otterburne originated simply with the banter arising out of a not unfriendly trial of personal prowess, in which Hotspur was unhorsed, and Douglas, possessing himself of his lance and pennon, taunted him to come and take it from his tent. This of course developed a battle, for both sides gathered their men together to secure or prevent such a result. Froissart says—"Of all the battailes and encountrynges that I "have made mencion of heretofore in all this my story, great or small, this "battaile that I treat on now was one of the sorest and best foughten, "without cowardes or feynte hartes."

Twice or thrice did the young rival leaders meet face to face in mortal combat; and the popular tradition is that Douglas fell by the hand of the former. At least so says the old ballad of Chevy-Chase, which has been supposed to refer to this. And there is something very touching in what ensued.

> "The Perse leaned on his brande
> And sawe the Douglas de;
> He took the dede man by the hande
> And said, 'Woy's me! for thee
> To have saved thy lyffe I wolde have pertyd with
> My landes for years thre;
> For a better man of harte, nore of hande,
> Was not in all the north countre.'"

In 1402 the Scots made a plundering expedition under Hepburn as far as the borders of Durham, and returning with their booty, were overtaken at Nesbitt Heath by the Earl of Northumberland and some of the northern lords, completely defeated, their commander taken prisoner, and "no less than 10,000 of their number slain."†

House of Percy, vol. i. * p. 109, † p. 205.

To avenge this, a second expedition of 12,000 men was led across the Border by Archibald, Earl of Douglas, and met and defeated by Hotspur at the heights of Homildon, near Wooler Douglas and the Earl of Fife were taken prisoners, and of the thousands that had crossed the Border but a few hundreds are said to have regained their native soil

It was evidently to the interest of both countries to restrain, if possible, this wanton and useless strife, and Edward I stipulated with Robert Bruce that there should be Wardens of the Marches on both sides On the Scottish side Bruce appointed Lord James of Douglas, who fulfilled his trust with great fidelity On the English side Edward divided the frontier among three Wardens, of the west, the middle, the east Marches, and installed Robert de Clifford as the first Lord Warden, 1296

The authority of the Warden was of a mixed nature, military and civil He was generalissimo of the forces, to give command, to place and appoint watchmen, to fire beacons, and give alarm on the approach of the enemy He had power to muster "all defensible men between sixteen and "sixty," marshal them in thousands, hundreds, and twenties, armed as billmen and archers, and to commence hostilities or conclude conditions of peace He took cognizance of all breaches of the Border laws, imprisonments, robberies and spoils, cutting timber, sowing corn, depasturing cattle, and hunting out of proper boundaries He had a council, composed of discreet borderers, to assist him in holding courts and sessions for the redress of grievances, could pursue a thief within six days, in "hot trod," with hue and cry, and had power of life and death

On one occasion the Earl of Northumberland (1528) held a court-warden at Alnwick, and beheaded nine and hanged five men for march-treason and felony, and soon after overtook and slew William Charleton of Sholyngton, "the hyed rebell off all the Howthlawes," and hanged four of his accomplices in chains at different places *

Not the least of his onerous duties was the reconciling of differences and patching up quarrels amongst the nobles and gentlemen themselves, even as it was across the Border, for Scott tells us—

"While Cessford owns the rule of Carr,
And Ettrick boasts the line of Scott,
The slaughtered chiefs, the mortal jar,
The havoc of the feudal war,
Shall never, never be forgot"

Lay of the Last Minstrel

His dignity was so great that in 1382 Sir Matthew Redmayne, deputy-governor of Berwick, refused admission to "time-honoured Lancaster" himself into the town, and the earl afterwards justified the act in the King's

* *House of Percy*, vol 1 p 388

presence, as having the royal authority not to "suffer any manner of person, "lord or other, to enter into cytie, towne, or castell in Northumberland, "without he were herytor of the place;"* and, 1403, Sir William Clifford, acting under the same, viz., Henry Percy, first Earl of Northumberland, refused to surrender Berwick to the King's officers, except under certain conditions.† When Henry, sixth Earl of Northumberland, arrested Wolsey at Cawood, he silenced the cardinal's plea that as a member of the see apostolic he was not under any temporal authority, with these words, "When I was sworn Warden of the Marches, you yourself told me that "I might with my staff arrest all men under the degree of the King, and "now I am stronger, for I have a commission so to do."‡

Under ordinary circumstances, therefore, this was a position of great responsibility, to which the King would not be likely to appoint a man on account of high connections and rank, but of proved integrity and ability. But these were specially troubled times. Flodden had been fought (1513), when James, brother-in-law to Henry VIII., and the flower of the Scottish nobility, perished miserably. Margaret, his widow, had married within a year the Earl of Angus, and was immediately deposed from her office as Regent. The late King's cousin, the Duke of Albany, had been called in as her successor, and endless dissension had been the result. Unhappily the Queen had compromised her character with Albany, and identified herself with him against Angus. Eventually Angus was exiled, and Albany fled; and when Henry interposed to reconcile the contending factions, assuring them that he desired nothing but the real welfare of Scotland, the Estates defied him to do his worst against them.

The Borders on each side were wasted with the usual recklessness; and when Albany returned from France with 6,000 French men-at-arms, a second Flodden was looked for, and Lord Dorset, Lord Latimer, the Earl of Northumberland, Darcy, Clifford, and all the gentlemen of Yorkshire, hastened to the rescue. But Albany lacked courage, his heart failed him, and after attacking Newark he retreated, to the disgust of the gentlemen of the Border, who tore the badges of their craven Regent from their breasts and dashed them on the ground. "By God's blood," they cried, "we "will never serve you more. Would to God we were all sworn English!"§

And so the danger subsided for the time: but only for a time. Margaret's waywardness and intrigues kept the country continually unsettled, and a war with England was always imminent. In 1528 the young King James began to assume the active duties of the Crown, and aggravated, rather than soothed, the existing irritation with England by identifying himself with the papacy as opposed to the Reformation, favouring the Pope

---

House of Percy, vol. i. * p. 134, † p. 230, ‡ p. 415. § *History of Scotland.* Sir Walter Scott.

and the Emperor rather than the allied English and French, and, rejecting Henry's efforts at conciliation, supported the Irish rebels against him In 1532 this unhappy alienation developed into war, and the Earl of Northumberland and Sir Thomas Clifford read to the Scotch lords, at the sword's point, those lessons of moderation which had been vainly urged with gentleness After a struggle of a year and a half peace was made, and Henry even offered to make James Duke of York, and include him in the line of inheritance

But James, alarmed at the protests of the clergy against accepting any favour from the arch-heretic, temporised with the offer, and excusing himself, on the score of inconvenience and distance, from meeting Henry at York, sailed over to France in May, 1536, and married Magdalen de Valois on the new year's day following During the next two years matters did not improve Margaret's dissensions with her husband, Methuen, which culminated in a divorce, giving endless trouble and anxiety to Henry, who sent Sir Robert Sadler to ascertain her real condition He spent a night at Darlington on his way, and in a letter to Cromwell describes the disturbed and excited condition of the people there, summing up his description in these terse words—"I assure your lordship that the people "be very tickle"

In 1537 Magdalen died, and James almost immediately married Mary, daughter of the Duke of Guise, a link which bound the country to France and the papacy, and in May following English spies in Edinburgh reported that an army was being prepared to co-operate with an invading force from France Sir Ralph Sadler again came north as ambassador to remonstrate, and the Duke of Norfolk advanced from York to Berwick, and to this combined display of reason and force James submitted Henry again implored his nephew to meet his overtures with the frankness with which they were made, and for two years, at least, there was peace

During these trying circumstances we can well understand that a firm hand and a loyal heart was needed for such a post as "Captain of the town "and castle of Berwick-upon-Tweed, and Warden of the East Marches "towards Scotland," and if Henry found such a man, as no doubt he did in Sir William Eure, we can well understand that in 1544 he should have created him a baron of the realm

But Henry's debt of gratitude was not confined to Sir William Eure only His eldest son, Sir Ralph Eure, had been appointed constable of Scarborough Castle, and in 1536 the famous conspiracy, called "The "Pilgrimage of Grace," commenced—a reaction provoked by the late drastic measures of the King, to restore, at least in some degree, the faith and practice of the pre-Reformation times It would be beside my purpose to trace in detail the progress and development of this movement The spark seems to have been kindled at Louth on Sunday, October 3rd, 1536, where Heneage, the commissioner appointed to examine into the condition of the churches and clergy, found himself on his arrival surrounded by a mob armed with belts and staves ("the stir and the noise arising hideous"), and compelled to swear to be true to the Commons.

The prompt measures of Lord Hussey of Sleaford and Lord Shrewsbury eventually prevailed, and the result of a gathering at Lincoln Cathedral, on October 13th, was that the country gentlemen persuaded the people to trust the King, who had said they were misinformed as to the character of his measures, and to wait and see.

But the smouldering embers were soon to be fanned into a blaze. John, Robert, and Christopher Aske, three Yorkshire gentlemen, whose mother was the daughter of John Lord Clifford, the stout old Lancastrian slain at Towton, having spent a short time cub-hunting with their brother-in-law, Sir Ralph Ellerkar, of Ellerkar Hall, separated to return to their duties and homes. Robert, *en route* to London, where he was a barrister in good practice, after crossing the Humber at Welton, found himself in the midst of a party of rebels at Appleby, who forced him to take the oath and become their leader. Flattered by their attentions, or convinced by their grievances, he put himself at their head, recrossed the Ouse, and having satisfied himself by a hasty visit to Lincoln, where he found the people again excited by the answer which the Duke of Suffolk had brought from the King, he went back at full speed, persuaded that an opportunity now presented itself which could never occur again.

That night beacons blazed throughout Yorkshire, and all Yorkshire was in movement. At Beverley, William Stapleton, a friend of Aske's, was, in a similar manner, forced by the excited crowd to be their leader; while Lord Darcy of Templehurst (an old man, who had won his spurs under Henry VIII., and fought against the Moors by the side of Ferdinand), temporised by merely putting out a proclamation and shutting himself up with twelve followers in Pontefract Castle, and took no further steps to secure peace and order. The conflagration now spread swiftly, and seemed likely to extend over the whole north.

Lords Darcy, Lumley, Scrope, Conyers,—Constable of Flamborough, the Tempests, Bowes, Fairfax, Strangeways, Ellerker, Sir John Bulmer, Mallory, Lascelles, Norton, Monckton, Gower, Ingleby, responded; only the Cliffords, Dacres, Musgraves, refused to come in to the confederacy. Scarcely one blow was struck anywhere. Skipton Castle alone in the West Riding held out for the Crown, although the whole retinue of the stout Earl of Clifford abandoned him, leaving him with some eighty people; together with Christopher and John Aske, who having rescued Lady Eleanor Clifford and her little children from Bolton Abbey, brought them in safety within the walls of the castle And Sir Ralph Eure did the same at Scarborough, defending it against the rebels with his household servants only, and subsisting for nearly twenty days on little more than bread and water

Who can say how much the unswerving loyalty and undaunted bravery of these gallant men contributed to check the apparent triumphant development of that movement which had such a speedy and ghastly end

Henry rewarded Sir Ralph by making him commander-in-chief of all the forces guarding the Marches towards Scotland And his services were soon called into action

In October, 1542, the Scotch began their customary depredations on the Border, and Sir Ralph Bowes, who had crossed the Marches in pursuit of a party of them, fell into an ambuscade at Halydon Rigg, and was taken prisoner—Hume says (vol iii p 198) with Sir Ralph Eure, Sir Brian Latoun, and some other persons of distinction War was now inevitable The Duke of Norfolk crossed the Tweed and wasted the country for nine days, and 10,000 Scotchmen crossed into the Marches of Cumberland to waste the country in revenge, but only, bewildered, to retreat before Sir Thomas Wharton, Lord Dacre, and Lord Musgrave, and a few hundred farmers, and perish ignominiously in Solway Moss

James, on hearing this, sickened of mortification and despair He went languidly to Falkland, and when the birth of his daughter, afterwards known as Mary Queen of Scots, was announced to him, he only said—"The de'il go with it! it will end as it begun It came from a lass and will "end with a lass," and falling back into his old song, "Fie! fled Oliver? "Is Oliver taken? All is lost!" in a few more days he moaned away his life.

Henry, on this, made another conciliatory effort, and (offering to betroth his little child Edward to Mary, release the prisoners of Solway Moss, the Earls of Casilis and Glencairn, Lords Maxwell, Fleming, Somerville, Oliphant, and Grey, Sir Oliver Sinclair, and two hundred gentlemen) he proposed substantial conditions of peace

Cardinal Beton was safely immured in Blackness Castle Arran was Regent The power had passed from the clergy to the laity, and as Knox said, "the situation was a wonderful providence of God" But Beton was soon again at liberty, for Ralph Sadler, Henry's ambassador, found himself involved in the conflicting bickerings and claims of Beton and Arran The Scotch ambassadors to Henry, Glencairn and Douglas, returned, indeed, with encouraging assurances, but the ecclesiastical influence, and the national antipathy of the Scots to their southern neighbours, prevailed The English ambassador and his retinue were insulted The Cardinal himself sent a hostile message to Sir Ralph Eure at Berwick, threatening to challenge him to single combat, to which Eure replied, signifying his entire pleasure at the prospect, and offering to return to Edinburgh to meet him sooner than balk the Cardinal's wishes.

Early in 1544 war again broke out, and Henry sent a fleet of 200 vessels and an army of 20,000 men to invade Scotland by landing at Leith. The Court fled to Edinburgh. Lord Eure, with 4,000 men, came in from Berwick, having marked his way by a broad track of desolation, where abbey and grange, castle and hamlet, were buried in a common ruin. Edinburgh was fired, Holyrood pillaged, and the country for seven miles round was wasted; and then the main army was transported from Newcastle to Calais, leaving a considerable number of men on the Border, under Eure and Lord Wharton, to continue the work of destruction. What that was may be gathered from the returns of the Wardens of the Marches between July and November, 1554:—"Towns, homesteads, barnekyns, parish churches, "fortified houses, burnt and destroyed, 192; of Scots slain, 403; of prisoners "taken, 816. The spoil amounted to over 10,000 horned cattle, 12,000 sheep, "1,300 horses, 850 boles of corn." Scott says (*Border Minstrelsy*, vol. iv. p. 197) "Eure burned the town of Broomhouse, with its lady (a noble and aged "woman, says Leslie) and her whole family." Lord Eure continued through the winter his desolating inroads. Jedburgh and Kelso were ravaged. Coldingham was taken, and Arran disgracefully beaten back when he tried to recover it by assault. Eure and Sir Brian Layton vauntingly promised to conquer the whole country south of the Forth.

But what the Scots could not attain by open attack they accomplished by stratagem. A party of Scots (pretending to be confederates with the English) brought information to Berwick that the Regent was lying with a small force at Melrose, and might be surprised. Eure started on Feb. 25th, 1544, with 4,000 men; reached Melrose, the Regent retiring as he advanced; and, disappointed of his expected assistance from the Earl of Angus there, Eure vented his irritation by desecrating the tombs of the princely ancestors of the earl. Then he continued his pursuit, the Regent still retreating, until, wearied and disheartened, he began to return from Melrose to Jedburgh, across Ancram Muir.

Hitherto the Douglas had at least affected goodwill towards Henry, but this insult, combined with a quarrel which Eure had lately had with Sir George Douglas, had turned the tide. Henry had promised to Eure and Layton all the lands which they could conquer in Merse and Teviotdale. "I will write the instruments of possession upon their own bodies with sharp pins and in blood-red ink," exclaimed the Earl of Angus, the chief of the Douglas, "because they destroyed the tombs of my ancestors in the "Abbey of Melrose," and co-operating with Arran, the Regent, he was reinforced by Leslie of Rothes, with 300 men, and the laird of Buccleuch.*

* *Tales of a Grandfather.* Sir Walter Scott.

By the advice of this experienced warrior, Angus withdrew from the height which he had occupied, and marshalled his forces behind it, upon a piece of low flat ground called Panier-heugh The spare horses, which had been sent to an eminence in their rear, appeared to the English to be the main body of the Scotch in the act of flight Under this persuasion Eure and Layton hurried precipitately up the hill, and found, to their surprise, the phalanx of Scottish spearmen drawn up in firm array upon the flat ground below The Scotch in their turn became the assailants The English were taken by surprise, and found themselves attacked on all sides by enemies who appeared to have risen out of the morass At the same time the 2,000 Scottish borderers who had submitted to Eure, and formed part of his force, perceiving that their countrymen would be victorious, threw away their red cross badges, and fell upon the English, to make amends for their late desertion of the Scottish cause The English broke and fled in utter disorder, leaving their commanders to their fate Eure, Layton, Lord Ogle, and 200 more were killed, and a thousand prisoners paid for their cowardice by the ransom which was wrung from them * So perished the gallant Sir Ralph, and his body was buried in the Abbey of Melrose, which he had so ruthlessly desecrated and finally burned

As an illustration of the grim justice of Henry VIII, amongst the prisoners was Thomas Read, a London alderman He had declined to contribute his share to the "benevolence," as it was called, which the King had demanded of the citizens of London For this act of insubordination the King ordered him to be seized, and sent him to Eure, with directions that he should be compelled to serve as a soldier, and subjected to all the rigour and hardships of the service, that he might know what soldiers suffered whilst in the field, and be more ready another time to assist the King with money to pay them The luckless alderman escaped from his unwelcome experience with life, but his heavy ransom, combined therewith, taught him a lesson which he probably never forgot

Angus professed, even after this, to remain true to the English cause, and when threatened with the anger of Henry he exclaimed, "Is our good "brother offended that I am a good Scotchman—that I revenged on Ralph "Eure the abusing of the tombs of my forefathers at Melrose? They were "more honourable men than he, and I ought to have done no less Will "King Henry for that have my life? Little knows he the Skirts of "Kernetable I will keep myself there from his whole English army"†

The spot where the battle was fought was also called Lillyard's Edge, Scott says (*Tales of a Grandfather*, vol 1 p 225), because a beautiful young maiden called Lillyard followed her lover from the little village of Maxton,

* *Border Minstrelsy* Sir Walter Scott † Froude's *History of England*

and when she saw him fall in battle, rushed herself into the heat of the fight, and was killed after slaying several of the English. The old people point out her monument, broken and defaced. The inscription is said to have been legible within this century, and to have run thus:—

> "Fair maiden Lillyard lies under this stane,
> Little was her stature, but great was her fame;
> Upon the English loons she laid many thumps,
> And when her legs were cutted off she fought upon her stumps."

That it was a sanguinary battle Scott has indicated in his poem on the "Eve of St. John," where he says:—

> "He came not from where Ancram Moor
> Ran red with English blood;
> Where the Douglas true, and the bold Buccleugh,
> 'Gainst keen Lord Evers stood."

Four years after, Lord Eure died, and was succeeded by Sir Ralph's eldest son, William, whose mother was Margaret, daughter of Ralph Bowes, of Streatlam Castle, Durham. His first marriage, with Mary, daughter of Lord Darcy, celebrated at Eynsham, Oxon, when he was eleven and she only four years old, was dissolved thirteen years afterwards, 1554, by decree at Durham. He seems to have succeeded to the office held by his father and grandfather, as, 6th Edward VI., he was appointed Warden of the Middle Marches towards Scotland; and, 4th and 5th of Philip and Mary, and 1st of Elizabeth, Captain of Berwick-on-Tweed. His second wife was Margaret, daughter of Sir Edward Dymoke, of Scrivelsby, Champion of England. He left a sum of money to his son to build a house at Jarrow, but it seems never to have been carried out.

In 1544 the cell of Jarrow had been granted to William, Lord Eure, by the Crown, and the property remained in the family until 1627, when William, Lord Eure, conveyed it to Henry Gibb, of Falkland, Gentleman of His Majesty's Chamber.*

Lord Eure's two sons were both distinguished men. The eldest, we are told, was born at Berwick Castle, 28th Sept., 1558, at eight o'clock in the morning, and christened the following Monday in the parish church, Mr. Christopher Nevill acting deputy for his brother Henry, Earl of Westmoreland, and Thomas, Earl of Northumberland.† He was made Warden of the Middle Marches 1586, when 28 years of age; and Sheriff of Yorkshire 1594; and I conclude that he conducted the difficult duty of maintaining order on the Borders with satisfaction to Queen Elizabeth of England and James of Scotland, for the former continued him in that office until her death, seventeen years after.

---

* Surtees' *History of Durham*, vol. ii. p. 73. † MS. Lord Harlech.

When James VI of Scotland assumed the throne of England, the office became no longer necessary The borderers on each side of the Scottish boundary wall became, at least outwardly, friendly, and the "Moss "Troopers"--no longer having the pretext of national hostility, and living simply for themselves by plunder, and by the black mail which they compelled the inhabitants to pay for their safety—became common objects of terror and detestation, and were eventually exterminated, chiefly by the efforts of Lord William Howard ("Belted Will") and Charles Howard, Lord Carlisle, whose mother was Mary Eure, eldest daughter of Sir Ralph's eldest son

The King, therefore, having previously employed Lord Eure as ambassador to the Emperor Rudolph II, and also to Denmark, appointed him Lord President of the Council in the Principality of Wales, 1616—a similar position, though, then, one comparatively of "otium cum dignitate," but which in days gone by had been as difficult and troublesome * For the Marches of Wales were supposed to have been settled by the Saxons to prevent the incursions of the British, or Welsh, and those who obtained seigniories therein by right of conquest were termed Lord Marchers of Wales The chief officer amongst them for the government was a Warden Edward IV acquired Ludlow Castle, the stronghold of the Mortimers, through his grandmother, Lady Anne Mortimer, sister of Edmund Mortimer fifth Earl of March, and some years after his accession to the throne repaired the castle, and made it the Court of his son the Prince of Wales, who was sent hither (as Hall relates) "for justice to be done in the Marches "of Wales, to the end that by the authoritie of his presence the wild "Welshmen and evil-disposed persons should refrain from their accustomed "murthers and outrages" And Sir Philip Sydney (some years afterwards) observed, that since the establishment of the Lord President and Council the whole country of Wales had been brought from their disobedience and barbarous incivility to a civil and obedient condition, and freed from those sports and felonies with which the Welsh had annoyed them But the young Prince, of course, was never Lord President, as he was murdered at thirteen He seems only to have been sent to give importance to Alcock, successively Bishop of Rochester, Worcester, and Ely, the first President, who certainly was surrounded by a most stately Court Besides a Vice-President—probably Lord Rivers—the Council comprised a Lord Chancellor, Lord Treasurer, Lord Keeper of the Privy Purse, Lord Treasurer of the King's Household, Chancellor of the Exchequer, Principal Secretary of State, with the Judges of Assize for the counties of Salop, Gloucester, Hereford, and Monmouth, the Justices of the Grand Session of Wales, the

* *History of Ludlow*

Chief Justice of Chester, and Attorney and Solicitor-General, and many of the neighbouring nobility, with a number of subordinate officers.

The sword of State borne before him is still in possession of Earl Powis. Alcock was the first of a long succession of magnates, which lasted until the days of William and Mary, 1689, when the Court was dissolved at the humble suit of the gentlemen and inhabitants of the Principality of Wales, by whom it was represented as an intolerable grievance.*

Arthur, Prince of Wales, son of Henry VII., resided there after his marriage with Catherine of Arragon, and died there.

Amongst the Presidents many illustrious names occur.† Lord Eure succeeded Edward Lord Zouche, who died and was buried in a vault close to the wine cellar, which gave rise to the following epigram by Ben Jonson :—

"Whenever I die, let this be my fate,
To lie by my good Lord Zouche;
That when I am dry, to the tap I may hie,
And so back again to my couch."

Lord Eure retained the appointment from 1607 to 1616, and does not appear to have found it altogether a bed of roses, for in the Cotton MS. there is a letter of his, probably addressed to the Earl of Salisbury, commencing: "It doth not a little grieve me to have occasion to relate to your "lordship the generall disobedience, many meetings and combinations "against the government of the Court in the Principality of Wales." He marvels that "the grave Bishop of Hereford" should combine with "the rest of the gentlemen of that countie to their principal agent, "Sir Herbert Croft, to challenge the free action and inheritable libertie of "the laws of the realme." "Worcester groweth," he says, "almost as "vehement as Herefordshire, by means of Sir John Packington, now High "Sheriff of the countie. The Deputy Lieutenants there, as also in Here- "fordshire, do refuse once to visit me, so that I do forbear to grant them "my deputations till I see better conformitie." And the letter concludes with a postscript: "I beseech your lordship let me know whether by your "favour I may obtain at his Majesty's hands the place of second justice in "circuit with Mr. Barker, for my brother, Sir Francis Eure."

Whatever may have been the result of the former part of the letter, he seems to have been successful in his request, as we shall see by-and-by. During his short tenure of office, though he (for some reason not stated) "being then absent, the creation of Prince Charles of Wales to the Princi- "pality of Wales and the earldom of Chester, was celebrated here with "unusual magnificence on November 4th, 1616." A long description thereof, printed by Nicholas Okes, 1616, is extant.

* Todd's *Milton*. † *History of Ludlow*.

In it Sir Francis Eure is duly mentioned as one of the justices. It seems to have consisted of a stately procession of all the officials of the Council and Court, "having another company of waits and good concerts "of musicke, as cornets, sagbuts, and other winde instruments, playing "and sounding all the way before them; a great voley of shott was dis-"charged by the muskettiers and calivers, which so pierced the ayre with "the great noyse of drummers and sound of trumpets, fifes and flutes, and "other instruments, as the like in these parts has not been seen, to the great "admiration and rejoicing of all the spectators." To the church they proceeded, where, after prayers and psalms, "one Mr Thomas Picorn, a "grave divine and worthy preacher, made a very learned sermon of an hour "and a half long, on Psalm lxxii. 1." Then to the market-place, where the scholars of the school "pronounced" several speeches from a platform. Thence to the court-house, where Sir Thomas Chamberlayne, Chief Justice of Chester, "made a long oration in praise of the prince, "whereunto all the "people with a loud voice prayed, and cried Amen, Amen." Then, "being "full one of the clocke in the afternoon," to the castle, where there was a great feast provided, "with excellent musicke, and drinking to the happie "health and prosperitie of our said gracious Prince of Wales." After which the day closed with "evening sacrifice" at the "chappell, when much "rejoicing was within doors, and excellent musicke of voyces in singing "many psalms and new anthems within the said chappell." All the banners used were then "orderlie placed in the said chappell, where they "now remain as remarkable trophies of that solemnitie."

And the following morning they all reassembled there to hear another "very learned sermon preached by Master Thomas Kaye, the King's "chaplaine attending the Lord President and Council, on Ps. cxvi. 12, 13." After which "every man returned to their home, the musicke, ringing, "and bonfires continuing, to the great comfort of all his Majesty's said "loving and faithful subjects, all the said day."

Lord Eure seems to have resigned the same year, and died the year following. His first wife, Mary, daughter of Sir John Dawnay, of Sessay, died in 1612, and was buried in Ludlow Church, where her monument, in black and white marble, is on the south side of the chancel. His second wife, Elizabeth, daughter of Sir John Spenser, of Althorp, and widow, first, of George Cary, Lord Hunsdon, and second of Sir Thomas Chamberlain, only survived him twelve months, dying 1617.

Lord Gerard and Lord Northampton succeeded him; after whom John, first Earl of Bridgwater, was appointed, in succession, Lord President in 1633. In his tenure of office occurred that which has shed an undying halo on the office, and on the Castle of Ludlow, viz., the performance of Milton's "Masque of Comus." Lord Bridgwater being appointed Lord President of Wales, entered upon his official residence with great solemnity, attended by a large concourse of the neighbouring nobility and gentry, May, 1633. Amongst the rest came his children—Lord Brackley, Mr. Thomas and Lady Alice Egerton. They had been on a visit at the house of a relation in Herefordshire, and in passing through Haywood Forest were benighted, and the Lady Alice was even lost for a short time, or, as the poet rendered it :—

> "And all this tract that fronts the falling sun
> A noble peer of mickle trust and power
> Has in his charge, with temper'd awe to guide
> An old and haughty nation, proud in arms:
> Where his fair offspring, nursed in princely lore,
> Are coming to attend their father's State
> And new entrusted scepter, but their way
> Lies through the perplexed paths of this dreer wood,
> The nodding horrors of whose shady brows
> Threat the forlorn and wandering passenger."

Milton must have been very young at the time he composed the "Masque," founded probably on Fletcher's "Faithful Shepherdess," an arcadian comedy recently published, and on the story of "Circe," the subject of a mask, written by William Browne, and performed by the students of the Inner Temple, 1615. The music to *Comus* was written by Henry Lawes, a vicar-choral of Salisbury Cathedral, who himself acted the part of "the attendant spirit, afterwards in "the habit of Thysis." Lady Alice, aged 13, acted "the Lady;" Lord Brackley, aged 12, "the first Brother." Thomas Egerton performed the part of "the second Brother." The "Masque" was performed at Michaelmas, 1634.

Charles I. was splendidly received and entertained here on going to pay a visit to Lord Powis; and also stayed a night here in his flight from Wales during the unhappy Civil War. In 1646 the castle, garrisoned for the King, was delivered up to the Parliament, and was a few years after shorn of its magnificence, its stately furniture being inventoried and sold. There is something rather touching in some of the details of its ancient splendour and the prices they fetched, *e.g.*—"Suite of old tapestry "hangings, containing in all 120 ells, at 2*s.* per ell, £15; two pictures, the one "of the late King, the other of his Queen (probably by Vandyke), 10*s.*"

Lord Carberry was appointed Lord President at the Restoration, under whom Butler enjoyed the office of steward, and in an apartment over the gateway of the castle is said to have written his inimitable "Hudibras."

Gerard, Earl of Macclesfield, was the last.

In 1659 the office was abolished, and since then the castle has gradually fallen into decay.

Sir Francis Eure died in 1621, having married as his second wife Ellen, daughter and co-heir of William Wynne-Maurice, of Clenneny, county Salop, and widow of Sir John Owen, secretary to Sir Francis Walsingham.

By her he had one son, Compton Eure, who died 1666, *sine prole*, but the property passed to her son by her first husband, Sir John Owen, Governor of Conway Castle for Charles I., and through his descendants to the Ormesbys, and thence to the Gores, and is now possessed by William Ormesby-Gore, Lord Harlech. The old house has been pulled down, but in the modern mansion of Brogyntyn there is an old oak mantelpiece on which are carved the arms of Eure.

Sir Ralph Eure probably built the great house at Malton, which was erected in the reign of James I.; but if it be so, he probably overbuilt himself, as in 1609 he sold his property at Ingleby to Sir D. Foulis. His son William, fourth Lord Eure, made a Knight of the Bath on the coronation of James I., further depreciated the property by selling Witton to Sir Richard Forster, and Jarrow to Henry Gibbs, and got into serious trouble with regard to his property at Malton, for Gardiner tells us, in his *History of England* (vol. vii. p. 232), that "Lord Eure had fallen into debt, "and had executed a deed surrendering his estates to feoffees, in order that "they might be sold for the benefit of his creditors. When the feoffees, "fortified by an order from the Court of Chancery, attempted to take pos- "session of the family mansion at Malton, he peremptorily refused them "admission, garrisoned the house, and stood a siege. Layton, the sheriff, "finding himself helpless, appealed to Wentworth, who at once ordered "cannon from Scarborough to be brought up. But it was not till a breach "had been made by these guns that the stout old lord submitted." This happened in July, 1632. An order in the Commons journals, 1645, on Lord Eure's petition, allows him 40*s*. a week out of his own estate.*

He died in 1646; his eldest son, Ralph, who had married Katherine, daughter of Thomas, Lord Arundel Wardour, being killed in a duel, 1635, leaving one son, William, who only survived his grandfather six years, dying as fifth Lord Eure, 1652. When, therefore, the great rebellion broke out we cannot expect to find the names of the heads of the family taking prominent part therein, but, as usual, the name of Eure is not wanting in a great national movement, and the younger branches of the family seem to have participated actively therein, though (as is commonly the case) on different sides.

William Eure (younger brother of the Ralph killed in the duel) seems to have held an honourable position in the Royalist army, for he was knighted, and was colonel of a regiment of horse at the battle of Marston Moor, July 2nd, 1644, where he was killed. We know nothing of the part which he took therein, but his body was buried in York Minster on the 7th. There is something touching and significant in the simple entries of the register of burials of himself and his brave companions in arms;—

---

* MS. Canon Jackson.

Sir Ffrancis Armytage ..	June 12, 1644.	Captain Stanhope ..	July 3, 1644.
Colonel Biron	" 17 "	Colonel W. Evers ..	" 7 "
Major Huddlestone ..	" 17 "	Colonel Charles Slingsby	" 9 "
Colonel Steward	July 2 "		

Of these Sir Henry Slingsby in his diary mentions two, "Sir Philip Biron" (who had the guard at the Manor House), killed while leading some men into "the bowling-green, whither the enemy had gotten"; and "a kinsman, "Sir Charles Slingsby," "slain in ye field at Marston Moor, after our horse "was gone,"—I suppose in Rupert's wild pursuit of the Parliamentary horse, by Wilstrop Woodside. His body "was found and buried in York "Minster."

His cousin, Thomas Eure, son of old Sir Ralph's youngest brother, Sir William (a major in this Sir William's regiment of horse), was slain at Newbury, 1643. His sister Margaret was married to Sir Thomas Howard, fifth son of "Belted Will," who was slain at Pierce Bridge, Durham, 1642. And others there are of the name whom it is impossible to identify. Gardiner (vol. ix. p. 173) mentions Lieut. Eure, "a Catholic officer," who refused to accompany the Devon men to church when halting at Wellington, July 12, 1640, and was murdered by them, the population sympathising with the perpetrators and the crime; and another Isaac Eure, whose name appears amongst the signatures to the death-warrant of Charles I.

In *The History of the King-killers* he is curtly described as "an obscure "traitor, said to have been of an ancient family in Yorkshire." Noble, in his *Lives of the English Regicides* (vol. i. p. 203), says that he was of the ennobled family of the Barons Eure, in Yorkshire. He seems to have had a command in the Parliamentary army, and in May, 1648, took Chepstow Castle, killing Sir Nicholas Kemish and taking 120 prisoners, for which he received a letter of thanks from the Parliament. In the same year he was made the instrument for executing the most daring stroke of policy which Cromwell had yet devised. The siege of Colchester had just terminated, with the wanton murder of Sir Charles Lucas and Sir George Lisle—that indelible blot on the otherwise blameless reputation of Lord Fairfax. The army was now triumphant, and Cromwell (intending to carry out extreme measures as regards the King) was anxious to get him from the protection of the Parliament into the hands of the army. He therefore persuaded the council of general officers to send a remonstrance to the Parliament, complaining of their treaty with him, and demanding his punishment for the blood spilt during the war. At the same time they advanced with the army to Windsor, and sent Colonel Eure to seize the King's person at Carisbrook. In the *Memorials of the Civil War*, by Henry Cary (vol. ii. p. 60), there is a letter from Col. Hammond, the Governor, to the Speaker, reporting the arrival of Colonel Eure with a letter from "the General Council of the

"Army," directing him to repair to head-quarters, and Colonel Eure to secure the person of the King (using force if necessary), and to bring the King over the water

Colonel Hammond says that he recognises the authority of the Generals over him, but he felt that "to the matter of their directions I ought not to "give obedience to any save the Parliament alone, who had entrusted me, "and alone had power to do so" He had, therefore, resolved to go to head-quarters, Colonel Eure accompanying him, and in the meantime acquainted the Speaker "that you may take such further order, in an affair "of so high concernment, as to your wisdom shall seem best"

The House ordered a letter to the General, acquainting him that his orders and instructions to Colonel Eure were contrary to their resolutions and instructions given to Colonel Hammond, directing him to recall the said orders, and set Colonel Hammond at liberty to return to his charge in the Isle of Wight But Cromwell and the Generals paid little attention to the Parliamentary order—indeed, the plan was carried out before Parliament could interfere *

Mr Davenport Adams, in his *White King* (vol i p 81), says, quoting from *Cooke's Narrative*, that Hammond left three officers, Major Rolfe, Captain Bowerman, and Captain Hawes, strictly enjoining them to prevent the King's removal, but that in his absence Colonel Cobbett arrived with a strong body of horse and foot, which so alarmed Colonel Cooke that he appealed to Rolfe as to their intentions, who professed ignorance,—then to Bowerman, who said that he was no better than a prisoner in his own garrison, who had already threatened him with death, and that all that he could do was to obtain the removal of extra sentinels in the King's very chamber-door, who was almost suffocated with the smoke of their matches

Sir Thomas Herbert, who lies buried under the site of St Crux Church, in his *Memoirs of the last Two Years of the Reign of Charles I*, probably knowing nothing of all this, gives a touching account of the manner in which it was accomplished He says that a Lieutenant-Colonel Cobbett came to Newport with a commanded party of horse, with orders to apprehend Hammond as "too much of a courtier," but that he, "being premonished, "evaded him, though very narrowly," and that Cobbett "made an abrupt "address to the King, letting him know that he had orders to remove him "from Newport" Herbert gives a graphic account of the poor King's bewildered reluctance to submit, specially as Colonel Cobbett declined to give his authority, or to state "the place he was to remove the King unto"

At length he submitted, and, after a sorrowful parting with the Duke of Richmond, Lord Hertford, and other members of his Court, entered a coach with Mr Mildmay, Mr Herbert, and Mr Harrington, though when

* Clarendon's *History*, vol iii p 182

"the Colonel offered to enter the coach uninvited, His Majesty, by opposing "his foot, made him sensible of his rudeness, so as with some shame he "mounted his horse and followed within guard."

The coach, by the Colonel's directions, went westward, towards Worsley town in Freshwater Isle, "where, after resting an hour, the King "embarked in a vessel and crossed that narrow sea in three hours, and "landed at Hurst Castle—a wretched place, joined to the land by a narrow "neck of sand, covered with small loose stones and pebbles, upon both "sides of which the sea beats—the air noxious by reason of the marish "grounds that were about, the unwholesome vapours arising from the "sargassos and sea-weeds, and the fogs that those marine places are subject "to. The room, too, in which the King eat was neither large nor light- "some, at noonday in that season requiring candles;" and the only place of exercise the neck of sand, "about two miles in length, but a few paces in "breadth." Here the King was content to walk, "much delighted," in his marvellous equanimity in trouble, "with the sea prospects, the view of the "Isle of Wight, and the sight of the ships of all sizes daily under sail."

To his honour be it said that though frequently urged to make his escape, which would have been very easy, Charles positively refused, having given his word to the Parliament not to attempt the recovery of his liberty during the treaty.*

Noble says that Eure was rewarded for what he had done by being appointed governor of Hurst Castle; but Herbert does not mention his name as such, though he speaks of "the governor;" and Noble adds that £200 was voted to him by the army. Eventually Eure was appointed one of the judges at the King's trial, and was constant in his attendance, omitting being there only on the tenth, twelfth, and eighteenth days.

In 1649 he proceeded to Ireland with his regiment, where he distinguished himself at the taking of Drogheda and Tredagh. Cromwell, in his report of *The Storm of Tredagh* to Lenthall, the Speaker, says—"A "great deal of loss in this business fell upon Col. Hewson's, Col. Castle's, "and Col. Ewer's regiments, Col. Ewer having two field-officers in his "regiment shot." *Cromwell's Letters and Speeches* (Carlyle), pt. v. p. 54. "In "this kingdom," Noble says, "he died possessed of a large estate, procured "him through the patronage of Cromwell, whose devoted creature he had "always been, and whom he had served in his vilest offices." Happily thus he escaped the terrible retribution meted out to the surviving regicides at the Restoration. It is a bloody page of history, which one reads with reluctance and closes with readiness, but of which one presumes not to judge. Men's minds had been highly wrought in the effort to obtain ends and to defend persons very dear to them. If severe measures seemed just

* Hume's *History of England*, vol. v. p. 272.

on one side, who can wonder that retaliation seemed the same to the other side when they came into power? The actors have long passed to a fairer tribunal than earth can afford We can but contemplate with respect and reverence the firmness with which Cavalier and Roundhead were ready to meet death, even in its most revolting form, in defence of what they felt to be right, whether on the field of battle, the scaffold at Whitehall, or the gibbet at Tyburn

On the death of the lad William, fifth Lord Eure, 1652, George, grandson of Sir Francis Eure, brother of old Sir Ralph, inherited the title, the property going to his cousins, the daughters of Sir William, killed at Marston Moor Of the former little is known He sat in Cromwell's Parliament as member for the North Riding (1654), of which Parliament Hume says "In this notable assembly were some persons of the rank of "gentlemen, but the far greater part were low mechanics—fifth monarchy "men, anabaptists, antinomians, independents—the very dregs of the "fanatics," of which "Praise God Barebone," a leather-seller in London, being an active member, procured for it the *sobriquet* of "Barebone's "Parliament" (*History of England*, vol v p 35)

After a short and useless existence, amidst the derision of the people, they were peremptorily dissolved by Colonel White with a party of soldiers Lord Eure died 1672, some years after the Restoration, having, I conclude, been included in the act of indemnity, for certainly a seat in Barebone's Parliament could not have involved him in the fate of the regicides

His brother Ralph succeeded him as seventh and last Lord Eure, and took his seat in the House of Lords 4th February, 1672, and died April, 1707 The family must, indeed, have fallen into very reduced circumstances, for in Glover's *Visitation* it is said that in early life he was a woollen-draper in London with his brother Sampson Le Neve, in his *Memoranda*, says—"He had not above £100 per annum Before the title came to him, he was "journeyman to a woollen-draper at £20 per annum and his diet" And the great house at Malton also passed away, for the two daughters of Sir William Eure (killed at Marston), co-heiresses—one of whom married Thomas Danby, of Farnley, Yorkshire, first mayor of Leeds, who was killed in a tavern in London, 1667—and the other, Mary, married William Palmes, of Lindley, Yorkshire—quarrelled respecting the occupation of it And in 1665, under a writ of partition, the family mansion was pulled down (Henry Marwood being the sheriff), and, stone by stone, was divided between the unyielding sisters (Glover's *Visitation*, p 626) In 1712, William Palmes sold the manors of Old and New Malton, together with the lodge and entrance gateway, to Sir Thomas Wentworth, from whom they have descended to the present Earl Fitzwilliam *

* *History of York and North Riding* (Whellan & Co), vol ii. p 211

But scanty traces now remain of the successive epochs of grandeur which this hill has witnessed. Some tumbled hillocks mark the lines of the Roman camp. The railway cutting has ploughed deeply into the ground close by where a massive stone bastion had stood, and, in process of digging, many interesting Roman remains were brought to light.

The roadway beneath is still skirted by ponderous masonry, which was probably part of the Norman castle on the flat brow above. It is easy to trace the site of the grand Jacobean house, built in the days of his prosperity by Ralph, third Lord Eure. It must have extended round three sides of a quadrangle (similar to Cobham Hall in Kent), facing west, with pleasant prospect of the valley beneath, watered by the Derwent, and the wooded hills beyond. The entrance gateway, abutting on the Malton high-road, still stands in the old boundary wall, though it is partially bricked up, and the stone pilasters on each side are much dilapidated. But the gatehouse, preserved, I suppose, for their residence by the family of Palmes, and used, since the property was acquired by the Wentworths, as an agent's residence, has lately been beautifully restored and much increased by Mr. and Lady Mary Fitzwilliam.

The gateway itself, through which ponderous coaches once rumbled, has been converted into a most charming hall. Above the curiously-carved wooden mantelpiece are still the arms of Eure, quartering Eure, De Vere, Tyson, and Aton; and the ceiling groined above.

A lesser sitting-room is panelled with grand Jacobean panelling, probably brought from the old house. Pillars, in pairs, break into separate panels the wainscoting around the room; elaborately-carved pilasters support the mantelpiece, which consists of four bas-reliefs in carved oak, illustrating the history of Jonah. On the walls hang several pieces of armour, which probably belonged to the family of Eure. The panelling of some of the rooms is handsome and of a later date, probably the eighteenth century, indicating that the building was used, for some time at least, as the residence of the proprietors.

The parish register in Old Malton Church contains a few entries of interest concerning a race which has passed away:—

1610.—Samuel Brittain, servant to the Honourable Sir William Eure, Knight, was buried ye 6th day of January.

1620.—Nicholas Biays, steward to ye Rt. Honourable Lord William Eure, gent., and Margaret . . . . of . . . . were married ye twentieth day of August.

1646.—The Right Honourable William, Lord Eure, was buried (as it was said) the eight and twentieth day of June.

1652.—The Right Honourable William, Lord Eure, was interred June 25th.

The Honourable Frances Eure, daughter to the Right Honourable William, Lord Eure, deceased, was interred Nov. 26.

1653.—William Tyson, son of James Tyson, of ye Spittal, was buried Sep. 14.

1666.—Mary Palmes, daughter of William Palmes, Esq., was buried ye fifth day of October.

1669.—Guy Palmes, the son of William Palmes, Esq., was buried the 5th day of September.

1670.—Catherine Palmes, daughter of William Palmes, baptised.

There is also an entry purporting to be a "copy of the names of ye "such well-disposed persons as did voluntarily contribute to the repairs of "the parish church of Old Malton, being much ruined in ye Civil Wars "from 1648 to 1671, with their several contributions received and dis-"posed, anno domini 1671-1672." Amongst the names appear William Palmes, Esq., £5, Mrs. Palmes (his wife), £5.

And so, it seems to me, God raises up nations, families, and individuals from small beginnings to great positions, possessions, and opportunities. They do the work appointed for them (sometimes voluntarily, oftentimes unconsciously), and then bring their years to an end like a tale that is told. They pass away, and are no more seen; "and the place thereof knoweth them no more."

The Constables

The fifth window west of the north side of the nave gives us another similar coat, viz., quarterly gules and vair over all, a bend or.* This is probably the shield of William Constable, sub-dean of this Minster in 1483, and archdeacon of Cleveland in 1481.

The name Constable seems to have been in this, and in other instances thereof, derived from the office, the origin of which is lost in remote antiquity. Edmonson, in his *Complete Body of Heraldry*, tells us that from the very commencement of the "feudal system" each prince appointed two great officers to act under him—the constable and the marshal. There seems some little difficulty as to the exact etymology of the name, but the probability is that the former is a corruption of "Comes Stabulæ," or Lieutenant of the Horse, being analogous to the office in the Court of the Roman Emperor of "Magister Equitum," or Master of the Horse. The derivation of marshal is not so easy, but it is possibly a corruption of "maer," or mayor, and "sola," which in German signified the King's Court, and would, therefore, imply that he was "magister domus regiœ," and, as such, the principal officer for ordering the Court. In fact, to these two officers was committed the assembling and leading of the army, the supervision that every baron not only attended personally, but also brought such quota of soldiers as by his tenure he was bound to furnish, that they were properly armed, and stayed their appointed time. The constable and marshal also allotted their places of encampment, appointed and superintended their

* See coloured illustration.

duties, issued directions for the necessary supply of provisions, and were responsible for the good order and efficiency of the army in general.

Canon Raine says that the marshal was the farrier, and that he has seen the seal of a Johannes Marescallus with a horse's shoe in the middle.

When William the Conqueror came to England he established these offices, as well as those of the High Justiciar, the Seneschal or Steward, the Chamberlain, the Chancellor, and the Treasurer, who formed also his Council, with whom also he consulted in all matters affecting the welfare of the realm. The duties of the constable and marshal, however, affected the camp and Court, and were multifarious, honourable, and confidential. On the march, in advance, the marshal, having a white flag displayed before him, led the van; the constable had charge of the main body and rear. In retreat, the constable conducted the forward, the marshal the rear. In encampment, the marshal's duty was similar to that of a quartermaster-general in modern times. Every evening the marshal posted the watch; the constable rode the rounds and gave the watchword. All foragings and incursions were jointly directed by them, but the former rode out with the party, the latter remained in camp. The marshal punished all military offenders, but military courts, or courts-martial, were held by the marshal and constable jointly.

In their civil capacities they had also great rank and powers, as officers of State and of the household. The constable was in close personal attendance on the King; the marshal regulated the economy of the household, officers and affairs. In all processions the constable, bearing in his hand his mace, attended next to the King's person; the marshal, bearing his rod, was next to or in the same line with the constable. Both the constable and marshal had their diet in the great hall of the King's court, and at meals the latter sat on the right hand of the steward. On the establishment of the King's Exchequer the constable and marshal were two of the principal officers of the court. The former was witness to the King's writs, together with the justiciar; the marshal took all summonses under the King's seal, and defaulters were arrested by the constable and committed in custody of the marshal.

The muster-rolls of the army were in their custody, and all payments of soldiers were made by them to the barons or others, according to the number which they were bound to produce. The conduct of legal trials and decisions by duel or single combat, and the exercise of feats of arms in jousts, tilts, and tournaments, were under the control of the constable and marshal.

Edward IV. gave the office of chief constable to Sir John Tiptot, Earl of Worcester, and invested it with unparalleled powers. He was to take cognizance of and proceed in all cases of high treason; to hear, examine, and conclude them, even summarily and plainly, without noise and show of judgment, "on simple inspection of fact." He was to act as the King's vicegerent, without appeal, and with power to inflict punishment, fine, and other lawful coercion, notwithstanding any statutes, acts, ordinances, or restrictions made to the contrary. By this supreme and irresponsible judicature many Lancastrians were doomed. The Earl of Oxford and his son, and four others, were beheaded by Tiptot in 1462. Twelve of the prisoners taken at Hexham, in 1464, were condemned and executed in the same summary manner at York; and Sir Ralph Grey, the defender of Alnwick, was in the same year tried by Tiptot, and beheaded in the King's presence.*

As such multifarious duties multiplied and developed, the constables were empowered by their patents to appoint deputies to act for them in the Exchequer and elsewhere, and eventually throughout England. In the reign of Henry III., 1252, constables were nominated to hundreds and townships, to secure the conservation of the peace; and amongst the eleven Articles presented by the Parliament in 1309 to Edward II., in reply to his demand for money, was a complaint of the illegal jurisdiction of the constables of the Royal Castles in common pleas.†

Ralph de Mortimer, who accompanied William, Duke of Normandy, to England, and took Edrich, Earl of Shrewsbury, and his lands and castle of Wigmore, was the first constituted constable of England by the Conqueror, and the office remained for the most part hereditary amongst his descendants until the 13th year of the reign of Henry VIII., when Edward, Earl of Stafford, was attainted and beheaded, and the office of Constable of England reverted to the Crown.

The office of marshal was in like manner hereditary. In 1138 Gilbert de Clare, lord of Striguil, was made Earl of Pembroke by King Stephen, and also seized in fee of the office of Marshal of England, and it continued amongst his descendants until 1297, when Roger Bigod, Earl of Norfolk, dying without issue, it reverted to the Crown. In the 9th of Richard II. it was conferred on Thomas de Mowbray, Earl of Nottingham, and continued amongst his descendants until the death of Richard, Duke of York, second son of Edward IV., when it again reverted to the Crown, and was granted in succession to many, until the reign of Charles II., when on Oct. 19th, 1672, Henry Howard, Baron Howard of Castle Rising, and Earl of Norwich, was constituted hereditary Earl Marshal of England, with whose descendants the office and title still remain, though the duties are confined to the patronage of Heralds' College, and some special offices at the Coronation.

It is difficult, perhaps impossible, to say what were the original duties of the deputy constables in their several spheres. Probably at first arbitrary and powerful, with responsibility only to their chief, but when the office

* *Stubbs' Const. Hist.*, vol. iii., p. 302. † Stubbs, vol. ii., pp. 296–351.

reverted to the Crown, they would become responsible directly to the King, and as time went on and their office was multiplied, it decreased in power and importance, until of the parish constable it might truly be said, "Magni stat nominis umbra," for, though his duties were humble, they were of the same character, viz., the preservation of peace and the administration of justice. But in ancient times it must have been an office of great dignity as well as power, and we can well imagine those who had once attained to it perpetuating the name of the office as a surname for themselves and their descendants.

The same name does not, therefore, imply the same family, and the different coats-of-arms carried by persons called "Constable" shew that their families are the survivors of various bygone holders of the office. There are two distinct families of Constable in Yorkshire, both represented in the Minster. The one, bearing barry of six or and azure, viz., the Constables of Burton Constable, and the Clifford-Constables of Tixall, Staffordshire; and the other, bearing quarterly gules and vair, with a bend, differenced in some instances, viz., the Constables of Flamborough, Everingham, Otley, Dromondby, and Wassand.*

The first of the latter family was William, who was living about 1260. He seems to have been the only son of Robert de Lacy, who obtained from his elder brother, Roger, the lordship of Flamborough, which they had inherited many generations before from their maternal ancestor Nigel, created by William the Conqueror premier baron of the palatinate of Chester and constable of Chester. William seems to have held the office of constable of Flamborough, and in consequence the office became the name of the family and his descendants.

His son, Sir Robert, was knighted at a grand festival at Whitsuntide, with some three hundred others, by King Edward I., in the 34th year of his reign, "in order to augment the glory of his expedition into Scot-"land;"† and his son, Sir Marmaduke, was High Sheriff of York, 40 and 41 of Edward III., as well as Member of Parliament for the county, his descendants for five generations enjoying, in succession, the same honours. Sir Marmaduke, the nephew of the archdeacon, whose wife was a daughter of Lord Fitzhugh, was in France under King Edward IV., and at the taking of Berwick, of which he was made captain. He shared with his sons in the glory of Flodden, being then 71 years of age, for his distinguished services at which he received an autograph acknowledgment from King Henry VIII. He survived the dangers and fatigues of this chivalrous expedition for four years, and died at Flamborough, 1518, aged 75. His body rests within the chancel, and on the tomb above it there is a long and quaint inscription commemorating this patriotic feat.

Few tourists who visit Flamborough Head stop to visit Flamborough

* See coloured illustration. † Foster's *Yorkshire Pedigrees.*

Church, the driver of the carriage which conveyed me there, some time ago, did not even know where it was, though he had driven through Flamborough many times And yet the quaint old church is worth a visit, not only for the sake of Sir Marmaduke's tomb, but also for the exquisitely beautiful rood screen and loft The latter has been placed against the west wall, the better to preserve its delicate tracery, which is an elaborate specimen of the perpendicular period, and, in the graceful carving of the vine and foliage, equal to anything of that date in England

Robert, the eldest of the four brothers, Marmaduke, William, and John—who with him were all knighted on the field of Flodden—succeeded his father He married a daughter of Sir William Ingleby, of Ripley, and eventually, taking part in the rising in Lincolnshire under Lord Hussey, was attainted and beheaded at Hull, and his body hung in chains over the Beverley Gate, Flamborough, and thirty-five manors in Lincolnshire being forfeited to the Crown His son, Sir Marmaduke, however, served Henry VIII in his wars, was with him at the siege of Teroven, and knighted by him at Lisle In the first year of Edward VI he was made a knight-banneret in the camp of Roquesborough, by the Earl of Surrey, and died in the second year of Queen Elizabeth, having married Elizabeth, only daughter of Lord Darcy The good Queen Bess restored Flamborough to his son, Sir Robert, who was knighted by the Earl of Sussex in 1570, in the expedition to Scotland to help King James VI against the Hamilton faction I am sorry to be obliged to add that he committed bigamy by marrying Dorothy, daughter of Sir John Widdrington, while his wife, Dorothy, daughter of Sir William Gascoigne, was still alive His son Robert succeeded him, circa 33rd year of Queen Elizabeth, and his son Sir William was knighted for his services under the Earl of Essex, in Ireland, 1599 James I created him a baronet, but in the succeeding reign he espoused the cause of the Parliament, was a colonel in the Roundhead army, and his name appears in the warrant for the execution of Charles I He died during the Commonwealth, 1655, and was buried in Westminster Abbey He left no children, but the family name and honours were carried on by his kinsman, Sir Philip, descended from Sir Marmaduke, one of the four brothers knighted at Flodden Sir Philip was created a baronet by Charles I in 1642, and after suffering severely in the Royal cause, died 1664 His great-grandson, Sir Marmaduke, fourth and last baronet, died unmarried, 1746, when the baronetcy became extinct, and his estates passed to William Haggerstone, grandson of his only sister, Anne, who married William Haggerstone, second son of Sir Thomas Haggerstone, whose wife was Margaret, daughter of Sir Francis Howard, of Corby

And so the long and gallant race of Constable of Flamborough terminated, and nothing now remains of their ancestral hall, in which so many distinguished generations had lived and died, but a fragment of an old and crumbling tower, in the midst of the modern village of Flamborough

The Constables of Wassand are a younger branch of this family, being descended from Sir William Constable, who purchased the estate of Wassand in 1531. He was the fifth son of Sir Robert Constable, who died in 1488, by Agnes, daughter of Sir Roger Wentworth. Amongst the "funeral monuments" effaced at the repavement of the Minster, Drake mentions, on the middle choir, east end, "a blue stone," having an inscription to Marmaduke Constable, of Wassand, in Holderness, husband of Elizabeth Shirley, who deceased 12th October, 1607.

In the fourth light of the great window of the north choir transept there are several figures of the family of De Roos, the donors of this window, amongst them there is a figure of a lady kneeling, probably Margaret, daughter of Sir John Constable, who married Sir John Roos, and on her gown appears barry of six or and azure. The same device may be found on the second window east on the south side of the nave, where there is a shield bearing barry of eight or and azure, impaling gules a cross patoncée or,* probably Sir Robert Constable, who married Avice, daughter of Sir Roger de Lascelles. These are the arms of the other race bearing the name of Constable, descended from Ulbert, son of the Constable who fought on the side of the Conqueror at Hastings, and who married Evenburga de Burton, an heiress, from whence they have been ever styled the Constables of Burton Constable. In the time of Edward I. Sir Simon Constable assumed these arms of his grandmother, Ela d'Oyri, in lieu of his paternal bearing, viz., Or a fesse compony argent and azure, in chief a lion passant gules. He seems to have had the confidence of the King, as he was deputed by him, with Walter de Fauconberg, to hold an inquisition "ad quod "damnum" at Marton, in Holderness. His son, Sir Robert, who died 10th year of King Edward III., 1336, married Avice, daughter of Sir Roger de Lascelles, and coheiress with her three sisters, viz.: Johanna, wife of Thomas de Culwenne, of Workington, Cumberland; Matilda, wife of Sir William Hilton, of Swine; Theofania, wife of Ralph FitzRanulph.

In 1620 Sir Henry Constable was made Viscount Dunbar by James I., but the title became extinct on the death of his grandson, William, fifth Viscount Dunbar. He married Elizabeth, eldest daughter of Hugh, second Lord Clifford, of Chudleigh (who after his death became the wife of Charles Fairfax, of Gilling), and bequeathed his estates to his nephew, Cuthbert Tunstall, son of his sister Cecily, who had married Francis Tunstall, of Skargill. Cuthbert Tunstall appears to have married his aunt's sister, viz., Amy, fifth daughter of Hugh, Lord Clifford, but on his line becoming extinct the property passed to his great nephew, Sir Thomas Clifford, who had been created a baronet in 1803, at the special request of Louis XVIII. He assumed the name of Constable, and is represented therein by his grandson now.

* See coloured illustration.

PLATE 4.

LUTEREL.

FURNIVAL.

WALWORTH.

DE BOHUN.

CLARE.

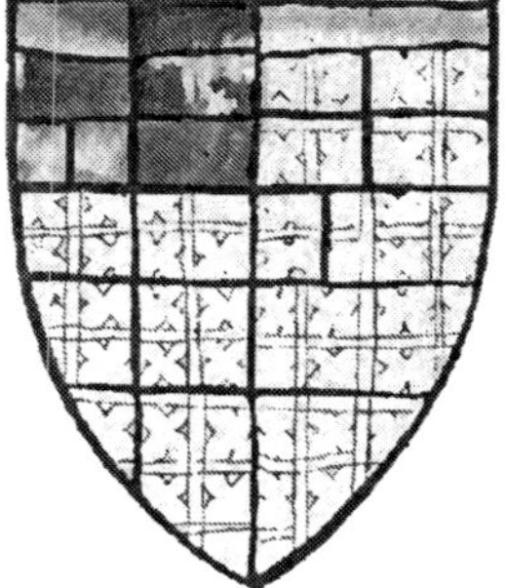
OLD CLARE.

The Luterels

A small shield in the central west window of the vestibule to the Chapter House gives another illustration of the bend, in which the charges are in the field, and not on the bend itself, viz, azure, a bend between six martlets argent * Drake gives these as the arms of Tempest, which are generally argent a bend between six martlets sable They may be a variety of this coat, and if so, are probably the arms of Sir Richard Tempest, born 1356, who married Isabel, daughter and heiress of John le Gras, of Studley His granddaughter married Richard Norton, of Norton Conyers

They are more probably the arms of Luterel, which Papworth gives in the same tinctures The family of Luterel was descended from one of the Norman chiefs who accompanied William the Conqueror to England Sir Geoffry de Luterel married Frethesant, second daughter and co-heiress of William Paganel, lord of Irnham, whose arms (gules a cross patoncée ermine) are in the sixth window from the west, on the north side of the nave.

In the 36th year of the reign of Henry III, Alexander, king of Scotland, married Margaret, the eldest daughter of King Henry, at York Minster, on St Stephen's day, 1251, and upon collection of the aid on this occasion, "Andrew Luterel (probably son of the above) answered for fifteen "knights' fiefs, the number belonging to the barony of Hooton" And he is also mentioned as making a similar contribution at the marriage of Prince Edward with Alianora of Castile Geoffry Luterel, his son, died insane, and his brother Alexander died (a crusader) in the Holy Land His son Sir Geoffry was summoned to perform military service against the Scots in the reign of Edward II, though he does not appear to have been ever summoned to Parliament He married Agnes, daughter of Sir Richard Sutton, of Sutton and Worksop, co Notts, whose arms (argent a fess between three buglehorns, stringed sable) are in the seventh window of the north aisle of the Choir

Sir Robert de Luterel was companion-in-arms of Edward I in Wales, and is mentioned in the muster-roll at Worcester, July 1st, 1271, again at Devizes, 1282, at Westminster, 1287, and at Darlington, 1291 He was summoned to Parliament as Baron Luterel, of Irnham, 1296, and died possessed of Irnham, in Lincolnshire, and Hooton Paganel, in Yorkshire His grandson, Sir Andrew, third Baron Luterel, married Beatrice, daughter of Sir Geoffry Scrope, Lord Scrope of Masham, and I should fancy that these are his arms The estates and barony afterwards passed through the families of the Hiltons, Thimlebys, and Conquests Eventually an heiress brought the manor to Henry, eighth Lord Arundale of Wardour, through whose daughter it passed to the Cliffords

* See coloured illustration

The Furnivals.

There is one other similar coat which I must mention before leaving the subject of the bend, and that is on the sixth window east on the south side of the nave: Argent a bend between six martlets gules—Furnival.*

Gerard de Furnival came into England from Normandy (says Burke); and Powell, in his *History of Wales*, tells us that N. de Furnival, with Bartholemew Mortimer, Roger de Lacy, and others, accompanied Richard I. and fought with him in the Holy Land. His grandson, Thomas, went there on a pilgrimage, and was slain by the Saracens, and his body brought back and buried at Worksop.

Another, Thomas de Furnival, had summons, 22nd Edward I., to attend the King and advise on the affairs of the realm, and having done so, was despatched, with a full equipment of horse and arms, on an expedition to France. In June, 1295, he was summoned as a baron, and in 1300 we find him mentioned amongst the knights at the siege of Caerlavrock. The chronicler quaintly describes him thus: "With them marched the handsome "Thomas de Furnival, who (when seated on horseback) does not resemble "a man asleep. He bore six martletts and a red bend in a white banner." He was one of those who "sealed" the letter to Pope Boniface in February, 1301, in which he is styled "Lord of Sheffield." In the 7th and 8th of Edward II. he again served in Scotland. His name appears amongst those summoned to Parliament from 23rd Edward I., 1295, to 6th of Edward III., 1332, *i.e.* 37 years. He died Feb. 3rd, 1332, aged 70.

Conspicuous as he evidently was, from his quaint *sobriquet*, in the field, he was even more remarkable for the important benefits which he conferred upon his dependants at home. At Sheffield he was long remembered as "the great grantor," for he emancipated his tenants from their vassalage; he established a regular municipal court, with trial by jury; and instituted a market and fair in his demesnes. In these quiet times we can very little estimate the inestimable blessing of such wise, liberal, and truly beneficent conduct, in those turbulent days of violence and oppression. His record is that of the truly brave and strong, who is daunted by no dangers, and dares to protect and strengthen the weak, and maintain peace, justice, and purity around them.

He married first Joan, daughter of Hugh le Despencer, and secondly Elizabeth, daughter of Sir Peter de Montfort, of Beaudesert Castle, Warwickshire, and was succeeded by his son Thomas, created a baron during his father's lifetime, and styled "Thomas de Furnival, junior."

He had also three daughters—Maud, wife of John, Baron Marmion; Katherine, who married William de Thweng; and Eleanor, the wife of Peter, Baron de Mauley.

---

* See coloured illustration.

Thomas de Furnival, jun, had two sons, Thomas and William, who succeeded as third and fourth barons The latter died 1383, leaving one only daughter, Joan, who married Thomas Nevill, brother of Ralph, first Earl of Westmoreland, who was summoned to Parliament 7th Richard II, 1383, as "Lord Furnival" He died 1406, leaving one surviving daughter, Maud, who married, 1408, Sir John Talbot, second son of Lord Talbot, a great general under Henry V, with whom he acquired a splendid reputation

In the following reign, however, he was attacked by Joan of Arc, "the Maid of Orleans," near Patay, in 1429, when his army was entirely routed and he taken prisoner After four years he was ransomed, and, again distinguishing himself, was created (1443) Earl of Shrewsbury and Earl of Waterford He was also made Lord Chancellor, and eventually Lieutenant of the Duchy of Aquitaine He captured the city of Bordeaux, and from thence proceeded to the relief of Chastillon, where he was slain (fighting, sword in hand) by a cannon ball, 20th July, 1453, in the eightieth year of his age

His remains were brought to England and interred at Whitchurch, in Shropshire The church was burned down and rebuilt in the days of Queen Anne, but in the wall of the new church was placed a tablet, stating that his remains had been deposited there Within the last few years the church has been "restored," when the wall was opened, and from it taken a small box, about three feet long (something like a gun-case), in which were found the bones of the great captain carefully and methodically packed His body had evidently been dismembered for facility of carriage in those days of difficult travelling I need scarcely say that they were reverently and carefully replaced, and rest once again within the wall, with the ancient inscription to mark the spot —

"Orate pro anima prænobilis domini, domini Johannis Talbot, quondam Comitis
"Salopiæ, Domini Furnival, Domini Verdon, Domini Strange de Blackmere, et Marescelli
"Franciæ, qui obiit in bello apud Burdenos vii Julii MCCCCLIII"

Shakespeare (*Henry VI*, part i act iii scene iv), as usual historically inaccurate, represents Lord Talbot as having been created Earl of Shrewsbury before he was taken by Joan of Arc The address, however, of the young King seems appropriate to this warrior's acknowledged reputation —

"Welcome, brave Captain and victorious Lord!
When I was young (as yet I am not old),
I do remember how my father said
A stouter champion never handled sword
Long since we were resolved of your truth,
Your faithful service, and your toil in war
Yet never have you tasted our reward
Or been reguerdon'd with so much as thanks,
Because (till now) we never saw your face
Therefore, stand up and for these good deserts,
We here create you Earl of Shrewsbury
And in our coronation take your place"

The title of Furnival remained merged in that of Shrewsbury until 1626, when the seventh earl died, leaving only three daughters, two of whom died without issue. The youngest, Alethea, married the Earl of Arundel, and the barony of Furnival became merged into that of Norfolk, until 1777, when it fell into abeyance between two heiresses, and so continues, the present Lords Stourton and Petre having equal claims thereto.

Furnival's Inn in London was originally the mansion of the Lords Furnival. Stowe mentions William Furnival, Knight, who had in Holborn two messuages and thirteen shops, as appeareth by record, in the reign of Richard II.

It was, however, an Inn of Chancery in the 9th of Henry IV., and was sold, early in Elizabeth's time, to the benchers of Lincoln's Inn, who appear to have formerly had the lease of it.

In Charles I.'s time the greater part of the old Inn described by Stowe was taken down, but the Gothic hall was standing in 1818, when the whole was rebuilt by Mr. Peto.

Two famous names in English history are associated therewith: one, Sir Thomas More, who was "reader by the space of three years and more" in this Inn, and, in more modern days, Charles Dickens, who lived here from shortly after entering the Reporters' Gallery (1831).

Here, in 1833, he wrote his first published piece of writing, which appeared in the January number, 1834, of the old *Monthly Magazine*. Down these dark stairs he went, and dropped his paper, as he himself has described, stealthily—one evening, at twilight, with fear and trembling—into a dark letter-box, in a dark office, up a dark court in Fleet Street.*

And he has also told us of his agitation when his paper appeared in all the glory of print. "On which occasion," he says, "I walked down to "Westminster Hall and turned into it for half an hour, because my eyes "were so dimmed with joy and pride that they could not bear the street, "and were not fit to be seen there."

He had purchased the *Magazine* at a shop in the street; and exactly two years after, when the younger member of a publishing firm called upon him here in his rooms in Furnival's Inn with the proposal that originated *Pickwick*, he recognised in him the person he had bought that *Magazine* from, and whom before or since he had never seen.

Here, too, Mr. N. P. Willis, in company with Mr. Macrone, a young publisher, who had just purchased the conditional copyright of *Sketches by Boz* for £150, visited "the young paragraphist for the *Morning Chronicle*," as he calls him, and thus describes his visit:—

"In the most crowded part of Holborn, within a door or two of the "Bull and Mouth Inn, we pulled up at the entrance of a large building

---

* Foster's *Life of Dickens*.

"used for lawyers' chambers I followed by a long flight of stairs to an "upper storey, and was ushered into an uncarpeted and bleak-looking "room, with a deal table, two or three chairs, and a few books, a small "boy and Mr Dickens, for its contents I was only struck at first with "one thing (and I made a memorandum of it that evening, as the strongest "instance I had seen of English obsequiousness to employers), the degree "to which the poor author was overpowered with his publisher's visit "I remember saying to myself, as I sat down on a rickety chair, 'My good "'fellow, if you were in America with that fine face and your ready quill, "'you would have no need to be condescended to by a publisher' "Dickens was dressed very much as he has since described Dick Swiveller, "minus the swell look His hair was cropped close to his head, his "clothes scant, though jauntily cut, and (after changing a ragged office- "coat for a shabby blue) he stood by the door, collarless and buttoned up, "the very personification, I thought, of a 'close sailer to the wind'"

Here, too, he had his first interview with Mr Hogarth, from Mr Black of the *Morning Chronicle*, whose daughter he afterwards married, and who eventually agreed with him that he should write a series of articles in the *Evening Chronicle*, at a salary of seven guineas per week

Here, too, Mr Hall, of the firm of Chapman and Hall, negotiated with him the plan of *Nicholas Nickleby*

Here were spent the days of his early married life, and from hence, after the birth of his eldest son, Jan 6th, 1837, he removed to 8, Doughty Street

And here, thirty-two years after, he came, no longer the unknown "paragraphist for the *Morning Chronicle*," but the successful popular man of literature, at the close of his prosperous career His friend Mr Field, who had shewn him great kindness in America, was now his guest at Gad's Hill At his request, he visited with him some of the scenes of his early life—the cheap theatres, the poor lodging-houses, the thieves' quarters—and, for the last time, mounted the staircase, and stood in that eventful room at Furnival's Inn

In twelve months he had passed to his rest "Statesmen, men of "science, philanthropists, the acknowledged benefactors of their race, may "pass away and yet not leave the void which is caused by the death of "Charles Dickens" So wrote *The Times* immediately his demise was announced, and added—"Westminster Abbey is the peculiar resting-place "of English literary genius, and amongst those whose sacred dust lies "there, or whose names are recorded on the wall, very few are more "worthy than Charles Dickens of such a home Fewer still, we believe, "will be regarded with more honour as time passes and his greatness "grows upon us"

Who will not ratify these eloquent words, or justify my humble endeavour to associate his memory with the memories of the brave and good who have lived and died amongst us, and whose achievements adorn our Minster!

WALWORTH.

On the first west window on the north side of the Choir we find another variety of the bend, viz., Gules a bend raguleé (*i.e.* embattled) argent, between two garbs or,* which introduces us to a name not only associated with the Minster, but illustrious in the history of England, viz. Walworth.

Surtees, in his *History of Durham*, says—"There was a family who "bore the name, but they had no land *here*," *i.e.* Walworth, a village about nine miles from Darlington, on the Stockton and Darlington line, where there is a ruin of a castle, built *temp.* Queen Elizabeth by Thomas Jennison, and where James I. rested April 14th, 1603. The Walworths, however, are mentioned as owning land in Preston in Skerne, Great Burston, and Darlington; and there is another Walworth in the county of Surrey, one of seventeen manors in the hundred of Brixistan (Brixton) given by Edmund Ironsides to his jester, Hitard, who (*temp.* Edward the Confessor) made a pilgrimage to the Holy Land, and, before starting, went to the Church of Christ in Canterbury and presented it. At the dissolution (time of Henry VIII.), the King placed a dean and twelve prebendaries there in lieu of the prior and monks.†

In 1396 Margaret Walworth is mentioned in the Bishop of Winchester's registry as lady of the manor, probably lessee under the priory; and in 13th Edward IV., 1474, Sir George Walworth died "seized" of it.

Two members of the family of Walworth (probably belonging to the northern race of that name) were canons of York, viz., John de Walworth, who, in 1349, was prebendary of Salton, annexed to the priorate of Hexham; and Thomas Walworth, who, in 1406, was collated to the prebend of Langtoft, and was vicar-general and chaplain to Archbishop Scrope. He was buried in the Minster. He had also been prebendary of Stillington and Bugthorpe, and was rector of Hemingbrough.

His will is recorded in the *Testamenta Eboracensia*, in which he bequeaths "Parvum portiforium meum" (*i.e.* my pocket breviary) "cum "quo sepulcrum Domini nostri Jesu Christi peregre visitavi," which shews that he had performed a pilgrimage to the Holy Land—almost the only fact which we know of his life.

---

* See coloured illustration. † Manning's *History of Surrey*, vol. iii. p. 265.

He also bequeathed "Unam peciam" (piece) "deauratam, quæ "quondam fuit Domini Willelmi Walworth militis fratris mei defuncti," which shews that he survived his brother, who was none other than the illustrious Walworth, Lord Mayor of London, whose presence of mind saved Richard II, and indeed the whole nation, from the excesses of one of the most formidable popular risings which ever took place in this country

Riley, in his *Memorials of London and London Life*, 13th and 15th century (*Longman*, 1868), mentions two others of the same name, viz, Philip Walworth, who was chosen sergeant of the chamber, 1377, and John Walworth, a vintner, who had a tavern in Fleet Street, near the hostel of the Bishop of Salisbury

Stowe, in his *Survey of London* (vol ii p 571), mentions a Thomas Walworth who in 1399 attended, with the abbot of Westminster, when Thomas Samestin "did obedience to the Archbishop of York at York "Place," the ancient London residence of the Archbishops, given to the see by Walter Gray, and confiscated by Henry VIII (when Cardinal Wolsey fell), named "White Hall," and appropriated as a royal residence in lieu of the palace of Westminster, destroyed by fire

These memorials by Riley are compiled from the ancient *Letter-books* of the city of London, folio volumes, in manuscript, on parchment, commencing with the reign of Edward I and continuing to 1416, when journals of the proceedings of the court of aldermen supplied their place Their quaint, graphic language makes them specially interesting, and they were the sources from which Stowe made the collections which have immortalized him *

Riley gives us some very interesting details about the life of this important historical character William Walworth was apprenticed to John Lovekyn, stock-fishmonger (*i e* salt fishmonger), and succeeded him as alderman of Bridgeware, London, on "Monday next after the feast of "St Martin," in the 42nd year of Edward III, 1368

In 1370 he was elected sheriff, and his name is mentioned in the same year as one of the aldermen who, with "an immense number of the "commonalty, for certain reasons convened in the chamber of the Guild-"hall, London, assented to the addition of a certain sign called a molet" (mullet) "in the common seal of the city of London, and the same stands "or is placed in a small port," (gateway) "which is in the same seal, "beneath the feet of St Paul"

In the 3rd of Richard II, 1379, he is represented as living in the parish of St Michael, Crooked Lane, London

Thornbury says† that he lived on the spot where Fishmongers' Hall now stands, at the foot of London Bridge, where he carried on his business

* Loftie's *History of London*, vol i p 188 † *Old and New London*, vol. ii p. 1

as a fishmonger, and that the building comprised a wharf, a loft, and a tower built by him.

In the 9th Edward III., 1374, he was elected mayor of London; and in 1377, a temporary enactment having been passed that aldermen should be chosen yearly, and should not hold office two years in succession, he vacated his office as alderman, but was re-elected the following year.

Municipal life, however, does not seem to have been, in those days, a bed of roses, any more than, I suppose, it is in the present day; for in that same year "he made plaint" by his attorney, before the mayor and corporation, that a certain Alice, wife of Robert Godrich, did come to his house and did "horribly raise the hue and cry upon the said William, as "though against a thief, and without cause, calling him a false man, and "imputing to him that he had unjustly disinherited her of £20 value of "land yearly, and that, by his mastery, he had unjustly detained the afore-"said Robert in prison for that reason, to the great scandal of the "offices which the said William had held in the city aforesaid, and to his "own damage of £100.

"The persons, however, before whom she was tried for this, acquitted "him, and for her lies and slanders the mayor and aldermen sentenced "her to have the punishment of the pillory called 'the thewe,' for such "women provided, to stand upon the same for one hour in the day, with "a whetstone in the meantime hung from her neck; and that the said "William should recover against the said Robert and Alice 40 pounds as "his damages, taxed by the court.

"And thereupon," we are told, "came here the said William, begging "and entreating the said mayor and aldermen that the punishment of "the pillory might be remitted to the said Alice, that the payment of "the sum of money might be put in respite during the good behaviour of "the said Alice, and that she might be released from prison." *

Which requests were immediately granted at Walworth's intercession—and we shall not deem this the least noble trait in his chivalrous character.

Yes; and had I space I could recount many quaint instances of the rough and ready way in which justice was administered by the worthy alderman and those associated with him, for men's lives or persons, rather than their liberties, paid the penalties of their evil deeds. Prisons there were few, and they wretched dens of misery, where the unhappy prisoners lived, and often starved, at their own charges, or pined away and died from jail-fever, the result of the malaria arising from many closely confined in ill-ventilated and undrained dungeons. Never, till John Howard arose some three hundred years later, was anything done to mitigate them; and,

* Riley.

in the meantime, the prisoners were subjected to the lash,—the rope,—the axe,—and the pillory, in which they stood with their heads and hands fixed in a sort of frame, while the rabble pelted them with mud and filth, or jeered and mocked at them

There was some method and reason, then, in the summary justice of those days, for Robert Colyer, of the county of York, being convicted in 1375 before the mayor of stealing a fillet of pork and two fowls, was sentenced to stand for one hour in the pillory, with the fillet and fowls aforesaid round his neck, and John Bernard, of Bishops Hatfield, 1380, who was tried before William Walworth, mayor, and the aldermen, for selling eight sacks of charcoal, each one bushel short, was sentenced to stand in the pillory until all the sacks were burned beneath him, and another man, who had sold a stinking capon, was sentenced to stand in the pillory for an hour, with the unsavoury fowl suspended under his nose John Penrose, a taverner, being found guilty of selling unsound wine, it was ordered that "the said John Penrose shall drink a draught of the said "wine which he sold to the common people, and the remainder of such "wine shall then be poured on the head of the said John, and that he "shall forswear the calling of a vintner in the city of London for ever, "unless he can obtain the favour of our lord the King as to the same"

But the mayor and aldermen in those days could inflict graver punishments than these, and John Barry, 1339, being caught with the mainour (*i e* the stolen goods in his hand), consisting of one surcoat of appel-blome and one coat of blanket, value one mark, burglariously stolen in the night, was incontinently hanged And William Hughot, 1387, having struck John Rote, an alderman, who attempted to prevent him assaulting one John Elyngham, and commanded him, "as an alderman of the city "and an officer of our lord the King, to desist from his wicked and evil "conduct, and surrender himself to the peace of our lord the King," was sentenced to lose his hand, and "an axe was immediately brought into "court by an officer of the sheriffs, and the hand of the said William was "laid upon the block, there to be cut off," and but for the kind intercession of the said John Rote, the sentence would have been immediately carried out

But I must proceed with my story In 1380, the 4th year of Richard II, William Walworth was again elected mayor, and during his second year of office occurred the event which has rendered his name famous throughout posterity

Without entering at too great length into the collateral history of these times, I may remind you that the weak King Richard II sanctioned the "demand for a great taxe," as Stowe says, "which afterwards was the "cause of a great disturbance" The great tax was a levy or a poll-tax of "five shillings and eightpence on all religious persons," and "every person, "man or woman, fourpence to the King."

The great disturbance arose from his accepting "from divers courtiers, "desirous to enrich themselves with other men's goods, a great summe of "money for the farme of that which they gather," and which they proceeded to collect by "handling the people very sore and uncourteously."

This was resented by the people of Essex; and Sir Thomas Bampton being sent down to enquire into the matter, they took all the "clerks of "the said Thomas Bampton, and chopped off their heads, which they carried "before them on poles."

At the same time, a certain Sir Simon Burley excited the wrath of the people at Gravesend by an act of cruel extortion on one of their number, whom he carried off and shut up in Rochester Castle, which the populace at once assaulted, and released the man of Gravesend.

And having then elected as their leaders Jacques or Jack Straw, a second priest, and a certain Wat Tyler, of Maidstone (a man described by Walsingham—"*Vir versutus et magno seusu preditus*"), they marched to Canterbury, forced the mayor, bailiffs, and commons of the town to swear that they would "be true to King Richard and the lawful commons of "England," and proceeded towards London.

The spark of rebellion, thus kindled, was fanned into a conflagration by an event which happened almost at the same time, at Dartford, where one of the tax-collectors grossly insulted the daughter of one John Tyler (a kinsman, I conclude, of Wat), who being hastily summoned by the neighbours from a house in the town which he was tiling, rushed home with his "lathing-staffe in his hand," and when the collector answered him with "stoute words and strake at him, he smote him with his lathing-staffe "that the brains flew out of his head."

Then the tumult burst all bounds, and the excited people surged on towards London, joining their brethren from Canterbury on Blackheath. The contagion spread throughout the country like wildfire—in Sussex, Hertford, Essex, Cambridgeshire, Norfolk, Suffolk, &c.—marked with those unreasonable excesses inseparable from such spasmodic movements.

"They took in hand," says Stowe, "to behead all men of law, as well "apprentices as utter barristers and old justices, with all the jurors of the "country whom they could get into their hands. They spared none whom "they thought to be learned; especially if they found any to have pen and "ink, they pulled off his hood, and all with one voice of crying—'Hale "'him out and cut off his head!'"

"Pinched, ground, and starved, as they had been in the name of the "law, they fell at once on the instruments of their oppression."—*Froude.*

The destruction of all records and the confiscation of all property, ecclesiastical and lay, completed their programme. And so from all parts they surged onwards towards London, the Essex men gathering on this side of the river, the remainder at Blackheath

Richard, with his hereditary courage, would have at once proceeded from the Tower to meet them and hear their complaint, but being dissuaded by his chancellor and treasurer from what they deemed an act of folly, he departed to Windsor On hearing this the vast multitude marched on London

Sir William Walworth, fearing for the safety of the city, proceeded at once to London Bridge, "fortified the place, caused the bridge to be drawn "up, and fastened a great chain of iron across, to restrain their entry"

In retaliation they destroyed certain houses in Southwark which were the property of Walworth, "brake down the houses of the Marchelsea and "loosed the prisoners, while the men of Essex went to Lambeth, a manor "of the Archbishop of Canterbury, and spoiled and burned all the goods"

On this the bridge-keepers "were constrained for fear to let it down "and give them entry" Over the bridge they passed peaceably enough, not interfering with religious persons who were earnest in procession and prayer for peace, but, calling upon the citizens to join them, they proceeded to the Savoy, the palace of the then unpopular John of Gaunt, Duke of Lancaster ("the which," says Stowe, "there was none in the "realme to be compared in beauty and stateliness"), and setting fire to it, burned it to the ground The King seems to have returned to the Tower, and seeing the conflagration spreading on all sides, he "demanded "of his council what was best to do in that extremity, but none of them "could counsel in that case"

The garrison, too, of six hundred warlike men, furnished with armour and weapons, expert men in arms, and six hundred archers, seemed stricken with panic, as well as the council with perplexity, for Stowe quaintly remarks—"all which did quaile in stomache"

Indeed, they set open the gates and allowed the multitude to enter, who defiled the King's apartments, and, proceeding to the chapel, found Simon of Sudbury, Archbishop of Canterbury and Chancellor of England, kneeling before the altar He rose to meet them "Welcome, my children," he said, "I am he that you seek, though no traitor and no oppressor" They rushed upon him His chaplain held up the Corpus Dominicum They flung him aside and dragged their prisoner, unresisting, across the court, and through the Tower gates to Tower Hill As he appeared, there rose a yell from the crowd not like any human shout, but like a "scream "from Satan's peacocks,"—*vocibus pavonum diabolicis*,—swords flashed over his venerable head "What means this?" he said "What have I done? "If you kill me, the Pope will lay you under an interdict" "Pope and "interdict, go to their own place!" was the answer "Thou art a false "traitor, lay down thy head." The archbishop was most eloquent—eloquent, it was said, above all Englishmen of his day. He pleaded hard, but it availed nothing. A ruffian struck at him. "Ah, ah!" he cried, putting his hand to the wound in his neck, "it is the hand of the Lord." The next stroke severed his fingers and cut an artery. At last, with eight blows, they hacked the head from the body, and left him in dust and blood.* The skull of the murdered prelate is still preserved in Sudbury church.

These, surely, were trying circumstances to test the courage of any man, and Richard shewed himself equal to the occasion; he resolutely determined to meet the people. This time he succeeded, because he set about it in the right way, *i.e.* not going to consult half-hearted, time-serving counsellors, but going direct to ask God's blessing and direction, solemnly and devoutly, before he started.

The King, we are told, that same day, after dinner, attended by about 200 persons, went to the abbey of Westminster, where "he devoutly prayed "and offered," which being done, the King made a proclamation "that all "the commons of the county which were in London should meet him in "Smithfield," and rode thither with his people. After the contemptible cowards and cravens which his Court had already shewed themselves to be, it was a plucky thing to do.

And the first onset did not seem very encouraging, for Wat Tyler's reply from the head of the great multitude, "in forme of battaile," to the King's messenger offering them peace, was that "peace be desired, but "with conditions of his liking," which he would mention the following day.

Three times did the King send terms of peace to him, each time altering the conditions, with the endeavour to please him, but with no avail. Then, fearing that another night should increase the pillage and bloodshed, he sent Sir John Newton, one of his own knights, "not so "much to command as to entreat him to come and talk to him about his "own demands."

On this Wat Tyler came, leisurely riding on his horse "a slow pace, "and came so near to the King that his horse's head touched the crop "of the King's horse," Thornbury says, throwing up his dagger in the air, and venturing to take hold of the King's bridle.

The King calmly and peaceably answered his somewhat coarse demands, when Tyler turned on Sir John Newton, bearing the King's sword, and ordered him to dismount in his presence. The gallant knight replied in scornful terms, and in a moment each man's dagger flashed from its sheath.

Again the King intervened in the cause of peace, and "commanded "the knight to light on foot and deliver his dagger" to Tyler; but the

* Froude. *Short Studies on Great Subjects. Annals of an English Abbey.*

demagogue, still dissatisfied, demanded his sword also, which the knight stubbornly refused to give up, saying it was the King's sword "By my "faith," said Wat Tyler, "I will never eat till I have thy head," and would "have run on the knight"

At that critical moment Walworth intervened, invoking the King's authority "not to permit a noble knight so shamefully to be murdered "before his face," which the King boldly gave, and "commanded the "mayor to set hand on him" But Tyler furiously struck at the mayor with his dagger, upon which Walworth drew his "baselard" and grievously wounded him in the neck, and knocked him backwards on his horse with a blow on the head, while an esquire of the King's house drew his sword, and wounded him "even unto death"

Wat Tyler, as he fell from his horse, cried to the commons to avenge him,—in a moment every bow was bent,—in another moment a frightful massacre would have taken place, but the King, "showing both wisdom "and courage, pricked his horse with his spurs," and rode alone straight in the face of this menacing line of rough and determined men, bristling with arrows pointed directly at him, and without flinching (surely in the strength of that courage which is the result of prayer, for it is the grace of God), he calmly said—"What a work is this, my men? What mean you "to do? Will you shoot at your King? Be not quarrelous, nor sorry for "the death of a traitor and ribald I will be your King, I am your captain "and leader, follow me into the field, there to have whatsoever you will "require"

And wheeling his horse round, led them into "the open field" The armed multitude stood silent for a moment, then followed with that sudden submission which the roughest natures will shew under the influence of true magnanimity and presence of mind The soldiers that were with him, we are told, also followed, "not knowing whether they would kill the King "or be in rest and depart home with the King's charter"

But Walworth's task was not done Ere the people could recover the surprise at the fall of their leader, and raise a shout of vengeance, he had put spurs to his horse, and, with only one servant, "riding speedily "into the city," soon returned with a number of armed men, whom he had implored to come and rescue the King from being murdered

But the danger of strife was passed Disheartened by the loss of their leader, not knowing whether these were not the advance-guard of a still greater number, and perhaps touched by the King's kindness, gentleness, and courage, the whole multitude laid down their arms, fell on their knees, and asked for pardon, which the King as readily granted, giving them the charter of their liberties, which he had already signed, and in spite of the earnest entreaties of some of his lately cowardly attendants to wreck their vengeance upon them, allowing them to depart to their homes in peace, without one of them being injured

Then came Walworth's reward The King required him to put on a bascinet, to which the worthy mayor demurred, saying he was but a merchant and lived by his merchandise, "but the King answered that he "was much bound to him, and therefore he should be made a knight," and then the King "took a sword with both hands, and, strongly and with "a good will, strake him on the neck, confirming a similar honour upon "three other citizens, knights for his sake, in the same place"

"And so the King, with his lords, and all his company, orderly entered "the city of London with great joy" What he thought of the stirring scene through which he had passed may be gathered from his answer to his mother, to whom with filial affection he went immediately on his return to the Tower "Ah, fair son," she said, "what great sorrow have I suffered for "you this day" "Madame," he answered, "I know it well, but now rejoice "and thank God, for I have this day recovered mine inheritage and the "realm of England, which I had nearhand lost"

So ended a great national crisis I am no advocate of bloodshed, or apologist for wrong-doing in any man or any class of men In the dim retrospect of such a far-distant event in English history we can discern alike provocation and retaliation, equally to be condemned and deplored But the actors in this great scene which I have endeavoured to sketch out before you, have long ago passed into His presence by whom alone actions are and can be rightly weighed, weighed against circumstances, of which we can know nothing, of temperament, education, surroundings, and a thousand things different and peculiar to each

There let us leave them, but the lesson which is taught us as a nation, not only here, but again and again throughout the pages of history, is that in all communities of men there are latent elements of discord, and they are wise and true citizens who so recognise and deal with them, both in themselves and in their fellows, that the sparks thereof may be diverted into the calm light of peace, instead of being fanned into the lurid flame of anarchy and strife

Yes, and for ourselves personally, God give us grace to brace ourselves in Him for our difficulties in life, not once in a lifetime, like Richard, but continually And God send many more like Sir William Walworth, who will support another in time of need and difficulty, and enable him to stand firm in spite of weak friends, and in the face of overwhelming dangers

I find Walworth mentioned* as keeper of Croydon Park, but I do not know whether it was an additional honour in consequence of his conduct

* Thornbury ii 441

He died 1383, and was buried in the north chapel by the choir in the church of St Michael's, Crooked Lane, now pulled down

His monument, defaced in the time of Edward VI, was renewed by the fishmongers, June, 1562, with his effigy in alabaster, richly gilt, at the cost of William Parvis, fishmonger, who dwelt at "The Castle," New Fish Street The epitaph ran thus—

"Here under lyeth a man of fame,
William Walworth called by name,
Fishmonger he was in lyfftime here,
And twise Lord Maior (as in books appear),
Who with courage stout and manly myght,
Slew Jack Straw in King Richard's syght,
For which act done and trew contend
The King made him knight incontinend,
And gave him arms (as here you see)
To declare his fact and chivalric
He left this lyff the year of God
Thirteen hundred, four score, and three odd"

He left money to relieve the prisoners in Newgate, and founded, in the said parish, a college for a master and nine priests He also augmented with one mill, one dovecote, and 140 acres of land, the chapel of St Mary Magdalene at Kingston, which his old master, John Lovekyn (to whom he had been apprenticed as stock-fishmonger), had founded There is something rather touching in this kindly act of remembrance on his part for one in whose honourable steps he was treading, and to whom, perhaps, he felt he owed much of his success in life Indeed, by his epitaph in Kingston church, Master Lovekyn seems to have been as worthy a person, in his generation, as Walworth

"Worthy John Lovekyn, stock-fishmonger, of London, here is layd,
Four times of the city Lord Mayor he was if truth be sayd—
Twice he was by election of citizens then being,
And twice by the commandment of his good lord the King
Chief founder of this church in his lifetime was he,
Such lovers of the commonwealth too few there be
On August the fourth, thirteen hundred and sixty and eyght,
His flesh to earth, his soul to God went streyght"*

The religious institution which these good men had established for the poor did not survive the dissolution In 31st Henry VIII, Charles Carew, the last master, was attainted of felony, probably some act against the Six Articles, and died 1540, it is not improbable that he suffered capitally In 1st Edward VI, 1547, the institution was dissolved, and came to the Crown †

* Thornbury, vol i p 335 † Manning's *History of Surrey*

Though the monument of Walworth in the church of his burial has passed away, three memorials of him still remain at Fishmongers' Hall (the third in succession, rebuilt by Roberts, 1831)

First, the dagger, or, as Stowe calls it, the "baselard," which is preserved in a glass case in the drawing-room, and is undoubtedly a weapon of the period, though, in 1731, a publican in Islington pretended to possess the actual poignard

Secondly, on the stairs, there is a statue of Walworth by Pierce, with a dagger in his hand, and beneath the statue this inscription —

> "Brave Walworth, Knight, Lord Mayor, that slew
> Rebellious Tyler in his alarms,
> The King, therefore, did give (in lieu)
> The dagger to the city arms
>
> In the 4th year of Richard II, anno Domini" (1381)

It would be an unpardonable act of heresy to profess any doubt on this subject within the precincts of Fishmongers' Hall, but here I may venture not only to repeat, but to prove, the improbability, if not impossibility, of the statement

In the "letter-books," which I have already mentioned, it is recorded that on the 17th April, 1384, in full congregation holden in the upper chamber of Guildhall, London, and summoned by William Walworth, mayor, it was agreed and ordered that the old seal of the office of mayoralty of the said city should be broken, seeing it was too small, rude, and ancient and unbecoming, and derogatory from the honour of the city, and that another new seal of honour which the same mayor had had made, should in future be used for that office, "in place of the other"

"In the new seal (from *Historical Account of the Guildhall*, by E Price, *Stowe and Strype*, vol 1 p 506), besides the figures of Peter and Paul, "beneath the feet of the said figures a shield for the arms of the said city "is perfectly graven," &c The record continues —"Therefore the old "seal of the office was delivered to Richard Odyham the chamberlain, who "broke it, and in its place the said new seal was delivered to the mayor, to "use the same as his office of the mayoralty should demand and require"

On these arms the dagger appears, and Wat Tyler was not slain until the 15th of June following The dagger is really a short sword, emblematical of St Paul, the patron saint of the corporation

It is curious that Walworth should have been associated with two alterations in the city seal, once, as I have already mentioned, in 1376, and once in 1384 This may account for the legend, but as the insertion of so trifling an addition as a mullet was only done with the consent of a full meeting of the corporation, and recorded in the letter-book, it is not likely that such an honourable augmentation as the dagger of Walworth could have been added after the new seal had been adopted, in 1384, without some similar record being made thereof.

And the other relic of Walworth consists of a pall, which is carefully preserved at Fishmongers' Hall, and is said to have been made to do honour to his burial. Through the courtesy of the chief clerk, I have been permitted to see it, but it is far beyond my power adequately to describe it, so as to give any idea of such a triumph of taste and needlework.

It consists of a centre slip, about 12 feet long and 2½ feet wide, and two shorter sides, each 8 feet 11 inches long by 1 foot 4 inches wide, and when laid over the corpse it must have totally enveloped the coffin, but without corner falls, like our modern palls. The central slip is a piece of gold brocade, of a very elaborate pattern and costly material. The end pieces consist of very rich and massively-wrought pictures in gold and silk of St. Peter in full pontificals, supported by angels burning incense; their wings are radiant as peacock feathers; their outer robes gold raised with crimson; their under dress white shaded with blue. The faces are finely worked in satin, and they have long yellow hair.

The side pieces are divided into three portions. On the centre, in each side, figures of Christ and St. Peter, superbly and elaborately wrought, and, on either hand of them, the fishmongers' arms, richly and properly emblazoned, supported by mermen and mermaids, the former clad in gold armour, the latter in white silk thread beautifully worked, with superb jewels hanging from their necks.

It is indeed a splendid specimen of ancient art, and well worthy of a visit. I am told that there are similar palls belonging to many of the great London companies, and that the pall of the Vintners' Company equals if not eclipses it in beauty.

But having laid my hero to rest under such a costly coverlet, there I must leave him; like another hero whose life and actions are not above criticism, "after he had served his own generation, by the will of God he "fell on sleep and saw corruption." And we must each in our time endeavour so to act that the same may be said of us.

The Hothams.

The name of Hotham has been already incidentally mentioned in the foregoing pages, but it is right that it should receive more definite notice, as it is associated with more than one interesting incident in English history. According to the Hotham pedigree, Sir John de Trehous, who served under William the Conqueror at the battle of Hastings, had a grant of the manor of Hotham, county of York His descendant, of evil memory, Peter de Trehous, having married Isabella de Turnham in reward for his nefarious transaction with King John, divided his property between his two sons—Peter, I suppose the eldest, obtaining his mother's estate of Mulgrave, and John receiving his paternal estate of Hotham From henceforth the name of Trehous was abandoned, and as Peter and his descendants are known under the name of Maulay, John and his descendants are known by the name of Hotham, but both sons assumed the arms of their maternal grandfather, Nigel de Fossard The younger differenced the bend sable with three mullets argent *

John de Hotham married a daughter of Baldwin de Wake, about which family I shall have much to say by-and-by, and had three sons The youngest, Edmund, married a Grindall, and had a son, Sir Galfrid or Geoffry de Hotham, who in 1331 founded the monastery of St Austin, called the Black Friars, in Hull Hadley, in his *History of Hull*, from which I have derived much of the following information, says that "The "building was so large that it took up half the street, and was decorated "with fine gardens, fountains, and courts" About three years after its foundation, Sir Richard Hotham, his son and heir, agreed to take the charge of the fee-farm rent of thirteen shillings and fourpence upon himself and his heirs, provided that the prior and friars would always pray for the souls of himself, his wife Avicia, and all their posterity Five years after, the mayor and corporation made a similar composition in favour of themselves and their successors About the same time John de Wetwang bestowed many messuages and tenements upon the monastery It flourished in great plenty and magnificence until the dissolution of the religious houses, when, in the name of religion, the abuse of these good gifts devoted to God was corrected by their absolute confiscation to gratify mere worldly greed and rapacity

The second son, William, was prior-provincial of the Friars Preachers in England, and a person of great piety and learning Educated at Merton College, Oxford, in 1298, he was intimately associated with Edward I in his intended expedition to Palestine, and with Queen Eleanor in the management of her affairs The same year he had letters of credence to the Pope, and the following year he was preferred to the Archbishopric of Dublin, having been consecrated abroad He died, however, the same year, August 28th, at Dijon, and his body was buried in the church of the Dominicans in London † The eldest, John or Alan, married Maud, daughter of Robert Lord Strafford, and had two sons

John, the younger, was ordained priest at York 1274, and in 1311 is mentioned as one of the King's clerks, probably through the influence of

* See coloured illustration † Canon Raine MS

his uncle, as well as of the well known Peter de Gaveston, in whose service he was In 1306 he held a stall at Dublin, and in 1309 was presented to the living of Rowley, Yorks, and, three years after, to that of Cottingham in the same county, with Ashfield, Notts, in commendam, and the prebend of Stillington in the Minster In 1310, 2nd Edw II, he went to Ireland as Chancellor of the Exchequer, and the same year was "Escheator ultra et infra Trentam" In 1313 he was sent to Ireland by the King as special envoy to treat with the rebels, and again the following year to counteract the intended invasion of the Scots In 9th Edward II he was made Chancellor of the English Exchequer, and the same year was consecrated Bishop of Ely In 1316 he went as ambassador to the Pope, the following year he was made Treasurer of the English Exchequer, and, in 1319, Lord High Chancellor of England In the autumn of that year he assisted Archbishop Melton in raising and leading the "posse comitatus" of Yorkshire to resist the Scots at Myton, and only escaped from that disastrous field by the swiftness of his horse On Nov 8th, 1324, he was made an ambassador to treat with Robert de Brus *

In January, 1327, on the death of Edward II, a council of regency, consisting of twelve persons (five prelates and seven temporal peers), was appointed to hold office during the minority of Edward III, and Hotham was again made Lord Chancellor, but he only consented to hold the office till a settlement of the kingdom should take place, and he finally resigned it on the 1st of March following †

In 1328 he assisted Archbishop Melton to marry Philippa of Hainault to the young King Edward in York Minster The King had kept his Christmas here with great state and hospitality, and before the solemnity of the festival was ended, Lord John of Hainault arrived with his beautiful niece and a very numerous attendance On January 22nd, being Sunday, the eve of St Paul's conversion, the ceremony took place ‡ The magnificence of the espousals was heightened by the grand entry of a hundred of the principal nobility of Scotland, who had arrived in order to conclude a lasting peace with England, cemented by the marriage of the King's little sister Joanna The Parliament and Royal Council were likewise convened at York, and the flower of the nobility then in arms were assembled round the young King and his bride

One would fain idealize what the Minster was at that time, and what a brilliant *cortege* thronged its aisles—very different, indeed, from what we see it now The old Norman choir of Archbishop Roger was then standing, but the new transepts of Walter de Gray and John le Romaine, the glory of our Minster, were in all the freshness of their recent completion The present nave was probably only partially finished, and perhaps the chapter-house but rising from the ground The great central tower then

* Raine MS † Lord Campbell's *Lives of the Chancellors* ‡ Drake

lacked the lofty lantern which now crowns it, and no western towers finished the west end, but many of the windows must have been sparkling with painted glass and all, in its partially developed splendour, not only already beautiful, but kindling bright anticipations of its future glory Who does not wish to recall the scene therein on that winter day, when amidst flashing steel, and gay silks and rich velvets, and costly furs, glistening tapers, fragrant incense, and solemn voices, one of the fairest brides of earth entered on a married life of forty years, in which she attained to a high ideal of wife, mother, and Queen, and at the close of which, extending her hand from her death-bed, she joined it once again, for the last time, to the right hand of King Edward, overwhelmed with sorrow, saying in faltering accents, "We have, my husband, enjoyed our "long union in happiness, peace, and prosperity"

Yes, and there is one touching memorial of that tender but chequered wedlock yet remaining in the Minster—the recumbent figure of Prince William of Hatfield, their second son, born at the royal hunting-lodge in Hatfield Chase, near Doncaster, and, dying while still a child at York, probably when Philippa was resident here during the King's absence in France, 1346–7, was buried in the north choir aisle of the Minster Who that has eyes to see can fail to discern in that still beautiful figure, albeit defaced during succeeding generations, not only the evidence of the sculptor's art and taste, but the token of a fond mother's care and love, or fail to feel, as he recalls the fate of his brothers, that the most appropriate epitaph thereof are the words of Scripture—"Taken away from the evil to come"

Surely the good bishop's prayer and blessing were abundantly answered But he had long before passed to his rest, having died, after being stricken with paralysis and bedridden for two years, in 1336

The high offices which Hotham filled enabled him to amass a princely fortune, which he dispensed in a princely manner His benefactions to the Church and to his family in Yorkshire were many

In 1327 he bought and settled on the bishops and church of Ely divers lands and tenements, including a vineyard, in Holborn, adjacent to his manor there He probably built the noble chapel of St Mary at Ely, and in 1322, when the great central tower fell upon the choir, destroying two bays, he rebuilt them at the cost of £2,000, and they still remain the noblest portion of that magnificent cathedral

His body was buried in the middle thereof, but the sumptuous tomb, with its effigy of alabaster and splendid sculpture, is now gone—only a slab of marble, inlaid with a brass plate engraved with his arms, marks the site of his last resting-place

Godwin says of him that he was "Prudens sapiens sed admodum "indoctus" *

* Canon Raine MS

The eldest son, Peter, married a daughter of Thomas Staunton, by whom he had several children His eldest son, John, was created a Knight of the Bath, which Order, Camden says, is of great antiquity, and, according to Anstis, was conferred as early as William the Conqueror *

He was also summoned as baron of the realm 8th Edward II, 1296, though Dugdale says, "after this John, none of his descendants had the "like summons"

His grandson, John, married again into the family of Stafford, and had an only child, Alice, who married twice Her second husband was Sir John Trussel, her first husband was Hugh le Despencer, son of Edward le Despencer, whose father was the Hugh le Despencer commonly called "the younger," who was executed by order of Queen Isabella, wife of Edward II, at Hereford, November 28th, 1326 The family tradition is that Hugh the husband of Alice was also executed that same year, and that in consequence of this, the ancient arms of the family of Hotham were changed by Thomas Hotham, the great-uncle of Alice, with the advice of the Bishop of Ely

This is possible, though Hugh must have been a very young man at that time Perhaps he was his grandfather's esquire, and perhaps, because of his relationship, involved in the same fate by that "angry and outrageous "woman" But I can find no evidence of this, or that any one was executed at the same time, except Simon de Reading, late marshal of the King's house, who was "hanged on the same gallows, but ten foot "lower" † Alice, too, must have been very young, as she did not die until forty-three years afterwards, viz 1370—perhaps only lately married But they had two children, Hugh, and Anna who afterwards married Edward Boteler, and they would be entitled, as their mother was an heiress, to quarter the arms of Hotham with the family coat of Le Despencer And if we realize the horror and execration with which the Le Despencers were then regarded, we can imagine how any family coat associated therewith would be accounted as utterly disgraced For Holinshead says he was "drawn in his own cote armour, about the which there "were letters embrodered plaine to be read conteining a parcell of the "52nd Psalm 1–7" In the Harleian MS we are told (vol 1 p 89), "She "made her poor condemned adversary, in strange disguise, attend her "progress He was set upon a poor lean deformed jade, and clothed in "a tarbrace—the robe in those days due to the basest of thieves and "rascals—and so was led through all the towns and villages with trumpets "sounding before him, and all the spiteful disgraces and affronts that they "could devise to cast upon him" Dallaway mentions Hugh le Despencer as one of the few instances of those who suffered the indignity of being compelled to appear in tabards with their arms reversed

* *Encyclopædia Heraldica* W Berry † Stowe

We can therefore imagine Thomas Hotham, of Scorborough, now the head of the family, consulting with his aged uncle, the bishop, and deciding to renounce the old coat and adopt a new one. If so, what more natural than that Thomas Hotham should suggest the arms of his mother, Matilda, a daughter of Robert de Hilton, a baron of the realm temp. Edw. I. (about whom I shall have much to say by-and-by), who bore argent two bars azure, and that the bishop should suggest the arms of his mother, Maud, daughter of Robert Lord Strafford, by Alice, daughter of Thos. Corbet, of Shropshire, who bore Or a corbeau or raven sable? Her brother was also made a baron by Edw. I.; but on the death of her nephew, John, third baron—*sine prole*—she, and her sister Elizabeth married to Edmund de Cornwall, became co-heiresses, and thus entitled to bear the arms of Corbet, which her daughter would inherit and impale. An illustrious coat indeed in those days, for the device of the raven is said to have been granted to Robert Corbet, grandfather of Alice, by Richard I., at the battle of Acre, so that it would be specially valued by her descendants, and incorporated in any coat which they might bear.

And thus the new, *i.e.* the present coat of Hotham, could be formed, viz., the bars of Hilton becoming barry of argent and azure, and the corbeau of Corbet being placed on a canton at the most honourable corner of the shield—the method employed when it was desired to give significant reference to some allied coat.

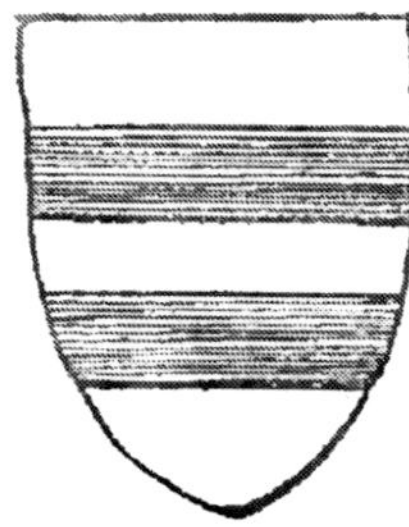
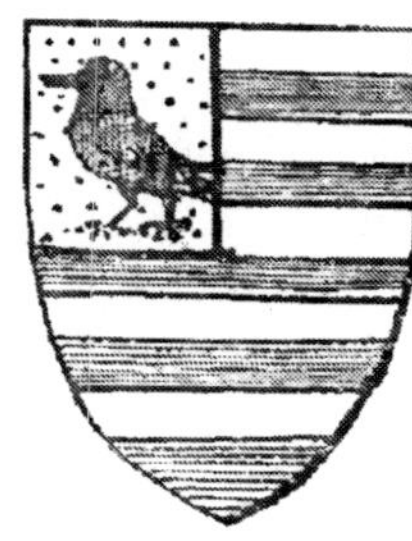

And this, I think, is confirmed by the fact that Bishop Hotham undoubtedly bore the coat, for it was illuminated on the south wall of the choir at Ely, and the colours rigidly adhered to by Dean Peacock when Ely Cathedral was restored. It was considered by those at work upon the re-illumination that the old colours were coeval with the masonry, viz. 1336, the year of the Bishop's death. Wharton, in his *Anglia Sacra*, quoting from the *Continuatio Historiæ Eliensis*, in the Lambeth Library, by Robert Steward, the last prior and first dean of Ely, 1522–1577, says, "Arma Johannis Hothum sunt barrulæ octo partium azuræ et argenteæ, in uno cantone aureo unus mertellus sable." And

Cole, writing to Bentham, the Ely historian, 1766, mentions the same arms as existing in the church of Ditton, near Cambridge, in the Diocese of Ely

But Hugh, Alice's son, and his sister died without issue, and in a little while the Le Despencers recovered their prestige, and have ever since been regarded as a noble and honourable house, with which it is an honour to be connected

The elder branch thus died out, the younger still flourishes, and long may it continue to do so For many generations, the central line thereof, which is all that I can mention here, filled honourable positions, and made worthy alliances amongst their neighbours Eight successive generations attained to the dignity of knighthood during a period when that was a token of meritorious service in the field

Sir John Hotham, born 1458, was knighted at Flodden in 1513, and died 1524

On the news of the death of Queen Elizabeth reaching Hull, March 27th, 1603, Christopher Hildyard, John Hotham, and Launcelot Alford, Esq , and others, joined in commission with the mayor, recorder, and aldermen, who with great solemnity, preceded by music, went in procession to the market-place and proclaimed King James I , and this is the first mention I find of one who played a part of no little importance, not only in his family history, but in the councils of his country

In 1617 his Majesty came to York, and was lodged at the Manor House During his stay Lord Sheffield, the Lord President of the North, entertained him at a banquet at Sir George Young's house, in the Minster Yard, built on the site of the house of the Treasurer, and now known as Gray's Court After the banquet, Mr Hotham and seven others were knighted by the King

In 1635 he was Sheriff of the county, and very active in the rigorous collecting of the ill-advised tax of "ship money," imposed by Charles I Up to this time he had been a staunch Royalist, but possibly this may have shaken him in his attachment, for in 1639, when he was elected Member for Hull, he was examined by the Council and committed to the Fleet for refusing to answer questions concerning the transactions of Parliament Clarendon says (vol ii p 476)—"His particular animosity against the Earl "of Strafford first engaged him in that company"

That same year Charles visited Hull, and was received with great state by the mayor and corporation I suppose that he thus saw the capabilities of its situation, for when war broke out with Scotland, 1640, Lord Strafford by his orders directed the town to be immediately put in a posture of defence, and eventually sent Sir Thomas Glemham to be the governor of the town To this the corporation demurred, representing that by the charter of Edward VI the mayor for the time being was the governor, and that to admit another was a breach of their privilege But Strafford was not a man to "take no for an answer" He persisted in his purpose, and threatened to come down himself to enforce it, on which the corporation reluctantly acquiesced, and delivered the keys of the town to Sir Thomas, who took the command of the garrison, then consisting of 1,000 men However, when Charles relinquished his project of subduing the Scotch, Sir Thomas Glemham vacated his office and returned the keys to the mayor

But matters became more unsettled, and the breach between the King and Parliament wider, every day Both parties began to turn their attention towards the strong places and seaports of the kingdom, and the Earl of Newcastle came down, under the name of Sir John Savage, and tried to persuade the mayor to give up the town to him, but he was discovered and insulted by young Hotham, and returned to London Charles then conceived the design to seize the magazine at Hull with the assistance of the gentlemen of Yorkshire But the Parliament got wind of it, and Sir Henry Vane, by their order, wrote to Hull, and the corporation put the town in a posture of defence Soon after, the Commons sent a message to the Lords demanding that some of the trained bands of Yorkshire should be put into Hull under Sir John Hotham, then a Member of Parliament, with orders not to deliver up the place or the magazine without the King's authority, signified by both Houses To this the Lords consented, and young Hotham was sent immediately to Hull to execute this order, till his father's arrival a few weeks after with eight hundred of the militia of the county But the mayor was suspicious, and shut the gates, drew up the bridges, charged the cannon, refused them admittance, threatening to treat them as enemies if they did not remove further off And so they remained, until an express having been sent to London, an order arrived from the Parliament, upon which Hotham and his forces were received without further delay

But Charles was bent upon gaining Hull, and on April 22nd, being at York, he sent the Duke of York, the Elector Palatine, Lords Newport and Willoughby, Sir Thomas Glemham, and others, who entered the town on a market-day without being observed, and were hospitably received and entertained by the mayor and governor The following day being St George's day, they were invited to dine with Sir John, when the King suddenly arrived some four miles off, accompanied by about 300 men, and sent Sir Lewis Dives to the governor to say that he designed to dine with him Sir John Hotham, surprised and alarmed, hastily consulted with Alderman Pelham, his brother member, and ordered the gates to be closed, the bridges drawn up, the guns loaded, and the men to stand to their arms, and sent a messenger to the King beseeching him to forbear coming.

However, Charles arrived at the Beverley gate about eleven o'clock, and summoning the governor, demanded admittance. What actually took place has been variously reported. There can be no doubt of this, that Sir John declined to open the gates, but whether because he said it would be a breach of his trust to both Houses, or because the King had too great a train, it is difficult to say; probably in the excited, nervous discussion he said both. There is also a difference of opinion as to whether he offered to admit the King with twenty horses only, and the King stipulated for thirty. No doubt it is true that "the gentleman, with much "distraction in his looks, talked confusedly of the trust he had from the "Parliament, and then fell on his knees, wished that God would bring "confusion upon him and his, if he was not a loyal and faithful subject to "his Majesty; but in conclusion declined to suffer his Majesty to come "into the town." *

Clarendon adds—"The man was of fearful nature and perplexed "understanding, and could better resolve upon deliberation than on a "suddain: and many were of opinion that if he had been prepared "dextrously beforehand, and in confidence, he would have conformed to "the King's pleasure: for he was master of a noble fortune in land, and "rich in money, of a very ancient family, and well allied: his affections to "the government very good, and no man less desired to see the nation "involved in a civil war than he: and when he accepted this employment "from the Parliament, he never imagined it would engage him in "rebellion: but believed that the King would find it necessary to comply "with the advice of his two Houses, and that the preserving that magazine "from being possessed by them would likewise prevent any possible "ruptures into armes." All this may be very true, but I cannot conceive any position more difficult than that in which he was placed.

However, the King then summoned the mayor and demanded admittance, but he "with a heavy heart drew near, fell upon his knees, "and, shedding tears, answered that he could do no more; protesting that "he would let him in if it was in his power, but that he could not do it, "there being a guard over him, the inhabitants, and at the gates, which "were kept by the soldiers ready armed, with orders to put any to death "who should attempt to open them. †

After this the duke and his party, who were still in Hull, passed out and joined the King; and at five o'clock the King, having again made an ineffectual appeal to the governor to open the gates, proclaimed him a traitor by two heralds he had brought with him, commanded the corporation to reject his jurisdiction, and finally ordered those within to

* Clarendon's *History of the Rebellion*, vol. i. p. 397. † Hadley's *History of Hull.*

throw the traitors over into the ditch "Of all which there was no notice "taken, except some expressions of disloyalty and contempt expressed by "Sir John Hotham to the King, who then withdrew to Beverley," and from thence the following day returned to York The Lords and Commons declared the said proceedings to amount to a high violation of the privileges of Parliament, and indemnified that worthy person employed by them

The gentlemen of the north offered to raise a force and take Hull by assault, but the King preferred to make Sir John Hotham and his conduct the subject of an acrimonious correspondence between the Parliament and himself

On the 12th of May, 1642, however, the King summoned the gentry of Yorkshire, represented to them that, from the late action of Sir John Hotham, countenanced by Parliament, he had reason to apprehend danger, and desired them to form a guard for his person, which they did to the extent of a troop of horse and a regiment of 600 foot taken from the militia, which were placed under the command of the Prince of Wales Soon after, he determined on a fresh attempt on Hull, and removed to Beverley with 3,000 foot and 1,000 horse The town was closely blockaded, the water supply diverted into the Humber, and 200 horse sent into Lincolnshire to intercept all provisions, and two forts were built at Hassel Cliff and Paul, to guard the Humber

Sir John, on the other hand, took every precaution for the safety of the town, and, his messengers to Charles, requesting him to desist from his purpose, being detained, he ordered the sluices to be drawn, the banks of the Humber and the Hull to be cut, and thus flooded the country The contest was now actively carried on by both sides A ship with reinforcements and provisions evaded the blockade and reached the town, some Royalist officers were captured in an open boat and imprisoned, the cannon of the Royalists played on the town, and were answered by the guns on the walls Anlaby was attacked, the Royalists expelled, and their magazine in the great barn of Mr Legard blown up, the Earl of Newport being knocked senseless off his horse into a ditch by a cannon ball, and nearly drowned Sir John on the one hand did his best to inflame the minds of the Parliamentarians by reports of intended incendiarism and cruelty, and the King, on the other hand, inveighed against Sir John in the remonstrances which he addressed to the neighbouring country However, it soon became evident to the King that his forces were inadequate for the object which he had undertaken, and it was desirable to find some other way This was brought about by accident Lord Digby had come over from the Queen in Holland, disguised, with communications to the King On his return he was captured with Colonel Ashburnham in a "fly boat" by one of the Parliament ships, and carried into Hull

An excellent French scholar, he acted the part of a sea-sick Frenchman so admirably that the crew were entirely deceived, and left him to himself while they carefully guarded the other On reaching Hull he told one of the guards in broken English that he desired to speak to the governor, as he could disclose some secrets relative to the King and Queen Hotham received him in the presence of a large company, and, in spite of his own knowledge of French, and of many of those around him having only lately come from France, he was quite deceived by Lord Digby's voluble statements of the French service and his experiences therein

At length he asked for a private interview, to which Hotham, afraid of assassination, demurred, but he withdrew with him into a large bay window, where they would be out of earshot To his surprise, the supposed Frenchman asked him in good English if he knew him Sir John said "No" "Then," replied Lord Digby, "I will try whether I know Sir John "Hotham, and whether he be the man of honour I take him to be," and at once revealed himself to him Hotham, taken aback and apprehensive lest the others should discover him, accepted the confidence reposed in him Postponing further communication for the present, he called the guard and ordered them to take the prisoner away to safe keeping Then, turning to the company, he said that the Frenchman was a shrewd fellow, and understood more of the Queen's counsels and designs than any could suspect, though he had not as yet elicited such clear information as he hoped in a few days to send to the Parliament

The result of a secret interview next day was that Lord Digby skilfully wormed himself into Hotham's confidence,—painted such an exaggerated picture of the Royal cause,—the certainty of its speedy triumph,—the honours in store for its friends,—the destruction of its enemies,—and so worked on Hotham's fears and ambition, that he consented to give Lord Digby a free pass to York, where he could assure the King that if he would only appear before Hull with one regiment he would, after sufficient show of resistance to save his reputation, open the gates But his subordinates proved very ill disposed to favour such a purpose, specially his son, and though Charles came to Beverley, Digby found the governor, on his next secret interview, less sanguine Eventually Sir John abandoned the plan, and acted with increased activity against the Royalists, sending out his son to ravage the country, until encountered and defeated by Sir Thomas Glemham on the wolds above Malton, he was forced to retreat But again sallying out with him, he committed terrible devastations in Lincolnshire and Yorkshire

However, another influence arose from his own side, for the Parliament, feeling that there ought to be a commander-in-chief in the north, sent down Lord Fairfax, and thus virtually superseded Hotham, who resented this as a slur on his late eminent services, and was cordially supported by his son Mutually exasperated, they opened secret communications with the Earl of Newcastle, at whose suggestion Captain Hotham went to the Queen in Holland to treat for the surrender of the town At her direction, Lady Bland came over to Hull to confer with Sir John, and tried to tamper with Mr William Stiles, the vicar of the High Church, but the worthy ecclesiastic was too prudent to commit himself to any such dangerous course, and simply pointed out to her the inexpediency of clergymen and ladies *interfering in matters of state*

But Digby came again, and eventually clenched the matter by shewing Hotham some intercepted letters of Fairfax in which his destruction had been resolved upon In fact, the Parliament had "smelt a rat" from the evident abatement in young Hotham's zeal, and other circumstances which had been brought to their knowledge, and, adopting a similar policy, persuaded a kinsman of Sir John's, a staunch Puritan, to ingratiate himself into his confidence, and having elicited his secret design, to betray it to them

On this, Captain Hotham was ordered to march with his troop to Nottingham, where he was at once arrested by Oliver Cromwell, then only a colonel in the forces, and committed to the castle, but he, sending his servant, John Kaye, to the Queen, effected his escape On his arrival at Hull a council was called by Sir John, and a complaint made to the Parliament of his son's false accusation and imprisonment But their only answer was to direct Captain Mayer, of the *Hercules* man-of-war, then lying in the harbour, to consult with Sir Matthew Boynton (Sir John's brother-in-law) and the Mayor, and bring Sir John, Captain Hotham, and their adherents prisoners to London

Captain Mayer on this sent 100 men before daylight, surprised the castle and blockhouse, overpowered Colonel Lyard, and, assisted by 1,500 of the inhabitants and soldiers, secured Captain Hotham and placed a guard on the governor's house Sir John, however, escaped by a back way, borrowed a horse of a man whom he met in the town, and started for his house at Scorborough Finding no ferry-boat either at Stone Ferry or Waghen, he rode on to Beverley, where he found seven or eight hundred mounted men in arms, and was immediately arrested by their commander, his nephew, Colonel Boynton, sent by Sir Matthew for that very purpose, who taking hold of his horse's bridle, said, "Sir John, you are my prisoner, "and though I revere you as my relative, I am obliged with reluctance to "waive all respect on that account and arrest you as a traitor to the "state" After an ineffectual effort to escape by dashing through the soldiers, he was knocked off his horse by a blow from a musket on the head, and conveyed bleeding and wounded into Hull Soon after, together with his son and Sir John Rhodes, he was placed on board the *Hercules*, conveyed to London, and committed to the Tower

On Dec 1st, after remaining several months prisoners there, father and son were brought to trial at the Guildhall before the Earl of Manchester and others The proofs against them were many and full, not the least being a packet of letters found in the carriage of the Earl of Newcastle after the ill-advised battle on Marston Moor, on July 3rd, which Rupert, in defiance of earnest remonstrances, had insisted on forcing, and from which the Earl had fled himself, leaving his "Whitecoats" to be hacked to pieces by the Roundheads They were both convicted and condemned to death Sir John presented a petition for pardon to the House, which the Lords accepted, but the Commons negatived without debate On his way to execution, however, a reprieve arrived, and he was taken back to the Tower The House of Commons indignantly resented this, passed a vote that no reprieve should be granted to any person without the consent of both Houses, and ordered that the lieutenant of the Tower should proceed to the execution of Sir John Hotham, according to the sentence of the court-martial

On January 1st, 1644, Captain Hotham suffered death on a scaffold erected on Tower Hill, and shewed great courage on the occasion, protesting that he had not been guilty of treason to the Parliament, who were the principal authors of rebellion by waging an unjust war against their sovereign and fellow subjects

On the morning of the following day, fixed for his execution, Sir John procured a motion to be made in his behalf before the Commons A debate ensued, and the time fixed for the execution was delayed to two o'clock, but the motion was rejected, and having "suffered "his ungodly confessor, Peters, to tell the people that 'he had revealed "'himself to him and confessed his offences against the Parliament,'"* his head was severed from his body

At Dalton Holme, the residence of Lord Hotham, there are two touching relics of this tragical episode in the family history I suppose that when the sad news reached Scorborough that sentence of death had been pronounced, the afflicted family would naturally be anxious to do anything in their power to shew their respect for their father and brother, and they therefore sent up two fine-linen cloths to receive their heads when they were severed from their bodies The cloths are long and narrow, of very good but rather coarse material, probably "homespun" woven into a rude damask, the product probably of some local loom Perhaps they were cherished treasures of a generation already passed away—choice portions of the family "lingerie" which had hitherto been only brought out on "high days and holidays," when special honour should be done to persons

* Clarendon

or events. Now, they are the simple tokens of that love which trouble only increases and which no axe can sever or extinguish. Whether they were used for the purpose for which they were sent I cannot say. Untarnished by stain of blood, they seem, in their spotless whiteness, types of the spirits cleansed from the defilements of human frailty and restless ambition, and at peace with God.

The names of Sir John and his son are not recorded in the list of those buried at the Tower, so I conclude that their bodies were brought to Scorborough and laid in the family burying-place.

Captain Hotham's son, John, succeeded to the baronetcy, and seems to have been governor of Hull in 1689, during the troubles of the early years of James II. He married Elizabeth, only daughter of Viscount Beaumont, and had several children, all of whom died without issue except one, Elizabeth, who married William Gee of Bishop Burton, great-grandson of Sir William Gee, one of the Council of the North, whose wife was a daughter of Archbishop Hutton, and who is buried under a stately monument in the south choir aisle of the Minster.

The eldest son, John, succeeded his father, and married, but dying without issue, 1691, the direct line of Hotham from the first wife of the decapitated Sir John failed, and the baronetcy now reverted to a distant cousin, Charles Hotham, grandson of the second wife, Anne, daughter of Ralph Rokeby.

Whether Sir John had had any quarrel with him, or whether he regarded half-blood as no relationship, I cannot say; but he left the whole of the property to his mother, at her free disposal. Fortunately Lady Hotham was both high-principled and unselfish. She immediately sent for Sir Charles, and told him that she felt the great responsibility laid upon her, and was anxious to do the best for the family honour, as for her own immediate kith and kin. If, therefore, he would marry her granddaughter, Bridget Gee, she would make over the whole estate to him, only retaining an annuity of £500 for her life.

Sir Charles, who was a young officer of dragoons, at once acceded, not doubting of his success with the young lady; but, to his surprise, on communicating to her his wishes, he was quietly but firmly refused. Perplexed and crestfallen he returned to Lady Hotham and told her what had occurred. She replied that she learned with great regret the failure of what had been the cherished wish of her heart, but as she could not control another's affections, and as he had shewn himself ready to comply with her wishes, she was determined that the family should not suffer, and therefore would make over the estate to him, without that condition, leaving him free to marry whom he pleased. But he had a real affection for his young cousin, and venturing to make another appeal, was at once accepted,—in what language I cannot say, but in words which told him that while she would not be his wife for mere mercenary considerations, she cordially reciprocated the love which he so evidently entertained for her

And there is yet another equally touching episode recorded of their younger son, Beaumont Hotham When he arrived at man's estate he went out to Holland to seek his fortune, and became clerk in the house of a wealthy merchant, who was so much pleased with his intelligence and industry that he offered to receive him into partnership if he would marry his daughter But Beaumont Hotham had already fixed his affections on Frances, daughter of William Thompson of Humbleton, and declined the offer The merchant, however, pleased with his constancy, agreed to receive him into partnership nevertheless. But a commercial crisis soon after arose, and, being involved in the famous "South Sea Bubble," the house of business failed Young Hotham returned to England, a penniless man, only to learn on reaching home that his intended wife had been stricken with the small-pox, that frequent scourge of former generations, and had quite lost her beauty "I loved her for herself," he replied, "and "am as ready to marry her as ever" The marriage proved a long and happy union, and a letter is still preserved, in her handwriting, to him absent from home, when stricken with a mortal sickness, which testifies to the integrity of her character

Their three sons inherited their parents' worth Sir Charles, the eldest —who inherited the baronetcy from his cousin Sir Charles, gentleman of the bedchamber to Frederick, Prince of Wales, dying without issue—became a General in the army and a Knight of the Bath John, the second, who succeeded him in the baronetcy, attained to be Bishop of Clogher William, the third, rose to be an Admiral of the Blue, and was created Baron Hotham for his gallant victory over the French squadron, March, 1795 Beaumont, the youngest, was appointed one of the Barons of the Exchequer, and inheriting the titles of his elder brothers, they have passed through his descendants to the present generation

Waller.

But the Bend was sometimes diminished one-half its size and called a bendlet. This was again sometimes divided into two parts, called cotises, which were sometimes borne with a bend between, or sometimes with some heraldic charge or charges placed bendwise between them.

We have no illustration in glass or stone of this in the Minster now. It was in former days illustrated on a cushion, which has long since passed away; but the historical associations connected with the armorial bearings are so interesting that I cannot allow them to pass away too, but must do what I can to rescue them at least from oblivion.

In Torre's history of the Minster we find the following entry:—"On an old cushion in the quire is embroydered these coats, viz.,

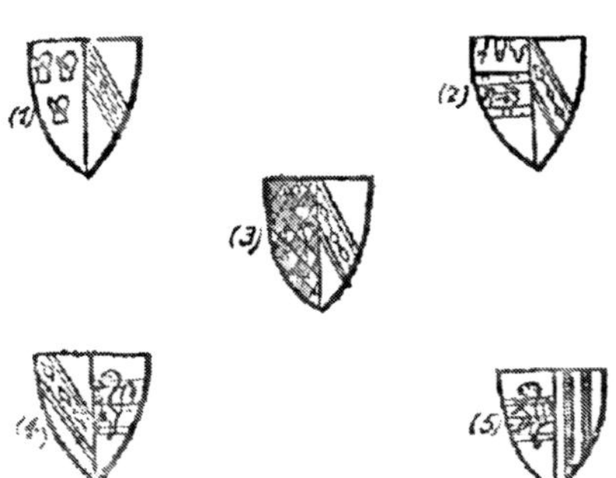

"(1) B, 3 left-hand gauntletts Or, "impaling sable 3 leaves in bend "argent between two cotices O.

"(2) Argent a lyon passant gules "inter 3 barrs sable, thereon 3 be-"zants, and 3 bucks' heads cabossed "sable in chief impaling as No. 1.

"(3) Lozengy gules and varrie im-"paling as No. 1.

"(4) Sable 3 leaves in bend argent "between 2 cotices O, impaling a "lyon rampant sable debruised by 3 barrs gemelles gules.

"(5) The last, impaling paly of 6 Or and B, a canton ermine."

The cushion itself probably perished when the choir was burned, and therefore we have no clue, from this crude illustration and vague description thereof, as to its date or history; we can only surmise as to that. But heraldry enables us to say that 1, 2, 3 of these shields represent female members, and 4 a male member of the Waller family and the families into which they had married; and shield 5 represents the alliance made by some member of one of these families.

The arms on shield 3 seem to be the arms of De Burgh. Those on shields 4 and 5 may be the arms of Maude, for I am assured that there was no such connection with the family of Fairfax, and there was an old Yorkshire family of Maude located at West Riddlesden, which bears the same charges, though differently tinctured. Torre mentions that a certain "Timothy "Maude, M.A., clerk upon the Archbishop's collation, was admitted to this "prebend of Holme Archiep: then vacant by the resignation of Wm. Lister "next preceding, A.D. 1622." The shield, then, No. 5 may be his arms impaling the arms of his wife, Strelly or Shirley, for here again the charges are the same, though the tinctures are different. I am disposed to think that the arms are Shirley, because, in his account of the "Funeral Monuments" of the Minster, Torre says that there was a stone "in the middle choir" to Marmaduke Constable of Wassand, husband of Elizabeth Shirley, who died 1607 So that the Shirleys were evidently connected with York The previous shield, charged with the arms of Waller impaling Maude, may be the arms of his sister, who had married a Waller And possibly Mrs Waller and Mrs Maude may have worked the cushion together—or perhaps the former only, as the achievements of the Waller family are most noted At any rate there is no doubt about the first shield,—it contains the arms of Fane impaling Waller And we find that George Fane, Esq , of Badsell, in the county of Kent, who served the office of sheriff of that county in the 4th and 5th of Philip and Mary, married Joan, daughter of William Waller, of Groombridge

And though it is not easy to understand how the cushion with these arms became connected with York Minster, it is very easy to understand how George Fane and Joan Waller became connected with each other, for Badsell was a fine old mansion in Tudeley parish, now in ruins, but on the entrance-gate there is still the crest of the Fanes, with the date 1581, and Groombridge, the residence of the Wallers, is close by So it was natural there should be an alliance between the two families

I do not know how far George Fane was in favour of Queen Mary At any rate, by his holding the office of sheriff, he dissembled his dislike, even if it were not an evidence of his loyalty His son Thomas, however, boldly expressed his dissatisfaction, and was involved in the rebellion of Sir Thomas Wyatt against her, committed to the Tower, attainted of high treason, and only pardoned and set at liberty after he had been ordered for execution I have seen it somewhere stated that he was so young and good-looking that her Majesty was persuaded not to cut off such a handsome head Queen Elizabeth knighted him, and he married Mary Nevill, daughter and heiress of Lord Abergavenny, who on her father's death claimed the barony of Abergavenny, which was disallowed by the House of Lords, who, however, restored to her, by letters patent, the barony of Le Despencer, which her father had also held, and she retained the ancient castle of Mereworth, close by Thither Thomas Fane went to live, and the old house at Badsell naturally fell into decay, and there his descendants remained (his son having been created Earl of Westmoreland) until 1762, when John, the sixth earl, who had served under Marlborough, died childless, and the title of Le Despencer and the castle of Mereworth went to his nephew, Sir Francis Dashwood, of West Wycombe, the son of his sister, Lady Mary, and the family of Fane retained, with the title of Westmoreland, only Apethorpe in Northampton, which was brought by Mary, daughter and heiress of Sir Anthony Mildmay, when she married the first Earl of Westmoreland

To return, however, to Joan Waller. The history of her family, as indicated in their armorial bearings, is very interesting. The shield is sable, between two cotises or, three walnut leaves argent. This demonstrates the foreign extraction of the founder of the family, for Wal is another form of Walshe or Welche, which simply means a foreigner, *i.e.* one who was not of the Teutonic race.

The walnut is a native of Persia and China, and when first introduced into England it was called "nut," or *the nut par excellence.* But in the fourteenth century it had acquired the name of the ban-nut, from its hardness, and is so mentioned in a metrical vocabulary of that date:—

"Appel-tree, peere-tree, hazel-nute, banne-nute, fygge."

At the same time it had also acquired the name of walnut. "Hæc "Avelana; *Anglicé,* walnut-tree" (vocabulary, fourteenth century). And so Lyte says that the tree is called "the wal-nut and walshe-nut tree." *

Probably, therefore, Alured le Waller, who died in 1183 (*temp.* Hen. II.), or one of his progenitors, was a retainer in the train of some Norman knight, and was known as Alured the Foreigner, or Alured le Waller, which in due time became the family name of his descendants; and when the arms were granted, such a device was chosen (according to the practice of "canting heraldry," to which I have already alluded) as would express the name.

However, Alured's son was Master of the Rolls to Edward III. for thirty years; and from his only brother, Henry, sprang John Waller, who added to the large estates which the family had already acquired in Kent and Sussex, by purchasing from the Clintons the estate of Groombridge, which had once been the property of a younger branch of the ancient family of Cobham, of Cobham in Kent.

His son, Richard, was a soldier in the army of Henry V. when, on St. Crispin's day, 1415, was fought the famous battle of Agincourt.

Fabyan, who lived at the latter end of the same century, in his *Chronicles* shews the wonderful disparity of the forces engaged, men slain, and prisoners taken, on that eventful day. He speaks of King Henry V. as "hauynge in his companye of noble men y[t] myght fyght, not passynge "the nombr of vii M (7,000). But at those dayes the yomen had their "lymmes at lybertie, for their hosen were then fastened w[t] one poynt, and

* *Plant-lore and Garden-craft of Shakespeare.* Rev. H. Ellacombe.

"theyr jackes were longe and easy to shote in, so that they might drawe "bowes of great strentgth and shote arowes of a yerde longe, besyde the "hedes Upon the morrow, the Kynge caused dyuers masses to be songyn "The nyght before, the Englysshe hoost was occupied in prayer and "confession

"And that done, with a comfortable chere ordered his people as they "should fight, hauynge unto them good and comfortable words, and so "abode ye comyng of theyr enemyes, which of dyuers writers were and "are remembered to be aboue xl M fyghtynge men" (40,000)

He estimates the relative loss of that eventful day as follows — "But of Frenchmen were slayne yt day, after Englysshe wryters, over yt "nombr of x M (10,000), of the Englysshe hoost were slayne the Duke of "Yorke and with hym iiii C men (400)

"At the sayd batayll was taken prysoners the Duke of Orleance, "the Duke of Burbon, ye Erles of Vendosme, of Eur, of Rychemont and "Bursigaut, then marshall of Fraunce, with many other knyghtes and "esquyres, which were tedyous to name, to the nomber of xxiii C (2,300) "and aboue, as wytnesseth ye boke of mayres

"And in this batayl were slayne of the nobles of Fraunce the Dukes "of Barre, of Alanson, and of Braban, viii erles, and barons above lxxx, "with other gentylmen in cote armours to the nombre of iii M (3,000) "and aboue" *

Charles, Duke of Orleans, conspicuous amongst these French nobles, though only twenty-five years of age, had been married six years before to Isabel of Valois, the girl-widow of Richard II On the death of her husband she had been detained a close prisoner at Havering-atte-Bower, where she remained until her father had acquiesced in Henry's preposterous claim to retain her jewels and dower, for the sake of restoring to her the peace and comfort of her early home without further delay Strange as it may seem, Henry IV, having caused her husband to be murdered, and taken from her all her dower and jewels, was anxious to betroth her to his son, Henry, Prince of Wales, afterwards Henry V

And there can be no doubt that the young Prince really loved the beautiful girl-widow, and wooed her with great pertinacity But, faithful to the memory of her murdered husband, these offers she sternly and scornfully refused

In the month of July, 1402, Isabella, who had not then completed her fifteenth year, landed in her native country, and three years afterwards defeated the overtures which the English king was even then making to the Royal Council of France (viz, that if her hand was bestowed on his son he would abdicate the throne in his favour), by marrying her cousin, the young Prince Charles of Orleans

* Fabyan's *Chronicles*, p 581

Shortly after his marriage the unhappy feud which had existed between his father, Louis, Duke of Orleans, brother of Charles VI., and his relations, the Dukes of Burgundy, culminated in the assassination of the former. During the life of his uncle, Philip "the Bold," the growing virulence of these dissensions had long been foreboding something of the sort, but on the accession of his cousin, John "the Fearless," to the dukedom, it speedily came to pass. Louis, on obtaining, by an intrigue with the Queen Isabel of Bavaria, the regency of the kingdom from his crazy brother, adopted as his device a hand grasping a club full of knots, with the motto (insinuating the sentiment with which this was regarded by the opposite party), "I envy it."

The Duke of Burgundy, on the other hand, adopted as his device a carpenter's plane, with the Flemish motto, "Je poud," "I plane," *i.e.* "I hold "the means of smoothing the knotted club;" and this he speedily illustrated by appealing to the Parliament, which at once represented to Charles, through his most trusted counsellors, the folly of committing the government to so young a man. On which the King withdrew it from the Duke of Orleans and restored it to the Duke of Burgundy.

In April, 1404, Duke Philip died, and for a time it seemed, from the mutual civilities which passed between them, that harmony had been re-established between the cousins. But on November 23rd, 1407, as the Duke of Orleans was proceeding from the Queen's to the King's apartments, mounted on a mule, accompanied by only two gentlemen and a few valets, he was suddenly assailed by ruffians hired for the purpose by the Duke of Burgundy, headed by one D'Hacquetonville. "I am the Duke of Orleans," he cried, as a sudden blow from a battle-axe missed his head and severed his right hand. "It is you whom we seek," responded the assassins with wild exultation, as they swept him from the saddle and cut him limb from limb, exclaiming, as they completed their bloody work, "See if the knotty mace has not been well smoothed by the plane." *

Valentine Visconti, the Duke of Milan's daughter, was at Château Thierry when she heard of her husband's murder. Gathering all her family round her, she started at once and rode to Paris through the roughest winter known for several centuries. Beautiful and loving, the softness of her nature had given place to poignancy of grief and fierce thirst for vengeance. Dismounting at the door of the hostel of St. Paul, she passed at once with her family to the royal presence, and falling down at the feet of the King, surrounded by his princes and council, demanded the immediate punishment of her husband's murderer. The whole court was moved, and justice immediately promised by the Chancellor in the King's name. But the Duke of Burgundy was successful and powerful, and months passing away in empty promises and delays, her spirit sank under an

* *Tales of a Grandfather* (France). Sir Walter Scott.

overwhelming sense of misery and despair. On the black hangings of her chamber she had embroidered the words, "Rien ne m'est plus; plus ne "m'est rien" ("nought have I more; more hold I nought"): and then on the following December she died of a broken heart.*

The unfortunate Duke Louis and his Duchess Valentine had been very extravagant, and the young Duke Charles found himself encumbered with enormous debts. In order to discharge these honourably, he pledged or sold a quantity of jewels, and refused to take advantage of any pretext, however legally valid, that would lessen the amount.

In memory of his father's death he caused two rings to be made, on one of which was engraven the words, "Dieu le scait" ("God knows it"), and on the other, "Souvenez vous de" ("Remember").

Two years afterwards a reconciliation took place, by the King's command, in the church of Our Lady at Chartres, and Charles and his brother forgave their father's murderer, and swore peace upon the missal, though it was done under protest, and "pour ne pas désobeir au Roi."

But the shadows again gathered, and after a union of only three years, Isabella died a few hours after the birth of her little daughter, eventually Duchess d'Alençon, in 1410.

The tender attachment of the duke for his young wife is touchingly expressed by a poem which he wrote, entitled *J'ai fait l'Obsèques de Madame*, *i.e.* "Madame of France," her title as eldest daughter of the King and wife of the second Prince of France. The following is a translation thereof:—

"To make my lady's obsequies
My love a Minster wrought,
And, in the chantry, service there
Was sung in doleful thought.
The tapers were of burning sighs
That light and odour gave;
And grief, illumined by tears,
Irradiate her grave.
And round about, in quaintest guise,
Was carved, 'Within this tomb there lies
The fairest thing to mortal eyes.'

"Above her lieth spread a tomb
Of gold and sapphires blue;
The gold doth shew her blessedness,
The sapphires mark her true.
For blessedness and truth in her
Were livelily portrayed,
When gracious God, with both His hands,
Her wondrous beauty made.
She was, to speak without disguise,
The fairest thing to mortal eyes.

* Guizot's *History of France*, p. 176.

"No more, no more! My heart doth faint
 When I the life recall
Of her who lived so free from taint,
 So virtuous deemed by all;
Who in herself was so complete,
 I think that she was ta'en
By God to deck His paradise,
 And with His saints to reign;
For well she does become the skies,
Whom while on earth each one did prize,
The fairest thing to mortal eyes." *

Five years of widowhood (even though for state reasons he had entered on a second marriage with Bona, daughter of Bernard, Count d'Armagnac) had not, we may believe, extinguished the grief of such a mourner; and we can well imagine that he took little part in the vain-glorious merriment which Shakespeare describes as pervading the French host the night before the battle.

Perhaps his only longing was that he might by an honourable soldier's death escape from the troubles of life, and find rest with her whom he had so tenderly loved, in the paradise of God.

But the morning came, and with the morning came the battle, which, as the French herald had tauntingly assured Henry the night before, was to result in such a facile victory to France. And foremost amongst the nobles of France was Charles, Duke of Orleans, at the head of his 500 lances, with the arms of his house (Azure three fleurs-de-lys or, and a label of three points argent) emblazoned on the pennon which fluttered over his head, and on the shield which he held to his left side.

I need not tell the old familiar story of Agincourt over again. How the French, vainly confident in their superior numbers, advanced with impetuous valour upon the English archers, who, sheltered behind fixed pallisadoes, safely plied them from that defence with a shower of arrows which nothing could resist. The clay soil, moistened by some rain which had lately fallen, hampered the movements of the cavalry, already impeded by the crowd of men-at-arms on foot who thronged their ranks; the wounded horses disordered their lines; and the rapidly increasing heaps of dead and dying men hindered them in the narrow compass in which they were pent from recovering any order. The whole army was soon a scene of terror, confusion, and dismay. At the command of Henry, the archers threw down their bows, and rushing upon the enemy with their battle-axes, supported by the men-at-arms from behind, covered the field with wounded, dismounted and overthrown, and secured the victory for the English king.†

* Agnes Strickland. *Isabella of Valois.* † Hume.

As soon as the terrible strife had ceased, the first thought of the chivalrous King was to care for the wounded, and to secure such prisoners as might be left helpless on the field. Amongst many engaged in this generous duty was the young English archer, Richard Waller, who, attracted by a faint moan, or by a moving limb, drew out from beneath a heap of the mangled bodies of the slain in the fearful slaughter which had ensued, Charles, Duke of Orleans. Life was not extinct, and, by the efforts of his preserver, he was brought back to an unwelcome existence. As soon as the rank of his captive was discovered, Richard Waller took him at once to the King, who received his lately triumphant, but now fallen, rival with dignified courtesy, and directed that he should be treated with every consideration. On the way to Calais, Henry sent him bread and wine (and bread was then a luxury in the English camp) from his own table, but Charles would neither eat nor drink; nor were his miseries alleviated by a personal visit from the King, who assured him that God had fought against the French on account of their manifold transgressions.

After a tempestuous voyage, in which many of the French nobles declared that they would rather endure another Agincourt, they landed in England; and eventually the triumphant conqueror and his brave army entered London, amidst the clashing of bells, and the shouting of the multitude, and waving banners and scattered flowers. But there was one sad heart amidst all that jubilant multitude, one unwilling participator in that great national pageant—Charles, Duke of Orleans.

Of course, according to the custom of those days, a prisoner could only be liberated by a ransom; and for such a prisoner the ransom must be high, and 300,000 crowns were named as the price of his liberty.

Until the time of its payment, he was committed to the charge of his captor, Richard Waller, who had been knighted, and who received, in addition, the permission to have the shield of his captive, Azure three fleurs-de-lys or, over all a label of three points argent, added to his crest, a walnut tree, with this appropriate motto, "Hæc fructus virtutis."

The generous captor did all in his power to make his country home agreeable to his unwilling guest. The old house, if not entirely rebuilt, was very extensively enlarged and improved. There were frequent hawking and hunting parties, and no lack of money or books. Indeed, the duke, who was no mean poet, wrote several of his most beautiful compositions here. A chivalrous friendship grew up between him and Sir Richard; and Charles so far succeeded in acquiring the language of his host that he wrote a roundel in English. He took an interest in the parish church of Speldhurst.

The building itself was destroyed by lightning many years ago, and rebuilt in memory of the safe return of Prince Charles, afterwards Charles I., from his expedition to Spain; but the arms of the Duke of Orleans still adorn the porch.

He remained at Groombridge for some years, and was then removed to the Tower, where he completed his long captivity in England of twenty-five years. Broken and defeated, France could not easily raise so large a sum as 300,000 crowns.

But Henry V. really preferred his prisoner to the money, for he had married Katherine of Valois, the sister of the young widow who had rejected him, and had thus become brother-in-law to his prisoner, the Duke of Orleans. If the Dauphin died, Henry was assured of the Crown of France, should Charles of Orleans die without male issue; and hence, to gain that summit of the ambition of the Plantagenets, his relative was detained, if not "in durance vile," at least in durance disagreeable. For he said in after years to his son-in-law, the Duke d'Alençon, "I have had "experience myself; and in my prison in England, for the weariness, "danger, and displeasure in which I there lay, I have many a time wished "that I had been slain in the battle when they took me." *

Henry of Agincourt had been dead many years, and the French had recovered nearly the whole of France (thanks to Joan of Arc and to the duke's natural brother, the famous Bastard of Orleans) before Charles's day of liberation came.

One by one the sons of Charles VI. dropped off, leaving no heir to the Crown, and his life became every year more precious. At length deliverance was at hand from a quarter least expected. The vengeance of God had fallen upon the murderer of the late Duke of Orleans.

In 1419 "John the Fearless" had himself been murdered in retaliation by Tanneguy Deuchatel, at Montereau, in the very presence of the Dauphin, afterwards Charles VII. † His son, "Philip the Good," resolved to pay the ransom of the man whose father had been assassinated by his father, and fallen a victim to the house of Burgundy. And he did not rest until, some twenty years after, his noble and generous purpose was carried out, and Charles of Orleans was free.

When he arrived in Paris he found his second wife, Duchess Bona, dead; his daughter, whom he had left a child of five years old, a woman of thirty. Reasons of state compelled him reluctantly to begin life again. He married, for his third wife, Mary of Cleves, by whom he had a son, called Louis in remembrance of his father, who lived to mount the throne of France, and who is known in history as Louis XII.

---

* Mrs. Streatfeild. † Guizot.

In the British Museum there is still a magnificent copy of Charles's poems, given by our King Henry VII to Elizabeth of York on their marriage, and on one of the pages there is a large illumination, which is almost a history of the latter part of his imprisonment Here is a view of London with all its spires—the river, passing through the old bridge, busy with boats One side of the white Tower has been taken out, and we can see, as under a sort of shrine, the paved room in which the duke sits writing He occupies a high-backed bench in front of a great chimney Red and black ink are before him, and the upper end of the apartment is guarded by many halberdiers with the red cross of England on their breasts On the next side of the Tower he appears again, leaning out of a window and gazing on the river Doubtless there blows just then "a pleasant wind "from the land of France," and some ship is coming up the stream Is it the "ship of good news"? Another scene represents him at the door embracing a messenger, while a groom stands by holding two saddle-horses And, yet further to the left, a cavalcade defiles out of the Tower The duke is on his way at last to "the sunshine of France"

The following quaint extract is from *The Paston Letters* The letter is written by Robert Repps, dated All Saints' day, Tuesday, 1st November, 1440, 19th Henry VI, addressed "To my Right Reverend and Right "Honourable Master, John Paston, be this given

"Salvete se Tytyings [tidings] The Duk of Orleyaunce hath made "his oath upon the Sacrements, and usyd it (never for to bere armes agenst "England) in the p'sence of the Kyng and all the lordes excepting my "Lord Glouc' and in p'oying [proving] my sayde Lord of Glouc' agreyed "nevr to hys delyvraunce, gwan [when] the masse began he toke hys "barge God gef grace the seide Lord of Orleyaunce [Orleans] be trewe, "for this same weke shall he toward France"

"NOTE Henry V, on his deathbed, had ordered that this duke should "not be released *till a peace with France was concluded*, and the Duke of "Gloucester not only now protested against his enlargement, but had his "protest recorded"

Groombridge remained the home of the Wallers for more than a century In 1516 died John Waller, leaving two sons, William, whose daughter, Joanne, married George Fane of Badsell, already mentioned, and John, who was ancestor of the Wallers of Beaconsfield, from which branch was descended Edmund Waller the poet

William was sheriff of the county in the reign of Henry VIII, and died 1555 His grandson, Walter, was knighted, and died leaving two sons George, who married Mary, the daughter of Richard Hardres, and had one son, Sir Hardres Waller, born 1604, major-general in the Parliamentary army, and one of the regicides, for which he was, after the

Restoration, tried and condemned, but was, "through the King's mercy, "pardoned," and resided at Castletown near Limerick.

The other son, Thomas, married Margaret, sister of Henry Lennard, Lord Dacre. He, too, was knighted, and made lieutenant of Dover Castle in the reign of James I. But he alienated the home of his fathers to Thomas Sackville, Earl of Dorset, who died suddenly 1608. His grandson, Richard, sold the estate to John Packer, Clerk of the Privy Seal to Charles I., who rebuilt the little chapel, as I have mentioned, and placed this inscription over the door:—"D. O. M. S. Ob felicissimum Caroli "Principis ex Hispaniis reditum sacellum hoc. DD 1625. I.P."

His son, Philip, was the friend of John Evelyn, and married the daughter of Sir Robert Berkeley of Spetchley, "that honest judge," as Evelyn calls him, "who, when the Puritans burned down his house at "Spetchley, nothing daunted, converted his stables into a dwelling, and "lived there with content, and even dignity, to the end of his days."

Under the advice of Evelyn, who had just returned from his foreign tour, and was enamoured of the classic style of architecture, the old stronghold of Groombregge was rased to the ground, and the present mansion, in the form of an H, built in its stead. His grandson, Philip, died 1697, leaving one son and two daughters. The former had no children; the latter, marrying, entitled their heirs to the place and manor.

I suppose there were disagreements as to its possession, for, eventually, it got into the court of Chancery, and having been purchased by William Camfield, was sold on his death, in 1781, to Robert Burges, from whom it descended to the late Rev. Mr. Saint, who once kindly received me at this most interesting house, and to whose daughter, Mrs. Charles Streatfeild, I am indebted for much of the information concerning the Wallers.

The old broad deep moat still remains, abundantly supplied with water by a trout-stream which flows through the garden, and falls, in a picturesque cascade, through an archway leading to the moat.

Traces of the ancient structure may be observed in the basement of the house, which, with its wide portico supported by pillars of stone, depicted in the background of the portrait of Philip Packer within, exhibits all the characteristics of the Stuart period.

The garden still bears its ancient character. It is enclosed on all sides with brick and stone walls, mellowed into a variety of beautiful tints by time, and by the soft grey lichen with which they are covered. The stately walks, the broad green terraces, the trim hedges of yew and laurel, carry the mind back to the time when Evelyn planned and laid out the gardens and walked therein. It is indeed, what he has himself described, "a pretty, melancholy seat, well wooded and watered."

The shady trees, the green meadows, all add an aspect of grace and beauty to this bijou mansion, snugly nestled under a steep wooded hill

The railway is close by, but few passengers, as they rush through the station, or hear "Speldhurst!" called out in the usual incoherent lingo of railway officials, have any idea how much picturesque beauty or historic interest and sweet sentiment are at hand

It is instinct with touching memories, not the least of the gallant prisoner and his brave captor, who met as enemies, lived as friends, and now rest in peace

"The knights are dust, their good swords rust,
Their souls are with the saints, we trust"

De Bohun

The shield of De Bohun* supplies an illustration of great heraldic and historical interest

As regards the former, it is not only an example of the division of the bend into cotises, which are one-half of the bendlet (itself one-half of the bend), but it is also an example of compounding arms, *i e* of an usage practised in the early days of heraldry (before "marshalling" or arranging complete coats-of-arms on one shield by quartering was established), when the desired combination was made by forming a new composition from all the charges of the several shields, or from the most important and characteristic of them †

The founder of the De Bohuns as an English family, was a Humphrey de Bohun, one of the fortunate adventurers at Hastings, known amongst his companions, the close-shaven Normans, as "Humphrey with the beard" (Dugdale) His son married Matilda, daughter of the feudal baron, Edward de Sarum, descendant of William de Longespee, son of Henry II and Fair Rosamond, whose arms were six lioncels rampant

Their son, Humphrey, steward and sewer to Henry I, married Margeria, one of the co-heiresses of Milo, Constable, and Lord of Gloucester and Hereford, who bore gules, two bends, the one or, the other argent Their grandson, Henry de Bohun, was in 1199 made Earl of Hereford by charter of King John He thereupon adopted as his arms a coat compounded by dividing the gold bend into four bendlets, and cotised the silver bend by placing two of them on either side thereof, grouping three of the six lions of Sarum also on either side.

Henry de Bohun married Maud, sister and co-heir of William de Mandeville, Earl of Essex, and with her he acquired the cognizance of the Mandevilles, so frequently afterwards associated with the De Bohuns (viz

---

* See coloured illustration † Boutell's *Heraldry*

a swan, close, argent, beaked and legged or, gorged with a crown, and chained of the last), together with the earldom of Essex, and the manor of Enfield near London.

Edward I. granted a license for a weekly market to be held here, which, in the reign of James I., had acquired the name of the "Court of "pie powder."

Richard II. granted to the inhabitants certain exemptions of the tolls for their goods; and, in 1347, Humphrey de Bohun procured the King's license to fortify his manor-house at Enfield. The site of this original manor-house has long been a subject for antiquarian research, for Camden says that "almost in the middle of the chase there are the ruins and "rubbish of an ancient house, which the commoner people from tradition "affirm to have belonged to the Mandevilles, Earls of Essex;" and, from the traces of the site still left, it must have been of considerable extent, as, when measured in 1773, one side of the moat was 150 feet.

Humphrey, second earl, was a crusader, and fought, together with his eldest son, Humphrey, who died *vita patris*, on the side of the barons against the King at the battle of Evesham, 1265.

In 1243 he founded an Augustinian convent in London, the site of which is where Broad Street falls into Throgmorton Street, and is now known as "Austin Friars." Humphrey himself was buried here; also Edward Bohun (or Stafford), Duke of Buckingham, beheaded 1521.

It was granted at the dissolution to William Paulet, first Marquis of Winchester; but the church was retained, and granted by Edward VI. to the Dutch nation in London to have their service in, by whom the building is still held. The marquis built a house there known as Winchester House, and only pulled down in 1839. He lived to a great age, and during the reigns of nine sovereigns. When asked in his old age how he had contrived to get on so well with them all, he said, "By being a willow, "not an oak." *

His grandson, Humphrey, third earl, was Lord High Constable, and attended Edward I. in Scotland, as did also his son Humphrey, fourth earl, who was present at the siege of Caerlaverock. The old poet "Walter of Exeter" thus describes him:—"A rich and elegant young man. He had "a banner of deep blue silk, with a white bend between two cotises of gold, "on the outside of which he had six lioncels rampant." He mentions him also at the conclusion of the siege, as accompanying the royal banner with his own banner, by established rights, as constable.

His seal also appears appended to the letter of the barons to Pope Boniface. He married Elizabeth Plantagenet, daughter of the King and widow of John, Earl of Holland.

* *Walks in London* (Augustus Hare), vol. i. p. 277. Walford's *Greater London*.

He seems, however, to have been rather fickle in his allegiance, for in the succeeding reign (Edward II) he joined Thomas Earl of Lancaster, in his insurrection for the redress of certain grievances and the banishment of the King's favourites

After the murder of Piers Gaveston a reconciliation was effected between him and his brother-in-law, Edward II, who sent him from York to guard the Marches of Scotland He was with the King at the battle of Bannockburn, where he was taken prisoner when flying from the field after the English army had been routed He was eventually exchanged for the wife of Robert Brus, who had been long in captivity in England He joined Thomas of Lancaster again, however, and having forced the King to agree to their demands, published the edict for the banishment of the Despencers in Westminster Hall He was ultimately slain at the battle of Boroughbridge, March 16th, 1322, five years after the death of his wife, who was buried at the abbey of Walden, in Essex, where many of the De Bohuns are interred In the journal of the Archæological Institute (vol ii p 338) his will is printed, made at Gosforth, near Newcastle, on his way to Scotland His body was buried at York

John, his eldest son, seems to have been early invalided, and died He was succeeded by his brother Edward, who was one of those who accompanied Edward III, his first cousin, when, by the connivance of Sir William Elland, governor of Nottingham Castle, he was admitted at midnight through a subterranean passage, long disused and forgotten, to the apartments inhabited by Queen Isabella and her paramour, Mortimer They found him conversing with the Bishop of Lincoln and a number of his friends, but, though stout resistance was made by Sir Hugh Turpleton and Richard Monmouth, he was overpowered and taken away, while the voice of Isabella was heard from a neighbouring chamber exclaiming, "Beau fils, beau fils, ayez pitie du gentil Mortimer!" Mortimer was afterwards hung, either on the elms or under the elms, on the banks of the Ty-bourn or Tyburn—the first execution on that afterwards notorious spot —the gallows being removed here from St Giles pound, which continued to be the place of the public execution for 450 years, the last criminal suffering there being one Ryland, who was hung for forgery, 1783 (Walford's *Old and New London*)

Edward died without issue His younger brother, Humphrey, the sixth earl, was one of the warlike companions of Edward III, and he assisted at the celebrated feasts and jousts which the King held in London in honour of Elizabeth Montacute, Countess of Salisbury, daughter and co-heir of Lord Mohun of Dunster, with whom the King was much smitten, and when, under circumstances which I need not repeat, "the order of the "Garter was established," and Camden says of this old story, "Hæc vulgus "perhibet, nec vilis sane hæc videatur origo, cum nobilitas sub amore jacet"

The author of *Heraldic Anomalies* gives another reason. He says Edward III., being engaged in a war with France for the obtaining of that Crown, in order to draw into England great multitudes of foreigners with whom he might negotiate for aid and support, appointed a tournament to be holden at Windsor, in imitation of King Arthur's round table, at which all his illustrious guests were to be entertained.

But King Philip of France, suspecting his design, caused a like tournament to be proclaimed in his own dominions, which, meeting with success, proved a counter-mine to Edward's original plan, and induced him to turn his thoughts from it to the institution of a new order of knighthood. To signify the purity of his intentions, and to bring shame on those who should put any malignant interpretation on his proceedings, he chose for his motto, "Honi soit qui mal y pense"—which is not ill-treated in the dramatic poem on the institution, to be found in Dodsley's collection, thus—

> "Ashamed be he who with malignant eye
> So reads my purpose."

The Earl never married, and was succeeded by his nephew, Humphrey, who married Joan, daughter of the Earl of Arundel, but died young, at the age of thirty-two, leaving only two daughters, Eleanor and Mary, sole heiresses of his estates, valued at 5,000 nobles a year. Eleanor was married to Prince Thomas of Woodstock, son of Edward III., Earl of Buckingham, and, in her right, Earl of Essex, and subsequently Duke of Gloucester. If Mary died childless, the whole of the estates would devolve upon his posterity, and he was quite alive enough to his interests to keep her unmarried.

He, therefore, having obtained permission from his elder brother, John of Gaunt, her guardian, to have her under his control, placed around her the nuns of the order of St. Clare, and took all possible pains to give her mind a religious bias. But he went on a warlike expedition to France, and during his absence John of Gaunt conceived the idea that the young lady would make an excellent wife for his son, Henry Earl of Derby.

But how to accomplish this,—for Mary had been left under the care of her sister, the Countess of Buckingham, the person of all others least likely to promote the success of the scheme, at Pleshy Castle.

Pleshy Castle was another, and perhaps the principal, among the many seats of the Earls of Essex and Hereford, and for this reason, I suppose, had become the residence of the elder sister. It, or rather the ruin of it, is situated in Essex, near Romford. It had been a fortress in the time of the Romans, and its stupendous keep, wide ditch, and magnificent bridge of a single arch, still remain. Its site is high and its prospect agreeable, from which it is said to have derived its name "Castellum "de Placeto." The father of the late Earl had added 150 acres to the park, which, down to 1516, was called "the great park" And it is recorded that when Queen Elizabeth was here, she had a new chariot (purchased in France by a clerk sent over for that purpose), to enable her to roam about at pleasure therein

Here the young lady was, her brother-in-law fondly imagined, safely immured But Lady Mary Fitz-Alan, their maternal aunt, was induced to enter the plot, and she, having paid the ladies a visit at Pleshy Castle, persuaded the younger one to accompany her to Arundel Castle, the residence of her uncle There John of Gaunt, Duke of Lancaster, and his son, the Earl of Derby, were already guests, and the young and inexperienced girl was soon fascinated by the young man, who is described as then a gay and gallant youth, endowed with every accomplishment A few days effected a sudden revolution in the destiny of Mary de Bohun, and the destined nun became the bride of one of the handsomest cavaliers in Europe

Vehement, though fruitless, was the indignation of the Earl of Buckingham when, on his return, he discovered the trick which his brother and nephew had played upon him, and it is said that he "became melancholy, "and never loved the Duke of Lancaster as he had before done"

The Earl and Countess of Derby lived at Peterborough Castle, where her literary attainments and love of music, and her skill in playing the guitar, rendered her very popular Minstrels, whether English or foreign, were always welcomed when they presented themselves before the gate, and handsomely rewarded for their performance *

Four sons and two daughters were born in the course of a brief but happy wedlock, but, soon after the birth of the two daughters, Philippa, the countess, died in July, 1394, at the early age of 26

Four years later, 1398, "Old John of Gaunt, time-honoured Lancaster," was dead, the weak and unfortunate Richard II was deposed, and the Earl of Derby elevated to the throne as Henry IV

His after-life and character seem rather a contrast to the tenderness and love of that young wedded life Perhaps it was as well for Mary de Bohun that she was thus early "taken away from the evil to come," for she was a good woman, distinguished for her devotion to her religion, and her memory was fondly cherished by her son, Henry V Two months after his accession to the throne, he caused an image of her, newly devised and made, to be placed over her tomb at Leicester, and in the higher, nobler traits of his character, I venture to trace qualities derived from his mother Perhaps, if she had lived, she would have supplied the influence which was so terribly lacking in his earlier years At any rate we may condone, for the want of this, that course of conduct which seems so unworthy of the heir of a throne

---

* *History of Blanche, daughter of Henry IV* (E Green), vol iii p 306.

But I doubt whether the lot of her elder sister, Eleanor, was more enviable, for her life, if prolonged, must have been a very troubled one.

On November 12th, 1385, Richard II. made his uncle, her husband, Duke of Gloucester, by girding him with a sword and placing a cap upon his head, at Hoselow Lodge in Tividale.* But his ambitious disposition caused him to take advantage of the dissatisfaction created by his nephew's indolent, low, and dissolute habits.

He courted the friendship of every one actuated by private resentment and disappointment, and encouraged the vulgar prejudices of those who compared the military glories of the late reign with the sensuous inactivity of the present. According to Froissart, he proposed to Roger Mortimer, Earl of March, whom Richard had declared his successor, to place him at once on the throne; and, when he declined the project, he resolved to divide the kingdom between himself, his two brothers, and the Earl of Arundel.

His treason, of course, leaked out, and King Richard, becoming acquainted with his designs, acted for once with something like his father's promptitude, though with a treachery alien to his generous nature.

He rode over from Havering-atte-Bower, as it were on a hunting party, and came to Pleshy, where the duke resided, about five o'clock. The duke, who had just newly supped, hearing of his coming, met him, with the duchess and children, in the court, and ordered a table to be prepared for the King's supper. In the course of the meal the King casually informed his uncle of a great gathering of the Londoners about to take place the following day, when the Dukes of Lancaster and York would be present, and at which he desired his counsel. He invited him to ride on with him that night to London, leaving his steward to follow with his train, so that they might discuss the matter on the way together. The unsuspecting Duke complied, and, with only seven servants, accompanied the King.

Richard rode at a rapid pace, avoiding the ordinary road, and taking the route by Bondelay and Stratford. When near the latter place, he set spurs to his horse, leaving his uncle behind. At the same moment the Earl Marshal with a band of men appeared from an ambuscade, seized him (calling in vain upon the King, who rode on unheeding), carried him to the river close by, placed him on board a ship which was lying in the Thames, and conveyed him to Calais.

There he was immured in the castle, and, Froissart says, murdered one night after dinner by four men "suddenly casting a towel round his "neck and strangling him."

John Hall, a servant of the Earl Marshal, who was afterwards hanged at Tyburn in the 1st year of Henry IV., for his share in the matter, declared

* Burke's *Extinct and Dormant Peerage.*

that he was instigated thereto by the Duke of Norfolk and Edward Plantagenet, Earl of Rutland (afterwards Duke of York), who assured him that "the King had given charge that he should be smothered," and that the Duke of Gloucester was brought to a "certain hostel called Prince's "Inn," and there smothered between two feather beds

His body was conveyed to Pleshy for burial in a tomb which he had prepared during his lifetime, and, later, removed to Westminster Abbey, and interred upon the south side of the shrine of Edward the Confessor

He left one son, who was imprisoned by the King in the castle of Trim in Ireland, and who died at Chester, on his way to London, after his release by Henry IV

Anne, his daughter, married two brothers in succession, Thomas and Edmund, Earls of Stafford, by the latter of whom she had a son, the ancestor of a long line of Dukes of Buckingham, and thirdly, William Bouchier, Earl of Eu in Normandy, from whom the late Duke of Buckingham, and many others, have derived their claim to bear the Plantagenet arms.

Lady Eleanor, his widow, died a nun, 3rd October, 1399, having survived her sister five years,—thankfully seeking refuge in the cloister from troubles and sorrows which, common to all stations and all times, seem specially sharp and bitter in the rough times of which we are speaking

The property at Enfield was inherited by her sister Mary, and thus became vested in the Crown, and annexed to the Duchy of Lancaster

In the reign of Henry VIII, the house was retained as a royal residence Here Edward VI was living while Prince of Wales, and was hailed by the Scottish prisoners, after the defeat of Solway Firth, as the future husband of the infant Princess Mary of Scotland, eventually the unfortunate Mary Queen of Scots

Truly "man proposes and God disposes" How differently would the history of England have been written had this project come to pass, had that young, precocious life been spared to ascend the throne of England, had that frivolous, but not unkindly, nature been united to one whose vigorous character and strong religious convictions might have influenced her for good, and saved her—from the unhappy life which afterwards awaited her,—from her weakness under the temptations of unprincipled and designing libertines,—and from the hard, rancorous persecutions of narrow-minded, intolerant men

From hence Edward went to London on his accession to the throne The Earl of Hertford dates his letter to the Council "From Envild this "Sunday night att xj of the clok," and says, "We intend the King's "Ma'tie shall be a-horsbak to-morrow by xj of the clok, so that by iij we "trust his Grace shall be att the town"

Here, when Edward was dead, the same Earl of Hertford confidentially communicated to the Master of the Horse his intention to assume the office of Protector, in contravention of the late King's will, which had designated eighteen executors with equal powers.

Here Elizabeth resided from September 8th to 22nd, and again from July 25th to 30th, 1564, and again in 1568, and received a visit from Katherine Parr, the house having been settled upon her when princess by her brother, Edward VI.

But in 1608 a great part of the house was demolished to build the palace which James I. was erecting at Theobalds—that earthly paradise, in his eyes, for which he had lately exchanged King's Hatfield with Robert Cecil, first Earl of Salisbury, second son of the great Lord Burghleigh.

From 1600 to 1623 it was leased to Lord William Howard. In 1629 it was granted by Charles I. to Edward Ditchfield, and afterwards conveyed by him to Sir Nicholas Raynton.

In 1660 it was the residence of Dr. Robert Uvedall, master of the grammar-school, celebrated in those days as a botanist.

As a prophylatic against the plague he used (and apparently with success) the following "preventive." He "caused a brick to be put into "the fire overnight, and the next morning, when red-hot, poured a quart "of vinegar on it, and placed it in the middle of the hall floor, the steam "of which was received by the whole family standing round. They then "went to prayers; afterwards, locking up the house, walked to Winchmore "Hill, and on their return went to school. By this precaution not one of "the family caught the infection."

What still remains of the house is almost obscured from public view by houses and shops built in front of it, and bears nothing externally to denote any semblance of the residence of royalty.

The interior preserves some vestiges of its ancient magnificence, viz., part of a large room with its fine fretted panels of oak, and its ornamental ceiling with pendants of four spreading leaves and enrichments of the crown, the rose, and the fleur-de-lys; and also a chimney-piece of stone, beautifully cut, and supported by Ionic and Corinthian columns, decorated with foliage and birds, and the rose and portcullis crowned with the arms of France and England quarterly in a garter, and the royal supporters, a lion and a dragon. Below is the motto, "Sola salus servire Deo: sunt "cætera fraudes," with the monogram E. R., clearly that of Edward VI. Upon another part of the chimney-piece are the words, "Ut ros super "herbam, est benevolentia regis" ("The King's favour is as the dew upon "the grass"—*Prov.* xix. 12).

Let us say "Amen" to the pious aspiration of the young prince, and add this, as expressing our sentiment after considering the vicissitudes of these once great families—

"Sic transit gloria mundi."

THE CHEVRON.

"None of the ordinaries have so uncertain an origin as the chevron," says Dallaway (*Heraldic Enquiries*), "which is so called from its expansion like the roof of a "house, to which etymology Legh inclines when speaking of a person who bore "three chevronells: 'the auncestor of this cote hath builded three grete houses "'in one province.' It has likewise been referred to the tiara or head-dress of "women, but the *Glossary* of Furetiere confirms the above."

CLARE.

THE shield of Clare, then, Or three chevronels gules,*—which may be noticed in the *vestibule*, third window, west; *Chapter House*, north and north-east windows; *Nave*, south side, second window, east,—opens a subject of great historical and local interest. I do not know to what "houses" Legh alluded, but as this represents the combination of three great houses, he probably supplies the significance of the charges thereon, and it is interesting to notice it.

Richard Fitzgilbert, Earl of Brion in Normandy, whose grandfather, Geoffry, was natural son of Richard I., Duke of Normandy, came over with the Conqueror, and receiving as his share many manors in Surrey, Essex, Cambridgeshire, as well as ninety-five in Suffolk, one of which was the Manor of Clare, from which he was styled Richard de Clare, he exchanged his castle of Brion (or Brionne) with the Archbishop of Canterbury for the town and castle of Tonebruge in Kent, now called Tunbridge. This is the *first house*. He would seem to have borne for his arms, Argent, on a fess azure, three cross crosslets fitchée of the field.

This view of the subject is, I think, borne out by the fact that on the tomb of Richard de Clare, his grandson, second Earl of Pembroke, surnamed Strongbow, in Christ Church Cathedral, Dublin, there is a recumbent figure of a man in armour of banded ringmail, and on "the head a peculiar "carveliere or coif de fer—a skull-cap of steel, curiously indented at the "apex." The knees are protected by nine genouillières of plate. The spurs are broad-rowelled; and on the heater-shaped shield, carried on the left arm, is the above device, which were probably the arms of Fitz-Gilbert.

* See coloured illustration.

The Rev. James Graves, the writer of three articles in the *Gentleman's Magazine* for 1865, devotes several paragraphs to prove that this could not have been the original figure, because it does not bear the three chevronels of De Clare, but that it is a figure from a monument of the Earl of Desmond, which was at Drogheda, removed here by Sir Henry Sydney, Lord Deputy, in 1562, when the roof, south wall, and part of the body of the church fell, demolishing Earl Richard's monument so completely that another effigy had to be substituted for the original one. Papworth, however, gives these arms to "Clare Pembroke, Strongbow, *i.e.* Gilbert and "Richard de Clare, Earls of Pembroke, 1138–76."

His son Gilbert, who seems to have been alternately the friend and the enemy of William Rufus, married Adeliza, daughter of the Earl of Claremont; by which alliance, I conclude, he added the *second house*, and possibly thereby acquired the arms, Argent a Canton gules, which are always known as "Old Clare," and which are in the nave, north side, second window, west.* He seems to have been created Earl of Hertford, and his brother Gilbert, Earl of Pembroke, by King Stephen in 1138.

Sandford, in his *Genealogical History*, p. 220, speaking of Lionel, third son of Edward III., Duke of Clarence, who had married Elizabeth de Burgh, "having also with her the honour of Clare, in the county of Suffolk, as "parcel of the inheritance of her grandmother, Elizabeth, the sister and "co-heiress of the last Earl Gilbert de Clare," says he distinguished "his "arms by a label of three points argent, each charged with a canton "gules; argent a canton gules being a coat attributed to the Clares, and "is placed in the first quarter with three chevrons, as appeareth upon the "covering of a tomb of Gilbert de Clare, Earl of Gloucester, in the abbey "at Tewksbury."

Richard de Clare, Earl of Hertford, great-grandson of Richard, first Earl, married Amicia, the second of the three daughters (co-heiress and survivor) of William Earl of Gloucester, which would make the *third house*. Several of the shields at Tewksbury carry three clarions, which are always attributed to Robert Earl of Gloucester, natural son of Henry I., who married Maud, the daughter of Fitz-Hamon, Lord of Gloucester, the founder of the Abbey, and whose granddaughter and heiress married Robert de Clare, fourth Earl of Hertford.

These, then, would represent the three houses; and it is quite possible that Gilbert de Clare, fifth Earl of Hertford, when on the death of his two aunts, Isabel and Mabile, he became Earl of Gloucester, in right of his mother Amicia, assumed this new coat in token of his having united in himself the three houses of Tonebruge, Clermont, and Gloucester.

* See coloured illustration.

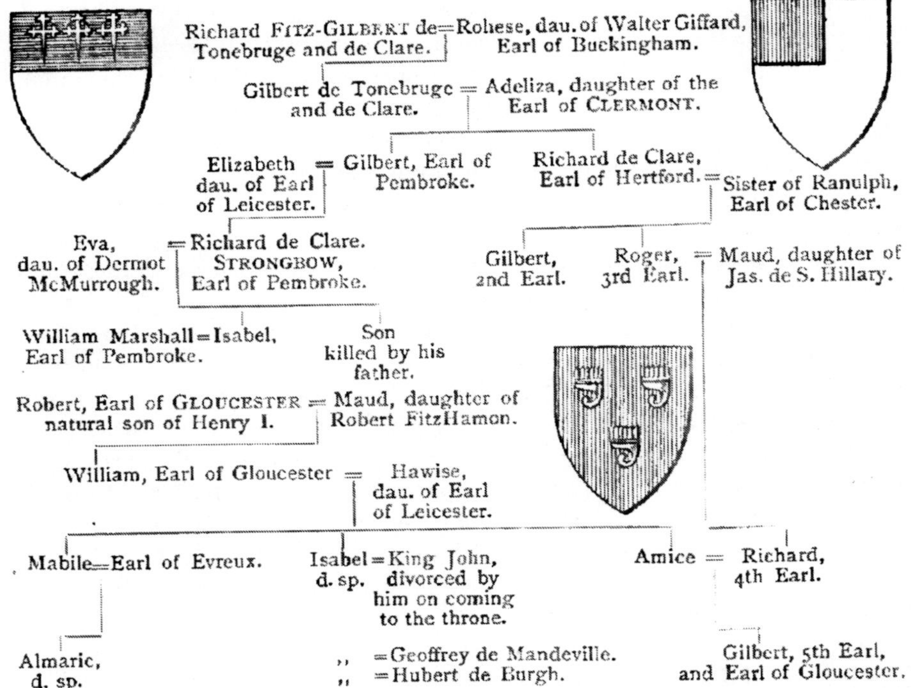

Gloucester also claims to be the resting-place of Strongbow, for there is an inscription on the wall of the chapter-house there to this effect:—"Hic jacet Richardus Strongbow, filius Gilberti, Comitis de Pembroke." However, wherever he was buried, his line seems to have ended with him, and his title and property to have gone to William Marshall, who married his only daughter, Isabel. He had one son, of whose untimely fate the following story is recorded.

"Being a youth of seventeen, who, frighted with the numbers and "ululations of the Irish in a great battle, he ran away, but being after-"wards informed of his father's victory, he joyfully returned to congratulate "him. But the severe general, having first upbraided him with his "cowardice, caused him to be immediately executed by cutting him in "sunder with a sword."

This is alluded to in the epitaph said to be on the tomb of Strongbow in Dublin:—

> "Nate ingrate, mihi pugnanti terga dediste
> *Non mihi, sed genti, regno quoque terga dedisti.*"

Of the elder branch, Gilbert de Clare, Earl of Gloucester, was amongst the principal barons who took up arms against King John, and was appointed one of the twenty-five chosen to enforce the observance of Magna Charta.

He died in 1229, and was succeeded by his son, Richard de Clare, who married Maude, daughter of John de Lacy, Earl of Lincoln. The Earl of Gloucester seems to have been employed on some important missions by the King, and was one of the barons assembled in Westminster Hall when Boniface, Archbishop of Canterbury, with other prelates, pronounced a solemn curse against all who should henceforth violate Magna Charta. His memory is rather notorious for a "mauvais pleasantrie" upon an unfortunate Jew, who having fallen into a cesspool, declined to be pulled out because it was the Jewish sabbath; upon which the Earl forbade him to be pulled out the following day because it was the Christian sabbath, and so the conscientious Israelite perished.

The Earl himself died the next year, 1262, having been poisoned at the table of Peter de Savoy, the Queen's uncle, with Baldwin, Earl of Devon, and others.

His son, Gilbert de Clare, seventh Earl of Hertford and third Earl of Gloucester, married Alice, daughter of Guy, Earl of Angoulesme, and niece of the King of France. He seems at first to have taken part with the barons against Henry III., who besieged and captured his castle at the battle of Lewes. However, the King was defeated, and surrendered himself prisoner to the Earl of Gloucester.

Becoming, however, dissatisfied with Simon de Montfort's conduct, he connived at the escape of Prince Edward (who had generously given himself up in exchange for his father) by supplying him with a swift horse to mount after he had tired out his own and his attendants' in previous races, and returned to his allegiance. He commanded the second brigade of the royal army at the battle of Evesham, which restored the kingly power to its former lustre. His future allegiance was, however, fickle, until his demands were satisfied by the confirmation to him of his paternal estates.

On the death of Henry he boldly stepped forward, and placing his hand on the heart of the deceased monarch, lying in state at Westminster, swore fealty to the absent Prince Edward in the Holy Land, joined in the proclamation of Edward I., and was one of those who received him on landing from the Holy Land, entertaining him with great magnificence at Tonbridge Castle. Thirteen years after, he divorced his wife Alice, the French princess, and married, at Westminster, in 1289, Joane of Acre, daughter of the King (*Archæologia Cantiana*, vol. xvi.).

After the defeat and death of the Earl of Leicester, Gilbert de Clare had become decidedly the first peer in the kingdom. Matthew of Westminster tells us that he was only inferior in power and dignity to the King himself; and Edward was anxious to form a substantial bond of union between himself and his restless subject.

The Earl, as a token of his loyalty, resigned into the King's hands the whole of his estates in England, Wales, and Ireland, which were re-settled on Joane and her children But the King, considering that by his marriage he became third in succession to the Crown, required him to take an oath of fidelity towards himself and his son Edward, a deed being drawn up to this effect, and six bishops affixing their seals thereto

After their marriage the bride and bridegroom left his court, much to the disgust of the King and Queen, who kept back part of the bride's wardrobe in consequence, and lived at St John's Priory in Clerkenwell, where, in 1265, Edward had spent his honeymoon, and of which Fitz-Stephen, who wrote 1190, says—"In the north of London are choice "fountains of waters, sweet, wholesome, and clear, streaming forth among "glittering pebbles, one of which is called Fons Clericorum, or Clerk's-"well, because in the evening the youths and students of the city are "wont to stroll out thither to take the air and taste the waters of the "fountain" A priory of the knights of St John of Jerusalem stood there, also a priory of nuns Cromwell, in his history of Clerkenwell, says that possibly England hardly offered a scene more rich in picturesque situation On every side but that of the city was spread wooded hills, whilst the river Holeburne (Holborn), whose banks were then clothed with vines, wound amongst romantic steeps and secluded dells towards the west At the dissolution the nunnery became the property of the Cavendish family, and the priory was sold to John Dudley, Viscount Lisle, for £1,000 (Thornbury, *Old and New London*, vol ii)

After a short married life the Earl died 1295, at the castle of Monmouth, aged fifty-five, and was buried at Tewksbury

In one short year after the death of the Red Earl, his young widow, the Princess Joane, contracted a clandestine alliance with Ralph de Monthermer, a young and handsome esquire who had been in the service of the late Earl, and requesting for him knighthood at her father's hands, the old King broke out into a furious invective at her hasty mesalliance, committed the bridegroom to Bristol Castle, and seized his daughter's estates At her urgent entreaties, however, supported by the kind offices of Anthony Bek, Bishop of Durham, he relented, released the young squire, took him into his service, and, as he shewed much valour in an expedition with him in Flanders, created him (1307) Baron Monthermer Moreover, he restored Tonbridge Castle to his daughter, and sent the young Prince Edward, her brother, to be there under her care What characteristic traits of this warm-hearted, high-spirited man!

But there must have been something very conducive to love-making in the stately halls and shady glades thereof, as Eleanor de Clare, the eldest daughter, speedily married Sir Hugh le Despencer, the eldest son of the great baron of that name, whose castle of Mereworth was not far distant; while Elizabeth, another daughter, contracted a secret marriage with one Theodore de Verdun,—which second mesalliance so enraged the King that he put him into Bristol Castle, from whence he in like manner was liberated by the intercession of the now favourite Monthermer.

And as regards Margaret, the third daughter,—Piers de Gaveston, a handsome Gascon youth, had been selected by the King as a companion and friend for his son Edward, and was with him at Tonbridge. A high-spirited, thoughtless boy, he encouraged rather than controlled the prince in his wildness; and having instigated him to break into the park of Bishop Langton, of Coventry, and kill some deer, was banished the country, while Edward returned to his sister at Tonbridge. However, in 1307 the King died, and Edward, now Edward II., lost no time in recalling his former friend. Can we not imagine at whose tender pleading? for, as soon as he returned, he was married to the Lady Margaret, and created by the King at the same time warder of the vast estates of his young brother-in-law, Gilbert de Clare, Earl of Gloucester, with the earldom of Cornwall.

There is something very sad and touching in the after-history of these young people. The next year the young Earl of Gloucester married Maud, daughter of Richard de Burgh, Earl of Ulster—a very promising and suitable alliance. But in six years, viz., June 24th, 1314, the disastrous battle of Bannockburn took place, where, fighting in behalf of his uncle and King amidst the *elite* of the knights of England, he fell pierced by a score of lances. Sandford (in his *Genealogical History*) says that "the Scots would "gladly have ransomed him, but he had that day neglected to put his "surcoat of arms over his armour. King Robert Bruce caused the bodies "of Earl Gilbert and Sir Robert Clifford to be sent to King Edward, "being then at Berwick, to be buried at his pleasure, demanding no reward "for the same."

This Sir Robert, Baron de Clifford, had married Maud, daughter and co-heiress of Thomas, brother of the late Earl of Gloucester, so that the young men were cousins,—and this honourable treatment of the bodies of his foemen is a generous trait on the part of the chivalrous Bruce.

Nothing is further told us in history of his young widow. Their only son, John, died in infancy; and her brief and brilliant married life is shrouded in loneliness and sorrow. Alas! how many such sad entries of blighted love and disappointed anticipations are contained in the pages of history, indicating troubled lives which command our attention and sympathy, even though they have long since sunk to rest.

With the death of Earl Gilbert the male line of the Earls of Clare, Hertford, and Gloucester ended, and the Tonbridge estate and the earldom of Gloucester passed to Eleanor the eldest, who had married Hugh le

Despencer He assumed the title, but his tenure thereof was short-lived indeed Like Gaveston, he was a favourite with Edward II, and, like him, rightly or wrongly, peculiarly obnoxious to the people of England, who attributed much of the King's folly and extravagance to the influence which they had over him And Edward seemed to take every opportunity of exasperating them by publicly shewing his attachment Rich presents, even the very regal jewels, were showered upon them

The troubled lives and tragic ends of these unfortunate brothers-in-law are incidents so well known to all readers of history, that there is no need here to enter into them at any length

Mr Wadmore, in his paper, "Tonbridge Castle and its Possessors and its Lords," in *Kent Archæologia* (vol xvi), says that Gaveston accompanied his brother-in-law, the Earl of Gloucester, to Scotland, and was present at Bannockburn Stowe, however, records his death as happening before that date

At any rate, the confederate barons, under Thomas of Lancaster, soon rid the country of him, for seizing him at Scarborough Castle, whither Edward sent him for safety during his absence from York, they sent him to Dedington, near Oxford, where he was captured and eventually beheaded on Blacklow Hill, close to Warwick, 1312, by Beauchamp, Earl of Warwick, whom he had formerly, in a jeering way, called "the black hound of "Arden," leaving one daughter, Joane, who died young, and the widow married Sir Hugh de Audsley, who assumed the earldom of Gloucester, with the possession of the Tonbridge estates

Hugh Le Despencer, whom Henry had made constable of the Tower, was then made chamberlain in his place At first he was popular with the people, "because they knew the King hated him" But Stowe says of him that "he was in body very comely, in spirit proud, and in action most "wicked," and speedily became, with his father, who was devotedly attached to him, the object of suspicion and hatred He was present with the King in Scotland at the time of Bannockburn, and shared his flight

In 1320, he and his father were banished, and, returning the following year, were committed to the Tower by the King, but in 1322 were received again into favour, the elder being made Earl of Winchester at York, where the King held his Parliament at Easter Two years after (1326) the Queen, being now in open rebellion against the King, and with Mortimer, "of great power under her son's banner, persecuting his father," caused the elder Le Despencer to be "drawn and hanged in his armour at Bristol" And soon after, the younger Le Despencer, being "brought bound before her by "certain Welchmen," at Hereford, he was hanged on a gallows thirty feet high, and beheaded and quartered, Simon Reding being hanged on the same gallows, but "ten feet lower" He left several children, by whom his title was carried on, until his great-grand-daughter, on the death of her nephew, carried the title by marriage to Richard Beauchamp, Earl of Worcester and Baron Abergavenny, whose daughter carried it into the family of Nevill.

Elizabeth, the third daughter, retained the honour and castle of Clare for her portion, from whence she was better known as "the Lady of Clare." She married John de Burgh, the god-son and heir of the Earl of Ulster, and brother of Maud, the wife of her brother Gilbert. John died in 1313, in the lifetime of his father, and soon after his eldest brother, leaving one son, William. Elizabeth married, secondly, Theobald de Verdon, by whom she had an only daughter, Isabel, married to Henry, Lord Ferrers of Groby; and thirdly, she married Roger Damory or D'Amorie.

From the year 1313 to 1321, Elizabeth de Clare spent her life at Clare Castle, and would seem to have been a lady of much culture and beneficence, for she was a most munificent benefactress to the college at Cambridge, which the Chancellor Richard Badow and the University founded in 1326. She made numerous grants to it, provided it with a code of statutes, and changed its name from University Hall to Clare College.

Her son William, Earl of Ulster, married Maud, daughter of Henry Plantagenet, Earl of Lancaster, younger brother and heir of Thomas Earl of Lancaster, beheaded at Pontefract. The Earl of Ulster was murdered (1333) by Thomas Fitzpatrick, Mandeville, and others, leaving by her one daughter, Elizabeth de Burgh; and his widow married Sir Ralph Stafford.

Elizabeth de Burgh married Lionel, the third son of Edward III. Born at Antwerp in 1338, where the King was keeping his Court as Vicar of the Empire and head of the Confederate League of Germany.

Of a Flemish mother, the Prince was a true Fleming, and in due time grew to be nearly seven feet in height,—and being athletic in proportion, was a champion of which any country might be proud. Sandford says that he was betrothed to Elizabeth de Burgh when he was three years old, and that the marriage actually took place when he was fourteen (1353). He was created Earl of Ulster in right of his wife, who died in 1363, leaving him with one child, Philippa, and was interred in the chancel of the Augustine Friars at Clare. His father also made him *custos* of the kingdom of England during his absence from the realm, and in 1362 created him Duke of Clarence, on which occasion he distinguished his arms by a label of three points argent, each charged with a canton gules, the old coat of the Clares. Four years after the death of his wife he married Violanta, daughter of Galasius II., Prince of Milan; and five months after, Sandford says, "having lived with this new wife "after the manner of his own country, forgetting or not regarding his "change of ayre, and addicting himself to immoderate feasting, spent and "consumed with a lingering disease, he departed this life at Alba Pompeia, "1368"

Philippa, at whose baptism John Thoresby, Archbishop of York, had stood godfather, was, at the death of her father, thirteen years of age, and was married by the King to Edward Mortimer, third Earl of March, who enjoyed, with her, the earldom of Ulster and the lordships of Clare, Connaught, and Trim His daughter Elizabeth was the wife of the famous Hotspur, and his son, Roger Mortimer, Earl of March, who on his seal styled himself also Earl of Clare, married Eleanor Holand, daughter of Thomas Holand, Earl of Kent

The Earl of March died in the prison at Trim, where he had been confined for almost twenty years, on suspicion, by Henry IV, leaving no issue

His sister, Anne, had married Richard of Coningsboro, Earl of Cambridge, second son of Edward Langley, Duke of York, fifth son of Edward III

He was made Earl of Cambridge by Henry V in the second year of his reign, but the next year (1414) he conspired with Henry, Lord Scrope of Masham, then Lord Treasurer, and Sir Thomas Grey, to plot the King's death, and make his brother, Edward, Earl of March, King, and was beheaded in consequence, with his fellow-conspirators, at Southampton, and his head and body interred in the chapel of God's house He carried as arms —France and England quarterly, a label of three points charged with three torteaux, within a border argent, charged with ten lions rampant, purple, marking his descent from the house of Castile and Leon

By him Philippa had issue Richard, Earl of Cambridge, who married Cecily Nevill, and succeeded his uncle Edward, slain at Agincourt, as Duke of York He was slain at the battle of Wakefield, his head placed on the walls of York, and his titles descended to his son Edward, Earl of March, who eventually became Edward IV, and were thus merged in the Crown

His arms seem to have consisted of France and England quarterly, without any border, and label of three points charged with nine torteaux

There is a significance worth noticing in the assumption by Lionel Plantagenet of the title of Clarence, and not Clare, for the family of Clare used that name as their surname, and never as their title They became Earls of Hereford, Gloucester, and Pembroke, but never took any rank or title from the honour of Clare, which gave them their name If any one of the family was called "Comes Clarensis" (*e g* William de Warren, Earl of Surrey, was called "Comes Warrensis"), this meant "the Earl residing "at Clare," and not "the Earl of Clare" Lionel of Antwerp, having married in 1354 Elizabeth, heiress of Clare, from her grandmother Elizabeth, in 1362, was created, probably at Edward III's jubilee, not Duke of Clare, but Duke of Clarence, Dux Clarentiæ, or Dux Clarensis And the word Clarence or

Clarentia meant the territory of which he was feudal chief, and which comprised not merely the castle in Suffolk and its dependants, but a large portion of the fairest lands south of the Trent. In addition to his fiefs in Wilts, Devon, Cambridge, and Kent, the founder of the family had thirty-eight lordships in Surrey, thirty-five in Essex, and ninety-five in Suffolk (*Bury and West Suffolk Archæological Association*, 1853, vol. i.). His grandson added to this the earldom of Hereford and extensive possessions in Wales. Indeed, when Gilbert the Red married Joane Plantagenet, there was scarcely a county in the breadth of England, south of the Trent, which did not own the influence of the great Clarensis.

Those who owed obeisance or fealty to the mighty lord seneschal of Clare were called Clarencels; and the extent and dignity of these vast possessions may be estimated from the fact that, there being two principal heralds—Norroy King of Arms, *i.e.* of the north men, and Surroys King of Arms, *i.e.* of the south men—the latter was changed to Clarencieux, or King of Arms of the Clarencels, probably at the time when the dukedom was granted and those vast possessions became absorbed into the *personnel* of the Crown.

One member of this distinguished family was a member of our Minster, viz. Bogo de Clare, younger son of Richard de Clare, and brother of Gilbert de Clare, who married Joane of Acre. He was instituted Treasurer of the Minster September 28th, 1287, and died in 1294, during which time the building of the chapter-house was probably commenced, if not completed; and I cannot help thinking that he was instrumental therein, if not to be regarded as the actual founder thereof.

According to our modern ideas, the records which are extant about him do not indicate a man of very high spirituality, and are rather inconsistent with our conception of a mediæval ecclesiastic; but it was a rough, if ready time, lacking generally the refinements which in our days seem inseparable from real religion, and when men, who were not absolutely absorbed in the cloisters, discharged many secular duties, not only political, but military.

The chapter-house, too, seems identified with the secular rather than spiritual side of the great institution of York, and therefore likely to be the work of a man whose reputation is more closely connected with the former than the latter. And even if, as Canon Raine says, "he left an "evil name behind him," for that very reason he might have been anxious to do something in the way of benefiting the Church, which would be recognised as some sort of atonement for his excesses or shortcomings: or he may have bequeathed some part of the wealth which he had amassed, and which he could scarcely have exhausted on his own pleasures, for this purpose. At any rate, the chapter-house and vestibule windows contain many shields, not only of the Clare family itself, but of the royal family and other families with which they were closely associated or related at this time, and this fact, combined with the certainty that Bogo de Clare filled the office of the treasurer, gives, at least, a very strong presumption for this view of the matter

As regards the vastness of his wealth, Canon Raine has shewn his greed to have been almost insatiable On the strength of a dispensation which he had received from Martin IV, who had made him one of his chaplains, he accumulated an almost incredible amount of preferment, viz. Calham in Ireland, Leverington, diocese of Ely, Cheveley and Simondburne, and to make up the sum of 400 marks in annual rent, Higham, diocese of Salisbury, worth 30 marks per annum, St Peter's, Oxford, the same, Kilkhampton, diocese of Exeter, Eynesford, diocese of Cambridge, worth 20 marks, Swanscombe, diocese of Rochester, worth 20 marks, moiety of the church of Dorking, worth 20 marks, Dunmow, diocese of London, worth 40 marks, Polstead, worth 30 marks, and Saham, diocese of Norwich, worth 30 marks, Rotherfield, diocese of Chichester, ditto, a moiety of the church of Doncaster, worth 25 marks, Llanderon, diocese of Llandaff, worth 10 marks, Fordingbridge, diocese of Winchester, worth 40 marks, Acaster, diocese of York, worth 10 marks

In 1290 Archbishop Romanus makes the following return to Archbishop Peckham of the preferment which Clare held in the northern province — Treasurership of York, worth 600 marks per annum, prebend of Masham, in the same church, worth 300 marks, church of Hemingborough, worth 250 marks, Settrington, worth 100 marks, Pickall, Richmondshire, worth 60 marks

In 1283 he was also holding the deanery of Stafford, a pension of 50 marks from the prior and convent of Durham, the rectory of St Andrew, Walpole, Norfolk His total annual income is estimated by Canon Raine at not less than £50,000 per annum, according to the present value of money He was, of course, an absentee as well as a pluralist, and kept "an army of bailiffs and receivers to enforce and collect his dues," and equally, of course, the goods of the Church nominally under his care suffered through his neglect

"The officers of York Minster told with horror how De Clare's "creatures allowed the sacred vestments in the treasury to be taken out "and used by women in childbed The *Lanercost Chronicle* relates that "the only reredos at the church of Simondsburne was made of wattles "besmeared with cow-dung"

A curious document, throwing some light upon the character of Bogo de Clare and the domestic history of his times, has been discovered in the MSS under the custody of the Master of the Rolls, and has been transcribed by the Rev. C. Hartshorne, and published in the journal of the British Archæological Association (vol. xviii., p. 67), 1862. The document in question is called "Rotulus de expensis Hospicii "Bogonis de Clare," during the twelfth year of Edward I. (1284). The roll seems to be imperfect at the beginning and end, as it abruptly commences with an entry upon Monday, the feast of the apostles Philip and James, at Ruthin, near which place Bogo must have been previously, and ends at Lincoln.

Some of the items are curious as indicating the manner of life and travelling in those days. On Tuesday, at Conway, they were as follows:— "In bread, two shillings; in wine, sixteen pence; in eggs, two-pence half-"penny; in butcher's meat, two shillings and seven pence; in goat's flesh, "three pence; in potage, one penny; in salt, a farthing; in plaice for those "who fasted, eight pence; in hay and forage, twenty pence; in one quarter "of oats, three shillings; in salt fish, two pence; in wood, three pence; "in candles, two pence; in mending a boat for conveying the harness "over the water, and for carriage of the harness, for stabling, and for "horses, sixpence; in the dinner of the lord and family at Denbigh, two "shillings and a penny halfpenny."

The journey on from Conway, Tuesday; Bangor, Wednesday; Carnarvon, Thursday to Saturday; thence Oswestre, Shrewsbury, Newcastle-under-Lyne, Derby, Nottingham, to Axholme-in-the-Isle, where a payment of four pence occurs "for wood to dry the clothes of my lord, on account "of the great rains." Eventually they come to Lincoln, where the ordinary expenses are increased by six pence (in *pisce de dulce aqua*) for fresh-water fish, and eight pence, ale. Thence they journey back to Carnarvon in fifteen days, at the rate of two shillings per diem, where he sojourned, waiting the will of the King and Queen, from the day of Pentecost, 1284.

Amongst his expenses here are, "for parchment purchased for the "rolls of account, and for making letters, six pence; for six pounds of "wax, of which were made candles and torches for the lord, two shillings "and three pence."

Another account, from the feast of St. Gregory to the feast of St. Michael here following, 13th Edward I., 1284, shews that he set out from Thacham towards London. They travelled with twenty horses, fourteen grooms, and one page.

At Maidenhead, where they supped, bread cost sixteen pence; wine, tenpence; and the same sum for a pike, "lupus aquaticus;" a letter, two shillings and a halfpenny; beds, five pence; wood and charcoal, seven pence three farthings.

But when Bogo de Clare reached London, he entertained, on Saturday the vigil of Pentecost, according to his confidential attendant, Walter de

Reyny (afterwards Archbishop of Canterbury), the following distinguished company —Lord Edmund de Mortimer, Lord William de Mortimer, Lord Roger de Mowbray, Lord Robert de la Warde, Lord John de Clinton, Lord Roger de Molton, Lord Henry de Kokington, Lord Roger de Beltofte, Gilbert de Clifton, Henry de Ludlow, and others *

The consumption of ale amounted to eleven shillings, but there was no wine Of fish they had conger, plaice, soles, costing eight and six pence, pike and barbels, costing seven shillings, lampreys, six shillings and eightpence, besides "morue" and stork fish No meat is mentioned, it being, I suppose, fast-day The total expense amounted to fifty-five shillings and eight pence

On the following day the same guests again dined, with the exception of Lord Roger de Mowbray

This being the feast of Pentecost, ten sextaries of wine were drunk they had beef, veal, white pudding, two sheep from the store at Dorking, geese, kids, fowls and pigeons, together with all the essential parts of a good dinner Forty horses also were fed, and there is an entry for (besides their provender) a pudding, or mash ("sagimen") for them

On the following day, Bogo entertained Henry de Kokington and William de Lamborn, Clerks of the Exchequer, and others Also on Tuesday and Thursday he received his friends to dinner, amongst them Roger de Aspal, the Prior of Striguil, and Roger de Mowbray On the Sunday following, Roger de Mowbray and all his family dined with him, and again on the Monday, with two merchants from Germany Again we have an entry of pork and mutton from Dorking

On Tuesday, many of the Court were at dinner, and in the evening Bogo de Clare departed from town towards Brentford

On the back of this expense roll there occurs, amongst others, the following curious entries —"For a chaplet of flowers, bought for John de "Belchamp on the day of Pentecost, four pence half-penny For two rings "bought and given to Lady Margaret la Rouse and her daughter, by "the precept of the lord, at London, four and six pence

"For one hat of felt bought for the lord and given to Edward Mortimer, twenty pence

"On the Sunday, on the feast of the Holy Trinity, in an oblation "of the Lord Edmund de Mortimer and his Lady, and their knights and "companions of the lord in London, according to the precept of the lord, "eight pence In alms given at the same time, twopence For a chest "brought to hold the spoons of the lord, sixpence Paid to William Pilk, "jester, of Sarum, two shillings"

* The title "Lord" here is the translation of "Dominus," not indicating a Peer, but a term of respect

The expense roll also contains a full account of the ceremonies and expenses connected with the funeral of John de Wortley, who seems to have been assistant to Walter de Reyny, the head of his household. The entire cost came to three pounds three shillings and fourpence, which was disbursed principally amongst ecclesiastics, *e.g.* "Paid to 12 Clerks, saying "the Psalter for the soul of John de Wortley, eighteen pence, of whom "six took 12 pence, because they said both day and night, and the rest "took six pence, because they took it only by night. Five wax-lights for the "Monastery of the Holy Trinity, at London, for the lord of the aforesaid, "at the hands of Walter de Reyny, at the command of the lord." After other similar charges, "To the Clerks of the Parish for twice beating the "whole of the bells, two pence. Also for tolling the great bell of St. Paul's, "six pence. Also to the common porter of the bell for divulging his death, "six pence. For carrying wax-lights inside the church, four pence. For "carrying the coffin in which the body was deposited, one penny. In "making the sepulchre, four pence. For half a hundred of wax, twenty-"three shillings and six pence. For making it into square wax-lights, and "for the driver and for the horse, and for the carriage of wax-lights, "and for bringing the herse: in all, four and four pence. For incense, "three pence; earthen jars a penny; for a chest, six pence. Also for a bed "brought for Jordan to lie upon before John de Wortley, for six nights, "six pence. Also for a certain woman from Swaneschamp, keeping him "by the command of the lord, two shillings. Also in an oblation the "day of his death, seventeen shillings and four pence."

Canon Raine also records that he presented a wonderful jewel case to the Queen of France (I suppose the aunt of his brother's first wife), in the shape of a car on wheels, and it was made of ivory, silver, and gold.

All these details not only throw light upon the domestic life of that period, but indirectly testify to the character of Bogo de Clare, presenting him to us as the friend and associate of some of the greatest in the land. Hospitable in his entertainments, munificent in his presents, and kind and generous towards the memory of those who had served him faithfully.

In another roll, however, of the same period, called the "coram rege" roll, of the 13th year of the reign of Edward I., in the barbarous jargon called Latin employed in the law courts at that time, perhaps less creditable traits of character are recorded: they were evidently deemed culpable even in those rough times; in our own they would probably be regarded as unpardonable.

It appears that "the Prior of the Holy Trinity in London, and "Bogo de Clare, were attached to answer to our Sovereign Lord the King, "Peter de Chavel, the King's seneschal, Walter de Fanecourt, the King's "marshal, Edmund Earl of Cornwall, and the Abbot of Westminster, upon "this ground, that when the said Earl of Cornwall had come at the "King's mandate to this Parliament of London, and was passing through "the middle of the greater Hall of Westminster, where everybody of the "kingdom and peace of our Lord ought, and has a right to pursue his "ease and business lawfully and peaceably, free from any citations and "summonses, the aforesaid Prior, at the procurement of the said Bogo de "Clare, on the Friday next before the feast of the Purification of the blessed "Virgin in this year, did, in the hall aforesaid, serve a citation upon the "aforesaid Earl, that he should appear at a certain day and place before "the Archbishop of Canterbury" This was regarded as a flagrant interference with the liberty of the subject, notwithstanding that the aforesaid Edmund Earl of Cornwall was his brother-in-law, having married his sister Margaret, and the following severe penalties were claimed in consequence, viz £10,000, for "the manifest contempt and disparagement "of our Lord the King," £1,000 to the Abbot of the aforesaid church, for damage done to his exemption by the Court of Rome from the jurisdiction of Archbishops or Bishops, besides some compensation, not stated, to the seneschal and marshal, for the "manifest prejudice of their office," and in conclusion, "£5,000 to the aforesaid Earl for damage done to him" Bogo and the Prior appeared before the court, acknowledged their fault, pleaded their "ignorance that the place was exempt," and threw themselves upon the King's mercy They were forthwith committed to the Tower, to be kept in custody at the King's pleasure, but (as we may easily conjecture) with a short term of "durance vile," and by the payment of a mitigated fine, so powerful and influential a personage as Bogo de Clare soon escaped this little difficulty

But he does not appear to have been able to keep himself or his household out of hot water In Hilary term, 21 Edward I, we find him again before the court, being attached to answer to one John de Valeys, clerk, concerning this, viz, "that when the said John, upon Sunday in "the feast of Trinity last past, in the peace of our Lord the King, and on "the part of the Archbishop of Canterbury, had entered the house of the "aforesaid Bogo in the city of London, and then and there had brought "down some letters of citation to be served, certain of the family of the "aforesaid Bogo did cause the said John, by force and against his will, "to eat the same letters and the seals appended thereto, and then and "there did imprison, and beat and evilly intreat him, against the peace "of our Lord the King, and to the damage of the said John of £20, and "also in contempt of our Lord the King of £1,000" To this Bogo pleaded that only a general complaint had been laid of his family, and no distinct individuals named, as is wont De Valeys being interrogated "if the said Bogo either did or instruct any trespass?" replied in the negative; but says that the offence was committed by some of the family, of whose names he is totally ignorant. The King (*i.e.* I suppose the Court), adjudged that the trespass was an egregious outrage upon Holy Mother Church, and an open violation and contempt of the King's sovereignty, and ought not to be unpunished, and that he ought to be accountable for any transaction which transpired under his roof, and at the hands of those who fed at his table. Whereupon all the family of Bogo de Clare were brought up, excepting Henry de Brabant, John Denham, Roger de Berkham, and some others (the actual perpetrators, I suppose), who had escaped and fled beyond the seas. "The jurors examined divers "knights and clerics, and others of the family of the said Bogo, and find "that it was done without his cognisance, precept, or assent." He was, therefore, "hailed to answer at the King's pleasure, when the real per-"petrators of the offence might be discovered." In the interview the above-named delinquents were outlawed, and writs issued to the various sheriffs for their apprehension.

The name of Bogo de Clare is associated with Merton College, Oxford, as well as York Minster; but how far Bogo was or was not a benefactor of Merton College, it is difficult, perhaps, to decide. The facts are these: Walter de Merton, when Chancellor in 1260, obtained from Richard, Earl of Gloucester, as his feudal superior, a charter, empowering him to assign his manors at Farley and Malden, in Surrey, to the Priory of Merton, for the support of scholars "residing at the school." The expression is not very clear, but it probably meant exhibitioners to be entertained at the University of Oxford. In 1266, a royal charter was issued by Henry III., giving to the College, then settled at Malden, the advowson of St. Peter-in-the-East, for impropriation with all the chapels appertaining to it, one of which was that of St. Cross, now Holywell Church (*History of Merton College:* Broderick).

At that time it would seem to have been part of the preferment, as already mentioned, of Bogo de Clare, who is recorded not only to have claimed but exercised "la haute justice" there, by causing a thief, named Bensington, to be hanged on his own gallows, by his own bailiffs. Walter de Chauncey is mentioned in the archives of the College as having been sometime "Baillive to Bogo de Clare, Lord of the Manor of Holy-"well," as being Rector of St. Peter-in-the-East.

It would seem that Bogo de Clare died somewhere about 1296, for in the Exchequer Pleas roll, 24 and 25 Edward I., "Nicholas, Bishop "of Sarum, is attached to answer Percival de Ast and Thomas de Estwyk, "executors of the will of Bogo de Clare, deceased, in part payment of "debts which the said executors owe to the Lord the King for the said "deceased, on the plea that he may pay them £122 9*s.* 8*d.*, which he "owes for the fruits of the churches, formerly belonging to the said Bogo, "of Tacham and Chievele (Thatcham and Chieveley), which fell into the "hands of the said Bishop, after the decease of the aforesaid Bogo—"Edward 23rd" Probably, therefore, he had only the tenure for life granted to him by the King, and at his death, provision was made therewith for the lodging and support of the scholars from Malden, which was the commencement of Merton College

The armorial bearings of the College testify to the founder having been a retainer of the Clare family, as they are —Or, three chevronels per pale azure and gules, *i e* the arms of Clare differenced

Anthony Wood says (p 36) of this house —"After some small time "of the endowment of it, there was one Bogo de Clare (kin to the Earl "of Gloucester), who gave to it the Church of St Peter-in-the-East, "Oxford, the Chapel of Wolvercote, and the Chapel and Lordship of "St Cross (now known by the name of Holywell), with all the appurten-"ances and liberties thereunto belonging, which he held of the gift of "King Henry III, and which were valued really at £40 per annum The "said Bogo de Clare, and others of that house, were so great benefactors "to this house, that it is supposed the College imitated them in the bearing "of their arms, for, whereas the Clares bear Or 3 chevrons gules, the "College bore the same, only counterchanging the chevrons per pale gules "and azure, and for the great respect the College owed to that family "did set up their arms in many places of the College, besides in the "Chancel of St Peter-in-the-East, the Chapel of Wolvercote, and Holywell"

We now go back to Hugh de Audley, the husband of Margaret, second daughter of the "Red Earl," and widow of Piers Gaveston He, however, sided with the Earl of Lancaster, and was taken prisoner with him at the battle of Boroughbridge, but being treated with indulgence on account of marriage with the King's niece, and, perhaps, his relationship to Gaveston, he was not beheaded with the good Duke

His estates were seized, but restored in 1327, the first year of the following reign Some years after he was summoned to Parliament as Earl of Gloucester, and died in 1347, leaving one only daughter and heir, Margaret, married to Lord Stafford, the eldest son of Edmund Lord Stafford, by Margaret, daughter of Ralph Lord Basset, of Drayton

THE STAFFORDS.

Our attention is called to this very family of Stafford by the second window west of the north side of the Choir, where we find the arms of Stafford, Or a chevron gules, impaled with the arms of Roos, three water bougets argent, viz.: Beatrix, the eldest daughter of this Ralph Lord Stafford, who married—1st, Maurice Fitz Thomas, son and heir of the Earl of Desmond; and 2nd, Thomas Lord Ros, of Hamlake.*

Ralph Lord Stafford was created Knight of the Bath in the 17th year of Edward II., and in the first year of the following reign accompanied Edward III. to Scotland. He was one of his companions when, the year following, he entered Nottingham Castle by the secret passage, and captured Roger Mortimer, Earl of March. He distinguished himself in various other expeditions in Scotland and France, and his administrative capacity appears to have been equal to his skill as a military commander and diplomatist. He commanded the van in the great English victory of Crecy; and it is to him and Sir Reginald Cobham that history owes the record of the slain, which was returned by them and the three heralds who searched the field, as eleven great princes, eighty bannerets, twelve hundred knights, and over thirty thousand men of all arms. After this he was accredited as ambassador to treat with the Cardinals of Naples and Claremont, as to the conclusion of the war between Edward III. and Philip de Valois, King of France. On his return he was created a Knight of the Garter.

In 1352, he was appointed on a commission at York, together with the Bishop of Durham and Lords Percy and Neville, to settle the terms of peace with Scotland; on the accomplishment of which he was created Earl of Stafford, with a grant of 1,000 marks per annum, until lands equivalent thereto could be assigned to him.

His further services were in France and Ireland; and after a life spent in the service of his king, he died 1373 (46 Ed. III.), aged 67. There is something touching, as well as appropriate, in the following epitaph, recorded in a contemporary MS., now in the Bodleian:—"Eodem anno "ultimo die mensis Augusti obiit nobilissimus Comes Staffordiœ Radulphus "nomine, apud Tunbrig, homo quondam validus, fortis, audax, bellicosus, "in armis strenuus; senio confectus, longo squalore maceratus."

Hugh, his only son, succeeded him, and followed in his steps. From 1360 to 1370 he was on Prince Edward's staff, and, in the next eight years, engaged in Flanders, Brittany, and the siege of Berwick.

Having accompanied Thomas of Woodstock to Calais, he returned to join the King in his expedition to Northumberland, accompanied by

* See coloured illustration.

PLATE 5.

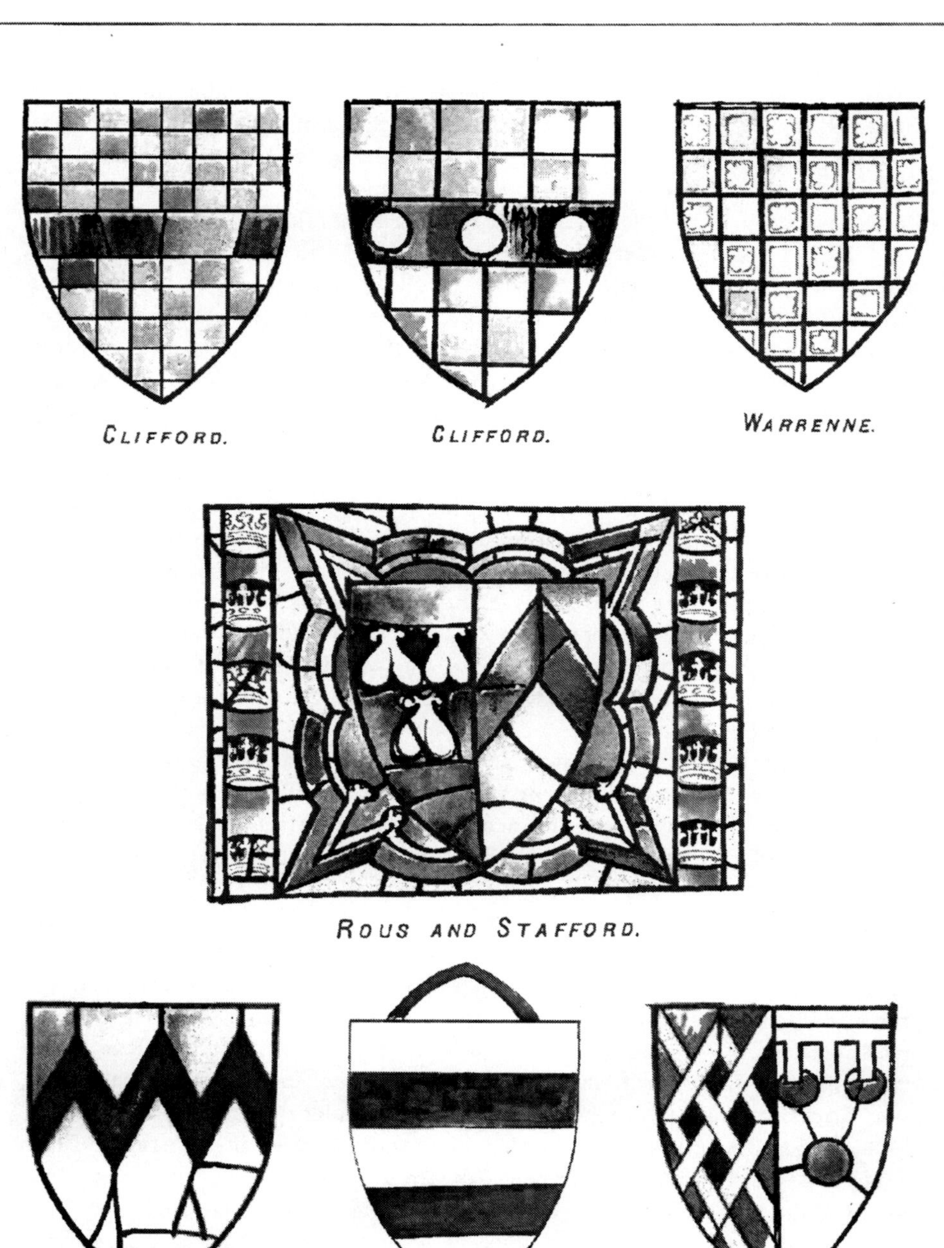
CLIFFORD.
CLIFFORD.
WARRENNE.
ROUS AND STAFFORD.
VAVASOUR.
HILTON.
HARINGTON AND COURTENAY.

his son Ralph, who was murdered (1385) while proceeding to Scotland, by John Holland, the Queen's half-brother (as I have related in the history of the Wakes) The Earl's daughter Joane was married to Thomas Holland, Earl of Kent, so there was a close relationship between them

This sad event so affected the father, that he threw up his military position, and started on a pilgrimage to Jerusalem, and died on his way back at Rhodes, 1387

In his will he bequeathed a gold ring with a diamond, to his sister, Lady Roos, to Joane, his daughter, a gold fermail with a heart His eldest son, Thomas, did not long survive him He was succeeded by his brother William, who, in his turn, was succeeded in a few months by his brother Edmund, who married his eldest brother's widow, Ann, daughter of Thomas of Woodstock, Duke of Gloucester, and co-heir of her mother, Eleanor, daughter and co-heir of Humphrey de Bohun, Earl of Hereford, but in 1403, July 21st, he was slain at the battle of Shrewsbury His son, Humphrey, was but a child at his death, but when he grew up he identified himself with the cause of Henry VI, was with him when he was crowned King in Paris, followed his changing fortunes to Calais, landed with him at Dover, and in 1441, was appointed Captain of the Town of Calais, under the style of "Earl of Buckingham, Stafford, Northampton and Perch, "Lord of Brecknock and Holderness, Captain of the Town of Calais"

In the 23rd year of Henry VI he was created Duke of Buckingham, and in the 28th year, Constable of Dover and Queenborough Castles Very shortly after the Duke of York assembled an army in Wales, while the Duke of Warwick suddenly landed at Sandwich with Salisbury and the Earl of March (eldest son of the Duke of York) Part hastened to London, under Cobham and the Earl of Salisbury, to overawe Lord Scales, governor of the Tower, the rest marched on with an army of 25,000 men, to meet the King at Coventry He, however, with the Dukes of Gloucester and Buckingham, removed from thence, and strongly entrenched themselves at Northampton

The result is thus tersely summed up by Fabyan (*Ch* p 636) —

"Whereupon the sayde lordes beynge enfourmyd, sped them thyther-"warde, and so y^t^ upon the IX daye of Iulet (1460), bothe hostys there "mette and foughte there a cruelle batayll, but after a longe fyght the "vyctory fell unto the erle of Salesbury and the other lordys upon his "partye, and the kynges hoost was sparbled and chasyd, and many of "his noble men slayne, amonge the which was ye duke of Buckyngham, "the erle of Shroysbury, the vycount Beaumoude, ye lorde Egremonde, "with many other knyghtis and esquyers, and the kyng taken in the "felde"

By his wife, Anne, daughter of Ralph Nevill, Earl of Westmoreland, the Duke left seven sons and five daughters. His eldest son, Humphrey, Earl of Stafford, who had married Margaret, daughter and co-heir of Edmund Beaufort, Duke of Somerset, was slain at St. Albans, leaving two sons.

Henry, the eldest, now second Duke of Buckingham, with Humphrey, his brother, were committed by Edward IV. to the care of Anne, Duchess of Exeter; and on coming of age, played a conspicuous part in the history of the period. Dugdale (*Baronage*) tells us that before entering the maelström of political strife, he sent his trusty servant, Pershall, to Richard Duke of Gloucester, in the north, assuring him that he was ready to come to his assistance with a thousand friends, but stipulating for the Earldom of Hereford, and the ample manors of his kinsman, for so doing. Shakespeare, in his play of *Richard III.*, graphically pourtrays how Richard despised him, and how Buckingham became his tool.

"My other self, my counsel's consistory, my oracle, my prophet, my "dear cousin, I, as a child, will go thy direction,"* the King says, when speaking to him; but when, soliloquising, he speaks of him, and Hastings, and Stanley, as "so many simple gulls."* On the other hand when Hastings announced that the Queen, with the Duke of York, have taken sanctuary, Buckingham suggests to Cardinal Boucher: "Lord Cardinal, "will your Grace persuade the Queen to send the Duke of York unto his brother presently?" And on his hesitating to undertake such a task, he overcomes his scruples with taunting words:—

"You are too senseless obstinate, my Lord;
Too ceremonious and traditional;"
* * * * * *
"Oft have I heard of Sanctuary men,
But Sanctuary children ne'er till now."

When the child has been brought, and, ere he goes with his brother to the Tower, makes some precocious remarks to Gloucester, the Duke of Buckingham seeks to exasperate the Lord Protector against the Queen, by saying to him:—

"Think you, my Lord, this little prattling York
Was not incensed by his subtle mother,
To taunt and scorn you thus opprobriously?" †

He sets on Catesby to sound Lord Hastings "How far he stands "affected to our purpose."‡

He is present at the Council at the Tower, and assures Hastings "you and he are near in love,"§ and yet, when Catesby has reported that "he will not desert his master's child," stands by while Gloucester, in a simulated burst of rage, orders Hastings to instant execution.

* Act II. Sc. 1. † Act I. Sc. 3. ‡ Act III. Sc. I. § Act III. Sc. 4.

In the following Scene (5) we find him agreeing with Richard to play the hypocrite, and (when the Lord Mayor enters) he palliates to him the hasty execution, as though Richard were innocent thereof, he assures him concerning Hastings, "The subtle traitor this day had plotted in "the council-house to murder me and my good Lord of Gloucester," adding —

> "Yet had we not determined he should die,
> Until your Lordship came to see his end,
> Which now the loving haste of these his friends
> Somewhat against our meaning, hath prevented'

In another Scene he tells Richard how he had enlarged to the citizens on his virtues—

> "Your discipline in war, wisdom in peace,
> Your bounty virtue, fair humility,
> Indeed left nothing fitting for your purpose
> Untouched, or slightly handled in discourse"

And that when—

> "Some ten voices call'd 'God save King Richard!'
> Thus I took the vantage of those few—
> 'Thanks, gentle citizens and friends,' quoth I,
> 'This general applause and cheerful shout
> Argues your wisdom and your love for Richard!'"

He, too, suggests to Richard how he should come forth to meet the Lord Mayor and aldermen —

> "And look you get a prayer-book in your hand,
> And stand between two Churchmen, good my Lord,
> For on that ground I'll make a holy descant"*

And then, when the Lord Mayor comes in, draws invidious comparisons between Richard and the late King, and says —

> "Ah, ah! my Lord, this prince is not an Edward,
> * * * * * * *
> Not sleeping to engross his idle body,
> But praying to enrich his watchful soul
> Happy were England would this virtuous prince
> Take on himself the sovereignty thereof,
> But, sure, I fear, we ne'er shall win him to it" †

As they have arranged, Richard appears "between two bishops," and in reply to earnest entreaties from Buckingham that he would accept the Crown, he pleads —

> "Yet so much is my poverty of spirit,
> So mighty, and so many, my defects,
> That I would rather hide me from my greatness"

* Act VII Sc 7 † Act VII Sc 7

Buckingham again professes to remonstrate with him, and says:—

> "*Then, good my Lord, take to your royal self*
> This proferred benefit of dignity;
> If not to bless us and the land withal,
> Yet to draw forth your noble ancestry
> From the corruption of abusing time,
> Unto a lineal true-derived course."

Even this seems not to convince him. Richard replies:—

> "Alas, why would you heap those cares on me?
> I am unfit for state and majesty.
> *I do beseech you, take it not amiss:*
> I cannot, nor I will not yield to you."

Upon this, Buckingham pretends to go off in a huff with the citizens, threatening to

> "plant some other on your throne
> To the disgrace and downfall of your House."

But Catesby now seems to intercede:—

> "Call them again, sweet prince, accept their suit;
> *If you deny them, all the land will rue it.*"

Then Richard affects to yield:—

> "Will you enforce me to a world of cares?
> Well, call them again, I am not made of stone,
> But penetrable to your kind entreaties,
> Albeit against my conscience and my soul."

Buckingham returns, proclaims him King, and Richard retires saying to the Bishops:—

> "Come, let us to our holy work again."

However, a quarrel quickly springs up between this worthy couple. Shakespeare represents Richard instigating Buckingham to murder young Edward, and Buckingham declining to proceed any further until he receive

> "The gift for which your honour and your faith is pawned,
> The Earldom of Hereford, and the moveables
> Which you have promised I shall possess."*

Richard banters him, and puts him off by saying:

> "I am not in the giving vein to-day."

This seems to open Buckingham's eyes to the man he has to deal with, and his own position—

> "And is it thus? Repays he my deep service
> With such contempt? Made I him King for this?
> O let me think on Hastings: and be gone
> To Brecknock, while my fearful head is on."

---

* Act IV. Sc. 2.

Dugdale says (*Baronage*, p 168, 9) that (on his reminding the King of his promise) he signed a brief to that effect less than a month after his coronation Holinshead tells us that (through some coolness between himself and the King) Buckingham retired to Brecknock, and commenced plotting with Morton, Bishop of Ely, to place Henry of Richmond on the throne

Richard first tried to bring him back with promises, then with threats, and Buckingham, taking alarm, raised an army in Wales, and marched on Richard at Salisbury

But while they waited for the flooded waters of the Severn to subside for their crossing, his army melted away Buckingham fled, and Richard having offered £1,000 for his arrest, he was betrayed by Humphrey Bannister, his servant But the King declined to pay the money, grimly remarking that "He who would betray so good a master, would be false "to all others"*

Taken to Salisbury, and examined by the King in council, on the morrow (without any arraignment of peers) he was beheaded in the market-place Shakespeare says, on All Souls day, and puts these very appropriate words into his mouth on his way to execution (alluding to his words in Act II Sc 1) —

"This is the day, which (in King Edward's time)
I wished might fall on me, when I was found
False to his children, or his wife's allies
This is the day, wherein I wished to fall
By the false faith of him whom most I trusted
This, this All Souls day, to my fearful soul
Is the determined respite of my wrongs,
That high All-seer, which I dallied with,
Hath turned my feigned prayer on my head,
And given in earnest what I begged in jest
Thus doth He force the swords of wicked men
To turn their own points on their masters' bosoms
Thus Margaret's curse falls heavy on my neck—
'When He,' quoth she, 'shall split thy heart with sorrow,
Remember, Margaret was a prophetess'—
Come, sirs, convey me to the block of shame,
Wrong hath but wrong, and blame the due of blame"†

By Catherine, his wife, daughter of Richard Widvile, Earl Rivers, he had issue three sons Edward, his heir, Henry, afterwards Lord Wiltshire, who married Muriel, sister, and eventually heiress, of John Grey, Viscount Lisle, and Humphrey, who died young

Edward Stafford, third Duke of Buckingham, is another of those characters which stand out prominently on the page of history, and he is one of the four main characters in Shakespeare's play of *Henry VIII*

---

* Atkyn's *Gloucestershire* † Act V Sc 1

Professor Gervinus, in his *Shakespeare Commentaries*, page 819, very justly and fully delineates his character. "In the character of the Duke of Buckingham, we look again," he says, "on the age of the great armed "nobility, with their pretensions and rebellions, which were the soul of "the history under the houses of York and Lancaster, though (in this play) "the physiognomy of the age seems wholly changed compared to the "character of that earlier epoch. The noise of arms has ceased, the "prominent personages are men of education, mind, and well-won merit. "The Duke himself has kept up with the change of the time; he is not "merely an ambitious man of the sword, he is learned, wise in council, "rich in mind, and a fascinating orator."

We are told that he appeared in arms against the Cornish men who befriended Perkin Warbeck; that he was a constant companion of King Henry VIII. in his revels at Greenwich and Richmond, and, on one occasion, declined jousting with him. On another the King gave him a horse. Shakespeare makes Henry say of him:—

"This gentleman is learned, and a most rare speaker,
To nature none more bound: his training such
That he may furnish and instruct great teachers,
And never seek for aid out of himself."*

One of the gentlemen (in Act II. Sc. 1) comparing him with Wolsey, says:—

"All the commons
Hate him perniciously, and, o' my conscience,
Wish him ten fathoms deep: this Duke as much
They love and dote on: call him bounteous Buckingham,
The mirror of all courtesy."

His object seems to have been (with Norfolk, Surrey, and Abergavenny) to maintain the old authority of the nobles, as against Wolsey, who is a thorn in their eyes. Buckingham regards it insufferable that

"This butcher's cur is venom-mouthed, and I
Have not the power to muzzle him:
* * * * * * *
A beggar's book
Outworths a noble's blood.
* * * * * * *
This holy fox,
Or wolf, or both, for he is equal ravenous
As he is subtle: and as prone to mischief
As able to perform it."†

He was only watching his opportunity to denounce to the King

"This top proud fellow,
Whom from the flow of gall I name not, but
From sincere motions, by intelligence
And proofs as clear as founts in July, when
We see each grain of gravel, I do know
To be corrupt and treasonous."

---

* Act I. Sc. 2. † Act I. Sc. 1.

Atkyns, in his *History of Gloucestershire*, says —"His haughty spirit "and contemptuous slighting of Wolsey did contribute to his ruin The "Duke was presenting the basin after dinner, on his knees, for the King "to wash his hands, and when the King had done and was turned away, "the Cardinal sportingly dipped his hand in the basin, whilst the Duke "was on his knees The Duke resented it as an affront, and rising up "poured the water into the Cardinal's shoes, who being nettled at it, "threatened the Duke to sit on his skirts The Duke, therefore, next "day came to Court without skirts to his doublet, and the King demanding "the reason of it, he told the King that it was to avoid the Cardinal's "anger, for he had threatened to sit upon his skirts The Duke had his "jest, but the Cardinal had *his* head"

And this *denouément* was precipitated by a domestic incident Finding his tenants clamorous, in Kent, against the exactions of his steward or surveyor, Charles Knevett, he summarily discharged him, and wrote to Sir Edward Nevill to procure him another bailiff for Tonbridge This so infuriated Knevett, that he divulged certain conversations respecting the succession to the Crown which he stated to have been held by his late master and one Hopkins, a Carthusian monk, of Hinton These words were repeated to Wolsey, which (Act II Sc 1) he repeats to the King himself Henry was at that time without male heir, and "Buckingham was the next heir in the Beaufort branch of the Lancastrian "House if the King died without issue" Knevett says

"First it was usual with him, every day
It would infect his speech, that if the King
Should without issue die, he'll carry it so
To make his sceptre his"*

And further states, as a proof of his reckless disloyalty

"Being at Greenwich
After your Highness had reproved the Duke
About Sir William Blomer,
'If,' quoth he, 'I for this had been committed
As to the Tower, I thought I would have played
The part my father meant to act upon
The usurper Richard, who being at Salisbury,
Made suit to come in his presence, which if granted,
As he made sunblane of his duty, would
Have put his knife into him"

The King exclaims

"He is attached
Call him to present trial, if he may
Find mercy in the law, 'tis his, if none,
Let him not seek't of us by day and night
He's traitor to the height"

---

* Act I Sc 2

And being summoned from Tonbridge, he was, on entering London, arrested in his barge on the Thames by Sir Thomas Marney; his attendants were dismissed and led on foot to the Tower (*Arch. Can. Tower of London*, vol. ii., p. 355).

At his trial, Shakespeare says this was confirmed by

> "Sir Gilbert Peck, his chancellor, and John Court
> Confessor to him; with that devil monk
> Hopkins, which made this mischief." *

Hopkins is said to have repented in the part he took, and to have died of grief.

Buckingham does not seem to have denied this, though he imputes bribery in the betrayal of his confidence: "My surveyor is false: the o'er "great Cardinal hath showed him gold;" † and hearing his sentence passed upon him with much feeling by the Duke of Norfolk (Act II. Sc. 1), Shakespeare says: "He shewed a most noble patience;" and Dugdale records this touching speech from him: "My Lord of Norfolk, you have "said as a traitor should be said to; but I was never one. I nothing "malign you for what you have done for me; but the eternal God forgive "you my death, as I do. I shall never sue to the King for life, howbeit "he is a gracious prince, and more grace may come from him than I "desire. I beseech you, my Lord, and all my fellows, to pray for me."

Shakespeare represents his passage from the hall of judgment to execution, and fills his mouth with sentiments in harmony therewith. He condemns no one. He forgives all. He desires the prayers of all.

> "You few that loved me,
> And dare be bold to weep for Buckingham:
> His noble friends and fellows, whom to leave
> Is only bitter to him, only dying;
> Go with me, like good angels, to my end,
> And as the long divorce of steel falls on me,
> Make of your prayers one sweet sacrifice,
> And lift my soul to heaven." ‡

He speaks of himself as "half in heaven," and utters this noble aspiration for the King:

> "May he live
> Longer than I have time to tell his years:
> Ever beloved, and loving, may his rule be;
> And when Old Time shall lead him to his end,
> Goodness and he fill up one monument."

After attending service in the chapel, he was led to the scaffold, and died calmly, August 17th, 1520, amidst the regrets of all.

---

* Act II. Sc. 1. † Act I. Sc. 1. ‡ Act II. Sc. 1.

His remark "more grace may come of him than I desire," seems to express his expectation that, though he would not plead for himself, some one else might plead for him, and in Act III Sc 2, Surrey (who had married his daughter) taunts Wolsey, after his fall, with having prevented this—

"Thy ambition,
Thou scarlet Sin, robbed this bewailing land
Of noble Buckingham, my father-in-law
The heads of all thy brother cardinals
(With thee and thy best parts all bound together)
Weighed not an hair of his Plague of your policy!
You sent me deputy for Ireland
Far from his succour, from the King, from all
That might have mercy on the fault thou gavedst him
Whilst your great goodness, out of holy pity,
Absolved him with the axe"

Which Wolsey with indignation denies However, that such denial was not generally accepted is evident from the exclamation of the Emperor Charles V when he heard of the Duke's death "A butcher's dog hath "killed the finest Buck in England" A bill of attainder followed the execution, and all his honours became forfeited, and with the last Duke sunk for ever the splendour, princely honour, and great wealth of the ancient and renowned family of Stafford

The King granted, however, some of the manors in the county of Stafford to his son, Henry, who, in the first year of Edward VI, was summoned to Parliament as Baron Stafford, and who died, esteemed for his learning and piety, 1562, leaving his estates to his brother Henry, who succeeded him Edward, his brother, succeeded him, who seems to have made a mesalliance For in 1595, Rowland White, writing to Sir Robert Sidney, says "My Lord Stafford's son is basely married to his mother's "chambermaid" His grandson, Henry, fifth Baron, died, unmarried, in 1637, and then—such are the strange vicissitudes of fortune—the title reverted to Roger Stafford, the grandson of the Duke of Buckingham, but he, having fallen into great poverty, had lived in obscurity under the name of Fludd, his mother's brother being a servant to Mr John Corbett, in Shropshire At the age of 65, he felt quite unequal to assume the position and dignity which had come to him, and having petitioned Parliament, he was allowed by Charles I to surrender to him the said Barony of Stafford, which title the King then granted to Sir William Howard, the younger son of the Earl of Arundel, and to Mary his wife, the sister of the late lord, creating them Baron and Baroness Stafford, by letters patent, with remainder to their heirs *general*, and two months after he advanced Lord Stafford to the dignity of a viscount

Viscount Stafford was one of the five Roman Catholic peers—Arundel, Powys, Belasyse, Petre, and Stafford—arrested on the charge of being implicated in the supposed "Popish Plot" in the days of Charles II., on the information of Titus Oates. They were sent to the Tower, and Viscount Stafford alone placed upon his trial. Incapacitated by age, and inferior in abilities to making a strong defence, he could scarcely obtain a hearing at a trial the evidence adduced at which fills us with indignation for the honour of the land.

To the lasting shame of Lloyd, Bishop of St. Asaph, who knew the truth, he forbore to speak in contradiction of a perjured witness, Tuberville.

By a majority of thirty-two of his fellow peers, each laying his hand upon his breast and appealing to his honour, Stafford was found guilty and condemned to death. The crowds of spectators which gathered on Tower Hill showed their opinion by baring their heads when he denied his guilt on the scaffold, and crying out that they believed his word. With his last breath he predicted that the time would come when his injured honour would be vindicated. Eight years after, that virtually came to pass, for his widow was created Countess of Stafford for life, and his son Earl of Stafford.

In 1762 the earldom became extinct by the death of the Earl's grandson, John, 4th Earl, *s.p.*; but in 1824 the iniquitous attainder of 1680 was reversed, and Sir George William Jerningham, the lineal descendant of the beheaded Viscount, through his daughter Mary, was restored to the barony of Stafford.

Let us close this foul and blotted page in England's history; and while we condemn not the actors who have rendered their account at the bar of perfect and unbiassed Justice, let us not neglect the warning which bids us remember how easily religious prejudices may be aroused and fanned into acts of violence and bloodshed, against even the noblest and purest of the children of God.

THE FESS.

THE next Heraldic charge which I shall notice, the FESS, so called from the Latin "fascia," French "face," has been taken of old (according to Leigh) "for a girdle of honour, occupying the third part of the shield," though its width varied very much, and rarely if ever attained that proportion. It represented a part of the dress of no little importance.

Even the ordinary girdle, which must, indeed, have been indispensable in days when garments were of a loose and flowing and sometimes voluminous character, was of the costliest material, and occasionally ornamented with jewels. The monumental effigies of our early sovereigns and their consorts, have representations of girdles of elaborate workmanship, and probably rich substance. The girdle of King John's effigy at Worcester Cathedral was gilt, and in the inventory belonging to him mention is made of a belt or girdle wrought with gold and adorned with gems. In the reign of Edward III., girdles ornamented with gold or silver are strictly prohibited to all persons under the estate of knighthood, or not possessed of property to the amount of two hundred pounds per annum. Those who came within the latter class were permitted to wear girdles reasonably embellished with silver. Similar prohibitions respecting the ornamentation of girdles with gold, silver, or silk, are to be found in all the sumptuary laws down to the sixteenth century.

Several of the figures in the organ screen, which I assume represent the costumes of the date of Henry IV.–VI., have girdles which are evidently intended to represent good material and workmanship. That of Henry I. has a broad band, richly ornamented, which may have been a belt, or simply a band to keep the robe or cloak together.

But the next figure, King Stephen, has a very remarkable belt or girdle, which is probably intended to represent pieces of metal fastened together side by side, the ends being bent over at right angles, and ornaments adorned with some simple device.

The statue of Henry V. is girt with a very rich and beautiful girdle, ornamented in the centre with a representation of the Pelican vulning herself, or as it is termed, "the Pelican in her piety." This forms a charge

in the arms of Pelham, and also of Corpus Christi College, Cambridge, founded 1351, and Corpus Christi College, Oxford, 1516. It is not mentioned amongst the royal badges, and therefore I am disposed to regard it here, as in these two latter coats, as having simply a religious significance.

On the dress of Richard I. will be noticed a representation of an aulmoniere, sometimes called an alner, *i.e.* a bag, pouch, or purse. It is mentioned in the *Lay of St. Launfal*—

> "I will give thee an alner
> Made of silk and gold clear."*

It was more or less ornamented, and generally hung from the girdle by long laces of silk and gold; here it seems attached to the dress.

The girdle, therefore, was evidently an important and honourable part of the costume, and, for that reason, might well be regarded as finding its expression in the Fess. But besides the girdle, there seems to have been another belt of far greater significance. Even the belt of knighthood, or "le ceinture noble," which appears not to have been worn by anyone under the rank of knight, and which, by its excessive magnificence, imparts a marked character to the costume of the period, ranging from the middle of the reign of Edward III. to the end of that of Henry VI. It was not worn round the waist but encircled the hips, and always formed part of the costume, alike over the "coat hardie" in hall and at banquet, as over the "jupon" in the lists, or the field of battle. It was made

* Planche's *History of Costume*, vol. i., page 23.

sometimes of leather or velvet, on which metal plates were fastened, more or less closely together, richly gilt, elaborately ornamented with roses or other objects, and frequently enamelled or set with precious stones. At other times, it was wholly made of square plates of metal linked together, which were called tàsselle, or tasseaux. The touching and graceful

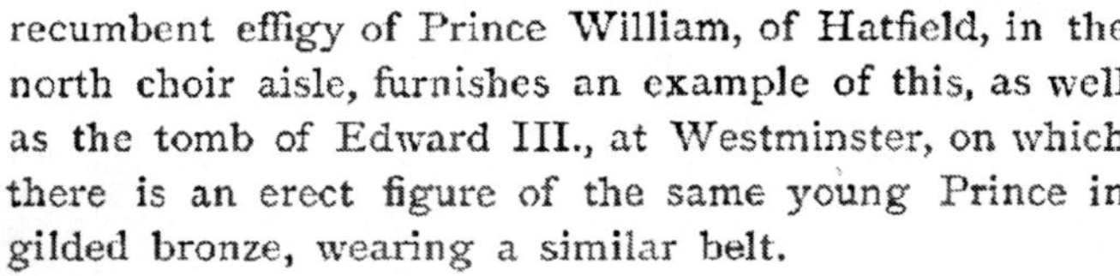

recumbent effigy of Prince William, of Hatfield, in the north choir aisle, furnishes an example of this, as well as the tomb of Edward III., at Westminster, on which there is an erect figure of the same young Prince in gilded bronze, wearing a similar belt.

When the knight was armed, his sword was affixed to this on the left side, and his dagger on the right, and the "ceinture noble" was kept in its place by an auxiliary belt which passed round the waist. Thus the "ceinture noble, the conferring of which was "the mode of investiture on the creation of a knight,"* was not merely a sword-belt, but the belt or token of knighthood with which he was girded when knighted, and was only utilized as such when on occasion required. Thus in a deed of Philip, King of France, to Peter du Cheuin, his valet, dated 1313, is—"Quem hac instanti "die Dominica ordinavimus, disponente Deo, militari "cingulo decorare:"—"Whom this very Lord's Day "we have designed, God willing, to decorate with the "military girdle." And in the *Close Rolls*, 36 Hen. III., m. 31, preserved in the Tower, there is this interesting record of the knighthood of the young King of Scotland, by Henry III., on Christmas day, 1252, at York, previous to his marriage with the Princess Margaret, Henry's daughter, the day following:—

"Mandatum est Eduardo de Western, quod cum festinatione requirat "pulchrum gladium et scandberg ejusdem de serico, et pomellum de argento "bene et ornate cooperiri, et quandam pulchram zonam eidem pendi "faciat ita quod gladium illum sic factum habeat apud Ebor de quo Rex "Alexandrum Regem Scotiœ illustrem cingulo militari decorare possit "in instanti festo nativitatis Dominicœ. Teste Rege. apud Lychfield "xxi. Novembr. Per ipsum Regem." "It is commanded to Edward of "Westminster that with speed he require a fair sword with scabbard of "silk and pouch of silver, to be well and ornamentally made, and that "he make a fair belt for the hanging of the same, so that he may have "the sword so made at York, with which the King may be able to "decorate the illustrious Alexander, King of Scotland, with the military

* Meyrick, vol. i., p. 190.

"girdle, on the approaching festival of the birth of our Lord. Witness, "the King at Lichfield, 21st day of November. By the King himself." *

The recumbent figure of Brian Fitzalan, at Bedale church, shews a loose belt, evidently of leather, embossed with lions' heads, from which the sword hangs. The brass of John Gray, at Chinnor, Oxfordshire, shows the "ceinture noble" as on the tomb of Prince William at York, with the sword and dagger affixed thereto.

Tennyson, in the *Holy Grail*, p. 42, thus idealizes such a belt:—

> "But she the wan sweet maiden shore away
> Clean from her forehead all that wealth of hair
> Which made a silken net-work for her feet;
> And out of this she plaited broad and long
> A strong sword belt, and wove, with silken thread
> And crimson, in the belt a strange device,
> A crimson grail within a silver beam,
> And saw the bright boy knight and bound it on him."

It is not surprising then that an accoutrement so honourable, and given sometimes under such honourable circumstances, should pass into a device, and be assumed by those who desired to exhibit and to perpetuate in their descendants the distinction which they had received. Sometimes they adopted the whole belt, sometimes only portions of the belt; so the house of Pelham still carries a buckle as an armorial bearing, granted by Edward III. to their ancestor John de Pelham, who assisted to take captive John, King of France, at the battle of Poictiers, 1356. To Sir Denis de Morbie, a knight of Artois, the King gave his glove; to Sir Roger le Warr and Sir John de Pelham he surrendered his sword; and in remembrance of the exploit the former assumed the "crampet," or termination of the scabbard, the latter the buckle of the sword belt.

THE CLIFFORDS.

The first shield bearing the fess which I shall notice, is that of Clifford: Chequy or and azure a fess gules.†

Under what circumstances the Cliffords obtained those arms I cannot say, but there is much interesting significance in that chequered, or chess-board field, about which I must first say a few words.

Brand, in his *Popular Antiquities*, says that "the Earls of Warenne "and Surrey, in the reign of Edward IV., possessed the privilege of licensing "houses of entertainment, and that thus they were called 'The Chequers,' "or had the chequers marked upon them." I can find no reasonable confirmation for this; though the three balls which hang over the pawn

---

* Hewitt's *Ancient Armour*. † See coloured illustration.

broker's shop are, no doubt, derived from the arms of the great Italian family of Medicis, which had the monopoly of receiving goods in pledge, when the system was first started in Italy, centuries ago More probably the chequers were marked up outside to encourage travellers to enter, with the prospect of obtaining their favourite amusements.

Chess is, no doubt, one of the oldest popular games extant, but there were also other games beside chess, played on a chess or chequered board, for in Riley's *Memorials of London and London Life*, p 395, we find "Nicholas Prestone and John Outlawe were attached to make "answer to John Atte Hill, and Wm his brother, for cheating" It appears that the two former invited the two latter to play at *tables*, or chequers, commonly called quek, for money, and bringing them to the house of the said Nicholas, in Friday-street, produced "a pair of tables, on the outside "of which was painted a chequer board, that is called a quek" The game "at the tables," played with dice upon the inside of the board, probably resembled our backgammon, that on the outer side, or the *chequers*, was probably played with rounded pebbles rolled upon the squares, the one party staking on the white squares, the other on the black, perhaps similar to the game called "checkstone" at a later date Finding that they were losing money at *the tables*, the said tables were then "turned" (hence the proverbial saying of 'turning the tables'), "and "the complainants played with the defendants at quek When they had "lost 39*s* 2*d*, their suspicions being aroused, they examined the board, and "found it to be false and deceptive, seeing that in three-quarters of the "board all the black squares were depressed below the white, and in "the remaining quarter the white below the black, and the dice were also "found to be false Hence, after a scuffle, Nicholas Prestone and John "Outlawe were brought before the mayor and aldermen, and sentenced to "refund the money which they had won, restore a cloak which they had "stolen in the scuffle, stand in the pillory for one hour in the day, while "the false board was burnt underneath them, and then be imprisoned in "Newgate until the mayor and aldermen ordered their release"

A similar case is quoted as occurring in 5 Richard II, A.D 1382, with similar consequences

Chatto, in his *History of Signboards*, says "In or near Calcot's alley, "Lambeth, was formerly an inn or house of entertainment, 'The Chequers.' "In the year 1454, a license was granted to its landlord, John Calcot, to "have an oratory in the house, and a chaplain for the use of his family "and his guests, as long as his house should continue orderly and "respectable, and adapted to the celebration of divine service"

He also adds "The chequers is the most patriarchal of all signs "It may be seen even on houses in exhumed Pompeii On that of Hercules, "*e.g.* at the corner of the Strada Fallorina, they are painted lozengewise, "red, white, and yellow, and on various other houses in that ancient city "similar decorations may still be observed."

Dr. Lardner, in his *Arithmetic*, p. 44, says that "during the Middle "Ages it was usual for merchants, accountants, &c., to appear on a covered "*banc*" (*i.e.* an old English word meaning seat). "Before them was placed "a plain surface, divided into squares. This latter was called an exchequer ". . . . and the calculations were made by counters placed upon its "several divisions. A money-changer's office was generally indicated by a "sign of the chequered board suspended. This sign afterwards came to "indicate an inn, probably from the circumstance of the innkeeper also "following the trade of money changer, a coincidence still very common "in seaport towns."

But the chequered shields represent, probably, that the founders of the family were members of the Court of Exchequer, "called," says Madox, in his *History of the Exchequer*, "scaccarium, from *scaccus* or "*scaccum*, a chess-board, because a chequered cloth was anciently wont "to be laid on the table in the court or place of that name. From the "Latin cometh the French word exchequier, and the English from the "French." The original object of the chequered cloth being to assist calculation, like the ancient abacus, which, in some form or another, seems to have been used from time immemorial. The Greeks and Romans certainly used it; the Russians use something of the sort still; while in China (where the whole system of measures, weights, &c., is decimal), the "shawnpah," as they call it, is used with marvellous rapidity.

"The King's Exchequer," says Theodore, "was anciently a member "of his Court, and was wont to be held in his palace. It was a sort of "subaltern court, partly resembling (in its model) that which was called "Curia Regis, for (in it) the King's barons and great men (who used to "be in his palace, near his royal person) ordinarily presided, but sometimes "the King himself. In it the King's chief justices, his chancellor, his "treasurer, his constable, his marshal, and his chamberlain, performed "some part of their several offices."

Madox divides the business of the Exchequer (during the period between the Conqueror and the reign of King John) under the head of revenues, causes, non-litigious business, and matters of public policy. The members were called the Barons of the Exchequer. Lysons says that "this court," which he calls 'the Upper Exchequer,' "is supposed to have "been in existence in the time of the Anglo-Saxon kings, but was not "established at Westminster until after the Conquest. Previously it was "itinerant, or accompanying the King's Court and progresses; and this "continued until the reign of Henry III., when the expense and "inconvenience of the removal of the Court from place to place, whither-"soever the King went, occasioned it being permanently established in "Westminster by the great Charter of 2 Henry III, instead of following "the movements of the Court As regards the 'Lower Exchequer,' the "King's treasury was anciently at Winchester, where William Rufus "found his father's heaps of gold and silver"

The reparation of the treasury house, in the time of Henry III, is also mentioned, and thither the treasure was carried from London by the sheriffs in the same reign There were, besides, some subordinate receipts or places of revenue, called also Exchequers, one was at Worcester, others at Nottingham, Shrewsbury, and York

Near Aylesbury is situated, in one of the most lovely spots amidst the Chiltern Hills, a beautiful old English mansion, called "Chequers," which, the same Lysons says, was originally the residence of John de Saccariis King John had a palace in the immediate vicinity, and this may have been the abode of one of the officers of the *Upper Exchequer*, or "Aula "Regia," or, perhaps, one of the treasuries of the *Lower Exchequer*, of which the said John had the charge

There are several families which carry a shield, the field of which is chequy, in different colours, and many which have the field of one "tincture" only, but the "ordinaries" thereon (*i e* chevron, bend, fesse,) chequy, *e g* the Royal House of Stuart, Or, a fesse chequy argent and azure Only Warren and Clifford, however, are clearly represented in the Minster There is in the south-west window of the Chapter House a shield, much defaced, which may be chequy Or and gules, in which case it would represent the arms of Hubert Vaux, created Baron of Gillesland by William the Conqueror His granddaughter, Maud, *temp* of Henry III, married Thomas de Multon, whose great-granddaughter, Margaret, married Ranulph, summoned to Parliament as Baron Dacre, 1321 His arms, three escallop shells, are in the south transept of the choir, and his descendant was the Lancastrian general whose death—by a "bird-bolt" shot at a venture by a boy from a tree,—contributed to the disastrous defeat of that party at the battle of Towton

Or, it is possible that this shield may have had a chief ermine in addition, in which case it would be the arms of Tateshall In the reign of Henry III, Sir Robert de Tateshall, by his marriage to Joan, daughter and co-heir of Robert Fitzranulph, Lord of Middleham, became possessed of the manor of Well and Snape with Crakehall and Bedale, in the North-Riding of Yorkshire He died in 1297, and was succeeded by his son, Robert de Tateshall, who was summoned to Parliament 1299–1302, and died 1303 He served King Edward I in the expedition to Gascony and in the wars of Scotland He was present at the siege of Caerlaverock, and was a party to the Barons' letter to the Pontiff, 1301

But now to turn our attention to the House of Clifford. The arms, chequy, or and azure a fesse gules, may be found in several places, viz.:—

In Glass.—Chapter House: north-west window.
Nave: south side, fifth window east.
Nave: north aisle, eighth window west, on one of the tabards of the figures in the border of the centre light.
Choir: south side, sixth window east, with 3 bezants on the fess.
In Stone.—North Choir: transept, south side.
Choir: north side, sixth window west.

Not only, however, do the arms thereof adorn our walls and windows, but the body of one member at least of the family rests within our precincts. At the east end of the Lady Chapel lies a black marble slab, the remains of a monument which—shattered by the falling beams at the fire which burnt the greater portion of the choir in 1829—has been lately restored by the present Duke of Devonshire. Whom does it commemorate? Frances Clifford. Truly a lady worthy of our sympathy and our interest, for she was the widow of Henry the last Earl Clifford, the intimate friend and companion of Thomas the great Lord Fairfax, whom he playfully addressed as "Worthy Father Tristram," until the civil war broke out, and even the staunchest friends were ranged on opposite sides and bitterly estranged from each other.

And so Lord Clifford Earl of Cumberland "heartily espoused the "Royal cause, yet not being in any degree active or of a martial tem- "perament," according to Clarendon; nevertheless, in his cousin Lady Anne's estimation, he was "a tall and proper man, a good courtier, a brave "horseman, an excellent huntsman, with good skill in architecture and "mathematics." In 1643 he came to York, probably to escape from the disturbed condition of his own country, Craven, and died in one of the Prebendaries' houses "of a burning fever," that same year. His body was buried in Skipton church amidst the clash of arms; for even there the Roundheads, under General Lambert, were hotly besieging the castle, which was stoutly held against them for three years under Sir John Mallory, the governor, a most valiant soldier. In three months his widow followed him, borne down with sorrow, and by the care and anxiety "which those "troublous times brought her;" and we can understand why, at such a time, her body was laid here instead of being buried by her husband.

Like many another life, her sorrows seem, perhaps, the greater because of the bright promise of her early days. She was the daughter of Robert Cecil, first Earl of Salisbury, second son of Queen Elizabeth's celebrated High Treasurer, Lord Burleigh, and a far more distinguished man than his elder and half-brother Thomas who succeeded his father. This Robert rose to be Secretary of State to the virgin Queen, which post, however (according to his letter to Sir John Harington, the poet), he found to be not altogether easy or agreeable "Good knight," he said, "rest content, and give heed to one who hath sorrowed in the bright "lustre of a Court, and gone heavily on even the best seeming fair ground "'Tis a great task to prove one's honesty and yet not mar one's fortune "You have tasted a little thereof in our blessed Queen's time, who was "more than a man, and in truth, sometimes, less than a woman I wish "I waited now in your presence chamber, with ease at my food and rest "in my bed I am pushed from the shore of comfort, and know not "where the winds and waves of a Court will bear me I know that it "bringeth little comfort on earth, and he is, I reckon, no wise man that "looketh this way to heaven"

His wife was Elizabeth, daughter of William Brooke Lord Cobham, and in the old gate-house at Bolton Abbey there is a charming picture, by Lucas Van de Heere, of this same William Brooke and his wife and her sister, standing behind a table covered with fruit and toys, at which are seated six children playing with a parrot and a monkey—four boys and two little girls

Of the four boys, one of them, the unhappy Henry Lord Cobham, (though made by Queen Elizabeth Lord Warden of the cinque ports) was arraigned by James I for participation in the alleged treason of Sir Walter Raleigh, attainted, deprived of all his property, and tortured by being brought on the scaffold and then taken back to linger fourteen more years in the Tower (while his heartless wife, Lady Kildare, was enjoying herself at Cobham, and contributing little or nothing to his support), until his death in 1618 Another, George, implicated with him in the same conspiracy, was beheaded on Tower Hill, 1603

The elder little girl grew up to become Countess of Salisbury, and probably gave this picture to her daughter, Frances, when she made an equally grand marriage and became the wife of Henry Lord Clifford, heir to the earldom of Cumberland

But her bright prospects were clouded, and her anticipations were disappointed Her three sons died, and, one by one, her natural expectations that her children would inherit and carry on the name and lineage of this noble house Her only daughter, Elizabeth, married Richard Boyle Viscount Dungarvan, eldest son of the first Earl of Cork an alliance which, for some reason or other, sorely displeased the young lady's uncle, Thomas Wentworth Earl of Strafford Some said because he was jealous of him, others because he disapproved of the manner in which he, as Deputy of Ireland, knew that the Earl of Cork had enriched himself with Church lands This, however, had doubtless produced family dissensions, and aggravated the feud which had raged ever since the death of George third Earl in 1605, between his daughter and heiress Lady Anne, and her cousins, Francis the late Earl, and Earl Henry. Troubles, too, without, were gathering and increasing. In 1641, the Earl of Strafford was beheaded; Earl Henry's duties as Lord Lieutenant of the Northern counties and governor of Newcastle, were becoming intolerable through the incursions of the Scotch and the vacillation of the King.

No wonder that, two years later (1643), she penned this touching entry in her account-book, containing the items of the expenses of her husband's funeral, viz., some £240: "Disbursed since the 11th day of December, the "yeare aforesaide, on which day it pleased God to take the soule of my "most noble Lord out of this miserable, rebellious age: I trust, to His "eternal joyes;" and, conscious that this great family was now extinct, and that its great estates must be divided and go to other families, she passed to that land where "the weary are at rest," within three months.

And it was, indeed, a great inheritance, which had accumulated through successive generations, and remained vast in extent and value, in spite of the reckless extravagance of some of its last possessors. And Whitaker, in his "*History of Craven*" (from which I quote) has given abundant details thereof.

The founder of the family, Fitz-Ponz, had come over in the train of the Conqueror, and received the castle of Clifford, in Herefordshire, as well as the office of Castellan of York Castle, where the almost only remaining fragment—the keep—still retains the name of Clifford's Tower; and also the hereditary privilege which, in after days, they more than once hotly contested, viz.: that of carrying the city sword before the King whenever he visited this ancient city.

In the thirteenth century, Roger de Clifford married Isabel Veteripont, daughter and co-heir of Richard Veteripont, Lord and Hereditary Sheriff of Westmoreland; by which marriage the castles of Pendragon, Brough, Appleby, and Brougham, and the intervening district, seventy miles in length, became the property of the Cliffords.

In the fourteenth century Edward II. transferred the Barony of Skipton—which his father had dishonestly wrested from John de Eshton, rightful heir to Aveline de Fortibus Countess of Albemarle, and which he himself had given to his short-lived favourite Piers de Gaveston—to Robert de Clifford, who afterwards fell at Bannockburn, June 24th, 1314, and in that family it continued, with the exception of a single attainder, for five hundred years.

Perhaps, too, in recognition of his martial services, the King granted to the Cliffords the honourable heraldic augmentation of three spiked heads of clubs, called "holy water sprinkles," which appear on their arms.

In the fifteenth century, John ninth Lord Clifford, known as the "Black Lord Clifford," married Margaret Bromflete, daughter and heiress of Sir Henry Bromflete, and brought into the Clifford family the title of Baron Vesci, and great estates at Londesborough

And, finally, in the sixteenth century, Henry Clifford, first Earl of Cumberland, by his marriage with Lady Margaret Percy, on the demise of her brother, Henry Earl of Northumberland, acquired the whole Percy *fee*, equivalent in extent to half of Craven While to complete their superiority in that district, Henry VIII, at the time of the dissolution of the monasteries, granted to him the priory of Bolton, with all the lands thereto belonging, in the parish of Skipton, together with the manor of Storithes, Heslewood, Embsey, Eastby, Conondley, &c, and the manor of Woodhouse, which last belonged to the dissolved priory of Marton

Truly, a goodly inheritance, not only in extent but in value, for though every portion thereof had not been brought under cultivation, yet even from the wide tracts of forest there was something more substantial to be gained than the pleasures of the chase They were under the charge of bailiffs, who (in each bailiwick, as it was called) had their staff of foresters, verderers, regarders, agistors, and woodwards, who collected and annually accounted for the profits of waifs, agistments, pannage (*i e* money for the pasturage of hogs on the acorns, &c), husset (*i e* French "houset," holly, the croppings of which formed a principal article of winter fodder for cattle as well as sheep, and was valuable, as appears from an entry in Henry Younge the forester of Barden's book, A D 1437 "Of hussett sold to the amount of "iv iiis viii[d]"—at least £50 of our money), also of bark-croppings, turbery, and bee-stock For in the old economy of the forest, wild bee-stocks were always an object of attention, and in France, as well as in England, officers called Bigres or Bigri, perhaps from apigeri, were appointed specifically for pursuing the bees and securing their wax and honey And it is to be remembered that those rugged districts, now stripped of their woods, are spoken of in the compotus of Bolton as far from destitute of timber The manor and chase of Barden comprised 3,252 acres The forest of Skipton, which comprised an area of six miles by four, or 15,360 acres, seems to have been enclosed from very early times with a pale,—a practice, indeed, introduced by the Norman lord Here the mast-bearing and bacciferous trees, particularly the arbutus, were planted, and herein were nourished the stag, the wild boar, the fallow deer, the roe, and the oryx (or the wild bull), which, indeed, during the winter were fed with beans, even as the few remaining deer above Bolton are fed still There was many a "toft "and croft" also, as they were called (*i e* a homestead with a space of clear ground around it), where sheep browsed among the brushwood and glades

And so the forest furnished support for those who dwelt in it, either by fair means or foul. Fair means: as, when John Steining, the keeper, saw my "lord that now is, with his company, hunt in Rilstone, and hound "30 brace of deer, both horned and not horned, and kill all they might, "both red and fallow." Or when "Old Lady Clifford," (as Launcelot Marton, lord of Eshton, one of her gentlemen, says,) "would hound her "greyhounds within the said grounds of Rilstone, and chase deer, and bring "them away at her leisure." Also when "Master John Norton gate leave "of my olde lord for a morsel of flesh for his wife's 'churching,' and had "half of a 'grete fat stag,' which Robert Gorton hunted and killed, and "'had the shulders and the ombles' for his trouble."

And foul means: as when, in 1499, Will Gyzeley was bound in penalty of £40 "conditional to save harmless the deer and woods of Henry Lord "Clifford;" or when, in 1546, "James Horner, of Beamsley, enters into "recognizances with two sureties to be of good abearing to my lord's deer "within Craven;" and when, in 1575, "Thomas Frankland, of Michels Ing, "Gent., for killing and destroying deere, as well tame as wild and savage, "in Litondale and Longstroth," was required to yield himself as prisoner into the castle of Skipton, there to remain during the Earl's pleasure.

The record does not proceed to say whether he complied with this summons, but if his doing so involved his being immured in the gloomy dungeon—which I saw, until the guide blew out his lamp, and then, verily, there was a darkness which might be felt—he was a wise man if he kept away, or fled the country.

Yes, then as now, country gentlemen quarrelled over their game, and frequent strife took place between the Cliffords and the Nortons; and a grave complaint is made by the same Master Marton that Master Norton, "to draw my Lord of Cumberland's deer into his ground, hath made a "wall on a high rigge beside a quagmire, and at the end of the wall he "hath rayled the ground, so that it is destruction to my Lord's deer as "many as come." And Whitaker tells us that, after 300 years, vestiges still remain on Rilstone Fell of this very ground, and of the cunning of Master Richard Norton.

And the castle of Skipton, though not, as we have seen, the only residence, was, at least, the principal residence of the Cliffords, and though, perhaps, as such, its size a little disappoints one's expectations, it is a goodly building, and well worthy of examination as one of the few remaining specimens of a feudal baron's castle of the olden time.

The outer wall of the castle, which encloses a space about 650 feet long by 300 feet wide, is pierced by a massive gateway, comparatively modern, bearing the arms of Henry fifth Earl of Cumberland, by whom it was possibly rebuilt, the parapet above being perforated with the family motto: "Desormais" (henceforth).

The western, or more ancient portion of the castle, which stands back some 150 feet from the gate, and which was probably erected by Robert de Clifford, who entertained Edward II on October 1st and 2nd, 1323, is about 60 yards in length, with irregular sides, each corner flanked by a massive round tower The northern wall stands on the brink of a perpendicular rock washed by a torrent, to the bed of which from the battlements is 200 feet In the glen beneath was the pleasure-ground of the Cliffords, consisting of fish-ponds, walks, &c Within is the inner or conduit court, shaded by an ancient yew tree, said to have been planted here in 1642, in the place of one destroyed by the siege, but which, however pleasant in summer, must have rendered the rooms, the windows of which all look into the very picturesque court, inconveniently dark during the rest of the year The banqueting hall, on the north side, is a fine lofty room, 50 feet by 28 feet, with the kitchen on the one side and the withdrawing room on the other, and there are many other rooms—one said to have been tenanted by Mary Queen of Scots, whose visit here is very apocryphal, and one called "Fair Rosamond's inner chamber," who, however, had been dead and buried years before Skipton Castle came into the hands of her family

The eastern portion, about 160 feet long, and flanked by a massive octagonal tower, was built by Henry first Earl of Cumberland, in 1536, for the reception of Lady Eleanor Brandon, who married his son Henry, 1537 As daughter of Charles Brandon Duke of Suffolk, and his wife Mary, sister of Henry VIII, and widow of Louis King of France, such an enlargement of the castle was deemed necessary "The Lady Eleanor's "grace," says Whitaker, "appears to have been received by the family "(who, no doubt, were proud of such an alliance), with the honour of "royalty, and a long gallery was then considered as a necessary appendage "to every princely residence" The long gallery has, however, been cut up into bedrooms, the old pictures have been removed to Appleby Castle, and there is nothing of interest in this part of the building, except the upper room in the octagonal tower, hung with ghastly but good tapestry, representing the tortures of the Inquisition, used as a bedroom by Lady Anne Clifford, Countess of Dorset and Pembroke, the last of the direct line of the Cliffords, during her residence here

Three curious inventories are extant, which give us some idea of the furnishing thereof at different periods of the tenancy by the Cliffords

In that of 1572, taken after the death of the second Earl, there is a curious list of "My Lord's app'ell"

The ordinary habit of a nobleman at that time consisted of a doublet and hose—a cloak, or sometimes a long gown, sometimes a short gown with sleeves

Amongst many items, mention is made of "a black velvet gown "with a black laice furred with squyrels, and faced with jenets furr, some- "thing decayed;" "one single gowne of black sattan garded with velvet, "very olde;" "one black velvet jacket imbrothured with silver and faced "with luserdes, and furred thorowly with whyte lambe;" "a black velvet "jyrkine, with golde lace, having xvi. buttons enamelled black, lined with "sarcenet, very olde."

Here, also, are mentioned his robes as Knight of the Garter: "a "kyrtle of crimson velvet, and a robe of blew velvet, and a hode, &c."

Also "a hole horse harness, for a trapper, sett with whit and blew, "and enamelled;" another harness of red velvet, containing six pieces; and one other harness of "black velvet imbrothured with silver gilt, "cont'g vii. pieces;" "iii. paynes of cloth of gold, and ii. of tawny "velvet, with a redd dragon lokyng forthe of a whit castell, mad of "sylver tys-say," the crest of the Cliffords. "Item iii. rydynge hatts, one "of cremsyn velvet, with a golde bande;" another of "tawney velvet "with a golde bande, and laced with silver laice;" "one murreon (morion), "covered with cremesyn vellvett and laid with lacce of golde;" and so on.

A small stock of "app'ell in a cheist," probably belonging to Lady Eleanor Brandon, is also mentioned; "a frenge gowne, with a long trayne "of black satten, edged with black velvet;" "a purple satten gowne, "playted with five pieces of gold aglets garded with velvet, faced with "grayn coloured sarcenet;" "a kirtle of cremesyn damask, with one "over bodie of satten of bridges, and welted with cremyson velvett;" "one pair of sleeves of black velvett, of the French fac'on;" "ii. parre "of velvet shoys, grene, redd, and white." This, of course, is only a portion, but enough for a specimen of a lady's wardrobe in those days.

But it is noticeable that, though everything was strong and costly—velvet, satin, sarcenet, gold lace and fur—yet many articles are described as old and worn. A wardrobe at that time lasted for a life and more, and was handed down from generation to generation.

Of the rooms, only two bedchambers are mentioned, which seem to have been entirely destitute of what we should deem necessary furniture, only a "coppard," and one stool. Not a glass, a carpet, or even a chair, appears in any of the rooms; but the beds must have been magnificent, and, judging from "federbedds, beds of down," bolsters, pillows, blankets, &c., very comfortable.

In "La Strange Chamb'r" (*i.e.* the state bedchamber), the tester of the bed was of "tynsell and black vellvett with armes, having curtains of "sylke with frynges."

In the "corner chamb'r," the tester was of "black vellvett and tynsel, with curtaynes of silk, and frynges of silke and golde."

In the "great well chamb'r," the tester was of "grene tawnsy vell-"vett and tynsell, with armes on, and also curtains of grene and yalowe "sarcenett, and frynges of silk"

Several pieces of hangings are mentioned with "Adam and Eve," "The Distruccon of Troye," "The Storie of David," and "Hunting and "Hawking" thereon, and "carpetts" are mentioned, one called a "coucher," but they seem to be for tables (*i e* covers)

A certain, though not considerable, amount of plate is mentioned—"bowles," "cupps," "playtes," "great saltes," with "dragons" and lybard-"heads," and with "percullions and the rose graven"

The stock of cattle and horses is also mentioned, the latter seem to have been named from friends, or those from whom they had been purchased "Grey Clifford," "White Dacre," "Sorell Tempest," "Bay Middleton" The list, too, of "cassens," "yron slyngges," "deculverons," "harquebers," "corsletts," "lawnces," "briganteens," "mawles," "battell axes," seems to shew that the castle was well armed, and that the arms were well disposed throughout the building

About twenty years later, viz 1591, another inventory was made, which mentions at least some articles of furniture the drawing chamber has "three hangings of arrisworke, bought of Mr Yorke, one hanging or ' counter point of forcet worke, with Clifford armes, two cheares of estate "of clothe of silver, three long quisheons, suited to the same, one low "stoole, suitable, five buffetts covered with crimson velvet, and five with "grene velvet" Hangings of dornix (perhaps damask) are mentioned

During the twenty years, paintings had found their way to Skipton, for "in the wardropp were xiii Herculas pictures, and xxiii Vislereus"

The list of books in the "high court" (the library of the castle), was certainly not very extensive "1 booke of Bocas, 1 greatt owld bowke, "1 great bowke or grele for singing, 1 trunk of wickers covert with lether "with bowks and scrowles in"

The pantry contained "sylv spoones, vi., knives ii. case, and iv "glasses, ii gilt with one cover, trenchers, iv dozen"

Upon the death of the last Earl, in 1643, another inventory was taken, which indicates a further advance, not only in the quantity but the quality of the furniture Amongst many other things, we find mentioned in the great hall "7 large pieces of hangings with the Earl's arms at "large in every one of them, and poudered with the severall coates of the "house, 1 fayre brass lantern, 1 iron cradle with wheells for charcoal" (*i e* a movable grate, the fumes from which should escape through the cupola above) The "alms tubb," from which the oatmeal would be doled out to the poor The "Church Bible and Booke of Common Prayer"

"In the parler 1 oval table, 1 side boarde, 1 payre of organs, 1 harpsicon

K 2

"In the byllyard chamber and terrayce: one byllard board, the "picture of our Saviour and Virgin Mary, 12 pictures in black and "whyte, 3 landskippes in frames, 16 mappes of cities and shires.

"In the great chamber: 12 high chayres of green damask, 2 grene "carpets, 2 large window curtaynes of grenet, 8 pictures. Item: 1 Turkey-"work carpet, a large one.

"In the closet: my Lady Frances' gettorne, and 2 trowle-madams, "or pigeon-holes.

"In the music room: 1 great picture of the Countess of Cumberlande, "1 statue of her grandfather Burleigh, in stone."

In this inventory fifty-seven apartments are named—the best rooms hung with arras; the better beds with silk or velvet.

There appears to have been but one looking-glass in the house, in the Earl's room. The plate had been sent to York, I suppose for safety, but ineffectually, for the countess of Cork, the Earl's sole heiress, "complains in another paper that, at the surrender of the city, she had "effects taken from her to the amount of £1,500, contrary to the articles."

The household books, which have been preserved, contain many quaint entries illustrative of the customs of the times, and, I am afraid I must add, the extravagance of the family.

In the first year of the seventeenth century, the income from the Craven and Londesborough estates was about £2,000, the expenditure £3,000, and sometimes nearly double; but they were as generous as they were hospitable, and allowed ten per cent. upon all bills not paid the first year.

The household consisted of thirty servants, and the money was spent in wines, journeys, clothes, presents, and tobacco. Claret, sack, and muscadine, they consumed in such quantities that it is only reasonable to suppose that the upper servants had their share at least of the first. For tobacco they paid 18*s*. per lb., the best, and inferior, 12*s*.

The following items which I have selected, will throw a curious light upon the comparative value of things in those days and ours:—"Five "hundred oysters, 2*s*. 6*d*. Halfe toone of wine for my lord, £8 5*s*. 0*d*. "For 31 trootes, eles and ombres, 1*s*. 6*d*. Paid to William Townley for "6 lb. and 1 oz. of pepper, for baking a stagg sent to Grafton, for another "sent to Westmorland and Cumberland for the assizes, 18*s*. 6*d*. For ¼ lb. "of sugar which Sir Stephen Tempest had in wyne, 5*d*." Sugar, therefore, cost 1*s*. 8*d*. per lb., as the value of money at that time went.

The price of a fat wether was scarcely that of 2 lbs. of sugar. "4 chickens and 24 eggs, 1*s*. 6*d*.; 45 eggs, at 5 a penny, 9*d*.; 4 lbs. of "butter, 1*s*. 4*d*.; 10 burden of rishes against the judge coming, 20*d*.

If food was cheap clothing was expensive: "A suite for my lord of "fyne Spanish cloth, laced with 3 gould and silver laces, with silk stockings, "garters, roses, and all things belonging thereunto, £60 8*s* 7*d* A bever and "gold band, £3 16*s* o*d* 11 payre of whyte kidd gloves, and 2 paire of "stagg's leather, one plain, three trim'd with gold lace and plush, £1 9*s* 2*d* "A malmouth capp, tufted with plush and gold lace, 18*s*" A single suit for Henry Earl of Cumberland, 1632, cost £154 4*s* 9*d*

A great amount of money went in travelling About the year 1620, Lord Clifford paid £88 3*s* 9*d* in travelling to London, a journey which occupied eleven days In 1635 he went to Ireland by way of Scotland, and the journey cost £312 4*s* 7*d* A few of the items are curious "To "two pipers at Carlisle, 3*s* For a merlin that went to my ould lord, "£1 o*s* o*d* To my lord at cards, 10*s*"

"By my lorde's appointment, to my Lord Clifford, my Lady Clifford, "my Lady Margaret, and my Lady Frances, to each of them in gold "10 twenty-shilling pieces, as new year's gift, XLIII L Paid Sir William "Paddie for his opinion in prescribing my lord a course for taking of "phisicke, £3 6*s* o*d*"

1620 "For two paire of tongs and two fyre-shovels for my Lord "Clifford's chamber, and for my little Miss her chamber For a warming "pan, 7*d* For the poor prisoners at Ludgate, and to the poore, all along "the way as his lordship went to the Tower To Mr Gill, the barber, "who did trimme my lorde before his lordship went to court, 6*s*"

In 1622, Feb 28th "Paid this day for the charges of Mr Jonas, "Mr Tailor, the Parson, Mr Edward Demsay, Cornelius Atkinson, &c "Two footmen and seven horses going to Skipton with the bodie of my "little sweete maister, Mr Charles Clifford, when he went to be buried, "the sum of four pounds, and what we gave on the way to the poore in "coming and going"

Of the festivals of this family there are few memorials, but it may be interesting to give some items of the finery and good cheer of the wedding of George Clifton to Mary Nevill, of Chevet, "21st year of the "reign of our Sovereign Lord King Henry VIII, 1530," in the records of the Cliffords, with which I will close this rather protracted portion of my subject

The dresses of the happy couple were rather funereal, viz, "the "bridegroom a gown of velvet 2½ yards £1 10*s* o*d*, richly trimmed with "skins, together with a jacket and doublet of black satin at 8*s* per yard" The lady was also clad in black satin Bridesmaids are not mentioned, but there are "3 black velvet bonnets for women," at 17*s*, 30 white lamb skins at 4*s*, two ells of white ribbon, for tippets, at 1*s* 1*d*, a pair of mytten sleeves, white satin 8*s*, and a wedding-ring of gold 12*s* 4*d*, six yards of white damask at 8*s*, so there was some white, then The total expense of their dresses was £30 16*s* 1*d*, and the dinner which followed, £61 8*s* 8*d*

The wedding feast of her sister, Elizabeth Nevill to George Rockley, seems to have lasted for a week, and to have been very sumptuous. The *menu* of the first day is as follows:—"First course:—First, brawn with "mustard served alone with malmsey; *item*, frumetty to pottage, a roe "roasted for standart, peacocks 2 of a dish, swans 2 of a dish, a great "pike on a dish, conies roasted 4 of a dish, venison roasted, capon of "grease 3 of a dish, mallards 4 of a dish, teals 7 of a dish, pyes baken with "rabbits in them, baken oringe, a flampett, stoke fritters, dulcetts 10 of "a dish, a tart. Second course:—Martens to potage, for a standart 2 "cranes of a dish, young lamb whole roasted, great fresh sammon gollis, "heron sewes 3 of a dish, bytters 3 of a dish, pheasants 4 of a dish, a "great sturgeon goil, partridges 8 of a dish, stints 8 of a dish, plovers 8 of "a dish, curlews 8 of a dish, a whole roe baken, venison baken, red and "fallow, a tart, a marchpane, gingerbread, apples, and cheese stewed with "sugar and sage."

The arrangements for the evening were as follows:—"First a play, "and streight after the play a maske, and when the maske was done, then "the bankett, which was 110 dishes and all of meat, and then all the "gentlemen and ladyes danced; and this continued from Sunday to the "Saturday after,"—except Friday and Saturday, when there was only fish. Expenses of the week for fish/and flesh, £46 5*s*. 8*d*.

Three hogsheads of wine, two white, the one red, one claret, costing £5 5*s*., with barley-malt for beer, £6 18*s*. 8*d*., seem to have been the amount of liquor provided.

But it is time we turned from the possessions of the Cliffords to the Cliffords themselves, and though in so long a line they are not all heroes, there were at least some of them who, for weal or woe, deserve a recognition as having taken active part in some of the most stirring incidents of our national history.

Of Clifford, the castellan of York Castle, there is little to be said. It is reported that his name was originally Fitz-Punt, or Ponz, and that coming on with the Conqueror, he acquired the name and castles of Clifford, in Herefordshire, by marriage with the heiress thereof, and that, on being appointed Governor of York, he built the ancient tower of the castle which to this day bears his name.

But to an early member of this family, probably his granddaughter, Fair (and I am afraid I must add frail) Rosamond, an unenviable notoriety is attached. She is said to have been the daughter of Walter de Clifford, a baron of the marches of Wales, of so turbulent a character that when one of the King's officers endeavoured to serve a writ upon him, he enforced the luckless official "to eate the King's writ, wax and all."

His daughter is said to have been educated at the nunnery of God stow, where she probably became acquainted with Henry II, as that monarch resided constantly at the Palace de Bello Monte (now Beaumont Street), built by Henry I, 1153, just outside the then city walls, and here also his legitimate son Richard Cœur de Lion was born

Without adopting all the stories current about this young lady, it is evident that Eleanor of Guienne was not likely to tolerate such a rival, and that the King should endeavour to conceal her from her jealous eye, first (if tradition is true) at Ludgershall, near Aylesbury, where there is still a lane called "Rosamond's way," and then in a carefully secluded bower at Woodstock, where, in what is now called Blenheim park, Fair Rosamond's well is still shewn, so called from a tradition that this rill supplied her bath during her residence hereat Indeed, when Sir John Vanbrugh was employed by the great Duke of Marlborough to build his palace here he pleaded to be allowed to preserve the "ancient remains" of Rosamond's bower, but Duchess Sarah was an imperious and suspicious lady, and imagining that he had an eye to it as a residence for himself, or to spite him, on the plea of saving £200 for its repair ordered it to be swept away, 1709

Local tradition says that Fair Rosamond accepted neither the poison nor the dagger which the indignant Queen offered her, but that she retired to the nunnery where she had been brought up, and ended her days in penitence, worshipping, from time to time, in the crypt of St Peter's in the East, Oxford, and eventually was buried by her parents beneath the high altar

"Her body then they did entombe
When life was fled away,
At Godstowe, near to Oxford towne,
As may be seen this day"

King John, with more charity than one is inclined to ascribe to him, or to vent his spleen, is said by Lombard to have erected a costly monument with this inscription

"Hic jacet, in tumulo, Rosa mundi, non Rosa munda
Non redolet, sed olet qua redolere solet"

It would be difficult to give a correct interpretation of this little distich, preserving at the same time the particular imagery of the Latin, but it is not quite clear whether the writer intended it in praise or in blame, whether he would gracefully whitewash the not altogether unquestionable memory of the departed, or cunningly express his opinion as to her real character If the former, and he is to be regarded as speaking with that charity which covereth a multitude of sins, perhaps the following would be an appropriate rendering —

"Here lies enshrined, within this little tomb,
A Rose of earth, not one of spotless bloom;
Noways remarkable midst Human flowers,
But just like others in this world of ours."

If the latter, it may be thus rendered:

"Here lies in grave, foul Rosamond, not fair,
A Rose of dust, not beauty, whose fragrance rare,
Erewhile so sweet, would now pollute the air."

Or,

"Here lies enshrined, within this little tomb,
A Rose of earth, and not of spotless bloom;
No longer perfumed, now consigned to earth,
Fœtid, like all decay of mortal birth."

But Stowe records that when Hugh, Bishop of Lincoln, came to Godstow in 1491, and entered the church, "he was so shocked by the "sight of her tombe in the middle of the quire, covered with a pall of "silke, and set about with lights of wax, that he ordered that her remains "should be taken up and buried without the church 'lest Christian religion "should grow in contempt.'" Perhaps the stern justice of the mitred ecclesiastic was as right as the charity of the royal layman. At any rate, the spirit had passed, we trust, to find in another world the forgiveness she had humbly sought here; and she had left behind her two noble sons, Richard Long-épée, Earl of Salisbury, and Geoffry Plantagenet, eventually Archbishop of York. They alone, of all Henry II.'s children, were a comfort to him.

The latter is said to have been his favourite son; and Canon Raine, in his *Lives of the Archbishops*, has given a touching account of the monarch's death-bed in the castle of Chinon. "The head and shoulders "of the sick man were resting on his son's breast, who was driving away "with a fan the flies that buzzed around his father's face, while a knight, "at the end of the bed, held to his bosom his master's feet. The eye "of the enfeebled monarch opened and fell upon his son. He told him "that, though base born, he had been a truer child to him than all his "rightful children. Should his life be spared his filial affection should "not be unrewarded. He bade him prosper and be blessed. His eyes "closed, but when he heard the expressions of grief which his son was "unable to repress, they opened again. Henry was dying, but he knew "him, and faltered out his wish that he might be Bishop of Winchester "or Archbishop of York; blessed him for the last time, and gave him, as "a final token of his affection, a ring of gold, and a ring with a noble "sapphire which he had worn and regarded as a talisman."

After this he passed away, and Geoffry committed his remains most reverently to the tomb in the church of Fontevraud.

Thither Richard, it is said, came, gazed upon the face of his injured sire for the last time, groaned in spirit, and prostrating himself on his knees beside the corpse in unavailing penitence, uttered words which have been so touchingly rendered by Mrs Hemans —

"Thy silver hairs I see,
So still, so sadly bright,
And, father, father, but for me
They had not been so white!
I bore thee down, high heart, at last,
No longer couldst thou strive
Oh, for one moment of the past,
To kneel and say Forgive!"

Space fails me to dwell on all the distinguished members of this illustrious house, for each generation seems to have provided its quota to the valiant and patriotic men of England, ready to do and die for what they felt best for their country

Robert, the first Lord, son of Roger and Isabel de Vipont, co-heiress of Roger de Vipont Lord of Westmoreland, was the comrade and friend of Edward I He was present with him at the siege of Caerlaverock The rhyming chronicler of that exploit, Walter of Exeter, describes him in glowing terms, ending with the words "If I were a damsel I would give "him my heart and person, so great is his reputation" He seems to have taken a very active part in the siege, and when it surrendered he was appointed governor of the castle, and his banner placed on its battlements His seal appears amongst those of the barons attached to the letter to Pope Boniface, 1301 In it he is described as "Castellanus de Appleby, and in the thirty-fourth year of Edward I he received, in recognition of his services with Agmer de Valune against Robert Bruce, the grant of the borough of Hartlepool and of all Bruce's lands For him he held the border fortress of Carlisle against the Scotch, and from him, on his death-bed at Burgh-on-the-Sands, 1307, he received the solemn charge to be loyal to his son, and preserve him from the evil influence of Piers Gaveston

He fulfilled the latter by joining Lancaster in putting the insane favourite to death, and the former by sacrificing his own life in the disastrous battle of Bannockburn, June 24th, 1314, aged forty, when the English were defeated and Edward II escaped with difficulty to Berwick

An old chronicler says of him that he "always soe kept the King's "favour that he lost not the love of the nobility and kingdom" Loyalty to his sovereign, and fidelity to his country, were his distinguishing characteristics

His son Roger followed, with indifferent success, in his father's footsteps Anxious to deliver the unhappy Edward from the power of his new favourites the Spencers, he and other barons conspired with Thomas of Lancaster, in his castle at Pontefract; and Sir Wm. de Pakington, an old chronicler, says that he "toke out his dagger and sayd he would kill him "with his oune hande in that place, except he would go with them."

But the battle at Boroughbridge was disastrous to their cause; the barons were beaten, Lancaster himself and many others were taken prisoners, and executed at Pontefract. Holinshead says that "Clifford was "hanged in yron chaines at York." Sir Matthew Hale says "that by "reason of his great wounds, being held a dying man, he was respited, "and that he died a natural death, 1327."

Two members of the House of Clifford held office in this Minster during the fourteenth century. Richard de Clifford—son of Thomas de Clifford, younger brother of Roger fifth Lord—Dean of York from 1397 to 1401, and afterwards Bishop of Worcester, Bishop of London, and Cardinal. He enriched the fess with a mitre stringed argent, and added a border of the second. John de Clifford, probably his uncle, was treasurer of the Minster, 1374. He may have borne the coat with the augmentation of three bezants, significant of his office, which appears amongst the coloured illustrations.

Thomas, the sixth Lord, was the dissolute friend of Richard II.

John, the seventh, a faithful and brave comrade of Henry V. With fifty men-at-arms and 150 archers he joined the King in France, and, made a Knight of the Garter for his services, fell, when only thirty-three years of age, at the siege of Meaux, 1422.

His son Thomas, eighth Lord, at the outbreak of the War of the Roses, in 1455, threw in his power and influence with the Lancastrians; and in the last act of his play of *Henry VI.*, part ii., Shakespeare, or at any rate the writer of that play, represents him sharply taunting the Earl of Warwick for his disloyalty to Henry VI., in the King's presence, and then, shifting the scene to St. Albans, introduces Warwick vehemently desiring to avenge this insult by single combat—

"Clifford of Cumberland! 'tis Warwick calls,
And (if thou dost not hide thee from the bear)
Now, when the angry trumpet sounds alarm,
And dead men's cries do fill the empty air,
Clifford, I say, come forth and fight with me!
Proud northern Lord, Clifford of Cumberland,
Warwick is hoarse with calling thee to arms."

Richard Duke of York, however, interferes, and insists on fighting with Clifford, slays him in the encounter—according to Whitaker they were first cousins—and departs. Young Clifford, as he is called (*i.e.* John, by his father's death ninth Lord Clifford), comes in, laments his father's death, and resolves upon a vengeance of ruthless extermination:—

"Wast thou ordained, dear father
To lose thy youth in peace, and to achieve
The silver livery of advised age,
And (in thy reverence and thy chair-days) thus
To die in ruffian battle? Even at this sight
My heart is turned to stone, and while 'tis mine
It shall be stoney
"York not our old men spares,
No more will I their babes, tears virginal
Shall be to me even as the din to fire,
And beauty (that the tyrant oft reclaims)
Shall to my flaming wrath be oil and flax
Henceforth I will not have to do with pity
Meet I an infant of the House of York,
Into as many gobbets will I cut it
As wild Medea young Absyrtus did
In cruelty will I seek out my fame,
Come, thou new ruin of old Clifford's House!"

The great dramatist was scarcely accurate in the first part, for Thomas Lord Clifford could not have been more than forty-one at this time But the son's passionate anger at his father's death is true to nature, specially in family quarrels

And certainly he soon evidenced in action what he is here made to express in word, for the battle of St Albans took place May 22nd, 1455, and the battle of Wakefield followed, December, 1460 The Duke of Somerset commanded the Lancastrian force, while Lord Clifford and the Earl of Wiltshire each had charge of a strong reserve concealed from the main body The Duke of York was drawn from his stronghold, Sandal Castle, by the taunts of Queen Margaret "All men," said he, "would cry wonder, and report dishonour that a woman had made a "dastard of me whom no man could even to this day report as a "coward, and surely my mind is rather to die with honour than to live "with shame Advance, my banners, in the name of God and St George" But the unsuspected ambushes assailed his rear when he attacked the main body Thus surrounded, his forces were literally hacked to pieces, and he and all his chief leaders were slain

Lord Clifford carried out his determination only too ruthlessly Meeting the Duke's son, the young Earl of Rutland, hurrying from the bloody scene, he repelled his tutor Aspall, who appealed to him for protection, and, as the rancorous memories of St Albans filled his breast, "By God's "blood," he said, "thy father slew mine, and so will I thee and all thy "kin," and plunging his dagger into his heart, he said to the chaplain, with a scornful leer, "Go, bear him to his mother, and tell her what thou "hast seen and heard"

The great dramatist of Stratford has vividly portrayed this scene (*Henry VI.* part iii., Act i. Sc. 2). Rutland speaks, as the soldiers are approaching,—

"Ah! whither shall I fly to escape their hands?
Ah! tutor, see where bloody Clifford comes!

Enter Clifford and soldiers.

"*Clifford.*—Chaplain, away! thy priesthood saves thy life.
As for the brat of this accursed Duke,
Whose father slew my father, he shall die.

"*Tutor.*—Ah! Clifford, murder not this innocent child,
Lest thou be hated both of God and man."

The youth pleads with Clifford to spare his life:

"Ah! gentle Clifford, kill me with thy sword,
And not with such a cruel, threatening look.
Sweet Clifford, hear me speak before I die;
O, let me pray before I take my death,
To thee I pray; sweet Clifford, spare me."

He reminds him of his own one son, and implores him, as he desires God's blessing on him, to spare his life, but in vain. The savage answer is returned, "Thy father slew my father, therefore die."

I am afraid that Shakespeare in these words only too faithfully idealized the wanton cruelty of this passionate, revengeful act, of which the cutting off of the Duke of York's head and placing it on Micklegate Bar encircled with a paper crown was but a natural sequel, and far more likely to be his act than, as Shakespeare represents it, the act of Queen Margaret.

Clifford's own end came soon, for, on the eve of the battle of Towton he was slain by a bird-bolt in the neck, in a skirmish at Dinting Dale.

Truly, as the old chronicler says of him: "For this act was Lord Clifford accounted a tyrant and no gentleman." It was a black deed, even according to the standard of those days, and "Blackfaced Clifford" was the title not unjustly bestowed.

His son Henry was spared the divine retribution which poor young Rutland had forecasted for him, and—carried off by his mother while still a child, to Threlkeld, in Cumberland, the residence of her second husband, Sir Lancelot Threlkeld—his very existence was carefully concealed; and, placed under the charge of the shepherds, he grew up in the rank of a simple shepherd, ignorant of his title and possessions, a stranger to the luxuries and pleasures of his rank, inured to hardships and privations, and utterly unlearned, except in the book of nature always before him. Wordsworth thus describes him:—

"Our Clifford was a happy youth,
And thankful through a weary time
That brought him up to manhood's prime
Again he wanders forth at will,
And tends a flock from hill to hill
His garb was humble, ne'er was seen
Such garb with such a noble mien
Among the shepherds' grooms no mate
Hath he, a child of strength and state,
Yet lacks not friends for solemn glee,
And a cheerful company
That learned of him submissive ways,
And comforted his private days
To his side the fallow deer
Came and rested without fear,
The eagle (lord of land and sea)
Stooped down to pay him fealty
He knew the rocks which angels haunt,
On the mountains visitant,
He hath kenned them taking wing,
And the caves where fairies sing
He hath entered, and been told,
By voices, how men lived of old
Among the heavens his eye can see,
Face of things that is to be,
And (if men report him right)
He could whisper words of might"

For twenty-five years Clifford remained in concealment, but when the union of the opposing factions of York and Lancaster was effected by the marriage of Henry VII with Elizabeth, daughter of Edward IV, in 1486, he emerged from his concealment, and petitioned for the restoration of his title and estates So Wordsworth, in his *Song at the Feast of Brougham Castle*, says —

"From town to town, from town to town
The red rose is a gladsome flower,
His thirty years of winter past,
The red rose is revived at last!
She lifts her head for endless spring,
For everlasting blossoming
Both roses flourish, red and white,
In love and sisterly delight
The two that were at strife are blended,
And all old troubles now are ended"

Lord Clifford was thirty-one years old when he entered on his estates, but his early training had ill-disposed him to take any prominent position in the world Loving seclusion and the companionship of the quiet and retiring, he fixed on one of the most sequestered spots on his estate, Barden Tower, and, adapting it for his residence, devoted himself to the study of astrology and alchemy with the monks of the adjacent priory of Bolton

Hartley Coleridge says of him: "Because he was an illiterate man "it does not follow that he was an ignorant man. He might know many "things well worthy of knowing without being able to write his name. "He might learn a great deal of astronomy by patient observation. He "might know where each native flower on the hills was grown, what real "qualities it possessed, and what occult powers the fancies, the fears, or "the wishes of men had ascribed to it. The haunts, habits, and instincts "of animals, the notes of birds and their wondrous architecture, were to "him instead of books; but, above all, he learned to know something of "what man is in that condition to which the greater number of men are "born, and to know himself better than he could have done in his "hereditary sphere. And amidst such lovely surroundings and such con-"genial society his life passed peacefully and blamelessly away, in strange "contrast to that of his father."

He was twice married, first to Anne, daughter of Sir John St. John; second, to Florence daughter of Henry Pudsey; and he had one daughter, and a son who succeeded to his title and estates, but not to his good example.

Only twice did he leave the retirement he loved so well: once when he led his men against the Scots when they invaded England, 1497; and again, when sixty years of age, he led a force of Craven yeomen to battle on Flodden Field, 1513.

In that engagement he had a principal command, and helped materially to turn the fortunes of the day.

"From Pennygent to Pendle Hill,
From Linton to Long Addingham,
And all that Craven coasts did till,
They with the lusty Clifford came.
All Staincliffe hundred went with him,
With striplings strong from Wharlédale,
And all that Hauton hills did climb,
With Longstroth eke and Litton Dale,
Whose milk-fed fellows, fleshy bred,
Well brown'd, with sounding bows upbend.
All such as Horton Fells had fed
On Clifford's banner did attend."*

He survived the battle ten years, and died in 1523, aged seventy. His place of sepulchre is unknown. Let us believe that "all that was "mortal" of such a gentle and gallant man rests under the (now) turf-clad aisles of Bolton priory, amidst the streams and glades which he loved so well.

* From *Metrical History of Flodden Field*, said to have been written by Richard Jackson, school-master, of Ingleden, about fifty years after the battle.

His son Henry, with whom he had lived on bad terms for many years, succeeded Gay, dissolute, extravagant, the friend of Arthur Prince of Wales, eldest son of Henry VIII, he sobered down by married life,—*i e* by the influence of good wives, who, thank God, are not yet improved off the face of the earth, and still hallow, elevate, and adorn the lives of many Englishmen of all degrees in life

In three years' time he was created Earl of Cumberland, and journeyed to London at prodigious expense to be installed in his new dignity

The total cost of my lord's outfit was £87 5*s* 3*d*, which brought to its modern value is a very considerable sum, and contains so many "gerdles "of russet velvet, shoes, girdles, &c, including robes of crimson velvet and "ermine, and a bugle horn tipped with silver, at 6*s* 8*d* the ounce," that we can well imagine it

His retinue consisted of thirty-three servants, who with him rode to London Old liveries were discarded, and his train arrayed anew in laced coats faced with satin and embroidered with the cognizances of the family Five days they were in riding to London, and five weeks and one day they remained there, and he stayed at Derby place, now the Heralds College Altogether the entire expenses amounted to £376 9*s*, or about £1,500 present value Seven years after he was made Knight of the Garter, that crowning dignity of England's nobility

I should not have mentioned all this if the sequel had not shown that he was worthy to be a man whom the King delighted to honour For in 1536 occurred the rebellion called the "Pilgrimage of Grace," the occasion of which I have already mentioned in the history of the Eures, and how Robert Aske, second son of Aske of Aughton, on the Derwent, being taken by the rebels and compelled to take the oath, eventually put himself at the head of the movement in Yorkshire, and being joined by Sir Thomas Percy, marched to Pontefract Castle, and compelled Lord Darcy to surrender, and, with the Archbishop of York, to take the oath

From thence they sent to the Earl of Cumberland, requiring him to join them, but he answered, as he afterwards proudly wrote to the King, that though 500 gentlemen retained at his cost had forsaken him, he would continue the King's subject and defend his castle, in which he had great ordnance, against them all

Froude says that in 1536 "Skipton Castle alone in Yorkshire now "held out for the Crown" He had but a mixed household of some eighty persons left to garrison the castle, but though the rebels surrounded it, he stoutly kept them at bay

But there was yet another and even more imminent danger His wife and three children and several other ladies were staying, when the insurrection burst out, at Bolton Abbey, and the insurgents, finding that they could not reduce the castle by fair means, threatened that, if the attack failed the next day, they would bring them in front of the castle, and insult them in the very presence of the Earl. This was a brutal threat, but, at that day, no villainy was impossible. It was clearly an imminent danger, and there was no time to be lost.

Robert Aske had two brothers, Christopher and John. They had remained loyal, and, with forty of their retainers, made their way to their cousin, the Earl of Cumberland, and threw themselves into the castle. In the dead of the night, Christopher, with the Vicar of Skipton and a groom and a boy, stole through the camp of the besiegers, crossed the moors with led horses by unfrequented paths, and reaching Bolton Abbey under cover of the darkness, brought all the party safely back and into Skipton, "so "close and clean," says the old chronicler, "that the same was never mis-"trusted nor perceived till they were safe within the castle." Proudly the little garrison looked down, when the day dawned, from the battlements upon the fierce multitude howling below in baffled rage.

This staunchness of the Earl of Cumberland, supported by the Dacres and the Musgraves, the Eures, and the Earl of Northumberland, held the rebels in check until the Earl of Shrewsbury, with the King's troops, could force the passes of the Don and cross the swollen river, when, after a conference between the leaders on both sides, the rebellion melted away. Martial law was proclaimed. Aske was beheaded at York, Darcy at London, Constable at Hull, and the gallows made short work of many of their companions. But it was the Earl of Cumberland who first stayed the rising tide, and saved the country, perhaps, from a civil war; and we are not disposed to grudge him the reward of his courage and loyalty, which he received from the King a short time before his death, viz., a grant of the priory of Bolton, with all the lands belonging thereto, in the parish of Skipton, with the manors of Storithes, Heselwood, Embsey, Eastby, Con-onsby, &c., and the manor of Woodhouse, which had belonged to this dissolved monastery of Marton.

I say nothing concerning the policy or equity of Henry VIII. in thus laying hands on Church property; but, at least, it was better to give it to a gallant and independent gentleman than to any of the crowd of sycophants and timeservers, mere creatures without any definite faith or principle, who cringed before the arbitrary, wanton, reckless King, that they might obtain some share of the spoil to gratify their selfishness or ambition, with little heed for the houses of God, for the purity of whose worship they professed to be so deeply concerned.

His son Henry succeeded him, and passed his life in comparatively quiet times. At sixteen years of age he had been made a Knight of the Bath at Anne Boleyn's coronation, and in 1537—during his father's lifetime also—he married Lady Eleanor Brandon, daughter of Charles Brandon Duke of Suffolk, by Mary Queen Dowager of France, daughter of Henry VII It was in honour of this lady, and in recognition of her royal descent, that the gallery which I have already mentioned was built at Skipton Castle

This Earl died in 1570, but in the previous year, 1569, on the insurrection of the Earls of Northumberland and Westmoreland, he assisted Lord Scrope in fortifying Carlisle against them This, which was one of the movements which disturbed the reign of the good Queen Bess, is known as the "Rising of the North," and was intended to secure the liberation of Mary Queen of Scots, her marriage with the Duke of Norfolk and recognition as next heir to the Crown, the deposition, and probably death, of Cecil, and the restoration of the "old religion," as it was called

The Earl of Cumberland again stood firm to his allegiance, but nearly the whole of Yorkshire was in their favour, and his neighbour, Richard Norton, of Norton Conyers and Rilstone, amongst them Wordsworth, in his poem of *The White Doe of Rylstone*, has touchingly portrayed the scene when the old man, resisting the counsel of his eldest son Francis, determined to go forth with his other sons and retainers They compelled the Earls of Westmoreland and Northumberland, who were hesitating to take action, to assemble at Raby Castle, thence they marched to Durham, where, on November 14th, Northumberland, Westmoreland, Sir Christopher and Sir Cuthbert Neville, and old Richard Norton, strode within the cathedral with sixty followers, armed to the teeth, behind them Norton, with a massive gold crucifix hanging from his neck, and carrying the old banner of the pilgrimage of grace,—the cross and streamers and the five wounds They overthrew what they called "the communion "board," tore the English Bible and Prayer Book to pieces, replaced the ancient altar, and caused Mass to be sung with all solemnity They then proceeded on their way to Tutbury, where Queen Mary was confined, but at Clifford moor, near Wetherby, they found themselves opposed in front by the royal army, under the Earl of Sussex, and in the rear by Sir George Bowes, so they retreated to Raby Castle Sir George Bowes threw himself into Barnard Castle, where he was soon captured by the rebels, who also besieged and took Hartlepool, where they hoped to receive reinforcements of Spaniards from the Low Countries

Queen Elizabeth, ever suspicious, dispatched Sir Ralph Sadler to look after the Earl of Sussex, who still tarried at York, but as soon as the Earl was joined by the Lord Admiral, Lord Hunsdon, and the Earl of Warwick, with 12,000 good men and true, he marched northward The insurgents, disappointed in their expectations of receiving reinforcements,—

"Neville is utterly dismayed,
For promise fails of Howard's aid;
And Dacre to our call replies,
That he is unprepared to rise,"

—fled in all directions; 500 horse and 300 Scottish horse escaped into Lidderdale. The Earl of Westmoreland and his wife, Egremont Ratcliffe, and some others, escaped to the Netherlands. The Earl of Northumberland, with Norton, Makinfield, Tempest, and a few companions, crossed the border into Scotland, and put themselves under the protection of the Humes, Scots, Kerrs, and other border clans. But the Regent Murray bribed Hector Graham, of Harlow, and he betrayed the Earl of Northumberland into his hands, by whom he was confined in the same rooms in Lochleven Castle which had been occupied by Mary.

In May, 1572, he was delivered up to Elizabeth, and after having been carried along the line of his rebellion to Durham, to Raby, and to his own house at Topcliffe, he was beheaded August 22nd, in the Pavement, at York, and his headless body buried beneath the pavement of the now ruined church of St. Crux. About 600 artizans, labourers, or poor tenant farmers, were hanged in the different towns through which the insurrection had passed, and some at York. The great estates of the Earl of Westmoreland, with his castles of Raby and Brancepeth, were confiscated, and he died, after years of exile, in great poverty abroad.

Wordsworth in his poem describes Norton and his sons brought to the castle here:—

"I witnessed when to York they came,
What, lady, if their feet were tied!
They might deserve a good man's blame;
But marks of infamy and shame—
These were their triumph, these their pride."

Francis visits his father in prison, is reconciled to him, and promises to obtain the sacred banner and "lay it on St. Mary's Shrine" at Bolton Priory.

"Then Francis answered fervently,
'If so God will, the same shall be.'
Immediately this solemn word
Thus scarcely given, a noise was heard,
And officers appeared in state
To lead the prisoners to their fate.
They rose; embraces none were given,
They stood like trees when earth and heaven
Are calm. They knew each other's worth,
And reverently the band went forth.
They met (when they had reached the door)
The banner, which a soldier bore,
One marshalled thus with base intent,
That he in scorn might go before,
And holding up this monument,
Conduct them to their punishment.

So cruel Sussex (unrestrained
By human feeling) had ordained
The unhappy banner Francis saw,
And with a look of calm command,
Inspiring universal awe,
He took it from the soldier's hand,
And all the people that were round
Confirmed the deed in peace profound
High transport did the father shed
Upon his son, and they were led,
Led on, and yielded up their breath
Together died, a happy death!"

And Richard Norton's property, too, was confiscated, and committed first to Sir Stephen Tempest, but eventually, second year of James I, it was granted to the Earl of Cumberland, and these lands, which are in the centre of their barony, and the scene of many contentions throughout previous generations as regards "forest rights" and killing deer, were added to their estates

Of "Ryleston's old sequestered hill" little remains save the site, the little chapel which adjoined the manor-house has disappeared, and the old bells also, on one of which was the motto of the Nortons, "God us ayde," and of which Wordsworth beautifully says

"When the bells of Rylstone played
Their Sabbath music,—'God us ayde,'
That was the sound they seemed to speak"

But on the side of Rylstone Fell still stand the remains of an old tower, built it is said by Richard Norton —

"High on a point of rugged ground,
Among the wastes of Rylstone Fell,
Above the loftiest ridge or mound
Where foresters or shepherds dwell,
An edifice of warlike frame
Stands single—Norton Tower its name,
It fronts all quarters, and looks round
O'er path and road, and plain and dell,
Dark moor, and gleam of pool and stream,
Upon a prospect without bound" *

George Clifford, eldest son of Earl Henry, who succeeded him, unlike his predecessors was devoted to the sea, and it is needful that we should say a few words concerning him, not only because his life illustrates an interesting epoch in English history, but also to rescue the reputation of a brave and distinguished man from unmerited calumny

Dawson speaks of him a "buccaneer," amongst the *Worthies of Old Skipton*, and Whitaker says of an entry in his diary recording that after

* *White Doe of Rylstone*, canto v

the burning of an Indian town on November 5th, "'the sixth day we "'sarvyd God, being Sunday,'—surely the barefaced religion of the "present day is more tolerable than such sanctified iniquity."

The truth is, as Davenport Adams tells us in his interesting book, *England on the Sea*, that piracy, as we should call it now, was not only recognized but utilized under the Tudors, for regular navy there was very little.

During the reign of Edward VI. and Mary, at one time young Catholic, and at another young Protestant gentlemen, rebelling against the ecclesiastical status, went down to the sea in ships, for occupation and livelihood. They hung about the French harbours, and creeks, and bays of the Irish coast, with the rough, wild crews they had gathered together. When England was at war they were recognized as commissioned privateers; when at peace they were tolerated by the Government, from the certainty that at no distant time their services would be again required. During the Marian persecution, Canns, Killigrews, Tremaynes, Strangwayses, Throgmortons, Horseys, and Cobhams—men belonging to the first families, became roving chiefs. On Elizabeth's accession they came back to the service of the Crown; and thus, as the modern gentleman keeps his yacht, so Elizabeth's loyal burghers, esquires, or knights, whose inclination lay that way, kept their ambiguous cruisers, and levied war on their own account when the Government lagged behind its duty.

Spain was at this time the dominant power, if not of the old world certainly of the new, and the increasing strength of their navy, necessary to secure their acquisitions across the Atlantic, seemed to Elizabeth and her wisest counsellors to threaten the liberty of this nation. That a rigidly defensive policy was not a safe policy they were also of opinion, as was specially evident to the great circumnavigator of the world, Francis Drake; and he, in conjunction with Sir Philip Sidney, laid before the Queen in council a plan for weakening the resources of Spain, by attacking her settlements in the West Indies and Spanish Main. As old Fuller quaintly puts it: "It was resolved by the judicious of that age the way to humble "Spanish greatness, was not by pinching and pricking him in the low "countries, which only emptied his veins of such blood as was quickly "refilled; but the way to make it cripple for ever, was by cutting off the "Spanish sinews of war, his money, from the West Indies. In order "whereunto this Earl set forth a small fleet at his own cost, and adven-"tured his own person thereunto, being the best born Englishman that "ever hazarded himself in that kind." And that they were not ineffectual is evident from the angry protest addressed by the Spanish ambassador to Queen Elizabeth. "Your mariners rob my master's subjects on the seas, "and trade where they are forbidden to go; they attack our vessels in "your very harbour, and take our prisoners from them, your preachers "insult my master from their pulpits, and when we apply for justice we "are answered with threats"

The Armada was the stupendous effort made by Spain to crush at once and completely the nation whose aggressive acts were becoming intolerable At this time there were only thirteen ships above 400 tons, and in the whole fleet, including cutters and pinnaces, not more than thirty-eight vessels of all sorts carried the Queen's flag When Lord Howard, of Effingham, with two ships of his own, joined Sir Francis Drake in Plymouth roads, and his squadron (for all the western privateers had rallied to his flag), Hawkins met them with four or five, London contributed thirty At all the seaports from Hull to Bristol, wealthy noblemen and patriots of all grades fitted out ships at their own cost, the Netherlanders contributed twenty barques, so that by the middle of July England had at sea, for the purpose of national defence, a fleet of nearly 200 vessels, conveying 15,785 mariners and fighting men, being, as compared with the Spaniards, in the proportion of one to two They were ill-equipped, and scantily supplied, but they were Englishmen, determined to defend their native land "Let her Majesty trust no more to Judas-like kisses," wrote Howard to Walsingham "Let her defend herself like a noble and mighty "Princess, and trust to her sword, and not to their word, and she need "not to fear, for her good God will defend her" And the sequel shewed that he was right "Afflavit et dissipantur"—"the Lord sent His wind and "scattered them"—were the significant words engraved on the medal struck to commemorate what has not been inappropriately called "England's "Salamis"

"What Wolsey and Henry had struggled for," says Mr J R Green, "Elizabeth had done France was no longer a danger, Scotland no longer "a foe Instead of hanging on the will of Spain, England had fronted "Spain and conquered her She now stood on a footing of equality with "the greatest powers of the world A new and lasting greatness opened "before her on the sea She had sprung at one bound into a great sea "power"

"Among the naval adventurers who distinguished themselves during "Queen Elizabeth's reign," says Southey, "there was no one who took to "the sea so much in the spirit of a northern sea-king as the Earl of Cumberland"* He took a prominent part in the destruction of the Spanish Armada (in 1588), and commanded the Elizabeth Bonaventure, and in one engagement specially, off Calais, greatly distinguished himself In consequence of this he was commissioned by the Queen to sail in the "Golden Lion" to the South Seas, and, subsequently, he commanded the

* *Lives of the British Admirals*, vol III

"Victory," and, eventually, small fleets of vessels were placed under his command, with varied results, but in which he always showed courage and seamanship. Fuller, the historian, says quaintly of him (as he was known to dabble in commerce), "His fleet may be said to be bound for "no other port but the port of honour, though touching at the port of "profit in passage thereto."* He seems to have been a man of considerable intellectual capacity, for he was passionately fond of mathematics, and the patron and friend of Spenser. Queen Elizabeth shewed him many marks of favour, and made him a Knight of the Garter in 1592. On one occasion, when her Majesty dropped her jewelled glove, Clifford picked it up and presented it on bended knee, but the Queen graciously desired him to keep it, and he had it covered with diamonds, and wore it in future, on great occasions, in his hat. He was one of the peers who sat in judgment on Mary Queen of Scots, and died worn out by hardships, anxieties, and wounds, aged forty-seven.

Of his brother Francis, who succeeded him as the fourth Earl, there is little to be said. He was an easy, improvident, but otherwise comparatively blameless man, who had the rare good fortune to die at eighty, in the same room in which he was born. His daughter married Mr. Wentworth, afterwards Earl of Strafford. He says of him, in his letter to his son, "Mr. Wentworth is an earnest, and seemeth to be a very affecc'onate "suiter to y'r sister. He hath beene here altogether for these three weekes "past, and remaines here still. Yo'r sister is lykewyse therewith well "pleased and contented. His father and I are agreed of all the con-"ditions. We shall onley want and wish yo'r compaine at the marriage, "which is, I thinke, not lyke to be long deferred. God blesse them."

But he lived to see dark days overtake the young couple, for when he died, in January, 1640, Lord Strafford had become the object of popular hatred, in spite of the vigilance, activity, and prudence of his eight years' government as Lord Lieutenant of Ireland. The universal discontent which prevailed in England all pointed towards him, and before the close of the year he was impeached, viz., November 11th, and beheaded in the March following. The following items from Earl Francis' son's steward's book, are significant of great anguish and sorrow, which must have been gathering round the old Earl's last days.

"To the doorkeepers at the Parliament House on the 17th day of "my Lord of Strafford's trial, 10 v.

"For wateridge to the town when his Lordship went to take leave "of my Lord of Strafford, the daye afore he was executed.

"Mem.—The 12 Maii that his Lordship came from Parlyment the "Earle of Strafford suffered."

* *History of Craven*, Whitaker.

There is little now to add. Of this son, Henry, the fifth and last of the Earls of Cumberland, I have spoken at the commencement of this memoir, and need add nothing more. Loyal to the Crown like all his race, he sank to his rest two years after the death of his brother-in-law Strafford, and six years before the death of the King; and with him expired, not only the title of Earl of Cumberland, but the "House of "Clifford," for his great estates were divided between his daughter, Lady Elizabeth, who had married the Earl of Burlington, and her cousin the daughter of the sailor Earl, Lady Anne, who had married, first, Richard Sackville Earl of Dorset, and secondly, Philip Herbert Earl of Pembroke. Through the former, the estate of Bolton "Abbey," as it is called, and the estates in Craven, have passed by marriage into the Cavendish family, and are owned by the Duke of Devonshire. Through the latter, Skipton Castle and the estates in Cumberland passed to her eldest daughter Margaret, who married John Tufton second Earl of Thanet, and is now owned by Sir Richard Tufton, created 1851 Lord Hothfield.

The ancient barony of "de Clifford" (being to heirs general) has passed through several families, and the title is now borne by a scion of the House of Russell. Lord Clifford, of Chudleigh, still represents a collateral branch descended from Sir Lewis Clifford, son of Roger, fifth Lord Clifford in the days of Edward III. The direct male line, however, which had lasted from father to son for more than six hundred years, terminated with the death of Henry the fifth Earl.

But the castle of Skipton still stands, an object of interest to the antiquary and the lover of the picturesque; and over its embattled gateway is still emblazoned in large stone letters the ancient motto of the family, in Norman French, "DESORMAIS." It is a motto for the present as well as for the past, as full of life and significance for us now, as for each member of the family of Clifford during those 600 years; for tersely and yet significantly it expresses a sentiment which is never out of date, never out of fashion.

For what is it? "From henceforth!" Surely this is a clear purpose as to the future, and a firm determination to act thereon at the present, whatever the past may have been. It is something more than the old Latin adage, "Nil desperandum;" something higher than the old English proverb, "Better luck next time." It expresses for the whole life that which St. Paul expresses for the religious phase of life, when he says: "Forgetting those things which are behind, and reaching forth unto those "things which are before, I press to the mark for the high calling of "God in Christ Jesus." It is the man, undaunted by the past, undismayed by the future, bracing himself to fresh efforts, irrespective of any failures or discouragement, realizing that the opportunities of life are still before him, and determined, whatever he may have done in the past, to grasp them and profit by them. No dreamy speculations as to the future, no useless laments over the past; but clear, calm apprehension, resolute determination, and vigorous action.

Perhaps to many a member of this noble race these words shone forth like a load-star from the fluttering banners above their heads, or from the stone wall before their eyes—keeping ever before them the stern reality of life, the momentous issues of the present moment, and the folly of being discouraged by the past—cheering them in their seasons of bewilderment, sustaining them in their hours of defeat, and stimulating them to be other and better men in the future than ever they had been before.

It is a motto not only for the House of Clifford but for every House. Wipe out any craven recollections from your memories; put down the foot firmly which is faltering; stretch out the hands which are hanging down; utilize the opportunities and abilities which yet remain to you, as you have never done before; and (leaving it to Providence to decide whether you shall be in the fore-front of the men of your time, or only be one "in the ranks" of your generation) adopt, as the motto of your future life, this, which is as worthy of men clad in broad cloth or in fustian now, as it was of mail-clad warriors and stout Yorkshiremen in buff jerkins and steel morions, and put forth your powers—*and do your best.*

The Warrennes.

Before proceeding to deal further with the Fess, I would keep your attention to the chequy field as being the arms of the House of Warrenne,* to which I have already alluded (page 68).

I now proceed to trace the history of the descendants of the elder son, William de Warrenne, Gualterius de Santo Martino, Earl of Warrenne, leaving the descendants of the younger son Ralph, or Reginald Earl of Mortimer, to be dealt with further on.

Gualterius de Sancto Martino, Earl of Warrenne, was, as I stated, created by William Rufus, Earl of Surrey, and married the daughter of Hugh Earl of Vermandois. He probably built the castle at Conisborough. Immediately before the Conquest it had belonged to Harold the Earl.† Under what circumstances it became the property of his father I cannot say, but it is mentioned in Domesday Book amongst the first Earl's estates in Yorkshire. Earl Warrenne evidently took it as it stood, and seated himself in the English "Aula," having about him the

* See coloured illustration. † Clark's *Mediæval Military Architecture.*

twenty-eight Vills which, either in whole or in part, were appended to it Possibly it was given to William de Warrenne by the Conqueror, not so much as a reward for his bravery as for his consanguinity, for he had certainly married Gundred, the daughter of Matilda, William's wife There is no doubt of that, for in the Charter (dated 1085) of the Priory of Lewes, which William de Warrenne founded, 1078, he states his donations to be for the salvation of the souls, amongst others, of Queen Matilda, mother of his wife (matris uxoris meæ), but antiquaries, as M Planché shews in his *Conqueror and his Companions*, are at issue as to her father, and it seems doubtful as to whether she was the daughter of William or the child of a previous marriage, and thus sister to Gherbod the Fleming, to whom William gave the earldom of Chester an unaccountable act of generosity on any other hypothesis Or was she the child of Matilda before her marriage? That age was not an epoch of refined morality, and William, an illegitimate son himself, would probably not allow such a consideration to prevent his forming an advantageous alliance with the daughter of the powerful Count of Flanders We have no record of Matilda's frailties, though she certainly meted out strong measure to one who did not return her advances, for Brihtric, the son of Algar, surnamed Meaw (snow) from the extreme fairness of his complexion, an Anglo-Saxon Thegn, having come to her father's Court, she fell desperately in love with him, and offered herself in marriage, but, receiving a cold rebuff from one whose heart was, perhaps, already pre-occupied, she took the first opportunity after becoming Queen of England to persuade her husband to confiscate the lands of the unfortunate Thegn, and drag him to Winchester, where he died in a dungeon However, Gualterius was her grandson, and the Lord of Conisborough

What a grand position! Standing high above the bank of "the "gentle Don," about half-a-mile below its reception of the Dearne, in the midst of a fine sylvan amphitheatre—fitting seat, as its name "Conings-burgh" implies, of Saxon royalty An isolated knoll of rock or gravel, rising, at about 400 feet from the river, to the height of 170 feet Here he built the curtain wall of the enciente, and much of the lower gate-house, together with a hall, kitchen, and lodgings within the area of the old Saxon earthworks It was probably not until a century later that the keep was added What a glorious building still, as it rears its lofty form above the ruins around, a vast cylinder of stone, supported by six massive buttresses, sixty feet in diameter The walls fourteen feet thick at the first floor level, twenty feet from the ground (where the only entrance is to be found—a narrow door at the top of a long straight flight of narrow steps), decreasing to twelve feet at the summit Who, without interest and emotion has examined or climbed up this stately ruin; or peered down into the domed vault, some ten feet deep and twenty-two feet in diameter, with neither loop-hole nor lateral recess of any kind, no seats, nor vents, nor sewer, with a well said to be 105 feet deep in the centre!—perhaps the castle store; perhaps the prison. Four storeys rise above it, each connected by a staircase in the thickness of the wall. The first, devoted to provisions; the second, furnishing the ordinary room for the constable or lord, and his family and guests. The men sleeping there, the ladies in the room above, with the beautiful little oratory opening out of it, thirteen feet by eight feet, fourteen feet high; the roof groined in stone, the ribs ornamented with chevron pattern, the bosses carved with the cross moline or with flowers, the half-shafts of the pillars against the wall terminating in caps delicately carved, and becoming more enriched towards the east. On each side a small quatrefoil window. At the east end, one single narrow round-headed light. Above it the topmost floor, probably covered once with a high conical corniced roof, under which was, probably, the kitchen, and the lodging of the small garrison of some twenty men.*

Who can enter this stately building without wishing to know something of its antecedents,—the hands which reared it,—the generations which dwelt in it,—until, roofless and dismantled, it was left to be the refuge of owls and bats!

Earl William† seems to have been a brave and loyal man, and worthy of the confidence of the King which allowed him to commence such a fortress, impregnable in those simple days. He faithfully adhered to his sovereign, and when King Henry I. lay on his death-bed at Lyons, in France, he was one of five earls who, with other great men, attended him, and afterwards accompanied the body of the King to its burial in Reading Abbey. He was a munificent benefactor to the Church, completing the chancel at Castle-acre, and giving many grants and tithes to the religious houses. Amongst others, he gave a church to St. Mary, at Southwark, attesting his gift by laying his knife on the altar, as is attested in the deed of gift: "Unde donavi de manu mea, per quendam cultellum super "altare ejusdem ecclesiæ positum."

So Hugh Lupus gave an estate to the abbey of Abingdon, and so, in those early illiterate days, Dr. Gale tells us, in his *Disscrtation on the Ulphus horn in our Minster*, conveyances were made "nudo verbo absque "scripto vel charta," the granter delivering to the grantee some movable which was known to belong to him. And Earl William, of course, carried a knife. Chaucer, in his *Reve's tale*, illustrating the pre-eminence of Yorkshire handicraft even in those ancient days, says:

"A Shefild thwitil bare he in his hose."

* Clark. † *Memoirs of the Ancient Earls of Warren and Surrey*, Rev. John Watson, 1782.

He was buried with his wife in the Priory Church, at Southover, near Lewes An account of the discovery of their coffins on making the railway is given in *Archæologia*, vol xxxi

His son William succeeded him He was a supporter of Stephen in his struggles against the Empress Maud, and, together with Gilbert de Clare and other famous knights, ran away at the battle of Lincoln, Candlemas day, 1141, where Stephen was defeated and taken prisoner, "as soon as they saw their own side shrink" He seems to have then changed sides, but with equal unsuccess, for he was taken prisoner by Stephen when he defeated Maud's army near Winchester

The Earl engaged in one of the Crusades, and died abroad, Lord Lyttelton says, when the French were defeated by the Turks after their leaving Laodicea, his heart only being brought to England and buried at Lewes. Watson says of him "He was a man who may be said not to "have been a favourite of fortune, for he had the ill-luck to be always "on the losing side, though when he joined it there was an appearance "of its being the stronger"

He married Adela, or Ela, daughter of William Talvace Earl of Ponthieu, and left one daughter, his heiress, Isabel, who married William de Blois, third and youngest son of King Stephen, who is said to have been "Dapifer Regis Angliæ," *i e* steward of the King's household He attended Henry II in his expedition against Thoulouse, and died there, October, 1160 At his decease Isabel married Hameline Plantagenet, natural son of Geoffry Earl of Anjou, and, therefore, illegitimate brother of the King

He supported Henry in his disputes with his sons, but carried the sword of state before Richard at his coronation, and was one of those who had charge of the 70,000 marks of silver raised for his ransom. He granted to the Church of St Mary, of York, thirty wether sheep, and to the free burgesses of Wakefield a toft of an acre of free burgage for sixpence rent per annum, with liberty of free trade in all his lands in Yorkshire, and leave to take from his wood of Wakefield dead wood for fuel Isabel died, 1199, the Earl, 1202, leaving two children, William, his successor, and Adela, married to Sir William Fitz-William Lord of Sprotborough Earl William's memory is still cherished amongst the good people of Stamford, as the donor to that town of the two meadows—in which he saw from the castle walls two bulls fighting,—in order that annually, on St Brice's day, six weeks before Christmas, a bull may be baited for the diversion of the inhabitants

I do not know whether the barbarous custom prevails, but in the *History of Stamford*, 1822, it is mentioned and defended as "an opportunity for display of personal courage"

Earl William is, however, to be remembered for other things than that. He seems to have been a man of great influence with King John, and to have used it for some purpose. In 1213 he was one of four great barons who bound themselves by oath to see that the King performed what the Pope had determined. In 1215 he was joined in commission with Archbishop Langton and others, for the safe conducting of all who should come to London to implore the King's pardon for their offences. At Runnymede, he was one of those who appeared on the King's side, and one of the few counsellors by whose advice and persuasion the King put his seal to the Magna Charta. He was one of those selected to see that the King carried out his promises; and was also a witness to the Charter which John gave to the archbishop at the Temple for confirmation of the rights of the Church and the clergy of England. In 1216, when John, by his persistent ill-conduct had made himself odious to the people, he sided with the barons, and Louis the son of the King of France, against him; but as soon as John was dead, he swore allegiance to Henry III. Peter Langtoft calls him "The gode Earle of Warrenne." He was present at Henry's coronation, and, in the ninth year of his reign, one of the witnesses to his confirmation of the two great charters of the realm at Westminster. In 1227 he joined the discontented barons against the King, but it is a token, not only that he had been again received into royal favour, but was trusted by the people, that, in 1237, the King, putting from him such counsellors as were disliked, admitted him with the Earl of Ferrers and Fitz-Geoffrey in their room. He established a house for the Crutched Friars in Reigate, and died 1240.

His first wife was Maud, daughter of William de Albini Earl of Arundel; his second wife, Maud, daughter and co-heiress of William Mareschal Earl of Pembroke, and widow of Hugh Bigod Earl of Norfolk. The arms of Mareschal, Per pale or and vert, a lion rampant gules—may be seen in the east window of the chapter-house. His natural son, Griffin de Warrenne, married Isabella, sister of Robert de Pulford, and their son John married Audela, daughter and heiress of Griffin de Albo Monasterio (or Blanch Minster), whose arms, argent fretty gules, are in the small quatrefoil of the south-west window of the chapter-house.

John, the eldest legitimate son of Earl William, but five years of age at his father's death, succeeded him. When only thirteen he attended the Parliament held in London, which sharply rebuked the King, Henry III., for his many and high exactions of clergy and laity. Six years after he joined the King at Guienne, and when, in 1258, the barons came to Oxford to compel the King to submit to the provisions they made, he was one of twelve lords elected on the King's part to settle matters with them, and he refused to consent to them. In the forty-sixth year of Henry III.

he was again acting on the King's behalf, but the following year he sided with the barons, and was elected one of their chief captains with Simon de Montfort, though, under Prince Edward's influence, he soon returned to his allegiance He defended Rochester against the Earl of Leicester, and was with the King when the barons defeated him at Lewes, and served in the van of the royal army with Prince Edward But, if the truth must be told, he did not distinguish himself therein, but deserted at the commencement of the battle with the Earl of Pembroke, and fled, first to Pevensey Castle, and from thence to France Their flight is thus quaintly alluded to by Peter de Langteft

"The Erle of Warrenne, I wote, he 'scaped over the se,
And Sir Hugh Bigote als with the Erle fled he"

This, probably, was not so much from cowardice as to ingratiate himself with the barons, who, he foresaw, would have the supremacy However, he failed in his object, for when he returned the following May, he found that they had already declared his estates forfeited, and given them to the Earl of Clare This induced him, once more, to change sides, and he confederated with the Earl of Gloucester for the restoration of the King's power, and was present with the royal forces at the battle of Evesham, after which his possessions were restored to him

In 1269 he became involved in some dispute about his land with Henry de Lacy Earl of Lincoln, and prepared to establish his claim by force of arms, but the King, hearing of it, interfered, and referred the cause to his justices to hear and determine, who decided in favour of the Earl of Lincoln Two years after he had a similar disagreement with Alan Lord Zouche, which, in like manner, was decided against him in the courts of law Upon which he grievously assaulted the Baron and his son, in Westminster Hall, and mortally wounded the former As Robert of Gloucester describes it

"Suththe ther was at Londone a lute destance, Ich wene
In yer of grace tuelf hundred and sixti and tene,
So that the Erl of Wareine slou atte verste touche,
Bivore the justises atte Benche, Sir Alein de la Souche" *

This was too flagrant a disregard of the royal prerogative to be passed over, and Earl Warrenne fled to his castle at Reigate Thither he was pursued by Prince Edward, to whom he humbly submitted, and was fined 10,000 marks, afterwards reduced to 8,000, and he and fifty of his followers concerned in the fray were ordered to walk on foot from the New Temple to Westminster Hall, and swear before the justices that they had acted from heat and passion, and not from *malice prepense*

* *Siege of Caerlaverock*, pp 94, 131

On the death of Henry III., he was one of those who went up to the altar at Westminster Abbey and swore allegiance to Edward I., then fighting against the Saracens. Four years afterwards he shewed that he could be as independent as he was loyal. Edward, in order to raise money, required all those who held any lands or tenements of him, to come and shew by what right and title they held them, that by such means these possessions might return to him by escheat as chief lord of the same, and so be sold or redeemed again at his hands. Great was the dissatisfaction expressed on all sides at this, but few dared to resist the King's will. At last the Earl was summoned to answer, and he appeared before the justices. Being asked by what right he held his lands, he suddenly drew forth an old rusty sword, "By this instrument," sayd he, "doe I hold my landes, and by the same I intend to defende them. "Our ancestours, comming into this realme with William the Conquerour, "conquered theyr lands with the sworde, and wyth the same will I defende "me from all those that shall be aboute to take them from me. He did "not make a conqueste of this realme alone, our progenitors were with him "as participators and helpers with him." The King wisely understood from this the nature of his action, and proceeded no further. "So that," Holinshed concludes, "the thing which generally shuld have touched and "bene hurtfull to all men, was now sodeinly stayed by the manhood and "couragiouse stoutenesse only of one man, the forsaid earle."

Hence the ancient motto of the family,

"Gladio vici, gladio teneo, gladio tenebo."

It gives some idea as to the powers of the barons in those days, to find him disputing with the King, not only about the rights in Sussex, but claiming to have his coroners, prison, market, fair, tronage, pesage, a certain toll called thurtol in Stamford and Grantham, without license or will of the King. He claimed also gallows, assize of bread and beer, and of measures, pleas de vetito namio, and for shedding of blood, and waif at Coningsburgh. And on inquisition, his claim was allowed without question.

The following extracts, quoted in Guest's *History of Rotherham*, show that these powers were not only claimed but exercised :—"Richard (steward "to Earl Warrenne) imprisoned Beatrice, who was wife of William the "tailor at Rotherham, at Wakefield, for a whole year, because she had "impleaded the said Earl for a certain tenement in Grisbrook, and they do "not know how she was set free. The said Richard made devilish and "miserable oppression (*i.e.* heavy charges and rates), as it will appear by "the roll of ministers."

"Also they say that Nigel Drury, constable of the castle of "Conisbrough, seized, in the town of Roderham, six stones of wool from "a certain chest which belonged to a certain woman who was hung at

"Conisburgh, and carried off the same wool against the inhibition of the "bailiffs of the said town of Roderham"* He does not seem, therefore, to have been a popular character, and in an old poem called *Richard of Almasque*, he is thus spoken of —

> "By God that is abovv ous he deede muche synne,
> That let passe over see the Erl of Warynne,
> He hath robbed Fnglelonde the mores ant the fenne,
> The gold and the silver ant y-boren henne" †

Dugdale, in his *Summonses to Parliament*, attributes to him the establishment, in the Parliament held 23rd Edward I, of the custom of sending burgesses to Parliament The Earl's spirited conduct seems, however, only to have delayed the attack upon himself, for, shortly after (7th Ed), his rights in Sussex were impeached before John de Reygate and his associates, the justices' itinerants in the county of Sussex, but the "jurat," consisting of six knights and six lords of towns, confirmed the claims of the Earl Likewise at Lincoln and Scarborough similar attacks were made on his rights in Lincolnshire and Yorkshire, but, Mr Watson says, "upon an "inquisition being taken it does not appear that anything was found for "the King" And therefore I suppose that Edward, feeling that he could neither coerce nor reduce his powerful baron, deemed it the best policy to enlist his support, and accordingly we find him taking the leading part in Edward's proceedings in Scotland I shall treat of these generally under Royal Heraldry It will suffice now to notice the details thereof specially associated with Earl Warenne

Alexander III, King of Scotland, having died childless, the crown of Scotland devolved upon his granddaughter Margaret, the child of his daughter, who had married Eric, King of Norway. Edward conceived the idea of uniting the two kingdoms together by the marriage of "the maid "of Norway," as she was called, to his son Edward, Prince of Wales, and a treaty having been agreed to by the Scotch for this purpose, Warrenne was employed, A D 1290, by the King to obtain a guarantee from them for the due performance of the marriage He was actually in Scotland, on his way to Orkney to meet the young Queen, when tidings arrived of her death. Had she lived, "the Union" would have taken place at once, but God had ordained that three centuries of bloodshed and strife should ensue before the happy consummation thereof

When in 1296 Edward received at Berwick‡, which he had taken by storm, Balliol's formal renunciation of his homage to him, he treated his letter with angry contempt, exclaiming "Ha! ce fol felon, tel folie faict!

* Answers returned by Jury to inquisition as to certain abuses Rotuli Hundredorum, 1st Ed 1276, printed by Records Commission, 1812, p 110

† *Old Yorkshire*, 2nd series, p 179 ‡ Tytler's *History of Scotland*

"S'il ne voult venir à nous, nous viendrons a lui;" and immediately sent the Earls of Warrenne and Warwick to recover the castle of Dunbar, which the garrison had treacherously surrendered. With 1,000 horse, 10,000 foot, and 100 men from the army of the Bishop of Durham, Warrenne defeated 1,500 horse and 40,000 foot, and defeated the Scots, who had come to its rescue, pursuing them seven or eight miles, almost to the forest of Selkirk; and when he had finally routed the Scotch forces—captured Roxburgh, Jedburgh, Stirling, and Edinburgh,—Balliol having surrendered was stripped of his royal robes, spoiled of crown and sceptre, and compelled to stand as a criminal before the King with a white rod in his hand. Warrenne was then appointed Regent of Scotland, General of all the forces north of the Trent, with his residence at Bothwell Castle, and with him were associated Cressingham, an ecclesiastic, as Chief Treasurer, and William Ormesby, Chief Justice.

On the Scots rising in arms under the famous William Wallace, second son of Sir Malcolm Wallace, of Ellerslie, in 1297, Warrenne received the King's orders to raise the militia in the northern parts and chastise the insurgents. Warrenne at once sent his nephew, Henry de Percy, at the head of an army of 40,000 foot and 300 horse, to Galloway, who surprised the Scotch at Irvine, and compelled them, divided amongst themselves, to capitulate and promise hostages, while Wallace, in anger and disgust, retired with a few tried and veteran followers to the north. But the Scots were irresolute and contradictory—too jealous to act with Wallace, they were too proud to submit to Warrenne. Only William Douglas and the Bishop of Glasgow submitted, meanwhile the great number allied themselves with Wallace. Edward was dissatisfied, superseded Warrenne, and appointed Brian Fitzalan Governor of Scotland in his stead. Smarting under this indignity, and, in consequence, more than ever at variance with Cressingham, the treasurer, a proud and violent churchman, who preferred the cuirass to the cassock, Warrenne marched with his army towards Stirling, and on reaching the south bank of the river Forth, spanned by a long, narrow wooden bridge, he found that Wallace had already occupied the high ground on the other side, above Cambuskenneth. Lennox, the Steward of Scotland, was with the English army, and asked Warrenne to delay the attack until he had attempted to bring Wallace to terms. He failed in his purpose, and a scuffle arose between foraging parties, which, but for the command of Wallace to wait until the morning, would have drawn on an engagement that night. The morning was already far advanced before Warrenne rose from his bed and drew up his army in battle array. Wallace had not, however, been idle; he had tampered with his English soldiers, drawn away his Scotch, acquainted himself with the numbers of his men, and matured his measures Warrenne ordered his infantry to cross the bridge, but another delay arose owing to a fancied overture from Wallace for peace, but none came, and two friars, sent to him to propose terms, brought back a scornful refusal "Return to your friends and tell them we came "here with no peaceful intent, but ready for battle, and determined to "avenge our own wrongs, and set our country free! Let your masters "come and attack us, we are ready to meet them beard to beard"

Sir Richard Lundin—a Scottish knight, who had with his followers joined the army of Percy at Irvine, and was, therefore, well acquainted with the country—urged him not to try the bridge, but to send part of his army by a ford which he offered to shew, while the rest occupied the bridge in front Warrenne hesitated "Why do we protract the war and "spend the King's money?" cried Cressingham, in a taunting voice, "let "us pass on as becomes us, and do our duty" Stung by this reproach, Warrenne ordered the advance Sir Marmaduke Twenge led half the army over the bridge, and charged the Scots at the top of the hill, but Wallace seized the opportunity and despatched a portion of his men, occupied the foot of the bridge dividing the English force, while he himself charged from the high ground, and thus assailing Twenge and Cressingham in front and rear, threw them into confusion Many were slain, many drowned attempting to swim the river on their horses, to rejoin Warrenne The standard bearers, and a body of men who crossed the bridge to their relief, were cut to pieces Sir Marmaduke Twenge set spurs to his horse, and driving him into the midst of the enemy, with his nephew and armour-bearer, cut his way through the thickest of the Scottish columns and rejoined the English Lennox threw off the mask, and with his followers attacked and plundered the flying English Cressingham was killed, his body mangled, his skin torn from his limbs, and made, it is said, into garters for the soldiers, and a sword-belt for Wallace Half the English army was cut to pieces Warrenne breaking down the bridge left Twenge in command, and promising to return within ten weeks in case of need, rode with such haste to Berwick that his horse died, and putting that place in defence proceeded to London to consult with Prince Edward, the King being still abroad As soon as the King could sign a truce with the French, he returned to England, summoning all the nobility to meet him with their forces at York, in the Octave of St Hilary, 1298, to help the Earl of Warrenne On the day appointed there was a great muster of the most powerful nobles The Earl Marshall, the great Constable of England, Earls of Gloucester and Arundel, Lord Henry Percy, John de Wake, John de Segeair, and many others, bringing 2,000 heavy cavalry, 2,000 light horsemen, and 100,000 foot With such a reinforcement Warrenne relieved Roxburgh—hardly pressed by the Scots—and occupied Berwick

There Edward ordered him to remain until he could join the army himself; and summoning the whole military power to meet him at York at Pentecost, he advanced from there to the rendezvous he had appointed his combined forces at Roxburgh, on the feast of St. John the Baptist.

With a vastly increased force he proceeded by moderate marches into Scotland, laying waste the country and defeating the Scotch at Falketh. The following year he again invaded Scotland, encamped in Annandale, captured Lochmaben, and attacked the castle of Caerlaverock, the principal seat of the family of Maxwell from the time of Michael Canmore, and now held by the staunch Sir Eustace de Maxwell, ancestor of the Maxwells Earls of Nithsdale, and Baron Herries, of whom the present Lord Herries, of Everingham, Yorkshire, is the lineal representative. Situated near Dumfries on the north shore of the Solway Firth, at the confluence of the Nith and Locher, "Caerlaverock was so strong a castle," says the old poet, "that it did not fear a siege, therefore the King came himself "because it would not consent to surrender." *

Its shape was like a shield, for it had only three sides, all round, with a tower at each angle. One of them was double; one so high, so long, and so large, that under it was the gate and the drawbridge. To the west and north it was surrounded by an arm of the sea, so that no creature born could approach without putting himself in danger of the sea. To the south there were numerous dangerous defiles of wood and marshes, ditches where the sea is on each side of it, and where the river reaches it; and therefore it was necessary for the host to approach it towards the east, where the hill slopes. On the 10th July, 1300, Edward reached Caerlaverock with his forces. By the 12th of that month he had taken it by storm, and advanced to Dumfries. Such a brilliant achievement, we can well understand, elicited the admiration and applause of the world, and it is not surprising that it should have at once become the theme of a poem which doubtless was afterwards sung by many a minstrel, as during the long winter evenings the family and household gathered round the blazing logs in the castle hall, to listen to the prowess of the good King Edward and his knights. This poem, written by Walter of Exeter, a Franciscan Friar, a contemporary, is preserved amongst the MSS. in the College of Arms, and within the last few years has been printed by Sir Harris Nicholas. It is far too long to quote here. It contains the names and banners of all the knights, and short, quaint, epigrammatic notices of each, some of which I have quoted from time to time. The progress of the siege, the simple weapons of offence, the bows, crossbows, and espingalls; the terrible Robinet, worked by Brother Robert, which sent numerous stones without cessation from dawn to evening; and three other terrible engines erected by him, very

* *Siege of Caerlaverock*, Sir Harris Nicholas.

large, of great power, and very destructive, so that whenever the stones entered, neither iron cap nor wooden target could save from a blow, as well as the individual acts of heroism—are tersely and graphically described, and the poem concludes with the capitulation of the garrison, to the number of sixty, who were beheld with much astonishment, but they were kept and guarded till the King commanded that life and limb should be given them, and ordered to each of them a new garment

Earl Warrenne seems to have commanded the second squadron on this occasion, and he is thus described by the poet —"John, the good Earl of "Warren, held the reins to regulate and govern the second squadron, as he "who well knew how to lead noble and honourable men His banner was "handsomely chequered with gold and azure" The Scotch, fairly unnerved by Edward's successes, seem to have implored the protection of the Pope, upon which Boniface addressed a haughty letter to Edward, and claimed the kingdom of Scotland Winchelsea, Archbishop of Canterbury, arrived while the King was still encamped at Caerlaverock, bearing this document, and presented it to Edward in the presence of the nobles and Prince of Wales, with a few words of suitable admonition, observing that Jerusalem would not fail to protect her citizens, and to cherish, like Mount Zion, those who trusted in the Lord Edward broke out into a paroxysm of wrath, and swearing a great oath, exclaimed, "I will not be silent or at rest, "either for Jerusalem or Mount Zion, but so long as there is breath in my "nostrils will defend what the world knows to be my right" The Archbishop retired, but was soon sent for by the King, who, in milder and more dignified terms, assured him of his respect for the Pope, but that he could not give an answer to such a grave letter without holding a council with his nobility On his return to England he summoned a Parliament at Lincoln, February 12th, 1300, and caused the Pope's bull to be read to the earls and barons assembled After great debates, a spirited reply was drawn up to the Pope, with one hundred and four seals appended to it, denying that Scotland had ever belonged to the Church of Rome, asserting that it was an ancient fief of the crown of England, that the Kings of England had never answered for their rights or temporalities to any ecclesiastical judge, adding that they would not permit the King, even if he were willing, to do such an unheard-of thing, or so far to forget his royal rights, and humbly and reverently entreating his Holiness to permit the King to possess his rights in peace, without diminution or disturbance The first seal is that of the Earl of Warrenne Two authentic transcripts of this document are preserved at the Heralds' College, and it was engraved by the Society of Antiquaries, 1729, and printed in the *Archæologia* It is most valuable to the antiquary, as showing the arms of those days, and is frequently referred to throughout this book

The castle appears to have remained in the possession of the English for many years, and Sir Eustace to have joined the English interest. But afterwards he associated himself with Robert Bruce, and having defended it successfully against another attack of the English, demolished, himself, its fortifications, lest it should eventually fall into their hands.

Edward pushed his conquests to the furthest part of Scotland, and during this time Earl Warrenne's services were continued as a commander in his army. In 29 Edward I. he was appointed, conjointly with the Earl of Warwick, to treat with the King of France for a peace between England and Scotland. In 1304, the 32nd year of Edward I., he died at Kennington, and was buried before the high altar at Lewes, and the following quaint epitaph engraven on his tomb:—

> "Vous qe passez ov bouche close,
> Priez pour cely ke cy repose;
> En vie come vous estis jardis fu,
> Et vous tiel serretz come je su.
> Sire Johan Counte de Gareyn gyst ycy,
> Dieu de sa alme eit mercy.
> Ky pur sa alme priera,
> Trois mill jours de pardon avera."

According to Langtoft his death took place as he was returning with Edward from Scotland, after the capture of Stirling:—

> "Upon Brustwik opon Humbre ther he mad sojoure,
> Sir Jon of Warenne that ilk tyme gan deie;
> His body was redy then in grave for to leie.
> After the enterment the Kyng toke his way,
> To the south he went through Lyndesay"—

to Lincoln, where he kept his Christmas with great ceremony and rejoicing.

His son William married Joan, daughter of Robert de Vere, Earl of Oxford, but was killed at a tournament at Croydon during his father's life, and buried at Lewes. Stowe suggests foul play. "He was," he says, "by the "challenger intercepted and cruelly slain." John, his grandson, succeeded him at eighteen, only to close this ancient lineage under a dark cloud of dishonour and unhappiness. That same year the King offered him his granddaughter Joan, daughter of Henry Earl of Barr and his daughter Eleanor, in marriage. Such an honour could not be refused; but like many similar marriages, specially in early life, it was unsuccessful. It brought him into brilliant positions;—we find him accompanying the Prince of Wales in an expedition against Robert Bruce, in 34 Edward I., and with Edward I. when he died on his way to Scotland the following year. In 1308 he accompanied Edward II. to France, to marry the French King's daughter Isabel, and again to Scotland with him against Robert Bruce.

Then came a quarrel between him and his royal cousin For, having been affronted by Piers Gaveston, the King's favourite, at a tournament at Wallingford, he associated himself with Thomas of Lancaster and others similarly aggrieved, and never rested till the obnoxious favourite had been captured at Scarborough Castle, and beheaded at Warwick by the Earl of Warwick, whom Gaveston had once tauntingly called "the black boar of "the Ardennes" Nor were matters mended by his matrimonial dissensions, for his wife, the King's cousin, bearing no children, he divorced her, and cohabited with one Maud de Nerford, the daughter of a Norfolk knight Two years after (1317) he carried off Alice de Laci, the wanton wife of Thomas Earl of Lancaster, who at once divorced her, and proceeded, in revenge, to demolish the Earl of Warrenne's castle of Sandal, near Wakefield, and waste his manors on the north side of the Trent This probably alienated Warrenne from the Lancastrian party, and induced him to seek reconciliation with the King, for in 13 Edward II he was again with him in Scotland, and two years later he did him signal service and indulged his own revenge by making a flank movement across the river at the battle of Burton-upon-Trent, and thus assisting materially in the King's victory over Thomas of Lancaster He was also present when, four days afterwards, the unfortunate Earl of Lancaster—having been again defeated, by Sir Andrew de Harcley, at the battle of Boroughbridge—was arraigned in his own hall at Pontefract Castle, before the King, and sentenced to lose his head, which immediately was put in execution on the Monday next preceding the Festival of the Annunciation of the Virgin Mary

On the death of Edward II he was taken into favour by his son Edward III He was with him in Scotland at the battle of Halidon, and soon after assisted his relative Edward Balliol against the Scots, receiving from him in recognition of his services the earldom of Stratherne Two years afterwards he was again with the King, in an attack made upon the Scotch both by sea and land, entering Scotland by Berwick as the King did by Carlisle

On June 30th, 1347, he died, and was buried under a raised tomb before the altar at Lewes Having no legitimate children the hereditary honours became extinct, and as regards his property, "knowing that— "according to the custom of those days—it would not descend to his illegiti- "mate children, except it was estated in trust, he gave by special grant the "inheritance of all his lands to the King and his heirs, with the intent "to have a re-grant to his unlawful issue in tail"* This was accomplished, and in 9 Edward II he had a re-grant to himself for life Then he made a settlement for Maud de Nerford and the children which he had by her, still extant in the patent rolls of 10 Edward II, consisting of all his

* Watson

estates on the north side of the Trent. Out of the rest he provided for his sister Alice, wife of Thomas Fitz-Alan Earl of Arundel, who died seized of the castle and manor of Castle-acre, Lewes, Reigate, and many other estates belonging to the Warrenne family, and thus the arms of Warrenne have been emblazoned amongst the quarterings of the Howard family to this day. And so the House of Warrenne ended, and the great castle at Conisbrough passed into other hands.

In his illegitimate children John, Thomas, William, Joan, Catherine, and Isabel, we have no particular interest at York, except, perhaps, William, whose arms—chequey or and azure a chief argent—are carved in stone upon one of the pillars of the ancient nave of Trinity Church, Micklegate, but I do not know what was his connexion therewith.

We can well understand, therefore, that the arms of Warrenne should be found in the Minster, and that they should be associated with those who were his relatives or friends. Hence they may be noticed in—

> The Vestibule of the Chapter-house, on the west side, with Percy Plantagenet, Roos, and Clare; and on the east side with Nevill and Fauconberg.
>
> In the north window of the Chapter-house they appear twice, with Clare and Plantagenet, &c.
>
> Again in the north-east window.
>
> They are carved in stone on two shields in the south side of the Nave.
>
> They appear in the glass of the fourth and eighth windows west in the north side of the Nave.
>
> And are emblazoned on the tabard of one of the figures in armour in the border of the eighth window west of the north aisle of the Nave.

The Wakes.

The BAR, though never carried alone, is a diminutive of the Fess, occupying one-fifth of the field. In the fifth window east on the south side of the nave, and on the wall beneath, are two shields associated with a very interesting history, viz.: Or, two BARS gules, in chief three torteaux, which are the arms of Wake.* Dr. Trollope (Bishop Suffragan of Nottingham), in a paper read before the Lincolnshire Architectural Society, has given us a most interesting account of one of that name. What a strange, wild epoch was that in our national history when the Saxon dynasty was yielding to the Norman power, and William the Conqueror, with his fierce band of barons and retainers, was grasping with an iron hand the fair possessions of the Saxon inhabitants, putting the lives and liberties of those who resisted them into great jeopardy, and establishing, not without blood and cruelty, the thraldom of a new and foreign despotism. No doubt there were many who refused to submit themselves, and all that they held dear, to such an

* See coloured illustration.

iron yoke, many who found a speedy result to their independence in the headsman's axe or the gallows-tree, but the name of one—and probably the most conspicuous of them, one who made a gallant though futile effort to help his countrymen—has come down, Hereward the Saxon, or as he was generally called by the Normans, Hereward "the Outlaw," by the Saxons, Hereward "the Wake," *i e* the watchman, Lord of Bourne He was born about 1047 His father was Leofric, Lord of Bourn, who was distinguished through his services in the field, and his munificence towards Croyland Abbey His mother was Ediva, a descendant of Oslac "the Pincerna," or cup-bearer to King Ethelwolf, and his uncles, Brand and Godric, were successively abbots of Peterborough Hereward's vigorous and independent character shewed itself by various precocious acts in his early youth, which made his residence at home unwelcome, and sent him a wanderer amongst friends and relations in different parts of the country With each he distinguished himself by some act of giant strength and indomitable courage one time killing a bear which had broken its chain, to the terror of the household, at another, chastising in single combat a boasting Irish prince who had impugned the courage and skill of the English, at another time rescuing unhappy prisoners who were already bound to have their eyes put out, then carrying off a captive bride and restoring her to her lover, then rescuing a fallen fellow-soldier from the enemy in an expedition to Flanders, and vanquishing a noted knight who was esteemed a very lion in valour

On his return to Bourn (1068), he found that the people were groaning under their Norman masters, his father's house in the hands of the invaders, and his brother's head nailed above the door In a moment, he was in the midst of these unwelcome intruders, the head of the minstrel who was regaling them with insulting songs about Hereward's family was rolling on the floor, and after a fierce struggle the heads of sixteen were exposed in their turn, as their young victim's head had previously been, to public gaze The Isle of Ely had for some time afforded a retreat for all Saxons as were impatient of Norman rule Thither Edwin and Morcar, native princes, thither Stigand, the primate, and several Saxon bishops had come, and thither Hereward went at their call to take the supreme command of their little scanty forces, and to help them amidst the swampy pools and marshes to resist, with sturdy heart and firm reliance upon God, any force which might be sent against them For a long time Hereward kept the enemy at bay, in spite of the floating causeway which they made to reach them, and which sank under the weight of their arms, in spite, also, of the witch whom they sent to curse him, and who was destroyed by the blazing sedge and rushes Disguised as a potter Hereward visited the Norman camp, and having slain one of the royal guards in the very presence of the King, escaped, in spite of all their efforts to take him. Even William admired his prowess, and but for Earl Warrenne would have made peace with him.

But treachery did what valour could not accomplish, and the crafty monks, thinking to make better terms with the Normans, pointed out the way to the camp of refuge to the Earls of Warrenne and Clare. From amidst the awful carnage which ensued, however, Hereward escaped to Northamptonshire, devastated the forest with fire and sword, carried on a system of guerilla warfare, and for several years resisted the whole force of the Conqueror. But like many another warrior, invincible in war, he was conquered by love. His wife Turfrid having retired to a convent, the fair Alftrude consented to be his second wife only if he would make peace with the King. Of course he did so after many and unavailing protestations, and, as of course also, the fiery spirit, unsubdued, blazed out again at some provocation from his Norman neighbours, fighting manfully against overwhelming assailants, he fell.

It was a wild, desultory life,—a life like Samson's in some respects,—a life of spasmodic efforts unsupported, to protect the weak against the strong, and to save the peaceful and unoffending from the power of the invader. He did not hinder the inevitable progress of the Norman rule, but he did his best to provide at least temporary alleviation. He made himself a name which, even at this long distance, is associated with courage and magnanimity; and in more than one instance the same name has added lustre to the future history of that nation whose destinies he was not suffered to mould according to his pleasure.

In the reign of Henry I. the name of Wake again appears on the page of history, though it is impossible to say whether or not Hugh Wac or Wake who married Emme, daughter of Baldwin FitzGilbert, was lineally descended from him. Baldwin de Wake assisted at the coronation of Richard I., and his daughter married Peter de Trehous, whose name I have already mentioned in the history of the family of Mauley.

John Wake was summoned to Parliament as a baron, 1295. His name occurs in the Parliament 26th of Edward I., but he is not mentioned in the Caerlaverock roll, nor amongst the signatories to Boniface VIII.; but he was one of the commissioners appointed with the Archbishop of York to see to the fortification of castles in Scotland. His son, Thomas Wake, the second baron, is mentioned in the Parliament 12th and 15th of Edward II., and obtained license to make a castle of his manor-house at Cottingham, near Hull. He married Blanche, eldest daughter of Henry Earl of Lancaster, son of Thomas Earl of Lancaster, beheaded at Pontefract, who was the eldest son of Edmond, surnamed "Crouchback," brother of Edward I. Her mother was Maud, daughter and heir of Sir Patrick de Chaworth, Lord of Kidevelly, the elder branch of the family whose arms, impaled with Scrope, are in the south transept of our choir.

Baron Thomas became also Governor of Jersey and Constable of the Town, but he died without issue, 1349. His sister and sole heir, Margaret, married Edmond of Woodstock, younger son of Edward I. King of England, by his second wife Margaret, daughter of Philip III. of France. He was created Earl of Kent "per cincturam gladii," by Edward II., his half-brother, 1321, but in 1329, the fourth year of the reign of King Edward III., he was arrested on a charge of high treason and beheaded at Winchester, "after he had stood on the scaffold from noon until five "in the evening expecting the deadly stroke which no one could give "him, till a base wretch of the Marshalsea was sent who performed it."* His widow Margaret survived until September 29th, 1349. His two sons, Edward and John, died, the latter 1349, without issue, and his only daughter, Joan, being for her admirable beauty called "the fair maid of "Kent," succeeded as Lady of Wake, and Countess of Kent in her own right.

"Joan the fair maid of Kent, was" (says Mr. James, quoting from Dugdale in his *Life of Edward the Black Prince*, vol. ii., p. 298) "when a "mere child affianced to Thomas Holland. During his absence from "England, the Countess of Salisbury, under whose charge she had been "left, either ignorant of the previous engagement or stimulated by the "prospect of great wealth and an alliance with the royal family, caused "a contract to be drawn up between her and her eldest son. When the "young lady, however, came to a marriageable age, she was claimed by "the Lord Holland, and the dispute was brought before Clement VI., who "after long investigation decided in favour of Lord Holland, and the "second contract was annulled." But inasmuch as she did not marry Sir Thomas Holland until she was twenty-five, it is possible that Miss Agnes Strickland's account† is true, and that, in spite of any contract which her parents had made for her, a long and early attachment existed between her and the Black Prince. But Queen Philippa had a great objection to her son's union with his cousin because of her "flightiness," and even Froissart condescends to chronicle some scandalous stories concerning her, but she was beautiful, and rich, and a countess in her own right, and we can therefore make allowance for no little jealousy amongst the ladies and gentlemen of the Court, which would vent itself in the usual way.

However, at twenty-five, I suppose she began to despair of the royal consent, and therefore gave her hand to Sir Thomas Holland. But in 1360 he died, having that year assumed the title of Earl of Kent and been so summoned to Parliament, leaving her with three sons and a

* See *Royal Heraldry*. † *Life of Philippa of Hainault*.

daughter. In the following year, 1361, she married the Black Prince. Rymer says: "Joan married the Prince a few months after the death of "her husband." James, quoting from Barnes, tells us that the Prince went to her to plead the cause of one of his friends, and then first discovered that he himself was in love with her. He adds that the marriage was hastened on by the King, to whom it gave the greatest satisfaction. Agnes Strickland speaks as if the Queen had given a reluctant consent. Probably she saw that the Black Prince would not marry anyone else, and as it was very undesirable that the heir apparent should remain unmarried, they made the best of it. However, Joan at last secured the prize for which her love and ambition had long been yearning. Wife of the handsomest and most popular man in England, and he Prince of Wales, with every possibility of one day being Queen of England, with boundless wealth and acknowledged beauty, what a pinnacle of earthly glory and happiness to have attained!

Five years after, 1366, her son Richard was born, and in 1369 Queen Philippa, who had been permitted to see the child of her best beloved Edward, died. History is silent as to the character of their union, but with such a man it ought to have been a happy one. Froissart says concisely of him: "The valiant, gentle Prince of Wales, was the flower of all chivalry "in the world at that time;" and if suffering of body in his closing days prompted him to be cruel towards the inhabitants of Limoges, that by no means seems to have been the character of his life. Kind, gentle, liberal, just even to his enemies, he must have made his home happy; and when we read that his friend the Captal de Buch died of grief on hearing of his death, we can imagine the distress of his widow. He died at Berkhamstead Castle, on Trinity Sunday, June 8th, 1376, of a disease which in those days of surgical knowledge was incurable, and which rendered the latter years of his life "one sad prolongation of suffering."

Queen Philippa had then been dead six years. Edward III., sinking into his dotage, was clouding the close of his gallant life with an unworthy intimacy with one Alice Perrers, "late damsel of the chamber to our "dearest consort Philippa, deceased."

There was a great feeling of jealousy against John of Gaunt, who was supposed to be aiming at the Crown; so Joan probably did not remain at Berkhamstead Castle, which for many years was tenanted by Robert de Vere, Marquis of Dublin and Duke of Ireland,* and probably returned to Aquitaine, the duchy of which had been given to the Black Prince by his father, and where she had passed most of her married life.

However, the year following, 1377, Edward III. died, and Richard II., only eleven years old, came to the throne. I cannot say how far, under

* *History of Berkhamstead* (Rev. J. W. Cobb).

these circumstances, she was responsible for his education Certainly he was brought up in the most ruinous personal indulgence and unconstitutional ideas of his own infallibility, but Hume says* that the Earls of Kent and Huntingdon, his half-brothers, were his chief confidants and favourites, and Miss Agnes Strickland mentions as traits of his vivid and enduring affection for his family, which was the redeeming trait of his character, that "the "distress and terror to which he saw his mother reduced by the insolence of "Wat Tyler, was the chief stimulant of his gallant behaviour when that "rebel fell beneath the sword of Walworth," and that on the occasion of his marriage, 1382, to Anne of Bohemia, the King's mother accompanied the bride to Windsor, "where they were very happy together"

However, their happiness was not long to last In 1385, soon after the death of Wycliffe, whom Anne had befriended, and during the absence of the King in Scotland, Ralph Stafford, eldest son of Hugh second Earl of Stafford, was murdered by the King's half-brother, Sir John Holland Stafford is represented as a peerless chevalier, adored by the English army, and, for his virtuous conduct, in high favour with Anne, who called him her knight He was, moreover, actually on his way to London, with messages from the King, encamped near Beverley, to the Queen, when the fatal encounter took place The ostensible cause of the murder was likewise connected with the Queen, for Froissart states that the archers of Lord Stafford, when protecting Sir Meles, a Bohemian knight then with the army, who was on a visit to Queen Anne, slew a favourite squire belonging to Sir John Holland, and to revenge a punishment which this man had brought upon himself, Sir John cut down Lord Stafford without any personal provocation Sir John was half-brother and boon companion of Richard II, but his loving nature was no doubt wrought upon by the indignation of his wife and the passionate grief of the old Earl of Stafford, as well as the popular outcry at the death of a man so distinguished and highly esteemed, and as soon as John Holland emerged from the shrine of St John of Beverley, whither he had fled for sanctuary, the King ordered him to be arrested, and condemned him to death But on the other hand the Princess of Wales earnestly pleaded with the King for the life of her son, and Richard's weak, undecided nature, wrung by piteous solicitations from both sides, and vexed and pained at what had taken place, for four days was unable to make up his mind what to do On the fifth day, Joan, unable to endure the suspense any longer, died of a broken heart at the royal castle of Wallingford, and then, with his characteristic impulsiveness, Richard, when too late to save his mother, pardoned the criminal "Her corpse," says Sandford, "(embalmed and

* Vol ii, p 255

"wrapped in lead) was ordered to be honourably entombed in the church "of the Friars Minors, at Stamford."

In the *History of Stamford* (published by John Drakard, 1822) we are informed that this was in accordance with her will, dated August 7th, 1385, in which she desires to be buried in the chapel of their Hospital, near the grave of Thomas, Earl of Kent, her husband. That will was made, then, nine years after the death of Edward the Black Prince. Perhaps in the lonely hours of her second widowhood her mind went back to her first married home; or perhaps there is here an indication of the truth of the story that Thomas Holland had been her first lover, the hero of her childhood's days, before considerations of rank or earthly prospects enter the young head, and the boy lover is, for the time, at least, the ideal of perfection. If so, how natural, when the brightness of a very sunny day had waned, and shadows of life were gathering, how natural to wish that the weary body should rest, not under or near the great tomb at Canterbury, but once again at *his* side, and in the quiet stillness of the cloisters await the resurrection.

This John de Holland, however, eventually made his peace with the King through the intervention of the Duke of Lancaster, and was received into favour. In 1397 he was advanced by Richard II. to the Dukedom of Exeter, made Chamberlain of England and Governor of Calais. In the first year of Henry IV. he was deposed from the title of Duke of Exeter, and beheaded at Pleshy, in Essex (Sandford's *Genealogical History*), "upon the third day after the Epiphanie, in the year 1400, for seditious "conspiracy against the life of King Henry," on the very spot where the "Duke of Gloucester was arrested by Richard II., which was in the base "court of the castle of Pleshey, that he might seem to be justly punished "for the Duke's death, of which he was thought to be the principal "procurer, and he lyeth buried in the Collegiate Church there."

He married Elizabeth, second daughter of John of Gaunt, sister to Henry IV. His eldest son, Richard, died without issue, 4 Henry V. His second son, John, was, in the twenty-second year of Henry VI., restored to the title, and distinguished himself as a gallant soldier and able administrator in the reign of Edward V. and VI.; but his only son Henry, having fought bravely for the Lancastrians at Towton and Barnet, escaped to France, where, after wandering about destitute and bare-legged, begging his bread for God's sake, he died, his body being found in the sea between Calais and Dover, but the cause thereof was never ascertained (13 Edward IV. 1473).

And the family of the eldest son, Thomas Earl of Kent, was even shorter-lived. He himself served in the retinue of his gallant step-father the Black Prince, and was held in high estimation by Richard II.

He married Alice Fitz-Alan, daughter of Richard Earl of Arundel Five of his six daughters made great marriages, and he was succeeded at his death in 1397, by his eldest son Thomas His prosperity was brief, for he was attainted by Henry IV, and beheaded by the populace at Cirencester, 1400, leaving a widow Joane, daughter of Hugh Earl of Stafford, but no children

His brother Edmund succeeded him in his honours and estates, and seems to have been loyal to Henry IV, as he was appointed by him a commissioner to treat for peace with the Duke of Brittany, but on the 15th September, 1407, he received a mortal wound in the head by an arrow when besieging the castle and isle of Briak, and died leaving no issue by his wife Lucy, daughter of the Duke of Milan, and the Barony of Wake has been in abeyance ever since But the family of Wake was not extinct with the death of the last of the Hollands, but has continued to this day in the descendants of Sir Hugh Wake, brother of John Wake first Baron Wake He is described as Lord of Deeping, in Lincolnshire, and of Blisworth, in Northamptonshire *

In the reign of Henry VIII there was a Wake living at Cottingham Castle, who had a very beautiful wife, and who on receiving an intimation that the King was at Hull and intended to honour him with a visit, burnt his house, preferring the loss thereof to the risk of the King's admiration, and later still there was in the seventeenth century, William Wake, son of John Wake, who became Archbishop of Canterbury There is an interesting story told in the *Spectator*, No 313, with reference to John Wake, with which I will conclude my notice of this family —

"Everyone who is acquainted with Westminster School knows that "there is a curtain which used to be drawn across the room to separate "the upper school from the lower A youth happened by some mischance "to tear the above-mentioned curtain The severity of the master, "Dr Busby, was too well known for the criminal to expect any pardon for "such a fault, so that the boy, who was of meek temper, was terrified to "death at the thought of his appearance, when his friend, who sat next to "him, bade him be of good cheer, for that he would take the fault on "himself He kept his word accordingly As soon as they were grown "up to be men the Civil War broke out, in which our two friends took "opposite sides one of them followed the Parliament, the other the Royal "party As their tempers were different, the youth who had torn the "curtain endeavoured to raise himself on the Civil List, and the other "who had borne the blame of it, on the military The first succeeded so "well that he was in a short time made a judge under the Protector. "The other was engaged in the unhappy enterprise of Penruddork and

* Bishop Trollope

"Groves, in the west. I suppose, Sir, that I need not acquaint you with "the result of that undertaking. Everyone knows that the Royal party "was routed, and all the heads of them, among whom was the curtain "champion, imprisoned at Exeter. It happened to be his friend's lot at "that time to go the western circuit. The trial of the rebels, as they "were called, was very short, and nothing now remained but to pass "sentence on them, when the judge, hearing the name of his old friend, "and observing his face more attentively, which he had not seen for "many years, asked him if he was not formerly a Westminster scholar. "By the answer he was soon convinced that it was his former generous "friend, and without saying anything more at that time, made the best of "his way to London, where employing all his power and interest with the "Protector, he saved his friend from the fate of his unhappy associates. "The gentleman whose life was thus preserved by the gratitude of his "schoolfellow, was afterwards the father of a son whom he lived to see "promoted in the Church, and who deservedly fills one of the highest "stations in it."

A note adds: "The gentleman here alluded to was Colonel Wake, "father to Dr. Wake, Bishop of Lincoln, and afterwards Archbishop of "Canterbury. As Penruddork, in the course of the trial, takes occasion "to say 'he sees Judge Nicholas on the bench,' it is most likely that he "was the judge of the assize who tried the Cavalier."

THE HILTONS.

The shields which adorn the walls of "the Vestibule" of the Minster are all painted in the same tincture, so that it is impossible to say accurately to whom they belong; but there is one, consisting of two bars,* which is at least worthy of conjecture, for this may be the arms of Mainwaring, the founder of which family, Ranulphus, a noble Norman in the train of William the Conqueror, received for his share of the spoil, Peure, or Over Peover, in Cheshire, and sixteen lordships contingent thereto; but I can find nothing to connect this family with York. Powell, in his *History of Wales*, gives these arms to William Maudit, who he tells us fought under King Louis against Henry III., in Lincolnshire, 1217, associated with Saere Quincey Earl of Winchester, Henrie de Bohun Earl of Hereford, Gilbert de Gaunt Earl of Lincoln, Robert Fitzwalter, Richard Montfychet, Gilbert

* See coloured illustration.

de Clare, William Mowbray, William Beauchamp, William de Colvill, and others, and as the arms of several of these are in the Minster, it is possible that this cognizance may have been his

In the Caerlaverock roll, one John de Lancaster is mentioned, whose arms were argent two bars gules, on a quarter of the second a lion passant guardant or Dugdale says of him that "he was in that expedition made "into Scotland, being in the retinue of Brian Fitz-Alan, of Bedale, in "Yorkshire" Harris Nicolas says that he was the descendant of the Governor of Lancaster Castle in the reign of Henry II, and that, 22 Edward I, he was summoned by the King to attend him with horse and arms into France These facts seem strongly to associate these arms with him, the quarter mentioned being probably an augmentation of honour, viz, one of the royal lions, granted to him in recognition of his personal services and perhaps valour in the field Who can say what deed of prowess may have merited such a distinction at the hands of a Plantagenet? He seems indeed to have continued in the royal favour, for he was one of the King's sergeants for the county of Cheshire in the reign of Edward III, and died *s p*, 1334, when his barony became extinct

But as this shield is close to the window bearing the arms of Luterel, I am disposed to assign them to Godfrey de Hilton, who bore argent two bars azure, and who married Hawisia, daughter of Andrew Luterel, and died 1459, having released all his rights in Winestead and Swine to his nieces Isabel and Elizabeth, the former of whom married Robert Hildyard, whose descendant still owns the property there Godfrey de Hilton was grandson of William de Hilton and Matilda, daughter of Roger de Lascelles, of Kirby Underknoll William de Hilton received, as his younger son's portion from his father Robert de Hilton, lord of Hilton in Durham, these same lands in Winestead and Swine, which he had inherited from his grandmother Beneta, daughter and heiress of Gilbert Tyson, lord of Bridlington and Malton

There is much that is very quaint and interesting about this family of Hilton First they bore as their crest Moses' head, horned or radiated The conventional representation of the Divine glory which flickered on his face and made it shine The statue of Moses by Michael Angelo, at Rome, is an instance of this There is an engraving in *Surtees* of the arms on Hilton Castle, on the banks of the Wear, near Sunderland, surmounted with a helmet richly mantelled, bearing Moses head in profile "The horns resemble," he says, "poking sticks," but I should say, the horns on the head of a snail The Hiltons were also amongst the families whose ancestors used supporters from ancient times (see page 72) But, in addition, they bore the title of baron, not from any peerage created by the Crown, or from any summons to Parliament,—for though Robert de Hilton, 1303–5, and Alexander de Hilton, 1332–5, had such summons, according to Dugdale, it was never repeated to any of their descendants,—but given either by the general courtesy of the country, from the long and immemorial existence of the family in a "gentle" state, long before the creation of barons either by writ or summons, or else with reference to the rank which the Hiltons undoubtedly held as barons of the Bishopric (like the Vernons, Fitz-Hughs, Masseys, and others, barons of the Palatine Earl of Chester, which Hugh Lupus had power from the Conqueror to constitute and create*), sitting with a sort of provincial peerage in the great council of their Ecclesiastical Palatine, and possessing some degree of controlling or consulting power. There is ample evidence of such a Chamber of Peers in many episcopal charters, &c. The name of Hilton always stands first in every episcopal commission. In 1669 Mr. Arden complains to Miles Stapleton of the unseemly pride of Dean Carleton and his daughters, inasmuch as the Dean had seated himself above the Baron at Quarter Sessions, and the young ladies had crowded themselves into a pew in the Cathedral before Baron Hilton's daughters.

The antiquity of the family was deemed so great that it was reputed by popular tradition to have sprung from a northern rover, who wooed and won a fair young Saxon dame, with all her lands and towns, under the disguise of one of Odo's ravens. The playful fancy of Mr. Surtees has elaborated this into a metrical romance, which I have not space to quote entire, in which he describes how Harold the son of Eric fell beneath the withering spell of the witches, and was sentenced to wander as a raven,

> "Till lady, unlike thing I trow,
> Print three kisses on his brow."

Edith is the daughter of a knight slain in the crusade,

> "And she is left an orphan child,
> In her gloomy hall of the woodland wild."

In "her saddest mood" she climbs the bartizan stair, and from the summit of the tower, watches

> "A raven on the wing,
> Circling round in airy ring;
> Hovering about in doleful flight,
> Where will the carrier of Odin alight?
> That seems to be her willow-wand.
> For he trusted the soft and maiden grace,
> And tries to smooth his raven note,
> And sleeks his glossy raven coat,
> To court the maiden's hand;
> And now, caressing and caressed,
> The raven is lodged in Edith's breast."

---

* Ormerod's *History of Cheshire.*

The sequel is easily imagined —

> "That maiden kiss hath holy power
> Over planet and sigillary hour,
> The Elfish spell hath lost its charms,
> And a Danish knight is in Edith's arms
> And Harold, at his bride's request,
> His barbarous gods forswore,
> Freya, and Woden, and Balder, and Thor,
> And Jarrow, with tapers blazing bright,
> Hailed her gallant proselyte"

But there was another legend connected with the Hiltons, even a certain visionary inhabitant called "The cauld lad of Hilton," who was seldom seen but heard nightly by the servants who slept in the great hall, showing his capricious temper by breaking the plates and dishes, and hurling the pewters in all directions when they had been left tidy, and by arranging everything with the grandest precision when that apartment had been left in disarray At length his pranks becoming unbearable, it was determined to make an effort to get rid of him, and in accordance with the acknowledged specific as to dealing with brownies, a green cloak and hood were laid before the kitchen fire, while the domestics sat up watching at a prudent distance Sure enough at twelve o'clock the sprite glided in, stood by the glowing embers, surveyed the garments very attentively, tried them on, frisked about, cut somersaults and gambadoes, and as the crow of the first cock was heard, twitched the mantle tightly about him and departed, uttering as his valediction —

> "Here's a cloak, and here's a hood,
> The cauld lad o' Hilton will do no more good"

But tradition said that "the cauld lad of Hilton" was no mere brownie, but the disembodied spirit of a certain groom lad whom one of the old barons of Hilton had slain in a moment of wrath or intemperance Impatient that his horse did not come to the door at the time appointed, he went to the stable, finding the boy loitering, he seized a hay-fork and struck him, though not intentionally, a mortal blow He covered his victim with straw till night, and then threw him into the pond, where the skeleton of a boy was (in confirmation of the tale) discovered in the last baron's time Certainly on the 3rd of July, 1609, an inquest was held before Master John King, coroner Wardœ de Chestre, of which the following record remains "Inquisitio super visum corporis Rogeri Skelton ibi "jacentis mortui Jurati presentant quod Robertus Hilton de Hilton, Gen, "die et anno supradictis inter horas 8 et 9 ante meridiem, falcans gramen "cum quadam falce, Anglice a Syth, ad valorem cxx^d. quam ipse in manibus "suis tenuit, eundem Rogerum stantem a tergo casu infortunii cum acie "ejus falcis, Anglice the Scyth point, percussit super dextrum femer ejusdem

"Rogeri unam plagam mortalem longam unius pollicis et lat' duor pollic, "ex qua plaga idem Rogerus eadem hora mortuus ibidem obiit, et quod "casu non aliter, &c." A free pardon for the above manslaughter appears on the rolls of Bishop James, date 6th September, 1609, so that there is a very matter of fact explanation to what has naturally been enshrouded in mystery and romance.

But the Hiltons seem to have been habitually a little high-handed in their dealings with others; and the monks at Wearmouth made frequent complaints of the grievances sustained at the hands of these very lay and haughty barons. Amongst others, "William Hylton and divers of his "servants came to Monkwearmouth the Saturday before Palm Sunday, and "assaulted William Ingham, master of Wearmouth, and layd on him his "hands in the quere of tye saide kirke in violence, and poul'd off his "hode, to great shame and reproof."

Amongst other baronial appendages, the Hiltons were amongst the last to keep a domestic fool. The Baron, on one occasion returning from London, amused himself with a homeward saunter through his own woods and meadows. At Hilton footbridge he encountered his faithful fool, who, staring at the gaudy laced suit of his patron, in the newest metropolitan fashion, made by some southern tailor, exclaimed: "Wha's fule now?" I wonder whether this was the same baron who (1630), previously to leaving home for one of those metropolitan excursions, made his will:—"In the name, &c. . . . Because I am at this instant, God assisting me, "intending to goe for London, and that no mortall man is certain of his "safe return." A curious indication of the insecurity of travelling which has been so minimised in our more favoured days.

Henry Hilton, who died 1630, was a captain in the State service under Prince Maurice of Orange, and is mentioned in Bishop Neil's letters as "an experienced soldier that had borne office in the field," and was made "Muster Master" of the trained bands of the county. His inventory seems to have been small, though characteristic, viz.: "a target, "muscat, bandeloor, and head pece, £1;" he had "£33 in apparell, one "wine peece, and four silver spoons;" the rest of his wealth corn ("£100 "in the staggarth), and nowte bestiall, his wyve's stock."

But, like many old families, the decadence of the Hiltons came at last. Henry Hilton, who succeeded his father Robert Hilton, 1607-8, and died 1640, seems to have been a half-witted, melancholy creature, living at Billinghurst, in Sussex, in strict retirement, having married a daughter of Sir Richard Wortley, and dying at Mitchell Grove, in the same county of Sussex, 1640. He made a will leaving his property in trust to the Lord Mayor and four senior aldermen of the city of London, for certain charitable bequests to parishes in the county of Durham, orphan children

PLATE 6.

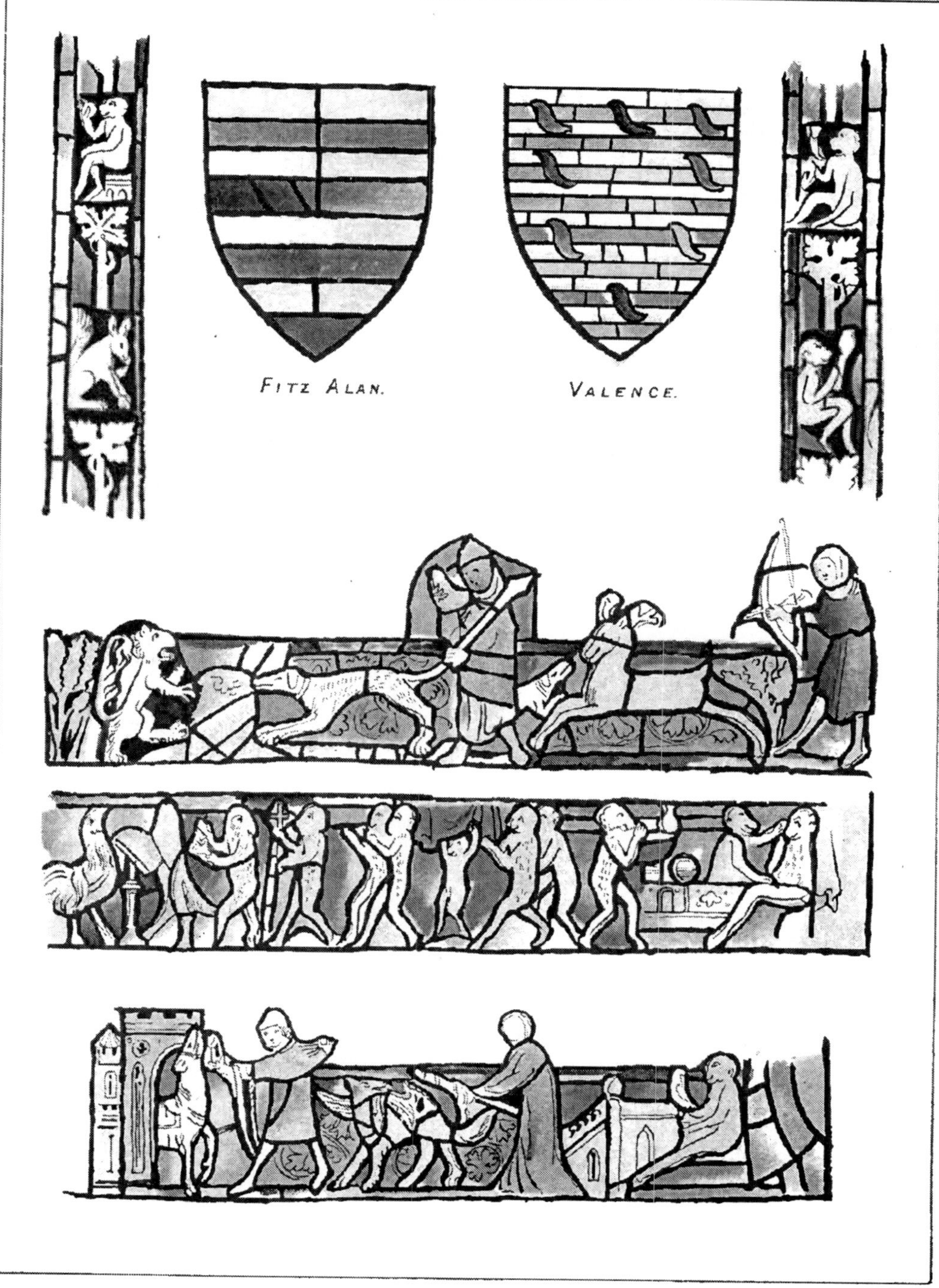

in London, &c, appointing Lady Jane Shelley his executrix, and desiring to be buried in St Paul's Cathedral After twenty years of litigation a compromise was effected, by which the estates were restored on condition of the payment of the legacies, but the property had been plundered and wasted during the civil war, by the armies of Newcastle and Lesley, and the family were sadly impoverished when at last the inheritance became their own again, and retreated, without degradation of blood or honours, into the quiet ranks of private gentry

In 1723, Anne, daughter and heiress of Baron John Hilton, married Sir Richard Musgrave, to whom John Hilton devised his property, on condition that he assumed the name of Hilton only About 1750 he sold the whole of the estates under an Act of Parliament His granddaughter and heiress, Eleanor, married, 1769, William Jolliffe, of Petersfield, and his descendants are the Hylton-Jolliffes of the present day

---

FITZALAN AND POYNTZ

When the shield is divided into an equal number of bars it is called barry, and the first which I shall notice is barry of eight or and gules, *in the south-west window of the vestibule, and in the chapter-house* * Whose arms are these? Well, they may be the coat of Brian Fitzalan or Hugh Poyntz

Brian Fitzalan was descended from Alan Rufus, one of the younger sons of Eudo Earl of Brittany He (Alan) was one of the chief and principal advisers of William to undertake the conquest of England He commanded the rear-guard at the battle of Hastings Three years afterwards he was employed at the siege of York, which Edwin Earl of Mercia and his brother Morcar, with Waltheof, the governor, bravely defended After six months' siege it was subdued, and William, by the advice of Matilda, rewarded him with the possessions of Edwin, and created him an earl He died unmarried, and was interred at Bury St Edmunds, 1089 He was succeeded by his brother,† Alan Niger, from whom Stephen the monk, driven out of Whitby and Lastingham by William de Percy, obtained a grant of St Olave's minster and four acres in York, and converted it into a monastery William Rufus afterwards built another monastery further south, and dedicated it to St Mary Alan Niger died 1093, and was succeeded by his brother Stephen, who died 1137, aged 90, and directed that his heart should be buried at St Mary's, York He left two sons—Alan, who married Bertha, daughter and heiress of Conan Duke of Bretagne, their son Conan, in consequence, succeeding to both titles, and Brian, who married Agnes, granddaughter and heiress of Scolland, lord of Bedale

* See coloured illustration

† Clarkson's *History of Richmondshire*

His grandson was Brian Fitzalan, of whose arms in the Minster I am speaking He seems to have been a brave warrior and a man of great distinction, for he was one of the eight knights who had their special stations and periods of duty at the castle built by Alan Rufus as a place of security for himself and followers from the incursions of the Angles and Danes, and called by him Riche-mont (Richmond), as being the more fruitful and stronger portion of his territory The town grew up around it, the adjoining territory called by the Bretons "the land of Fontenay" being given to the burgesses in 1145 by Alan, third earl It must—according to the mode of warfare at that time—have been a strong and impregnable fortress, towering up on an almost perpendicular rock upon the banks of the Swale It was encompassed with a wall six feet thick and 650 yards long, embattled, and strengthened at intervals with lofty square towers, two or three storeys high, some of them had open galleries on the outside of the inner wall, supported by stone brackets, as means of communication between the upper apartments, to which there was no admission from the rooms below Against this wall, after the manner of Norman castles, were placed the habitations of the owner and his warlike retainers, and there was a great central tower, called Robin Hood's tower, beneath which was the chapel dedicated to St Nicholas There was also the keep, a great square tower of hewn stone in courses, 54 feet long by 48 feet wide at the base, and other towers called the Barbican or watch tower, the Garden tower, and the Cockpit tower

To maintain this fortress, his followers and retainers had to keep "castle guard" at the castle, and perform military service at appointed periods in discharge for the lordships and manors which he had with a liberal hand distributed amongst them The circumference of the castle wall seems to have been divided into eight portions, each allotted to a trusty knight and his retainers, and marked with their standards

Standard 1 Or a chief indented azure (over the chapel of St Nicholas, on the east) Ranulphus, son of Robert, lord of Middleham His great-grandfather, Ribald, received the manor of Middleham from his brother Alan Rufus, and his father, Robert, built the castle there, receiving in addition, from his kinsman Conan, the forest of Wensleydale, and marrying Helewisia, daughter and heiress of Ralph de Glanville, lord of Coverham Ranulphus, who died in 1251, had a son, Ralph, by Mary, daughter of Roger Bigot, Earl of Norfolk, and Ralph, having married Anastasia, daughter of William Lord Percy, left one daughter, Maria, who married Robert de Nevill, lord of Raby, and carried Middleham into that family, to be in after-times the residence of the great Richard Nevill, Earl of Warwick, surnamed "the king-maker"

Standard 2, Barry of ten or and gules (in the court before the great tower) was held by Alan, son of Roaldus the Constable, whose father had the sobriquet of "Musard the dreamer," and whose descendant in the reign of Edward III sold his possessions to Henry le Scrope, lord of Bolton

Standard 3, Barry of six or and gules, was in the great hall of Scolland, and was held by Brian Fitzalan, lord of Bedale, of whom I have already spoken, and of whom more hereafter

Standard 4, Vair, argent and azure, a fesse gules (between the kitchen and the kennel) was assigned to Torphinus, whose granddaughter and heiress married John Marmyon, who assumed these arms Marmyon is a name rendered famous by Walter Scott's stirring poem of the doings, or misdoings, of one of that family

Gall, the Norman, who was attendant on William the Conqueror at the battle of Hastings, mentions that "in the said battle there was a noble "baron called Roger Marmyon, in whom the Conqueror placed great "confidence, and who (like a good and valiant chevalier) fought so well and "acquitted himself so ably in that battle, that he deserved afterwards to "have great possessions in England for his prowess" Clarkson does not say whose those estates were, but Sir Walter Scott tells us concerning his hero, that the heralds at Norham

"Hailed him as lord of Fontenaye,
Of Lutterward and Scrivelbaye,
Of Tamworth Tower and town"

Burke says that Robert (not Roger) Marmyon, lord of Fontney, came over with the Conqueror, and received from him the feudal lordship of Tamworth and Scrivelsby, to be held in grand sergeanty, to perform the office of champion at the King's coronation His grandson, Robert, married twice Robert, his eldest son by the first marriage, inherited these two estates, which passed, early in the fourteenth century, through his granddaughters (failing male issue), as follows —Tamworth to Baldwin de Freville, Lord Freville, and Scrivelsby (with the office of Champion of England) to Sir John Dymoke Robert, his eldest son by the second marriage, had the manors of Wintringham and Coningsby, in Lincolnshire, and married Amice Fitzhugh His grandson, John, was created a baron by writ of summons, 1294, but his male issue failed in the fourth generation, and Avice (sister of Robert, third and last Baron Marmyon, who died 1335) married Sir John Grey, Lord Grey of Rotherfield, whose granddaughter Elizabeth, by marrying Henry Lord Fitzhugh, brought the estates to the family of Fitzhugh

The battle of Flodden was fought 1513, more than one hundred years after the estates were separated As far as we know, the abeyance had never terminated in favour of any of John's descendants, and the barony is in abeyance still Nor had the estates been reunited, so that mythical person in the poem could not have been feudal lord of Tamworth and Scrivelbaye, and the gift "of a chain of twelve marks' weight" to the heralds who uttered such a fiction, was to "requite" an empty "courtesy" indeed.

Standard 5, Azure, three chevronels interlaced and a chief or (on the west part of Scolland, near the kitchen) was held by Randolph, grandfather of Hugh, whose posterity retained the name of Fitzhugh.

Standard 6, Sable a saltire or (near the court of the tower at the east part, on the outside of the walls), was assigned to Conan the son of Elias, who seems, from this coat, to have been ancestor of the family of Clarevaux.

Standard 7, Argent, a cross engrailed sable, was the station of the chamberlain (on the east part of Scolland, near the oven). There were three chamberlains—Robert, Ernald, and Ralph, who (I suppose) shared the duties thereof. The arms are those of Conan de Kelfield.

Standard 8, Argent on a fess sable, three bezants (west part of the greater chapel): Thomas de Brough, seneschal.

There is something very interesting in these quaint details of days gone by; and who that has ever visited Richmond (one of the most lovely spots in the north), would not strive to picture it in his imagination in its pristine glory, towering up above the stream and forest. Its battlements, decorated with the banners which showed that the good knights were at their station; glittering with spear, and helm, and shields, and re-echoing with the clang of a barbaric, but nevertheless picturesque, panoply of war.

Brian Fitzalan had, then, a noble heritage for those days, which he further increased by his marriage with Anne, daughter of John Baliol, lord of Barnard Castle, and in right of his mother, Devorgilda, Countess of Huntingdon, for a time King of Scotland. Brian Fitzalan was also a great favourite with King Edward; he accompanied him in the wars in Wales, and brought great assistance to him in Scotland, was present at the siege of Caerlaverock, and is described by the chronicler thereof as "full of "courtesy and honour."

He was summoned (23rd Edward I.) to Parliament at Carlisle, and continued to be summoned for seven years until his death (30th of Edward I.). He was buried with his wife on the south side of Bedale church. The monumental effigies which covered their grave are said to be amongst the "finest sepulchral memorials in England," but are now placed on the north side of the tower arch. Their daughter Agnes married Gilbert de Stapleton, and their daughter Catherine married John, Lord Grey of Rotherfield, amongst whose descendants the property was divided.

Brian Fitzalan must have been a man great in station and noble in character; and this consideration throws some light upon an incident recorded of him of which there is, if I mistake not, an illustration in the

Minster Amongst the seals attached to the Barons' letter to Pope Boniface (see page 293), is the seal of Brian Fitzalan, but the charges thereon are evidently a device, for no shield appears On a square were engraved two birds, a rabbit, a stag, and a pig or boar, with the legend *Tot capita tot sentencie*

In the north aisle of the nave there is a window, next to the bellfounders' window, which has a similar device For in the borders of the window (unlike the others which are composed of armorial bearings, probably the ensigns of the donors), only a strange medley of monkeys, and men, and dogs, and other animals and birds appear *

I venture to attribute this window to the gift of Brian Fitzalan, and thus to account for these fanciful representations In the Caerlaverock roll it is stated "The handsome Brian Fitzalan, full of courtesy and "honour, I saw with his well-adorned banner of barry of gold and red, "which was the subject of dispute between him and Hugh Poyntz, who "bore the same, neither more nor less, at which many and many "marvelled" This was, indeed, something more than an infraction of courtly etiquette, for arms were not assumed at pleasure, but granted by the Heralds College, under the authority of the Crown, and, as we have noticed in the Scrope and Grosvenor contest, very tenaciously held and defended.

Hugh Poyntz (or Pons or Poinz or Pointz) was son and heir of Nicholas Poyntz, of Cory Malet, Somerset † His lineage was second to none, either as regards antiquity of origin and nobility of descent, or as regards the illustrious deeds with which his ancestors had been associated

William, Count of Eu, had, by his wife Esseline, four sons, two of whom accompanied the Conqueror to England—William, who was Count of Soissons, and Pons, or Pontz There is absolutely no trustworthy record of the leader of the Norman army, and there are at least ten different lists all professing to be the roll of Battle Abbey, and each differing from the other

Robert Wace, an Augustinian monk of Bayeux (born 1100), frankly acknowledges his inability to give all the names of the barons present But John Brompton, abbot of Jorvaux, 16th Henry VI, in his rhyming chronicle gives a list (on what authority he does not say) of 240 names, amongst which he mentions Merle and Mowbray, Pounchardon and Pomeray, Gornay and Courtenay, Longevil and Longespay, Hainstlaing and Turnay, Payns and Pontelarge, Husec and Husay It has been suggested that the "*a*" in Payns is a clerical error of the copyist, to which the Brompton MS in the British Museum seems to give confirmation However, Pons had five

* See coloured illustration

† Sir John Maclean's *History of the Family of Poyntz*, Atkyn's *History of Gloucestershire*

sons—Drogo, Walter, Richard, Osbert, and Simon—of whom Richard, on the death of his elder brothers, styled himself Fitz-Pons. His eldest son, Walter, married the heiress of the Castle of Clifford, and assumed the name.* Simon, also called Fitz-Pons, inherited the manor of Swell, and was amongst the benefactors of Tewkesbury. His son, Pontius Fitz-Simon, who held eight knights' fees in the honour of Gloucester, afterwards *Signavit se cruce cum Rege Ric.*, or, in other words, became a crusader with Richard I.

His great-grandson Hugh married Helewisia, coheiress of Wm. Malet, baron of Cory Malet; and his son Nicholas inherited not only his mother's property but also that of her sister Mabel, wife of Hugh de Vivonia. He also held the manor of Tokington as well as Swell, and the manor of Sutton *in capite* of Gilbert de Clare, Earl of Gloucester. He married Elizabeth, daughter of Timothy Dyall, by whom he had one son, Hugh Poyntz. He did homage for the barony he held of the King (2nd Edward I.), and was summoned to a muster at Worcester, 1277, to punish Llewelyn Prince of Wales, by invading his country. Again, in 1282, the Welsh having broken into rebellion, and murdered Lord Clifford, the King's justiciar in Wales, Hugh Poyntz was summoned to Rhuddlan Castle, and was probably at the great battle fought in December, 1282, in which the English were completely victorious, Prince Llewelyn slain by a common soldier, and two thousand of his men destroyed. In the following year he was also serving with the King when Prince Edward (Llewelyn's brother), who had escaped, was captured and cruelly put to death. And the following year we find him attending the Parliament summoned at Shrewsbury.

In 1294 he was with another army, collected to march into Wales, at Worcester, and was summoned to Parliament as a baron, 1295. He was also with the King at the battle of Dunbar, 1296, when the Scots were defeated with great slaughter, which led to the formal surrender by Baliol of the regal dignity. And finally we find his name on the Caerlaverock roll, when in 1300 Edward determined to invade Scotland again, and assembled his army at Carlisle to attack that famous castle. He also was amongst the barons who signed or rather sealed the letter to Pope Boniface, though the actual seal used seems to have been that of his son, "S. Nicholai "Poyntz;" and his name appears amongst the barons summoned to Parliament, as late as 1st Edward II., 1307, when he died. He married Margaret, daughter of Sir William Pavelly, and left one son, Nicholas, who married Elizabeth, daughter of Sir Edward de la Zouche. His grandson Nicholas left two daughters—Amicia, wife of John Barry, who had no issue, and Margaret, wife of Sir John de Newburgh, of Lulworth. But Nicholas was never summoned to Parliament. He is known to have dissipated his patrimony, and it is possible that having thereby alienated his *tenure* without the King's license, the barony by *tenure* lapsed to the Crown.

* See page 256.

So if Brian Fitzalan was a great man, Hugh Poyntz was a great man too, and as they were both members of the Parliaments which were summoned at York, it is probable that they were both here during the building of the nave and chapter-house, and gave windows thereto, and it is certain that between this mighty baron of the south and the great baron of the north there must have been considerable jealousy, and a vigorous claim, on either side, to the exclusive monopoly of the same arms. Brian Fitzalan, as a Yorkshireman, would be strongly supported by kindred and neighbours on his own soil, but Hugh Poyntz, though living in the south, was related by kindred to the powerful houses of Clifford and Zouche, and was numbered amongst the retainers of the great family of Clare, Earl of Gloucester, whose arms are in the windows close by.

It may seem a trifling matter to us now: it was a grave matter then—a matter grave enough to stir men's angry passions of jealousy, and provoke bloodshed and feuds, a matter, as we see in the Scrope and Grosvenor case, weighty enough to occupy three years, and the testimony of two hundred of the bravest and wisest in the land. It was a matter, as we have seen in the Hastings' case, which might entail imprisonment for life upon a costly lawsuit. But it came to none of these, and, if I interpret Brian Fitzalan's quaint motto aright, his was the wise counsel which kept the peace. He would not cause a schism amongst the King's soldiers, when the King and the country needed their united power against the enemy. He could not bear arms borne by another, or fall back on some other family quartering, leaving these to his rival, so he adopted the third course—good-humoured philosophy, ridiculed and caricatured, as strutting cocks or foolish apes, his opponents, and dismissed all further consideration of the vexed question from his mind with the wise aphorism, *Tot capita tot sentencie* ("So many heads, so many opinions.")

If I am right, the arms in the chapter-house and the quaint fantastic bordure in the nave,* express—in characters so distinct that he who runs may read it—that which is a truism for all time, and the more general recognition whereof would not only shew genuine wisdom in those who hold it, but soften many a hot controversy, smooth many ruffled feelings, and allay many a rising tempest, which, Fitzalan has shewn us, it is the part of true courage not to excite or aggravate, but to subdue.

Perhaps you may be disposed to question whether the arms which I have been describing are the arms of Fitzalan, and to assert that they are the arms of Poyntz. Well, don't let us quarrel over it. Let us keep our own opinions and be content: yes, and maintain this policy, not only as regards the windows, but all which concerns the Church. Better, peace than discord, aye, and braver far the peace-maker and the peace-holder than the noisy, reckless, sharp-tongued, vehement partizan. And as

* See coloured illustration.

Fitzalan seems wise to us to have thus acted concerning what appears in our eyes so very trifling, so too, hereafter, shall many things appear which we are sorely tempted now to regard as of the utmost importance, and, for the sake thereof, to break the peace, if not each others' heads.

Dare to be firm, to be patient, and to keep your temper, and the clouds will disperse and the noise subside, and that which is really great and valuable will not be overthrown, but will abide for ever.

The Vavasours.

The shield of Vavasour—Or, a fesse dancette sable*—has a twofold claim to a foremost place in any book on the Heraldry of the Minster, not merely because of its heraldic interest, but as representing a Family to which we are indebted for much of the very material of our great fabric.

As regards the former, the charge is not only a variety of the fess, but it is a specimen of what is called "Canting Heraldry" and "Armes "Parlantes." We have reason to believe that in genuine Heraldry every charge had its distinct significance, indicating some quality in the character of the original holder, or some meritorious action done by him. "Canting Heraldry" indicated, by some device, the name of the individual, punning upon it or playing upon it, and representing it not in words but in forms; hence arises the term—when such a device was used beside the arms or apart from the arms—"rebus." "Non verbis sed rebus loquimur."

The introduction of this practice seems coeval with Heraldry itself. In the earliest roll of arms extant, *temp.* of Henry III. (1240–1245), nine illustrations of this occur, *e.g.* "Geoffrey de Lucy: de goules a trois "lucies d'or; Thomas Corbett: d'or deux corbeaux noir." In another roll of Edward II. they are still more abundant—"Sire Johan Heringaud: de "azure, crusule de or, a vi harengs de or; Sire Adam Martel: de sable a iij "martels de argent; Sire Peres Corbet: de or a un corbyn de sable; "Sire Thomas Corbet: de or a iij corbyns de sable; Sir Odynel Heron: "de argent a iij herons de azure;" and so on. The arms of Castile and Leon, *temp.* of Edward I. as shewn in eighth window west, nave, north aisle, were a castle and a lion. The arms of Grenada, a pomegranate.†

The old Yorkshire family of Foulis carried three leaves (feuilles). The arms of Sykes are three "fountaines,"—a syke, in the northern dialect, signifying a spring, or rather that kind of well which was sunk within the precincts of the camp; and the arms of Pigot, or Picot, of Clotherholme, which appear on one of the pillars of the nave of Ripon Cathedral, are three mill picks, two and one.

---

* See coloured illustration. † *Curiosities of Heraldry* (Mark Antony Lower).

But in many instances actual letters were introduced into the shields. The ancient family of Toft bore argent a chevron between three text "T"s sable; and Thurland three Greek taus, *i.e.* "T," on a chief indented. Sometimes the meaning of the letters is not so apparent, for the family of Kekitmore bore three text "S"s, viz. "S.S.S." gules;* sometimes they applied to sacred things, *e.g.* Archbishop Sudbury carried, argent on a cross azure, the letter "M" crowned or; the city of Rochester, Or on a cross gules, the letter "R" of the field, or sometimes the letter "X" surmounted by the letter "I" sable. The priory of Bridlington carried, per pale sable and argent, three Roman "B"s counter-changed.

The charge on an ancient seal of the Vavasours seems to have been originally a peculiar variety of this practice, for it is neither a simple letter nor a simple device, but the fess twice indented so as to form a letter "M." Since then, however, the indentations have been increased, so that the simple meaning of the charge has been rendered very indistinct. But the legend round tells us that it is the seal of Magerus (or Malger, or Mauger) le Vavassur.

Two considerations at once arise therefrom. First, what was a vavasour? secondly, who was Mauger the Vavassur, or Vavasour?

As regards the former, there is some little difficulty in accurately tracing the details of an office which has long gone out of vogue. According to the *Imperial Dictionary*, the etymology of the word is as follows:—"The word vassal seems to have meant what we now term a subordinate, "just as vaslet, or varlet, was applied to a boy between the ages of seven "and fourteen years, after which he became an esquire." Hallam says: "In ancient days a vassal was a feudatory, or tenant holding lands under "a lord, and bound by his tenure to feudal service." †

According to the feudal system, all land was vested in the King, and all landholders held of him by service of "grand sergeanty," or "petit sergeanty," as I have shewn on page 62. Every baron, therefore, was a vassal of the King. A vavasour seems to have been a vassal of a vassal, *i.e.* va-vasour, holding land of him on exactly the same terms as he held them of his lord. A position inferior indeed to the baronage, but next to it, with many subordinate retainers, tenants, and villeins. Hallam, in vol. i., p. 149, further says: "In France all who held lands "immediately depending upon the Crown, whatever titles they may bear, "were comprised in the order of barons. To these corresponded the

* Guillim. † Hallam, *Middle Ages*, vol. ii., p. 555.

"valvasores majores, and capitanei of the empire. In a subordinate class "were the vassals of this high nobility, who upon the continent were "usually termed vavassours: an appellation not unknown though rare in "England. The chatilaines belonged to the order of vavassours as they "held only arriere fiefs; but having fortified houses from which they "derived their names, and possessing complete rights of territorial justice, "they seemed to raise themselves above their fellows in the scale of "tenure. But after the nobility of chivalry became the object of pride, the "vavassours who obtained knighthood were commonly styled batchelors, "those who had not received that honour fell into the class of squires "or damoisaux."

Lord Lyttelton, in his *Life of Henry II.*, tells us: "Sir Henry "Spelman says that a mesne tenant who had more than a single knight's "fee was called a vavassour, which he thinks was a degree above knights, "yet we generally find that name applied to any vassal who held a "military fief of a tenant-in-chief of the Crown."

Chaucer, however, in his inimitable *Canterbury Tales*, has given us a portrait from which we can form a very fair opinion for ourselves as to his status and quality. He says that he was a Frankelein (*i.e.* according to Tyrwhit,* classed with, but after, the miles and armiger). His beard was white as the daisy,—his complexion ruddy,—liking his morning sop,—the very son of Epicurus, esteeming simple delight to be truly perfect happiness. Having a large house he was a very St. Julian for hospitality in his country. Bread and ale were always on his board. His house was never without baked meat of fish and flesh, so that it may be said to have snowed meat and drink there. It was not only plentiful but of every conceivable dainty, changing with the seasons. Sad was his cook if his sauce was not piquant and pungent and his utensils ready; for all day long his table, fixed in the hall, always stood ready covered. He was chairman of the sessions and very often knight of the shire (*i.e.* M.P. for the county). A knife and a silk purse hung at his girdle, which was as white as morning milk. He had been the sheriff and the contour, or coroner (*i.e.* the head of the Hundred-court summoned by the constable). In fact there was nowhere such a worthy Vavasour. However, the poet shall speak for himself:

"A Frankelein was in this companynie,
White was his berde as is the dayesie.
Of his complexion he was sanguin.
Wel loved he by the morwe a sop in win.
To liven in delit was ever his wone,
For he was Epicures' owen sone,

* *Canterbury Tales of Chaucer*, Thos. Tyrwhit, 1798.

That held opinion, that plein delit
Was veraily felicite parfite
An housholder, and that a grete was he,
Seint Julian he was in his contree
His brede, his ale, was alway after on,
A better envyned man was no wher non
Withouten bake mete never was his hous,
Of fish and flesh, and that so plenteous,
It snewed in his hous of mete and drinke,
Of all deintees that men coud of thinke,
After the sondry sesons of the yere,
So changed he his mete and his soupere
Ful many a fat partrich hadde he in mewe,
And many a breme, and mary a luce in stewe
Wo was his coke, but if his sauce were
Poinant and sharpe, and redy all his gere
His table dormant in his halle alway
Stode redy covered alle the longe day
At sessions ther was he lord and sire,
Ful often time he was knight of the shire
An anelace and a gipciere all of silk
Heng at his girdel, white as morwe milk
A shereve hadde he ben, and a countour—
Was no wher swiche a worthy vavasour"

Such may be the portrait of Malger, who possibly came over in the train of William de Perci, 1067 (*i e* the year after the Conquest), whose name appears not in the roll of Battle Abbey, and there is no evidence that he took part in the battle of Senlac, but for some reason he was highly in favour with the Conqueror Indeed, Mr Fonblanque, in his *Annals of the House of Percy*, suggests that William de Perci had been one of the Norman colonists who came over and established themselves during the days of Edward the Confessor, and that he had married Emma de Port, daughter of Gospatric Earl of Northumberland, and heiress of Seamer, near Scarborough, then an important seaport, and a large district of the lands adjacent Her fellow-countrymen gave Perci the sobriquet of "Al-Gernons," *i e* "aux moustaches," or "a la barbe," on account of his hairy face, which, under the more euphonious form of Algernon, remains a family name to the present day Guizot (*History of France*) says that Edward, "having passed 27 years of exile in Normandy, returned "to England, almost a stranger to the country of his ancestors, and far "more Norman than Saxon in his manner, tastes, and language He was "accompanied by Normans whose number and prestige, under his rule, "increased from day to day" Mr Fonblanque further suggests that he had retired to Normandy to tide over the approaching complications, and returning when William's power was established, the Conqueror found it expedient to conciliate him with large gifts At any rate, in 1085 he possessed in capite no less than eighty-six lordships in the North Riding, in fact the Percy fee, which was in the deanery of Craven, was equal to 17,400 statute acres, and must have comprised a considerable number of the 30,000 knights' fees (*i.e.* two hides, or two hides and a half of land), "into which," Madox says, "the Conqueror had divided the country, and "which entailed the obligation of furnishing the King with one armed "soldier for forty days in each year."

In Domesday-book—a book of the general survey of England, commenced by William's order, 1085, and completed 1086, by Commissioners—this entry occurs:—"Izelwode, Gamel, and Ulf, had three carucates of "land to be taxed where there may be two ploughs. Malger now has it "of William, himself one plough there, and three borders with two ploughs." So Malger, or Mauger, was probably one of the suite of William de Perci (and these probably constituted the two knights' fees which his grandson, William, is recorded to have held of William de Percy, the third baron, 1187). At any rate, in 1184, Maud de Percy, his daughter, widow of William de Newburgh, Earl of Warwick, endowed the Church of our Lady at Tadcaster, and the Chapel of Hazelwood, with a carucate of land in her birthplace, Catton; and a yearly pension in consideration of the performance of perpetual masses for the souls of her husband and family. The grants being made—in wording which indicates the quasi-royal state in which the Percy heiress lived—"by the advice of the Lord Vavaseur, "and other of our faithful lieges, and of the whole court." (*Monast. Angl.* vol. v., p. 510.)

In 1234, in a litigation between Richard de Percy and his nephew William, the latter was attached to answer, *inter alia*, that he had distrained William la Vavasur, and allowed him to do homage to him. So that from this we gain some idea of the position of the earliest member of the Vavasour family, and their relative connection with the Percies.

In 1070, Thomas, a wealthy Norman, Canon of Bayeux, and chaplain to the Conqueror, was appointed Archbishop of York, "upon coming to "which," says his friend Hugo, the cantor or precentor of York, "he "found the church despoiled by fire, and commenced to rebuild it from "its foundation." Mr. Brown says* that "on examining the remains that "still exist of this once splendid edifice, the material is not of the oolite "limestone nor coarse sandstone used in the more ancient buildings, but "of the magnesian limestone which is found in and around Thievesdale, "near Tadcaster; and it is probable that the material came from there, "and was granted to the Norman archbishop by William de Percy."

In 1137, however, the cathedral was burned down (Stowe says), together with St. Mary's Abbey and 39 churches, and for nearly 40 years lay in ashes. Probably some sort of building was erected in the ruins, for,

* *History of York Minster.*

from the lesson appointed in the York breviary to be read at the commemoration of St William, during the primacy of Geoffry Plantagenet, there appears to have been another fire after the death of Archbishop William The origin of the fire is thus recorded: "It happened that "on a certain dark night the flame from the torch of a careless watchman "set fire to the city From this conflagration proceeded a globe of fire "which ran along the middle of the street consuming everything in its "way, encompassed the house of prayer in which the holy body rested" (i e of the archbishop), "and by its fiery assault laid it waste, not only "unroofing it, but reducing to ashes or desolate charcoal the furthest "building of the temple"

On the death of William, Roger of Pont l'Eveque was appointed archbishop, 1171, and he at once commenced to rebuild the choir, and Walter de Percy, Lord of Rougemont, descended from a younger son of Alan de Percy, placed his forest at Bolton Percy at the entire disposal of the archbishop, for the supply of whatever timber might be required, as long as he lived* I conclude that the grant of stone, previously granted by the head of the house of Percy, was continued, at any rate his vavasour was determined not to be lacking in seasonable generosity, for in Dugdale's *Monasticon Anglicanum* there is a grant from Robert le Vavasour, giving, granting, and confirming, for a pure and perpetual alms to God and the blessed Peter, and to the church of York, for the health of his soul and the souls of his wife Julian and his ancestors, "a full and free passage "through the ancient and customary paths and ways, without any "impediment and contradiction in going and returning along Thievesdale, "which is my own free tenure, for what shall be sufficient for the fabric "of the said church, as often as they shall have occasion to rebuild or "enlarge the said church"† I suppose that, at that time, the quarry did not belong to him, or that, being only vavasour, he had no right to give the substance of the soil, but that he had the right to certain tolls for passage which he generously waived on behalf of the church Those ancient and customary paths and ways would scarcely include any portion of the great Roman road from Calcaria to Eboracum,—though it was probably paved, and there would be a tolerable level transport of about eleven miles,—for the waggons of those days were rude and cumbersome, and, at the end, the stone would have to be ferried over the river At that time York had only a very narrow, rickety, wooden bridge, which, when Archbishop William entered York in 1154, broke down under the weight of the crowd which followed The stone bridge, for the erection of which Archbishop Walter Gray granted a brief in 1235, would, like its predecessor, be only a narrow pack-horse bridge for horses and pedes-

* *Annals of the House of Percy* † Brown's *York Minster*

trians, such as still remain entire at Wilberfoss, or, in modern times widened for carriages, at Harewood, and many other parts of the county. Probably, therefore, the stone was floated in flats and barges down the Wharfe to its junction with the Ouse, and then towed up the stream to the "Stanegate landing,"—which Mr. Davies* tells us existed at the bottom of Common Hall Lane, close to the Guild House of St. Christopher, now the Mansion House,—and from thence dragged on sledges up Stonegate to the Minster. For in 1421 there is an entry in the Fabric rolls:† "For "the carriage of 120 tuntygyht of stone from the quarry, at Thievesdale, "unto the water of Tadcaster, by Robert Hardy, by tuntygt, 4*d.*; and "by carriage of the same by ship from Tadcaster unto York, by John "Blackburn, at 6*d.* each tuntygyht; and for sledding 40 tuntyght of "Bramham stone from the Ouse to the cemetery" (*i.e.* churchyard round the Minster) "by John Bell, and others, 11*d.* each tuntyght."

However, the family of Vavasour was increasing in dignity as time advanced. Sir Robert became high sheriff of Notts and Derby, and received from King John free warren in Werverdale, or Wharfedale, so that he might there make a park if he pleased. His daughter, too, had married Fulke Fitz-Warin, an eminent baron; and his son, Sir John, further increased his property and position. He obtained free warren in Wodehall, Sikelinghall, Addingham, and Scarcroft; and married Alice, daughter of Sir John Cockfield, by his wife Nicholaa, daughter and co-heiress of Jordan de St. Mary, who must have herself been a substantial heiress, for her son, Sir William, is recorded to have done homage for all lands and tenements which his mother held of the King.‡

It would only be natural that, under such circumstances, the social position of the family would change, and that they would emancipate themselves from the condition of vavasour, and become lords of the soil, instead of mere mesne tenants of the Percies, by enfranchising their tenures for some lump sum. For though the spirit of feudal tenure established so intimate a connection between the two parties, that it could be disposed of by neither without requiring the other's consent, the vassal's feud could be alienated on payment of fines to the lord.§

Having, however, made the sobriquet by which they had been known, familiar and respected amongst all their neighbours, they retained it as a name, like the Constables, after they ceased to fill the position. For I find that Sir John is recorded as having *given* to the abbots and convent of St. Peter's, Howden, stone from his quarry in Thievesdale; indicating, I think, that he now possessed the fee simple of the land, and could do as he pleased with the soil. And this, I think, is confirmed by the facts that in 1291, when the nave was commenced, Sir Robert

* *Walks about York*, p. 25.
† Brown's *History*, p. 222.
‡ *Yorkshire Pedigrees* (Forster).
§ Hallam, vol. i., p. 130.

Percy gave a special grant of free passage by water from Tadcaster to York, with permission to load or haul from his land on their passage down the Wharfe, thereby implying that the stone was no longer his, though he still retained the right of the river, and also that, in 1302, the Dean and Chapter of York recorded their acknowledgment of the liberality of Sir William Vavasour, Kt, in having given stone from his quarry in Thievesdale, for the repair of the house in which the precentor of the church lived *

And as they now had the power, so they seem to have inherited the will, for both the grant of free gift of stone by Percy, and of free carriage by Vavasour, were, as far as I know, continued by the Vavasours, and never withdrawn There are no actual documents to prove it, that I am aware of, but there is reason to believe that the large proportion of the stone of York Minster, used in its grand development from 1070 to 1470, which is of the same quality, viz, magnesian limestone, came from the same quarry at Thievesdale And I suppose that the Percies in like manner continued their grant of timber, and that in each successive increase of the building the forest of Bolton Percy was free for all wood required And thus we can understand why Percy and Vavasour should stand side by side over the west door, with Archbishop Melton's hand raised over them in blessing (not, indeed, the present modern figures, but the figures which they have replaced), the former bearing a log of wood, the latter an ashlar of stone—emblematical of their special gifts

"Arcades ambo," no longer lord and vavasour—landlord and tenant—but equal in social rank, and equal in the commendable purpose of devoting their goods, which God had given them, to His glory and the development and beauty of His sanctuary But the work was not finished then, for the glories of the grand perpendicular choir, only commenced in his successor's time, were then still in the quarry of Thievesdale and the forest of Bolton Percy

From this period, however, the gift seems to have been supplemented, from time to time, both by offerings and purchase When Thoresby was about to commence the building of the Ladye Chapel, he gave, July 20th, 1361, the materials of "a certain Hall with a chamber adjoining," which seems all that remained of an archiepiscopal manor house, at Sherburn, originally provided for the see by Archbishop Walter Gray, but which, says Archbishop Thoresby, "had been suffered to go to ruin in the time "of his predecessor, to be applied to the more speedy finishing, through "God's favour, of the same "† The site can still be traced at a spot called "Manor Garth," in a large meadow known as Rest Park, between Sherburn and Cawood The outer and inner moats still remain It

* Drake's *History of York*, pp 111–115 † Brown's History, page 149

seems to have been rebuilt by Archbishop George Neville, for he obtained a license from the King to fortify and make a fortress of his Manor of Rest, *circa* 1374–1392. Archbishop Rotherham was living there in 1500, but it was finally dismantled, and sold under the Act for the Sale of Dean and Chapter Lands, 1647.*

There is also mention of instruments at the quarry at Stapleton, viz., "mallietez, gavelockes, and weges," and, 1419, of a payment of £10 to "Sir John Langton, knight, and lord of Huddlestone, for five rods of quarry "bought of him at the same place, and one rod given to the fabric:" this seems to have been carried by cart unto the water: and in 1460 "paid in pence for one pipe of wine £3 6*s.* 8*d.*, given to Sir John Langton, "knight, for the renewal of the indenture touching certain bounds of the "quarry of Huddlestone.

William Barker, of Tadcaster, 1403, by will bequeathed to the fabric of the Cathedral Church of the blessed Peter, of York, "the carriage by water of one shipful of stone."

Timber seems to have been also bought and given. In 1471 there is an entry of "eighty-one large oaks bought, and a large quantity of "thick boards;" and there are entries of similar purchases at Ryther, and elsewhere. The Abbot of Selby, in 1418, gave four trees to the new library. In 1421, the Archbishop gave twelve trees, and eight batons of oak were given by the Earl of Northumberland from Spofford wood, and eight large oaks from Topcliffe; and in 1465 there is an indenture for eighty years which had lasted and expired, "to be renewed to Master "William Maltster, prebendary of Fenton, for two acres of land and its "appurtenances lying in the field of Huddlestone, near Sherborne in "Elmet, to be used as a quarries for the fabric of the Cathedral Church "for a further term of nineteen years."

The rate of wages in 1371 was as follows:—the masons were arranged according to their wages into seven classes, viz., fifteen at 3*s.* per week; five at 2*s.* 9*d.*; one at 2*s.* 7*d.*; one at 2*s.* 6*d.*; four at 2*s.* 4*d.*; five at 2*s.*; four at 1*s.* 8*d.*; and the church found tunics, aprons, gloves, clogs, and gave occasional potations and remuneration for extra work.†

And thus we find that each separate section of the building of the Minster is adorned with the arms of Vavasour, thereby indicating that they were substantial contributors to each portion thereof.

No arms, indeed, appear in the transepts, for at that period Heraldry was in its infancy, and confined strictly to military ensigns; but in the nave the arms appear twice in stone on the north side, and once in stone and in glass in the first and second windows east of the south side of the central aisle, and on the window six east of the south nave aisle,

* *History of Cawood* (Wheater). † Brown, pp. 168, 217, 222, 223, 248, 250.

beside being on the outside of the west end next to the figure of Vavasour On the outer wall of the east end of Thoresby's Ladye Chapel we are told similar statues once stood, though they have now passed away In the south transept of the choir—the commencement, probably, of Scrope's work—the arms appear again, and finally, highly decorated, as deserving special honour, at the extreme west end of the north side of the choir,* which indeed marks the completion of the building

And we can understand this, because as the Vavasours rose in importance they became closely associated with the Plantagenet kings, who, as we shall see in the chapter on Royal Heraldry, made York their residence, and had the interests of the Minster so thoroughly at heart Sir William, Sir John's son, having been keeper of the castles of Bolsover, Harston, and Nottingham, in the reign of Henry III, had license from Edward I to castellate his dwelling at Hazelwood a significant token of confidence on the part of the King in his fidelity In the twenty-second year of his reign Sir William accompanied him in an expedition into Gascony, and also in the twenty-seventh, twenty-ninth, and thirty-second years of his reign he was with him in Scotland His name is recorded amongst the knights at the siege of Caerlaverock, where he served in the squadron commanded by the Earl of Lincoln Walter of Exeter in his poem thus describes him

"E de celle mesme part Fu Guillemis li Vavasours, Ki d'armes neest muet ne sours Baniere avoit bien conoissable De or fin oue la daunce de sable"	"And also of the same division Was William le Vavasour, Who in arms is neither deaf nor dumb He had a very distinguishable banner Of fine gold, with a dauncet of sable"

In 20th of Edward I, he is said to have purchased of the King for thirty marks two houses in the parish of St Martin, Coney Street, which belonged to Bonomy the Jew, when the Jews were expelled from the city This was the conventional way of repudiating the obligations incurred by the barons for loans upon their lands from the Hebrews, to raise a cry against them, and, expelling them from their midst, recover the title-deeds, which, for better security, were often deposited in the Minster

No doubt the barons were very rapacious, but, perhaps, "Simon of "York" and his brethren were not a little usurious However, probably Bonomy had a pleasant residence, and garden sloping down to the river, which for such a trifling consideration the rising nobleman of the neighbourhood was glad to obtain, and where, no doubt, he entertained his companions in arms and friends, on many occasions on their frequent passages through York to and from Scotland, and at other times He built the chapel at Hazelwood, which, in consideration of his liberality to the Minster, was

* See illustration at the end of this Memoir

made extra-parochial by charter from Edward I, dated 29th April, 1286, afterwards confirmed in 1452 by Henry VI, and the zenith of his prosperity was reached when, in 25th Edward I he had summons to Parliament as one of the barons of the realm He died in 8th year of Edward II His wife was Nicholaa, daughter of Sir Stephen Walens

His eldest son, Walter, by whom he was succeeded, was also distinguished in the Scotch wars In 34th of Edward I he went with him to Scotland, and in the 8th of Edward II was with those who assembled at Newcastle to resist the incursions of the Scotch On his father's death he was summoned to Parliament, but he died *sine prole*, and the privilege of the baronage was never continued to any others of the family He was not happy in his marriage, for Alianora his wife, daughter of Sir Thomas Furnival, was charged with intriguing with Peter de Mauley (4th), as I have already mentioned on page 106, and, being convicted by a commission issued by the archbishop in 1313, was enjoined to do penance His arms, as I have already stated, were in the Mauley window He had two brothers Sir Henry, whose son married one of the family of Fitzhugh, and Sir Robert, who was a benefactor to the abbey of Fountains, and in 1322 was one of those who, with Henry de Scargill and others, "harried Parlington, "turned out Hugh le Despencer, le pere, and pulled his house down about "his ears"* He was knighted by King Edward III when on service in France

There is little further to be said of general interest concerning individual members of the Vavasours They continued to maintain their position amongst the county families, and intermarried with several of them, while cadet branches of their own house took root in various places, and were, or are, represented still by the Vavasours of Copmanthorpe, Dennaby, Acaster, Spaldington, Willitoft, Belwood, Kippax, Skarrington, and also in Devonshire and Ireland Wise in their generation, they seem to have evaded the burning questions of the day, and devoted themselves to careers of unobtrusive usefulness amongst their own people John Vavasour, in the sixteenth century, married Julian, daughter of John Aske, of Aughton, but they were never drawn into the "Pilgrimage of Grace" or the "Rising of the north," or any combinations disloyal to the Crown Indeed, Thomas Vavasour was an officer in the navy during the time of Queen Elizabeth, and commanded the "Foresight" in that gallant fleet when "At Flores, in the Azores, Sir Richard Grenville lay" Mistress Anne Vavasour, maid of honour to Queen Elizabeth—and of whom Sir John Stanhope, writing to Lord Talbot, 1590, says "Our new mayd, Mrs Vava-"sour, flourishethe like the lilly and the rose"—was a daughter of Henry Vavasour of Copmanthorpe Her strange infatuation, however, for old

* Wheater's *History of Sherburn*

Sir Henry Lee, one of the Queen's "challengers," ruined her fair prospects, and brought her to a dishonoured grave in Quarrendon church, near Aylesbury Sir Thomas Vavasour was a loyal supporter of King Charles, and made a baronet by him, although he had to pay, for his recusancy, a composition of £150 per annum His eldest son raised a regiment of horse for the King's service, and fought under the Duke of Newcastle. His second son, William, served in the same regiment, and his youngest son, Thomas, was slain at Marston Moor, 1644 *Ex parte regis*

In the *Calendar of State Papers*, vol. 1638, the following mention is made of the eldest son of Sir Thomas Vavasour, Knight, of Copmanthorpe, Sir Charles Vavasour, of Killingthorpe, county Lincoln, created a baronet, 1631, who died unmarried, 1665 —"Bishop Morton, of Durham, "to Sir Charles Windebank " "He (Thomas Morton) thought I might "do well to appoint Sir Charles Vavasour colonel for this county, who "without any condition or expectation of payment, until the day of action, "in his true zeal in his Majesty's service, was willing to undertake it, "notwithstanding whatsoever hazard of his life " His younger brother William was also created a baronet, and slain when serving as major-general to the King of Sweden, at the siege of Copenhagen, 1659, *sine prole* *

In vol 1639, p 34, of the *Calendar of State Papers*, there is mention of a Nicholas Vavasour, who was a son of Nicholas Vavasour, of Waltham, Essex —"Bond of Nicholas Vavasour, of St Andrews, Holborn, stationer "Francis Mitchell, of Thoydon Garison, Essex, gentleman, and Patrick "Winch, of Waltham Cross, Essex, gentleman, in £500, conditioned for "the said Vavasour at the Council board upon three days' warning, "to answer such matters as shall be objected to against him." What those matters were we may gather from the following extract from vol 1639, p. 526 —"The Duke of Northumberland, Lord General and Lord "Admiral of England, to Sir Thomas Roe " "I have, according to your "desire, provided well for Capt Minore, having made him Lieutenant-"Colonel to Vavasour" (Nicholas, colonel)

On the Feast of the Purification, February 1st, 1829, the disastrous fire took place, by the act of a lunatic, one Jonathan Martin, which consumed the internal fittings and the roofs of the choir, seriously damaged the walls and pillars, and left the lately beautiful building a hideous ruin Amongst the first to tender assistance towards the restoration was the late Sir Edward Vavasour, who sent "with an offer of stone from the "quarries from which the church was built, £25 " This truly enlightened and liberal act of hereditary munificence was cordially accepted, and Brown records in his *History of York Minster* that the stone required for

* *Yorkshire Pedigrees*

the repairs was obtained from the quarries of Huddlestone and Tadcaster, "and also from the old quarry of Thievesdale, which was allowed to be "freely used for the occasion by its late possessor, the Hon Sir Edward "Vavasour, in addition to his donation of £25"

What is remarkable, I think, is that only one member of the family should have been buried in York Minster, viz, Henry, son of John Vavasour, of Newton, who died December, 1522 And that, though there have been many ecclesiastics in the family, none of them should have risen to high places in the Chapter This, of course, would have been impossible since the Reformation, but it might be reasonably anticipated during at least the four preceding centuries But the race of Vavasours have not been left without their reward for the liberality of their ancestors, in ancient days, to the interests of the Church of Christ Having thus largely provided for the worship of others, they have themselves enjoyed the privilege of undisturbed worship in their own church When the great ecclesiastical reform burst upon the nation, under Henry VIII, no hand was stretched out either to deprive them of, or to tamper with, what they held dear From the day when Edward gave the charter to St Leonard's Chapel to the present time, the ritual and doctrine have remained, almost if not quite unique in England, unaffected by any of the passing changes

To the honour of the race be it spoken, the name of Vavasour never appears amongst the names of the ruthless persecutors during Queen Mary's reign, but with pain it must be admitted that during the bitter retaliation of succeeding generations, more than one member of the family suffered fine, imprisonment, and death, simply for conscience sake Not even the worthless informer, Robert Bolron—who endeavoured in the north to follow the example of the infamous Titus Oates in the south—ventured to accuse them of more than this, no treasons or conspiracies were laid to their charge, they suffered in patience, and the testimony of history to the House of Vavasour, so far as I can decipher it, is expressed in the words of the poet—

> "*Along the cool, sequestered way of life,*
> They held the noiseless tenour of their way"

While beneath the pavement of, and in "God's acre" which surrounds, their house of prayer, the bodies of successive generations lie awaiting the resurrection of the dead Their graves have never been disturbed, or their sepulchres rifled While the ashes of many have been scattered to the winds, their bones still lie where loving kinsfolk and weeping friends placed them It seems as if a special providence had preserved to them at least this haven of rest

Who would wish it otherwise? Who would demur to the justice of such a recompense, at least, for a past liberality towards God, which has been a blessing to men for nearly a thousand years? What a countless multitude have worshipped in the great House which they so largely helped to build,—differing indeed in the apprehension and expression of what they believed, for each, however sincerely, only knowing in part,—yet all, we trust, hereafter to find their animosities quenched and their shortcomings forgiven, when they meet together, seeing no longer as in a glass darkly, but beholding their common Lord and Saviour face to face, and knowing each other and Him, even as they are known, in "the "building of God, the House not made with hands, eternal in the "Heavens."

VALENCE.

But the shield was not only varied by increasing the number of bars, but by placing distinct charges upon them. Amongst these I think the most beautiful is that of Valence, which may be found in stone and glass upon the north side of the nave, viz. Barry argent and azure, an orle of martlets gules.*

William de Valence, the first of the family, was son of Hugh le Brun, Count of the Marches of Acquitaine, by Isabel, daughter and heiress of Aymer Count of Angoulesme, and widow of King John. We know little of William save that he was created Earl of Pembroke by his half-brother, Henry III., but his son, Aymer de Valence, who succeeded him, plays rather an important part in the history of that day. Summoned to Parliament as a baron 25 Edward I., he seems to have had the precedence of all other barons. He was sent as a commissioner into Flanders to ratify an agreement between the King and Florence Count of Holland; and likewise as ambassador to France to treat for peace. His name is mentioned amongst the barons at the siege of Caerlaverock,

* See coloured illustration.

but the chronicler confines his notice of him to a pun upon his name. "Le Valence Aymars li Vaillans" In the following year he was a party to the barons' letter to the Pope, and in 34 Edward I, besides obtaining grants of the castles of Selkirk and Traquair, he was constituted guardian of the Marches of Scotland, and entrusted with the sole command of the English forces which had been levied against Robert Bruce, whom he vanquished, pursued into the castle of Kildrummie, and, failing to find him, put his brother Nigel and all the garrison to death

"Edward I on his death-bed," Holinshed says, "charged the Earls "of Lincolne, Warwike, and Penbroke, to foresee that the foresaid Peers "Gavestone returned not againe into England, least by his euill example "he might induce his sonne the prince to lewdness, as before he had "alreadie donne" Gaveston, however, returned in spite of them, was loaded with honours by Edward II, and created Earl of Cornwall, and, to shew his contempt for Valence, nicknamed him, in derision of his tall stature and pallid complexion, "Joseph the Jew" But Valence was true to his charge, and in the 3rd year of Edward II joined the Earl of Lancaster against Gaveston, and petitioned the King that he might be rendered incapable of ever holding any office Edward, however, conducted his favourite to Scarborough Castle, and leaving him with sufficient forces for its defence marched into Warwickshire, whereupon Valence, supported by Earl Percy, then constable of York Castle, attacked the castle at Scarborough so vigorously that Gaveston thought it wise to surrender This he did on the promise that his life should be spared, and both Valence and Percy solemnly pledged themselves to this effect, but as soon as the obnoxious favourite was in their hands he was sent off to Warwick Castle, and beheaded on Blacklow Hill, about a mile from the town of Warwick, without any form of trial whatsoever

The King's wrath was naturally very vehement at the death of his favourite, but, now that the hated Gaveston was dead, the attachment of the people to the King's royal person was so loyally manifested, that his anger was appeased, and he received back into favour even the principal actors in this summary act Valence was appointed (in the 7th year of his reign) Custos and Lieutenant of Scotland until the arrival of the King For the apparent union of all parties in England, after the death of Gaveston, seemed to restore the kingdom to its native force, and to open a prospect of reducing Scotland and bringing the war still carried on with Bruce to a happy conclusion

Edward roused himself to a great effort, and assembled forces from all quarters Vassals from Gascony, mercenaries from Flanders, rude adventurers from Ireland and Wales, ready to give their services at any time with the prospect of certain prey Stowe says "Never afore that "time was seen the like preparation, pride, and cost in the time of warre" In all 100,000 men confident of an easy victory

Bruce, equally determined, though with a far smaller force, 30,000 in all, was besieging Stirling, whose governor, Philip de Mowbray, had at last promised to capitulate, if, before a certain day, he were not relieved—

"And they took terms of truce—
If England's King should not relieve
The siege ere John the Baptist's eve,
To yield them to the Bruce" *

Bruce, therefore, awaited Edward's arrival there, and chose the field of battle, with all the skill and prudence imaginable, at Bannockburn, about two miles distant On his right flank he had a hill, on his left a morass called "Halberd's bog," in front a rivulet, the "Bannock-burn," and along the banks deep pits were dug and sharp stakes planted in them carefully covered over with brushwood and turf The standard he pitched in a stone having a round hole for its reception, thence called the "Bore "stone," fragments of which, carefully fenced with iron rails, still remain on the top of the small eminence called "Brocks Brae," to the south-west of St Ninian's

On the evening of June 3rd, 1314, the English army arrived at the ground, and immediately Sir Robert Clifford, with a body of 800 horsemen, endeavoured to make a flank movement through the low grounds, and throw themselves into Stirling Castle They had nearly succeeded, when they were seen by the quick eye of Bruce, who angrily exclaimed to Randolph, "Thoughtless man, you have suffered the enemy to pass," and the trusty lieutenant immediately dashed forward with his men to repair his fault or perish As he advanced, the English cavalry wheeled to attack him, but he drew up his troops in a circular form, with their spears resting on the ground and protruding on every side At the first onset, Sir William d'Eyncourt, an English commander, was slain, but the English, superior in numbers, hemmed in the Scots on every side Douglas, seeing the jeopardy, earnestly besought Bruce to let him go to their relief "You shall not "move from your ground," said the King, "let Randolph extricate himself "as best he may I will not alter my line of battle, and lose the advantage "of my position" But the impetuous Douglas was not to be gainsaid, and wringing a reluctant consent from Bruce, he galloped off, only, however, to find that the English were already falling into disorder, and that the stubborn perseverance of Randolph had prevailed over their impetuous courage "Halt!" he cried, "those brave men have repulsed the enemy "Let us not diminish their glory by sharing it"

* *Lord of the Isles*, canto vi, 4

Immediately after this a single combat took place between Bruce and Sir Hugh de Bohun, the issue of which not only decided that preliminary skirmish, but had great effect upon the battle the following day

Sir Walter Scott, in his *Lord of the Isles*, canto vi, gives a graphic and stirring account thereof Edward is riding down his line, drawn up in battle array—

"O gay, yet fearful to behold,
Flashing with steel and rough with gold
And bristled o'er with bills and spears,
With plumes and pennons waving fair,
Was that bright battle front For there
Rode England's King and peers"

The sight of Bruce similarly engaged, stirs the King's anger, who exclaims

"Still must the rebel dare our wrath?
'Set on him—sweep him from our path!'
And at King Edward's signal, soon
Dashed from the ranks Sir Henry Boune,
Of Hereford's high blood he came,
A race renowned for knightly fame
He burned before his monarch's eye
To do some deed of chivalry
He spurred his steed, he couched his lance,
And darted on the Bruce at once
As motionless as rocks that bide
The wrath of the advancing tide,
The Bruce stood fast,—Each breast beat high,
And dazzled was each gazing eye,—
The heart had scarcely time to think,
The eyelid scarce had time to wink,
While on the King, like flash of flame,
Spurred to full speed the war-horse came!
The partridge may the falcon mock,
If that slight palfrey stands the shock—
But, swerving from the knight's career,
Just as they met, Bruce shunned the spear
Onward the baffled warrior bore
His course—but soon his course was o'er!
High in his stirrups stood the King,
And gave his battle-axe the swing
Right on de Boune the whiles he passed
Fell that stern dint—the first—the last!
Such strength upon the blow was put,
The helmet crushed like hazel-nut
The axe shaft, with its brazen clasp,
Was shivered to the gauntlet grasp
Springs from the blow the startled horse!
Drops to the plain the lifeless corse!
First of that fatal field, how soon,
How sudden, fell the fierce de Boune!

This act was hailed with acclamation, but, as Scott renders it,

"His broken weapon's shaft surveyed
The King, and careless answer made
'My loss may pay my folly's tax,
I've broke my trusty battle axe'"

Two large stones, at the north end of the village of Newhouse, about a quarter of a mile from the south part of Stirling, still mark the place of this memorable skirmish Scott says

"That skirmish closed the busy day,
And couched in battle's prompt array,
Each army on their weapons lay"

The night was passed very differently in the two camps Stowe records the testimony of one "Robert Paston, a Carmelite Friar, being present and taken of the Scots 'Ye might have seen the Englishmen "'bathing themselves in wine There was crying, shouting, wassailing "'and drinking, with other rioting far above measure'" On the other side, ye might have seen the Scots quiet, still, and close fasting, the even of St John the Baptist, labouring in love of the liberty of their country "In the morning, however," he says of the English host, "the army of "the Englishmen coming out of the west, the sun rising casting his beams "on their golden targets, bright helmets, and other armour, gave such a "reflection as was both wonderful and terrible to behold"

Gilbert de Clare, Earl of Gloucester, the King's nephew, who commanded the left wing of the cavalry, irritated by some galling remarks of the King the day before, rushed on the attack, and with his men was immediately entangled amongst the concealed pits, and thrown into disorder. He was slain, and Sir James Douglas, who commanded the Scotch cavalry, giving them no time to rally, drove them from the field, and pursued them in the sight of their own infantry

After this the fight was commenced in earnest Froissart says each Scottish soldier had a little horn, on which, at the onset, they made such a horrible noise as if all the devils in hell were among them Scott seems to indicate that pipes were actually played,—

"Responsive from the Scottish host,
Pipe clang and bugle-sound were toss'd"

And a note affirms that the well-known Scottish tune, "Hey, tutti, tutti," was Bruce's march at the battle of Bannockburn For a time the fight was hotly contested

"Unflinching foot 'gainst foot was set,
Unceasing blow by blow was met
The groans of those who fell
Were drowned amid the shriller clang
That from the blades and harness rang,
And in the battle fell"

T 2

The concealed pits terribly hamper the movements of the assailants, but—

"Too strong in courage and in might
Was England yet, to yield the fight
Her noblest all are here,
Names that to fear were never known
Bold Norfolk's Earl de Brotherton,
And Oxford's famed de Vere,
There Gloster plied the bloody sword,
And Berkley, Grey, and Hereford,
Bottetourt and Sanzavere,
Ross, Montagu, and Mauley came,
And Courtenay's pride and Percy's fame,

Pembroke with these, and Argentine
Brought up the rearward battle line"

But the contest was at length decided by a stratagem on the part of Bruce, who had caused a number of waggoners and sumpter boys to be supplied with military standards, and to appear at some distance, as though a formidable body were marching to the relief of the Scots In the turmoil of the battle their real character could not be discerned, and on sight of them a panic seized the English, and they threw down their arms and fled, and were pursued with great slaughter for 90 miles, until they reached Berwick

In Blore's *Monumental Remains* two chronicles are quoted, speaking rather sarcastically of the Earl of Pembroke, Henry de Bellomonte, and other "magnates" who fled away from the battle on their feet But flight seemed to have become the order of the day, for the King himself set the example, and narrowly escaped capture, taking shelter in Dunbar, whose gates were opened to him by the Earl of March, and passing from thence by sea to Berwick Hardyng says,—

"Whiche kild was doune, saufe fewe that led the Kyng
To Dunbarre, then fleayd with him away
Ther was therle of Gloucester slain fleying,
The Lord Clifford and all the lordes that daye,
Therle of Herford to Bothuile fled his waye,
Therle Edmond of Arundell ard erle of Valence,
Therles of Warwike and Oxenford take at defence"

Happy had it been for him, perhaps, and for his after reputation, if he had fallen on the field of battle, and thus been spared—the after years of trouble and degradation which awaited him, when with "sobbes and "teares" he resigned his crown to the Bishops of Winchester, Hereford, and Lincoln, at Kenilworth,—the torments and insults inflicted upon him by Sir Thomas Barkeley and Sir John Maltravers,—and the inhuman cruelty of that awful night at Berkeley Castle, January 20th, 1327, when his piteous screams caused many in Berkeley, and also of the castle, as they themselves affirmed, "to take compassion thereof, and to pray for "the soule of him that was then departing the world" There is something very touching in the awful account which Stowe gives of his latter days, "guarded by a rabble of hell hounds," under the command of such monsters of iniquity as Barkeley and Maltravers It would shock your eyes and wring your hearts if I were to repeat his terrible details

Once again are the Psalmist's words illustrated "Thy loving correction shall make me great," and the fickle, sensual, trivial Edward becomes indeed a King, as he toils along the road to Bristowe Castle crowned with hay, mocked by the soldiers crying "Avaunt, Sir King!" His patient endurance elicits our sympathy and admiration, and we read, with reverence, the chronicler's testimony concerning him "This man being by nature strong to suffer pains, and patient, through God's grace, to abide all griefs, he endured all the devices of his enemies"

"Edwardum occidere nolite timere bonum est," was the sophistical advice to the infamous Isabel, from Adam de Orleton, the Bishop of Hereford If the comma be placed after "nolite," the translation is—"Do not consent to kill Edward, it is right to fear to do so" If the comma be placed after "timere," it would read thus "Do not yield to "fear to kill Edward, it is right to do so" Isabel chose the latter interpretation, and in so doing stained her hands with the murder of her husband, but delivered him from the hands of his persecutors, and ushered him into the presence of that Saviour where the weary are at at rest

Aymer de Valence, however, continued in the royal favour after the defeat of Bannockburn, and the following year—9th of Edward II—was sent on a mission to the Pontiff, and on his return was taken prisoner by a Burgundian called John de Moiller, who sent him captive to the Emperor, by whom he was detained in custody in spite of all King Edward's threats and entreaties, until the sum of £20,000 in silver was paid, said to be due to Moiller from the King for wages in his service However, the King recouped him for his losses on his return by making him governor of Rockingham Castle, and (in payment for sitting in judgment on Thomas of Lancaster, at Pontefract, four years after) he gave him several manors

In 1323 he accompanied Queen Isabella to France to endeavour to adjust the differences between Edward II and her brother, Charles the Fair, and lost his life at a tournament given by him to celebrate his nuptials with his third wife, Mary, daughter of Guy de Chastillon Count of St Paul's Some say he was murdered, others that he died of apoplexy, at any rate it was looked upon as a divine judgment for his participation in the death of Thomas of Lancaster, or, as Dugdale says, "by reason he had a hand in that affair"

He was buried with his father in Westminster Abbey, where a beautiful tomb on the south side of the sanctuary marks his resting-place By his death his estates were divided amongst his four sisters, and his title passed into abeyance Anne, who married Hugh de Baliol and two other husbands, but died without issue, Isabel, who married John, second Baron Hastings, whose grandson, Lawrence Hastings, was by royal favour declared (1339) Earl of Pembroke, Joan, who married John Comyn, and Margaret, who died unmarried

---

Mortimer

The place and circumstances of the death of Valence, however, are appropriately associated with the next subject for our consideration, viz, the House of MORTIMER, whose arms are in stone and glass on the south side of the choir, and furnish, perhaps, the most elaborate arrangement of a field barre, viz Barry of six or, and azure on a chief of the first two pallets between two esquires of the second, over all an inescutcheon argent *

It is difficult to reconcile conflicting statements, and thus to define accurately the origin of the title of Mortimer, but it would seem that the name Mortimer is derived from the Latin words "Mortuum mare," applied to a little district afterwards called "Vexin Normand," the extreme north-eastern portion of Normandy, between the rivers Oise and Epte, not far from Rouen, probably a tract of sedgy and marshy ground, ceded to Duke Robert of Normandy by Henry I of France Dugdale says that "Odo, "brother of Henry I King of France, having invaded Eurveux, Duke "William sent Roger (son or brother of William de St Martin Earl of "Warrenne), who had married his fifth daughter, Gundred, to resist his "attempt, who gave him battle near to the castle of Mortimer, and "obtained a glorious victory"

I conclude that in consequence of his defending this frontier castle, Duke William gave him the title, and perhaps the castle of Mortimer, but suspecting him of treachery he seems to have taken it from him and given it to his brother William, from whom it passed to his second son, Ralph, or Roger, "one of the chiefest commanders in his whole army "upon his first invasion of this realm," and shortly after that signal contest† he was sent into the marches of Wales to encounter Edrich Earl of Shrewsbury, who still resisted the Norman yoke He overcame him and received his castle of Wigmore as his guerdon There he founded an abbey of which his son Hugh, at the close of a warlike life, became a canon, and to which his son Roger, in recognition of his father's connection therewith, granted a spacious and fruitful pasture, saying to his

---

* See coloured illustration † Dugdale

steward, who remonstrated with him for parting with such a valuable portion of his inheritance "I have laid up my treasure in that field "where thieves cannot steal or dig, or moth corrupt" The piece of land was known ever after as the "Treasure of Mortimer"

Roger Mortimer, his grandson, in the time of Henry III, warmly supported the cause of the King against the barons, and was present at the battle of Lewes He commanded the third division of the royal army at the battle of Evesham, August 6th, 1265, and continued to the end of his days high in favour with Edward I, whom he entertained right royally at a grand tournament, at Kenilworth, on the occasion of the knighthood of his son

His grandson, Edmund, son of Sir Edmund, by Margaret, daughter of Sir William de Fendles, was rector of Hodnet, and treasurer of York Minster Possibly the arms in the window on the south side of the choir are his We know little of him, but his elder brother Roger, however, was the man who made the name of Mortimer famous, or infamous, as the paramour of Queen Isabella, the queen consort of Edward II In early days he was high in favour with Edward I, for it is recorded of him that he was not only present at the siege of Caerlaverock, but that, with William de Leyburne, he was "appointed to conduct and guard the King's son" He also signed the letter to Pope Boniface On Edward II's accession to the throne, Roger was promoted to many positions of importance, viz, the King's lieutenant, and justice of Wales, having all the castles of the Principality committed to his charge He was also made (2 Edward II) governor of Beaumaris Castle, and (7 Edward II) of Blaynleveng and Dinas Early in 9 Edward II, he was one of the manucaptors for Sir Hugh le Despencer, who was accused of having assaulted and drawn blood from Sir John de Roos, in the Cathedral Court of York, in the presence of the King and the Parliament

In the next few years he received even further tokens of the favour of the King, but in the 15th year of Edward II he sided with the Earl of Hereford in his quarrel against the Despencers, and having entered and burnt Bridgenorth, his Majesty declared him and others to have forfeited their lands Indeed, although he made his submission to the King, he was condemned for high treason, and sentenced to imprisonment for life in the Tower, but he made his escape from thence into France, where he associated himself with other English fugitives, united in their common hatred of the Despencers, and was, therefore, easily admitted to pay his court to Queen Isabella, when, as already mentioned, she arrived in France on a mission to her brother Whether they had met before I cannot say, but now "the graces of his person and address advanced him "quickly in her affections, he became her confidant and counsellor in all "her measures, and gaining ground daily upon her heart, he engaged her "to sacrifice at last to his passion all the sentiments of honour and "fidelity to her husband Hating now the man whom she had injured "and whom she had never loved, she entered ardently into all Mortimer's "conspiracies, and having got the young Prince of Wales into her hands,"* she engaged her brother in the same criminal purpose, viz, the ruin of the King and the Despencers, lived in declared intimacy with Mortimer, and when Edward, informed of these alarming circumstances, required her immediately to return, defiantly answered that she would never set foot in the kingdom till the Despencers were for ever removed from his presence and his councils This spirited declaration at once secured her popularity with the English people, and stimulated many traitorous conspiracies against him The King's half-brother, the Earl of Kent, joined her The Earl of Norfolk, the Earl of Leicester, and even Walter de Reynel, Archbishop of Canterbury, and many of the prelates expressed their approbation of the Queen's measures Having affianced the young Edward to Philippa, daughter of the Count of Hainault, and thus secured his assistance, she landed with Mortimer on the coast of Suffolk Edward II fled to the west The virtuous and loyal Bishop of Exeter was at once seized and beheaded The garrison of Bristol mutinied, and delivered up the elder Despencer (lately created Earl of Winchester) to the foreign forces of John de Hainault The venerable noble, now nearly ninety years of age, was instantly hanged on a gibbet, and his son soon after captured and beheaded, the Earl of Arundel put to death, and Baldock, the chancellor (a priest) expired under the cruel usage he received at Newgate Edward, as I have already mentioned, was eventually taken as he endeavoured to conceal himself amongst the mountains of Wales, and ruthlessly murdered The Queen and Mortimer were now triumphant

Mortimer caused himself to be advanced to the title of Earl of March, extorted from Edward innumerable grants of manors, castles, and lands, to gratify his insatiable greed, † insisted on receiving the same reverence as the King, claiming equal precedence The next year, 1328, at a Parliament held at Northampton under the auspices of Isabel and Mortimer, a treaty of peace was concluded with David Bruce, by which it was agreed that the Princess Joanna should marry his son David,—that all claims to allegiance from the Scotch should be given up,—all lands granted to Englishmen in Scotland surrendered,—and all charters, &c, seized by Edward I restored, including the "Ragman Roll," *i e* the acknowledgment of English supremacy signed by the late candidates for the Crown,—the Scottish Regalia,—"the black rood," supposed to be a piece of the true Cross,—and the stone from Scone Neither Edward nor the Earls of Kent and Lancaster would attend the wedding, which took place at Berwick

* Hume's *History of England* † Dugdale

The London populace positively refused to allow the stone to be taken from the Abbey And when it became known that Mortimer had received £20,000 from the Scotch to promote their wishes, a feeling of general indignation was kindled against him The Earl of Kent he speedily disposed of,* but the Earl of Lancaster was too wary to be entrapped, and too powerful to be seized The young King, however, stung with a sense of "his own dishonour and damage, as also the impoverishment of his people," consulted his own Council, and with the courage and resolution of a Plantagenet at once acted thereon, privately directing Sir William de Montacute to secure the assistance of Sir Humphrey and Sir Edward de Bohun, Sir Ralph de Stafford, Sir William de Clinton, Sir John de Nevill, of Hornby, and Sir William Eland

The Parliament had been summoned to meet at Nottingham Mortimer and Isabel forestalled the King's intention of taking up his abode in the Castle, by establishing themselves there with a strong guard of armed followers Conscious of the changing temper of the times and the muttering of the coming storm, the walls were strongly guarded, the drawbridge raised, the gates locked and barred, and the keys placed under the guilty woman's pillow But without avail

Sir William de Montacute and his comrades "drew unto them," says Stowe, "Robert Holland, who had of long time been keeper of the castle, "unto whom all the secret corners of the same were known" By his means the King and his friends were led "by torchlight, by a secret way "underground, in the dead of the night, which through the rock passeth "up with stairs to the room next the Queen's lodgings, which they by "chance found open" Here Mortimer, Henry Bishop of Lincoln, and others, were assembled The King remained outside, but the others rushed in, and killing in the scuffle Sir Hugh de Turpleton and John de Munmouth, seized Mortimer, and led him into the hall below, the Queen crying, "Bel "filz! bel filz! ayez pitie de gentil Mortimer" The keys of the castle were then delivered to the King, and "the next day, very early in the morning, "they bring Roger, and his friends taken with him, with a horrible shout "and crying—the Earl of Lancaster, then blind, being one of them that "made the showt for joye—towards London, where he was committed to "the Tower, and afterwards condemned at Westminster in the presence of "the whole Parliament, on Saint Andrew's even next following"

Sir Simon Burford and John Deverel, who were also taken in the Queen's ante-chamber, earnestly desired to disclose the particulars of Edward II's death, but they were not permitted to do so, lest they should implicate the Queen mother They were, however, taken with Mortimer to Tyburn, then called the Elms, and hung, being the first persons executed

---

* See *Royal Heraldry*

there After hanging on the gallows two days, Mortimer's body was removed and buried in the Grey Friars church, within Newgate

Very significant, but very just and very touching, was the King's conduct towards Isabella, consistent at once with the respect due to his mother, and the respect due to the law of God and man, which she had outraged She was sent to Castle Rising, in Norfolk, which, built by Wm de Albini, 1176, had been rented by her from the widow of the last Baron Montalt, during her regency, for £400 per annum Here she remained in close seclusion for twenty-seven years, until her death, on August 22nd, 1358, at the age of 63 "The Queen," says Froissart, "passed "her time there meekly," *i e* gave no further occasion for political or moral scandal Her health of mind, if not of body, was affected by what had taken place, and she was liable to severe fits of derangement, which had commenced while Mortimer's body hung for two days on the gallows

After two years the King returned to her the revenues of Ponthieu and Montrieul, originally granted to her by her murdered lord, as a token of his approval of her conduct, and when she had resided ten years at Castle Rising, he himself visited her, with his good Queen Philippa, and stayed some days Miss Strickland says "Once only did she leave "her seclusion, and that was to be present at a solemn act of State in "the Bishop of Winchester's great chamber, at Southwark, when Edward "delivered the great seal in its purse to Robert de Burghesh"

This is impossible, for Henry Burghesh, who succeeded Hotham as chancellor, was dismissed from office at the time of Mortimer's death Probably it was on an occasion which would naturally be deeply interesting to her, when Edward her son, on appointing Robert de Stratford chancellor, adopted a new great seal, quartering, for the first time, with the lions of the Plantagenets, the lilies of France, to which he was entitled through her, and which he now adopted as betokening his claim to the kingdom of France *

She also more than once received visits from her daughter Joanna, wife of David Bruce, King of Scotland, "who," says Wyntown, recording her visit to England, "came her mother and her brother to see" John Packington, clerk of Edward Prince of Wales, mentions the Queen-mother as being at Hertford Castle (which had been given to Joanna as her residence in England) with her daughter †

It was a long and, no doubt, a needed season of repentance for such a life not altogether inexcusable, perhaps, for she must have been sorely aggravated by the wanton folly of her husband in the early days of their married life, but nothing could justify the vindictive cruelty, to which she was, no doubt, a consenting party, inflicted upon him How-

* Campbell's *Lives of the Chancellors* † Green's *Princesses of England*

ever, she has passed to a juster tribunal than ours. *Requiescat in pace.* Strange choice! She was buried, by her own request, at the Grey Friars, London, by the side of Mortimer, with the heart of her murdered husband on her breast; and tradition says that at the same time the body of Joanna, Queen of Scotland, who had died in Hertford Castle, where she had lived since her separation from her husband (1360), was brought for burial, and that the funeral processions of the two Queens, one from the eastern and one from the northern road, entered the church by opposite doors at the same time. The royal biers met before the high altar, and there, after a separation of thirty years, the bodies of the evil mother and holy daughter were united in the same funeral rite.

But the Monastery of the Grey Friars, Newgate, has long passed away. Originally, it was one of the most important buildings in London; and was founded by the first Franciscans (who came over to England in the days of Henry III.) on a plot of ground next to St. Nicholas Shambles, given by John Ewin, a pious and generous mercer, who eventually became a lay brother. Its buildings were raised by the charity of various pious benefactors, and its glorious church was in a great measure built by Margaret, second wife of Edward I., who gave in her lifetime 2,000 marks, and by will 100 marks, towards building the choir. It became, perhaps for this reason, a favourite burial-place of the queens of England, as well as the usual place of interment for the foreign attendants of the Plantagenet queen's consort. "The Grey Friars church," says Penhant, "was reckoned one of the most superb of the conventual "establishments of London." "In 1429 the immortal Whittington built the "library, 129 feet long and 31 feet broad, with 28 desks and 8 double "settles. He gave about £400 for books, and Dr. Thomas Winchilsey, one "of the friars, £150 more, adding 100 marks for the writing out the works "of Dr. Nicholas de Lyra, in two volumes, to be chained there. Amongst "other benefactors, John Dreux, Duke of Brittany and Earl of Richmond, "gave £300 towards the church buildings, besides jewels and ornaments. "Mary, Countess of Pembroke, sent £70; and Gilbert de Clare, Earl of "Gloucester, twenty great oak beams, from his forest at Tunbridge, and £20. "The good Queen Philippa gave £62, and Queen Isabel, £70."*

Here was buried the heart of Queen Eleanor, mother of Edward I., who was married to Henry III. thirty-seven years, survived him nineteen years, and died 1291, at Ambresbury, where her body was laid, a nun. Beatrice, her second daughter, wife of John de Dreux Duke of Brittany, in France, and Earl of Richmond, in England, father of the benefactor above, was also buried here. "She died," says Augustus Hare, "when "she came over to the coronation of Edward I., 1272."

* *Walks About London*, Hare. Thornbury, &c.

The generous Queen Margaret, second wife and widow of Edward I was buried here, and Queens Isabel and Joanna, as I have mentioned Near them was laid Isabel Duchess of Bedford, the eldest and favourite daughter of Edward III, who was separated from her husband, Ingelram de Coucy, by the wars between France and England

John Hastings, the young Earl of Pembroke, slain by accident at a Christmas tournament, in Woodstock Park, 1389, was buried here Also John Duke of Bourbon, taken prisoner at Agincourt, and confined in the Tower for eighteen years Sir Robert Tresilian, Lord Chief Justice of England, and Nicholas Brembre, Lord Mayor of London, rapacious favourites of Richard II, were here interred after being hung at Tyburn

According to Hume, however (vol ii page 246), Tresilian at least does not deserve such a hard name Gloucester and his associates had forced Richard II to sign a commission transferring the sovereign power to him and thirteen other persons for a twelvemonth,—in fact abdicating Richard, obliged to submit, nevertheless submitted it at Nottingham to Sir Robert Tresilian, Chief Justice of the King's Bench, Sir Robert Belknappe, Chief Justice of the Common Pleas, Sir John Carey, Chief Baron of the Exchequer, Holt, Fulthorpe, and Bourg, inferior justices by whom he was advised that the late commission was derogatory to the royalty and prerogative of the King, that those who procured it were punishable with death, that those who compelled him were guilty of treason. But the Duke of Gloucester, Earl of Derby (soon after Henry IV), and the Earls of Arundel, Warwick, and Nottingham, persuaded Parliament to summon these judges and others before them, and without hearing a witness, examining a fact, or deliberating on one point of law, to pronounce them guilty of high treason, and Tresilian and Brembre were executed at once As far as we can judge of men's actions and motives at this distance of time, it appears to have been a most unjustifiable murder

Sir John Mortimer, too, was buried here,—a Yorkist hung by the Lancastrian party when Henry VI was but a child, and Thomas Burdet, also a victim of Yorkist cruelty, hung for speaking a few angry words about a favourite white buck which Edward IV had carelessly killed

What a list of noble and notorious dead! But the very place of their sepulchres can no longer be traced, nay, even the stately walls under the shadow of which their bodies rested have passed away, "and "like the baseless fabric of a vision, left not a wreck behind" For when the Reformation came and the brethren were dispersed and the buildings dismantled, Henry VIII gave the Grey Friars church to the city, to be devoted to the relief of the poor, and for some years it was used as a storehouse for plunder taken from the French Then, in 1552, the worthy Ridley, preaching before the young King at Paul's Cross, on mercy and charity, "made," says Stowe, "a fruitful and godly exhortation to the rich "to be merciful to the poor" The young King was touched, sent for the preacher, and a long interview took place between them, alone, in the great gallery of the palace of Westminster, the result of which was an autograph letter from the King himself to Sir Richard Dobbes, the Lord Mayor, urging the special claims of the poor in London This Ridley the same day delivered The day following his Worship invited the bishop, two aldermen, and six commoners, to discuss the same At this—I suppose I may say first of the many charity dinners which have since taken place—a report to the King was drawn up, upon which Edward acted at once, confirming his father's grant of the old Grey Friars monastery, endowing it with lands and tenements which had belonged to the Savoy, to the yearly value of £450, and other lands to the yearly value of 4,000 marks, exclaiming, as he signed his name, with his usual pious fervour "Lord, I yield Thee most hearty thanks that Thou hast given "me life thus long to finish this work to the glory of Thy name" In a month from that time the King was dead

Much of the building was demolished to adapt the old monastery to its new purpose, and in six months' time, so energetically did the Corporation carry out the late King's benevolent wish, 340 boys were admitted into "Christ's Hospital"

In 1545 Sir Martin Bowes, Lord Mayor of London (I hope not from Yorkshire), basely and stupidly sold the monuments and tombs for £50, and in 1660 the great fire completed the utter destruction of the whole fabric In 1673 the school was rebuilt by Sir Christopher Wren, Charles II founding an additional mathematical school And for more than 200 years the good work has gone on, an inestimable blessing from generation to generation to poor parents in training their children for the battle of life

But we live in days of change The quaint dress of the time of Edward VI, hitherto worn by the boys, is passing, or has already passed away New and more commodious premises are to be found elsewhere, the present buildings are to be demolished, and the tide of mammon, pure and unadulterated, is to sweep over a spot for so many centuries set apart for devotion or intellectual culture

The place where queens were laid at the close of life, and where Camden, the great antiquary-bishop, Bishops Stillingfleet and Middleton, Joshua Barnes, the Greek scholar, Markland, the critic and scholar, Richardson, the novelist, Samuel Taylor Coleridge, "logician, metaphysician, bard," Mitchell, the translator of Aristophanes, Leigh Hunt, William Henry Neale, master of Beverley School, James Schofield, the Regius Professor of Greek, a host of other distinguished men, and last, not least, Charles Lamb, with his "pensive, brown, handsome, kindly "face,"—the place where these men commenced the cultivation and development of their intellect, which has rendered their names illustrious in their country's records, shall know it no more

But the Mortimers must not be remembered only for the wicked actions and illicit intercourse with royalty of one of their line Sir Edmund Mortimer, the eldest son of Roger, was summoned to Parliament as Baron Mortimer, and to his son Roger Edward III reversed the attainder of his grandfather, restoring him to the earldom of March and his forfeited lands He accompanied the King to France, where he was knighted, and was eventually made constable of Dover Castle and warden of the Cinque Ports, so it is evident that he had redeemed the character of his family His son, Edmund, born 1532, further increased the family prestige by marrying Philippa, daughter and heir of Lionel Duke of Clarence, the third son of Edward III, whom I have mentioned on page 226 The Earl of March was member of the Privy Council to Richard II, and Lord Lieutenant of Ireland, of which he died governor in 1381 He left three sons, Roger, who succeeded him, Edmund and John, and two daughters, Elizabeth, married first to Henry Percy the famous "Harry "Hotspur," and second, to Thomas Lord Camoys, and Philippa, who married three times first, John Earl of Pembroke, second, Richard Earl of Arundel, third, John Poynings Lord St John

The Lord Mortimer mentioned in Shakespeare (1 Henry iv, act iii sc 1) is evidently Edmund, who married a daughter of Owen Glendower, for not only is Owen introduced, but his daughter also, of whom Mortimer says "My wife can speak no English, I no Welsh," but as he gracefully expresses it, there was, therefore, no lack of understanding between them

> "I understand thy looks that pretty Welsh
> Which thou pour'st down from these swelling heavens
> I too am perfect in, and but for shame,
> In such a parley would I answer thee
> I understand thy kisses, and thou mine,
> And that's a feeling disputation
> But I will never be a truant, love,
> Till I have learned thy language, for thy tongue
> Makes Welsh as sweet as ditties highly penn'd,
> Sung by a fair queen in a summer's bower,
> With ravishing diversion, to her lute"

Harry Hotspur is also introduced, and his death at the battle of Shrewsbury graphically rendered in the last act

Roger Mortimer married Alianor, daughter of Thomas Lord Holland, and was slain in Ireland by O'Brien and the Irish of Leinster, at a place called Kenlis It was to avenge his death that Richard II, who in the tenth year of his reign had declared him to be his successor, imprudently invaded Ireland, giving Henry of Bolingbroke, eldest son of John of Gaunt, opportunity to land in England, establish himself in his absence, and secure the Crown

His son, Edmond, was but six years of age at the time of his father's death, and was committed by Henry IV to the Prince of Wales, out of whose custody he was stolen by Lady de Spencer, but being discovered in Chittham woods, he was kept under stricter guard, for he was the rightful heir to the Crown, being the great grandson of Lionel, the third son of Edward III , whereas Henry IV was the son of John of Gaunt, the fourth son Burke says that he was frequently engaged in the wars of France, *temp* Henry V , and that in 1 Henry VI , he was Lord Lieutenant of Ireland Sandford, on the contrary, tells us that he was purposedly exposed to danger in a battle fought against Owen Glendour, and being taken prisoner, afterwards, by order of Henry IV , he was conveyed to Ireland, where he was confined for twenty years in the castle at Trim, and "there through extreme grief ended his life, and his corpse was brought to "England and entombed in the college of Stoke, near unto Clare, in the "county of Suffolke"

At any rate with him the male line of the family of Mortimer Earls of March closed, and the great estates, with the right to the throne and the barony of Mortimer, devolved upon his nephew, Richard Plantagenet, Earl of Cambridge and Duke of York, son of his sister Anne, who was married to Richard Earl of Cambridge, second son of Edmond of Langley Duke of York, and youngest son of Edward III This Richard was seized at Southampton in the third year of Henry V , and charged, together with Thomas Grey, of Heson, county of Northumberland, and Henry Scrope, of Masham, Yorkshire, with conspiracy to carry off young Edmond Mortimer into Wales, and there proclaim him King in opposition to Henry, whom they styled "the Lancaster usurper ' Being found guilty, Earl Richard earnestly petitioned for his life to Henry V , but in vain, and on the 6th August, he, together with Scrope and Grey, were beheaded, the Earl's head and body being interred in the chapel of "God's house," in Southampton Anne must have died some years before, for at the time of his execution he was married to Maud, daughter of Thomas Lord Clifford

His son by Anne Mortimer succeeded, as I have already said, to his mother's barony and estates He married Cicely Nevill, daughter of Ralph Earl of Westmoreland and Joane Beaufort, daughter of John of Gaunt He fell at the battle of Wakefield, or properly, Sandal, on the last day of December, 1460. His head, adorned with a paper crown, was presented to Queen Margaret of Anjou, and (by her direction, it is said) affixed upon Micklegate Bar, here in York In three months his son Edward IV , victorious after the battle of Towton, March 29th, 1461, ordered it to be taken down, and, with his body, hastily interred at Pontefract, and that of his son, the Duke of Rutland, murdered at the same time, to be buried with great solemnity in Fotheringay churchyard, by the side of the Duchess Cicely Here they rested until Queen Elizabeth's time, when she ordered the bones of father, mother, and son to be removed into the church This was but a becoming act towards her own ancestors for Edward IV's daughter, Elizabeth of York, married Henry Duke of Richmond, afterwards Henry VII, grandfather of good Queen Bess Yes, and through her aunt, Margaret, sister of Henry VIII and wife of James IV of Scotland, the barony of March has passed to our beloved Queen, who is still entitled to bear amongst her many quarterings, the shield which adorns our walls and window, of the historic house of Mortimer

THE WHITE HORSE
AT
UFFINGTON,
BERKSHIRE.

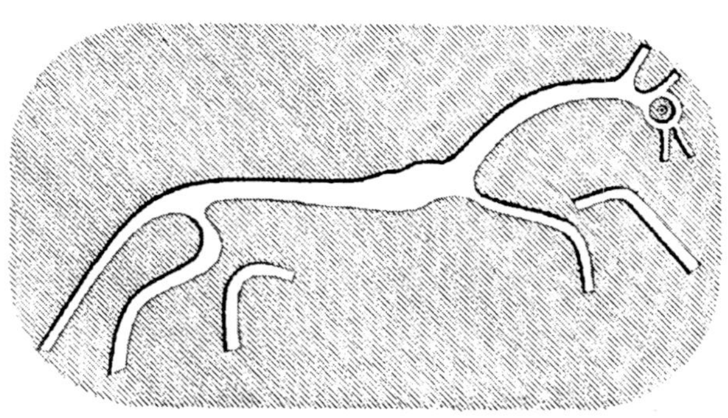

EXTREME LENGTH,
325 FEET.
ARCH: VOL. XXXI.

BAYEUX TAPESTRY
FROM
MONUMENTS DE LA MONARCHIE FRANCAISE
BERNARD DE MONTFAUCON.

ROYAL HERALDRY.

The ROYAL HERALDRY of the Minster occupies so large and prominent a portion of the achievements emblazoned both on stone and glass therein, that any volume professing to deal even with a portion of the subject would be incomplete without some adequate notice thereof, and specially when published under royal auspices. The consideration of the source and origin of the lions of England has kindled many and ingenious speculations on the subject, for there is really nothing authentic to be advanced thereon until we come to "the great seals" of the English monarchs. That the lions are the outcome of early traditional ensigns of nations, or individuals, is, however, more than probable, and it would be impossible, therefore, to deal with the subject without in some measure going over the same ground which I have already touched upon in the origin of heraldic achievements.

That the Saxons had a national emblem is evident from the rude and rather vague figure which is cut upon the turf on the hill side, above the little village of Uffington, in Berkshire, and still gives to that district the name of the "Vale of White Horse;"* for its existence before the Norman Conquest is evident from its mention in *Two Cartularies of the Abbey of Abingdon*, now in the British Museum; one of the date of Richard I., and the other Henry II., where the hill is mentioned as known by the name of the "White Horse Hill," in the time of Aldelm, who was the abbot from 1072–1084; and there is little doubt that it commemorates a victory of the West Saxons, under the command of King Alfred, over the Danes, in 871. Indeed, the worship of the horse was common to the Celtic and Germanic as well as the Sclavonic tribes. Sleipnir was the name of the eight-footed horse of Odin, and white horses were kept in hallowed groves of ash trees, which were reckoned by the Saxons amongst the sacred trees; hence Escrick or Ashridge, in Yorkshire and Bucks, and Ashbury (or Ashdown), near Uffington, as well as similar names throughout the country. These white horses were never desecrated by being put to any kind of labour. From these sacred horses it is probable that many of the

* See Illustration.

ancient heroes derived their names, of which Hengist and Horsa, those traditional if not historical leaders of the first Saxon invaders, furnish examples, those names being nearly synonymous.*

And it seems equally certain that if this was the standard of the nation generally, each individual king, when the land became divided into several kingdoms, had his own special device. At the battle of Assandun, where Eadmund Ironsides was defeated by Cnut, "the King "took the post," Freeman tells us,† "which immemorial usage fixed for "a royal general, between the two ensigns which were displayed over "an English army, the golden dragon, the national ensign of Wessex, "and the standard, seemingly the personal device of the King;" and that the Danes had also their national standard is evident from the same passage, which relates how Cnut had no mind to attack, and most likely wished to avoid a battle altogether; but the raven fluttered her wings, and Thurkill, overjoyed at the happy omen, called for immediate action. For the Danish raven, according to the story, opened its mouth and fluttered its wings before a victory, but held its wings down before a defeat.

Edward the Confessor is accredited with an actual coat-of-arms, viz., a cross between five martlets, to which I have already referred, page 29. The Bayeux tapestry‡ certainly gives indications that Harold, his successor, bore a distinctly heraldic device, for the shields of the soldiers are represented as bearing a dragon, probably the dragon of Wessex, of which he was the earl in succession to his father, Godwin. Freeman, in his *History of the Norman Conquest*, vol. iv., p. 61, says that "William sent to Pope "Alexander the fallen gonfanon of Harold, on which the skill of English "hands had so vainly wrought the golden form of the fighting man;" and that afterwards, when the abbey was to be founded on the very site of the battle, "the King bade that his church should be built on no spot but "where he had won his crowning victory . . . . the high altar of the "abbey of St. Martin should stand nowhere but on the spot where the "standard of the fighting man had been pitched on the day of Calixtus" (vol. iv., p. 401).

The shields of the soldiers of William also have indications of definite devices upon them; and William himself is represented bearing a gonfanon, on the head of which there is a distinct cross, which the writer of the paper in the *Archæologia*, xviii., 360, on the tapestry, calls the "Norman cross," and adds that "the colours thereof are argent, cross or, "border azure." These facts, if they do not give any definite information as to the heraldic devices of the Saxon kings, seem to me to suggest a

* *Archæologia*, vol. xxxi., p. 290. † *Norman Conquest*, vol. i., p. 390.

‡ See illustration.

1ST GREAT SEAL OF RICHARD 1ST

2ND GREAT SEAL OF RICHARD 1ST

SEAL OF JOHN EARL OF MORTAIGNE, AFTERWARDS KING JOHN.

SEAL OF EDMUND CROUCHBACK, EARL OF LANCASTER, SON OF HENRY IIIRD

3RD GREAT SEAL OF EDWARD 1ST

theory by which we may account for that which some time after the Norman Conquest became the armorial bearings of the English kings, and has continued ever since, viz, the three lions, or leopards passant

The only authentic information can be derived from the regal seals, and on those of William I and II, Henry I, Stephen and Henry II, the kings' are represented so that the devices on the convex sides, if any, are not visible The first device, even partially apparent, is on the first seal of Richard I, where the dexter half of the shield alone is visible, and on that there is a figure of a lion rampant, which may have had another or a similar figure on the sinister side, or may have been one of the six lioncels which I have already noticed on page 31 On his return from captivity, however, Richard seems to have had a second seal made, upon which he is represented on horseback, in his coat of mail, his helmet adorned with the Planta Genestæ, and on his shield are plainly represented the three lions passant guardant *

There are various theories to account for these lions That which I venture to add is based upon what I think I have established by facts already shewn, viz, that national ensigns, as well as individual devices, were in vogue at or about that time, *e g*—the white horse of the Saxon people, the golden dragon of Wessex, the "fighting man" of Harold, the raven of the Danes Sandford, in his *Genealogical History*, states on page 1 that "as tradition tells us, Rollo, the first Duke of "Normandy, is said to bear on his escocheon the same charge, affecting "as several other northern princes did, that sovereign beast the lyon" This shews, first, that the lion was the charge of the northern princes,—probably differenced by colour and attitude,—and secondly, that Rollo carried a lion, which accounts for one of the three, viz, the lion of Normandy He further mentions (page 59) concerning Henry II, "the "opinion of modern genealogists, who say that 'this Henry, before his "'marriage with Eleanor of Aquitaine, did bear gules two lions passant "'guardant or, and that the arms of Aquitaine being also a lion or, in "'a field gules, did add the same in his shield to his other two lions'" Now what was the second lion? Not, as Sandford seems to imply, a mere duplicate of the lion of Normandy, but, if the courteous reader will refer to the monumental plate of Geoffry Martel, Duke of Anjou, on page 31, he will see on the cap of the figure a lion passant, which I venture to recognize as the second lion, and which was probably the *national* ensign of Anjou, just as the lioncels on his shield are the device of the *family* of Martel If so, it is very likely that his son, Henry II, having assumed the Norman lion of his mother, the Empress Maud, the daughter of Henry I, and the lion of Anjou, the device of his father, Geoffry Martel,

* See illustration

should also add the lion of Aquitaine, the device of his wife Eleanor, daughter and heir of William ninth Duke of Aquitaine.

We cannot say for certain that Henry II. did so, because we cannot see the device on his shield; and the fact that both Richard and John in their early seals carried only two lions, may seem rather to indicate that it was not until Richard returned from the Crusade, where he probably became imbued with the spirit of heraldry then rapidly coming into vogue, that he fully expressed in the arms of his seal that which his father had already expressed in the legend round it—"Dux Normannor et "Aqitannor et Comes Andegavor," and, adopting one uniform attitude and tincture for the several lions, composed the cognizance of his family as it has remained to this day. All this is, of course, only another conjecture on my part; but I venture to think that its probability is very strongly supported by its harmony with the legend round the seal.

Richard, the second son of King John, seems never to have borne the Plantagenet arms; but having been created by his brother Henry III. Earl of Poictou and Cornwall, adopted for his cognizance a shield bearing the arms of Poictou, viz.: argent a lion rampant gules, crowned or, within a bordure sable bezantée of the ancient Earls of Cornwall. According to Torre this shield existed in the second window west on the north side of the nave; but it is not there now. On page 70, however, an illustration of this coat will be found dimidiated with Clare, being the shield of Richard's fifth son, Edmond, who married Margaret, daughter of Richard de Clare, and died at Ashridge, in Bucks, where he had built an abbey of the order "Bon hommes," leaving no issue. Sandford says: "I cannot "find as yet that arms of women were joyned in one escocheon with those "of their husbands of a more ancient date."

With that single exception all the Plantagenets down to the reign of Edward III. bore, gules three lions passant guardant or. When the Emperor Frederick married Isabella, sister of Henry III., he sent, amongst many other precious gifts, three leopards, significant of the royal arms of England.* The author of the *Metrical Chronicle of the Siege of Caerlaverock*, gives an animated description of the banner of Edward I. on that occasion:

"En sa baniere trois luparte	"In his banner three leopards
De or fin estoint mis en rouge	Of fine gold set on red,
Courant felloun fier et harouge	Courant, haughty, fierce, and cruel.
Par tel signifiance mis	Thus placed to signify
Ke ausi est vers ses enemis	That also towards his enemies
Li Rois fiers felouns et hastans	The King is fierce, haughty, impetuous,
Car sa morsure n'est tastans	For his bite is not slight
Nuls ki nen soit euvenimez	To those who inflame him;
Non porqant tot est ralumez	Nevertheless, soon is rekindled
De douce debonairete	His sweet graciousness
Quant il requerent se amiste	When they seek his friendship,
El a sa pais veullent venir."	And are willing to submit to his power."

* M. Paris, vol. ii., p. 416.

PLATE 7.

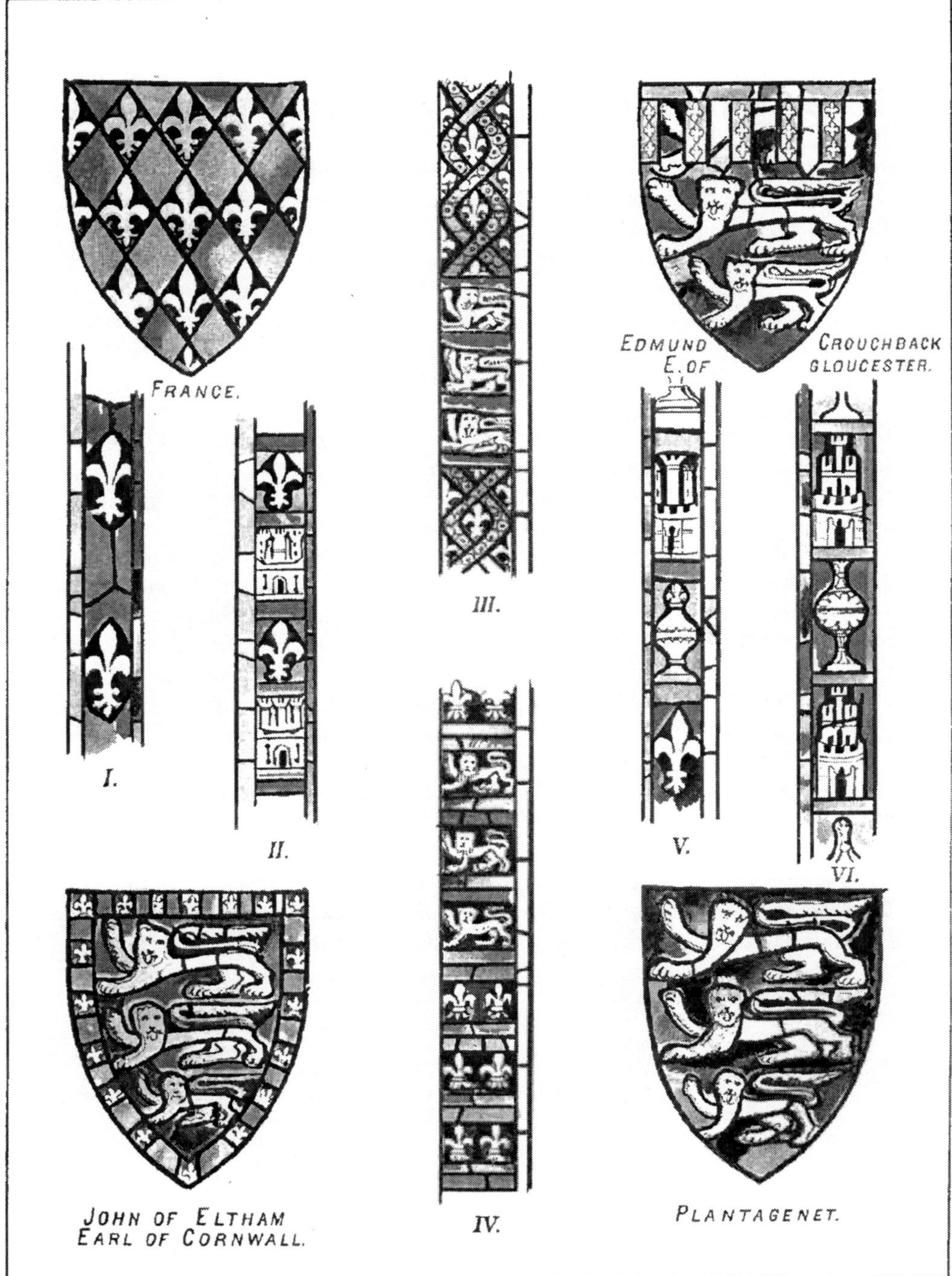

FRANCE.
III.
EDMUND
E. OF
CROUCHBACK
GLOUCESTER.
I.
II.
V.
VI.
JOHN OF ELTHAM
EARL OF CORNWALL.
IV.
PLANTAGENET.

I may add here that the term "leopard," or "lion leopardez," which is sometimes applied to the lions, has a purely heraldic significance, and is the word used for all lions "guardant," *i e* looking towards you *

But the interest attached to these arms in our Minster, and to the future development and differencing of them, depends not on the fact that they are mere conventional tokens of loyalty or court flattery in days gone by, but that they are, as it were, "footprints in the sands of time," indicating great national events and changes of which York was the centre of action, and commemorating those who, in various degrees, were actors in the great historic events which have contributed so much to make England what it is

In order to trace this we must begin with the reign of Edward I, "who," says Mr Green, "definitely abandoned all dreams of recovering "the foreign dominions of his race, to concentrate himself upon the con- "solidation and good government of Britain itself We can only fairly "judge his annexation of Wales, or his attempt to annex Scotland, if we "regard them as parts of the same scheme of national administration to "which we owe the final establishment of our judicature, our legislation, "our Parliament" †

York is little connected with the first, it is closely identified with the two latter

As regards the last, viz, *the establishment of our Parliament*, Green truly says of Edward I "He is the first English king since the Conquest "who loves his people with a personal love, and craves for their love back "again To his trust in them we owe our Parliament, to his care for "them the great statutes which stand in the forefront of our laws" He found the country distracted for the want of something like a real and adequate representation of the people, and he developed and consolidated the crude efforts which were ready to hand The great council of the Norman kings had simply consisted of all tenants who held directly under the Crown—the bishops, greater abbots, and great officers of the Court But these had become divided into "the greater" and "the lesser" barons, and as the ancient earldoms became extinct and lapsed to the Crown, "the lesser barons," who formed the bulk of the tenants of the Crown, desired, as their protection, to have associated with them the country gentry, freeholders, and substantial yeomen, rapidly rising into affluence through the long peace and prosperity of the realm, and the increased export of wool And the Crown itself desired it as a means of rendering taxation more efficient, but mistrusting the increased power thereby of the people, had temporized with them until what they required, as far as the country was concerned, was established in the previous reign (Henry III)

* *Tresor Heraldique*, Chas Segoing † *History of the English People*

by the provisions of Oxford, July, 1258; and afterwards as far as the towns were concerned, by Earl Simon de Montfort, who broke through older constitutional tradition, and dared to summon two burgesses from each borough to the Parliament of 1265.

Edward seems to have done willingly and generously what his predecessor had done grudgingly and reluctantly. He based the representation of the country by knights of the shire, upon the old county court, presided over by the sheriff; and freely accepting the representation of the boroughs, he admitted the burgesses, originally summoned to take part only in matters of taxation, to a full share in the deliberation and authority of other orders of the State. Finally, he developed the representation of the clergy from mere *ex-officio* members to elected members, and added to the bishops and greater abbots, all archdeacons, deans, or priors of cathedral churches, with a proctor for each cathedral chapter, and two for the clergy within the diocese. The Parliament thus organized was at first called in various places,—Winchester, Acton Burnell, Northampton, Oxford, &c.,—but eventually it was settled at Westminster.

The provisions of Oxford had enjoined that three Parliaments should be assembled every year, whether summoned by the King or no; but as far as I can discover, this formed no portion of Edward's plan, and he and his successors seem to have only called their Parliaments together when and where they needed their advice and support.

Under these circumstances it is very evident why, during the reigns of the first three Edwards, Parliaments were summoned, and summoned to York; for during that epoch the most vigorous efforts were made *for the assertion of English supremacy in Scotland.*

To comprehend the reason for this, we must remember that at the close of the thirteenth century, what we now call Scotland was an aggregate of at least four distinct countries. Saxony, now called the Lowlands, the space between the Firth of Forth and the Tweed, which had been the northern portion of the kingdom of Northumbria, reaching from the Humber to the Firth of Forth. The long strip of coast between the Clyde and the Dee had formed the country of Cumbria. The whole country north of the Forth and Clyde had acknowledged the supremacy of the Picts; and the little kingdom of Scot-land amongst the lakes and mountains on the south of Loch Lynne, founded centuries before, when a fleet of coracles had borne thither a tribe of the "Scots," as the inhabitants of Ireland were at that time called. In days gone by, these several kingdoms had banded together to resist their common enemy the Danes; and in the tenth century the direct line of Pictish sovereigns becoming extinct, the Scot king, Kenneth Mac-Alpine, who claimed to be their nearest kinsman, was raised to the vacant throne, and eventually the common throne gave its designation to the common realm, and it was termed Scotland.

The same policy, viz., protection against the Danes, had mutually animated the English kings and the kings of Scotland, and a common hostility to a common foe brought about a "commendation" by which the Scots beyond the Forth and the Welsh of Strathclyde, chose the English King, Eadward the Elder, "to father and lord."

In course of time the kingdom of Scotland grew in stability and dignity, the families of her kings became united to the families of the English and Norman kings. Malcolm married the sister of Eadgar Etheling, and Henry I. the Scottish princess, Matilda. Her brother, David, with his special sanction, married Countess Maud, the widow of Simon de St. Liz Earl of Huntingdon, and assumed the earldom. He afterwards assisted Matilda in her contest with Stephen, and he filled his Court with Norman nobles, such as the Bruces and Baliols, from the south, and was defeated at the battle of the Standard.

His son, Henry, who succeeded him, on condition of swearing allegiance to Stephen, had the earldom and honour of Huntingdon, with the borough of Doncaster and Carlisle, and this was held by succeeding kings until William the Lion transferred it to his youngest brother, David, the grandfather of Robert Bruce, and the great-grandfather of John Baliol.

In the reign of Henry II., William the Lion, being captured during the revolt of the English baronage, to gain his freedom consented to hold his Crown of Henry and his heirs. Richard I. allowed the Scotch to repurchase the freedom which they had thus forfeited, and in future the Scotch king did homage, with a distinct protest that it was rendered for lands which he held in fief within the realm of England. The English king accepted the homage with a counter protest that it was rendered to him as "over-lord" of the Scottish realm.

In 1249 Alexander III., grandson of William the Lion, became King of Scotland.* He was but a child, only eight years of age. His father was Alexander II., and his mother, Mary, daughter of Ingelram de Couci—a family so proud that they affected a royal pomp, and considered all titles as beneath their dignity. The "Cri de Guerre" of Ingelram was—

"Je ne suis Roy, ni Prince aussi
Je suis le Seigneur de Couci."

Henry III. had then been some thirty years upon the throne of England, and this seemed a golden opportunity for asserting his claim as "over-lord." Walter Bisset, a powerful Scotch baron, had murdered Patrick Earl of Athole, at a tournament near Haddington, and condemned for this to forfeit his estates and be exiled to Palestine, he fled to the English Court and

---

* Tytler's *History of Scotland*.

"Quhen Alysandye, oure Kyng, wes dede,
That Scotland led in luwe* and le,†
Away wes sons of ale and brede,
Of wyne and wax, of gamyn and gle,
Oure gold wes changyd into lede.—
Christe, born in-to virgynte,
Succour Scotland and remede
That stad‡ is in perplexyte."

These words touchingly express what must have been too true. Of the regency of six guardians, immediately appointed by the Parliament, the Earls of Fife and Buchan were speedily murdered. Robert Bruce and John Baliol, with their adherents, pushed forward their conflicting claims to the throne, and for two years open war raged between them. The States in their alarm turned to Edward, the late King's brother-in-law, to act as peacemaker, and by his advice and mediation compose the trouble of the kingdom. The King readily accepted their offer, saying to his most confidential minister as he did so: "Now the time is at last "arrived when Scotland and its petty kings shall be reduced under my "power;" and from that moment the distinctive policy of his reign became *the assertion of English supremacy in Scotland.*

The Bishops of St. Andrews and Glasgow, with Robert Bruce and John Comyn, were appointed by the Scotch regents to meet the Bishops of Worcester and Durham, and Earls Pembroke and Warrenne, at Salisbury, where the King privately communicated his own solution of the difficulty, viz., the marriage of the young "Maid of Norway" to his son Edward. The estates of Scotland, on the return of the commissioners, assembled at Brigham, near Roxburgh, and gladly accepted the proposal. The consent of Eric was also taken. A treaty was carefully drawn up,—the young princess was sent for,—the vessel arrived,—but only with the intelligence that she had sickened of a mortal disease at sea, and died at Orkney, September, 1290. Sorrow and despair overwhelmed the nation.

Edward saw his opportunity, and at once acting upon a private suggestion of the Bishop of St. Andrews, commanded all his barons and military tenants to meet him at Norham, June 3rd, 1291; and invited the clergy and nobility of Scotland to hold a conference with him there on the 10th of May. They gladly consented, but the first words of the justiciary, Roger Brabazon, must have struck a chill into their hearts, for it was the old story: "Our lord the King, for the due accomplish-"ment of his design, doth require your hearty recognition of his title "of Lord Paramount of Scotland."

They pleaded their inability to recognise such a claim while they had no recognised king, in whose presence such a challenge should alone be

* Love. † Tranquillity. ‡ Placed.

made. "By holy Edward!" exclaimed the King, "whose crown I wear, I will either have my rights recognised or die in the vindication of them!" What could they do? The utmost consideration which they could obtain from him was an adjournment of three weeks. His army had now arrived. His money and promises had already secured some, including the Regent Frazer. Bruce, and Baliol, and other competitors for the throne, were only too anxious to curry favour with him. They assembled again on Holywell Haugh, a green plain opposite to Norham. The same demand was made by the Bishop of Bath and Wells, the Chancellor of England, and submitted to without further discussion. "We agree to receive judgment from him as "our Lord Paramount. We are willing to abide by his decision, and "consent that he shall possess the kingdom to whom he awards it." On June 11th the four Regents of Scotland delivered the kingdom into Edward's hands, Gilbert de Umfraville, the Earl of Angus, being the only exception to such a craven submission. The great seal of Scotland was delivered to Alan, Bishop of Caithness, and Walter Agmondesham, his assistants, both Englishmen. The four Regents swore fealty, and a herald then proclaimed the peace of King Edward as Lord Paramount.

After some deliberation the claims of twelve competitors were reduced to three, viz.: John de Hastings, Robert Bruce, and John Baliol, the descendants of the three daughters of David Earl of Huntingdon,—the two former claiming each a third part of the kingdom; the last, as descended from the eldest daughter, claiming the entire sovereignty. On the 6th November, it was decided that the kingdom could not be divided; on the 17th, 1292, at Berwick, Edward finally decreed that the sole sovereignty should be awarded to Baliol. The great seal of Scotland was solemnly broken, and on the following day Baliol, in the Castle of Norham, swore fealty to Edward, who gave a commission to John St. John to perform the ceremony of coronation by placing the new monarch upon the ancient stone at Scone.

But the consequences of such a craven submission could not long be endured, for Edward, having at last obtained the object of his own and his predecessors' wishes, was determined that it should not become a dead letter. First, Baliol was summoned to appear before him on an appeal from Roger Bartholomew against the judgments of the Regents; then, on the appeal of Macduff against their decision as to his having seized the property of his great nephew and the earldom of Fife; and on each occasion he was treated with hauteur and contempt. Then Edward, having refused to obey a similar summons directed to him as Duke of Aquitaine, by Philip King of France, found his own territory seized and declared forfeited, and war was immediately declared to recover it. He at once summoned Baliol and the most powerful of the Scottish nobles to attend him in person, with their armed vassals; but, disgusted with his insolent and overbearing conduct, they treated his summons with scorn, and, assembling a parliament at Scone, engaged in a treaty of alliance with France, by which it was agreed that Baliol's son should marry the French king's niece, and that they should help each other in making war on England.

After a second and third refusal, together with the refusal of Baliol to attend his Parliament at Newcastle, and the investment of Carlisle by the Scotch, Edward advanced against Berwick and took it by storm, 1296. Edinburgh, Stirling, and Perth capitulated. Bruce joined the English army; Baliol surrendered, and was dethroned and with his son sent to the Tower. Edward declared the fief to be forfeited, and that the country had passed to its "over-lord." Earls, barons, and gentry swore homage in Parliament at Berwick to Edward as their king. The sacred stone on which their sovereigns had hitherto been crowned was removed from Scone to Westminster, and enclosed in a stately seat made for this purpose by his order, which became from that hour the coronation chair of the English kings; and the government of the new dependency was entrusted to Warrenne, Earl of Surrey, at the head of an English Council of Regency.

The humiliating consequences of such a state of things irritated and at last enraged the Scottish people. The nobles had shewn themselves mere cravens, and submitted. William Wallace, an outlaw knight, was of sterner stuff, and soon roused the lowlands into revolt. At the battle of Stirling Bridge, Sept., 1297, he defeated Warrenne, cut half his army to pieces,* and then reduced Stirling Castle, calling himself, in Baliol's name, "Guardian of the Realm," and invading Northumberland. Edward at once returned from Flanders and marched to the north, with the largest army that ever followed his banner, and transferring the Court of Exchequer and King's Bench from London, held a parliament in York, to which he summoned the Scotch nobility. They did not, however, attend, nor the clergy, but 70 representatives of the counties and 151 of the boroughs. Having obtained the necessary subsidies, he hastened onwards,—surprised Wallace,—forced him to fight a battle at Falkirk, July, 1298,—utterly defeated him, with great loss,—and retired. Wallace resigned. Comyn and Soulis, with Bruce and the Bishop of St. Andrews, were chosen by the Scottish barons to be governors of Scotland.

In 1299, Edward having assembled his Parliament in York,† made, from hence, another but ineffectual attempt; but in the following year he was more successful, as I have described on page 292. Eventually, in 1305, Wallace was betrayed by Sir John Menteith, condemned at Westminster, and executed at Smithfield. A parliament was then held in London, when the Scottish nation was represented by ten Commissioners, who conferred with twenty-one English Commissioners, and organised an

* See page 290. † *The Parliaments at York*, C. H. Harts-horne.

entirely new system of government for Scotland, by which, while the name of authority was given to the Scottish Commissioners who were to sit in parliament, the real power belonged solely to King Edward. The conquest and settlement of Scotland seemed complete

But the flames soon burst out again Robert Bruce, who had hitherto been on the English side, fancying that his claims had gained new force by the withdrawal of Baliol, commenced an intrigue with Lamberton, Bishop of St Andrews, and finding that it was discovered, fled for his life to his castle at Lochmaben In the Church of the Grey Friars, at Dumfries, he met John (called Red) Comyn, lord of Badnoch, and charging him with treachery in this matter, slew him on the spot, and assumed the Crown six weeks after, in the abbey of Scone (March 27th, 1306) Edward, exasperated on hearing this, determined on another expedition, convened a great gathering at Westminster on the Feast of Pentecost, where he knighted the Prince of Wales and 300 young esquires, and at the banquet which followed, vowed by the swan on the table before him, the emblem of constancy and truth, to inflict vengeance on the murderer himself, and marched towards the north Aymer de Valence, however, speedily routed the disorderly forces of the new monarch Bruce was compelled to flee, and noble after noble who had supported him were hurried to the block Edward, having advanced as far as Lanercost, ordered the Countess of Buchan, who had set the crown on the head of Bruce, to be exposed in an iron cage on one of the towers of Berwick, but he never arrived to complete the conquest, and expired at Burgh-on-the-Sands, July 7th, 1307

The cause of Bruce gained ground under his vacillating successor, Edward II, whose measures seem to have mostly evaporated in orders and preparations countermanded or disobeyed, while he himself was immersed in the pleasures of his Court, and engrossed by his infatuated fondness for his favourite Gaveston

Douglas rallied to the call of Bruce, and many of the Lowland nobles followed his example Edward, in 1309, summoned his parliament to meet him at York, to hold conference and treaty (*colloquium et tractatum*), and from thence made a feeble effort to repel the advances of the Scotch into England, but they evaded his army, and driving away their herds and flocks, compelled him to return to Berwick for fear of starvation to his forces Edinburgh, Roxburgh, Perth, and many other fortresses fell into the hands of the Scotch The clergy met in council, at Dundee, February, 1310, and owned Bruce as their lord, who at length invested Stirling, now the last fortress which held out for Edward On this the King, having reinforced his army, advanced to its relief, only to be utterly routed at Bannockburn on June 20th, and fly for safety to York Here he remained until the October following The Scotch crossed the Tweed on August 6th, and the King having issued writs for 4,000 men, and sealed letters patent for 8,800 marks in vain, and thus having neither men nor money to repel them, again summoned the parliament at York, which met and sat from September 9th to 27th, Aymer de Valence presiding, Edward avoiding the disgrace of meeting them by the plea of urgent business

In 1318, Edward again held his parliament in York, which sat for fifty-two days, on the same subject, viz, the intolerable aggression of the Scotch, which resulted in 5,000 footmen being sent against them, and an act being passed, long quoted as "the statute of York," containing important clauses for the due administration of justice

In 1319, the parliament again assembled here, and sat twenty-one days, eventually granting subsidies for carrying on the Scottish war, and Edward, rousing himself to make a great effort, besieged Berwick, already invested by the Earl of Lancaster, without success But while so engaged Randolph and Douglas made a diversion into England, ravaged the country as far as York, and utterly destroyed the ill-disciplined rabble brought against them by Archbishop William de Melton, and the mayor Nicholas Fleming, at Myton, after which Edward was glad to agree to a peace for two years

On the 20th of January following, he again called together his parliament at York on the same subject, and on the vexed question of homage for Guienne, and on May 2nd, 1322, they met here again for the last time in his reign, when the sentences on the Despencers were reversed, and, subsidies being granted, another great English army advanced to the north, but only to retreat for fear of starvation, for the Scots simply repeated their previous policy and left them unattacked, and a truce was concluded for thirteen years In 1323 Edward recalled Baliol to reside at court, when Bruce, with Douglas and Randolph, at once invaded the borders, defeated Edward at Byland Abbey, near York, and repeated their former tactics with more or less success until 1328, when the treaty of Northampton was concluded, by which the independence of Scotland was acknowledged, and Bruce recognized as king

In 1332 both Robert Bruce and Edward II were dead, and Baliol taking advantage of the minority of David Bruce and the discontent existing therefrom, snatched at the throne, and, supported by a body of disaffected nobles, defeated the King's army near Perth, and was crowned at Scone, while David fled helplessly to France On his acknowledging the suzerainty of Edward III, however, Baliol was at once driven by the Scots from his kingdom Upon which Edward III at once advanced to the north, and called together his parliament, at York, in December, 1332

Geoffrey le Scrope acted as the King's prolocutor The House adjourned, and the clergy, barons, and knights of the shires—each order separately—debated, on the King's request, to give him counsel and advice on the affairs of Scotland until the following Friday, when, all together, they resolved that, without the assistance of the absent members, they dared not advise the King The matter was adjourned to the following year Edward, however, at once besieged Berwick, and routed the Scotch force which came to its relief under Douglas, at the battle of Halidon Hill, restoring Baliol to his throne

For three years Edward continued his support in battle after battle against the despairing efforts of the Douglases, and other nobles who still adhered to the House of Bruce, during each of which the parliaments assembled in York, since which time, with the exception of the parliament held (1640) in the hall of the Old Deanery, from September 24th to October 28th, it has never again assembled in this ancient city In 1337 the outbreak of the war with France compelled Edward to withdraw his forces Baliol retired to the Court of Edward The freedom of Scotland was in fact secured From a war of conquest and patriotic resistance the struggle died into a petty strife between two angry neighbours which became a mere episode in the larger contest between England and France

But the Royal Heraldry of York Minster points also to this other critical epoch in English history, which thus commenced in the reign of Edward III, and, indeed, may be regarded as the aim and policy thereof—*the assertion of English supremacy in France* Up to this time the royal arms had been, as we have seen, the three leopards Now we find the shield divided into four, and the *fleurs-de-lis* occupying the prominent positions on the shield, viz, the first and fourth quarterings, the leopards of England relegated to the second and third, and this really indicates the reason for the commencement and continuation of which is called the Hundred Years' War, which lasted, more or less, from the time of Edward III to the reign of Henry VI

It is not uninteresting to notice what large portions of France and England were gradually welded together under one "over-lord," and how gradually and irrevocably they were, as completely, separated

As regards the former,—first, by conquest when "the Conqueror," by his victory at Hastings, acquired Wessex, East Anglia, and Northumbria, in addition to his patrimony of Normandy and feudal sovereignty of Bretagne Secondly, by alliance Anjou, Maine, and Touraine were added by the marriage of Geoffry Martel to the Empress Matilda, daughter of Henry I By his marriage with Eleanor of Aquitane, her son, Henry II, acquired Aquitaine and Poitou, which rendered him almost the sole possessor of the provinces of the south between the Rhone, the Loire, the Pyrenees, and the Bay of Biscay. Touraine, Poitou, Anjoumois, Saintouge, Guienne, Gascony, La Berri, La Manche, Le Limousin, and the greatest part of Auvergne belonged to him. The Count of Thoulouse did him homage for that province of which he had always defended the independence; and the possessions of the King of Aragon along the Mediterranean, from Perpiguan to the mouth of the Rhone, were placed by treaties of alliance in a sort of dependence on him. In fact, when John ascended the throne, the influence of England in France extended over forty-seven of the departments, while Philip Augustus hardly ruled over twenty.

Under the baneful *regime* of the appropriately nicknamed "Lackland," however, the disintegration commenced. By the foul murder of his nephew, Arthur, he lost the greater part of his French dominions at one blow, for the French king summoned him, as his feudal superior, to appear before him and answer the charge; and on his refusal took possession of the whole of Aquitaine with but little resistance from John, who returned to England, and by a treaty signed at Parthenay, in 1214, a truce for five years was agreed on between John and Philip Augustus, the condition of which was that the former should give up his possessions north of the Loire, viz., Normandy, Brittany, Anjou, Maine, and Touraine. So that Henry III., on his accession, possessed only Gascony and part of Guienne, though he probably held some castles and had some indefinite hold on parts of Poitou. In 1240 he demanded the restitution of Normandy, which was refused; and Simon de Montfort invaded Gascony, and eventually made himself governor of the province. But Henry quarrelled with De Montfort, intestine troubles ensued at home, and nothing more was done during this reign.

Edward I., on his return from the Holy Land, did homage to Philip III. in these vague but significant words: "My Lord the King, I do "homage for all the lands I *ought* to hold of you." In 1293 a dispute with France commenced by a quarrel between certain English and Norman sailors getting water for their vessels, which developed into sundry sea-fights between their rival ships, and culminated in Edward being summoned by Philip as his vassal to answer for injuries and rebellions committed. Edward not appearing, his dominions were declared forfeited, and the French attempted to take possession. Edmond, Earl of Lancaster, was sent to negotiate for peace, but, by means of the Queen and Queen-Dowager of France, was overreached, the French being allowed to garrison the six principal castles in the province, promising to evacuate them when the conditions were completed, which they eventually refused to do. War was declared, and an army made ready; but disturbances breaking out in

Wales and Scotland, the forces were diverted thither, and Guienne remained practically the only English possession

Nothing occurred during the following reign of Edward II, though a misunderstanding took place in consequence of Lord Basset demolishing a French castle built on English territory, but this was arranged by Isabella, who visited her brother for that purpose

In Edward III's time, however, a not unreasonable opportunity seemed to arise for not only regaining what had been lost, but acquiring the whole of France His mother had been the wicked, worthless Isabella, daughter of Philip the Fair, and sister of Charles le Bel, on whose death, without male issue to succeed him, Edward claimed the sovereignty in preference to Philip of Valois, son of Charles, the younger brother of Philip the Fair According to the ancient law of the Salian Franks, drawn up probably in the seventh century, no portion of really Salic land should pass into the possession of women, but it should belong altogether to the virile sex * This had, however, never been acted upon, owing to the uninterrupted male succession, until Isabella's brother, Louis le Hutin, having died without male issue, Philip the Long, his younger brother, claimed the throne in preference to his daughter, and was crowned at Rheims † But Edward was no doubt watching his opportunity to contest the matter, and it came A quarrel took place between the fishermen of the English "cinque ports" and the fishermen of Normandy, in which some 800 Frenchmen were killed, and Philip cited Edward before his Court at Paris for wrongs done to his suzerain, and seized Guienne as a hostage Edward, busy with war in Scotland and anxious to avert the conflict, offered to formally cede Guienne for forty days, but the refusal of the French King to restore the province left him no choice but war, and Edward, incited thereto by Robert Count of Artois, a fugitive at his Court from his brother-in-law Philip, boldly asserted his claim to the sovereignty of France in right of his mother, and on Oct 7th, 1337, proclaimed himself King of France

To strengthen himself, he formed an alliance (1340) with the people of Flanders, then under the sway of the famous brewer, Van Artevelde, head of the populace at Ghent, "and so a French prince and a Flemish "burgher prevailed on the King to pursue, as in assertion of his avowed "rights, the conquest of the kingdom of France King, prince, and "burgher fixed Ghent as their place of meeting for the official conclusion of "the alliance, and there, in January, 1340, the mutual engagement was "signed and sealed The King of England assumed the arms of France "quartered with England, and thenceforth took the title of King of "France" (Guizot's *History of France*, p 142)

---

* Guizot † Guizot's *History of France*

Lord Campbell, in his *Lives of the Chancellors*, vol. i., p. 234, tells us that "this year, on the occasion of the appointment of Robert de Stratford, "Bishop of Chichester, to succeed his brother John de Stratford as Chancellor, "the great seal was broken on account of a change in the King's armorial "bearings, and another seal, with an improved emblazonment of the *fleur-de-"lis*, was delivered by the King when embarking for France, to St. Paul, the "Master of the Rolls, to be carried to the new Chancellor." In fact, the arms of France were now for the first time quartered with the arms of England, and the great seal was on both sides thus circumscribed:—"Edwardus Dei "Gracia Rex Francie et Anglie et Dominus Hibernie." In the charter, however, to which the seal is affixed, he is styled, "Edwardus Dei Gracia Rex "Anglie et Francie"—giving England preference in the charter, and France in the seal.*

And this being so, it is interesting to inquire how this particular device became the cognizance of the sovereignty of France.†

This forms the subject of a long and elaborate article in the *Grand Dictionnaire Universel*, by Larousse. "Are they flowers of the garden, or "the irons of the lance or javelin, or crowns, or bees, or even frogs, which, "as certain authors pretend, adorn the banners of the original races of our "kings? How did the *fleur-de-lis* become the heraldic emblem of France "Bourbonienne?" These questions are discussed at great length. Some believe, he says, that in the fifth century the shield of France was brought by an angel to Clovis. Raoul de Preslis, in a discourse addressed to Charles V., says: "And so you carry the arms of three *fleurs-de-lis* in token "of the blessed Trinity, which were sent from God by His angel to "King Clovis, the first Christian king, for his battle against King Candat, "who was a Saracen, when before the battle took place in the valley the "mount was taken, and named Mount-joye, and this gives rise to your "battle-cry, 'Mount-joye St. Denis;' and in memory of this, the angel of "our Lord from heaven shewed to a hermit who lived close by that he "should erase from the shield of Clovis the three crosses which he had "borne hitherto, and put in their place three *fleurs-de-lis*."

Pere Daniel thinks that the *fleur-de-lis* was an extremity of an offensive weapon, lance or javelin, common to all Franks. Near Tivoli, he says, a statue of a Roman Emperor has been found, ornamented with *fleurs-de-lis*. In a mosaic portrait in the church of St. Vital of Ravenna, which is of the time of Theodora, wife of Justinian, she is represented with a crown in the middle of which is a *fleur-de-lis*. On the seals of the three first Othos they have crowns of *fleurs-de-lis*. The seal of the Emperor Rodolphe is *semée-de-lis*. The *fleur-de-lis* is also a Spanish royal ornament. St. Ferdinand, King of Castile and Leon, at the commencement of the 14th century, bore a crown ornamented with *fleurs-de-lis*.

* Sandford's *Genealogical History*. † See illustration page 349.

Claude Frankel, in his history of *l'Origin des Armoiries*, says that the blazoners of the shield of France, wishing to shew that the first French were derived from the Secambres, who inhabit the marshes of Frize, near Holland, Zealand, and Gueldre, gave to their kings the "*fleur-de-pavillee*" (which is a little yellow lily that grows near and in the marshes in the months of May and June), in a field of blue, which resembles the water which reflects the colour of the heavens Others say that they were frogs, given in disdain because we came from the Loire, and for that reason they call us "*crapaux franchons*" Jean de Fournes mentions having seen on a boss at a house in Nismes that which appeared to be *fleurs-de-lis*, but were frogs Another opinion is that Childeric I, having adopted bees as the badge of his nation, these, through faulty representation of painters and sculptors, became *fleurs-de-lis* Menestrier says that Louis VII "le jeune" adopted the symbol as illustrative of his cognomen "Florus," on account of his beauty He is represented on his seals with a flower in one hand and a sceptre in the other, and a lily is really a term for flowers generally Armorial bearings commenced to be emblazoned about this time It is very possible that he adopted the flower in his blazon, because it is called *fleur-de-lis*, *ly* in Celtic signifies king, which he diverted into *fleur-de-Louis*

The seal of Philip I, son of Louis le Jeune, is attached to a deed requiring the Abbey of St Martin, of Pontoise, to assume as a coat-of-arms a *fleur-de-lis* It is certainly true that before the age of Louis this was never used as an armorial bearing, though it may have been used as a device until, in an heraldic age, it was adopted as a blazon Pierre Larousse concludes by saying that of all these opinions that of Menestrier is the most probable, but not more than probable

What an interesting historical epoch, then, does the assumption of this device mark! The commencement of the final effort to accomplish the fond dream of royal ambition, the aim of political and matrimonial policy, yet the beginning of the end also of a decline, slow perhaps, but uninterrupted, complete, never to be recovered! At first all seemed to promise the former Crecy (August 25, 1346), with its awful carnage, and King Philip flying for his life, attended by only five barons, to the castle of Broye Calais the following month surrendered, and the key, as it were, of the province of Ponthieu, the dower of his grandmother Eleanor of Castile, attained Then, ten years afterwards, Sept 19th, 1356, the battle of Poictiers, and John, King of France, left almost alone upon the field, surrendering himself captive to Denis de Morbecque, with the request that he may be taken to the Prince of Wales Did not the dream seem already realised when "up the Strand," then a muddy country lane, through a concourse of exulting people, the Black Prince, mounted on a "little black "hackney," conducted the conquered king, on a white steed, with very rich furniture, to the palace of the Savoy as the place of his imprisonment; and Edward III. with Queen Philippa visited him there, entertained him sumptuously, and also, as Froissart quaintly says, "consoled him all in their "power." The ransom demanded for his release—three millions of crowns and the cession of Aquitaine—savour of terms proposed to a now prostrate enemy by a triumphant foe. One does not wonder that the French people were roused to the highest pitch of indignation when the Dauphin Regent received at Paris the text of the treaty which the captive king had concluded in London—the cession of the western half of France from Calais to Bayonne, with the immediate payment of four millions of golden crowns—and that the States-General should have rejected it. But Edward with a numerous army landed at Calais, and ravaging France to the very walls of Paris, demanded of the Dauphin, ensconced therein, the confirmation of his demands. But alas for the failure of royal expectations! He would neither fight nor sign, but having burned the suburban villages, compelled Edward, from fear of famine to his army, to agree to a compromise, May 3rd, 1360, by the treaty of Bretigny, by which Aquitaine ceased to be a French fief, with its surrounding provinces, but Edward renounced his claim to the crown of France, and gave up Normandy, Maine, Tourraine, and Anjou.

But all prospect of peace soon melted away. John the Good returned to France, only to come back to the Savoy on the inability to pay his ransom, and die there. Charles V., his son, smarting under the treaty, soon found an opportunity for war, by helping the Gascons and Aquitainians, irritated by the taxes which the Black Prince had laid on them to pay for his expenses against Bertrand du Guescelin and Henry Transtamara. Once again, June 3rd, 1369, Edward assumed the title of King of France, but his army failed to support his cause there. Charles recovered the greater part of the provinces which the English held, through Du Guescelin, now Constable of France. The Black Prince, after the ruthless destruction of Limoges, returned, stricken with death, to expire at Berkhamstead Castle June 8th, 1376. On June 21st the year following, Edward died, and the remainder of English territory simply melted away.

In 1415 Henry V. invaded France for the purpose of claiming the execution of the treaty of Bretigny, and defeated the French at Agincourt, October 25th. All seemed conceded to Henry at the peace of Troyes, May 21st, 1420, by which it was agreed by Charles that "immediately after our death, and from that time forward, the Crown "and kingdom of France, with all their rights and appurtenances, "shall belong perpetually and be continued to our son King Henry "and his heirs," but nothing practical came of it except the marriage of Henry with Catherine of France. On the death of Charles, two months after Henry V., the Duke of Bedford, Regent of France, caused a herald to proclaim "Long live Henry of Lancaster, King of England and "France," but Charles VII assumed the Crown, and war was resumed Joan of Arc for a time seemed to turn the tide of success against the English, but after her defeat and death, 1456, the young King Henry VI was crowned at Notre Dame, November, 1431, King of France

For a moment, the dream of English kings again seemed realised, but only for a moment During the succeeding twenty years Charles vigorously prosecuted the war The death of Bedford was a death-blow to the English cause Burgundy allied itself with Charles VII Paris surrendered to the King Lord Talbot, the bravest of English generals, in vain attempted to preserve Picardy, Maine, and Anjou Wading the Sonne with the waters up to his chin, he relieved Crotoy, and in the face of the French army Pontoise, but in vain Efforts of peace were made, first by the release of the Duke of Orleans, taken at Agincourt, then by the marriage of Henry VI to Margaret, daughter of Rene, titular King of Sicily and Jerusalem, and the cession of Maine and Anjou to him—an agreement which eventually cost Suffolk his head By the end of August, 1450, the whole of Normandy had been completely won back by the French Then followed the conquest of Guienne In three years Chastillon was taken, the brave Talbot slain in his efforts to relieve it Bordeaux capitulated shortly after, Oct 17th, 1453 The English had no longer any possessions in France but Calais and Guines The Hundred Years' War was over

The number of *fleurs-de-lis* was not originally defined, and the shield was termed *semée-de-lis*, but in the reign of Charles V they were limited to three, perhaps in the hope of distinguishing the shield of France from that of England This, however, was almost immediately adopted by the English kings, and appears on the great seal of Henry V, and though the last remnant of English supremacy was extinguished by the capture of Calais by the Duke de Guise, 1538, the lilies remained as the first quarter in the arms of England until the year 1707, when, on the accession of the House of Hanover, George I placed England impaling Scotland in the 1st quarter, France in the 2nd, Ireland in the 3rd, and Hanover in the 4th Upon the 1st of January, 1801, by royal proclamation, the French *fleurs-de-lis* were removed from the arms of England, Hanover placed on an inescutcheon, and the royal shield of England assumed the aspect with which we are all familiar as the "Royal Standard"

No motto appears on any of the Royal Heraldry of the Minster, but perhaps a notice thereof would be scarcely complete without a word thereon

The motto *Honi soit qui mal y pense*, belongs, as I have already said, page 213, to the Order of the Garter I have little to add thereon, save that further examination tends to throw increased doubt on the story of the Countess of Salisbury's garter Indeed, there is a difference of opinion as to which countess is alluded to therein. Milles, in his *Catalogue of Honour*, says that she was the daughter of William de Granson, and therefore Catherine, wife of William, first earl. Burke says that she was Elizabeth, daughter of Lord Mohun, therefore the wife of the second. Froissart* makes no allusion to this occurrence, but simply speaks of the Countess of Salisbury, and gives an account of the King coming to Werk Castle during Salisbury's captivity in France, and, having dispersed the Scottish army under King David, who were besieging it, being hospitably received by the fair countess and her son. She seems to have been virtuous as well as fair, and discouraged the King's attentions with so much prudence and dignity, that he left the castle astonished and disappointed.

I think that the outcome of a careful consideration of the history of the period amounts to this, viz., that Edward III., anxious to weld together a body of noble and gallant knights on whose loyalty and attachment to the Crown he might depend, utilized the popular memories of two of the most famous heroes of history, King Arthur and King Richard, for this purpose. As regards the former, tradition had asserted that Windsor was the very site of the fabled round table; and, therefore, Edward directed William of Wykeham, the great architect of the day, to build a round tower on the mound of the "upper ward," round the court within which the table might be set.† As regards the latter, viz., King Richard, tradition had also handed down (as indeed John Taylor, Master of the Rolls, mentioned in his address to Francis I., King of France, at his investiture, 1527),‡ that Richard I., in honour of his betrothment to Berengaria, instituted an order of twenty-four knights, who pledged themselves in a fraternity with the King to scale the walls of Acre; and that they might be known in the storming of that city, the King appointed them to wear a blue band of leather on the left leg, from which they were called "knights of the blue thong."

The fact that St. George was the tutelary saint of Aquitaine, and his name the war cry of the dukedom, accounts for the Order having been dedicated to him by King Richard and again by King Edward; and also for the chapel, originally built and dedicated by Henry I. to St. Edward the Confessor, being, on its rebuilding by Edward III., dedicated to St. George. The motto adopted seems to have been intended to convey a threatening and significant hint, viz., "Evil be to him that evil thinks "of *it*" (*i.e.* the Order), addressed in the first instance, to Philip of Valois, King of France, of whom Stowe also tells us—"The same time builded a "round tower in his country to the end he might allure the men of "warre of Germany and Italie, and so to keepe them from the King of "England's round table."

* Vol. ii., cap. 191, 2. † Loftie's *History of Windsor Castle.*
‡ *Memorials of the Order of the Garter*, Beltz.

On St George's day, 1343, the first chapter of the Order took place at Windsor, attended by the "twenty-four founders," and their wives, attired in the robes of the Order, for by its original statutes the latter were associated with their husbands Amongst the ladies, conspicuous for her beauty and the plainness of her attire, was the Countess of Salisbury

In 1358, the round tower was completed, and a great feast of the Order held within it The captive kings of France and Scotland came as guests, and sat one on each side of Edward III In the tournament which followed, John and David tilted in the lists The stout Earl of Salisbury was accidentally killed in one of the encounters, and his fair and virtuous wife retired at once into the deepest seclusion Her name being so prominently associated with the foundation of the Order, may, perhaps, account for a mere uncorroborated tradition

As regards the other motto, *Dieu et mon droit*, Sandford tells us that the first authenticated existence of that is, that it was carved in stone on Henry VIII's new buildings at the palace, at Whitehall, which he had taken from Wolsey, and which he adopted as his palace after the palace at Westminster was destroyed by fire

Supporters were introduced, according to Sandford, by Richard II He says, p 191 "He was the first of our kings that had his esctocheon "supported, as you may observe in his armes and those of St Edward the "Confessor, over the porch at the north door of Westminster Hall by him "erected, which are there (and in divers other places) held or supported "by two angels" But as supporters do not appear in the York windows I need not enter upon a long, though interesting, subject

The sovereigns of England never impaled the arms of their consorts, which was, however, done by the various members of their families, who differenced their arms according to their geniture, either by bordures or labels, sometimes of three points, sometimes five Sandford (p 127) quotes authorities to shew that the former marks the eldest son, the three points denoting father, mother, and self, the latter his eldest son, the two additional points indicate grandfather and grandmother Edward I, during the lifetime of his father, Henry III, differenced his arms with a label argent

It is not, perhaps, generally known that at his marriage his father created him Prince of Wales, with an exhortation to employ his youth in conquering the Principality of which he had rather prematurely assumed the title, and from that time to the present the Prince of Wales has always differenced his arms into a label of three points, generally argent, but in the Caerlaverock roll it is said of Edward II, then Prince of Wales—

> "He bore with a label of blue,
> The arms of the good king his father"

His brother, Edmond Crouchback, Earl of Lancaster, assumed a label azure, and afterwards charged it with nine *fleurs-de-lys* in honour of his second wife Blanche, Queen of Navarre. Of the younger children of Edward I., Thomas of Brotherton, Earl of Norfolk, being the eldest son of the second marriage, seems to have also differenced his arms with a label of three points argent. His younger brother, Edmond of Woodstock, Earl of Kent, assumed a bordure argent.

Edward III.'s younger brother, John of Eltham, Earl of Cornwall, assumed "a bordure of France," *i.e.* azure *semée-de-lys*, in recognition of his mother Isabel.

Of Edward III.'s sons, the Black Prince carried the label argent with three points; his wife Joan, "the fair maid of Kent," carried the arms of her father, Edmond Earl of Kent, but placed the label upon it in honour of her husband.

Lionel Duke of Clarence differenced his arms with the white label; but in recognition of his marriage with Elizabeth, the great heiress of De Burgh and of Clare, he distinguished it sometimes with the cross gules of the former, and sometimes with the canton gules of the latter.

John of Gaunt, the next brother, distinguished his white label with three points of ermine on each; but when he surrendered the kingdom of Castile, he bore three *fleurs-de-lys* on each point in right of his first wife Blanche, heiress of Edmund Earl of Lancaster. His children by his third wife, Catherine Swynford (*née* Roet), assumed the surname of Beaufort, from the place of their residence, and bore the royal arms with a bordure gobonnée azure and argent.

Edmond of Langley, Duke of York, his younger brother, carried nine torteaux on his label of argent; and Thomas of Woodstock, Duke of Gloucester, the youngest, surrounded his paternal coat with a bordure argent.

Richard II. impaled the arms of Edward the Confessor with his own, and granted to his half-brothers the same coat, with the distinction to the eldest, John Holland, Duke of Exeter, of a bordure of France, and to Thomas Holland, Duke of Kent, the youngest, a bordure argent.

Henry IV., as I have already said, reduced the number of the lilies to three. Of his younger children, Thomas of Lancaster, Duke of Clarence, adopted his grandfather's label, viz., argent charged with ermine, to which he added the canton gules of Clare.

His younger brother, John Duke of Bedford, dimidiated his label, the dexter portion being argent charged with ermine, the sinister azure charged with *fleurs-de-lys*, as borne by Edmond Crouchback first Earl of Lancaster. Humphrey of Lancaster, Duke of Gloucester, assumed first a bordure gobonnée argent and sable, afterwards a bordure argent.

PLATE 8.

EMPEROR OF GERMANY.

KING OF ROMANS.

PROVENCE.

CASTILE & LEON.

KING OF JERUSALEM.

I.

NAVARRE.

Edmond Tudor, son of Owen Tudor by his marriage with Catherine de Valois, widow of Henry V, obtained a grant of the royal arms, surrounded with a bordure azure, charged alternately with martlets and *fleurs-de-lys* or.

Richard Duke of York, the younger brother of Edward V, carried the argent label, and George Duke of Clarence, the younger brother of Richard III, carried the argent label, charged with the canton gules of Clare

I need not pursue this part of the subject any further, as this concludes the Royal Heraldry of the monarchs specially connected with the Minster, but the same plan continues to the present day The children of the sovereign have all differenced their arms with the label argent, the younger sons charging it with various devices

We have not specimens of all the shields which I have mentioned in the Minster

The Royal Heraldry of the nave and chapter-house practically commemorates Edward I and his family He is the central character intended to be honoured or represented wherever the family shield is seen, or the lions noticed, and eight members of his "kith and kin" are represented who participated in some way in the duties and pleasures of his life here, who were probably each of them personally present here, and also, probably, each contributed towards the building or ornamentation of the portion of the Minster which was in process of construction during his reign, and in which we know he took much interest and pleasure It will be most convenient, I think, to notice these persons in chronological order, and therefore we will commence with his *uncles*, represented by the two shields on the first west window, north aisle nave (coloured illustrations, plate 8), the former charged with the double-headed, the latter with the single-headed eagle

---

Frederick II

The shield of the double-headed eagle represents Frederick II, Emperor of Germany, who married Isabella, sister of Henry III He was the grandson of Frederick I, Barbarossa, monarch of the empire originally established when, on the division of the empire of Charlemagne, his grandson Louis, son of Louis le Debonnaire, was, by the treaty of Verdun, 843, made king of the Germans

In 887 this title ceased to be hereditary, on the deposition of Charles the fat, and thence became an elective monarchy under the title of Emperor In 962 the title of Emperor of Rome was assumed, and when a successor was elected in the Emperor's lifetime, he was called the King of the Romans. Not that the Emperor had any direct authority over Rome, which was exercised by the Bishop of Rome from the days when on the fall of the western empire he had been elected a Prœsule by the joint votes of the clergy, senate, and people, which governed Rome as an independent commonwealth, having its senate, consuls, tribunes, and forming its own alliances. Even when, in 541, Longinus, having abolished the Exarchs of Ravenna, sent an officer called "Dux," or Duke, who was changed every year, to each town or district, Rome retained its internal municipal administration and laws.

Pepin, 752–768, not only respected this, but having conquered Astolphus King of the Longobards, obliged him to give up the Exarchate of Ravenna and the Pentapolis, not to the eastern Emperor, but to the "holy church of God and the Roman republic;" and Charlemagne, though he assumed the title of "Patrician" of the Romans, confirmed and increased his father's donation.

Otho, when crowned as first Emperor of Rome by John XII., 962, swore to respect the authority of the Roman see, and not to encroach upon its temporal rights and possessions. He was acknowledged Emperor, and his son as King of the Romans; but the Pope remained lord of the Roman duchy as of a great Imperial feudatory, as in the time of the Carlowingians.

These facts throw light upon the origin and significance of the single and double-headed eagle. The former is evidently the continuance of that which was originally the insignia of the Roman people. The latter symbolical of the eastern and western Roman empires.

Frederick II., who was only four years old on the death of his father Henry, had been created King of the Romans in his cradle, but was not formally elected Emperor of Germany and crowned at Aix la Chapelle, until 1215. By his first wife he had a son, Henry, for whose marriage with Isabella of England negotiations had, in 1225, taken place, two years before her marriage with his father. His second wife was Iolante, daughter of John of Brienne, King of Jerusalem, who had gone to France for aid against the Mussulmans, in 1223, and whose title Frederick assumed, and at once prepared for a crusade. But it was not until 1227 that the Emperor actually started, when he only proceeded to the Morea, and abandoned the crusade; Pope Gregory excommunicating him in consequence, and laying his dominions under an interdict. The following year Iolante died, and Frederick determined to repeat his attempt in defiance of the Pope, who commanded the Patriarch of Jerusalem and the three orders of knights to oppose him; but Frederick persevered, and having made a treaty with Meledin, Sultan of Egypt, made his entry into Jerusalem, March 17th, 1229, and on the 18th of May placed the crown upon his own head, because no priest would even read mass. He returned soon after, leaving Richard Fellingher as governor of the country, which soon fell into a state of anarchy

The shield at the foot of plate 8, argent a cross potent between seven cross crosslets or, contains the arms adopted when, contrary to the advice of the bishops, after the storming of Jerusalem, 1099, it became the capital of a Christian kingdom which lasted to 1244, and Godfrey de Bouillon was elected the first king And, apart from their historical, they have this heraldic interest, viz, that this is the only recognized instance of metal being emblazoned upon metal They are, doubtless, inscribed on this window to represent the double regal dignity of Frederick being King of Jerusalem as well as Emperor of Germany In 1230, he forced the Pope to free him from the excommunication, and in 1234 negotiations were entered upon for a marriage between Isabella and himself Pope Gregory IX entirely promoted the union, not only by a bull, but also by a letter which he wrote to the French king, assuring him that the alliance would not be injurious to the interests of France, and early in the following year the necessary arrangements were satisfactorily completed

The union between Frederick and Isabella was neither very long nor very happy, though it began most brilliantly The fair bride* was richly dowered by her brother Henry III with 30,000 marks of silver, over and above plate, jewels, horns, and other things, according to what it was suitable for such a lady to possess and such a lord to receive, including fourteen dresses, three of silken cloth of gold, fur capes, two beds hung with Genoese cloth of gold, plate and jewelry, and the complete furniture of a private chapel

The Archbishop of Cologne, with the Duke of Brabant and Louvain, came to England to receive her Her suite included a chaplain, clerk, physician, and a complete set of servants, with a goodly train of noble matrons and damsels well exercised in all that pertained to their several departments, to attend and minister to her wants in regal fashion Her journey was indeed a royal progress Both at Antwerp and Cologne she received quite an ovation, and on reaching Worms was married in the Cathedral, July 20th, with great splendour, by the Archbishop of Mayence Four kings, eleven dukes, thirty earls and marquises, besides ecclesiastical dignitaries, being present, and, a month after, a splendid festival took place at Mayence But there, all her English attendants were dismissed, and she, a girl of twenty-one, was left alone with a husband past forty, who had already been married twice before, in a country of strangers

Frederick was a man of courage, energy, and high intellectual capacity, a poet, musician, and said to be the most learned prince of his

* Green's *Princesses of England*

time in Europe. He founded the University of Naples, and was a writer and translator of books, but not exactly suited for domestic happiness. His first act after the wedding was to degrade his son Henry, and imprison him in a castle in Apulia, where he died seven years afterwards. He was a freethinker, a patron and friend of alchemists and astrologers, and treated all that Isabella had been brought up to reverence, with biting sarcasms and contemptuous blasphemies. His personal life was grossly immoral, and his palace little better than a harem, where the Empress was expected to occupy the position of an eastern sultana. His reign was a series of intestine troubles, frequent wars, and incessant discord with the Holy See, by which he was eventually excommunicated. Isabella had three children—a daughter who died an infant, and a son Henry, who did not long survive her. She died December, 1344, in giving birth to another daughter, Margaret, who lived to marry Albert Lantgrave, of Thuringen, whose descendant of the fourth generation was made Elector of Saxony, and his offspring were the progenitors of the house of Saxe-Cobourg and Gotha, from which our Queen is descended. In 1245, Frederick himself was deposed, and died five years afterwards: it was said, poisoned by his illegitimate son Manfred, who, professing to govern the kingdom during the minority of Isabella's surviving son, endeavoured to establish his own authority.

Richard Earl of Cornwall, King of the Romans.

Discord and dissensions ensued, and the Pope, Innocent I., tried to tempt Richard Earl of Cornwall, the younger brother of Henry III., with the kingdom of Sicily, which Frederick had inherited from his mother Constance. He was wise enough to decline an honour which his brother foolishly accepted for his second son Edmond. But afterwards, not warned by the troubles which eventually ensued therefrom,—perhaps his wife, Senchia of Provence (see page 378), ambitious to be, like her two sisters, a queen, prompted him to this step, which seems contrary to his natural character,—Richard allowed himself to be chosen King of the Romans, which seemed to render his succession infallible to the Imperial throne; and to him I allot the shield bearing the single-headed eagle (plate 8). In 1258 he went over to Germany with a noble train, and was crowned with his wife upon Ascension Day, May 27th, King of the Romans and Almain, at Aix-la-Chapelle, by Conrad Archbishop of Cologne. On his great seal he pompously describes himself: "Richardus Dei Gratia Romanorum Rex "Semper Augustus." No doubt his great wealth—for it is said that he could spend 100 marks a day, *i.e.* £66 13*s.* 4*d.*, a mark being 13*s.* 4*d.*—had made the German princes select him as a candidate for the empire.

He spent vast sums in his election, and he carried over with him, according to Matthew Paris, some seven hundred thousand marks As long as his money lasted he had plenty of friends and partizans, but as soon as it was drained from him he found that there was no solid foundation to his power Senchia died 1261, and having no family ties there, he was glad to escape from the dissensions of his new kingdom and return "a poorer king than he went out an earl," and died at Berkhamstead Castle, which had been granted to him by his brother, 1272 He left one surviving son, Edmond, who in the absence of Edward I from England, was joint regent of the kingdom with Gilbert de Clare, Earl of Gloucester, whose sister Margaret he married in 1285 He founded on the Ash-ridge (or ridge of the ashes), in the forest near his castle, a college of the Bon Hommes, an Order under the rule of St Augustine, and supposed by Mosheim to have been a remnant of the Paulicians, to take care of a sacred relic, *i e* a particle of the Saviour's blood, which, according to Holinshed, he had found in a gold box amongst the relics of the ancient emperors in Germany Here he died, having been divorced from his wife for some years, leaving no issue *

He carried his shield, as Duke of Cornwall, suspended by a strap from an eagle's back, in allusion to his father having been King of the Romans This innovation is the first indicated of that custom which is now common in Austria and Prussia, of emblazoning the shield upon the eagle displayed

---

SPANISH ALLIANCES

The three shields, Provence or Aragon, Castile and Leon, and Navarre (plate 8), must first be *generally* noticed, as they form a group not only representing royal alliances, but the origin and development of those kingdoms of Spain which played such conspicuous parts in the middle ages †

The Roman dominion over the heterogeneous elements of Iberians, Celts, Phœnicians, Greeks, and Carthagenians, which composed the early inhabitants of Spain, practically came to an end A D 398, at the death of the Emperor Theodorus Soon after which the peninsular was overrun by swarms of barbarous nations—Vandals, Alans, Suevians and Goths, of which the latter obtained the supremacy for nearly four centuries, until Roderick the king having ravished Cava, daughter of Count Julian, the exasperated father invited Muza, lieutenant of Ulit, sole sovereign of the Moors, or Saracens, to come over from Africa and help him to avenge the insult inflicted on his family This he readily did, with 112,000 men, and

---

* *History of Berkhamstead*, Rev J W Cobb. † Mariana's *History of Spain*, 1699

after a battle at Xeres which lasted eight days, Roderick was defeated, and fled, and was either drowned or escaped to Portugal. The Moors overran the country, and for two and a half years held undisputed possession of Spain.

Then commenced a reaction on the part of a remnant of determined men who had fled for shelter to the fastnesses of the Asturias, and the mountainous districts of the Pyrenees. Here they found congenial spirits, for the inhabitants of the former love to derive their name from Ayster the Avenger, who after the siege of Troy had settled here, and whose descendants had never been conquered even by the Goths. The opportunity for action soon arrived. Four of their number daily met at a hermit's cell on Mount Uruela, for mutual consolation and consultation as to the best means of emancipating their country from its present misery. The good recluse happened to die, and the fame of his sanctity drawing together to his funeral 600 of the principal inhabitants, the four friends persuaded them to rise against their oppressors. Garcia Ximinides, one of their number, being chosen king, they marched at once against the Moors, and captured several towns, amongst them Sufa, the capital of Sobrave. Garcia was conspicuous by his red shield, and when his son, Garcia Iniquez, conquered *Navarre*, that was adopted as the name, and the plain red shield as the arms of the kingdom; and so it remained until nearly 500 years after, viz. 1212 A.D., when Sancho the Strong, King of Navarre, brother of Berengaria, wife of Richard I., together with the kings of Aragon and Castile, achieved a triumphant victory over the Moors. The allied forces had advanced to the foot of Sierra. The wily Moors occupied the pass of Lofa, the only passage; but guided by a shepherd, some said an angel, the confederate kings gained the summit of the mountains, fortified their camp, and then at their leisure swept down upon the camp of the Moors below, who had fortified their king's tent with bars and chains, and guarded it with the bravest of their forces. All day the Moors sustained the brunt of the attack, then fled, 200,000 of them, according to the ancient chronicler, being slain; and in memory of this victory of Navas de Tolosa, the King of Navarre added to the arms of his ancestors—viz. the red shield, with its cross ribs decorated with gold in honour of Garcia, termed an escarbuncle,—chains and an emerald in the middle, in token that he was the first who broke the chains which defended the citadel of the enemy's camp.

And in like manner the movement had rapidly spread. Agna, son of Eudo, in 710, having gained some towns from the Moors on the banks of the Aragon, was established by the King of Navarre as Earl of *Aragon*, subject to him. Taken from, and retaken by, the Moors several times, the country finally capitulated to Charlemagne and his son, Louis the Debonnaire, 801, and was established as an independent State, with the title Condado de Barcelona. Tradition says that one Geoffry, fighting amongst the leading warriors of the Emperor, presented himself before him at the close of the day to announce the victory. The monarch dipped his fingers in the blood flowing from the wounds of the gallant soldier, and drew them down the brazen shield which he held, and, commanding that he and his family should ever after bear that as the family achievement in honour of the memorable event, appointed him the first Conde de Barcelona.

The kingdom of *Leon*, in a similar manner arose to the west, when in 716, Pelagus the Goth, resenting the defilement of his sister by Muamza the Moor, stirred up the spirit of rebellion in the valley of the Congas, gathered 1,000 men in the cave of Cobadonga, defeated the Moors in a pitched battle, and proclaimed himself King of Spain. Then, six years after, having captured the city of Leon, he assumed the title of King of Leon, and the cognizance of a lion purpure on an argent shield; while under his sway were established the earls of *Castile*, named by the Moors "the land of the castles," from the number of fortresses erected on its frontier, who adopted for their arms, gules a castle or. In 1028, Sancho King of Navarre inherited the earldom of Castile, having married Da Nuna, sister of Garcia the Earl of Castile, and constituted it a kingdom. At his death he bequeathed Navarre to his eldest son Garcia; Castile, to his second son Ferdinand; Sobrave, to his youngest son Gonzalo; and Aragon, to his natural son Ramiro. Ferdinand conquered Bermuda King of Leon, annexed his kingdom, and united it with Castile and Navarre. At his death he also divided his kingdoms, giving Castile to his eldest son Sancho, and Leon to Alonzo. But on the death of the former they were again reunited in Alonzo, only to be divided again amongst his grandsons, and again reunited by the intermarriage of their grandchildren, Berengaria Queen of Castile, and Alonzo King of Leon.

Had these Christian kings only lived in harmony, the supremacy of the Moors—that hated but beneficent thraldom which initiated everything like civilization, art, and culture, in Spain—would soon have been overcome, instead of remaining until they were finally driven out by Ferdinand, 1492. But they quarrelled amongst themselves. "Bellum quam otium "malunt, si extraneus deest domi hostem quœrunt," said the old historian; and though Leon and Castile were united, Navarre and Aragon remained for many generations independent kingdoms, until the former was united to France by marriage with Philip the Fair, and the latter to Castile by Ferdinand and Isabella, who eventually welded them together with Grenada, the city of the Moors, into one kingdom.

But now to notice the individuals represented by these shields:

ELEANOR OF PROVENCE,

who is indicated by the shield containing the arms of *Aragon*, which were also the arms of *Provence*, for in 1137 Raymond Berenger, Conde de Barcelona, received from Ramiro, second King of Aragon, on his abdication of the throne, his daughter Petronilla as his affianced bride, and he governed the kingdom under the title Principe de Aragon. In due time the marriage was consummated, and their son, Alphonzo II., having two children, the elder in 1196 succeeded to the kingdom of Aragon, the younger to the county of Provence, which had "become "a possession of the House of Aragon in the beginning of the twelfth "century by the union of the Provencal heiress with the Pyrannean "king,"* and the honourable distinction assigned to Geoffry became thus the arms of the Count of Provence as well as of the kings of Aragon. His grandson, Berenger, had only daughters—Eleanor, who married Henry III. of England; Senchia, who married his brother Richard, Earl of Cornwall and King of the Romans; Marguerite, who married Louis IX. (St. Louis) King of France; and Beatrice, who married his brother Charles, Count of Anjou, who thus became Count of Provence. This shield, therefore, evidently indicates *the mother* of Edward I. But it also indicates an alliance with a country whose condition seems rather like an incident from Fairyland than a page of sober history.

"In the far south, where clustering vines are hung;
Where first the old chivalric lays were sung,
Where earliest smiled that gracious child of France,
Angel and knight and fairy, called Romance." †

"The Land of Song" part of the langue d'oc (as distinguished from the dialect spoken north of the Loire, where the affirmative being expressed by *oui*, was called the langue d'oui), free from the contentions of the Norman Princes which harassed the north, and the apprehensions of the Moors which disturbed the west and south, enjoyed in the 12th century an exceptional prosperity. How could it be otherwise? Snugly sheltered amidst the towering Alps from any wind but the mistral; with vine-clad slopes and terraces of olives and gardens and orchards, where the pomegranate, citron, orange, and almond ripen to perfection; the native place of the parent of the fairest, sweetest flower that blows—the rose of Provence; where the rivers are full of trout, eel, shad, and barbel, and the sea-coast yields sardine and anchovy. Of course the inhabitants quarrelled amongst themselves. All prosperous people do. But under the soft influence of that dreamy climate, yielding to many temptations which they ought to have conquered,

* *The Troubadours*, Rutherford. † *Legend of Provence*, Adelaide Procter.

wealthy and industrious, full of imaginative genius, art, and refinement—their panacea for all their failings was song. The form and rhythm of their songs were varied—the tenzon, the acrostic, the ballad, the frottola, the sonnet, the cobbole, the canzon. Every chateau, however petty, had its poet to write metrical histories, to satirize adversaries, to extol the family, to greet the wedding with a song and the funeral with an elegy, to play every conceivable instrument, and with perfect patience to endure every practical joke. Courts of Love, with president and council regularly appointed, gravely regulated all domestic scandals and differences, controlled matrimonial irregularities, and punished offenders. A Code of Love, containing 31 clauses, was drawn up, and four orthodox stages of love-making were laid down. Some were enrolled as cavaliers-servente—whose duties were to wait upon fair ladies, supply their wants, and protect them from harm. Some roamed the country as troubadours—free to come and go wherever they pleased, ever sure of welcome and hospitality, amongst the artisans or country-folk, at the hostelries, and at the great houses also. Sometimes, perhaps, their songs were unduly flavoured with satire and scandal, but many undertook their profession as a mission. "I see but one remedy for "all this mischief, and that is the art of the troubadour," said Vidal, as he strove with many to raise the tone of morality, if not religion.

It seems almost a dream in this prosaic age that such an effort should have been made. Well, the results were not, perhaps, altogether successful, though we have no reason to be ashamed of the reputations of the two fair sisters who were allied to our royal house. Eleanor and Senchia were tender, loving wives, and the former exhibited a firmness and courage which often supported her somewhat capricious and vacillating husband in his trials and difficulties. She filled the office of "Custos "regia vice regis," during his absence abroad, with dignity and vigour, and pawned her jewels when need required it, and if her beauty and luxuries sometimes emptied his purse, her resolution and decision as often replenished it, and forced even the reluctant citizens of London to pay their quota of "aurum reginæ" whenever she demanded it. The whole Court mourned the death of the gentle Senchia, 1261. The King passed to his rest, 1272, and eight years after, Eleanor retired to the convent of Ambresbury with her two granddaughters, Mary, daughter of Edward I., and Eleanor, daughter of the deceased Duchess of Bretagne. In 1284, according to Matthew Paris, "That generous virago Elianor, Queen of England, "mother of the King, took the veil and religious habit at Ambresbury." During the next seven years she maintained a close and tender intercourse with her son, often advising him on matters of state, and receiving from him the most dutiful and loving attention, and ever styling herself "Elinor, humble nun of the Order of Fontevraud." She died the year after Eleanor of Castile; and Edward is said to have borne, himself, both their hearts to London, and placed the former in the church of the Friars' Preachers, the latter in that of the Friars' Minors, now called the Minories.

ELEANOR OF CASTILE.

The shield of *Castile and Leon* is certainly the shield of Edward's *first wife*, Eleanor of Castile and Leon, who was the daughter of Ferdinand, King of Castile and Leon. His father was Alonzo IX., King of Leon; his mother, Berengaria, daughter of Alonzo VIII., King of Castile, who had married Eleanor, daughter of Henry II. of England. Berengaria's brother, Henry King of Castile, when quite a lad had married Malfada, daughter of the King of Portugal, from whom he was divorced, and soon after he was killed by a tile falling on his head from the roof of the palace. Upon this the Castilians elected his sister Berengaria as their Queen,—in preference to her eldest sister, Blanche, who had married a foreigner, Louis VIII. King of France; but Berengaria speedily resigned the Crown of Castile to her son Ferdinand, who, on his father's death, became King of Leon also. He first married Joanna, daughter of Simon Earl of Poictiers and Adelaide, daughter of Alice, daughter of Louis VII., King of France, whose repudiation by Richard Cœur de Lion in the preceding century had involved Europe in war. From her Joanna inherited Ponthieu, which at her death passed to her only child, Eleanor of Castile. Ferdinand's second wife was Beatrix, daughter of the Emperor Philip. This was considered, I suppose, a grand match, for Mariana tells us that "he was married in the "cathedral by the Bishop of Burgos, who, the day before, said mass in his "pontificalibus, during which the King knighted himself, there being none "worthy to perform that act as was the custom of those times."

Edward seems to have first made acquaintance with his fair cousin in 1255, when he came to the court of Alonzo X. (Eleanor's half-brother), on a mission from his father, probably to remonstrate about the treatment of his cousin Christina, daughter of the King of Denmark, by Alonzo. He had sent for her to become his wife in the place of his queen, Violante, whom he intended to divorce; but finding an unexpected prospect of a family by her, he repudiated the young lady, and compelled his brother Philip, Abbot of Valladolid, and Archbishop Elect of Seville, to renounce his priestly functions and marry Christina, who died soon after. I suppose that the young Prince Edward returned smitten, for when, soon after, war broke out between Henry III. and Alonzo, about Gascony, the union of the young people was proposed as the terms of peace; and the Bishop of Bath, and John Mansel, the King's secretary, having been despatched from Bordeaux with this purpose, they speedily returned with

Alonzo's consent inscribed in a scroll sealed with gold. In August, 1254, the marriage was solemnized with much splendour at Burgos, the young bridegroom being just fifteen, and the bride younger, at the time of their espousals.

They were young lovers, but lovers they must have been; for certainly lovers they were during their wedded life of thirty-six years, which then commenced. And never was lover more broken-hearted than when the gallant Edward turned back from his journey to Scotland, at the first tidings of the illness of his beloved Eleanor, only to find on his arrival at Hardby, near to Grantham, that she had already breathed her last at the house of a gentleman named Weston, November 29th. The King* had only left her at Hardby on the 20th, having journeyed thus far in her company, holding his Parliament at Clipston on October 27th, and enjoying the diversion of the chase, as appears from an entry in his wardrobe accounts of the payment of 6*s.* 8*d.* of the King's gift to Robert at Hall of Wyrardeston, "Quia navigavit in aquâ post cervum in quoddam stagnum in forestâ "de Pecco." All had been done which the rude medical skill of that time could suggest. "Magister Leopardus fisicus Reginæ," probably the Spanish physician sent from the King of Aragon, to whom she gave a silver cup, and who thus diagnosed her case—"Modicæ febris igniculo "contabescens," attended her. Henry de Montepessulano procured syrup and other medicines for the Queen's use from Lincoln, for 13*s.* 4*d.*, but to no avail. Sir Garcia de Ispannia, her father confessor, soothed her closing hours, and on the eve of the Feast of St. Andrew, 1290, her birthday, she entered into rest. In measured and stately procession the body, carefully embalmed, was carried, first to Lincoln, where all that was not embalmed was interred in the chapel of the blessed Virgin, at the Minster; thence by easy stages to Grantham, Stamford, Geddington, Northampton, Stony Stratford, Woburn, Dunstable, where the body, which had been met by the whole convent, "solemniter revestitus in capis," lay, one night, "in medio chori" of the Priory Church; thence on to St. Albans, Waltham, West Cheap, and Charing, the King, accompanied by the whole nobility, prelates, and other dignified clergy, going forth to meet it, and conducting it to the abbey where, "cum summa omnium reverentia et honore," it was finally laid in the Confessor's chapel, at the feet of her father-in-law, Henry III.

From thence the widowed King went to Ashridge, where he kept his Christmas, that holy festival—sweet in prosperity, yet sweeter still in sorrow; and on January 20th, proceeded to visit his aged mother, Eleanor of Provence, who died in the June following, in her seclusion at Ambresbury, comforted in her declining years by his daughter Mary, who, young

* *Archæologia*, xxix.

in life, had been professed with her in that house. In due time stately memorials arose. At Hardby, a chantry; at each of the resting-places a cross, erected by the best architects of the day, John de Bello, Richard de Stowe, Dymenge de Legeri, Michael de Canterbury, Richard and Roger de Crundale. William de Ireland and Alexander le Imaginator executing the sculpture. In London, the spot in the church of the Friars Predicants where her heart was deposited, was decorated by William de Hoo, William de Suffolk, Walter de Newmarch, and Walter le Durham. All these memorials, save Geddington and Waltham, have passed away; but her tomb at Westminster, though much defaced, still remains: exquisite in beauty, chaste in design, with the beautiful recumbent figure by Master William Torel, goldsmith, for which William Sprot and John de Ware furnished the metal, and Flemish coin to the amount of 476 florins were bought for the gilding. Shields, with the arms of Castile and Leon, England and Ponthieu, adorn the side of the tomb; and who can fail to read in the expression of that beautiful face of Grecian caste, the character given of her by Walsingham: "Fuerat nempe mulier pia, "modesta, misericors, Anglicorum amatrix omnium."

The most superficial reader of history must be acquainted with the many traits still extant of her pure and holy life. Much of it must have been spent here at York. It seems only appropriate, therefore, that so many of our windows should be adorned, not only with the family cognizance of the Castle, but with a badge which is significant of one of the most devoted acts of her married life, and which her husband, I venture to think, adopted and cherished in grateful commemoration of that most precious of all gifts from God—the unfailing devotion of a faithful and loving wife.

None need to be reminded that when Edward, as Prince of Wales, went to the Crusades, his young wife accompanied him, and shared his dangers and fatigue; or that he was nearly assassinated when besieging Acre, by a fanatic who had sought a private interview on the pretence of bearing a secret message from the Emir of Joppa. Edward, though taken at a disadvantage, lying on his couch, with his customary courage and promptitude parried the blow with his arm, felled his assailant to the ground with a kick on the breast, and, springing to his feet, killed him with a blow of a camp-stool. But the poignard had pierced his arm, and Camden quotes a story of Sanctius, a Spanish historian, that Eleanor promptly sucked the poison from the wound, which, after some threatening symptoms owing to the heat of the climate, was finally healed, according to Walter Hemingford, by the treatment and unguent applied by the surgeon of the Master of the Templars. What more natural than that Edward, in accordance with the custom of Crusaders to adopt some device significant of their having been in the Holy Land, should select something which would commemorate this? And what more appropriate than the covered cup or jar in which the ointment had been contained? And therefore, in the old Latin distich of the badges of the Plantagenets,* we cannot be mistaken in recognising this under the familiar Horatian expression, "Pistica nardus"

> "Est aper Edwardus, flos regum, pistica nardus,
> Sol solus lucens, rosa mundi, stella reducens"

Surely there is not only an interesting memory of the past, but a living meaning for the present and all ages, in this simple badge, singularly appropriate to the house of God, for it speaks not of the strife of war, but of love which no dangers of war can daunt,—of the noblest trait of a truly brave heart, grateful, tender affection,—of "the beauty and strength of a "woman's devotion,"—of the married life of those who were "lovely and "pleasant in their lives, and in their deaths were not divided," who enjoyed that chiefest of Divine blessings, which kings and peasants may alike participate in,—pure wedded life, which interrupted, not extinguished, by death, finds its perfect and eternal consummation in the paradise of God.

It is interesting to notice that some of the borders on plates 7 and 9 have only the Castle and pot of ointment, while one in plate 7 has the fleur-de-lis also, evidencing that the former were put up during the King's first married life, the latter during the second

---

JOANNA QUEEN OF NAVARRE

There is yet another Spanish shield to be accounted for, viz *Navarre* (plate 8), and I think we may safely attribute that to Jane, or Joanna, Queen of Navarre, wife of Philip the Fair, brother of Queen Margaret second wife of Edward I, and mother of Isabella, the wife of the Prince of Wales, afterwards Edward II She was the only daughter of Henry I, King of Navarre, by Blanche, daughter of the Earl of Artois, brother of Louis IX (St Louis), who afterwards married Edmond Crouchback, Earl of Lancaster (see page 392), she was, therefore, by birth second cousin to her husband Her only brother, Thibault, was killed when quite a child by an accident, 1273 His governor and nurse were amusing him by tossing him backwards and forwards, when he slipped through the hands of the former, and falling over the balcony was killed on the spot The horrified governor at once stabbed himself, and fell dead upon his body His bereaved father immediately proclaimed Joanna hereditary queen, in order to avoid any contention about the Salique law, and dying soon after, urged his widow to marry her as soon as possible to one of the French princes This she proceeded to carry out without delay, and as soon as possible removed

* Cussan's *Heraldry*

with her to the court of Philip III., where they were generously received, the child carefully educated, and in due time married to the Dauphin, afterwards Philip IV.*

Miss Sewell, in her *Popular History of France*, p. 132, says: "His "evil tendencies were aggravated by those of his wife Jeanne of Navarre, "who was as vindictive and cruel as himself." If so, that would account for the character of their daughter, Queen Isabella, who has been called, and not unjustly, "the she-wolf of France;" but as far as I can see, history does not bear this out. Her husband was prodigal in his testimony of esteem for his wife, in whom he had great confidence. He not only, when King, increased her territories of Brie and Champagne in 1288, but a few years later, when attacked by a dangerous malady, made a will in which he declared her the guardian of his children, and regent of the kingdom as long as she should remain a widow. She was herself highly cultured, and an enthusiastic patroness of the fine arts. She founded the celebrated college of Navarre, at Paris, and munificently remunerated the professors whom she established in it. She also built the town of Puente-la-Regna, in Navarre, an almshouse at Chateau Thierry, and several other places of public utility. Perhaps, like her fellow-mortals of all ages and stations, she was liable to gusts of temper, and failed always to control them in public; one instance at least of which is recorded. In 1300, when Philip had succeeded in his projects against Guy, Count of Flanders, by pouring an army into Flanders and compelling him to surrender himself as prisoner, he made a progress through the chief towns of the province, attended by a brilliant court. The Flemings, glad to be delivered from their late unpopular lord, welcomed them with festivities, at one of which, at Bruges, the ladies of the nobility and municipality appeared radiant with gay clothing and jewels; perhaps they eclipsed Her Majesty and her surroundings, for she somewhat tartly exclaimed: "I thought that I was the only queen here, but I find myself "surrounded by queens!"

By the wish of Philip III. she retained the government of Navarre, in which she shewed both energy and wisdom; for soon after her marriage she succeeded in expelling the Aragonese and Castilians from that kingdom, and established sub-governors to act under her directions both there and in Champagne; and when in 1297 the Count of Bar made an irruption into Champagne, she placed herself at the head of her troops, and marching to the attack, took the Count prisoner, and conveyed him in triumph to Paris. Judging from outward appearances her domestic life could not have been very happy, as Philip must have been a singularly overbearing and disagreeable person indeed. Dante calls him "the

* *Queens of France*, Mrs. Forbes Bush.

"pest of France." His interference with all classes at home was a source of constant annoyance. He aggravated the nobility by raising Ralph, his goldsmith, to their ranks, and allowing any persons, however low their condition, to purchase fiefs whereby they became barons. He exasperated his subjects, generally, by sumptuary laws regulating the number of dresses they were to have, and the expense of each dress. He settled how many dishes might be had for dinner and supper: one dish of soup and two dishes of meat being allowed for dinner at half-past eleven, and for supper between four and five o'clock in the afternoon; and when he found that they evaded the law by putting several kinds of meat into the same dish, he made a special law forbidding it.

In 1292 he took advantage of Edward being engaged with his wars in Scotland, to pick a quarrel with him on account of a disturbance between the French and English fishermen at Bayonne, and cited him as Duke of Aquitaine to appear before him. Edward sent his brother, Edmond Crouchback, to make a temporary arrangement until he was at liberty to attend to it. Philip insisted that Guienne should be given up to him in pledge for this, and then, having obtained it, pronounced the King contumacious, and declared all his fiefs in France forfeited. Of course war was proclaimed in 1294; but after some time, as no decisive advantage had been gained on either side, Pope Boniface made efforts for peace, and he was at length permitted to arbitrate in his private capacity, his decision being that each monarch should retain his possessions, and restore the ships and merchandise which had been seized during the war. He also proposed, as a guarantee for future peace, that Edward should marry the Princess Marguerite, Philip's sister, and the young Prince of Wales be affianced to Philip's little daughter, Isabel, then six years old.

In 1302 he quarrelled with Pope Boniface, threw his legate, Bernard de Saisset, Bishop of Pamiers, into prison, and ordered a bull issued by His Holiness to be publicly burned; then, summoning the States General, composed of the clergy, nobles, and deputies of the Commons, or *tiers etat*, he promulgated a stern defiance of the authority of the Pope. On this the Pope excommunicated him. Philip rejoined by accusing him of scandalous crimes. Boniface retaliated with a bull deposing him from his throne, and retired to Anagni, his native town, for rest during the heat of summer. Philip instigated William de Nogaret, a professor of civil law, and Sciarra Colonna, to make a rapid journey to Italy, raise an uproar at Anagni, storm the palace, and set fire to the church, where, on forcing an entrance, they found the unhappy old man awaiting the approach of his foes, seated on his throne, with the keys of St. Peter in one hand, and the cross in the other. Seizing him, they set him on a vicious horse, with his face to the tail, conveyed him to the common prison, and plundered his palace. In two days the people rose in his defence, rescued him, and led him back to his desolate home, while the people of Rome sent 400 horsemen to conduct him to the Vatican; but fear and mortification had crushed his bodily and mental strength, and he died about a month after, October 11th, 1303.

Philip now exerted himself to secure a successor who would be entirely subject to him; and having selected Bertrand de Goth, Bishop of Bordeaux, pledged him with six stipulations, five of which were specified, and the following year (1305) he was raised to the papal chair as Clement V. Queen Jane did not live to witness the fulfilment of the last mysterious pledge, for she died that same year at the Chateau de Vincennes, leaving, besides her daughter, then Queen of England, three sons, who were successively kings of France and kings of Navarre—Louis X., Philip V., and Charles IV. However, the time soon arrived when the last pledge was declared; and, soon after his accession, Clement summoned the grand masters of the military orders before him. The head of the Hospitallers refused, being already strongly posted in Rhodes. Jacques du Molay, the Grandmaster of the Templars, obeyed.

The sequel is well known to all readers of history. No doubt, now that the Crusades were over, the Templars had done their work. No doubt, that the sarcasm of Richard Cœur de Lion on his death-bed was true: "I leave my avarice to the monks of Citeaux, my luxury to the "Grey monks, my pride to the Templars." But pride, avarice, luxury, and immorality, would have had little weight with Philip. They had refused him admittance to their Order,—lent him money which he could not pay,—they were rich, and an easy prey. Every foul accusation which could be conceived was invented against them; every devilish device which could betray and convict them was practised. Du Molay, for the time, pleaded guilty, and was spared; the remainder, to some hundreds, were burnt or beheaded, and the Order dissolved. Then the conscience of the Grandmaster was touched, and protesting the innocence of his brethren, he bewailed and condemned his own cowardice and treachery. Without a day's delay, on March 20th, 1314, he was burnt to death on a little island in the Seine, in the very presence of Philip. The wood was wet, but from out the stifling smoke and sputtering flame came a voice, which said: "I call on thee, Clement, Pope of Rome, I call on thee, "Philip, King of France and Navarre, to appear, the one within forty days, "the other in less than a year, before the judgment-seat of God to answer "for the crimes done to me and my brethren."

On the 20th of April the Pope expired; on the 4th of November Philip was killed by a fall from his horse when hunting in the forest of Fontainebleau.

PLATE 9

BLANCHE OF CASTILE.
EDMOND OF WOODSTOCK.
EDWARD III.
BLACK PRINCE.
MORTIMER.
WAKE.

His three brothers, Louis X., Philip V., and Charles IV., reigned in succession. On the death of the youngest without male issue, Joanne, daughter of Louis X., and wife of Philip Count of Evreux, was crowned Queen of Navarre at Pamplona, in 1329. Her great granddaughter Blanche, was married, first to Martin of Sicily, and afterwards to John, son of Ferdinand of Aragon. The latter, after her death, made himself King of Navarre, with the title of John II. He was followed, 1479, by his daughter Eleanor, the wife of Gaston de Foix. After her death, Francis Phœbus, her grandson, was crowned, 1482. His sister Catherine, wife of Jean D'Albret, succeeded, 1483. The latter having fallen under the papal ban, Ferdinand the Catholic, 1512, seized the whole of what is now Spanish Navarre. The small portion on the French side of the Pyrenees being retained by Henry II., son of D'Albret, 1516. His grandson, Henry III. of Navarre, became Henry IV. King of France, 1589, and united non-Spanish Navarre to the French crown, 1607.

Blanche of Castile.

As regards this shield, it has been not a little difficult to arrive at any satisfactory explanation of the dolphins being quartered with the castles, and I know of no similar shield. I venture to identify it as belonging to Margaret, *the second wife* of Edward I., and to offer the following as a solution. The territory known as Dauphiné, formed, originally, part of the Regnum Provinciæ of the Roman Emperor, which, in the ninth century, was separated into two distinct kingdoms, that of Provence to the south, with Arles as its capital; and that of Vienne to the north, with Vienne as its capital. In the ninth and two succeeding centuries, the latter became broken up into principalities, the most important of which were the Lords of Albon, a little to the south of Vienne. First, they assumed the title of Counts of Vienne; afterwards, Dauphins, and their possessions were called Dauphiné. Why they chose this *sobriquet* I cannot discover, and can only conjecture. Heraldry had not then been established. I can only, therefore, assume that it had a Roman origin, for Tacitus speaks of "Vienna" as "Ornatissima ecce "Colonia valentissimaque Viennensium;" and Martial says of it:

> "Fertur habere meos, si vera est fama, libellos
> Inter delicias Pulchra Vienna suas."

It was, therefore, a city of culture, poetry, and song, the known characteristics of that region; and perhaps, therefore, associated with the fabled Arion: a famous lyric poet of Lesbos, and musician, who is said to have gone into Italy and made immense riches by his profession;

and, on his return to his country, to have been cast into the sea by the sailors of the ship, and saved from a watery grave by a dolphin, which, captivated by his music, bore him safely to Tænarus. Such a tradition, if Arion were associated with Vienne, would be sufficient to obtain for the country the name of Dauphiné, and for its ruler to assume the title of Dauphin.

In course of time Charles VIII., Dauphin of Vienne, had by his wife Margaret, daughter of Stephen Earl of Burgundy, a son and two daughters. The former succeeded as Guy IX. One of the latter, Beatrix, married the Count d'Auvergne, a tract of country on the opposite (*i.e.* western) bank of the Rhone. They had a son, who assumed the title of Dauphin through his mother, and from his time his successors holding the same petty canton of Auvergne, styled themselves Dauphins of Auvergne, and bore a dolphin in their arms. Henceforth there were two Dauphins, viz., of Vienne and of Auvergne. The latter territory being within the borders of Aquitaine, the Dauphin of Auvergne would simply hold his territory in fief from the Duke thereof.

In the year 1200 a treaty was concluded between John King of England and Philip King of France, in which it was agreed that Prince Louis, his eldest son, should marry Blanche, daughter of Alonzo King of Castile, and Eleanor, daughter of Henry II. of England and Eleanor the heiress of Aquitaine. John stipulating to give to his niece the province of Auvergne, which had long been contested between the crowns, together with a portion of 30,000 marks of silver. The Queen Dowager of England, Eleanor, heiress of Aquitaine, who, on resigning the vice-regency of England into the hands of King John, had retired to pass the close of her long life—now eighty years of age—in Aquitaine, journeyed from Mirabel in Poitou, to Valladolid, the palace of the Kings of Castile, and accompanied the French ambassadors with her granddaughter from thence to Normandy, where the wedding took place; and thus by her presence indicated her sanction of the cession of part of her patrimony for this purpose.* The armorial bearings of the bride would, therefore, naturally be the castle of Castile and the dolphin of Auvergne; but the title of Dauphin would become absorbed in her titles as Queen of France. Her husband, Louis VIII., died in 1226, leaving her with one son, who succeeded as Louis IX. Owing to the sterling good sense, courage, tact, and piety of his mother, he found, on attaining his majority, his kingdom uninjured by the intestine intrigues, plots, and insurrections of his minority, and, through her training and influence, acquired, by his life amongst his people, the *sobriquet* of "St. Louis."

* Green's *Lives of Princesses*, vol. i., p. 28.

When, therefore, Margaret, his granddaughter, married Edward I as his second wife, she would be entitled to bear not only the lilies of France, but also the arms of Castile and Auvergne, and, therefore, according to the practice then first coming into vogue, the latter are quartered on one shield

The window in which these arms are emblazoned (nave, south aisle fourth west), was probably erected by Archdeacon de Mauley (see page 103), and his object in inserting the three royal shields therein would be to compliment the King and his second wife, and therefore, for the former, he placed the lions of the Plantagenet, for the latter, two shields, one bearing the lilies of France, the other the arms of Blanche of Castile, and he did this, probably, because he felt that the Queen would appreciate such a recognition of her illustrious descent, not only from the kings of France, but also from the royal family of Spain The latter would be specially agreeable to her First, because commemorating one who had been so great a benefactress to her country and her dynasty, and whose name was still treasured with affection and reverence, not only by her descendants, but also by the people of France Secondly, because shewing that she (Queen Margaret) also had a Spanish descent, even higher than her predecessor Eleanor of Castile, as descended from the elder branch, for Blanche of Castile became eventually *de jure* heiress of the throne, her brother, King Henry, being killed by the fall of a tile from the roof of his palace, 1217, leaving no issue, though her younger sister Berengaria, wife of the King of Leon, was chosen queen because Blanche had married a foreigner

Queen Margaret, "the flower of France," was not unknown in Yorkshire during her residence in England It was on a hunting excursion from Cawood that she was compelled to tarry at Brotherton, where her first-born, Thomas, afterwards Duke of Norfolk, the progenitor of the house of Howard, was born She seems to have filled the office of peacemaker between the King and his foolish son Edward Prince of Wales, afterwards Edward II, one while, and then in behalf of Godfrey de Coigners, who had dared to make the gold crown for Robert Bruce, and again in behalf of the citizens of Winchester for allowing Bernard Pereres to escape Edward I, when dying, commanded his son to be kind to his little brothers Thomas and Edward, and, above all, to treat with respect and tenderness their mother, Queen Margaret She was present at Edward II's marriage with her niece Isabella, and at the birth of Edward III, soon after which she passed away peacefully at her residence, Marlborough Castle, and her body was laid in the church of the Grey Friars, London, which she had founded, now the site of Christ's Hospital Her best epitaph are the words of the old chronicler Piers Langtoft "Good withouten lack"

The sequel of the other Dauphinate of Vienne is soon told. In 1281 the Burgundian line dying out, the lordship passed to the house of "La Tour de Pin," which, in the person of Guiges VIII., was offered royal dignity by Louis the Bavarian. Guiges' successor, Hubert II., having lost his son, 1335, made over his lands to Charles of Valois, stipulating that the independence and privilege thereof should be maintained, and, in order that the title should not become extinct like the other, that the eldest son of the King of France should always bear the title of Dauphin.

Edmond Crouchback, Earl of Lancaster.

Edmond Crouchback, Earl of Lancaster (plate 7), was the second son of Henry III. and Eleanor of Provence, and therefore *younger brother* of Edward I. There is a legend that he acquired that *sobriquet* from his deformity, and that in consequence, though he was the eldest son, his brother Edward was in infancy preferred to his place. This is very unlikely, as there was a difference of six years between the births of the two children, so that the eldest son was already beyond the age of infancy, and must have been well known to all the Court. The term "Crouch-back" more probably indicated his wearing a crouch or cross on his back, in token of a vow made for him or by him, that he should go to Jerusalem. He was brought up at Windsor with his sister Beatrice, afterwards married to John of Bretagne. Four ladies in waiting, four sergeants-at-arms, a clerk, cook, washerwomen, seven valets, and five chaplains, forming their establishment, under the control of the constable of the castle. It is also mentioned in the rolls that wine and venison, with oaks for firewood from the forest, were supplied for their use, together with twenty-four silver spoons and twelve salt-cellars; and that a special order was given to the forester that Prince Edmond shall be permitted to hunt as often as he pleases in the forest, and carry away whatever he pleases.

In 1255, the Pope took the opportunity of the death of the Emperor Frederick II. to offer the crown of Sicily to Richard Earl of Cornwall; and on his discreet refusal, he offered it to Henry III. for his second son Edmond. Henry and Eleanor, delighted at the prospect of this acquisition of dignity for their family, immediately ordered a seal to be made, with the young prince enthroned, and crowned with the diadem of Sicily, bearing the orb and sceptre in his hands. But troubles with Scotland prevented their completing the acceptance by force of arms. Manfred, natural son of the Emperor, usurped the throne, and Henry contented himself with presenting his son in his royal robes at the opening of his parliament, and commending him to their liberality in these words —"Behold here, good people, my son Edmond, whom God in His gracious "goodness hath called to the excellency of kingly dignity How comely "and well worthy he is of all your favour, and how cruel and tyrannical "must they be who, at this pinch, would deny him effectual and season-"able help both with money and advice" *

In 1269, he assisted the King his father, Edward Prince of Wales, and the King of the Romans, to bear the bier of Edward the Confessor, and place it in St Edward's Chapel, the *chef-d'œuvre* of Gothic architecture in Westminster Abbey, which Henry III had been fifty years in building, and which was then completed

At the age of nineteen he was created Earl of Leicester, on the death of Simon de Montford at the battle of Evesham, and two years after, Earl of Lancaster, when Robert de Ferrers forfeited his titles and estates

In 1259 he is mentioned as meeting his sister Margaret, Queen of Scotland, at St Albans, on her way to London He seems at least to have made an effort to fulfil his vow, as he is mentioned, A D 1270, as arriving at Tunis with his brother, Edward Prince of Wales, and his wife, Eleanor of Castile, but only to find that St Louis King of France had died there shortly before, and that a truce for ten years had been made with the Saracens Edward endeavoured to rouse the French to proceed "But, my dearest lords," he urged, "have we not come here to destroy "the enemies of the Cross of Christ, not to compound with them? Far "be this from us Let us on,—the land is open before us,—and proceed "even to the holy city Jerusalem" But in vain the French pleaded the obligation of the truce, so they retired to Messina, where they were entertained by the King, Charles of Anjou, who had defeated Manfred at the battle of Benevento and established himself in his place, and whose wife, Beatrice of Provence, was sister to Queen Eleanor of England The following year they proceeded to Acre, where Edward was stabbed by the assassin whom he slew with a camp-stool After some days the surgeon, brought by the Master of the Temple, recommended incisions in the arm, which shewed unfavourable symptoms At which Eleanor lost her presence of mind, and bursting into tears, was unceremoniously carried out of the room by Edmond and John de Vesci, the former blandly remarking that it was better that she should scream and cry than all England mourn and lament After several unimportant skirmishes a truce for ten years, seven weeks, and ten days, was made, and in August 1272, Prince Edmond returned home On the eve of his departure for the Holy Land, however, he had been married—8th April, 1270—to Aveline, heiress of William de

---

* Matthew Paris

Fortibus, Earl of Albemarle, who died before his return. Her great-great-grandfather, William le Gros, Earl of Albemarle and Lord of Holderness, who died 1178, had married the only daughter of William Fitz-Duncan and Alice de Romille,—Cicely, who became heiress of the castle and honour of Skipton on the death of her brother William, drowned in endeavouring to leap over "the Strid" in the woods between Bolton and Barden. Wordsworth has immortalized the incident in his beautiful poem *The Force of Prayer;* and probably most of my readers have themselves recognized in the picturesque ruins of Bolton Abbey, how fully the agonized mother's charge was carried out—

> "Let there be
> In Bolton, on the field of Wharfe,
> A stately priory."

The wardship of Aveline, during her minority, had been granted by Henry III. to his eldest son, who, for the sum of £1,500, assigned the castle and barony of Skipton to Alexander King of Scotland, who married his sister Margaret. On the death of Alexander, 1286, it was granted, I conclude, to Crouchback, and, on his death, 1296, reverted to the King. Edward II. bestowed it on Peirs de Gaveston, and on his death to Robert de Clifford, in whose family it remained for 500 years. The death of Aveline, the young wife of the Duke of Lancaster, was almost immediately followed by the death of the King of the Romans, which so affected Henry III. that he sickened and died, Nov. 16th, 1272, committing England to the charge of Gilbert de Clare until the return of the Prince of Wales. Edmond is mentioned in the Cotton MS. as present at the coronation of Edward and Eleanor, and four years after he married for his second wife Blanche Queen of Navarre, daughter of Robert Earl of Artois, slain at the battle of Courtrai against the Flemings, 1302, brother to St. Louis King of France. Her daughter by her first marriage, Joane, married Philip the Fair, whose sister Margaret was the second wife of Edward I. This was a grand marriage, and in deference, I suppose, to his wife being a crowned head, he enriched his label with nine *fleurs-de-lys* from the shield of Artois.

Eleanor of Castile died October 28th, 1290, at Hardeby, near Grantham, and for some seven years Edward I. remained a forlorn and disconsolate widower. In 1294, however, he became violently smitten with Blanche, the daughter of St. Louis, and agreed with her brother, Philip the Fair, to give up the south-western portion of Aquitaine, his mother's inheritance, as a settlement on any posterity which he might have by her. But when he had completed the surrender of the province, Philip refused either to give his sister or restore it. Edmond, who seems to have been at the French Court negotiating the alliance, writes to his brother in great indignation, declaring that Philip had come into his chamber, and promised, on the faith of loyal kings, that all things should be as he supposed On this he had sent Master John de Lacy to Gascony, to render up to the people of the King of France the seizin of the land as afore agreed, and the King had sent the Constable of France to receive it, and that when the King withdrew his sister Blanche, the two Queens of France and Navarre had prayed him to give safe conduct to the King of England to come and receive back his land, and he had assured them of his intention, to do so Nevertheless, at the Council he had told them that he never meant to restore the territory Edmond concludes, however, by suggesting that the way out of the difficulty would probably be for him to take her younger sister Margaret instead However, Edward was not a man likely to submit tamely to such double-dealing, and a fierce war ensued, which lasted four years, at the end of which time they agreed to refer the matter to the Pope, who decided that Edward should give up Guienne or Gascony, and take Margaret, with the £1,500 left her by her father, and Peirs Langtoft indicates that he got the best of the bargain

> "Not dame Blanche the sweet,
> Of whom I now spake,
> But dame Marguerite,
> Good withouten lack"

And the marriage eventually took place at Canterbury, September 8th, 1299

Edmond Crouchback's eldest son, Thomas, had, in the meantime, made a great marriage with Alice, daughter and heir of Henry de Lacy, Earl of Lincoln, by Margaret, daughter and heir of William Longespée, Earl of Salisbury, but there was no issue of the marriage, and she proved a most profligate and abandoned character So, as his male line threatened to become extinct, he surrendered his estates to the King, on which a new grant was made of them to him 25th October, 1294, for life, with remainder to Edmond Crouchback, Earl of Lancaster, and the heirs of his body

In 1296, Edmond Crouchback went in command of an army into Gascony, and died at Bayonne, his body being brought to England and buried on the north side of the altar in Westminster Abbey, near to the body of his first wife, Aveline de Fortibus His tomb, surmounted with a triple canopy over a finely sculptured effigy of the Earl in chain armour, still remains, one of the largest and most elaborate in the building

The great estates and honours then passed to his son Thomas, who was condemned to death by Edward II in his own castle, at Pontefract, for having honestly endeavoured to carry out the injunction of the King's father As he had no children they passed to his brother Henry, whose daughter Blanche married John of Gaunt, who *jure uxoris* became Duke of Lancaster, and from whom our present Queen is descended, and thus inherits *the Duchy of Lancaster.*

Edmond Crouchback seems to have been a man of most winning and affectionate disposition. Evidently his father's favourite, he excited no jealousy in the heart of the noble Edward, his brother, "the greatest "of the Plantagenets." His earliest description among the records is that of "Edmond, the King's son," which, on the death of Henry and the accession of Edward I., was changed into "Edmond, the King's brother:" the same love, the same affection, continuing even to the end.

Next in chronological order in south-east window of chapter-house (see coloured illustration, plate 7) is the shield of

JOHN OF ELTHAM, EARL OF CORNWALL.

The life of John of Eltham was short but eventful. He was the second son of Edward II., born at the King's manor-house, Eltham, 1315, during the only happy period of the married life of Edward and Isabella, which lasted from the execution of Gaveston in 1312, to 1323, when the unhappy influence which the Despencers were exercising over Edward caused the final and fatal estrangement between man and wife. During those eleven years all their children were born: Edward, 1312; Eleanor, afterwards Duchess of Guildres, 1318; Joane de la Tour, 1322. The birth of the Prince of Wales had been the King's solace when smarting under the death of Gaveston. The birth of John happened as opportunely; for Edward, anxious to retrieve Bannockburn, had been again discomfited in his efforts against the Scotch, both by sea and land, by the vigour and courage of the Black Douglas. Edward had almost succeeded in landing his armaments at Dunybristle, but Sinclair, Bishop of Dunkeld, at the head of sixty of his servants, with only his rochet over his armour, rallied his panic-stricken countrymen, and seizing a spear from the nearest soldier, and crying "Turn, turn for shame, and let all who love Scotland "follow me!" headed the charge, and drove the English back to their ships with the loss of 500 men. Indeed, by an opportune diversion, Douglas had nearly captured the Queen, who had accompanied her lord as far as Brotherton. With 10,000 men he had almost arrived at the village, when one of his scouts fell into the hands of the Archbishop of York, and being forced by threats of torture to confess, the Queen had just time to escape to York, and from thence return to the south, where, shortly afterwards, her son John was born. The gratification of the King may be gathered from this entry in his household book: "To Sir Eubulo de Montibus for "bringing the first news to the King of the happy delivery of Queen "Isabella of her son John of Eltham, £100." The castle and honour of the peak, with the chase and appurtenances, amounting in annual value to £1,000, were assigned for the support of Prince John and his younger sister Eleanor, but they seem to have spent their childhood at the castle of Pleshy, in Essex, and Marlborough Castle, until 1325, by which time the renewed dissensions between the King and Queen had culminated in an open rupture.

The terrible scenes which followed of domestic dissension, impurity, violence, and murder, shadowed the young life of John of Eltham, brightened only by his brother's coronation at Westminster, at which his presence is mentioned, and brilliant marriage of true affection to Philippa of Hainault, in York Minster, where no doubt he was one of the brightest and comeliest of all that festive throng. But brighter days, which seemed dawning, were soon shadowed again, and the end speedily came. The King, his brother, in token of affection and confidence, created him Earl of Cornwall in the second year of his reign, and the following year appointed him custos of the kingdom, during his absence in France. Then two several efforts were made to arrange a brilliant marriage for him: first, with Joane, daughter of Ralph Earl of Eu, the year following with Mary, daughter of the Count of Blois, but for some reason neither were consummated. At last, in 1334, he was engaged to Mary, daughter of Ferdinand of Spain, Count of Lara, but the alliance had scarcely been formally settled in August, when, in October, "he deceased," says Sandford, "at St John's Town, the most remote part of Scotland," under what circumstances I cannot satisfactorily ascertain. Holinshed states that he accompanied his brother in his expedition to Scotland in 1233, which commenced with the siege and capture of Berwick, and culminated in the victorious battle of Hallidon Hill, over the forces of the Douglas. Perhaps he was mortally wounded in some one of the encounters or skirmishes which took place, at any rate he never returned alive.

Holinshed adds: "The Scottish writers affirm that he was slain by "his brother King Edward for the crueltie he had used in the West part "of Scotland, in sleaing such as for safeguard of their lives fled into "churches." This absolutely unsupported assertion from a hostile source is very improbable. Such a tragic episode could scarcely have taken place without being recorded in history, nor would such a character have been honoured by so sacred and honourable a sepulture. For his body was brought to Westminster Abbey, and there interred in St Edmund's Chapel. The stately monument reared over it still remains, deprived of its beautiful triple canopy, broken down in 1776, and removed by Dean Pearce, and many of the alabaster statuettes have been hopelessly mutilated, but the strong oaken screen preserved those on the south side from Puritan violence, and visitors who have the curiosity to peep between its solid stanchions may still see the figures of his murdered father, his wretched mother, and other members of his family. His own figure, also, still lies uninjured on the tomb; the feet rest on a lion, two angels support the head cushions, the coronet which encircles the helmet, with its alternate small and large trefoil leaves, is the earliest known example of the ducal coronet. The recumbent effigy is clad in armour; on the left arm is the shield, still decorated with his cognizance of the lions of England, with the bordure of France, in honour of his mother Isabel, and the calm, peaceful, noble face seems to indicate a character of gallant and kindly qualities—the "preux chevalier sans peur et sans reproche."

In the third east window, south isle of the nave (see coloured illustration, plate 9), and in stone on the north side of the choir, we find the shield of Edmond of Woodstock, Earl of Kent.

Edmond of Woodstock, Earl of Kent.

Edmond of Woodstock, Earl of Kent, was *the second son* of Edward I. by his second wife, Margaret of France, born at the Royal Palace, Woodstock, August 5th, 1301, when the King was, as usual, engaged in carrying on war in Scotland, and his nun-daughter, Mary, came from her cloister to bear her stepmother company at such a critical period. His lot was also cast amidst the conflicting and exasperating influence of the family quarrel, which disturbed his life and entailed on him an early and violent death. When only six years old, viz., 1307, his father died, and ten years after, his mother, leaving him and his elder brother, Thomas of Brotherton, executors of her will. In 1321 he was created Earl of Kent, *per cincturam gladii*, by his half-brother, Edward II., and about this time he married Margaret, daughter of John Lord Wake. So far so good; but about the same time the dissensions between his half-brother and his wife commenced, and he, not unnaturally, perhaps, sided with the latter. In fact, all the Plantagenets, at first, seem to have taken her side. To him, the ties of relationship to both were strong, but Isabella was his first cousin in whole blood, being the daughter of his mother's brother, Philip le Bel, King of France. His brother Thomas of Brotherton and his cousin Henry of Lancaster, sympathised with him. Immediately after the deposition of Edward II. and the coronation of his son, a Council of Regency was appointed, of which Thomas of Brotherton and Edmond of Woodstock, were members, under the presidency of Henry of Lancaster. The Queen made no objection, for practically they were powerless, as, having military power in her hands, she acted arbitrarily, with Mortimer, now Earl of March, as her prime minister, and Adam Orleton as her principal counsellor.*

* Walsingham.

In 1328, however, Isabella, accompanied by Mortimer, attended the marriage of her daughter Joanna, aged five years, to David Bruce, aged seven, at Berwick, but neither of the late King's brothers nor the Earl of Lancaster attended In fact an estrangement had already begun, and Mortimer's high-handed and outrageous conduct, as well as the heartless and unscrupulous manner in which Isabella made all the interests of the young King subservient to the caprices and ambition of her paramour, had roused their indignation Henry of Lancaster had already taken up arms, and put forth a manifesto calling for an enquiry into the late King's death, and her grasping rapacity Edmond of Woodstock, equally prompt in action though less cautious, was more easily disposed of He had had a real affection for his unfortunate brother, and was tormented now with remorse as to the part which he had taken towards him It was known that for some time he had been confined in Corfe Castle, and the confident belief of the neighbourhood was that he had never been removed from thence, and that the story of his murder at Berkeley Castle was a fiction Mortimer and the Queen caused a report to be circulated that he was still alive there, and masques and shows took place there, as though for the diversion of some great prince or king Edmond employed a friar to make enquiries as to the truth of this on the spot, who, having obtained admission to the castle, was shewn, at a distance, a person in the great hall, sitting at table, clothed in royal habiliments, with princely attendants, whose air and figure greatly resembled those of the late King, and he reported accordingly

The Earl of Kent fell into the trap thus cunningly laid for him, and being at Avignon consulted Pope John XXII upon this, who at once commanded him to help with all his power to deliver his brother out of prison On his return to England, without further enquiry or delay, he rode to Corfe Castle, and demanded of the governor, Sir John Daveril, to be conducted to the apartment of Sir Edward of Carnarvon, his brother The governor did not deny that he was there, but pleaded his inability to allow anyone to see him However, after many rich presents, he consented to deliver a letter which the Earl had brought for him, in which he stated that "I have unto me assenting all the great "men of England with all their apparrell (*i e* with armour) and treasure "exceeding much, for to maintain and help your quarrel so far forth that "you shall be king again as you were before, and hereto they have all "sworn to me upon a book, as well prelates as earls and barons" This was, of course, immediately conveyed to Isabella, and the Earl was at once arrested at Winchester, where the parliament was then assembled, and arraigned on the charge of high treason before the peers His own letter was the chief evidence against him, but he frankly confessed that a certain friar in London told him that he had conjured up a spirit, which assured him that his brother was still alive, and that Sir Ingram Berenger brought him a letter from the Lord Zouche requesting his assistance in the restoration of the late sovereign.

"On the morrow after the Feast of St. Gregory" he was arrested; on Sunday, March 13th, he was arraigned, and condemned to die on the morrow. "All that day," say the chroniclers, "the King was so beset by "his mother and the Earl of March that it was impossible for him to "make any effort to preserve his uncle from the cruel fate to which he "had been so unjustly doomed." And such was the feeling of the people, that the executioner himself stole secretly away, and the Earl of Kent had to wait upon the scaffold at Winchester Castle gate from noon till five in the evening, because no one could be induced to perform the office. At length, a condemned felon from the Marshalsea obtained his pardon on the condition of decapitating the unfortunate prince. His body was buried in the city, in the church of the Black Friars or Dominicans, who, together with two of the other mendicant orders, were accused of being accessory to the conspiracy, and with difficulty escaped punishment.

Væ victis. This is now a dry historical statement, yet who can read it without a thought of sympathy for the protracted suspense of that weary waiting, or the agony of the bereaved young wife and orphan children. The natures of those days were perhaps less keenly sensitive than ours, but such seasons must have been times of bitter anguish, which we, at least, are happily spared.

The Earl of Kent left two sons, Edmond and John, who each succeeded him, and died without issue, and one daughter, Joane, known as "the Fair Maid of Kent." During the lifetime of her first husband, Sir John Holland, her arms—gules three lions passant guardant or within a bordure argent—were impaled with the arms of Holland. On her brother's death, her husband was created Earl of Kent. Her two sons, Thomas, Duke of Kent, and John, Duke of Exeter, by the express wish of their half-brother, Richard II., carried the arms of France and England quarterly, impaling the arms of Edward the Confessor, and within a bordure, in the former instance argent, in the latter azure *semée-de-lys.* Her granddaughter Margaret, daughter of Thomas Earl of Kent, married Thomas Duke of Clarence, and her arms, the lions of England, with the white bordure, appear for the last time, impaled with his. Sandford says—"We have three examples of this particular bordure "being adopted as a difference by members of the Royal Family: first, "Edmond Earl of Kent; second, Thomas of Woodstock, Duke of Gloucester, "youngest son of Edward III.; and third, Humphrey, also Duke of Glou-"cester, youngest son of Henry IV.; which three princes being sent out of

PLATE 10.

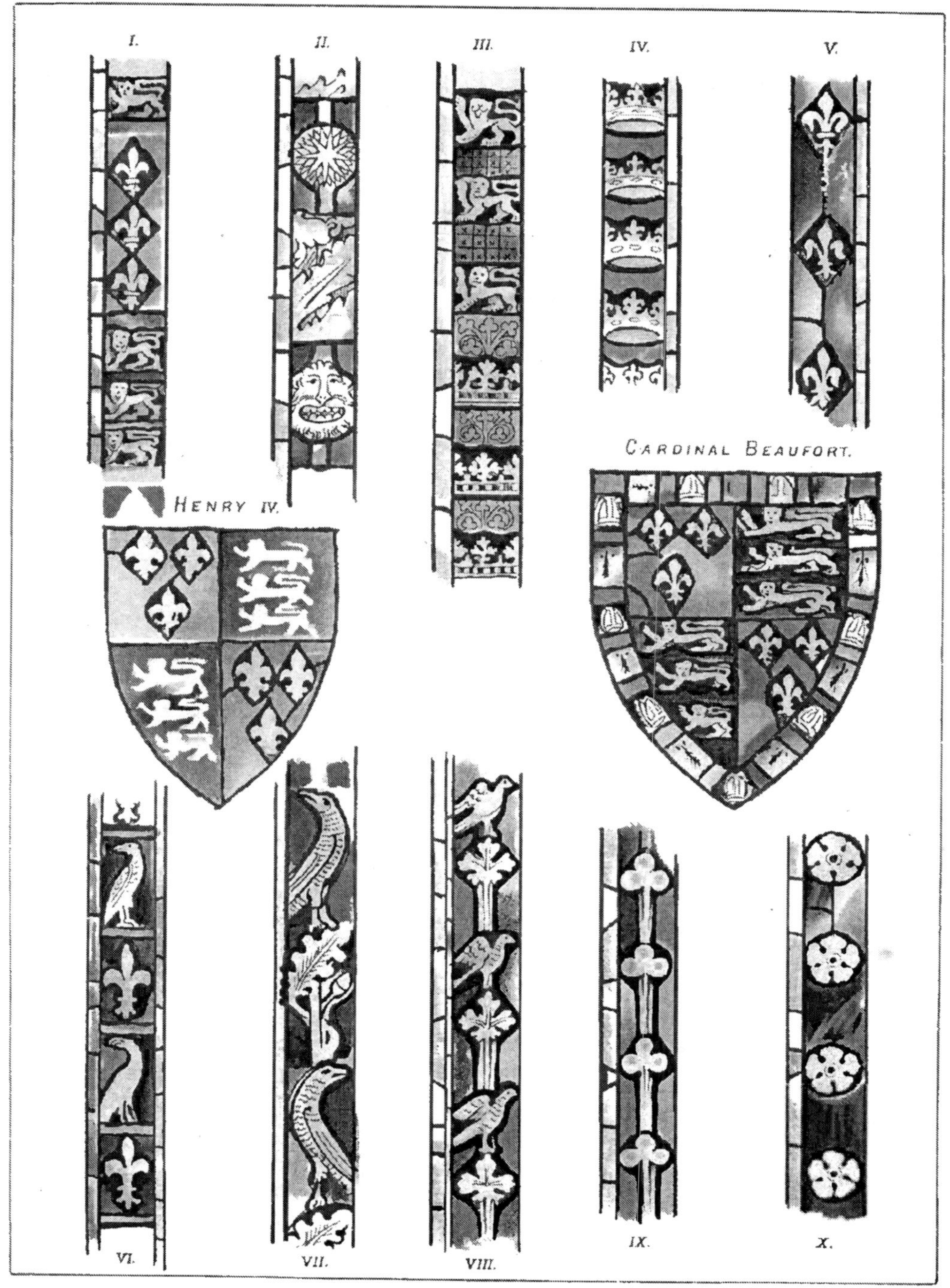

"the world by violent deaths (Edmond being beheaded, Thomas smothered, "and Humphrey poisoned) we will not positively aver was the reason why "the use of this bordure was declined by the youngest sons of our suc- "ceeding kings, but it is most certain that we find it not since about "any of their escutcheons"

There are no armorial bearings distinctive of Edward II, but it is probable that the figures, from the border of the first window east, in the north aisle of the nave, represented on the coloured illustration, plate 8, are intended for him and his wife Isabella, as this window was erected by Peter de Dene, his tutor, and the courtly ecclesiastic of that day This is very probable In the borders of the windows in the nave, viz 7 iii, we find the lions of England and the lilies of France, probably with reference to this alliance, and also 10 iii and iv, the triple coronets illustrative of the threefold sovereignty expressed on the great seal of Edward I and II —

"Rex Angliæ, Dominus Hiberniæ, Dux Aquitaniæ"

On entering the choir, we find in stone, on the north side (plate 9), the arms of Edward III, consisting of—as I have already explained—the lilies of France in the first and fourth quarters, the lions of Plantagenet second and third Opposite the same arms, with the white label, the distinction of the Prince of Wales, and, therefore, we may fairly assign them to the Black Prince In the window at the east end of the north choir aisle (plate 10), we have an instance of the first and fourth quartering, reduced from *semée-de-lys* to three *fleurs-de-lys*, which was adopted by Henry IV from Charles V, King of France, who had hoped thereby to make a distinction between the arms of France and England In the south-west spandril of the great tower, also, the same coat may be observed in stone In the borders of the windows we still find the lilies and the lions (plates 7, iv, 10, i), and the badges of the rival factions may be noticed in the second west window of the north aisle (10, x) of the nave, where we have the white rose of York, and the east window of the north aisle of the choir, where we have the sun of York (10, ii) In the rose window of the south transept, and in the mural decorations of the vestibule, we may also observe the red rose of Lancaster

---

CARDINAL BEAUFORT

There remains only one royal shield distinctly connected with the Minster, viz, that of Cardinal Beaufort on the south side of the choir * He

* See coloured illustration

was the second son of John of Gaunt, by Catherine Swinford, eventually his third wife. The match was not very creditable to him, and was "highly disdained," Sandford tells us, "by the Duchess of Gloucester and "Countess of Derby and Arundel, and other ladies of the blood royal."

Catherine was the daughter of Sir Page Roet (*alias* Guyen), king-of-arms, and widow of Sir Ottes Swinford, knight, and had been familiarly acquainted with the Duke of Lancaster in the time of his former wives, being guardianess to his daughters the ladies Philipe and Elizabeth, in their minority. As a recognition of her care in their education, the Duke granted her, by patent dated 27th December, 3 Richard II., the wardship of Bertrand de Sanneby's heir. He calls her—"Our most deare and beloved Dame Catherine Swinford," and three years later granted her an annuity of 700 marks. This was a valuable recompense at those times for such a service; but two years after the death of his second wife, Constance, daughter of Pedro the cruel, viz., 1396, he married her, and acknowledged his four children by her, viz., John, afterwards Earl of Somerset; Henry, of whom more by-and-bye; Thomas, afterwards Duke of Exeter; and Joan, who married, first, Thomas Ferrers, Lord of Wem, and second, Ralph Nevill, first Earl of Westmoreland. The year following he obtained an Act of Parliament by which they were made legitimate, and rendered capable of all ecclesiastical and civil honours and employments, the royal dignity excepted, being called therein Beaufort, from the Duke's castle in Anjou, the place of their birth, which came to the house of Lancaster with Blanche of Artois, Queen of Navarre, wife of Edmond, first Earl of Lancaster. Margaret, the mother of Henry VII., was granddaughter of John Beaufort, Earl of Somerset, the eldest son of Catherine Swynford. Hence the portcullis on the King's tomb at Westminster, the badge of the family, supposed to represent the portcullis of the castle gate at Beaufort, with this motto: "Altera securitas," which, true of the portcullis itself, was the plea, no doubt, of John of Gaunt, in days when the succession to the throne was most important, for legitimatising the children of his illicit intercourse.

Henry de Beaufort was appointed Prebendary of Thame, 1389; then of Riccall in this Minster, August 22nd, 1390; and next of Sutton, 1391, in Lincoln Cathedral; Dean of Wells, 1397; Chancellor of Oxford, 1397; Bishop of Lincoln, 1398; and he succeeded William of Wykeham as Bishop of Winchester, 1404.

Shakespeare, in his two plays of *Henry VI.*, has given us anything but an agreeable representation of his character, and a terrible account of his death, which Lord Campbell, in his *Lives of the Chancellors*, defends. Subsequent examination, however, of contemporary records has shewn this to be in a great measure exaggerated and without foundation; and Bishop

Stubbs, in his admirable *Constitutional History of England*, has, from them, traced an entirely different, and, I venture to think, far more accurate, character of him

During the reign of his half-brother, Henry IV, he seems to have lived on most intimate and affectionate terms with him, the fact that four years after his accession the King made him chancellor on the resignation of Stratford, 1403, and the year following translated him to Winchester, shews his confidence But he had an active enemy in Archbishop Arundel, who, on succeeding to the chancellorship, managed to introduce into the Act renewing the late King's legitimatising of the Beauforts, the clause "excepta dignitate regali," which was naturally resented by his brothers and himself As time advanced he drew closer to the Prince of Wales, whose tutor he was, and the Prince rewarded his attachment by taking his part when, on the death of Beaufort's brother, John, he declined, as executor, to pay a share of his estate of 30,000 marks to his widow, who had married Thomas of Lancaster

On the death of Henry IV, 1413, Henry V at once made him chancellor in the place of Archbishop Arundel, and Beaufort became to him the confidential friend and adviser which Arundel had been to his father, indeed, Beaufort generously lent him 21,000 marks towards his preparation for his expedition to France, which culminated in Agincourt In 1422 Henry died, significantly cautioning his brother Gloucester against allowing his selfish spirit to clash with the interest of the country His will, unfortunately, was indistinct, as he appointed therein John, his brother, sole guardian, but his intention evidently was that his two brothers, John Earl of Bedford, aged thirty-three, and Humphrey Earl of Gloucester, aged thirty-two, should together be guardians, with the Beauforts to preserve the balance Parliament decided that the elder should take charge of the portion of the kingdom in France, and the younger in England, and, during his brother's absence, be Protector, with a council containing five prelates, of which Beaufort was one The Earl of Bedford trusted the Beauforts, Gloucester was jealous of them and opposed them, and lost no opportunity of shewing it In 1423 the Earl of Bedford made Beaufort chancellor during his brother's absence, during which time the young King Henry first appeared in parliament, and Beaufort in his "opening speech enforced "the good qualities of a counsellor from the wonderful physical fact that "the elephant has no gall, is of inflexible purpose, and of great memory" But Gloucester on his return immediately picked a quarrel with him, on the ground that he had garrisoned the Tower with Lancastrians, and nearly raised a tumult endeavouring to keep him out For two years dissensions continuing, Beaufort resigned the seals in 1426, and absenting himself from the council went eventually to the Holy Land, from whence he returned in 1428, having been made by the Pope, Cardinal Legate. Gloucester immediately took violent umbrage at this, refused to receive him, and called upon him to resign the see of Winchester; but no action was taken thereon.

In 1429 Henry was crowned, first at Westminster, afterwards at Paris, by Beaufort, during which time Gloucester moved his expulsion from the council, and, assisted by a cabal of his own, seized his plate. When the Cardinal returned, he pleaded his justification before Parliament, which was accepted, and his plate, &c., restored, and Gloucester became entangled in a quarrel with his brother. In 1435 Bedford returned to France, and Gloucester immediately renewed his attack on Beaufort, which was aggravated, perhaps, by his second wife, Eleanor Cobham, being arrested on the charge of treasonable sorcery, and condemned by the two archbishops and Beaufort, to perpetual imprisonment. Beaufort seems now to have devoted himself principally to the education of the young King, "who," says Bishop Stubbs, "learned from him the policy of peace, though not of "government." Gloucester continued his impracticable conduct, which eventually involved him in a quarrel with the Parliament. In 1447 they assembled at Bury St. Edmunds, on account of the plague in London; and on Gloucester arriving he was ordered to his lodgings, placed under arrest, and died, probably of disappointment and mortification, in a few days.

There are no evidences that he died by violence, none to implicate Beaufort in his death, indeed he had no motive for it; but in six weeks, on the 11th of April, he himself passed away at the Wolvesley Palace, at Winchester. How far the circumstances of his decease justify Shakespeare's dramatic account may be judged by the testimony of an eye-witness: "As he lay a-dying, he had many men, monks and clergy "and laymen, gathered in the great chamber where he was, and there he "caused the funeral service and the requiem mass to be sung. During "the last few days of his life he was busy with his will. In the evening "before he died he had the will read over and corrected. The following "morning he confirmed it in an audible voice; then took leave and died, "leaving, after large legacies, the residue to charity." He had been munificent to the poor while he lived. He practically rebuilt and enlarged the Hospital of St. Cross, at Winchester, which, founded by Henry de Blois, in the twelfth century, for "men decayed and past their strength," had, after much perversion, been revived by William of Wykeham. Cardinal Beaufort added a distinct establishment, called "Nova domus Eleemo-"synaria nobilis paupertatis," for the support of two priests, thirty-five brethren, and two nuns, building the infirmary so that one end opens into the triforium of the church, in order that the sick in their beds might participate in the service.

How he was esteemed by the good King Henry VI, is evident from his words to the Cardinal's executors when they offered him the share of the residue, some £2,000, to which he was entitled "My uncle "was very dear to me, and did much kindness to me while he lived "the Lord reward him but do ye with his goods as ye are bounden, I "will not take them" Bishop Stubbs thus confirms these noble words "Henry spoke the truth Beaufort had been the mainstay of his house "For fifty years he had held the strings of English policy, and done "his best to maintain the honour and welfare of the nation That "he was ambitious, secular, little troubled with scruples, apt to make "religious persecution a substitute for religious life and conversation, "that he was imperious, impatient of control, ostentatious, and greedy of "honour, these are faults which weigh very light against a great politician, "if they be all that can be said against him It must be remembered "in favour of Beaufort, that he guided the helm of state during the period "in which the English nation first tried the great experiment of self-"government with any approach to success, that he was merciful to his "political enemies, enlightened in his foreign policy, that he was devotedly "faithful, and ready to sacrifice his wealth and labour for his King, and "that from the moment of his death everything began to go wrong, and "went worse and worse until all was lost"

So as we gaze upon his shield we recognize in the gobonnée bordure the token of an ignoble birth, but in the mitre and ermine which adorn it, the tokens of a holy and honoured life An escutcheon, then, not unworthy to decorate the House of God, to be associated with the achievements of princes, to be regarded by all generations of men, and to close this volume of heroic memories and gallant lives For what more noble than, in spite of hindrances of birth or station, to consecrate existence to our God, our Sovereign, and our Country, and leave a record which, in due time, after generations may honour and reverence, and which shall be acknowledged and rewarded at the last great day

GENERAL INDEX.

HERALDIC INDEX.

ARMS MENTIONED

LIST OF SUBSCRIBERS.

A

Aldam, W. ... ... Frickley Hall
Anderson, T. ... ... York
Annandale, R. C. ... Hull (7 copies)
Armytage, G. J., F.S.A. ... Clifton, Brighouse
Ashby, R. ... ... Scarborough
Aspinall, Rev. G. E. ... Southowram
Astley, Mrs. F. R. ... Chequers Court
Atkinson, S. ... ... Moor Allerton

B

Ball, Alfred ... ... York
Barran, H. ... ... Chapel Allerton
Barry, Miss ... ... York
Barstow, Miss ... ... Garrow Hill, York
Bath, The Marquis of ... Longleat
Batley, E. W. ... ... Albion Street
Bayly, Rev. Thomas ... Weaverthorpe Vicarage
Bedford, J. ... ... Leeds
Bedford, Rev. W. K. R. ... Sutton Coldfield
Bellerby, J. ... ... York
Benington, H. ... ... Wakefield
Benson, J. ... ... Burley-in-Wharfedale
Bethell, W. ... ... Rise Park
Blackburn, W. S. ... Leeds (2 copies)
Blaiklock, D. S.... ... Leeds
Blashfield, C. C. W. ... Skipton-in-Craven
Bligh, The Lady Isabel ... Fartherwell Hall
Bolton, The Lord ... Bolton Hall
Boston Public Library, Mass., U.S.A.
Bowman, W. P. ... ... Leeds
Braithwaite, W. S., M.S.A.... Leeds
Briggs, Thomas ... ... York
Bromley, C. ... ... Goole (2 copies
Brooke, Mrs. ... ... Brighouse
Brooke, Thomas ... ... Armitage Bridge
Brooke, Ven. Archdeacon ... Halifax
Brooke, J. A. ... ... Fenay Hall
Brown, Messrs. ... ... Hull
Brown, S. J. ... ... Loftus Hill
Brown, W. ... ... Arncliffe Hall
Bruce, S. ... ... Wakefield
Buckham, Rev. F. H. ... Kirby Grindalythe
Buckle, A., B.A.... ... York
Buckley, J. C. ... ... Headingley
Buckley, Rev. W. E., M.A. Middleton Cheney
Busfeild, W. ... ... Morland Hall
Butler, Hon. H. ... ... Eagle Hall, Pateley

C

Caldwell, Captain C. ... New Grange, Ireland
Caldwell, Mrs. ... ... " "
Calverley, E. ... ... Oulton Hall
Camidge, William ... York
Carter, F. R. ... ... Chapeltown
Cattley, B. ... ... York
Chambers, J. E. F. ... Alfreton
Chapman, George ... York
Chaytor, Lady ... ... Scrafton Lodge
Christie, Rev. J. J. .. Pontefract
Clark, G. T. ... ... Talygarn, Llantrissant
Clarke, J. ... ... Leeds
Clay, A. Travis ... ... Rastrick
Clay, J. W. ... ... Rastrick House
Close, J. ... ... York (5 copies)
Coles, T. H. ... ... Hyde Park, London
Comber, Thomas... ... Leighton, Chester
Constable, Thomas ... Manor House, Otley
Cookes, C. E. ... ... Richmond
Cookson, B. E. ... ... Settrington House
Cooper, Thomas P. ... York
Cordeux, Miss ... ... Harrogate (2 copies)
Crampton, W. T. ... Parcmont, Roundhay, Leeds
Cranbrook, The Viscount ... Grosvenor Crescent
Crossley, J. ... ... Halifax
Cust, Col. F. ... ... Harewood Bridge
Cust, Sir Charles, R.N. ... Onslow Square, London

D

Dale, J. B. ... ... Cleadon Meadows
Darnley, The Earl of ... Cobham Hall (3 copies)
Darwin, F. ... ... Creskeld Hall
Denham, J. ... ... Scarborough
Downe, Viscountess ... York
Duncan, T. ... ... Newall, Otley
Duncombe, The Lady Harriet Berkeley Square
Dykes, F. ... ... Wakefield

E

E. ... ... Leeds
Effingham, Countess Dow. of 57, Eaton Place, S.W.
Egerton, Mrs. Charles ... Solna, Roehampton
Egerton, Mrs. T. ... Whitwell Hall
Elsley, C. ... ... Thirsk
Ely, The Lord Bishop of ...
Emmett, J. ... ... Leeds
Empson, C. W. ... ... Hyde Park, W.
Eshelby, H. D., F.S.A. ... Birkenhead

F

Farrer, J — Oulton
Fisher, Edward — Newton Abbot
Foljambe, C G, M P — Cockglode, Ollerton
Forbes, C M — York
Ford, J R — Leeds
Foster, J — Glasgow
Fourness, J W — Leeds

G

Galloway, F C — Bradford
Gatty, Rev A., D D — Ecclesfield Vicarage
Gibbs, H H — Regent's Park, London
Glover, Very Rev Canon — Carlton, Selby
Gray, Edwin — Gray's Court, York
Green and Son, Messrs — Beverley
Green, Sir Edward, M P — Nunthorpe Hall
Greenwood, A — Leeds
Greenwood, H J — Birstwith Hall
Guest, W H — Manchester

H

Hailstone, E (The late) — Walton Hall
Hainsworth, L — Bradford (2 copies)
Hail, Miss — Sandal Grange (2 copies)
Hanson, Sir Reginald — 4, Bryanston Square
Hardcastle, C D — Leeds
Hardcastle, H — Clifton Green (2 copies)
Hargrove Rev C — Leeds
Harlech, The Lord — Brogyntyn
Harris, Miss — Oxton Hall
Harrison, W T — Southport
Hawke, The Lady — Wighill Park
Hogg, S — Charing Cross
Holt, James — York
Howard, Dr — Altofts, Normanton
Hudson, H A — Clifton, York
Hull Subscription Library — per A Milner
Hurst, A — NunthorpeAvenue, York

I

Ingilby, Lady — Ripley Castle

J

Jackson, Rev Canon — Leigh Delamere
Jarvis W — Charing Cross
Jebb, Rev H G — Firbeck Hall
Jessup, W S — Leeds
Johnson, B — York
Johnstone, Miss L G — Knaresborough

K

Kaye, W J — Edgerton, Huddersfield
Key, W H — Fulford Hall, York
Killingbeck, J — Kidderminster
Kirby, Rev R R — Chapel Allerton
Kitching, T R — Heworth
Knowles, A J — Leeds
Knowles, J W — York

L

Lawrence, Rev Canon, A F B — Birkin Rectory
Lawton, W — Nunthorpe, York
Leeds Library
Leigh, Rev N E — Kirkstall Vicarage
Lister, J — Shibden Hall, Halifax
Lister, S Cunliffe — Swinton
London Corporation Library
Longley, Sir H, K C B — London
Longstaffe, W H D — Gateshead
Loudon, W — Lincoln's Inn, London
Luden, C M — Bootham, York

M

Mackie, Colonel — Heath, Wakefield
Mann, W E — York
March, George — Thorner
Mason, C L — Leeds
Matterson, Dr (the late) — York
Maude, Miss Mary V — York
Meek, Sir James — Cheltenham
Melrose, J — Clifton Croft
Metcalfe, J H — Leyburn
Mexborough, The Earl of — Methley
Meynell Ingram, The Hon Mrs — Temple Newsam
Middleton, Gilbert — Leeds
Miles, J — Trinity Street, Leeds
Mills, Mrs — Bootham (2 copies)
Milne S Milne — Calverley
Milnes, S H — Wakefield
Morkill, J W — Killingbeck
Morley, Edwin — Leeds
Mostyn, The Lady Augusta — Gloddaeth
Moxon, R. — Pontefract
Munby, F J — Whixley

N

Newcastle Society of Antiquaries
Newnham, N J — Blagdon Court
Newton, Rev Canon H — Driffield
Nicholson, M — Middleton Hall
Nixon, Edward — Methley
Noble, T S — Museum, York
Norcliffe, Rev C B, M A — Langton Hall

O

Oldham Public Library — per T W Hand
Onslow, The Hon Mary — Richmond, Surrey
Ormerod, H, Esq — Rastrick
St Oswald, The Lord — Nostell Priory

P

Pashley, R — Rotherham
Peckitt, Lieut Col R W — Thornton-le Moor
Pemberton, R L — Seaham Harbour
Phillips, J W — Museum, Scarborough
Pickering, E H — York (2 copies)
Pitcher, M N — Stretford
Pitman, Rev E A B, F S A — Old Malton
Powell, F S, M P — Horton Old Hall

R

Radcliffe, Sir D. ... ... Thurstaston Hall, Birkenhead
Radford, G. ... ... Great Crosby, Liverpool
Ramage, J. ... ... Paternoster Row
Ramsden, Rev. W. F. ... St. Saviour's Vicarage, Leeds
Redhead, R. Milne ... Bolton-by-Bowland
Reed, W. ... ... York
Rhodes, J. ... ... Leeds
Richardson, W. R. ... Bromley, Kent
Ringrose, Rev. F. D. ... Frodsham Vicarage

S

Sampson, J. ... ... Coney St., York (5 copies)
Scott, J., Jun. ... ... Skipton
Scott, Joseph ... ... Leeds
Scrope, S. T. ... ... Danby Hall
Shaw, Miss ... ... St. Mark's, Leeds
Slingsby, F. W. ... ... Moor Monkton
Smithson, Messrs. ... Malton
Sotheran, H., and Co. ... London
Sotheran and Co. ... Manchester (2 copies)
Sotheran, Messrs. ... *Coney St., York (5 copies)*
Stansfeld, John ... ... Leeds (2 copies)
Stevens, B. T. ... ... Trafalgar Square
Stockdale, A. ... ... Huddersfield
Sutton, Rev. Edward ... Emley Rectory, Wakefield
Swallow, J. H. ... ... Halifax
Swinton, The Hon. Mrs. ... 19, Eaton Place, S.W.

T

Tait, Lawson ... ... Birmingham
Teal, J. ... ... Halifax
Telford, C. ... ... York
Terry, Sir Joseph ... York
Tetley, F. ... ... Weetwood, Leeds
Tew, T. W. ... ... Carlton Grange (2 copies)
Thompson, Richard ... Hob Moor, York
Tindall, Edward ... ... Knapton Hall
Tinkler, Rev. J. ... ... Arkengarthdale Vicarage
Todd, Joseph ... ... York
Turner, E. R. (His Honour Judge) ... ... Saltburn-by-the-Sea
Turner, Joseph ... ... Spencer Place, Leeds

V

Vincent, W. C. ... ... Boston Lodge

W

Walker, H. B. ... ... Leeds
Walker, Thomas ... ... Doncaster
Walker, W. T. ... ... York
Walsh, Rev. W. ... ... *Folkington Rectory*
Ward, Lieut.-Colonel ... Leeds
Watson, George ... ... Uppingham
Watt, E. ... ... Bishop Burton Hall
Wenlock, The Dowager Lady Escrick
Wentworth, Godfrey H. ... Woolley Park
Whitehead and Son ... Leeds
Whytehead, T. B. ... York
Wilkinson, Joseph ... York (2 copies)
Wilson, C. Macro ... Sheffield
Wilson, J. G. ... ... Darlington
Wilson, R. ... ... Leeds
Wood, Rev. Canon ... Headingley
Wood, R. H. ... ... Leeds
Woodd, Basil T. ... ... Conyngham Hall
Woods, E. ... ... York
Wurtzberg, J. H. ... Leeds

Y

Yarborough, The Earl of ... Brocklesby Park
Yates, James ... ... Public Library, Leeds
York, His Grace the Archbishop of
York Subscription Library... per Messrs. Sotheran
Yorke, Edward ... ... Bewerley Hall
Yorke, S. ... ... Erddig Park

RICHARD JACKSON, PUBLISHER, COMMERCIAL STREET, LEEDS.